Early American Women

Early American Women

A Documentary History, 1600–1900

Nancy Woloch
Barnard College

Wadsworth Publishing Company
Belmont, California
A Division of Wadsworth, Inc.

History Editor: Peggy Adams
Consulting Editor: R. Jackson Wilson
Editorial Assistant: Tammy Goldfeld
Production Editor: Donna Linden
Managing Designer: Carolyn Deacy
Print Buyer: Barbara Britton
Permissions Editor: Robert Kauser
Designer: Christy Butterfield
Copy Editor: Robin Kelly
Compositor: Thompson Type, San Diego, California
Cover: *Landscape with Shepherd and Shepherdess*, ca. 1745, artist unknown.
   Anonymous gift Otis Norcross Fund.
   Courtesy Museum of Fine Arts, Boston.
Printer: Maple Press

Photo Credits: Part I: Engraving of Washington's *Reception on the Bridge at
   Trenton*, on the way to his inauguration in 1789. Courtesy Library of
   Congress, Washington, D.C. Part II: Frontier family, 19th century.
   Courtesy State Historical Society of Wisconsin/Charles Van Schaick. Van
   Schaick Collection. Part III: The first graduates of Spelman Seminary,
   1887. Courtesy Spelman College, Atlanta, Georgia.
Text Credits: pp. 318–319: Reprinted by permission of The Harold Ober
   Agency; pp. 323–332: Reprinted by permission of The Tuskegee
   University Archives.

2 3 4 5 6 7 8 9 10—96 95 94 93

Library of Congress Cataloging-in-Publication Data
Early American women : a documentary history, 1600–1900 / [edited by]
   Nancy Woloch.
      p.   cm.
   Includes bibliographical references.
   ISBN 0-534-15102-7
   1. Women—United States—History—Sources.   I. Woloch, Nancy,
date.
   HQ1410.E15   1992
   305.4'0973—dc20   91-17829

Contents

Preface

"Why ought the one half of mankind, to vault and lord it over the other?" asked the anonymous author of an early American tract, *The Female Advocate* (1801). Unfurling her argument for women's education, the never-identified "matron of Connecticut" bombarded her readers with rhetorical questions. "Shall woman be forever destined solely to the distaff and the needle, and never expand an idea beyond the walls of her house?" she asked. "Shall the woman be kept ignorant, to render her more docile in the management of domestic concerns? . . . May not all the seeming differences between the sexes, be imputed solely to the difference of their education and subsequent advantage? . . . Is not a woman of capacious will and well stored mind a better wife, a better widow, a better mother, and a better neighbor; and shall I add, a better friend in every respect?"

The egalitarian convictions that impelled the "female advocate" have similarly infused the exploration of women's history. Since the 1960s, collective effort has produced an expansive field of inquiry. Historians of women have excavated a lost world of female experience, revealed the distinctive nature of that experience, created new chronologies to suit it, and offered interpretations to explain it. Like the embattled *Female Advocate*, women's history has also been committed to an agenda for change. A major target of such change, of course, is the discipline of history itself, and here women's history has had a major impact. Few areas of history, at least American history, remain immune to its achievements: Women's history has enlarged the terrain with which all historians must cope. But the relationship between this particular field and the rest of the discipline is now a two-way street. In many current studies, historians of women take pains to draw connections between aspects of women's experience and what might be called the larger picture. "The best women's history does not study women's lives in isolation," historian Louise Tilly observes in a recent article. "It endeavors to relate those lives to other historical themes, such as the power of ideas or the forces of structural change. In this way women's history has already changed our view of what matters in history."*

This collection of documents seeks to capitalize on the insights of recent work in women's history and to consider connections between women's lives and "other historical themes." The documents that follow by no means constitute a comprehensive history of early American women. Rather they focus on a series of discrete topics that figure prominently in this history. Within the topical limits imposed, I have sought to cover a diversity of women's experiences—for women's history is in fact several histories—and to suggest the impact of class, race, and region. I have also sought to present a variety of voices: women who reveal their own lives, women who describe the lives of other women, and men who record or discuss some facet of women's experience, or perhaps try to impart some piece of advice. Above all, I have sought to include a diversity of sources. Many of the documents in this book fall into the category of the private and informal: diaries, journals, correspondence, and personal narratives. Most of this material was never intended for public consumption, but rather directed at a limited audience of friends or family members, or perhaps not meant to be read by others at all. Other documents, aimed at a wider readership, fall into a more public category. These include tracts, speeches, declarations, circulating letters, institutional records, travelers' accounts, advice manuals, professional studies, newspaper and magazine articles, and other publications. A third type of documents comes from the public record, such as laws, wills, probate records, court records, and government reports. Through this variety of sources, I have tried to touch on the experience of both ordinary and exceptional women.

Under the assumption that what happened first was likely to affect what happened next, I have adopted a chronological format. Each of the three major sections in this book is devoted to a broad time span. Part I, on the seventeenth and eighteenth centuries, concerns primarily the movement of English traditions and institutions from the old world to the new. Part II, on the early nineteenth century, 1800–1860, involves some of the major developments—geographic expansion, economic change, class formation, voluntary association—with which women were involved. Part III, on the years 1860–1900, focuses on women's participation in public events—notably the Civil

---

*Louise Tilly, "Gender, Women's History, and Social History," *Social Science History* 13 (Winter 1989), p. 447.

War and the process of emancipation—and their movement into public life. Each chronological section comprises a group of topical chapters. Introductions to each chapter attempt to survey the history of the topic at hand, to anchor the documents that follow in time and place, and to present some relevant questions with which historians have been concerned. Headnotes to each document offer details about its author or origins, the circumstances under which it was written, and the audience for whom it was intended.

The use of documents has obvious advantages. At their best, primary sources are alive, direct, immediate, and vivid. They exude authenticity. These same documents, however, can be as laden with bias as interpretive narrative. Each document had its origins in a bygone time and should be regarded as a prism through which the values and concerns (often unfamiliar) of a particular era (often distant) are refracted. The anonymous "female advocate" of 1801, for instance, attuned to a distinctive climate of revolutionary-era ideas, sought not merely to assert "women's rights" but also to redress "women's wrongs," and above all to renegotiate the contemporary rules of the game under which women and men interacted.* Any given document, also, is likely to convey a specific writer's idiosyncratic or partisan slant on the subject in question. It may well be a vehicle through which narrowly personal views—or exceptionally prescient ones—are voiced. I am partial, for instance, to several of the documents that seem to anticipate, however inadvertently, the concerns of contemporary social historians—two examples are the selections written by Eliza Leslie (1856) and Mary Gay Humphreys (1896)—as well as to those documents offered by renegotiators such as the matron of Connecticut.

Finally, the selection of documents in this book is of necessity loaded. Despite all previous disclaimers, it is weighted in favor of the literate, often the highly literate. During the colonial era, approximately the first two centuries represented here, the vast majority of women lacked writing skills (more about this soon). Thereafter, female literacy made great strides. Still, throughout the nineteenth century, only a minority of people expressed themselves with ease through the written word. To depend heavily on women's voices, therefore, entails

---

*For an informative discussion on the history of women in the new nation and its social and political context, see Linda K. Kerber et al., "Beyond Roles, Beyond Spheres: Thinking About Gender in the Early Republic," *William and Mary Quarterly* 46 (July 1989), pp. 565–85.

reliance on a minority of women, usually educated women, who habitually conveyed their thoughts in writing. The schooled, propertied, and prominent—the pace-setters—are thus overrepresented. One last point: the documents offered here focus primarily not on "life-as-lived," though that is included, but on the cutting edge—on women who were involved in some new development or aspect of change. These caveats aside, I hope that I have presented important themes and suggested "what matters in history."

Acknowledgments

I am indebted to David Follmer for proposing that I undertake this book, and to Susan Ware, editor of *Modern American Women* (1989) for providing the format. Many thanks go to Eileen Glickstein, Director of the Barnard College Library, and Lucinda Manning, Manuscript Curator at the Teachers College library, Columbia University, for their assistance. Several historians have generously provided documents and advice. Let me thank Elizabeth Blackmar, Tim Gilfoyle, John Modell, Caroline Niemczyk, Rosalind Rosenberg, Herb Sloan, and Jack Wilson. For their perceptive reading of the manuscript, I am grateful to Jo Ann E. Argersinger, University of Maryland, Baltimore County Campus, and Lisa Wilson, Connecticut College, New London. My editors at Wadsworth have been congenial collaborators and models of competence. I am greatly indebted to Peggy Adams, acquisitions editor; Donna Linden, production editor; and Robin Kelly, copyeditor. Without their hard work, this book would not exist.

On a personal note, I would like to thank the members of the History Department at Barnard College for their collegiality and company over the past few years. I would also like to express gratitude to my family—to my sons, David and Alex Woloch, who shrewdly left home around the time I started this book, and to my husband, Isser Woloch, for his supportive interest in this project. To all of the above, many thanks for your time and your suggestions.

Early American Women

PART I

A New World:
The 17th and 18th Centuries

When Anne Bradstreet, a young Puritan wife, arrived in Boston harbor in 1630, she found "a new world and new manners, at which my heart rose [rebelled]. But after I was convinced that it was the will of God, I submitted to it." Few women in colonial America could record their response to emigration or any other experience, because only a minority could read or write. Studies of colonial literacy—usually measured by whether individuals could sign legal deeds or, alternatively, make "marks"—suggest that female literacy lagged behind that of men. Toward the end of the colonial era, in 1760, for instance, less than half of the women in Massachusetts, the most highly literate colony, could sign their names on wills, compared to some eighty percent of the men. Although many women who were unable to sign could probably read, historians estimate, female literacy was far from universal. Studies of female signing in other colonies suggest that well over half of white women lacked literacy, compared to smaller proportions of men. Among Indian and slave women, presumably few or none had the skills to leave written records.

The search for documentary evidence of colonial women's experience is therefore an imposing task. To present women's voices, it is tempting to rely on the output of the literate elite—those women who left letters and diaries, and occasionally (if rarely) publications. The women who produced such written records were usually Anglo-American women of some education and social status, and often related to important men. They were therefore singular and unrepresentative. To obtain information about ordinary women's lives, historians have had to delve into a far broader range of data than women alone were able to provide. Some information comes from the writings of men—from their letters, diaries, sermons, essays, and published observations. Some comes from the colonial press, with its wealth of announcements, advertisements, and local news. Some comes from

the colonial churches and their ministers, who may have recorded the activities of parishioners, especially their religious conversions, concerns, and disputes. And a vast amount of information about women's lives comes from the public records that colonists kept— from, for instance, county court proceedings, testimony in trials, marriage and separation agreements, indenture and apprenticeship contracts, and records of probate courts, which contain wills and household inventories.

Such documents, while offering far more than the experience of the literate elite, do not necessarily present a complete or accurate picture of colonial life, or of women's lives. Wills, for example, a favorite resource of historians, are a biased type of document. The vast majority of wills were left by men, whose view of family relationships they reflect. They also were left primarily by men with property to distribute. In the late colonial era, some two-thirds of men died without having written wills.

Other kinds of public records are also likely to be biased. At county court proceedings, for instance, a particular type of woman—the young, single, indentured servant, arrested for such crimes as theft or bastardy—was overrepresented. Documents concerning marriages also may convey misleading impressions. Separation agreements or decisions do not reflect the way that the majority of colonial marriages disintegrated, through the desertion of men. Few documents, moreover, present the experience of nonwhite women, which has been pieced together through information provided by such disparate sources as travelers' accounts and county censuses. Still, historians have used an impressive amount of ingenuity to mine the records that exist, whatever their liabilities, and to recreate the physical and social world of colonial women.

Chapter 1

Natives and Captives

*T*he Indians who inhabited North America during the era of European colonization left no written records. Their lives were described by those settlers and explorers who came in contact with them—along the Atlantic coast, in the Great Lakes region, and in lower Canada. These Europeans encountered a variety of Indian cultures. Eastern Indians belonged to hundreds of tribes and four language groups—Muskogean, Iroquoian, Algonquian, and Sioux. Their tribal customs differed, as did their social, political, and religious traditions. They were sometimes at war with each other, as well as with colonists who encroached on their land.

Yet, the Indians shared a common culture. All tribes had subsistence economies, dependent on hunting and farming. Most eastern Indians were agriculturalists, who supplemented their diets with game and fish. The clan was the basic social unit, and kinship the basis of economic and political relationships. Lineal ties and mutual obligations determined social arrangements. Farming tribes were often, though not always, matrilineal (lines of descent traced through mothers) and matrilocal (a husband joined his wife's family's household); in such tribes, women owned the fields and homes. All tribes adhered to a sexual division of labor. In general, men were responsible for hunting, fishing, diplomacy, and war; women took charge of agriculture, which kept them near their households and villages. Religious systems stressed the continuity of natural and supernatural; political systems were grounded in voluntarism, not coercion.

One further factor linked the eastern tribes during the first two centuries of colonization. All Indian societies changed in response to the intrusion of successive waves of European settlement. Laden with imperial goals and sophisticated weapons, the colonists also imported a heavy arsenal of European diseases—such as influenza, measles, smallpox, and typhus—to which Indians lacked immunity. Consequently, the steady arrival of settlers diminished Indian numbers, depleted their resources, disrupted their economies, threatened their traditions, and altered their day-to-day existence. Before the end of the seventeenth century, eastern Indians had been decimated by the colonization process. By the 1670s, for instance, New England Indians had dwindled to about ten percent of their precolonization numbers.

European encroachment undoubtedly affected Indian women's roles, apparently in ways both positive and negative. Among the hunting tribes, for instance, the economic importance of women may have risen, as the fur trade with Europeans expanded, because it was the women who cleaned hides. In southern New England, where European disruptions made warfare and diplomacy more important, women's status within their dwindling communities probably declined. Similarly, among the Iroquois, who adapted in part to European ways, women's position was no doubt affected by the abandonment of matrilineal traditions, the end of matrilocal living arrangements, the evolution of male-headed households, and the engagement of men in agriculture, traditionally a female pursuit.

Those Europeans who recorded their views of Indian life— explorers, colonists, traders, missionaries—were of course not trained ethnologists, as historian James Axtell has pointed out.* Some of their reports were colored by European expectations, a desire to spread Christianity, or sexual bias. Some commentators made invidious comparisons between colonists and Indians. Still, the accounts of these early observers, often based on years of experience, offered firsthand views of Indian life and gave prominent attention to Indian women. European reporters seemed especially interested in how women's roles among the tribes they encountered differed from those in European society.

---

*See the introduction to James Axtell, ed., *The Indian Peoples of Eastern America: A Documentary History of the Sexes* (New York: Oxford University Press, 1981).

Thus, they provided detailed descriptions of courtship and marriage, childbearing and child-rearing, and many examples of distinctive customs—such as abstinence in pregnancy and lactation, acceptance of premarital sexuality, the occasional practice of polygamy, and the simple dissolution of marriages, as when an Indian wife evicted her spouse's possessions. Indian work habits also interested the Europeans, although the sexual division of labor among Indians may have confused some reporters. Viewing Indian villages during times when adult men either were away on hunting trips or had recently returned from such trips, these Europeans saw mainly women at work and thereby concluded that women had been sentenced to lives of drudgery while men lolled about in idleness. Others corrected this misperception. Public life was another avenue of exploration. European observers were intrigued whenever women assumed prominent roles in tribal affairs, as either religious leaders or hereditary officials, or in formal government positions, as among the Iroquois.

The narratives of white women who were captured by Indians complement the reports of male observers by providing vivid and personal impressions of Indian life. Many of the 270 captives in northern New England between 1689 and 1730 were women, and subsequent captives were mainly women and children. Some were taken for ransom and some for adoption, or to replace clan members who had been killed recently. These captives lived for weeks, months, or even years among the tribes they described. Captivity narratives were hardly unbiased accounts; most were statements of religious faith written or dictated after release. Still, captives' views varied. This is evident, in the documents that follow, in the contrast between Mary Rowlandson's response to her Narragansett captors as "ravenous Beasts" and Mary Jemison's favorable reaction, after many decades, to the traditions of the Seneca Indians among whom she had spent most of her days.

All of the seventeenth- and eighteenth-century men and women—explorers, settlers, captives—who recorded their views of Indian life were speaking to an engaged audience. During the era of colonization, Europeans at home and abroad had an insatiable curiosity about the New World. Reports from the far-off American settlements reached an avid readership and went through many printings. Captivity narratives became a popular literary form in England and America. The accounts of the early observers, therefore, answer the questions that their contemporaries would have asked. Whatever the defects or limitations of these accounts, they retain the sense of curiosity and wonder with which they were written.

Narragansett Women

ROGER WILLIAMS, 1643

Roger Williams, *A Key into the Language of North America* (London: Gregory Dexter, 1643), pp. 95, 98–100, 146–51.

Separatist minister Roger Williams (ca. 1603–1683), advocate of "soul liberty," began studying New England Indians as soon as he arrived in Massachusetts Bay in 1631. He soon antagonized Puritan authorities by contending that the land covered in the Massachusetts Bay charter belonged to the Indians. After he was expelled from Massachusetts and founded Providence, Rhode Island, in 1636, Williams embarked on an extensive study of the nearby Narragansett Indians. Living among them, he learned their language—which he believed bore "some affinitie" to Hebrew and Greek—and wrote a dictionary of the language. This "key" to the Indians' tongue was a handbook of phrases, topically arranged, to which Williams added his observations of Indian life. It was published when he returned to England in 1643 to obtain a charter for Rhode Island.

In the following excerpts from his extraordinary book, Roger Williams describes aspects of marriage, childbirth, and women's work. Painless childbirth, for instance, suggested to Williams that Indian women had escaped God's curse on Eve. Polygamy, though rare, was desirable among Indians, he explained, because of women's agricultural wealth as well as the custom of abstinence during pregnancy and lactation. An idyllic picture of happy female agriculturists serves as a corrective to more derogatory comments made by subsequent European observers.

Of Mariage

Uskéne.	*A young man.*
Keegsquaw.	*A Virgin or Maide.*
Segaûo.	*A Widdower.*
Segoúsquaw.	*A Widdow.*
Wussénetam.	*He goes a wooing.*
Nosénemuck.	*He is my sonne in Law.*
Wussenetûock,	*They make a match.*
Awetawátuock.	

Obs. Single fornication they count no sin, but after Mariage (which they solemnize by consent of Parents and publique approbation publiquely) then they count it hainous fer either of them to befalse.

Mammaûsu.	*An adulterer.*
Nummam mógwunewò.	*He hath wronged my bed.*
Pallè nochisquaûaw.	*He or She hath committed adultery.*

Obs. In this case the wronged party may put away or keepe the party offending: commonly, if the Woman be false, the offended Husband will be solemnely revenged upon the offendor, before many witnesses, by many blowes and wounds, and if it be to Death, yet the guilty resists not, nor is his Death revenged.

Nquittócaw.	*He hath one Wife.*
Neesócaw.	*He hath two Wives.*
Sshócowaw.	*He hath three.*
Yócowaw.	*Foure Wives, &c.*

Their number is not stinted, yet the chief Nation in the Country, the Narrigansets (generally) have but one Wife.

Two causes they generally alledge for their many Wives.

First desire of Riches, because the Women bring in all the increase of the Field, &c. the Husband onely fisheth, hunteth, &c.

Secondly, their long sequestring themselves from their wives after conception, untill the child be weaned, which with some is long after a yeare old, generally they keep their children long at the breast:

Commíttamus. Cowéewo.	*Your Wife.*
Tahanawátu? ta shincommaugemus.	*How much gave you for her?*
Napannetashom paûgatash.	*Five fathome of their Money.*
Qutta, énada shoásuck ta shompaúgatash.	*Six, or seven, or eight* *Fathome.*

If some great mans Daughter *Piuckquom-paúgatash*, ten fathome.

Obs. Generally the Husband gives these payments for a Dowrie, (as it was in *Israell*) to the Father or Mother, or guardian of the Maide. To this purpose if the man be poore, his Friends and neighbours doe *pummanùm-minteàuguash*, that is contribute Money toward the Dowrie.

Nummíttamus.	*My Wife.*
Nullógana.	
Waumaûsu.	*Loving.*
Wunnêkesu.	*Proper.*
Maânsu.	*Sober and chast.*
Muchickéhea.	*Fruifull.*

Cutchashekeâmis?	*How many children have you had?*
Nquittékea.	*I have had one.*
Neesékea.	*Two, &c.*

Obs. They commonly abound with Children, and increase mightily; except the plauge fall amongst them or other lesser sicknesses, and then having no meanes of recovery, they perish wonderfully.

Katoû eneéchaw.	*She is falling into Travell.*
Néechaw.	*She is in Travell.*
Paugcótche nechaúwaw.	*She is already delivered.*
Kitummâyi-mes-néchaw.	*She was just now delivered.*

Obs. It hath pleased God in wonderfull manner to moderate that curse of the sorrowes of Child-bearing to these poore Indian Women: So that ordinarily they have a wonderfull more speedy and easie Travell, and delivery then the Women of *Europe*: not that I thinke God is more gracious to them above other Women, but that it followes, First from the hardnesse of their constitution, in which respect they beare their sorrowes the easier.

Secondly from their extraordinary great labour (even above the labour of men) as in the Field, they sustaine the labour of it, in carrying of mighty Burthens, in digging clammes and getting other Shelfish from the Sea, in beating all their corne in Morters: &c. Most of them count it a shame for a Woman in Travell to make complaint, and many of them are scarcely heard to groane. I have often knowne in one Quarter of an houre a Woman merry in the House, and delivered and merry againe: and within two dayes abroad, and after foure or five dayes at worke, &c.

Noosâwwaw.	*A Nurse.*
Noònsu Nonánnis.	*A sucking Child.*
Wunnunògan.	*A Breast.*
Wunnunnóganash.	*Breasts.*
Munnúnnug.	*Milke.*
Aumáúnemun.	*To take from the breast, or Weane.*

Obs. They put away (as in Israell) frequently for other occasions beside Adultery, yet I know many Couples that have lived twenty, thirty, forty yeares together.

Npakétam.	*I will put her away.*
Npakénaqun.	*I am put away.*
Aquiepakétash.	*Doe not put away.*
Aquiepokesháttous	*Doe not break the knot of*
Awetawátuonck.	* Mariage.*
Tackquiûwock.	*Twins.*
Towiû-ûwock.	*Orphans.*
Ntouwiú.	*I am an Orphane.*
Wáuchaûnat.	*A Guardian.*

Wauchaúamachick.	*Guardians.*
Nullóquaso.	*My charge or Pupill, or Ward.*
Peewaúqun.	*Looke well to him &c.*

Generall Observations of Their Mariage

God hath planted in the Hearts of the Wildest of the sonnes of Men, an High and Honourable esteeme of the Mariage bed, insomuch that they universally submit unto it, and hold the Violation of that Bed, Abominable, and accordingly reape the Fruit thereof in the abundant increase of posterity.

Of the Earth, and the Fruits Thereof, &c.

Obs.   The *Natives* are very exact and punctuall in the bounds of their Lands, belonging to this or that Prince or People, (even to a River, Brooke) &c. And I have knowne them make bargaine and sale amongst themselves for a small piece, or quantity of Ground: notwithstanding a sinfull opinion amongst many that Christians have right to *Heathens* Lands: but of the delusion of that phrase, I have spoke in a discourse concerning the *Indians* Conversion.

Aukeeteaûmen.	*To plant Corne.*
Quttáunemun.	*To plant Corne.*
Anakáusu.	*A Labourer.*
Anakáusichick.	*Labourers.*
Aukeeteaûmitch.	*Planting time.*
Aukeeteáhettit.	*When they set Corne.*
Nummautaukeeteaûmen.	*I have done planting.*
Anaskhómmin.	*To how [hoe] or break up.*

Obs.   The Women set or plant, weede, and hill, and gather and barne all the corne, and Fruites of the field: Yet sometimes the man himselfe, (either out of love to his Wife, or care for his Children, or being an old man) will help the Woman which (by the custome of the Countrey) they are not bound to.

When a field is to be broken up, they have a very loving sociable speedy way to dispatch it: All the neighbours men and Women forty, fifty, a hundred &c, joyne, and come in to help freely.

With friendly joyning they breake up their fields, build their Forts, hunt the Woods, stop and kill fish in the Rivers, it being true with them as in all the World in the Affaires of Earth or Heaven: By concord little things grow great, by discord the greatest come to nothing *Concordiâ parvæ res crescunt, Discordiâ magnæ dilabuntur.*

Anáskhig-anash.	*How, Howes.*
Anaskhómwock.	*They how.*
Anaskhommonteâmin.	*They break for me.*
Anaskhomwáutowwin.	*A breaking up How.*

The *Indian* Women to this day (notwithstanding our Howes, doe use their naturall Howes of shells and Wood.

Which they doe carefully upon heapes and Mats many dayes, before they barne it up, covering it up with Mats at night, and opening when the Sun is hot.

Sókenug. *A heap of corne.*

Obs. The woman of the family will commonly raise two or three heaps of twelve, fifteene, or twentie bushells a heap, which they drie in round broad heaps; and if she have helpe of her children or friends, much more.

Women's Lives Among the Delaware

JOHN HECKEWELDER, 1819

Rev. John Heckewelder, *History, Manners, and Customs of the Indian Natives Who Once Inhabited Pennsylvania and the Neighboring States*, ed. Rev. William Reichel (Philadelphia: Historical Society of Pennsylvania, 1876), pp. 154–61.

English-born John Heckewelder (1743–1823), a Moravian missionary, began working among American Indians in Pennsylvania in 1762. In 1771 he started his own mission among the Delaware Indians in Ohio, which he ran for fifteen years. Heckewelder's respected account of Indian life, based on his long experience, appeared in 1819 as the first volume of the *Transactions* of the American Philosophical Society, an outgrowth of Benjamin Franklin's "Junto."

In the following passages, Heckewelder presents Indian marriage as a male-dominated institution—not utterly dissimilar from the European or American institution of marriage, save for the option of simple divorce. He also refutes a prevalent notion that Indian women performed all of the drudgery while men loitered about at their ease. The topic of work roles among the agricultural tribes often baffled white observers because Indian women did the farming, a job that Europeans allotted to men. Some contended, therefore, that Indian women were more oppressed than the wives of colonists. Heckewelder, however, portrays Delaware women doing field work for a limited period each year, in the company of other women; Delaware men, he contended, worked more continuously and did more strenuous labor.

Marriage and Treatment of Their Wives

There are many persons who believe, from the labour that they see the Indian women perform, that they are in a manner treated as slaves. These labours, indeed, are hard, compared with the tasks that are imposed upon females in civilised society; but they are no more than their fair share, under every consideration and due allowance, of the hardships attendant on savage life. Therefore they are not only voluntarily, but cheerfully submitted to; and as women are not obliged to live with their husbands any longer than suits their pleasure or convenience, it cannot be supposed that they would submit to be loaded with unjust or unequal burdens.

Marriages among the Indians are not, as with us, contracted for life; it is understood on both sides that the parties are not to live together any longer than they shall be pleased with each other. The husband may put away his wife whenever he pleases, and the woman may in like manner abandon her husband. Therefore the connexion is not attended with any vows, promises, or ceremonies of any kind. An Indian takes a wife as it were on trial, determined, however, in his own mind not to forsake her if she behaves well, and particularly if he has children by her. The woman, sensible of this, does on her part every thing in her power to please her husband, particularly if he is a good hunter or trapper, capable of maintaining her by his skill and industry, and protecting her by his strength and courage.

When a marriage takes place, the duties and labours incumbent on each party are well known to both. It is understood that the husband is to build a house for them to dwell in, to find the necessary implements of husbandry, as axes, hoes, &c., to provide a canoe, and also dishes, bowls, and other necessary vessels for housekeeping. The woman generally has a kettle or two, and some other articles of kitchen furniture, which she brings with her. The husband, as master of the family, considers himself bound to support it by his bodily exertions, as hunting, trapping, &c.; the woman, as his *help-mate*, takes upon herself the labours of the field, and is far from considering them as more important than those to which her husband is subjected, being well satisfied that with his gun and traps he can maintain a family in any place where game is to be found; nor do they think it any hardship imposed upon them; for they themselves say, that while their field labour employs them at most six weeks in the year, that of the men continues the whole year round.

When a couple is newly married, the husband (without saying a single word upon the subject) takes considerable pains to please his wife, and by repeated proofs of his skill and abilities in the art of hunting, to make her sensible that she can be happy with him, and that she will never want while they live together. At break of day he will be off with his gun, and often by breakfast time return home with a deer, turkey, or some other game. He endeavours to make it appear that it is in his power to bring provisions home whenever he pleases, and his wife, proud of having such a good hunter for her husband, does her utmost to serve and make herself agreeable to him.

The work of the women is not hard or difficult. They are both able and willing to do it, and always perform it with cheerfulness. Mothers teach their daughters those duties which common sense would otherwise point out to them when grown up. Within doors, their labour is very trifling; there is seldom more than one pot or kettle to attend to. There is no scrubbing of the house, and but little to wash, and that not often. Their principal occupations are to cut and fetch in the fire wood, till the ground, sow and reap the grain, and pound the corn in mortars for their pottage, and to make bread which they bake in the ashes. When going on a journey, or to hunting camps with their husbands, if they have no horses, they carry a pack on their backs which often appears heavier than it really is; it generally consists of a blanket, a dressed deer skin for mocksens, a few articles of kitchen furniture, as a kettle, bowl, or dish, with spoons, and some bread, corn, salt, &c., for their nourishment. I have never known an Indian woman complain of the hardship of carrying this burden, which serves for their own comfort and support as well as of their husbands.

The tilling of the ground at home, getting of the fire wood, and pounding of corn in mortars, is frequently done by female parties, much in the manner of those husking, quilting, and other *frolics* (as they are called), which are so common in some parts of the United States, particularly to the eastward. The labour is thus quickly and easily performed; when it is over, and sometimes in intervals, they sit down to enjoy themselves by feasting on some good victuals, prepared for them by the person or family for whom they work, and which the man has taken care to provide before hand from the woods; for this is considered a principal part of the business, as there are generally more or less of the females assembled who have not, perhaps for a long time, tasted a morsel of meat, being either widows, or orphans, or otherwise in straitened circumstances. Even the chat which passes during their joint labours is highly diverting to them, and so they seek to be employed in this way as long as they can, by going round to all those in the village who have ground to till.

When the harvest is in, which generally happens by the end of September, the women have little else to do than to prepare the daily victuals, and get fire wood, until the latter end of February or beginning of March, as the season is more or less backward, when they go to their sugar camps, where they extract sugar from the maple tree. The men having built or repaired their temporary cabin, and made all the troughs of various sizes, the women commence making sugar, while the men are looking out for meat, at this time generally fat bears, which are still in their winter quarters. When at home, they will occasionally assist their wives in gathering the sap, and watch the kettles in their absence, that the syrup may not boil over.

A man who wishes his wife to be with him while he is out hunting in the woods, needs only tell her, that on such a day they will go to such a place, where he will hunt for a length of time, and she will be sure to have provisions and every thing else that is necessary in complete readiness, and well packed up to carry to the spot; for the man, as soon as he enters the woods, has to be looking out and about for game, and therefore cannot be encumbered with any burden; after wounding a deer, he may have to pursue it for several miles, often running it fairly down. The woman, therefore, takes charge of the baggage, brings it to the place of encampment, and there, immediately enters on the duties of housekeeping, as if they were at home; she moreover takes pains to dry as much meat as she can, that none may be lost; she carefully puts the tallow up, assists in drying the skins, gathers as much wild hemp as possible for the purpose of making strings, carrying-bands, bags and other necessary articles, collects roots for dyeing; in short, does every thing in her power to leave no care to her husband but the important one of providing meat for the family.

After all, the fatigue of the women is by no means to be compared to that of the men. Their hard and difficult employments are periodical and of short duration, while their husband's labours are constant and severe in the extreme. Were a man to take upon himself a part of his wife's duty, in addition to his own, he must necessarily sink under the load, and of course his family must suffer with him. On his exertions as a hunter, their existence depends; in order to be able to follow that rough employment with success, he must keep his limbs as supple as he can, he must avoid hard labour as much as possible, that his joints may not become stiffened, and that he may preserve the necessary strength and agility of body to enable him to pursue the chase, and bear the unavoidable hardships attendant on it; for the fatigues of hunting wear out the body and constitution far more than manual labour. Neither creeks nor rivers, whether shallow or deep, frozen or free from ice, must be an obstacle to the hunter, when in pursuit of a wounded deer, bear, or other animals, as is often the case. Nor has he then leisure to think on the state of his body, and to consider whether his blood is not too much heated to plunge without danger into the cold stream, since the game he is in pursuit of is running off from him with full speed. Many dangerous accidents often befal him, both as a hunter and a warrior (for he is both), and are seldom unattended with painful consequences, such as rheumatism, or consumption of the lungs, for which the sweat-house, on which they so much depend, and to which they often resort for relief, especially after a fatiguing hunt or warlike excursion, is not always a sure preservative or an effectual remedy.

The husband generally leaves the skins and peltry which he has procured by hunting to the care of his wife, who sells or barters them away to the best advantage for such necessaries as are wanted in the family; not forgetting to supply her husband with what he stands in need of, who, when he receives it from her hand never fails to return her thanks in the kindest manner. If debts had been previously contracted, either by the woman, or by her and her husband jointly, or if a horse should be wanted, as much is laid aside as will be sufficient to pay the debts or purchase the horse.

When a woman has got in her harvest of corn, it is considered as belonging to her husband, who, if he has suffering friends, may give them as much of it as he pleases, without consulting his wife, or being afraid of her being displeased; for she is in the firm belief that he is able to procure that article whenever it is wanted. The sugar which she makes out of the maple tree is also considered as belonging to her husband.

There is nothing in an Indian's house or family without its particular owner. Every individual knows what belongs to him, from the horse or cow down to the dog, cat, kitten and little chicken. Parents make presents to their children, and they in return to their parents. A father will sometimes ask his wife or one of his children for the loan of his horse to go out a hunting. For a litter of kittens or brood of chickens, there are often as many different owners as there are individual animals. In purchasing a hen with her brood, one frequently has to deal for it with several children. Thus, while the principle of community of goods prevails in the state, the rights of property are acknowledged among the members of a family. This is attended with a very good effect; for by this means every living creature is properly taken care of. It also promotes liberality among the children, which becomes a habit with them by the time they are grown up. . . .

It very seldom happens that a man condescends to quarrel with his wife, or abuse her, though she has given him just cause. In such a case the man, without replying, or saying a single word, will take his gun and go into the woods, and remain there a week or perhaps a fortnight, living on the meat he has killed, before he returns home again; well knowing that he cannot inflict a greater punishment on his wife for her conduct to him than by absenting himself for a while; for she is not only kept in suspense, uncertain whether he will return again, but is soon reported as a bad and quarrelsome woman; for, as on those occasions, the man does not tell his wife on what day or at what time he will be back again, which he otherwise, when they are on good terms, never neglects to do, she is at once put to shame by her neighbours, who soon suspecting something, do not fail to put such questions to her, as she either cannot, or is ashamed to answer. When he at length does return, she endeavours to let him see by her attentions, that she has repented, though neither speak to each other a single word on the subject of what has passed. And as his children, if he has any, will on his return hang about him and soothe him with their caresses, he is, on their account, ready to forgive, or at least to say nothing unpleasant to their mother. She has, however, received by this a solemn warning, and must take care how she behaves in future, lest the next time her husband should stay away altogether and take another wife. It is very probable, that if at this time they had had no children, he would have left her, but then he would have taken his property with him at the same time.

Iroquois Women in Government

PIERRE DE CHARLEVOIX, 1721

Pierre de Charlevoix, *Journal of a Voyage to North America*, 2 vols. (London: 1761
[Chicago: The Caxton Club, 1923]), 2:19–20, 23–27.

When Europeans compared Indian and white societies, they noted
that women sometimes inherited leadership roles in their tribes and
that, in the unique case of the Iroquois, some women played a prominent role in government. In practice, the formal authority that Iroquois tribes granted to women was subordinate to that of male chiefs
and the village council of elders. Still, the Iroquois matrons had a
legitimate voice in public affairs, which neither European women—
nor most other Indian women—could claim.

Pierre de Charlevoix (1682–1761), a Jesuit priest who traveled
from Quebec to the Gulf of Mexico, described the civic roles of Iro-
quoian-speaking Huron women in a letter to an unidentified woman
correspondent in 1721. Among these Indians, Charlevoix points out,
the role of chief was inherited through the female line. Older women
also played a special part in government. According to his account,
they could select and unseat male chiefs, serve as assistants to chiefs,
and oversee the public treasury. Debating issues separately, the women
also had their own representative, or orator, to express their views to
the all-male council of elders.

June 14, 1721

Madam,

After I had closed my last letter and given it to a person who was going down to
Quebec, I made myself ready to pursue my voyage, and accordingly embarked next
day; but I have not been able to get over, and through the neglect of those who
conducted me, am returned back to fort Pontchartrain, where I very much fear being
obliged to remain several days longer. These are disappointments we must lay our
account with, in travelling with Canadians who are never in a hurry, and who are very
careless in taking their measures. But, as we are to make the most of every thing, I
will take the opportunity of this delay, to divert you with beginning some account of
the government of the Indians, and their manner of proceeding in the dispatch of
public business. . . .

It must be agreed, Madam, that the nearer we view our Indians, the more good
qualities we discover in them: most of the principles which serve to regulate their

conduct, the general maxims by which they govern themselves, and the essential part of their character, discover nothing of the barbarian. . . .

In the northern parts, and wherever the Algonquin tongue prevails, the dignity of chief is elective; and the whole ceremony of election and installation consists in some feasts, accompanied with dances and songs: the chief elect likewise never fails to make the panegyrick of his predecessor, and to invoke his genius. Amongst the Hurons, where this dignity is hereditary, the succession is continued through the women, so that at the death of a chief, it is not his own, but his sister's son who succeeds him; or, in default of which, his nearest relation in the female line. When the whole branch happens to be extinct, the noblest matron of the tribe or in the nation chuses the person she approves of most, and declares him chief. The person who is to govern must be come to years of maturity; and when the hereditary chief is not as yet arrived at this period, they appoint a regent, who has all the authority, but which he holds in name of the minor. These chiefs generally have no great marks of outward respect paid them, and if they are never disobeyed, it is because they know how to set bounds to their authority. It is true that they request or propose, rather than command; and never exceed the boundaries of that small share of authority with which they are vested. Thus it is properly reason which governs, and the government has so much the more influence, as obedience is founded in liberty; and that they are free from any apprehension of its degenerating into tyranny.

Nay more, each family has a right to chuse a counsellor of its own, and an assistant to the chief, who is to watch for their interest; and without whose consent the chief can undertake nothing. These counsellors are, above all things, to have an eye to the public treasury; and it is properly they who determine the uses it is to be put to. They are invested with this character in a general council, but they do not acquaint their allies with it, as they do at the elections and installations of their chief. Amongst the Huron nations, the women name the counsellors, and often chuse persons of their own sex.

This body of counsellors or assistants is the highest of all; the next is that of the elders, consisting of all those who have come to the years of maturity. I have not been able to find exactly what this age is. The last of all is that of the warriors; this comprehends all who are able to bear arms. This body has often at its head, the chief of the nation or town; but he must first have distinguished himself by some signal action of bravery; if not, he is obliged to serve as a subaltern, that is, as a single centinel; there being no degrees in the militia of the Indians.

In fact, a large body may have several chiefs, this title being given to all who ever commanded; but they are not therefore the less subject to him who leads the party; a kind of general, without character or real authority, who has power neither to reward nor punish, whom his soldiers are at liberty to abandon at pleasure and with impunity, and whose orders notwithstanding are scarce ever disputed: so true it is, that amongst a people who are guided by reason, and inspired with sentiments of honour and love for their country, independence is not destructive of subordination; and, that a free and voluntary obedience is that on which we can always rely with the greatest certainty. Moreover, the qualities requisite are, that he be fortunate, of undoubted courage, and perfectly disinterested. It is no miracle, that a person possessed of such eminent qualities should be obeyed.

The women have the chief authority amongst all the nations of the Huron language; if we except the Iroquois canton of Onneyouth, in which it is in both sexes alternately. But if this be their lawful constitution, their practice is seldom agreeable to it. In fact, the men never tell the women any thing they would have to be kept secret; and rarely any affair of consequence is communicated to them, though all is done in their name, and the chiefs are no more than their lieutenants. What I have told your Grace of the grandmother of the hereditary chief of the Hurons of the Narrows, who could never obtain a missionary for her own town, is a convincing proof that the real authority of the women is very small: I have been however assured, that they always deliberate first on whatever is proposed in council; and that they afterwards give the result of their deliberation to the chiefs, who make the report of it to the general council, composed of the elders; but in all probability this is done only for form's sake, and with the restrictions I have already mentioned. The warriors likewise consult together, on what relates to their particular province, but can conclude nothing of importance which concerns the nation or town; all being subject to the examination and controul of the council of elders, who judge in the last resource.

It must be acknowledged, that proceedings are carried on in these assemblies with a wisdom and a coolness, and a knowledge of affairs, and I may add generally with a probity, which would have done honour to the areopagus of Athens, or to the senate of Rome, in the most glorious days of those republics: the reason of this is, that nothing is resolved upon with precipitation; and that those violent passions, which have so much disgraced the politics even of Christians, have never prevailed amongst the Indians over the public good. . . .

Each tribe has an orator in every town, which orators are the only persons who have a liberty to speak in the public councils and general assemblies: they always speak well and to the purpose. Besides this natural eloquence, and which none who are acquainted with them will dispute, they have a perfect knowledge of the interests of their employers, and an address in placing the best side of their own cause in the most advantageous light, which nothing can exceed. On some occasions, the women have an orator, who speaks in their name, or rather acts as their interpreter.

A New England Captivity

MARY ROWLANDSON, 1681

Charles H. Lincoln, ed., *The Narratives of the Indian Wars, 1675–1699* (New York: Charles Scribner's Sons, 1913), pp. 149–52, 158–61.

The most famous account of Indian captivity was written by Mary Rowlandson (ca. 1637–1710), a middle-aged minister's wife from Lancaster, Massachusetts. Taken during a Narragansett raid on her town in 1676, during King Philip's War—a failed effort by New England tribes to regain the land they had lost to the Puritans—Mary Rowlandson spent almost twelve weeks among her captors. Accompanying them on twenty "removes" (journeys) through northern New England, she covered about 150 miles on foot, until she finally was ransomed near her own village. She described this event in detail in her narrative.

A devout Puritan, Mary Rowlandson viewed her captivity as a test of faith. Convinced that God seemed to "order all things for his own holy ends," she analyzed her experience by seeking signs of divine favor. Puritan ministers, similarly, saw her "redemption" as a sign of God's favor toward the colonists' cause.

Mary Rowlandson was captured along with her six-year-old daughter, who soon died of a wound. Shortly after her capture, Mary Rowlandson's services were appropriated by one of the three wives of Quinnipin, a Narragansett chief who had participated in the raid on Lancaster. Resenting her status as a "servant," Mary Rowlandson especially resented her Indian mistress, Weetamoo, known to the English as Squaw-Sachem of the Pocasset, a sister-in-law of King Philip and one of his strategic allies during the war. A running theme in Rowlandson's captivity narrative is her ongoing battle with the formidable Weetamoo. Another theme is her continual hunger, which she staved off by begging and scrounging, as well as by trading items that she sewed or knitted. (Her Indian captors, it should be noted, were at this point in a desperate state of disarray and constantly on the move, as they attempted to both flee and fight their English enemies.) A third theme is Mary Rowlandson's attitude toward the Indians, whom she often regards as "murtherous wretches" and "ravenous beasts."

Sometimes she offers evidence to support this view and sometimes contrary evidence, of various acts of fairness or generosity.*

A final and paramount theme of the narrative is Mary Rowlandson's efforts to discern the will of God: why, for instance, did God enable the Indian enemy to survive and inflict injury on the English? Despite such questions, she managed to retain her faith throughout her ordeal. A clever and resourceful hostage, Mary Rowlandson proved outstanding as an expositor. Her vivid captivity narrative, first published in Boston in 1681, went through more than thirty editions and reached a huge audience over the decades. The following segments come from the latter part of the narrative, when the opportunity arises for her ransom by the colonists. Here, Mary Rowlandson describes the process of her "redemption," considers the Indians' survival techniques, and ponders some puzzling aspects of her captivity.

The Eighteenth Remove

We took up our packs and along we went, but a wearisome day I had of it. As we went along I saw an English-man stript naked, and lying dead upon the ground, but knew not who it was. Then we came to another Indian Town, where we stayed all night. In this Town there were four English Children, Captives; and one of them my own Sisters. I went to see how she did, and she was well, considering her Captive-condition. I would have tarried that night with her, but they that owned her would not suffer it. Then I went into another Wigwam, where they were boyling Corn and Beans, which was a lovely sight to see, but I could not get a taste thereof. Then I went to another Wigwam, where there were two of the English Children; the Squaw was boyling Horses feet, then she cut me off a little piece, and gave one of the English Children a piece also. Being very hungry I had quickly eat up mine, but the Child could not bite it, it was so tough and sinewy, but lay sucking, gnawing, chewing and slabbering of it in the mouth and hand, then I took it of the Child, and eat it my self, and savoury it was to my taste. Then I may say as Job, Chap. 6, 7, *The things that my soul refused to touch, are as my sorrowfull meat.* Thus the Lord made that pleasant refreshing, which another time would have been an abomination. Then I went home to my mistresses Wigwam; and they told me I disgraced my master with begging, and if I did so any more, they would knock me in head: I told them, they had as good knock me in head as starve me to death.

---

*Rowlandson's response to her Indian captors is examined in Mitchell R. Breitweiser, *American Puritanism and the Defense of Mourning: Religion, Grief, and Ethnology in Mary Rowlandson's Captivity Narrative* (Madison, WI: University of Wisconsin Press, 1991).

The Nineteenth Remove

They said, when we went out, that we must travel to Wachuset this day. But a bitter weary day I had of it, travelling now three dayes together, without resting any day between. At last, after many weary steps, I saw Wachuset hills, but many miles off. Then we came to a great Swamp, through which we travelled, up to the knees in mud and water, which was heavy going to one tyred before. Being almost spent, I thought I should have sunk down at last, and never gat out; but I may say, as in Psal. 94. 18, *When my foot slipped, thy mercy, O Lord, held me up.* Going along, having indeed my life, but little spirit, Philip, who was in the Company, came up and took me by the hand, and said, Two weeks more and you shal be Mistress again. I asked him, if he spake true? he answered, Yes, and quickly you shal come to your master again; who had been gone from us three weeks. After many weary steps we came to Wachuset, where he was: and glad I was to see him. He asked me, When I washt me? I told him not this month, then he fetcht me some water himself, and bid me wash, and gave me the Glass to see how I lookt; and bid his Squaw give me something to eat: so she gave me a mess of Beans and meat, and a little Ground-nut Cake. I was wonderfully revived with this favour shewed me, Psal. 106. 46, *He made them also to be pittied, of all those that carried them Captives.*

My master had three Squaws, living sometimes with one, and sometimes with another one, this old Squaw, at whose Wigwam I was, and with whom my Master had been those three weeks. Another was Wattimore,* with whom I had lived and served all this while: A severe and proud Dame she was, bestowing every day in dressing her self neat as much time as any of the Gentry of the land: powdering her hair, and painting her face, going with Neck-laces, with Jewels in her ears, and Bracelets upon her hands: When she had dressed her self, her work was to make Girdles of Wampom and Beads. The third Squaw was a younger one, by whom he had two Papooses. By that time I was refresht by the old Squaw, with whom my master was, Wettimores Maid came to call me home, at which I fell a weeping. Then the old Squaw told me, to encourage me, that if I wanted victuals, I should come to her, and that I should ly there in her Wigwam. Then I went with the maid, and quickly came again and lodged there. The Squaw laid a Mat under me, and a good Rugg over me; the first time I had any such kindness shewed me. I understood that Wettimore thought, that if she should let me go and serve with the old Squaw, she would be in danger to loose, not only my service, but the redemption-pay also. And I was not a little glad to hear this; being by it raised in my hopes, that in Gods due time there would be an end of this sorrowfull hour. Then came an Indian, and asked me to knit him three pair of Stockins, for which I had a Hat, and a silk Handkerchief. Then another asked me to make her a shift, for which she gave me an Apron.

Then came Tom and Peter,† with the second Letter from the Council, about the Captives. Though they were Indians, I gat them by the hand, and burst out into tears; my heart was so full that I could not speak to them; but recovering my self, I asked them how my husband did, and all my friends and acquaintance? they said, They are

---

*Weetamoo, to whom Mary Rowlandson refers as Wattimore or Wettimore.

†Two Christian Indians who conducted the negotiations for Mrs. Rowlandson's ransom.

all very well but melancholy. They brought me two Biskets, and a pound of Tobacco. The Tobacco I quickly gave away; when it was all gone, one asked me to give him a pipe of Tobacco, I told him it was all gone; then began he to rant and threaten. I told him when my Husband came I would give him some: Hang him Rogue (sayes he) I will knock out his brains, if he comes here. And then again, in the same breath they would say, That if there should come an hundred without Guns, they would do them no hurt. So unstable and like mad men they were. So that fearing the worst, I durst not send to my Husband, though there were some thoughts of his coming to Redeem and fetch me, not knowing what might follow. For there was little more trust to them then to the master they served. When the Letter was come, the Saggamores met to consult about the Captives, and called me to them to enquire how much my husband would give to redeem me, when I came I sate down among them, as I was wont to do, as their manner is: Then they bade me stand up, and said, they were the General Court.* They bid me speak what I thought he would give. Now knowing that all we had was destroyed by the Indians, I was in a great strait: I thought if I should speak of but a little, it would be slighted, and hinder the matter; if of a great sum, I knew not where it would be procured: yet at a venture, I said Twenty pounds, yet desired them to take less; but they would not hear of that, but sent that message to Boston, that for Twenty pounds I should be redeemed.

The Twentieth Remove

. . . The night before the Letter came from the Council, I could not rest, I was so full of feares and troubles, God many times leaving us most in the dark, when deliverance is nearest: yea, at this time I could not rest night nor day. The next night I was overjoyed, Mr. Hoar being come, and that with such good tidings. The third night I was even swallowed up with the thoughts of things, *viz.* that ever I should go home again; and that I must go, leaving my Children behind me in the Wilderness; so that sleep was now almost departed from mine eyes.

On Tuesday morning they called their General Court (as they call it) to consult and determine, whether I should go home or no: And they all as one man did seemingly consent to it, that I should go home; except Philip, who would not come among them.

But before I go any further, I would take leave to mention a few remarkable passages of Providence, which I took special notice of in my afflicted time.

1. Of the fair opportunity lost in the long March, a little after the Fort-fight, when our English Army was so numerous, and in pursuit of the Enemy, and so near as to take several and destroy them: and the Enemy in such distress for food, that our men might track them by their rooting in the earth for Ground-nuts, whilest they were flying for their lives. I say, that then our Army should want Provision, and be forced to leave their pursuit and return homeward: and the very next week the Enemy came upon our Town, like Bears bereft of their whelps, or so many ravenous Wolves, rending us and our Lambs to death. But what shall I say? God seemed to leave his

---

*The title of the colonial legislature of Massachusetts Bay.

People to themselves, and order all things for his own holy ends. *Shal there be evil in the City and the Lord hath not done it? They are not grieved for the affliction of Joseph, therefore shal they go Captive, with the first that go Captive.* It is the Lords doing, and it should be marvelous in our eyes.

2. I cannot but remember how the Indians derided the slowness, and dulness of the English Army, in its setting out. For after the desolations at Lancaster and Medfield, as I went along with them, they asked me when I thought the English Army would come after them? I told them I could not tell: It may be they will come in May, said they. Thus did they scoffe at us, as if the English would be a quarter of a year getting ready.

3. Which also I have hinted before, when the English Army with new supplies were sent forth to pursue after the enemy, and they understanding it, fled before them till they came to Baquaug River, where they forthwith went over safely: that that River should be impassable to the English. I can but admire to see the wonderfull providence of God in preserving the heathen for farther affliction to our poor Countrey. They could go in great numbers over, but the English must stop: God had an over-ruling hand in all those things.

4. It was thought, if their Corn were cut down, they would starve and dy with hunger: and all their Corn that could be found, was destroyed, and they driven from that little they had in store, into the Woods in the midst of Winter; and yet how to admiration did the Lord preserve them for his holy ends, and the destruction of many still amongst the English! strangely did the Lord provide for them; that I did not see (all the time I was among them) one Man, Woman, or Child, die with hunger.

Though many times they would eat that, that a Hog or a Dog would hardly touch; yet by that God strengthned them to be a scourge to his People.

The chief and commonest food was Ground-nuts: They eat also Nuts and Acorns, Harty-choaks, Lilly roots, Ground-beans, and several other weeds and roots, that I know not.

They would pick up old bones, and cut them to pieces at the joynts, and if they were full of wormes and magots, they would scald them over the fire to make the vermine come out, and then boile them, and drink up the Liquor, and then beat the great ends of them in a Morter, and so eat them. They would eat Horses guts, and ears, and all sorts of wild Birds which they could catch: also Bear, Vennison, Beaver, Tortois, Frogs, Squirrels, Dogs, Skunks, Rattle-snakes; yea, the very Bark of Trees; besides all sorts of creatures, and provision which they plundered from the English. I can but stand in admiration to see the wonderful power of God, in providing for such a vast number of our Enemies in the Wilderness, where there was nothing to be seen, but from hand to mouth. Many times in a morning, the generality of them would eat up all they had, and yet have some forther supply against they wanted. It is said, Psal. 81. 13, 14, *Oh, that my People had hearkned to me, and Israel had walked in my wayes, I should soon have subdued their Enemies, and turned my hand against their Adversaries.* But now our perverse and evil carriages in the sight of the Lord, have so offended him, that instead of turning his hand against them, the Lord feeds and nourishes them up to be a scourge to the whole Land.

5. Another thing that I would observe is, the strange providence of God, in turning things about when the Indians was at the highest, and the English at the lowest. I was with the Enemy eleven weeks and five dayes, and not one Week passed without the fury of the Enemy, and some desolation by fire and sword upon one place or other. They mourned (with their black faces) for their own lossess, yet triumphed and rejoyced in their inhumane, and many times devilish cruelty to the English. They would boast much of their Victories; saying, that in two hours time they had destroyed such a Captain, and his Company at such a place; and such a Captain and his Company in such a place; and such a Captain and his Company in such a place: and boast how many Towns they had destroyed, and then scoffe, and say, They had done them a good turn, to send them to Heaven so soon. Again, they would say, This Summer that they would knock all the Rogues in the head, or drive them into the Sea, or make them flie the Countrey: thinking surely, Agag-like, *The bitterness of Death is past.* * Now the Heathen begins to think all is their own, and the poor Christians hopes to fail (as to man) and now their eyes are more to God, and their hearts sigh heaven-ward: and to say in good earnest, *Help Lord, or we perish:* When the Lord had brought his people to this, that they saw no help in any thing but himself: then he takes the quarrel into his own hand: and though they had made a pit, in their own imaginations, as deep as hell for the Christians that Summer, yet the Lord hurll'd them selves into it. And the Lord had not so many wayes before to preserve them, but now he hath as many to destroy them.

But to return again to my going home, where we may see a remarkable change of Providence: At first they were all against it, except my Husband would come for me; but afterwards they assented to it, and seemed much to rejoyce in it; some askt me to send them some Bread, others some Tobacco, others shaking me by the hand, offering me a Hood and Scarfe to ride in; not one moving hand or tongue against it. Thus hath the Lord answered my poor desire, and the many earnest requests of others put up unto God for me. In my travels an Indian came to me, and told me, if I were willing, he and his Squaw would run away, and go home along with me: I told him No: I was not willing to run away, but desired to wait Gods time, that I might go home quietly, and without fear. And now God hath granted me my desire. O the wonderfull power of God that I have seen, and the experience that I have had: I have been in the midst of those roaring Lyons, and Salvage Bears, that feared neither God, nor Man, nor the Devil, by night and day, alone and in company: sleeping all sorts together, and yet not one of them ever offered me the least abuse of unchastity to me, in word or action. Though some are ready to say, I speak it for my own credit; But I speak it in the presence of God, and to his Glory.

---

*A reference to 1 Samuel 15:32 in the Old Testament.

Life Among the Seneca

Mary Jemison, 1824

James E. Seaver, *A Narrative of the Life of Mary Jemison*, 5th ed. (Buffalo, NY: Printing House of Matthews and Warren, 1877), pp. 60–63, 67, 69–70, 72–74.

Unlike Mary Rowlandson, the eighteenth-century captive Mary Jemison developed an extremely favorable view of her captors. Born en route from Ireland to Philadelphia in 1743, Jemison was captured as a teenager in 1755, by an attack party of six Indians and four Frenchmen, when she was living with her family on a farm on the Pennsylvania frontier. All of her immediate relatives were killed. She remained with the Seneca Iroquois tribe, to whom her captors sold or gave her, for the rest of her life. Many other "white Indians" who were captured as children refused, as Mary did, to return to white society.

A Seneca family adopted Mary Jemison as a replacement for a young male relation who had been killed recently. While in captivity, she learned the Indians' language and formed relationships with her adoptive relatives ("I was ever considered and treated by them as a real sister"). Married briefly to a Delaware Indian, Sheninjee, and then to another Indian, Hiakatoo, Mary Jemison had seven children. Over the decades, she turned down many offers of freedom from captivity, preferring to remain with her family and tribe. After the Revolution, when Mary Jemison was about eighty years old and living on a reservation in western New York state, she was interviewed by a minister, James E. Seaver, who published her story in 1824. Many subsequent editions appeared. In the excerpts that follow, Mary Jemison describes her experience of adoption, expresses her contentment with Indian society, and compares the work roles of Indian women to those of white women.

It was my happy lot to be accepted for adoption. At the time of the ceremony I was received by the two squaws to supply the place of their brother in the family; and I was ever considered and treated by them as a real sister, the same as though I had been born of their mother.

During the ceremony of my adoption, I sat motionless, nearly terrified to death at the appearance and actions of the company, expecting every moment to feel their vengeance, and suffer death on the spot. I was, however, happily disappointed; when at the close of the ceremony the company retired, and my sisters commenced employing every means for my consolation and comfort.

Being now settled and provided with a home, I was employed in nursing the children, and doing light work about the house. Occasionally, I was sent out with the Indian hunters, when they went but a short distance, to help them carry their game. My situation was easy; I had no particular hardships to endure. But still, the recollection of my parents, my brothers and sisters, my home, and my own captivity, destroyed my happiness, and made me constantly solitary, lonesome, and gloomy.

My sisters would not allow me to speak English in their hearing; but remembering the charge that my dear mother gave me at the time I left her, whenever I chanced to be alone I made a business of repeating my prayer, catechism, or something I had learned, in order that I might not forget my own language. By practicing in that way, I retained it till I came to Genesee flats, where I soon became acquainted with English people, with whom I have been almost daily in the habit of conversing.

My sisters were very diligent in teaching me their language; and to their great satisfaction, I soon learned so that I could understand it readily, and speak it fluently. I was very fortunate in falling into their hands; for they were kind, good-natured women; peaceable and mild in their dispositions; temperate and decent in their habits, and very tender and gentle toward me. I have great reason to respect them, though they have been dead a great number of years. . . .

Not long after the Delawares came to live with us at Wiishto, my sisters told me that I must go and live with one of them, whose name was Sheninjee. Not daring to cross them or disobey their commands, with a great degree of reluctance I went; and Sheninjee and I were married according to Indian custom.

Sheninjee was a noble man—large in stature, elegant in his appearance, generous in his conduct, courteous in war, a friend to peace, and a lover of justice. He supported a degree of dignity far above his rank, and merited and received the confidence and friendship of all the tribes with whom he was acquainted. Yet, Sheninjee was an Indian. The idea of my spending my days with him at first seemed perfectly irreconcilable to my feelings; but his good nature, generosity, tenderness, and friendship toward me, soon gained my affection; and, strange as it may seem, I loved him! To me he was ever kind in sickness, and always treated me with gentleness; in fact, he was an agreeable husband and a comfortable companion. We lived happily together till the time of our final separation, which happened two or three years after our marriage. . . .

I had then been with the Indians four summers and four winters, and had become so far accustomed to their mode of living, habits, and dispositions, that my anxiety to get away, to be set at liberty and leave them, had almost subsided. With them was my home; my family was there, and there I had many friends to whom I was warmly attached in consideration of the favors, affection, and friendship with which they had uniformily treated me from the time of my adoption. Our labor was not severe; and that of one year was exactly similar in almost every respect to that of the others, without that endless variety that is to be observed in the common labor of the white people. Notwithstanding the Indian women have all the fuel and bread to procure, and the cooking to perform, their task is probably not harder than that of white women, who have those articles provided for them; and their cares certainly are not half as numerous, nor as great. In the summer season, we planted, tended, and harvested our corn, and generally had all our children with us; but had no master to oversee or drive us, so that we could work as leisurely as we pleased. We had no plows on the Ohio, but performed the whole process of planting and hoeing with a small tool that resembled, in some respects, a hoe with a very short handle.

We pursued our farming business according to the general custom of Indian women, which is as follows: In order to expedite their business, and at the same time enjoy each other's company, they all work together in one field, or at whatever job they may have on hand. In the spring, they choose an old active squaw to be their driver and overseer, when at labor, for the ensuing year. She accepts the honor, and they consider themselves bound to obey her.

When the time for planting arrives, and the soil is prepared, the squaws are assembled in the morning, and conducted into a field, where each plants one row. They then go into the next field and plant once across, and so on till they have gone through the tribe. If any remains to be planted, they again commence where they did at first (in the same field) and so keep on till the whole is finished. By this rule, they perform their labor of every kind, and every jealousy of one having done more or less than another is effectually avoided. . . .

Our cooking consisted in pounding our corn into samp or hominy, boiling the hominy, making now and then a cake and baking it in the ashes, and in boiling or roasting our venison. As our cooking and eating utensils consisted of a hominy block and pestle, a small kettle, a knife or two, and a few vessels of bark or wood, it required but little time to keep them in order for use.

Spinning, weaving, sewing, stocking knitting, and the like, are arts which have never been practiced in the Indian tribes generally. After the revolutionary war, I learned to sew, so that I could make my own clothing after a poor fashion; but I have been wholly ignorant of the application of the other domestic arts since my captivity. In the season of hunting, it was our business, in addition to our cooking, to bring home the game that was taken by the Indians, dress it, and carefully preserve the eatable meat, and prepare or dress the skins. Our clothing was fastened together with strings of deerskin, and tied on with the same.

In that manner we lived, without any of those jealousies, quarrels, and revengeful battles between families and individuals, which have been common in the Indian tribes since the introduction of ardent spirits among them.

The use of ardent spirits among the Indians, and a majority of the attempts which have been made to civilize them by the white people, have constantly made them worse and worse; increased their vices, and robbed them of many of their virtues, and will ultimately produce their extermination. I have seen, in a number of instances, the effects of education upon some of our Indians, who were taken, when young, from their families, and placed at school before they had had an opportunity to contract many Indian habits, and there kept till they arrived to manhood; but I have never seen one of those but was an Indian in every respect after he returned. Indians must and will be Indians, in spite of all the means that can be used to instruct them in the arts and sciences.

One thing only marred my happiness while I lived with them on the Ohio, and that was the recollection that I once had tender parents, and a home that I loved. Aside from that recollection, which could not have existed had I been taken in my infancy, I should have been contented in my situation. Notwithstanding all that has been said against the Indians, in consequence of their cruelties to their enemies— cruelties that I have witnessed and had abundant proof of—it is a fact that they are naturally kind, tender, and peaceable toward their friends, and strictly honest; and that those cruelties have been practiced only upon their enemies, according to their idea of justice.

Chapter 2

Well-Ordered Families

I n the English colonies, the family was the basic agency of settlement, a fundamental economic unit, and an all-important social institution, whose health affected the larger community. As Puritan minister Cotton Mather declared in 1699, "*Well-Ordered Families* naturally produce a *Good Order* in other *Societies*." Well-ordered or otherwise, colonial families depended on women, who thereby played a vital role in the colonization process—not least of all by producing an abundant supply of younger colonists. Similarly, patterns of family organization shaped women's experience in colonial society.

During the seventeenth century, family life in New England and the Chesapeake offered startling contrasts. In early Virginia and Maryland, where women were few and life spans short, the family was at best a fragile institution. Of the 75,000 white people who immigrated to the Chesapeake between 1630 and 1680, about half to three-fourths were indentured servants who arrived as single individuals, and eighty percent of these servants were men. A harsh environment and rampant disease—such as typhoid, dysentery, and malaria—shortened their life expectancies. Four out of ten newcomers died within six years; men could expect to live to age forty-eight and women to forty-four, about a decade less than in England. Since sex ratios were so imbalanced, few male servants found wives. Those servants who married did so relatively late, after their indentures had expired, and their unions tended to be brief. Late in the century, for instance, half of the spouses in one Maryland county became widows or widowers within seven years. Of the four children such couples were likely to have, two died in childhood. Survivors, if orphaned, were left in the care of siblings, step-parents, or neighbors, or were put out to service by orphans' courts.

The minority of women who arrived in the early Chesapeake, almost all of whom were indentured servants, derived several benefits from these unfortunate circumstances. Since they were so vastly outnumbered by men, they had a far greater choice of spouse than did poor, young women left behind in England. In addition, Chesapeake husbands often left widows in control of their estates, a more liberal arrangement than practiced elsewhere. But such gains resulted mainly from the region's demographic defects—scarcity of women and high mortality. Only at the end of the century, when a native-born population arose—with greater immunity to disease and an equal number of males and females—did life spans lengthen and sex ratios become more balanced. The Chesapeake population soon began to grow primarily through natural increase, not through immigration, and family life achieved greater stability.

New England colonists, in contrast, had advantages over both their southern neighbors and kinfolk left in England. Unlike the Chesapeake newcomers, many immigrants to New England arrived in family units, which seemed to flourish there. A healthy environment, with access to land, adequate food, and relative scarcity of disease (compared to the Chesapeake) provided long life expectancies of sixty-five for men and slightly less for women. Marriages might have lasted a quarter of a century, large families were commonplace, and eighty percent of infants survived to maturity. Reproducing themselves at a prodigious rate, New Englanders created their own labor force and never depended on either indentured servants or slaves. Also, unlike their Chesapeake counterparts, they achieved a balanced sex ratio quite quickly, which facilitated their population boom.

Since Puritans viewed the family as the foundation of social order, New England authorities actively promoted family harmony. Feuding spouses, fractious offspring, and unruly servants might be hauled into court for disrupting domestic peace. Abuse of a wife by her husband was prohibited by law in 1672, "unless it be in his own defense upon her assaulte." Violence against husbands was similarly proscribed. Finally, in an effort to ensure domestic peace—as well as to keep women and children off the public dole—the Puritan colonies allowed divorce (see Chapter 4), thereby enabling some aggrieved spouses, usually deserted wives, to remarry and create new homes.

By the end of the seventeenth century, the demographic chasm between New England and the Chesapeake began to narrow, and the colonial population surged. New groups of immigrants, including the Scots-Irish, Germans, and other Europeans, infused the middle colonies and settled the southern backcountry. Still, from the late seventeenth century in the North and after 1720 in the South, native-born colonists outnumbered immigrants. By the time of the Revolution, only one out of ten colonists was foreign-born. These statistics, plus the high proportion of young people in the colonial population, testify to the family's achievement as an agency of colonization.

During the eighteenth century, women's family roles settled into a common pattern, allowing for variations of region and rank. The colonial family had its own hierarchy, as described by Puritan minister Benjamin Wadsworth in his famous sermon, "The Well-Ordered Family." Like the state, the family had one ruler at the helm, who supported and controlled other family members. Wives were subordinate to husbands by law (see Chapter 4), and daughters took second place to sons: For instance, they typically received smaller inheritances than their brothers did. Colonial women strove for success in their "station," centered around housewifery and especially child-rearing. On average, colonial women were married two years younger than their English counterparts and had six or seven children, compared to the four or five born to English wives.

As the eighteenth-century colonies became more like England, patterns of social stratification developed. A colonial elite gradually emerged on the eastern seaboard; kinship ties and family connections formed the basis of social rank and political influence. In New England and in the middle colonies, the elite included successful farmers and merchants. In the Chesapeake, it comprised planters who had large landholdings and who passed their wealth and prestige to their heirs. Well-off colonists, notably in the South, imitated the customs of the English gentry. In all regions, elite families built large houses in the Georgian style, imported English fashions and furnishings, and cultivated manners that would distinguish themselves from the lower orders.

Women of the eighteenth-century colonial elite—represented in the documents that follow by Eliza Lucas Pinckney of South Carolina and Esther Edwards Burr of Massachusetts and New Jersey—were on the cutting edge of social change. Often literate and educated, by colonial standards, they had less experience with household drudgery than did the typical colonial woman. Instead, they served as companions to their husbands and as domestic managers, child-rearers, and transmitters of values. They also maintained religious connections, established social contacts, engaged in friendships with peers, and laid the foundation for the tradition of the "Republican Mother" that emerged during the revolutionary era.

The ideal of the "well-ordered family," publicized in colonial sermons and advice literature, is reflected in the writings of these privileged women, as well as in the documents that reflect the lives of more ordinary women. But this ideal was honored in the breach as well as in practice. Many colonists evaded it, or, as was more likely to be the case for women, it eluded them. Impoverished widows, deserted wives, and illegitimate offspring dot the colonial landscape. Instances of sexual misconduct—adultery, fornication, and bastardy— as well as infanticide and other "enormous sinnes" fill colonial ledgers. Court records document marital frictions, domestic discord, and miserable unions. Southern newspapers contained almost as many advertisements for runaway wives as for fugitive servants and slaves. Still, for white women in the English colonies, the family, whatever its liabilities, remained the most important social institution, the major source of social gratification, and the locus of productive work.

Husbands and Wives

BENJAMIN WADSWORTH, 1712

Benjamin Wadsworth, *A Well-Ordered Family,* 2nd ed. (Boston, 1719),
pp. 22–59.

Colonial advice literature provides a guide to shared ideals, although
not necessarily to actual conduct. The most widespread form of advice
literature was probably the sermon, which could be given to several
audiences and circulated in print. The most fluent advice givers were
undoubtedly Puritan ministers, who instructed their congregations
twice a week on theological, political, and social matters. Few sermons
have achieved the posthumous popularity of *A Well-Ordered Family* by
Boston minister and one-time Harvard president, Benjamin Wadsworth. In this sermon, Wadsworth describes not the reality of Puritan
family life but the desirable type of relationships toward which his
congregation and reading audience might strive.

The ideal family, in Wadsworth's view, had several components.
First, like a society, the family was organized on hierarchical lines, with
the father at the head. Second, marital relations, while based on love,
affection, mutuality, and piety, were part of the power structure. Patriarchal "government" and wifely "obedience" were obligatory.
Third, although wives held only second place in the family hierarchy,
they were not without power, since they could exert authority over
children and servants. Finally, the ideal family was a harmonious unit,
one that would not offend God by disruptive outbursts. Here, *order* is
the pivotal word. As Benjamin Wadsworth proclaimed in another
sermon, "Tho *Tyranny* is burdensome and *hateful*, yet it's counted a
smaller evil than meer *Anarchy*, and confusion."* Domestic order, like
civil order, rested upon submission to authority and acceptance of a
degree of "Tyranny." The following segment of the sermon discusses
the mutual obligations of spouses.

---

*Benjamin Wadsworth, *Rulers Feeding and Guiding Their People,* cited in Harry S. Stout, *The New England
Soul: Preaching and Religious Culture in Colonial New England* (New York: Oxford University Press,
1986), p. 134.

Doctrine

Christians should endeavor to please and glorify God, in whatever capacity or relation they sustain.

Under this doctrine, my design is (by God's help) to say something about relative duties, particularly in families. I shall therefore endeavor to speak as briefly and plainly as I can about: (1) family prayer; (2) the duties of husbands and wives; (3) the duties of parents and children; (4) the duties of masters and servants. . . .

About the Duties of Husbands and Wives

Concerning the duties of this relation we may assert a few things. It is their duty to dwell together with one another. Surely they should dwell together; if one house cannot hold them, surely they are not affected to each other as they should be. They should have a very great and tender love and affection to one another. This is plainly commanded by God. This duty of love is mutual; it should be performed by each, to each of them. When, therefore, they quarrel or disagree, then they do the Devil's work; he is pleased at it, glad of it. But such contention provokes God; it dishonors Him; it is a vile example before inferiors in the family; it tends to prevent family prayer.

As to outward things. If the one is sick, troubled, or distressed, the other should manifest care, tenderness, pity, and compassion, and afford all possible relief and succor. They should likewise unite their prudent counsels and endeavors, comfortably to maintain themselves and the family under their joint care.

Husband and wife should be patient one toward another. If both are truly pious, yet neither of them is perfectly holy, in such cases a patient, forgiving, forbearing spirit is very needful. You, therefore, that are husbands and wives, do not aggravate every error or mistake, every wrong or hasty word, every wry step as though it were a willfully designed intolerable crime; for this would soon break all to pieces. . . .

The husband's government ought to be gentle and easy, and the wife's obedience ready and cheerful. The husband is called the head of the woman. It belongs to the head to rule and govern. Wives are part of the house and family, and ought to be under the husband's government. Yet his government should not be with rigor, haughtiness, harshness, severity, but with the greatest love, gentleness, kindness, tenderness that may be. Though he governs her, he must not treat her as a servant, but as his own flesh; he must love her as himself.

Those husbands are much to blame who do not carry it lovingly and kindly to their wives. O man, if your wife is not so young, beautiful, healthy, well-tempered, and qualified as you would wish; if she did not bring a large estate to you, or cannot do so much for you, as some other women have done for their husbands; yet she is your wife, and the great God commands you to love her, not be bitter, but kind to her. What can be more plain and expressive than that?

Those wives are much to blame who do not carry it lovingly and obediently to their own husbands. O woman, if your husband is not as young, beautiful, healthy, so well-tempered, and qualified as you could wish; if he has not such abilities, riches, honors, as some others have; yet he is your husband, and the great God commands you to love, honor, and obey him. Yea, though possibly you have greater abilities of mind than he has, was of some high birth, and he of a more common birth, or did bring more estate, yet since he is your husband, God has made him your head, and set him above you, and made it your duty to love and revere him.

Parents should act wisely and prudently in the matching of their children. They should endeavor that they may marry someone who is most proper for them, most likely to bring blessings to them.

Evangelical Child-Rearing

SUSANNA WESLEY, 1732

Eliza Clarke, *Susanna Wesley*, (Boston: Roberts Brothers, 1886), pp. 48–55, reprinted in Philip J. Greven, Jr., ed., *Child-Rearing Concepts, 1628–1861: Historical Sources* (Itasca, IL: F. E. Peacock, 1973), pp. 46–51.

For New England Puritans, child-rearing constituted a major part of family life. As Calvinists, Puritans adhered to the doctrine of infant depravity, which purported that children were born ignorant of all good and disposed to do evil. Parents were responsible not merely for their upbringing but for their very souls. In Puritan households, children were trained to be obedient and submissive, and their subjugation began in infancy. A major goal of Puritan parents was to break the child's will, a prerequisite for the youngster's ultimate submission to God.* Indeed, as John Wesley, the founder of Methodism, explained, "The will of a parent is to a little child in the place of the will of God."

For child-rearing advice, Wesley depended upon his own mother, Susanna Wesley (1699–1742), an Anglican of nonconformist background who lived in Lincolnshire, an area in eastern England from which many Puritans migrated to New England. Susanna Wesley raised a large family according to strict principles. In a 1732 letter to her son, who was about to set forth as an itinerant preacher in the new colony of Georgia, Susanna Wesley explained how she inculcated obedience among her offspring. Sadly, when fire destroyed the family home, the children were dispersed to neighboring households, where they apparently picked up some bad habits. Still, Susanna contended, parental authority prevailed. The mode of child-rearing that Susanna Wesley set forth with such clarity was commonplace among New England Puritans.

---

*For further discussion of Puritan child-rearing, see Edmund Morgan, *The Puritan Family: Religion and Domestic Relations in Seventeenth Century New England* (New York: Harper & Row, 1966), chaps. 3–4; John Demos, *A Little Commonwealth: Family Life in Plymouth Colony* (New York: Oxford University Press, 1970), chaps. 6, 9; Philip J. Greven, *The Protestant Temperament* (Knopf, 1977), chaps. 2–3; and David Hackett Fischer, *Albion's Seed: Four British Folkways in America* (New York: Oxford University Press, 1989), pp. 99–102.

Epworth, July 24,1732

Dear Son,

According to your desire, I have collected the principal rules I observed in educating my family.

The children were always put into a regular method of living, in such things as they were capable of, from their birth; as in dressing and undressing, changing their linen, etc. The first quarter commonly passes in sleep. After that they were, if possible, laid into their cradle awake, and rocked to sleep, and so they were kept rocking till it was time for them to awake. This was done to bring them to a regular course of sleeping, which at first was three hours in the morning and three in the afternoon: afterwards two hours, till they needed none at all. When turned a year old (and some before) they were taught to fear the rod and to cry softly, by which means they escaped abundance of correction which they might otherwise have had; and that most odious noise of the crying of children was rarely heard in the house, but the family usually lived in as much quietness as if there had not been a child among them.

As soon as they were grown pretty strong they were confined to three meals a day. At dinner their little table and chairs were set by ours, where they could be overlooked: and they were suffered to eat and drink [small beer] as much as they would, but not to call for anything. If they wanted aught they used to whisper to the maid that attended them, who came and spake to me; and as soon as they could handle a knife and fork they were set to our table. They were never suffered to choose their meat, but always made to eat such things as were provided for the family. Mornings they always had spoon meat; sometimes at nights. But whatever they had, they were never permitted at those meals to eat of more than one thing, and of that sparingly enough. Drinking or eating between meals was never allowed, unless in case of sickness, which seldom happened. Nor were they suffered to go into the kitchen to ask anything of the servants when they were at meat: if it was known they did so, they were certainly beat, and the servants severely reprimanded. At six, as soon as family prayer was over, they had their supper; at seven the maid washed them, and beginning at the youngest, she undressed and got them all to bed by eight, at which time she left them in their several rooms awake, for there was no such thing allowed of in our house as sitting by a child till it fell asleep.

They were so constantly used to eat and drink what was given them, that when any of them was ill there was no difficulty in making them take the most unpleasant medicine; for they durst not refuse it, though some of them would presently throw it up. This I mention to show that a person may be taught to take anything, though it be never so much against his stomach.

In order to form the minds of children, the first thing to be done is to conquer their will and bring them to an obedient temper. To inform the understanding is a work of time, and must with children proceed by slow degrees, as they are able to bear it; but the subjecting the will is a thing that must be done at once, and the sooner the better; for by neglecting timely correction they will contract a stubbornness and obstinacy which are hardly ever after conquered, and never without using such severity as would be as painful to me as to the child. In the esteem of the world they pass for kind and indulgent whom I call cruel parents, who permit their children to get habits which they know must be afterwards broken. Nay, some are so stupidly fond as in sport to teach their children to do things which in a while after they have severely beaten them for doing. When a child is corrected it must be conquered, and this will be no hard matter to do, if it be not grown headstrong by too much indulgence. And when the will of a child is totally subdued, and it is brought to revere and stand in awe of the parents, then a great many childish follies and inadvertencies may be passed by. Some should be overlooked and taken no notice of, and others mildly reproved; but no wilful transgression ought ever to be forgiven children without chastisement less or more, as the nature of circumstances of the case may require. I insist on the conquering of the will of children betimes, because this is the only strong and rational foundation of a religious education, without which both precept and example will be ineffectual. But when this is thoroughly done, then a child is capable of being governed by the reason and piety of its parents till its own understanding comes to maturity, and the principles of religion have taken root in the mind.

I cannot yet dismiss the subject. As self-will is the root of all sin and misery, so whatever cherishes this in children insures their after wretchedness and irreligion: whatever checks and mortifies it, promotes their future happiness and piety. This is still more evident if we further consider that religion is nothing else than doing the will of God and not our own; that the one grand impediment to our temporal and eternal happiness being this self-will, no indulgence of it can be trivial, no denial unprofitable. Heaven or hell depends on this alone; so that the parent who studies to subdue it in his child works together with God in the renewing and saving a soul. The parent who indulges it does the Devil's work; makes religion impracticable, salvation unattainable, and does all that in him lies to damn his child body and soul forever.

Our children were taught as soon as they could speak, the Lord's prayer, which they were made to say at rising and at bedtime constantly; to which, as they grew bigger, were added a short prayer for their parents, and some collects, a short catechism, and some portion of Scripture, as their memories could bear. They were very early made to distinguish the Sabbath from other days, before they could well speak or go. They were as soon taught to be still at family prayers, and to ask a blessing immediately after, which they used to do by signs, before they could kneel or speak.

They were quickly made to understand they might have nothing they cried for, and instructed to speak handsomely for what they wanted. They were not suffered to ask even the lowest servant for aught without saying "Pray give me such a thing;" and the servant was chid if she ever let them omit that word.

Taking God's name in vain, cursing and swearing, profanity, obscenity, rude, ill-bred names, were never heard among them; nor were they ever permitted to call each other by their proper names without the addition of brother or sister.

There was no such thing as loud playing or talking allowed of, but every one was kept close to business for the six hours of school. And it is almost incredible what may be taught a child in a quarter of a year by a vigorous application, if it have but a tolerable capacity and good health. Kezzy excepted, all could read better in that time than the most of women can do as long as they live. Rising out of their places, or going out of the room, was not permitted except for good cause; and running into the yard, garden, or street, without leave, was always esteemed a capital offence.

For some years we went on very well. Never were children in better order. Never were children better disposed to piety, or in more subjection to their parents, till that fatal dispersion of them after the fire into several families. In these they were left at full liberty to converse with servants, which before they had always been restrained from, and to run abroad to play with any children, bad or good. They soon learned to neglect a strict observance of the Sabbath, and got knowledge of several songs and bad things which before they had no notion of. That civil behavior which made them admired when they were at home by all who saw them was in a great measure lost, and a clownish accent and many rude ways were learned which were not reformed without some difficulty.

When the house was rebuilt, and the children all brought home, we entered on a strict reform; and then was begun the system of singing psalms at beginning and leaving school, morning and evening. Then also that of a general retirement at five o'clock was entered upon, when the eldest took the youngest that could speak, and the second the next, to whom they read the psalms for the day and a chapter of the New Testament, as in the morning they were directed to read the psalms and a chapter in the Old Testament, after which they went to their private prayers, before they got their breakfast or came into the family.

There were several by-laws observed among us. I mention them here because I think them useful.

First, it had been observed that cowardice and fear of punishment often lead children into lying till they get a custom of it which they cannot leave. To prevent this, a law was made that whoever was charged with a fault of which they were guilty, if they would ingenuously confess it and promise to amend should not be beaten. This rule prevented a great deal of lying, and would have done more if one in the family would have observed it. But he could not be prevailed upon, and therefore was often imposed on by false colors and equivocations which none would have used but one, had they been kindly dealt with; and some in spite of all would always speak truth plainly.

Second, that no sinful action, as lying, pilfering at church or on the Lord's Day, disobedience, quarrelling, etc., should ever pass unpunished.

Third, that no child should be ever chid or beat twice for the same fault, and that if they amended they should never be upbraided with it afterwards.

Fourth, that every signal act of obedience, especially when it crossed upon their own inclinations, should be always commended, and frequently rewarded according to the merits of the case.

Fifth, that if ever any child performed an act of obedience, or did anything with an intention to please, though the performance was not well, yet the obedience and intention should be kindly accepted, and the child with sweetness directed how to do better for the future.

Sixth, that propriety [the rights of property] be invariably preserved, and none suffered to invade the property of another in the smallest matter, though it were of the value of a farthing or a pin, which they might not take from the owner without, much less against, his consent. This rule can never be too much inculcated on the minds of children; and from the want of parents and governors doing it as they ought, proceeds that shameful neglect of justice which we may observe in the world.

Seventh, that promises be strictly observed; and a gift once bestowed, and so the right passed away from the donor, be not resumed, but left to the disposal of him to whom it was given, unless it were conditional, and the condition of the obligation not performed.

Eighth, that no girl be taught to work till she can read very well; and that she be kept to her work with the same application and for the same time that she was held to in reading. This rule also is much to be observed, for the putting children to learn sewing before they can read perfectly is the very reason why so few women can read fit to be heard, and never to be well understood.

Susanna Wesley

A Quaker Family

WILLIAM PENN, 1682

William Penn, "To Gulielma Penn and Children," in Jean R. Soderlund, ed., *William Penn and the Founding of Pennsylvania, 1680–1684* (Philadelphia: University of Pennsylvania Press, 1983), doc. 39, pp. 165–167.

Among Quakers (members of the Society of Friends) who settled the middle colonies, as among their Puritan neighbors to the north, child-rearing methods held great importance. For Friends as for Puritans, evangelism began at home: The family transmitted religious and community values to youngsters. As did the Puritans, Quakers valued domestic order. Ideally, in the Quaker household, anger would be suppressed, aggression contained, obedience encouraged, and self-will denied. Unlike their Puritan counterparts, Quaker parents sought to impose domestic peace through love. Siblings, for instance, were urged to treat one another with affection.

Quaker beliefs about family organization and child-rearing are evident in a letter written by William Penn (1644–1718), founder of Pennsylvania, to his wife, Gulielma, in 1682. Penn was about to depart on a trip to America, while Gulielma, then pregnant, remained in England with three young children. Penn had much advice to impart to his wife. Clearly, in the Quaker family as in other seventeenth-century English families, the father served as the major rule maker and source of authority. William Penn's advice, in this instance, covered both the short term (his expected absence) and the long-term possibility of permanent separation, should he never return.

To Gulielma, William Penn recommended diligence in worship, insulation from worldly influence, and frugal management ("live low and sparingly until my debts are paid"). Urging her to impose the Quaker mode of loving order on the household, Penn was most specific in his suggestions about child-rearing. The youngsters, then ages seven, four, and one, were, among other things, to obey their mother, cultivate love for one another, be educated at home, acquire habits of industry, and avoid "earthly" (non-Quaker) spouses. Still more detailed advice follows in messages (not printed here) to the children themselves about their future conduct in life. Of most interest in Penn's letter—in his very language—is the distinctive Quaker fusion of order, obedience, and authority with peace, love, and harmony.

Warminghurst, 4 August 1682

My Dear Wife and Children

My love, that sea, nor land, nor death itself can extinguish or lessen toward you, most endearedly visits you with eternal embraces and will abide with you forever. And may the God of my life watch over you and bless you and do you good in this world and forever. Some things are upon my spirit to leave with you, in your respective capacities, as I am to one a husband, and to the rest a father, if I should never see you more in this world.

My dear wife, remember thou was the love of my youth, and much the joy of my life, the most beloved, as well as most worthy, of all my earthly comforts. And the reason of that love was more thy inward than thy outward excellences (which yet were many). God knows, and thou knows it. I can say it was a match of providence's making, and God's image in us both was the first thing and the most amiable and engaging ornament in our eyes. Now I am to leave thee, and that without knowing whether I shall ever see thee more in this world. Take my counsel into thy bosom and let it dwell with thee in my stead while thou lives.

1st. Let the fear of the Lord, and a zeal and love to His glory, dwell richly in thy heart, and thou will watch for good over thyself and thy dear children and family, that no rude, light, or bad thing be committed, else God will be offended, and He will repent Himself of the good He intends thee and thine.

2dly. Be diligent in meetings of worship and business; stir up thyself and others herein; it is thy day and place. And let meetings be kept once a day in the family to wait upon the Lord, who has given us much time for ourselves. And my dearest, to make thy family matters easy to thee, divide thy time, and be regular. It is easy and sweet. Thy retirement will afford thee to do it, as in the morning to view the business of the house and fix it as thou desire, seeing all be in order, that by thy counsel all may move, and to thee render an account every evening. The time for work, for walking, for meals, may be certain, at least as near as may be. And grieve not thyself with careless servants. They will disorder thee. Rather pay them and let them go if they will not be better by admonitions. This is best, to avoid many words, which I know wound the soul and offend the Lord.

3dly. Cast up thy income and see what it daily amounts to, by which thou may be sure to have it in thy sight and power to keep within compass. And I beseech thee to live low and sparingly till my debts are paid; and then enlarge as thou see it convenient. Remember thy mother's example when thy father's public-spiritedness had worsted his estate (which is my case). I know thou loves plain things and are averse to the pomp of the world, a nobility natural to thee. I write not as doubtful, but to quicken thee, for my sake, to be more vigilant herein, knowing that God will bless thy care, and thy poor children and thee for it. My mind is wrapped up in a saying of thy father's, "I desire not riches, but to owe nothing." And truly that is wealth; and more than enough to live is a snare attended with many sorrows.

I need not bid thee be humble, for thou are so; nor meek and patient, for it is much of thy natural disposition. But I pray thee, be often in retirement with the Lord and guard against encroaching friendships. Keep them at arm's end; for it is giving away our power, aye, and self too, into the possession of another. And that which might seem engaging in the beginning, may prove a yoke and burden too hard and heavy in the end. Wherefore keep dominion over thyself, and let thy children, good meetings, and Friends be the pleasure of thy life.

4thly. And now, my dearest, let me recommend to thy care my dear children, abundantly beloved of me as the Lord's blessings and the sweet pledges of our mutual and endeared affection. Above all things, endeavor to breed them up in the love of virtue and that holy plain way of it which we have lived in, that the world, in no part of it, get into my family. I had rather they were homely than finely bred, as to outward behavior; yet I love sweetness mixed with gravity, and cheerfulness tempered with sobriety. Religion in the heart leads into this true civility, teaching men and women to be mild and courteous in their behavior, an accomplishment worthy indeed of praise.

5thly. Next, breed them up in a love one of another. Tell them, it is the charge I left behind me, and that it is the way to have the love and blessing of God upon them; also what his portion is who hates, or calls his brother fool. Sometimes separate them, but not long; and allow them to send and give each other small things, to endear one another with once more. I say, tell them it was my counsel, they should be tender and affectionate one to another.

For their learning, be liberal. Spare no cost, for by such parsimony all is lost that is saved; but let it be useful knowledge, such as is consistent with truth and godliness, not cherishing a vain conversation or idle mind, but ingenuity mixed with industry is good for the body and mind too. I recommend the useful parts of mathematics, as building houses or ships, measuring, surveying, dialing, navigation, etc.; but agriculture is especially in my eye. Let my children be husbandmen and housewives. It is industrious, healthy, honest, and of good example, like Abraham and the holy ancients who pleased God and obtained a good report. This leads to consider the works of God and nature, of things that are good and divert the mind from being taken up with the vain arts and inventions of a luxurious world. It is commendable in the princes of Germany, and [the] nobles of that empire, that they have all their children instructed in some useful occupation. Rather keep an ingenious person in the house to teach them than send them to schools, too many evil impressions being commonly received there. Be sure to observe their genius and don't cross it as to learning. Let them not dwell too long on one thing, but let their change be agreeable, and all their diversions have some little bodily labor in them.

When grown big, have most care for them; for then there are more snares both within and without. When marriageable, see that they have worthy persons in their eye, of good life and good fame for piety and understanding. I need no wealth but sufficiency; and be sure their love be dear, fervent, and mutual, that it may be happy for them. I choose not they should be married into earthly covetous kindred. And of cities and towns of concourse beware. The world is apt to stick close to those who have lived and got wealth there. A country life and estate I like best for my children. I prefer a decent mansion of a hundred pounds per annum before ten thousand pounds in London, or suchlike place, in a way of trade.

In fine, my dear, endeavor to breed them dutiful to the Lord, and His blessed light, truth, and grace in their hearts, who is their Creator, and His fear will grow up with them. Teach a child (says the wise man) the way thou will have him to walk; and when he is old, he will not forget it. Next, obedience to thee their dear mother; and that not for wrath, but for conscience sake. [Be] liberal to the poor, pitiful to the miserable, humble and kind to all. And may my God make thee a blessing and give thee comfort in our dear children; and in age, gather thee to the joy and blessedness of the just (where no death shall separate us) forever.

To Improve in Every Virtue

ELIZA PINCKNEY, 1750S

Harriott Horry Ravenel, *Eliza Pinckney* (New York: Charles Scribner's Sons, 1896), pp. 115–118.

Upper-class women in the eighteenth-century colonies were pioneers in shaping modern "middle-class" roles of the nineteenth century. Relieved of the household labor that dominated most women's lives in colonial times, they began to devote themselves solely to family affairs—to their obligations as wives, parents, and mistresses of the home. A prime example was Eliza Lucas Pinckney (1722–1793) of South Carolina, whose career was characterized by ambition and achievement. Daughter of George Lucas, a prominent English colonist in Antigua in the British West Indies, Eliza was born there and was educated in England. In 1739, George Lucas moved his family to Carolina. As a teenager, Eliza ran her father's three Carolina plantations while George Lucas returned to the West Indies to fight the French. She won a local reputation for her successful experiments planting indigo. In 1744 she married an older widower, Charles Pinckney, an important South Carolinian. Pinckney owned seven plantations, served on the governor's council, and was also the first English-trained lawyer in the colony. The couple soon had three children, to whose upbringing Eliza devoted the rest of her life, especially after Pinckney's death in 1758.

Each year in the early 1750s, when her children were young, Eliza wrote out a series of resolutions on her birthday, each list renewing the vows made in the last resolutions. She later stored away the list of annual resolves in a bundle labeled "papers belonging to myself onely." The resolutions, which follow, provided a pragmatic guide to conduct—a type of conduct quite similar to that which Eliza urged upon her younger siblings and offspring. Eliza Pinckney valued rationality and moderation. Opposed to religious enthusiasm and imbued with enlightenment values, she hoped, for instance, to "subdue every vice and improve in every virtue," to achieve a balance between extravagance and covetousness, to combine generosity with economy, and, overall, to "endeavor after a due medium." Significantly, Eliza enumerated all of the roles at which she planned to excel—as daughter, wife, mother, sister, mistress, friend, and "lover of all mankind."

I am resolved by the Grace of God asisting me to keep these resolutions which I have frequently made, and do now again renew.

I am resolved to believe in God; that he is, and is a rewarder of all that diligently seek him. To believe firmly and constantly in all his attributes, etc, etc. I am resolved to believe in him, to fear him and love him with all the powers and faculties of my soul. To keep a steady eye to his commands, and to govern myself in every circumstance of life by the rules of the Gospel of Christ, whose disciple I profess myself, and as such will live and dye.

I am resolved by the Divine will, not to be anxious or doubtful, not to be fearful of any accident or misfortune that may happen to me or mine, not to regard the frowns of the world, but to keep a steady upright conduct before my God, and before man, doing my duty and contented to leave the event to God's Providence.

I am resolved by the same Grace to govern my passions, to endeavour constantly to subdue every vice and improve in every virtue, and in order to this I will not give way to any the least notions of pride, haughtiness, ambition, ostentation, or contempt of others. I will not give way to Envy, Ill will, Evil speaking, ingratitude, or uncharitableness in word, in thought, or in deed, or to passion or peavishness, nor to Sloath or Idleness, but to endeavour after all the contrary Virtues, humility, charity, etc, etc, and to be always usefully or innocently imploy'd.

I am resolved not to be luxurious or extravagant in the management of my table and family on the one hand, nor niggardly and covetous, or too anxiously concern'd about it on the other, but to endeavour after a due medium; to manage with hospitality and Generosity as much as is in our power, to have always plenty with frugality and good Economy.

To be decent but frugal in my own Expences.

To be charitably disposed to all mankind.

I am resolved by the Divine Assistance to fill the several Stations wherein Providence has placed me to the best advantage.

To make a good wife to my dear Husband in all its several branches; to make all my actions Corrispond with that sincere love and Duty I bear him. To pray for him, to contribute all in my power to the good of his Soul and to the peace and satisfaction of his mind, to be careful of his Health, of his Interests, of his children, and of his Reputation; to do him all the good in my power; and next to my God, to make it my Study to please him.

I am resolved to make a good child to my Mother; to do all I am able to give her comfort and make her happy.

I am resolved to be a good Mother to my children, to pray for them, to set them good examples, to give them good advice, to be careful both of their souls and bodys, to watch over their tender minds, to carefully root out the first appearing and budings of vice, and to instill piety, Virtue and true religion into them; to spair no paines or trouble to do them good; to correct their Errors whatever uneasiness it may give myself; and never omit to encourage every Virtue I may see dawning in them.

I am resolved to make a good Sister both to my own and my Husband's brothers and sisters, to do them all the good I can, to treat them with affection, kindness, and good-manners, to do them all the good I can, etc, etc.

I am resolved to make a good Mistress to my Servants,* to treat them with humanity and good nature; to give them sufficient and comfortable clothing and Provisions, and all things necessary for them. To be careful and tender of them in their sickness, to reprove them for their faults, to Encourage them when they do well, and pass over small faults; not to be tyrannical peavish or impatient towards them, but to make their lives as comfortable as I can.

I am resolved to be a sincere and faithful friend wherever I profess'd it, and as much as in me lies an agreable and innocent companion, and a universal lover of all mankind.

All these resolutions by God's assistance I will keep to my life's end.

So help me O My God! Amen.

Mem^{dum}   Read over this dayly to assist my memory as to every particular contained in this paper. *Mem.* Before I leave my Chamber recolect in Gen.[1] the business to be done that day.

---

*Slaves.

Tied Hand and Foot

ESTHER BURR, 1756–1757

Carol F. Karlsen and Laurie Crumpacker, eds., *The Journal of Esther Edwards Burr, 1754–1757* (New Haven, CT: Yale University Press, 1984), pp. 189–196, 257.

Esther Edwards Burr, another member of the colonial elite, was, like Eliza Pinckney, notable for her male relatives. Born in 1732, Esther was the third child of Congregational Minister Jonathan Edwards of Northampton, Massachusetts, a leader of the Great Awakening. This fervent outburst of religious revivalism spread throughout the English colonies in the 1730s and 1740s. When Esther Edwards was twenty, she married the Reverend Aaron Burr, a Presbyterian minister and president of the College of New Jersey (later Princeton). Esther Burr soon became the mother of two. Her son, another Aaron Burr, was elected vice-president in 1800, when Jefferson won the presidency. Perhaps best known for his duel with Alexander Hamilton in 1804, Aaron Burr, Jr., was subsequently involved in a notorious scheme to undermine the nation. He was tried for and acquitted of treason in 1807. In her familial capacity, therefore, Esther Edwards Burr linked eighteenth-century revivalism with early national politics.

In women's history, however, Esther Edwards Burr is famous for her own achievement—an extraordinary journal, which she kept from 1754 to 1757 and sent in a series of letters to her best friend, Sally Prince of Boston. Sally responded with a similar journal. For those reared in the Puritan tradition, a journal was usually a private device for self-scrutiny, but here it served as a form of joint testimony to piety and friendship. The two young women, both minister's daughters, shared an intense commitment to evangelical religion and to one another. Admiration for the other's piety formed the basis of their mutual devotion. Through the interchange of journals, they shared their daily experiences, compared religious struggles, reviewed one another's spiritual progress, and strove to serve as exemplars of religious faith.* Esther Burr sent her last letter in the fall of 1757, just before her husband died. She herself died the following spring of

---

*The relationship between the two young women is discussed in the introduction to Karlsen and Crumpacker, eds., *The Journal of Esther Edwards Burr.*

an unidentified illness, shortly after receiving an inoculation for smallpox.

The following excerpts from the journal for 1756 concern Esther Burr's experience in the early (and, indeed, final) years of her marriage, when she was a young housewife and mother, first in Newark and then in Princeton. She was then caring for her daughter Sally, a toddler whom she raised with Puritan severity; giving birth to Aaron, who subsequently became a handful (a "little dirty, Noisy boy . . . sly and mischievous," Esther told Sally Prince in her final journal entry); and fulfilling her community responsibilities as the wife of a prominent man. Reverend Burr, who played the dominant role in the household, was often away from home on college business, as he was at the time of Aaron's birth. Throughout these segments—as throughout the entire journal—Esther Burr reveals her commitment to her calling, "matrymony" and motherhood. She displays her habitual religious enthusiasm and reiterates her devotion to Sally Prince, to whom she makes several suggestions about an ongoing courtship. In the final excerpt, from 1757, Esther Burr describes her encounter with a Princeton tutor, John Ewing, who derides the very idea of female friendship—an ironic touch in this exemplary display of attachment between friends.

Letter No. 20

[March 26, 1756]

I am my dear Fidelia yet alive and allowed to tell you so—I have been able to write nothing from the time of my confinement till now which is the 26 day of March and 7 weeks since I was delivered of a Son. *

I have but a short time to write and but little strength, tho' I have good will enough to write a quire of paper. I shall endevour to say as much as I can in as few words as possible for reasons that I shall give—I conclude you have received long since a Letter from Mr Burr informing you that I was unexpectedly delivered of a Son the sixth of Febry. Had a fine time altho' it pleased God in infinite wisdom so to order it that Mr Burr was from home. . . .

It seemd very gloomy when I found I was actually in Labour to think that I was, as it were, destitute of Earthly friends—No Mother—No Husband and none of my petecular friends that belong to this Town, they happening to be out of Town—but O my dear God was all these relations and more then all to me in the Hour of my

---

*Aaron Burr, Jr., 1756–1836; third vice-president of the United States.

distre[ss]. Those words in Psalms were my support and comfort thro' the whole. *They that trust in the Lord shall be as Mount Zion that cannot be mooved but abideth for ever*—and these also, *As the Mountains are found about Jerusalem so is the Lord to them that put their trust in him,* or words to that purpose—I had a very quick and good time—A very good layingin till about 3 weeks, then I had the Canker very bad, and before I had recovered of that my little Aaron (for so we call him) was taken very sick so that for some days we did not expect his life—he has never been so well since tho' he is comfortable at present.

I have my self got a very bad Cold and very soar Eyes which makes it very diffecult for me to write atall. Some times I am almost blind.

For my comfort and refreshment I received your No. 18. not long since. I think I never was so glad to have a Letter from you in my life. It did me good like a medicen. O that the Lord would reward you for all your kindness of this nature to me an unworthy Worm of the dust—With your Letter I received Mr Imries printed one,* for which I am much obliged, but cant now tell my thoughts but only this that I wish and pray that he may prove a True Prophet. O how comfortable is the thought that the glorious day is so near—O my friend this puts new life into me, altho' perhaps *you and I* may loose our lives in the cause—O that we may be fitted for the fiery Tryal and come forth as gold seven times tryed—I can write no [more] now for I am almost blind and have not time. I must lay down my pen a little while to recover my sight.

I wrote you word in my last which I sent away abut the 23 of Janry that Mr Burr was determined to see Boston this spring, but their is a meeting of the Trustees at the time he intended to set out so he is undetermined at present whether he can go or not, but I shall do all in my Power to remove all objections that seem to be in the way. If Mr Burr does go he will be at Boston by the latter end of April, and I hope, and beg, and pray that you will not fail to return with him. He depends upon it as I do fully.

I have seen Mr Prentice's [Minister Thomas Prentice's] sermon on the Earthquake and am greatly pleased with it—I want to know if Mr Prince has printed any thing on the same subject—I have also just seen Mr Byles's Poems.† I think they are the best that ever he printed.

I am greatly rejoiced to hear that the spirit of God is mooving amongst you and at the Eastward of you. I have no such good News to tell you, for never did People this way so give them selves up to wickedness. Sin has grown aparently within a year in this place—what our young people are coming to God only knows, but it seems as if nothing but swift distruction was in reserve for them—I can add no more—you have my heart is all I can say—Pleas to give my Duty to your honoured parents, and kind Love to all the Sisterhood and Miss Jenny.

> *I am, my dear friend, your most*
> *affectionate Friend and Sister*
> *Esther Burr*

Mr Burr sends Duty and Love etc.

---

*A book by the Reverend David Imrie.
†Minister Mather Byles's book of poems about natural disasters.

Letter No. 21

Newark, [April 3, 1756]
Saturday

Dear, very dear Friend

Not long since I sent you No. 20 by a cupple of schollars that belong to Newberry.* It was a broken business but the best and most I could send for reasons I have given you in it.

I have not been able to write since till now by reason of soar Eyes and a Presbytry that have been setting here this week—I am thro' the goodness of God on the recovery tho' tis by slow degrees—My little Son has got to be quite hearty—Ah—I thought it would be so if I began to write. Here comes somebody to *Pester* and to *Hinder*.

[April 4, 1756]
Sabbath

One A.M. Heard a stranger (Mr Burr and Mr Brainerd are both gone, Mr Burr is at Princeton) from those words of the Prophet Isiah, *Who hath believed our report*, and to whom has the Arm of the Lord been revealed—a good discourse. I am unwell so could not go out P.M.

[April 5, 1756]
Monday

Extreamly ingaged—what with prepareng for my spining frolick, and what with fixing out Sukey Shippen I am almost crazy. Mr Burr is just come home and has brought Doct Shippen with him for his Daughter, so goodby.

[April 6–9, 1756]

Teusday, Wednsday, Thursday and Fryday all devoted to spinning folks.

[April 10, 1756]
Saturday

I am almost wore up to the hub with so much spinning frolick, and poor Mr Burr for his part is quite sick with a bad cold and soar Eyes. Tis a general distemper throu the Town—I cant write I feel so quere—P.M. Governor and Lady made us a vissit.

---

*Students at the college who came from Newbury, Massachusetts.

[April 11, 1756]
Sabbath

A.M. Mr Burr preached to our young People. P.M. Mr Brainerd preached from those Words in Proverbs, *And thou mourn at the last saying how have I hated instruction etc.*, a very proper subject to inforce what was said in the forenoon—but Alas for me I feel dead under all.

[April 12, 1756]
Monday

Here are these Newbury scholars come back again and are not a going this 10 day. I would not care if you had my scrawls, and what is worse then all is they have left em at York locket up in a Chest, and I cant send it till they go.

Today Mr Burr is to set out for Princeton to the synod and Trustee-meeting and whether he is to go to Boston or not is quite unsertain till his return, and then if he does go he will set out the day after he comes home.

[April 13, 1756]
Teusday Night

I thought to have said a deal to you to day but behold the Court sets in Town, and I have had company from erly in the Morn till late in the Eve, and now I write with the Son at the Brest—When I had but one Child my hands were tied, but now I am tied hand and foot. (How I shall get along when I have got 1/2 dzn. or 10 Children I cant devise.) I have no help in the House except what is in our Ketchin and you know what that is—our young women are all Ladies and its beneath them to go out.

[April 14, 1756]
Wednsday Eve

I had just seated my self for writing this P.M. and company comes in—Tis *vacancy*, and I thought to have had a Vacancy as well as the scholars, but no such good luck for me. All I do say to you must be before Mr Burr comes home for he will be in such a hurry about geting away that I shall have hardly time to Breath—I cant help looking for you a little with Mr Potter and his Wife, but tis with fear and trembling—If you dont come this spring I shall dispare of ever seeing you in these parts, for if you M-a-r-r-y as I think you will before a nother spring I suppose we shall see no more of you in our world—Well tis a mighty strang piece of conduct of that sertain Gentleman—I wonder what ails him—I surspect he is bashfull. You must e'ne do the business for him—Tackle up your Chair and go a Courting, and bring the matter to an Issue, [so] that a body may know what to depend on—Its vastly uncomfortable to be hung up between the Heavens and Earth as it were Gibbeted—if Mr Burr goes to Boston he will do somthing in the affair you may be sertain, for you know he loves to be poking about matches.

(As I stept out of the Room Miss Sally gets this and has rumpled it [so] that tis not fit to send but you will excuse it—I scolded at her but she said she was a going to write.)

If Mr Burr goes I shall trouble you with some business. The things I want I will put on a piece of paper by it self—As for privacies I hant many and I guss I shant have time to write em so I will let 'em alone till you come. . . .

I have very lately heard good news from Long Island that their is an awakning in some parts their—O what a happy people should we be if God's Providences should Rouse us out of the deep sleep we seem to be fallen into. I cant but hope Mr Imrie is in the right. O how reviveing the thought—I long to see what he has Published. I am almost impatient about it.

[April 15, 1756]
Thursday Eve

Very affecting is Mr Alexanders death. He died very suddenly—he was you know a profesed Deiest and so he died, and now he knows how much he was out of the way— tis a remarkable time for sudden deaths. A Man at Elizabeth Town droped down in the street and expired in about an hour after. The sorrowfull accident that happened in York bay you saw in the news—their is Three persons in this place that lay upon the point of death and the Doc's cant tell what ails them, tho one of them seems to have the numb-palsy.

I have had company to dine with me to day and company at Tea—O I had almost forgot to tell you that Nancy Smith is married to Mr Hait. She will [be] a nigh neighbour to us at Princeton—*Cousen Joney Powel* her Brother is (I hear) very jellous of his Wife—just like the Man ant it? My Eyes are so very weak that I cant see to write any more so a good-nights rest to you.

[April 16, 1756]
Fryday Morn

I have heard from the synod that their is not a quorum of the Trustees so I guss Mr Burr will not go to Boston which will be a very great desappointment to me—I never had such a desire to have Mr Burr go anywhere in my life as I have to have him go to Boston this spring—You will never come here again if he dont go soon I am per- suaded—but for all I'll hope for the best till he comes home which will be today if the weather dont prevent which is not very good.

I saw Mrs Brown, Parson Browns Wife, and she desired her kind regards to you. She is a good creture, is often inquiring about you and speaking in your Praise.

11 o'Clock received No. 19 by Mrs Potter—I have read the Private papers and hant patience to read any more till I vent a little by writing—I never was so near being angry at you in my life. If you was her[e] I should sertainly Cuff you—Indeed my dear I think you are a little Proud—I have incouraged you in it two under a notion of

nobleness of mind, and greatness of soul but to be plain you have carried matter of this sort two far. *You have stood upon points two much, and two long,* and I should have told you so before if I knew as much as I do now. (You must pardon my severity for I am two warm about it but I cant bare to see you *murder your self*—it would have been better that Cats-paw had done it of the two.) Why you would not have the Man act like a fool would you? Well why will you oblige him to either become a fool or give up the affair, and without desighn in you two for you dont chuse nither—I am almost two vext to write—I wonder in the name of honesty what business you had to run a way time after time when you knew he was a coming—You may repent it when it is two late—for I dont know of such another match on all accounts not on all our shore.

You should consider my dear that he does not, nor cant know the reasons of your conduct—tis most likly that he thinks that you dislike him, or elce that you are a Mortal proud creture, which must sink you in his opinnion, and may lay a foundation for unhapyness all your days after Marriage for my dear no man likes a woman the better for being shy when she means the very thing she pretends to be shy off—not that you have ronged anybody this way but I think you are in a fair way to rong your self in such a way and can never be retrieved—Why should you cheat your self out of happynes all your days for the sake of a few nonsencical points—but I have done enough and two much. Tis time to tell what I think you should do for tis not right to blame and not tell how to amend, and hear I shall wait for Mr Burr [to] return and if he concludes not to go, shall consult togather and give you the best advice we can. If he goes I shall have no time to write any more but he [will] say all better then I can write.

P.M. 4 o'Clock

Now my zeal is a little coold I feel as I do after whping Sally pretty hard, and am affraid I have whiped her more then was needfull.

I have read all you was so good as to send me except the sermon of Mr Princes for which I am much obliged.

Every Letter I have from you raises my esteem of you and increases my love to you—their is the very soul of a friend in all you write—You cant think how those private papers make me long to see you. Tis impossible for one that has no better faculty of communicating then I have, to give you any Idea how full of those *petecular matters* I feel. I am like working Liquor, Bottled up that will sertainly burst unless it has vent soon, but I'll try to keep in till Mr Burr comes home.

With pleasure I have read the two Letters you sent me. They have raised the Ladies in my esteem greatly. They are handsomly wrote and what is more the spirit of a friend may be seen plainly—I hope Mrs Donaldson is happy in her Husband. She is a deserving Lady and I think if I am any judge she has more of a turn for friendship then Miss Kitty altho Kitty is a friendly creture.

Sally can speak quite plain—and Little Aaron begins to smile and play. He is a fine quiet Child—I never before knew you had such an aversion to marrying a Minnister. Well all helps along the main thing—I feel like a natural Fool. I cant gather my thoughts no more then I can gather the Wind that now blows. I am swallowed up in that same affair—the little Boy crys and I must mind him for all matrymony.

[April 17, 1756]
Saturday Morn

Mr Burr came home last night and today is to set out for Boston, preaches at Newyork tomorrow so hant time for anything but just to desire my kind Love to the freemasons—Mr Burr will say and do all about a sertain affair that is propor—To my great grief you tell me not to expect you this spring so I give you up for this World, but hope to meet you in a better. Till then I remain your most affectionat and sincere Friend, and as a token of it send you my best friend for a time, and hope after he has done you some good turns (this good turn is to see you married) you will return him to his and your

Esther Burr

April the 17, 1756

Pleas to procure for me the following things—

> 6 Fann Mounts—Two good ones for Ivory [sticks?].
> To Black and Wh[i]te—and two Wh[i]te ones.
> ¼ lb. of Gumarrabick and one large Pencil and one small.
> One Dz of Short Cake-pans.
> My Milk-pot altered to some shape or other.
> A pair of Correl Beeds.
> Some Codfish.
> Patterns of Caps not your airy caps. . . .
> Send me word how to cut Ruffles and handkercheifs.
> Send word how they make Gounds. . . .

Letter No. 22

[April 12, 1757]
Teusday A.M. 10 o'Clock

I have had a smart Combat with Mr Ewing about our sex—he is a man of good parts and Lerning but has mean thoughts of Women—he began the dispute in this Manner. Speaking of Miss Boudanot I said she was a sociable friendly creture. A Gentleman seting by joined with me, but Mr Ewing says—*she and the Stocktons are full of talk about Friendship and society and such stuff—and made up a Mouth as if much disgusted*—I asked what he would have 'em talk about—whether he chose they should talk about fashions and dress—*he said things that they understood. He did not think women knew what Friendship was. They were hardly capable of anything so cool and rational as friendship*—(My Tongue, you know, hangs pretty loose, thoughts Crouded in—so I sputtered away for dear life.) You may Guss what a large field this speach opened for me—I retorted several severe things upon him before he had time to speak again. He Blushed and seemed confused. The Gentleman seting by said little

but when did speak it was to my purpose and we carried on the dispute for an hour—
I talked him quite silent. He got up and said your servant and went off—I dont know
that ever I meet with one that was so openly and fully in Mr [Pope's] sordid scheam—
One of the last things that he said was that he never in all his life knew or [heard] of a
woman that had a little more lerning then [. . .] but it made her proud to such a degree
that she was disgusfull [to] all her acquaintance. P.M. Made two vissits—came home
and found my Aaron very unwell and a bad purging. The Bloudy-Flux is in Town which
gives me concern. Two Children have died of it and several more sick of it.

An Abominable Wickedness

ABIGAIL BAILEY, 1815

Ethan Smith, ed., *Memoirs of Mrs. Abigail Bailey* (Boston: Samuel T. Armstrong, 1815), pp. 31–35, 39–46 passim.

When marriage collapsed and the "well-ordered family" failed, colonial women faced severe problems. Married women had no independent legal existence, property rights, or control over their children (see Chapter 4). Divorce was rarely available, legal separations difficult to obtain, and financial support even more difficult to secure. Some of these problems are illustrated in the story of Abigail Bailey of New Hampshire (1746–ca. 1815). Seeking a companion of "meek, peaceable temper," Abigail at 21 married, instead, Asa Bailey, a man of harsh character who within three years engaged in "improper conduct" with a female servant. Asa subsequently became a revolutionary war soldier, a farmer and landowner, and a town official. Abigail had seventeen children. After twenty-two years of marriage, she discovered, though she strove "to disbelieve the possibility of such a thing," that Asa had begun an incestuous relationship with one of their daughters.

The first sign of trouble was when Asa insisted on taking the daughter in question, alone, on a proposed trip to the Ohio territory, ostensibly to buy land. When Abigail realized what was afoot, she threw Asa out; after initial resistance, he appeared to agree to her demands for a property settlement. Asa then tricked Abigail into taking a trip to New York state, severing her from her relatives, and deserted her there. After Abigail made her way back to New Hampshire, an arduous journey, she had Asa arrested—though only with the aid of her brothers, who accompanied her to a justice of the peace. At last Asa agreed to a property settlement, whereupon Abigail dropped her original charge of incest. After Asa left town, she finally gained a "bill of divorcement," put her younger children out as apprentices, and, according to the editor of her memoirs, lived happily until about age seventy. Asa, however, married again in New York and reportedly met extreme poverty, disgrace, and misery.

Abigail's children agreed to have her memoirs made public after her death, "viewing the finger of Heaven in these distressing scenes." The minister who published the memoirs hoped to illustrate the "horrid cruelty of which man is capable" and the role of faith in surmounting such cruelty. To contemporary readers, Abigail's story illustrates the lack of protection that "feme covert" status provided, the difficulties that married women could face when disaster ensued, and the virtual powerlessness of wives over their children's welfare.* In the excerpt that follows, Abigail Bailey describes her discovery of the incestuous relationship and her reaction to it. Of interest is the aura of female helplessness that permeates this account of male misconduct. Note, for instance, Abigail's resentment when the abused daughter refuses to testify against her father, and the editor's footnote explaining why Abigail was reluctant to turn to the law for assistance.

I have already related that Mr. B. said he would take one of our sons, and one daughter, to wait on him in his distant tour, before he would take all the family. After he had talked of this for a few days, he said he had altered his plan; he would leave his son, and take only his daughter: he could hire what men's help he needed: his daughter must go and cook for him. He now commenced a new series of conduct in relation to this daughter, whom he selected to go with him, in order (as he pretended) to render himself pleasing and familiar to her, so that she might be willing to go with him, and feel happy: for though, as a father, he had a right to command her to go, yet (he said) he would so conduct toward her, as to make her cheerful and well pleased to go with him. A great part of the time he now spent in the room where she was spinning; and seemed shy of me, and of the rest of the family. He seemed to have forgotten his age, his honor, and all decency, as well as all virtue. He would spend his time with this daughter, in telling idle stories, and foolish riddles, and singing songs to her, and sometimes before the small children, when they were in that room. He thus pursued a course of conduct, which had the most direct tendency to corrupt young and tender minds, and lead them the greatest distance from every serious subject. He would try to make his daughter tell stories with him; wishing to make her free and sociable, and to erase from her mind all that fear and reserve, which he had ever taught his children to feel toward him. He had ever been sovereign, severe and hard with his children, and they stood in the greatest fear of him. His whole conduct, toward this daughter especially, was now changed, and became most disagreeable.

For a considerable time I was wholly at a loss what to think of his conduct, or what his wish or intentions could be. Had such conduct appeared toward any young woman beside his own young daughter, I should have had no question what he intended: but as it now was, I was loth to indulge the least suspicion of base design. His daily conduct forced a conviction upon my alarmed and tortured mind, that his designs were the most vile. All his tender affections were withdrawn from the wife of his youth, the mother of his children. My room was deserted, and left lonely. His care

---

*The editor of a recent edition of Abigail Bailey's memoir stresses the sustaining power of religious faith. See Ann Taves, ed., *Religion and Domestic Violence in Early New England: The Memoir of Abigail Abbot Bailey* (Bloomington: Indiana University Press, 1989).

for the rest of the family seemed abandoned, as well as all his attention to his large circle of worldly business. Every thing must lie neglected, while this one daughter engrossed all his attention.

Though all the conduct of Mr. B. from day to day, seemed to demonstrate my apprehension, that he was determined, and was continually plotting, to ruin this poor young daughter, yet it was so intolerably crossing to every feeling of my soul to admit such a thought, that I strove with all my might to banish it from my mind, and to disbelieve the possibility of such a thing. I felt terrified at my own thoughts upon the subject; and shocked that such a thing should enter my mind. But the more I labored to banish those things from my mind, the more I found it impossible to annihilate evident facts. Now my grief was dreadful. No words can express the agitations of my soul: From day to day they tortured me, and seemed to roll on with a resistless power. I was constrained to expect that he would accomplish his wickedness: And such were my infirmities, weakness and fears (my circumstances being very difficult) that I did not dare to hint any thing of my fears to him, or to any creature. This may to some appear strange; but with me it was then a reality. I labored to divert his mind from his follies, and to turn his attention to things of the greatest importance. But I had the mortification to find that my endeavors were unsuccessful.

I soon perceived that his strange conduct toward this daughter was to her very disagreeable. And she shewed as much unwillingness to be in the room with him, as she dared. I often saw her cheeks bedewed with tears, on account of his new and astonishing behavior. But as his will had ever been the law of the family, she saw no way to deliver herself from her cruel father. Such were her fears of him, that she did not dare to talk with me, or any other person, upon her situation: for he was exceedingly jealous of my conversing with her, and cautioning her. If I ever dropped words, which I hoped would put her upon her guard, or inquired the cause of her troubles, or what business her father had so much with her? if I was ever so cautious, he would find it out, and be very angry. He watched her and me most narrowly; and by his subtle questions with her, he would find out what I had said, during his absence. He would make her think I had informed him what I had said, and then would be very angry with me: so that at times I feared for my life. I queried with myself which way I could turn. How could I caution a young daughter in such a case? My thoughts flew to God for relief, that the Father of mercies would protect a poor helpless creature marked out for a prey; and turn the heart of a cruel father from every wicked purpose.

After a while Mr. B's conduct toward this daughter was strangely altered. Instead of idle songs, fawning and flattery, he grew very angry with her; and would wish her dead, and buried: and he would correct her very severely. It seems, that when he found his first line of conduct ineffectual, he changed his behavior, felt his vile indignation moved, and was determined to see what he could effect by tyranny and cruelty. He most cautiously guarded her against having any free conversation with me, or any of the family, at any time; lest she should expose him. He would forbid any of the children going with her to milking. If, at any time, any went with her, it must be a number; so that nothing could be said concerning him. He would not suffer her to go from home: I might not send her abroad on any occasion. Never before had Mr. B. thus confined her, or any of his children. None but an eye witness can conceive of the strangeness of his conduct from day to day, and of his plans to conceal his wickedness, and to secure himself from the light of evidence.*. . .

I clearly saw that Mr. B. entertained the most vile intentions relative to his own daughter. Whatever difficulty attended the obtaining of legal proof, yet no remaining doubt existed in my mind, relative to the existence of his wickedness: and I had no doubt remaining of the violence, which he had used; and hence arose his rage against her. It must have drawn tears of anguish from the eyes of the hardest mortals, to see the barbarous corrections, which he, from time to time, inflicted on this poor young creature; and for no just cause. . . .

None can describe the anguish of my heart on the beholding of such scenes. How pitiful must be the case of a poor young female, to be subjected to such barbarous treatment by her own father; so that she knew of no way of redress!

It may appear surprising that such wickedness was not checked by legal restraints. But great difficulties attend in such a case. While I was fully convinced of the wickedness, yet I knew not that I could make legal proof. I could not prevail upon this daughter to make known to me her troubles; or to testify against the author of them. Fear, shame, youthful inexperience, and the terrible peculiarities of her case, all conspired to close her mouth against affording me, or any one, proper information. My soul was moved with pity for her wretched case: and yet I cannot say I did not feel a degree of resentment, that she would not, as she ought, expose the wickedness of her father, that she might be relieved from him, and he brought to due punishment. But no doubt his intrigues, insinuations, commands, threats, and parental influence, let her to feel that it was in vain for her to seek redress.

My circumstances, and peculiar bodily infirmities, at that time, were such as to entitle a woman to the tenderest affection and sympathies of a companion. On this account, and as Mr. B. was exceedingly stern, and angry with me for entertaining hard thoughts of him, I felt unable to do any thing more for the relief of my poor daughter. My hope in God was my only support. And I did abundantly and earnestly commit my cause to him. I felt confident that he would, in his own time, and as his infinite wisdom should determine, grant relief. . . .

I therefore had not known what to do better than to wait on God as I had done, to afford me strength and opportunity to introduce the means of his effectual control. This time I told him had arrived. And now, if God spared my life (I told Mr. B.) he should find a new leaf turned over;—and that I would not suffer him to go on any

---

Editor's note in the 1815 edition: The discreet reader will repeatedly wonder that this pious sufferer did not look abroad for help against so vile a son of Belial, and avail herself of the law of the land, by swearing the peace against him. Her forbearance does indeed seem to have been carried to excess. But when we consider her delicate situation at this time; her peaceable habits from youth; her native tenderness of mind; her long fears of a tyranical cruel husband; her having, at no time of her sufferings, seen all that we now see of his abominable character, as a reason why he should have been brought to justice; her wishes and hopes that he might be brought to reformation; her desires not to have the family honor sacrificed; and the difficulty of exhibiting sufficient evidence against a popular, subtle man, to prove such horrid crimes;— these things plead much in her behalf. After all, it will be difficult to resist the conviction, which will be excited in the course of these memoirs, that Mrs. B. did truly err, in not having her husband brought to justice. The law is made for the lawless and disobedient.

longer as he had done. I would now soon adopt measures to put a stop to his abominable wickedness and cruelties. For this could and ought to be done. And if I did it
not, I should be a partaker of his sins, and should aid in bringing down the curse of
God upon our family.

By this time Mr. B. had become silent. He appeared struck with some degree
of fear. He, by and by, asked me what I intended or expected to do, to bring about
such a revolution as I had intimated? whether I knew what an awful crime I had laid to
his charge? which he said could not be proved. He wished to know whether I had
considered how difficult it would be for me to do any such thing against him? as I was
under his legal control; and he could overrule all my plans as he pleased. I told him, I
well knew I had been placed under his lawful government and authority, and likewise
under his care and protection. And most delightful would it have been to me, to have
been able quietly and safely to remain there as long as I lived. Gladly would I have
remained a kind, faithful, obedient wife to him, as I had ever been. But I told Mr. B.
he *knew* he had violated his marriage covenant; and hence had forfeited all legal and
just right and authority over me; and I should convince him that I well knew it. I told
him I was not in any passion. I acted on principle, and from long and mature consideration. And though it had ever been my greatest care and pleasure (among my earthly
comforts) to obey and please him; yet by his most wicked and cruel conduct, he had
compelled me to undertake this most undesirable business—of stopping him in his
mad career; and that I now felt strength, courage and zeal to pursue my resolution.
And if my life was spared, he would find that I should bring something to pass, and
probably more than he now apprehended.

As to what I could prove against him, I told Mr. B. he knew not how much
evidence I had of his unnatural crimes, of which I had accused him, and of which *he
knew he was guilty.* I asked him why he should not expect that I should institute a
process against him, for that most horrid conduct, which he had long allowed himself
to pursue, and with the most indecent and astonishing boldness? I told him I well
knew that he was naturally a man of sense; and that his conscience now fully approved
of my conduct. . . .

Mr. B. now said, he was very sorry he had given me so much reason to think
such things of him; and that he had so far destroyed my confidence in him as a man of
truth. He then begged of me to forgive all that was past; and he promised that he
would ever be kind and faithful to me in future, and never more give me reason to
complain of him for any such conduct. I told him, if I had but evidence of his real
reformation, I could readily forgive him as a fellow creature, and could plead with God
to forgive him. But as to my living with him in the most endearing relation any longer,
after such horrid crimes, I did not see that I *could,* or *ought* to do it! He then anxiously
made some remarks upon the consequences of my refusing to remain his wife, and
seeking a separation from him. These he seemed unable to endure. I remarked, that
I well knew it was no small thing for a husband and wife to part, and their family of
children to be broken up; that such a separation could not be rendered expedient or
lawful, without great sin indeed: and that I would not be the cause of it, and of breaking
up our family, for *all the world*. But, said I, you have done all in your power to bring
about such a separation, and to ruin and destroy our family. And I meet it as my duty
now to do all in my power to save them from further destruction.

Chapter 3

The Colonial Economy

*A*ntipathy to idleness and exhortation to industry were commonplace throughout the colonies. Although land rich, these colonies were labor scarce, and no able-bodied worker was expendable. Women of all ages, therefore, became active participants in the colonial economy. The nature of their work varied according to rank, region, race, and status of servitude. It also changed over time, as the economy expanded.

As in England, the household was the major locus of women's work. Responsible for producing food, clothing, and household goods, the colonial woman faced a lifetime of labor. She cooked meals, planted vegetables, milked cows, fed pigs, preserved meat, knitted stockings, sewed garments, and produced such items as soap and candles. Differences of region and rank affected women's work. In a one- or two-room cabin on a newly carved out tobacco farm on the southern frontier, for instance, a woman helped out in the fields, slaughtered livestock, and chopped wood. Furnishings were so sparse that she had little of a household to maintain. In more settled areas, the variety of domestic labor increased, and specialized forms of production, such as running a dairy or spinning thread, emerged. Such household crafts, however, were never universal. In mid-eighteenth-century Massachusetts, about half of all households contained dairy equipment or spinning wheels, and fewer than one in ten had looms.

Household production sometimes extended into small-scale businesses. Housewives might sell or exchange the goods they produced, like homemade medicine or cosmetics. Spinsters and brewers (of cider or beer) were able to profit from their skills. Women also sold their services as seamstresses, nurses, and midwives. Those in cities ran shops, inns, taverns, boardinghouses, or dame schools. Just as married women customarily served as the surrogates for absent husbands, a propertied widow may have managed a deceased husband's trade, at least until grown sons replaced their mother. Widows worked as grocers and upholsterers, managed farms and mills, and became printers and blacksmiths. Some colonies granted "feme sole trader" status to married women so they could conduct business in their husbands' absence, or even in his presence (see Chapter 4).

The imprecise boundaries of women's work reflected a particular set of circumstances. The colonies had few skilled workers and a desperate need for labor, goods, and services. By the end of the colonial era, as the population increased and as parts of the colonies came more and more to resemble England, free women's commercial opportunities narrowed. Paid employment was increasingly limited to widows and spinsters, who usually took occupations connected in some way either to household production or to serving female clienteles; they worked as seamstresses, lacemakers, starchers, shop proprietors, or boardinghouse keepers. The married woman who sold her skills, like midwife Martha Ballard of Maine, combined services to her neighbors with services to her household.

The gradual growth of a market economy in the late eighteenth century also affected women's work roles at home. Some women became specialized producers. By the end of the century, many New England women, notably farm daughters, devoted most of their time to the home manufacture of thread and cloth. Late eighteenth-century farm women in Chester County, Pennsylvania, made dairy products for the Philadelphia market. By 1800 their households began to include springhouses or milkhouses and must have resembled small factories. Other women became consumers. Well-off housewives in towns or cities were able to buy some of the goods that homemakers once had produced themselves, such as cider, butter, cloaks, or hats, plus imported goods. They also depended on servants or slaves for the preponderance of household work.

Servants constituted a major source of female labor. A sizable portion of the work force in the colonies was young (as was most of the colonial population), single, and unfree. About half of all immigrants arrived as indentured servants, at first mainly in the South and later in the middle colonies. In the early Chesapeake, more women arrived as servants than as family members. Such servants, usually eighteen to twenty-five years of age, sold their labor for four to five years in return for transportation and maintenance. They faced arduous labor, high mortality, harsh discipline, and celibacy. Marriage of servants was prohibited, and penalties for pregnancy were severe. A pregnant female servant would be punished by fines and an extra period of service, in order to repay her master for the loss of labor. About one-fifth of female indentured servants in Maryland were convicted of bastardy.

In the eighteenth century, apprenticeship replaced indentured servitude as the major source of bound labor. Female apprentices often served far longer terms than did indentured servants. Daughters might be apprenticed at eleven or twelve years of age for up to ten years. Orphans, children of poor widows, and illegitimate youngsters might be bound out at any age. They exchanged their services for training in household skills, such as spinning; some learned to read. Masters assumed the cost of their upkeep.

Apprenticeship and indentures provided a temporary unfree status. Slavery did not. Although some of the first black women to arrive in Virginia may have served terms of indenture and achieved free status, southern slave codes of the 1660s and after defined black status as unfree. Slave women were few in number, because women were in a minority among slaves and slavery was slow to develop. In 1675, there were only about 5,000 slaves in the North American colonies, compared to 100,000 in the British West Indies. Slave ships that arrived in the Chesapeake in the 1700s typically carried two men to every woman. In the early eighteenth century, slave imports increased and slave populations began to reproduce themselves. Slavery had taken hold and thereafter expanded rapidly.

The status of black women was distinctive from the outset because, unlike white women, they commonly performed field labor. Before 1660, Maryland and Virginia levied taxes on anyone who worked "in the ground," a group defined as black and white men and "Negro women at least sixteen years of age." Economic decisions by planters determined the type of work slave women performed. The vast majority of colonial women slaves did field labor. One eighteenth-century Carolina planter expected slave women to do exactly the same work as men—to clear, plant, and harvest three acres in six months. On large plantations, at least some women might escape field work for housework, spinning, or weaving. However, they labored "under the Eye of the mistress," and enjoyed less independence than male artisans, who far outnumbered them. The most important feature of slavery, for women as for men, was its rapid growth. In 1720, only one in four Chesapeake planters owned slaves, but by 1770, over half owned slaves. By the time of the Revolution, slaves constituted one-third of the southern population and far more than that in South Carolina (70 percent), Virginia (47 percent), and Maryland (43 percent). Those slaves who lived on larger plantations began to benefit from more stable family life and more dense slave communities.

Many questions about women's work in the pre-industrial economy are now being explored. To what extent did women labor in all-women groups, as did female slaves on large plantations? To what extent were women's economic lives centered around interchanges with other women? To what extent did women exert economic leverage? The answer to this last question seems to be: to a very limited extent, primarily because married women lacked property rights (see Chapter 4). According to one recent study,* women controlled no more than five to ten percent of colonial wealth. Moreover, their access to wealth usually depended not on their own labor or enterprise but on who their male relatives were. Although vital to the household economy and active beyond it, women in general lacked control over family resources, rarely held real property, and probably remained marginal to economic decision making.

---

*Carole Shammas, "Early American Women and Control over Capital," in Ronald Hoffman and Peter J. Albert, eds., *Women in the Age of the American Revolution* (Charlottesville: University of Virginia Press, 1989), pp. 134–54.

A Household Inventory

MASSACHUSETTS, 1672

The Probate Records of Essex County, Massachusetts, vol. 2 (Salem: The Essex Institute, 1917), pp. 319–22.

To reconstruct the work of colonial women, historians have turned to household inventories—the detailed descriptions of estates that were submitted in court in order for a will to be proved valid and put into effect or, if a person died intestate, in order to divide an estate among heirs. Collectively, these inventories can reveal information about a given community, such as what proportion of women spun cloth. Inventories also offer information about women's work environments, especially if they record such data as the size of the home, its furnishings and utensils, the equipment used in household production, and the stores of supplies on hand.

In her study of early New England women, historian Laurel Thatcher Ulrich utilizes the household inventory of Francis Plumer, a Newbury, Massachusetts, farmer and weaver who died in 1672, in order to reconstruct the daily life of his wife, Beatrice Plumer. The Plumer estate was a moderately large one. Plumer owned some thirty-six acres, plus a house, a barn, an orchard, farm animals, and weaving equipment. The house, according to county records, contained "a chamber, parlour, another room, hall chamber, little chamber, dairy, and cellar." This was essentially a four-room, two-story house. The two upper rooms were used as storerooms; no doubt they were too cold to live in most of the year. The Plumers slept in the "parlour." "Another room," which contained pots, kettles, trays, and buckets, was probably a kitchen with a large fireplace in which Beatrice Plumer cooked.

Using the household inventory, Ulrich recreates the physical environment in which Beatrice Plumer worked and the work that she did. First, she cooked, baked, and preserved food. This included slaughtering animals and hanging flitches of bacon. Second, she milked cows and made cheese and butter in her dairy. Third, she went through the elaborate process of beer production—malting, mashing, and brewing.* Perhaps at one time Beatrice Plumer had used the

---

*Laurel Thatcher Ulrich, *Good Wives: Image and Reality in the Lives of Women in Northern New England* (New York: Knopf, 1982), pp. 18–24.

spinning wheel in the "hall chamber"—a storage room—or perhaps she was planning to stuff her feather supply into mattresses.

An unusual feature of the Plumer inventory is the document attached to it. Evidently, Beatrice had signed a prenuptial contract with Francis and later signed a postnuptial contract that reiterated it. Since Francis died intestate, this contract was important. It set forth what Beatrice would inherit if she survived him. Her inheritance included the estate of her previous husband (a house and land in Salem); a separate legacy from Francis Plumer (a room in his house, one-half of his orchard, and a portion of his land); and all of her personal possessions, listed in a separate inventory. The industrious Beatrice Plumer was clearly a well-off widow. For the conclusion of Beatrice Plumer's story, see Laurel Thatcher Ulrich, *Good Wives*, cited on page 69. For the rules of inheritance, see Chapter 4.

Estate of Francis Plumer of Newbury

Administration on the estate of Francis Plumer of Newbury, intestate, granted Feb. 20, 1672, to his sons Samuell and Joseph, by Mr. Samuell Symonds and Major Genrll. Denison, and they were ordered to bring in an inventory to the next Ipswich court. *Ipswich Quarterly Court Records, vol. 5, page* 191.

Francis Plumer dying intestate, administration upon the estate was granted to his son Samuell, who gave bond Mar. 25, 1673, for 500li. [500 pounds], with Wm. Sawyer as surety. *Ipswich Quarterly Court Records, vol. 5, page* 194.

Samuell Plumer, administrator of the estate of Francis Plumer, his father, brought in an inventory to the court amounting to about 412li. Court Apr. 16, 1673 ordered that the debts both to the widow and other men be first paid, and then the estate was to be divided, half to Samuell, the eldest son, and the other half to the other son and daughter. By agreement, Daniell Pearce, sr., Rich. Dole and John Knight, sr., were to divide the estate as equally as they could, the eldest son to have his choice of which half he would have. *Ipswich Quarterly Court Records, vol. 5, page* 196.

Inventory of the estate of Francis Plumer, deceased Jan. 17, 1672, taken Jan. 24, by Richard Knight, John Emery, Sr., Thomas Hale, Jr. and Anthony Somerby: the House, barne, orchard & sixteen acres of land adjoyning, being four four acre lotts with previledg of frehold, 120li.; twenty acres of salt marsh & meadow, 120li.; horse, 8li.; 2 mares, 2 colts, 8li.; four oxen, one yoake, 13li.; another yoake, 11li.; four Cows, 18li.; 2 yerling steers, 2 calfes, 5li. 10s.; five and twenty sheep, 12li.; His weareing Apparrell wth 2 pr. of bootes, 2 cushions, 3 hatts & a pr. of shooes, 17li.; four swyne, 2li.; in the chamber in Indian Corne about 20 bush., 3li.; A thousand of boards, 2 ladders, 4 formes, troughes, 3 hold posts & old timber of a house falne downe, 3li.; A long cart with wheels, stock bands, boxes, plow & Irons, yoaks & 2

Chaynes, 3li. 10s. In the shop, a weavers Loome with Gears, harnesses, &c. with 6 prongs, pitchforks, spade, shovell, Hooes, an Iron Barre, a frooe, Chissells, Augurs, Beettle, 3 wedgs, 4 axes, 5 Iron Hoopes, planes, files, an Iron vice, a woodden vice, short Crosscut saw, 2 handsawes, wimble stocks, wimble bitts, 2 sadles & bridles, 2 paire of scales & weights & many other tooles for Smiths tooles & carpenters Square, 14li. In the parlour: feather bed, bolster, 2 pillows, blanket, coverlet & bedsted, 7li. In the Hall: table, forme, cubbard & great chest, 3li. In another Roome: bed with 2 flock bolsters, pr. of blankets, Rug & Coverlet, 4li.; four paire of sheets, 3 pillow-bears, 1 holland pillowbeare, tablecloth, 7 napkins, a shirt, 4 peices of old sheets & 2 caps, 5li.; two paire of gloves & a remnant of kersy [coarse woolen cloth], 7s.; a small Iron kettle & Iron pot & Iron skillet, 4 peuter dishes, 2 basons, small flagon [bottle or container], pint pot, pint bottle, brasen candlesticke, tining dripping pan, 4 spoones & an old Iron kettle, 2li. 15s.; bible & 4 bookes, 16s.; 2 chayres, small table, 2 tramells, Grid Iron, smoothing Iron, spit, tongs, old fire shovell, bellows, chest, 3 paire of wooll cards, a welsh bill, 5 trayes, 2 bucketts, 9 trenchers, earthen pan, pitcher, woodden platter, 5 dishes, a paire of shooes, 4 Sacks, 2li. 15s. In the Hall chamber: 6 bushels of barly, 2 bushels of Rye, three bushels of wheat, 8 bushels of oats, a bushell of pease & beanes, 5 bushels of meale, 2 bushels of malt, 4li.; Three hayre seives, Ridder, seive, trowell, 4 old hogsheds, 3 barrells, meale trough, bottom of an old trunke, a fanne, 3 Raw sheep skins, a hogskin, A Reele, spining wheele, an old bedsted & lumber, 1li. 4s.; fifteen pound of wooll & 2 pd. & 1-2 of cotten wooll, 1li. 13s.; 2 pound of feathers, 4 pound of flaxen yarne & 2 pd. of tow yarne, 12s.; Grindstone, 7s.; Gun, sword, bullets, snapsacke, 1li. 10s.; two barrells, meshing tub, a halfe bushel & gallon & a pounding trough, 11s. 6d.; twelve pound of woollen yarne, 1li. 10s. In the little chamber: a great Tray, a trough, Syder presse, cheese press, cart rope, dungpot, old wheelbarrow, old sled, 2 tand skins, 1li. In the dairy house: 4 flitches & halfe of Bacon & a quarter of a barrell of porke, about 28 pound of cheese, 3 pound of butter, 2 barrells & a butter tub, 4li. 10s. In the Cellar: a peice of leather, a full Barrell of Syder, 2 empty barrels & an old Churne, 1li. 5s.; debts from Joseph Plumer, 6li.; from William Sawyer, 4li.; In larde, 10s.; total, 412li. 5s. 6d.

Attested in Ipswich court Mar. 25, 1673 by Samuell Plumer, the administrator.

Debts due from the estate to severall men, 33li. 8s. 9d.; to the widow, 35li.; total, 68li. 8s. 9d.; clear estate, 343li. 16s. 9d.

Debts due from the estate: to goodm. Pore, 18s.; for two bushels of wheat for the buriall, 10s.; to goodman March, 13s. 3d.; goodie Rendall, 3s.; goodman Person, 6s.; John Adkinson, 17s.; goodman Sumerbe, 17s.; goodman Ilsley, 4s. 6d.; Thomas haines, 2s.; goodman Perse, 4s.; the Constable for Rates, 17s.; goodman Emry, 15s.; Steven Grenleaf, 12s.; Peter Tapan, 15s.; Samuell Plumer, 4li. 6s.; Abram Adams, 4s.; Thomas Moyce, 1li. 15s.; John wels, 6s.; goodman Daves, 1li.; Joseph Palmer, 10s.; Marie duell, 2li. 10s.; goodman Mirick, 3s.; Richard dole, 4li. 10s.; Capt. Gerish, 4s. 6d.; Thomas hale, Sr., 6s. 6d.; Rich. Knight, goodm. Sumerbe, John Emry, Tho. Hale, 1li.; William Titcum, 2li.; to the widow upon a late agreement, 5li.; John Knight, 2li.

Agreement, dated Nov. 25, 1670, between Francis Plumer of Newbury and Beatrice, his wife, confirming the contract made before marriage that if Plumer should die before the said Beatrice, the latter was to have all the estate that was properly hers before marriage, and also to have the new room, half the orchard, half the apples, and her thirds of the land of said Francis during her life, also firewood out of said Francis Plumer's twenty acres near the little river and the garden as it is now enclosed. If said Beatrice deceased before him, that she should have power to dispose of what estate was hers before marriage to any of her relatives, and if anybody claimed any debts due from William Cantlebury,* deceased, said Beatrice's estate was to pay such debts and not the estate of said Plumer, her now husband.

Witness: Richard Dole and Anthony Somerby.

An inventory of the goods to belong to Beatrice, the wife of Francis Plumer or to her heirs: a horse & mare & cattell soe many as was prised to him at 35li. to be paid within one year after the decease of either the said Francis or Beatrice; two Ruggs, four blancketts, two paire of sheets of cotten & linnen, pr. of fine sheets of six yards a peice in them, one feather bed, one brass kettle, an Iron kettle, a paire of sheets more, one chest with a coffer with wearing linnen in them, petticoats, wascoats, two pillows, foure platters, a basen, pewter pint pott, a paire of old curtaines & vallens.

The house and land at Salem that was William Cantleburyes is the proper estate of the said Beatrice, and Francis Plumer has no interest in it as shown by the marriage contract between the said Francis Plumer and Beatrice; besides four cattell and four sheep, and also what is due by bills from Joseph Plumer, Daniell Thurston and Robt. Long, also Francis Plumer agreed not to require anything for keeping his wife's grandchild for the time past to this day.

Dated Nov. 25, 1670.   Francis (his mark) Plumer.

Witness: Richard Dole, Anthony Somerby.

Essex County Probate Files, Docket 22, 135.

---

*Beatrice Plumer's first husband.

Skilled Slaves in Maryland

THE MARYLAND GAZETTE, 1748–1763

The *Maryland Gazette,* 1748–1763.

The vast majority of Chesapeake women slaves throughout the colonial era worked as field laborers. To escape field work, slaves had to be trained as artisans or domestic servants. Such skilled slaves were useful only on the large plantations that developed in the eighteenth century. There, male slaves might be trained as shoemakers, blacksmiths, carpenters, coopers, masons, or personal servants. Women slaves might become household servants, such as cooks or nurses, or spinners and weavers.

Since the crafts open to men far outnumbered those open to women, fewer female than male slaves had the opportunity to escape field labor. In one Maryland county in the mid-eighteenth century, one out of twenty women slaves was a house servant, and a few more were spinners and weavers. Though small in numbers, these textile workers, usually trained in their early teens, were prime commodities on the local slave market.* Among the advertisements of women slaves in the *Maryland Gazette*, those for skilled young women were most prominent. This probably reflected the growing size of plantations. Only the wealthiest planters could train their own workers, as opposed to buying them. To others, who had recently expanded their holdings and now had to clothe a large number of slaves, the young women in the following advertisements must have been desirable purchases.

[April 27, 1748]

TO BE SOLD BY THE SUBSCRIBER, IN ANNAPOLIS
A brisk likely Country-born Negro Wench about 18 or 19 years of Age, who is a good Spinner; with a Child, about 18 months Old.

William Reynolds

Very good Nutmegs, by the Pound, or Ounce, to be sold by the same Reynolds.

---

*Allan Kulikoff, *Tobacco and Slaves: The Development of Southern Cultures in the Chesapeake, 1680–1800* (Chapel Hill: University of North Carolina Press, 1986), p. 405.

[December 21, 1748]

A Young Negro Wench, almost sixteen Years of Age, of a Strong, Healthy Constitution, and can do all sorts of Household Work. Enquire of the Printer hereof.

[December 20, 1749]

TO BE SOLD

A likely brisk, healthy Negro Wench, about Sixteen Years of Age, who Understands All Manner of Household Work. Enquire of the Printer.

[May 29, 1751]

TO BE SOLD

A likely, strong Negro Girl, about 16 Years of Age, fit for Plantation Work, or very capable of making a Good House Wench, having for some Months served as such in a small Family. For further Particulars, Enquire of the Printer Hereof.

[May 28, 1752]

TO BE SOLD BY PUBLIC VENDOR

At the House of Mr. Samuel Middleton, in Annapolis, on Wednesday the 10th Day of June next at 4 o'clock in the afternoon:

The Hull of a New Vessel lying now at the Town Dock, together with her Masts, and some of her Yards. . . .

Also at the same time will be sold a Blacksmith and a Wheelright, with their Tools; both being excellent workmen. Also a Collier and a Sawyer, who have each about 5 Yeares to Serve. . . .

Likewise a Country-born Negro Wench, About 27 Years of Age, very sober and healthy, and understands Household Business very well, with a Mulatto Boy about a year and a half old, who is the said Negro's Child.

Whoever is inclinable to purchase, on giving security (if required), may have two Months time for Payment.

[December 17, 1761]

TO BE SOLD BY THE SUBSCRIBER, being near Upper Marlborough, in Prince George's County, on the Second Day of January next, for good Bills of Exchange:

A Choice Parcel of Country-born Slaves, consisting of Men, Women, Boys, and Girls, all Young and healthy, chief between 10 and 20 years of Age; among these Slaves there are two Wenches about 16 or 17 Years of Age, who Understand Spinning and Knitting, and a young Fellow of 20 Years of Age, a good Plowman and Cartman.

The Sale to be on a Plantation near Mr. William Beall's.

William Parker

[October 20, 1763]

TO BE SOLD

A lusty likely healthy Mulatto Woman, aged about 23 Years, who has been brought up to Household Work, such as Washing, Ironing, Cooking, & C. For terms, enquire at the Printing Office.

[November 10, 1763]

TO BE SOLD TO THE HIGHEST BIDDER

About Sixteen Country-born SLAVES, consisting of one young Fellow, several Women, Boys, and Girls, Among them a good Cook Wench, two Women brought up to Waiting in a Family, & C. Likewise, a variety of genteel Household Furniture, too tedious to enumerate.

The Sale will begin on the Wednesday in Prince George's County Court Week, about Three O'Clock P. M. at the Subscriber's House.

Daniel Carroll

Apprenticeship in Pennsylvania

LIST OF INDENTURES, 1771–1773

"Record of Indentures . . . the City of Philadelphia, October 3, 1771 to October 5, 1773," *The Pennsylvania-German Society, Proceedings and Addresses*, vol. 16 (Lancaster, 1907).

In the eighteenth century, apprenticeship began to replace indentured servitude of immigrants as the major source of bound labor, although the two systems coexisted. Apprentices—usually native-born youngsters or teenagers—enjoyed a higher status than indentured servants. They could not be sold by masters, their working conditions were better than those of servants, and often their families paid their masters a fee in exchange for their vocational training. Apprenticeship, however, had different meanings for young men and young women. Male apprentices learned the "art, trade, and mystery" of skilled crafts. They became, for instance, carpenters, blacksmiths, tailors, masons, hatters, cordwainers, or boat pilots. Young women apprentices almost invariably learned the same craft: housewifery. The typical contract of an eighteenth-century female apprentice required that she be "taught housewifery, sew plain work, read in the bible, write a legible hand." Her term of service might be ten years or more.

The distinctions between male and female apprentices are evident in the Philadelphia record of "Individuals Bound Out as Apprentices, Servants, Etc." The following are representative samples of entries for 1771 and 1772.

Male Apprentices

Oct. 14, 1771

Bell, James
Indenture to Frazier Kinsley, Philadelphia
House carpenter, to be taught the art, trade, and mystery of a house carpenter, have two winters schooling, and be taught the first five rules in common arithmetic.
5 yrs. [term of service]

Oct. 5, 1771

Desher, Charles
Indenture to Abraham Hasselbery and his assigns, Philadelphia
To be taught the art, trade and mystery of a tin plate worker, and be found meat, drink, washing, and lodging only.
3 yrs., 6 mo.

Oct. 9, 1771

Cauffman, Jacob
Indenture to Thomas Atmore and his assigns, Philadelphia
Apprentice, to be taught the art, trade and mystery of a hatmaker and found in hats, to find him meat, drank, and lodging, the last six years and six months of the term.
7 yrs., 6 mo.

Oct. 21, 1771

Outerbridge, Rumsey White
Indenture to Joseph Dean, Philadelphia
Taught the art and mystery of a merchant and bookkeeping, found meat, drank, washing, lodging, apprentice[ship] free, the mother to provide sufficient apparel.
3 yrs., 6 mo.

Oct. 22, 1771

Brown, William
Indenture to John Duche and his assigns, Southwark
Taught the boatbuilder's trade, have three quarters evening schooling, found meat, drank, lodging, and working apparel, and at expiration have the tools he works with.
3 yrs., 2 mo., 23 d.

Oct. 22, 1771

Row, Jacob
Indenture to Philip Clumperg and his assigns, Philadelphia
Taught the business of a surgeon barber, read in the bible, write a legible hand, & cypher.
6 yrs.

Oct. 31, 1771

Hardie, Robert, Jr.
Indenture to Capt. Thomas Edward Wallace, Philadelphia
Taught the art, trade and mystery of a mariner and navigator, found meat, drink, washing, and lodging, his uncle to provide apparel.
5 yrs., 6 mo.

Female Apprentices

Oct. 21, 1771

Lynch, Mary
Indenture to William Faris and wife, Philadelphia
Taught housewifery, sew plain work, read in the Bible, write a legible hand.
9 yrs., 3 mo.

Nov. 4, 1771

Rone, Mary, Jr.
Indenture to Thomas Pugh and his wife, Philadelphia
Apprentice, taught housewifery, sew plain work, have one year schooling. To be found all necessaries and at the expiration have two complete suits of apparel, one whereof is to be new.
8 yrs., 10 mo.

Nov. 12, 1771

Inglis, Sarah
Indenture to John Kelly and his assigns, Philadelphia
Taught to read, write, and cypher, housewifery, and to sew.
10 yrs., 11 mo.

Nov. 14, 1771

Magere, Lydia
Indenture to Ann Paice and her heirs, Philadelphia
Taught housewifery, quilting, to sew and knit, have 9 months day schooling.
9 yrs., 4 mo., 11 d.

Jan. 23, 1772

Davis, Sarah
Indenture to William Logan and his assigns, W. Nantmeal twp., Northampton Co.
Apprentice, taught housewifery, sew, knit, spin, read in Bible, write a legible hand.
11 yrs., 6 mo.

June 23, 1772

Hughes, Jane
Indenture to William Snowden and Ann, his wife, Philadelphia
Apprentice, taught mantua [gown] maker's trade, have three quarters' schooling, in case of her death, the indenture to be void. To be found all necessaries and at expiration have one new suit of apparel, besides the old.
3 yrs. 9 mo. 13 d.

June 25, 1772

Woodward, Nice
Indenture to Joseph Johnson and his assigns, Southwark
Apprentice, taught housewifery, sew, knit and spin, read and write perfectly.
11 yrs.

July 21, 1772

Mannin, Elizabeth
Indenture to John Hilson, Philadelphia
Apprentice, taught housewifery and mantua maker's trade, and make bonnets and cloaks, have one year schooling. To be found all necessaries and at the expiration have freedom dues.
7 yrs. 6 mo. 14 d.

Sept. 29, 1772

Boyle, Mary
Jonathan Fell and wife, Warwick twp, Bucks Co.
Apprentice, taught housewifery, sew, knit, and spin, read in Bible, write a legible hand, and when she arrives at the age of twelve, give her one ewe. To be found all necessaries and at the expiration have two complete suits of apparel, one whereof to be new, and one spinning wheel.
9 yrs. 10 mo. 19 d.

Oct. 5, 1772

Brockington, Mary
Captain Thomas Powell and Wife, Philadelphia
Apprentice, taught housewifery and sew, time to go to school two years, the grand-father paying expense of schooling and the master to give such further schooling as will perfect her in reading and writing. To be found all necessaries and at expiration have freedom dues.
12 yrs., 9 mo.

Oct. 8, 1772

Adams, Abigail
Indenture to James Painter and his assigns, E. Bradford Co.
Apprentice, taught to read in Bible, write a legible hand, cypher as far and through the rule of multiplication, and spin, also housewifery.
14 yrs., 1 mo., 25 d.

Oct. 10, 1772

Anderson, Mary
Indenture to Benjamin Dismant and his assigns, N. Providence, Philadelphia Co.
Apprentice, taught to read in Bible, write a legible hand, sew, knit, spin and housewifery. To be found all necessaries and at the expiration have two complete suits of
apparel, one whereof to be new, a new spinning wheel, a cow, or £5 in money in lieu
of the cow.
14 yrs.

Adventure Schools

ADVERTISEMENTS, 1750s–1770s

Advertisements in the *Virginia Gazette, South Carolina Gazette, Pennsylvania Gazette,* and *New York Gazette or Weekly Post Boy,* 1751–1776.

Married or single, colonial women earned money from commercial ventures, including schools. Some ran dame schools, where small children learned to read though not to write or cipher. By the mid-eighteenth century, a new type of school for girls proliferated. Adventure schools catered to their clients' needs: They taught what the students wanted to learn. Their offerings sometimes included primary subjects such as writing and spelling, or secondary subjects such as grammar, geography, or French. The main courses taught at adventure schools, however, were "accomplishments," such as dancing, drawing, music, embroidery, enameling, quilting, lacework, and millinery work.

The following advertisements for adventure schools from the 1750s to the 1770s suggest their curricula and something about the entrepreneurs who ran them. Some schools were run by men, some by women, and some by family teams, such as husband and wife or father and daughter. One might question the qualifications of instructors like Anne Stockton, who attempted to open a tavern but suddenly shifted to teaching. Still, several of these schools—like that of James and Elizabeth Wragg, which operated for many years—were apparently successful businesses.

[*Virginia Gazette*, November 17, 1752]

John Walker, lately arrived in Williamsburg from London, and who for ten Years has been engag'd in the Education of Youth, undertakes to instruct young Gentlemen in Reading, Writing, Arithmetic, the most material Branches of Classical learning, and ancient and modern Geography and History; but, as the noblest End of erudition and Human Attainment, he will exert his principal Endeavors to Improve their Morals, in Proportion to their Progress in Learning, that no Parent may repent his Choice in trusting him with the Education of His Children.

Mrs. Walker, likewise, teaches young Ladies all Kinds of Needle Work, and makes Capuchins, Shades, Hats, and Bonnets, and will endeavor to give Satisfaction to those who shall honour her with their Custom.

The above John Walker, and his Wife, live at Mr. Cobb's new House, next to Mr. Coke's, near the Road going down to the Capitol Landing, where there is also to be sold, Men's Shoes and Pumps, Turkey Coffee, Edging and Lace for Ladies Caps, and four Gold Rings.

[Pennsylvania Gazette, April 1, 1751]

Isabel Hewet, in Macclenahan's Allay, the corner house, next to St. Paul's Church, Begs leave to inform the public that she intends to open a school for the instruction of young girls in sewing sundry kinds of needlework, such as white and colored seam, drawing and flowering, embroidery, and dresden work. Those who are pleased to intrust the above Isabel Hewet with their children, may depend on being carefully attended. Also all kinds of needlework, done at the said place, after the best and neatest manner, and at the most reasonable prices.

[New York Gazette or Weekly Post Boy, April 5, 1756]

Writing, Arithmetic, Merchants Accounts, Navigation, Mensuration, Surveying, Gauging, Dialing . . . &c. carefully taught by James Wragg, opposite to the Post Office, where there is Commodious Rooms for young Gentlemen and Ladies, to be instructed in any of the branches of the Mathematics, revised from those that are taught Writing and Arithmetic; Gentlemen, Sailors, and other, are taught navigation in a short time, and seasonable Evening School continues all Summer.

Elizabeth Wragg proposes, God willing, to open School, the first Monday in May, or before, as required; where young Masters and misses will be taught the first Rudiments of Learning. viz. A genteel behavior, Spelling, Reading, and Needle-Work.

Those that will be so Kind as to promote me in these my Undertakings, it will be esteem'd as a great Favour done to their

Humble Servant,
Elizabeth Wragg

[South Carolina Gazette, May 17, 1770]

A Boarding School

for the

EDUCATION OF YOUNG LADIES,

Will be opened the approaching Whitmonday, at the House

opposite the Rev. Mr. Cooper's in New Church Street,

BY MRS. DUNEAU

A Gentlewoman from England,

Who has brought up many Ladies of Rank and Distinction, having herself kept one of the genteelest Boarding-Schools About London.

Teaches the French and English Languages grammatically—Geography—History—and many instructing Amusements to improve the Mind—with all Sorts of fashionable Needle Work. Proper Masters will attend the young Ladies for their Dancing, Music, and Drawing; Writing and Arithmetic.

Agreeable Indulgence will be allowed for the Amusement and Encouragement of the young Ladies. Mrs. Duneau will be much obliged to the Gentlemen and Ladies, who please to Favour her with the Care of their Daughters Education; and has the Honour to subscribe herself,

Their most obedient humble Servant,
Elizabeth Duneau

[*Virginia Gazette*, February 27, 1772]

E. Armston (or perhaps better known by the Name of Gardner) continues the Schools at Point Pleasant, Norfolk Borough, where [there] is a large and convenient House proper to accommodate young Ladies as Boarders; at which School is taught Petit Point in Flowers, Fruit, Landscapes, and Sculpture, Nuns Work, Embroidery in Silk, Gold, Silver, Pearls, or embossed, Shading of all Kinds, in the various Works in Vogue, Dresden Point Work, Lace, Catgut in different Modes, Muslin after the Newest Taste, and most elegant Pattern, Waxwork in Figure, Fruit, or Flowers, Shell ditto, or grotesque, Painting in Water Colours and Mezzotints. . . . Specimens of the Subscriber's Work may be seen at her House, as also of her Scholars; having taught several Years in Norfolk, and elsewhere to general Satisfaction. She flatters herself that those Gentlemen and Ladies who have hitherto employed her will grant her their further indulgence, as no endeavors shall be wanted to complete what is above mentioned, with a strict attention to the Behavior of those Ladies entrusted to her Care.

Reading will be her peculiar Care; Writing and Arithmetick will be taught by a Master properly qualified; and, if desired, will engage Proficients in Musick and Dancing.

[*Virginia Gazette*, December 27, 1776]

Mrs. Neill (who for a considerable Time past, has lived in Colonel Lewis's Family, Gloucester County) purposes to open a Boarding School in Williamsburg for the Reception of young Ladies, on the Same Plan of the English Schools, provided a sufficient Number of Scholars engage, to enable her for such an Undertaking. She will instruct them in Reading, Tambour, and other Kinds of Needle Work, find them Board and Lodging, Washing &c. for one Guinea Entrance and thirty pounds a Year. The best Masters will attend to teach Dancing and Writing. She will also teach the Guittar. Those who choose to learn any of those Accomplishments [are expected] to pay for each separately. . . . As Nothing tends more to the Improvement of a Country than proper Schools for Education of both Sexes, she humbly hopes her Scheme will meet with Encouragement, and the Approbation of the Ladies and gentlemen of this State; and that those who choose to lend their Children will please to let her know as soon as possible, that she may provide accordingly for their Reception. . . . Direct for her at Col. Lewis's, Senior, in Gloucester, or at Mess. Dixon & Hunter in Williamsburg.

Mrs. Neill will take Day Scholars at one Guinea Entrance, and four Guineas per year.

A Maine Midwife

MARTHA BALLARD, 1785

"The Diary of Mrs. Martha Moore Ballard," in Charles Elventon Nash, *The History of Augusta: First Settlements and Early Days as a Town* (Augusta, ME: Charles E. Nash & Son, 1961 [originally published 1904]), pp. 240–44.

Martha Ballard's diary (1785–1812) reveals the experience of a married woman who pursued a vocation in pre-industrial America. Ballard began her career as a midwife in 1778, at age 42. She had just migrated from Massachusetts with her husband, Ephraim, and five children to the Maine river town that became Augusta. A year later she had her sixth and last child. In 1785, when she began her diary, Martha Ballard was fifty years old and a grandmother. The Ballard home was a busy workplace. Ephraim, a farmer and lumberer, ran a sawmill and also worked as a surveyor. Martha Ballard, similarly, had several careers.

First, she was a housewife. Throughout the period covered in the diary, Martha Ballard slaughtered livestock, spun flax, produced candles and soap, knitted clothing, pieced quilts, raised chickens, milked cows, fed pigs, and grew vegetables. Two teen-age daughters, Hannah and Dolly, and later a succession of hired girls, assisted her at home. Martha Ballard also ran a busy local practice as a healer and midwife. She advised the sick, treated the injured, dispensed remedies, and, most of all, delivered babies. Though sparsely settled, the region around Augusta grew quickly after the Revolution, and the high birth rate provided Martha Ballard with a steady clientele. Midwifery, in her case, involved forty to seventy house calls a year, some lasting a few hours and some a few days, and thirty or more annual deliveries.*

As the following segment of her diary for 1785 suggests, these deliveries occurred under varied circumstances. In some instances Martha Ballard arrived too late and the child had been delivered by a neighbor or competitor. Sometimes she joined forces with another midwife, like the respected Mrs. Winslow (August 11), or took charge after a delivery by a less trustworthy practitioner, like Mrs. Smith (November 11), who may have botched the job. Typically, a group of

---

*Laurel Thatcher Ulrich, "Martha Ballard and Her Girls: Women's Work in Eighteenth-Century Maine," in Stephen Innes, ed., *Work and Labor in Colonial America* (Chapel Hill: University of North Carolina Press, 1988), pp. 70–105.

women assisted in or was present at deliveries, as in the case of the Ballard's married daughter ("Daughter Town," July 23), or that of Mrs. Cowen (November 21). Although a doctor maintained a local practice, he appeared only rarely at childbirths.

Martha Ballard's detailed diary was at once a professional log, a family record, and a community record, because she was continually involved in the affairs of clients and neighbors and concerned with local happenings. The segment of the diary reprinted here comes from an edited and abridged version that was prepared for publication in 1904. The abridgement includes all records of births but excludes other information such as medical details, sexual references, and family problems.*

1785. July 23. Daughter Town unwell all day. Called her women together about two o'clock, afternoon; was safely delivered of a daughter at 7 o'clock, but somewhat weak. I sat up with her all night.

24. I left Mr. Town's at 10 o'clock in the morn; arrived at home about six.

25. I went to Doctor Cony for some medicine for Mrs. Stratton. Pollard stubbed his foot to-day.

26. I was at home all day; collecting herbs.

27. I went to Mr. Weston's to see Polly Adams, she being lame.

28. Mr. Leighton here. Informed that Mrs. Hersy was delivered of a son.

31. Old Mrs. Hawes and daughter, and sister Moore here at noon; they and many more people called after meeting. Mr. Ballard and I went to see them. . . .

August 1. Dolly rode a horse to plough.

4. Mr. Ballard went to survey for Mr. Dutch. Mrs. Church is ill. Mrs. Winslow with her.

10. I was called to Mr. Edson's to see his burnt foot; found it bad; drest it and left some salve. Augustus Ballard came for Alice.

11. Called to Mr. Church's about day. She being in travail; was delivered about 5 o'clock, p.m., of a daughter; the operation performed by Mrs. Winslow.

12. I was at Mr. Edson's; Doctors Williams and Colman there to see his foot, which he burnt.

19. I attended lecter [lecture]. Went from meeting to Mr. Suel's, to see Capt. Suel's foot, it being scalt. Drank tea there. James Moore called me from there to go to

---

*For portions of the original diary and interpretation of its contents, see Laurel Thatcher Ulrich, *A Midwife's Tale: The Life of Martha Ballard, Based on Her Diary, 1785–1812* (New York: Knopf, 1990).

Simmion Clark's wife, she being in travail; was safely delivered of a daughter at 11 o'clock, evening.

August 20. I came home from Mr. Clark's. Our men cleared the crick [creek] of sunken stuff.

21. Sunday. I went to meeting. The sacrament administered. Mr. Ballard and I partook.

22. Doctor Barton and wife came here; the Doctor went to Cobese (Cobbossee-contee).

23. Mr. Ballard and I, and sister Barton, Cyrus and Dolly and Pollard, went to see Norcrosses vessel launched.

25. Mr. Pollard, Weston, and Betsy Cheever here.

26. Doctor Barton came from Cobese, dined here. Went home to Vassalboro in the afternoon. I went to see them up the rips.

September 6. The town meeting to-day to hire Mr. Noble. Voted to hire him till March.

9. I went to Esqr. Howard's and Mr. Suel's to visit the sick. Mr. Suel made me a present of a calf-skin. I was called at 10 o'clock in the evening to Ezra Hodge's wife, she being in travail. I walked there in 20 minutes.

10. Mrs. Hodges was safely delivered of a daughter at 6 o'clock this morning. I returned home at ten.

11. Sunday. I got ready to go to Esqr. Howard's, and it rained and I put it by. Informed that Mrs. McMaster had got to bed, and her child was deceased. The funeral to-morrow.

12. I went to Esqr. Howard's to take care of Alvin Weeks and Polly Briant, who were sick of a fever. Capt. Nichols and Silas Eddy here from Oxford. I was called to Mr. Chamberlain's—his wife in travail. At about ten in evening John Comings came there after me to go to Benjamin White's of Winthrop, but I could not be dismist.

13. I was at Chamberlain's all day; she was delivered [at] six o'clock, afternoon, of a daughter.

14. Jonathan watched with Alvin Weeks at Esqr. Howard's.

15. Alvin Weeks departed this life in the night.

16. I attended funeral of Mr. Weeks. Tarried at Esqr. [Howard's] This night took care of Polly and Suck.

17. Came from the Fort and went to Chamberlain's, to see their babe.

20. Mr. Oriah Clark's wife here.

22. I was called to Mr. Leighton's, his wife being in travail. Left home at ten, forenoon; arrived there at two, afternoon. Found her safely delivered of a son, the operation by Solomon Leighton's wife.

26. Sherebiah Town came for me to go to Mr. Dexter's at Sebestacook. I left home at four o'clock, P. M.; arrived there a little before twelve. Found Mrs. Dexter very ill with the mumps; fixed her a remedy and she mended soon. I tarried there and at son Town's till October the sixth; then came home by water attended by Captain Hale and Sherebiah Town; they brought a barrel of fish from Mr. Stratton's pounds.

October 8. Daniel Robins has bruised his toe—it is painful; I put a poultis to it.

11. Called in great haste to Colo. Howard's, his wife and five children very sick; Samuel bleeding. Gave them Great Bitters. Wheeler sick at Esqr. Howard's.

13. Watcht at the Fort this night.

14. I came from the fort at ten. Went back again before night. Took a sleep fore part of the night. Sit up after two in Mrs. Howard's chamber.

16. I went to Colo. Howard's; tarried all night, and watcht. Mrs. Howard had a severe fever fit.

17. I tarried and helped move the sick, dress the blisters, &c.; returned home at noon. Brother Moore and Thomas Smiley here. Mr. Ballard went up with them to view a mill-spot.

19. Mr. Ballard went to Mr. Hersey's farm to the Hook, afternoon. Wilbra Stone sent here for camphor; I sent him an ounce of tincture.

21. Ephraim Town came here about day for me to go to Mr. Dexter's. We left here at 7 o'clock; arrived at Dexter's at afternoon; found his wife very ill. I removed the obstruction and delivered her safe of a fine daughter about the middle of the night. It stormed severely as I was on my journey.

22. I came from Dexter's. It rained. I called to see Polly Dudley who is extremely low and senseless. Dined at Doctor Barton's. Got to Fort Western at dusk, but could not cross the river by reason of the freshet. Tarried at Colo. Howard's; very kindly entertained; his family very sick yet.

23. I came over the river safe. Found Polly some more comfortable.

24. Mrs. Woodward dined here, then crossed the crick to go to Mr. Weston's. Mr. Hopkins and Mr. Stanley came in order to trim the mill. It thundered and rained in the night.

28. I left home about three o'clock, P. M. Went as far as Davis's store; was called to Colo. Howard's to assist Mrs. Pollard and Bisby lay out the corpse of his wife, just now deceased. His children yet very sick. I returned home a little after sunset.

30. Sunday. I came home from the fort about noon. Attended worship, afternoon. Mr. Jesse Koofe slept here; Samuel Bullen and Ephraim Cowen, also.

31. I was called at 10 o'clock in the morn in haste to Captain Jobe Springer's wife in travail, who was safely delivered at 2 o'clock, soon after my arrival there of a daughter. Left them both comfortable.

November 1. I was called to Mr. Weston's at 1 o'clock in morn. She being in labor; was delivered of a son at 7 in the morn. I returned home about one o'clock, afternoon. Polly Fletcher came to nurse Mrs. Weston. Mr. Ballard been with the court's committee on the roads from the river to Winthrop and west and to the country road eastward, which they have laid out.

November 7. Attended funeral of Peggy Margaret Howard who deceased yesterday.

8. I was at home all day very unwell. I tried to take a sweat last night but could not; this night went into a warm bed. Drank some hot brandy tody—sweat some.

10. Mrs. Edson here, 1 ounce salve for her husband's foot.

11. I was called at 5 o'clock this morn to Henry Babcock's, his wife being in travail. Arrived there about day-light—found her put to bed. The operation performed by Mrs. Smith. Mrs. Babcock, I found in severe pain, her complaints so great, and she very desirous I should inquire into the cause. I complyd, and found her greatly ingered [angered] by some mishap. Mrs. Smith does not allow that she was sensible of it; however her fix. Mrs. Babcock's distress was so severe we were apprehensive she was expiring; sent for Doctor Coleman. But Dr. Williams fortunately came in and prescribed remedies which afforded some relief. I left him there and returned home at 10 P. M.

12. I am at home. Doctor Williams called here on his return from Mr. Babcock's. Informs me that she is some more comfortable; he has hopes she may recover.

15. Mr. Ballard went to Cobese. I went to Mr. Suel's to visit his family; they were sick. There were a gang went to Samuel Dutton's and took John Jones.* Brought him to Pollard's; tarried till morn, when they set out with him for Wiscasset.

16. I heard that Captain Savage and Hersey were so heavy they overset their canoe and fell into the river.

17. It hath rained very much this day. The corn-mill ceased grinding till finished repairing.

20. I was called to Wm. Cowen's wife at 1 o'clock in morn; found her very unwell.

21. At Cowen's still. She unwell yet. Jonas Clark's infant had a fit; they called me to see it. Mrs. Cowen called her women together this evening; was safely delivered of a daughter about the middle of the night and is comfortable. Fee and medicines 10 shillings.

22. I returned from Cowen's. Mr. Ballard went to Doctor Cony's this afternoon to meet the select gentlemen [town officials].

24. Solomon Pollard went from here, went on board Captain Smith's [ship] bound for the West Indies.

25. I went to see Isaac Savage's youngest child, it being unwell. Mr. Sarls drank tea here, and took a raft out this crick this evening.

27. I did not attend divine service, but am going to visit Henry Babcock's wife who is sick. I find her some more comfortable.

28. Came home from Mr. Babcock's, and went to Mr. Weston's. Mr. Hamlen here to settle.

December 1. Mr. Crage's shop was consumed by fire.

6. The corn-mill set to going.

---

*A loyalist who had been expelled from town during the Revolution and, unfortunately for him, had returned.

December 9. Hannah Coole here. Informs of the death of Jabez and Reuben Moore's children. They were buried yesterday.

10. Mended my camblet gown. Mr. Ballard went to Wm. Pullin's. Brought home six fouls.

12. Called to Ben. Brown's wife. She being in travail, and was delivered of a son soon after my arrival.

13. I was called to see Dr. Colman. I watched.

14. I came from the Fort about noon. Left Dr. Colman exceeding low indeed.

15. Thanksgiving Day. I did not attend worship. Mr. Foster and wife, Mrs. Chamberlain. Theophilus Hamlen and Polly and Poll Savage, Hannah Woodward, and Eliphalet Robbins supt here.

16. I was at home all day. Mr. Ballard was surveying for Benjamin Brown.

17. A very rainy day. The freshet rose in the brook. Dutton's dam met with a breach which caused it to rise higher than usual. No great damage happened here.

18. A fine pleasant day. Mr. Hazelet performed divine service. I attended all day.

19. I have been at home this day. It is the anniversary of my marriage and thirty-one years since Mr. Ballard and I joined in wedlock.

20. Mr. Ballard been on the road by Hersey's.

21. Called to Mrs. Beaman, [she] being in travail—and was safely delivered of a daughter about midnight.

24. Mr. Ballard returned from surveying at Vassalborough (by desire of Esqr. Lovejoy).

29. Mr. Hallowell mended puter here for which he received 3 pecks of corn. Old Mr. Springer and wife here. Elizabeth Cosson, also. George Bolton has our horse—is gone to wedding of Daniel Savage, junior, and Betsy Peirce. Shubal Hinkley and widdo Robison are to be joined in wedlock this day.

30. Mr. French informed me of the death of Mrs. Stuart, who deceased this morn. Mr. Hinkley and lady went past here on their way home.

31. We were informed of the funeral of Mrs. Stuart at the Hook. Mr. Williams dined here. Says his wife is unwell. Children, I have been called to the birth of this year past, 28—seventeen of them were daughters. I have lost 42 nights' sleep this year past.

Chapter 4

Women and the Law

*E*nglish colonists brought with them a full array of English traditions, including legal traditions. Swiftly implanted in colonial soil, these traditions determined women's rights. Most important was the English tradition of common law, embracing judicial law and customary law. Under common law, a spinster or widow—a "feme sole"—was a legal individual, who could buy, own, and sell property, sue and be sued, make contracts, administer estates, and hold power of attorney. A married woman, or "feme covert," in contrast, lost her legal identity, which was merged with that of her husband. She could not sue, be sued, make wills, sign contracts, buy property, or sell it. The income that she earned, if any, belonged to her husband, as did her personal property and household goods. Any real estate that she brought to the marriage was under her husband's control. Similarly, the husband held custody of any children that the marriage produced, a practice that continued throughout most of the nineteenth century.

To English jurists, in the colonies as at home, the doctrine of coverture was a balanced, time-tried system under which a married woman gave up her legal identity in exchange for support and protection. "Even the disabilities, which the wife is under, are for the most part intended for her protection and benefit," wrote William Blackstone, whose *Commentaries on the Common Law* (1765) served as a handbook for early American lawyers. In what ways did coverture protect women? A husband was obliged, for instance, to support his wife. He was responsible for her debts, as well as for any crime she committed in his presence (presumably under his coercion). He could not cause her grievous injury, imprison her for long periods, or beat her to death.

Common law also offered some minimal protection of women's property rights. If a wife brought property to her marriage, for example, her husband could rent or use such property, but he could not sell it unless his wife agreed, alone, before a judge, to a deed of sale. Obviously, a wife could be pressured in some manner to give her consent. A more important type of property right was the dower right. Under common law, a man had to leave his wife at least a life interest in one-third of his real estate and one-third of his personal property outright. If he left no will, colonial courts insured his widow her dower right. This system protected both the widow and her community, which might otherwise have to support her. The dower could be affected by a colony's statutes. It was also a limited right. Life interest in a piece of property meant that the widow could not sell it or bequeath it but she was entitled solely to the income it produced—for example, the income from a piece of land farmed by her sons. In practice, the dower right offered most widows only minimal security and often left them very poor or dependent on relatives.

Common law, however, was not the whole story. Like her counterpart in England, the colonial woman had access to another legal tradition, equity law. Equity permitted some practices not sanctioned by common law. One example was the antenuptial agreement, a form of marriage settlement, which preserved for a married woman some control over the property she brought to the marriage and enabled her to bequeath it freely. In England, such agreements were made only by the very wealthy; in the colonies, they were used more often, typically by propertied widows embarking on new marriages. A different sort of option was the postnuptial contract, used either to reconcile feuding spouses or to separate them, with some provision for a wife's maintenance. Neither type of contract was a "right" but rather an agreement that depended on the assent of a husband or future husband. Equity law could mitigate coverture but provided no real escape.

Then, what happened to colonial women if a marriage fell apart—if a husband became abusive or simply vanished? In England, marriage was a sacrament, an indissoluble contract. Only the wealthy could obtain annulments through ecclesiastical courts or separations through special acts of parliament. Legally separated persons could not remarry. The colonies, however, provided some options. In Puritan New England, where marriage was a civil contract, the courts might grant divorces for such causes as desertion, prolonged absence, adultery, or bigamy, and the aggrieved spouse could then remarry. Such arrangements satisfied the Puritan desire to ensure family harmony, prevent destitution, and keep deserted wives and families off the public dole. Between 1639 and 1692, Massachusetts courts granted at least twenty-seven divorces.

"Absolute" divorce, divorce *a vinculo*, with the right of the injured party to remarry, was available only in New England. A more common remedy—though still rare—was divorce *a mensa et thoro*, a separation granted by a court or legislature, with no right to remarry but usually with an award of support to the injured party. Options for separation varied from colony to colony. South Carolina, for instance, prohibited all divorce, but its equity courts granted separations. In Pennsylvania, the assembly in 1705 authorized divorce *a mensa et thoro* in cases of adultery, bigamy, or sodomy. In New York and Virginia, this type of divorce might be granted for such causes as desertion, cruelty, adultery, or bigamy. But even divorce *a mensa et thoro* was an uncommon occurrence. After the Revolution, the new states enacted more liberal laws, providing for decrees of absolute divorce by the courts or assemblies, as in Virginia and Maryland.

Most colonial marriages that collapsed were ended not by law but by desertion, an illegal option used by both sexes but mainly by men. The deserted wife posed a legal problem; because she was legally nonexistent, she could not conduct business to support herself. As a "feme sole trader," however, the deserted wife could earn a living and spare the community the cost of her upkeep. In 1718, Pennsylvania passed a feme sole trader act to keep deserted wives and those left on their own for long periods off the public dole, as well as to pacify absent husbands' creditors. South Carolina's more liberal feme sole trader acts simply enabled wives to engage in business as feme soles.

The legal rights of free, white women in the English colonies, therefore, were determined by a combination of common law, equity law, and provincial statutes, which varied from one colony to another. (Each colony passed additional laws to regulate the conduct of indentured servants, slaves, and free blacks.) Colonial law, and the men who made it, sought neither to favor women nor to oppress them, but rather to preserve the interests of the community—by maintaining social order, preventing destitution, minimizing public expenditures, and facilitating the flow of capital. Overall, colonial legal practices were probably slightly more lenient toward women than English practices, especially in those colonies that had equity courts. To what extent was the protection of the law accessible to women? For an oppressed wife like Abigail Bailey (see Chapter 2), the law was clearly a last resort, and one to which she turned only with the help of male relatives. The prominent roles of women complainants or "accusers" in the best-known colonial courtroom scenes—witchcraft trials— may well give a misleading impression of women's clout in the legal arena. The women most likely to make court appearances were not complainants but those accused of crimes, such as theft or bastardy, as suggested in the county court records that follow.

The major significance of the English legal tradition that colonial women inherited was, in the end, its longevity. Although the revolutionary era marked the start of some changes, such as the wider availability of divorce, the common law doctrine of coverture, with modifications, remained intact. Firmly entrenched in the colonies, it survived long into the nation's maturity. Only in the mid-nineteenth century, when state legislatures began to enact married women's property rights acts, did the edifice of coverture start to crumble. The final demolition took more than a century.

An Antenuptial Contract

MASSACHUSETTS, 1653

Records and Files of the Quarterly Court of Essex County, Massachusetts, vol. 5, 1672–1674 (Salem, MA: Essex Institute, 1916), pp. 394–95.

When a couple signed an antenuptial contract, the bride retained some control over property that she brought to the marriage. She also retained the power to leave that property to whom she pleased. A well-off father might seek such a contract in order to provide for his daughter's support, if she became widowed. A propertied widow might insist on such an agreement with a prospective husband in order to retain control over whatever estate she had inherited from a previous husband.

In the following contract of 1653, Ann Allen, a Massachusetts widow, brought her dower right (or "thirds") to a new marriage, along with a sum of money that was intended for her six young children. Her prospective husband, Joseph Jewett, made some apparently minimal concessions: that on his death, Ann could regain the money intended for her children; that her oldest son would be sent to college and would receive a double share of inheritance; that all of her children would be supported; and that Ann could distribute among these children the household goods that she had brought to the marriage. The agreement even included arrangements for the raising of horses that Ann Allen had inherited. The document entered the court record twenty-one years later, when the youngest Allen son, Bozoon, sued the oldest Jewett son for not paying him his "portion," as stipulated in his mother's antenuptial contract.

Articles of agreement, dated Apr. 30, 1653, between Joseph Jewett of Rowley, merchant, and Ann, late wife to Capt. Bozoon Allen, deceased . . . ; Joseph Jewett, in consideration of a marriage shortly to be solemnized between him and Ann, widow of said Allen, and with receipt of her thirds and 600li., the children's portions, agreed in case of his death to leave the 600li. to his wife, and also agreed that his wife might dispose of 100li. during her life to her children by said Allen; that the eldest son should be brought up to learning, kept at a good school, found in diet, apparel, and books until he should be fitted for the University, and to be there maintained; that the other children should be brought up to learning and be supported until the age of twenty-one or marriage; that said Anne might give away to any of her children, a feather bed, bolster and pillow, with a bedstead, covering, pair of blankets, pair of fine sheets, five pillowbeers, curtains and wrought vallance, livery cupboard and cupboard cloth of needle work suitable for the vallance, two wrought cushions, two tables, one chair, two wrought stools, two trunks, two chests, two cases with glasses, one silver tankard, one silver bowl, six silver spoons, two gold rings, one silver dram cup, with the childbed linen in the trunk; that Joseph agreed to pay to Priscilla, the eldest daughter of said Anne 20li. over and above her portion; also that the mares which Captain Allen left, mentioned in the inventory, be allowed to run with their increase as the profit of that part of the double portion of John Allen until he came of age, and that said Joseph pay to John, Priscilla, Ann, Deborah, Isaac, and Bozoon Allen the portions their father left them in corn or cattle, when they become of age or are married, etc. Wit: Thomas Broughton, Thomas Buttolph, and Tho. Roberts. Acknowledged, 1 : 8 : 1653, before William Hibbins. Recorded, Feb. 3, 1653, by Edward Rawson, recorder. Copy made by Isa. Addington, cleric.

Divorce in New England

CONNECTICUT, 1655–1678

J. Hammond Trumbell, ed., *The Public Records of the Colony of Connecticut*, 3 vols.
(Hartford, CT, 1850–1859), 1:275, 301, 362, 379; 2:129, 292–93, 322, 326–28;
3:23.

Among all the colonies, only Massachusetts and Connecticut offered absolute divorce. Indeed, Connecticut offered only absolute divorce. During the seventeenth century, Connecticut's General Assembly served as both a legislature and an equity court, in which capacity it heard divorce petitions. In 1677, after granting divorces for twenty-two years, the assembly quietly passed a divorce statute, listing the justifiable causes: adultery, fraudulent contract, wilful desertion, or seven years' absence. Since this law ignored English law, Connecticut hoped that England would ignore the deviant statute, which it did.

During the seventeenth century, the typical Connecticut divorce recipient was a deserted wife, as indicated in the readings that follow (1655–1678). A major exception was Robert Wade of Seabrooke, whose wife's desertion, in the view of the court, was an exceptionally grievous act. In the eighteenth century, deserted wives continued to predominate among the colony's divorce petitioners, but the numbers of husbands complaining of desertion increased as did the numbers of wives who cited adultery in their petitions.*

The Connecticut Divorce Law,
Oct. 18, 1677

It is ordered by this Court that noe bill of divorce shall be granted to any man or woman lawfully married but in case of adultery, fraudulent contract, or willfull desertion for three years with totall neglect of duty, or seven years' providential absence being not heard of after due enquiry made and certifyed, such party shall be counted as legally dead to the other party; in all which cases a bill of divorce may be granted by the Court of Assistants to the agreived party who may then lawfully marry or be marryed to any other.

---

*For the changes in Connecticut divorce practices, see Linda Kerber, *Women of the Republic* (Chapel Hill: University of North Carolina Press, 1980), chap. 6.

Connecticut Divorce Cases

1655

This Courte considering the sad complaint of Goody Beckwith, of Fairefeild, in reference to her husbands deserting of her, doe declare y^t by w^{tt} evidences hath beene p^{r}sented to them of ye manner of her husbands departure and discontinnuance they judge that if the said Goody Beckwith, wife of Thomas shall uppon her oath testifie to the Magistrates that are shortly to keepe Courte at Strattford, that her husbands departure was as others have testified it to bee; and y^t shee hath not heard from him nor of him any wayes since hee deserted her, the said Magistrates may give her a bill of Divorce & sett her free from her said husband.

1657

This Court duely & seriously considering what evidence hath bene p^{r}sented to them by Robert Wade, of Seabrooke, in reference to his wives unworthy, sinfull, yea, unnaturall cariage towards him the said Robert, her husband, notwthstanding his constant & comendable care & indeavo^{rs} to gaine fellowship wth her in the bond of marriage, and that either where [were] shee is in England, or for her to live wth him here in New England; all wch being slighted & rejected by her, disowning him & fellowship wth him in that sollemne covenant of God betwene them, & all this for neare fifteene yeares; They doe hereby declare that Robert Wade is from this time free from Joane Wade, his late wife & that former Covenant of marriage betwene them.

1660

This Court orders, that in case Sarah North hear not of her husband by that ye seventh year be expired (he haveing bene absent six, already) that then she shal be free from her conjugal bonds.

1662

Bridget Baxter is by the authority of this Court, upon good consideration and solid reasons and evidenc, freed from her conjugall bond to her husband Thomas Baxter; and whereas the estate that her husband Baxter left with her is sold to pay debts, all excepting a bed and her wearing aparell, This Court doth prohibit all and every of the creditors to ye said estate for seizing, extending or any way troubleing ye remainder, until ye Court see cause to ye contrary.

1670

In answer to the petition of Hanna Huitt of Stonington, she haveing declared that she hath not heard from her late husband Thomas Huitt for the space of eight yeares and better, and the neighbours allso testifying that the sayd Huitt hath so long been absent and that they have not heard of him or of the vessell or company he went with since their departure, The Court haveing considered the premises, declare that she the sayd Hanna Huitt is at liberty to marry if shee see cause.

1676

This Court haveing considered the petition of Elizabeth Rogers, the wife of John Rogers, for a release from her conjugall bond to her husband, with all the allegations and proofes presented to clear the righteousness of her desires, doe find just cause to grant her desire, and doe free her from her conjugall bond to the sayd John Rogers.

1676

Upon the petition of Sarah Towle whoe hath been deserted by her husband above six yeares, without any care or provission made for supply of her or her child's maintenance by her husband, this Court declares that in case the said Towle shall have oppertunety to joyne herselfe in marriage with another man, she is left at liberty soe to doe without offence to the law or this Court.

1677

Upon the petition of Mary Murrain, the wife of Patrick Murrain, that she might be released from her conjugal tye to him, the Court considering of the same and findeing by the testimonies of sundry Deputies that he hath absented himselfe from her above six yeares, and hath not afoarded any thing towards her mayntenance as ever they heard of, besides other testimonies, and allso that he resolved never to see her more but wholly deserted her, the Court haveing considered the case doe find good reason to release her from her conjugall tye to the s^d Patrick Murrain, wth liberty to disspose herselfe in marriage, as God shall grant her oppertunety.

1677

Upon the petition of Elizabeth Griswould, the late wife of John Rogers, that she might have her children continued with her and brought up by her and not with John Rogers, he being so hettridox in his opinion and practice; the Court haveing considered the petition, and John Rogers haveing in open Court declared that he did utterly renownce all the vissible worship of New England, and professedly declare against the Christian Sabboth as a meere invention, &c. the Court see cause to order that the two children shall be and remayn with her the s^d Elizabeth and her father Mathew Griswould, to be brought up and nurtured by them (in the admonition and fear of the Lord) dureing the pleasure of this Court. And this Court doe order John Rogers to pay unto the sayd Elizabeth towards the mayntenance of his children, the sume of twenty pownds, to be payd five pownds a yeare, for fower yeares next followeing; and in case he fayle of payment, the reversion of the land by sayd John Rogers made over to Elizabeth his late wife, at Mamacock, is to be and stand for securety for the payment of the sayd sume of twenty pownds. [A sequel to the Rogers case of 1676.]

1677

This Court grants Experience Shepherd, the wife of Wm. Shepherd a release from her conjugall tye to the sayd Wm. Shepherd, he haveing deserted her with a resolve never to return to his wife againe.

1678

Upon the petition of Joanna Pember, the wife of Henry Pember, that she might be releassed from her conjugall tye to him, the Court haveing examined the case doe find it proved to ther sattisfaction that the sayd Henry Pember hath willfully deserted the sayd Joanna for the space of three yeares past and more, and that allso when he went away he declared he would com no more to her, and in his absence did take no care for her support and supply as appeares; and therefore the Court doe see cause to grant her a release from her conjugall tye to the sayd Henry Pember, with liberty to disspose of herselfe in marriage as she shall have opportunety.

Separation Decisions

MARYLAND, 1678, 1680

William Hand Browne, ed., *Archives of Maryland: Proceedings of the Council of Maryland, 1671–1681*, vol. 15 (Baltimore: Historical Society, 1896), pp. 206–7, 321–22.

Although absolute divorce was unavailable outside of New England, the opportunity existed for legal separation, through either postnuptial contracts or separation decisions imposed by courts. Requests for separation came most often from abused or abandoned wives who sought separate residences and alimony. Jurists were unsure of their power to require separate maintenance for wives without divorce, as this was not the practice in England. Still, they often sympathized with the plight of deserted or mistreated wives who had failed to obtain "protection" in marriage.

In Maryland, charges of cruelty, desertion, and nonsupport proved most successful in Courts of Chancery (equity courts), which made separation decisions. To these charges, wives sometimes added accusations of sexual misconduct, which were insufficient by themselves. On some occasions, marital disagreement sufficed as a cause for legal separation with separate maintenance. In the following cases, separations of feuding couples were decided by the Governor and Council of Maryland, acting as a court, in 1678 and 1680.

In the first case, which dragged on from 1676 to 1678, Robert Leshley brought his wife Elizabeth to court to clear his name of scandal. Elizabeth had accused him of buggery (sodomy) and demanded an allowance befitting the estate she had brought to the marriage. In court, the couple declared that they had resolved never to live together and Robert agreed to separate maintenance for Elizabeth, which the court imposed. In the second case, Elizabeth Tennisson claimed that she could not live safely with her husband and appealed for separate maintenance. John Tennisson denied cruelty but admitted lack of love, and his wife's request was granted. Both decisions were in the English tradition of divorce *a mensa et thoro*, although the term was not used. In both cases, the high annual alimony payments reflected the wife's social position and the contribution she had made at marriage to her husband's estate.

The Leshley Decision, 1678

Where came before them Robert Leshley and Elizabeth his wife according to appointm[t] by reason of a Peticōn [petition] exhibited [per] the s[d] Robert to the Governo[r] and the Governo[rs] warrant thereupon Dated the 5th instant, w[ch] said Peticōn & warrant foll: in ord[r] viz.

To the Hon[ble] Thomas Notley Esq[r] L[tt] Gen[ll] & Chiefe Governo[r] of Maryland

The Humble Peticōn of Robert Leshley Humbly Sheweth. That yo[r] Peticōners wife being a woman of an Implacable turbulent Spiritt has at severall times unjustly & wrongfully made Divers complaints and Accusations against yo[r] Pet[r] before severall of his Lo[pps] [Lordships] Justices of the peace of Calvert County but finding they tooke not the effect she hoped for, and that her Designe of procureing a considerable part of yo[r] Pet[rs] Estate to be allowed her for a maintenance with which she might live at her pleasure where she listed and quite Desert the family and concerns of yo[r] Pet[r] was wholly frustrated, she hath since very falsly injuriously & malitiously accused yo[r] Pet[r] of Buggery to the greate scandall & irreparable prejudice of yo[r] Pet[rs] creditt and reputation w[ch] he Does & alwaies shall Esteeme of greater price & value then his Life.

Wherefore yo[r] Peticōner humbly prayeth, that yo[r] Hono[r] will be gratiously pleased to grant him a Warrant, that she may be brought before yo[r] Hono[r] and her complaints & accusations against yo[r] Pet[r] heard and Examined before yo[r] Hono[r] whereby yo[r] Pet[r] may purge and cleanse himself of that grevious scandall cast upon him and that for the future he may live more peaceably & comfortably either with his said Wife or by allowing her such a maintenance as yo[r] Hono[r] shall ord[r] and Command.

And as in Duty bound he shall ever pray &c[a]

Upon heareing and Examination of the whole matter the Substance gathered from thence was that the Peticōner & his wife having had severall Differences betweene them w[ch] could not be composed Did severall Declare that they were fully resolved never any more to live together, She Desireing an allowance proportionable to what she had at her Intermarriage with him. He Declared himself willing to allow her such a reasonable maintenance as the Governo[r] and Councell should think fitt to award her with Due consideration had to his Capacity. The w[ch] at last they both referred to the Discretion of the Governo[r] and Councell to ord[r] therein what to them should seeme meete w[ch] they would submitt to.

The Governo[r] and Councell haveing Duely and maturely considered the p[r]misses Did ord[r] viz.

By the Governo^r and Councell

Whereas appeared before the Governo^r and Councell this Day Robert Leshley of Calvert County & Elizabeth his wife, and Did both jointly and severally openly Declare that for severall Differences betweene them both publick and private they were fully resolved never to cohabitt together again, and forasmuch as the said Elizabeth did Demand a reasonable maintenance to be allowed her by her s^d Husband, wch he readily consented to they both submitting themselves to the Discretion of the Governo^r and Councell to apportion the same as to them should seeme meete. It is Ordered.

That the said Robert Leshley pay or cause to be paid yearely and every yeare unto the said Elizabeth his wife for and Dureing her naturall life the just summe of two thousand pounds of tobacco for a maintenance and no more.

The Tennisson Decision, 1680

John Tennisson according to Summons of the 25th October last makes his appearance, Elizabeth Tennisson his wife at the same time also appeared and exhibited her Complaint to this board [personally] against her s^d husband for that she could not live peaceably and Quietly with him, but with a great deale of Danger and hazard to her [person], and therefore humbly prayed the allowance of a competent maintenance might be awarded her.

Whereunto John Tennisson replied Denying the allegations of his said wife and averring them to be altogether false malitious and unreasonable that he was ready and willing to receive her into his house and afford her a reasonable maintenance.

Both parties being heard and the Allegations on both sides duely examined and enquired into, and the said John Tennisson openly confessing that he could never entertain that love and respect for his said wife or neither afford her that countenance in his house as is [properly] due from a man to his wife, The following ord^r thereupon issued viz.

By the Lord Prop^ry & Councill

Maryl^d ss.   Whereas at a Councill held at the State house the second Day of November Anno One Thousand Six hundred and Eighty upon the complaint of Elizabeth Tennisson wife of John Tennisson of St. Maries County against her husband the said John Tennisson to this board this Day exhibited that she could not live peaceably & quietly with him but in Danger and hazard of her life, and therefore craved the allowance of a competent maintenance to be awarded her apart from her s^d husband, which complaint as also the Defence made by the said John Tennisson thereunto, and the allegations on both side duely heard and examined, The said John Tennisson alledgeing that he was ready and willing to take his wife home and to afford her a reasonable maintenance but withall openly and plainely acknowledgeing and confessing that he could never respect her soe as to love cherish countenance and maintaine her as a man ought to Doe his wife, all wch being Duely considered by this board it is this Day ordered.

That the said John Tennisson forthwith deliver unto his said wife or her ord^r one good bed and furniture called by the name of her owne bed, all her weareing apparell, and allow her yearely for the time to come three hundred pounds of meate, three barrells of Corne and one Thousand pounds of tobacco for and towards her maintenance dureing her naturall life to be paid and allotted her in such part and place of this Province as she shall Desire and appoint, and that the said John Tennisson give good security for his true pformance of what is hereby required of him before the Honble William Digges Esqr who is hereby Authorised and empowered (at such time as he shall think fitt) to summon before him the said John Tennisson and take of him such security as afores^d such as he shall approove of

Signed [per] ord^r
John Llewellin Cl Consil

Feme Sole Trader Acts

SOUTH CAROLINA, 1712 and 1744; PENNSYLVANIA, 1718

Thomas Cooper, ed., *The Statutes at Large of South Carolina* (Columbia: A. S. Johnston, 1836–1839), 2:593, 3:620. *Laws of the Commonwealth of Pennsylvania* (Philadelphia, 1810), 1:99–101.

The status of "feme sole trader" originated in London. It enabled married women to engage in business, independent of their husbands, and made them liable for their own business debts.* In most colonies, courts granted feme sole trader status on an individual basis, but two colonies enacted feme sole trader laws. Pennsylvania in 1718 offered feme sole trader status to women whose husbands would not support them—that is, wives of deserters, bankrupts, or men absent for long periods. Such women could engage in business as if they were feme soles, live off their earnings, support their children, and pay their own debts—and sometimes their absent husbands' debts.

South Carolina, in more liberal fashion, passed two laws that regulated women who engaged in business on their own. The first law (1712) made feme sole traders liable for their business debts. The second (1744) enabled such traders to bring suit in their own names. Unlike Pennsylvania, South Carolina did not limit feme sole trader status to women whose husbands were absent or bankrupt. Nor did South Carolina explicitly define *who* could be a feme sole trader. In practice, a husband's approval, tacit or written, was expected. The two liberal South Carolina statutes and the more restrictive Pennsylvania law follow.

An Act for the Better Securing of Debts Due from Any Person . . . and to Subject a Feme Covert That Is a Feme Sole Trader to Be Arrested and Sued for Any Debt Contracted by Her As a Sole Trader, 1712 [S.C.]

XII. Whereas several *feme coverts* in this Province that are sole traders, do contract debts in this Province with design

---

*Feme sole status is described in Marylynn Salmon, *Women and the Law of Property in Early America* (Chapel Hill: University of North Carolina Press, 1986), pp. 44–56.

to defraud the persons to whom they are indebted by sheltering and defending themselves from any suit brought against them by reason of their coverture, whereby several persons are defrauded of their just dues, for the prevention of which, *Be it enacted*, by the authority aforesaid, that any *feme covert* being a sole trader in this Province, shall be liable to any suit or action to be brought against her for any debt contracted as a sole trader, and all proceedings thereupon to judgment and execution as if such woman was sole and not under coverture, any law or custom to the contrary thereof in any wise notwithstanding.

Any Feme Covert, being a sole trader, liable to be sued as if sole.

An Act . . . to Empower and Enable a Feme Covert That Is a Sole Trader, to Sue for and Recover Such Debts As Shall Be Contracted with Her As a Sole Trader, and to Subject Such Feme Covert to Be Arrested and Sued for Any Debt Contracted by Her As a Sole Trader, 1744 [S.C.]

X. And whereas, feme coverts in this Province who are sole traders do sometimes contract debts in this Province with design to defraud the persons with whom they contract such debts, by sheltering and defending themselves from any suit brought against them, by reason of their coverture, whereby several persons may be defrauded of their just dues; and feme coverts, sole traders, are often under difficulties in recovering payment of debts contracted with them, by reason of the absence of their husbands, in whose name they are obliged to sue for all debts due to them, sometimes not being able to produce any power or authority from their husbands, *Be it therefore enacted* by the authority aforesaid, That any feme covert, being a sole trader, in this Province, shall be liable to any suit or action to be brought against her for any debt contracted as a sole trader, and shall also have full power and authority to sue for and recover, naming the husband for conformity, from any person whatsoever, all such debts as have or shall be contracted with her as a sole trader; and that all proceedings to judgment and execution by or against such feme covert, being a sole trader, shall be as if such woman was sole, and not under coverture; any law or custom to the contrary thereof in any wise notwithstanding.

Feme coverts, who are sole traders, may sue and be sued, naming the husband for conformity.

An Act Concerning Feme-Sole Traders, 1718 [Pa.]

Whereas it often happens that mariners and others, whose circumstances as well as vocations oblige them to go to sea, leave their wives in a way of shopkeeping: and such of them as are industrious, and take due care to pay the merchants they gain so much credit with, as to be well supplied with shop-goods from time to time, whereby they get a competent maintenance for themselves and children, and have been enabled to discharge considerable debts, left unpaid by their husbands at their going away; but some of those husbands, having so far lost sight of their duty to their wives and tender children, that their affections are turned to those, who, in all probability, will put them upon measures, not only to waste what they may get abroad, but misapply such effects as they leave in this province: For preventing whereof, and to the end that the estates belonging to such absent husbands may be secured for the maintenance of their wives and children, and that the goods and effects which such wives acquire, or are entrusted to sell in their husband's absence, may be preserved for satisfying of those who so entrust them, *Be it enacted,* That where any mariners or others are gone, or hereafter shall go, to sea, leaving their wives at shop-keeping, or to work for their livelihood at any other trade in this province, all such wives shall be deemed, adjudged and taken, and are hereby declared to be, as feme-sole traders, and shall have ability and are by this act enabled, to sue and be sued, plead and be impleaded at law, in any court or courts of this province, during their husbands' natural lives, without naming their husbands in such suits, pleas or actions: And when judgments are given against such wives for any debts contracted, or sums of money due from them, since their husbands left them, executions shall be awarded against the goods and chattels in the possession of such wives, or in the hands or possession of others in trust for them, and not against the goods and chattels of their husbands; unless it may appear to the court where those executions are returnable, that such wives have, out of their separate stock or profit of their trade, paid debts which were contracted by their husbands, or laid out money for the necessary support and maintenance of themselves and children; then, and in such case, executions shall be levied upon the estate, real and personal, of such husbands, to the value so paid or laid out, and no more.

II. *And be it further enacted,* That if any of the said absent husbands, being owners of lands, tenements, or other estate in this province, have aliened, or hereafter shall give, grant, mortgage or alienate, from his wife and children, any of his said lands, tenements or estate, without making an equivalent provision for their maintenance, in lieu thereof, every such gift, grant, mortgage or alienation, shall be deemed, adjudged and taken to be null and void.

III. *Provided nevertheless,* That if such absent husband shall happen to suffer shipwreck, or be by sickness or other casualty disabled to maintain himself, then, and in such case, and not otherwise, it shall be lawful for such distressed husband to sell or mortgage so much of his said estate, as shall be necessary to relieve him, and bring him home again to his family, any thing herein contained to the contrary notwithstanding.

IV. But if such absent husband, having his health and liberty, stays away so long from his wife and children, without making such provision for their maintenance before or after his going away, till they are like to become chargeable to the town or place where they inhabit; or in case such husband doth live or shall live in adultery, or cohabit unlawfully with another woman, and refuses or neglects, within seven years next after his going to sea, or departing this province, to return to his wife, and cohabit with her again; then, and in every such case, the lands, tenements and estate, belonging to such husbands, shall be and are hereby made liable and subject to be seized and taken in execution, to satisfy any sum or sums of money, which the wives of such husbands, or guardians of their children, shall necessarily expend or lay out for their support and maintenance; which execution shall be founded upon process of attachment against such estate, wherein the absent husband shall be made defendant; any law or usage to the contrary in any wise notwithstanding.

Malefactors and Complainants

MASSACHUSETTS, 1675–1680

Records of the Suffolk County Court, 1671–1680, Publications of the Colonial Society of Massachusetts, vol. 30 (Boston, 1933), pp. 603–1063 passim.

Women were active participants in the New England county courts, where they appeared in several capacities. Widows might claim parts of their dower rights or be sued for their late husbands' debts or serve as executrixes of wills. Wives occasionally served as attorneys for their husbands; colonies that accepted this practice did so on the grounds that a wife was legally an extension of her husband. Married or single, women might appear in court to complain about abusive treatment (see the charges brought by Judith Platts and Elizabeth Waters, in the reading that follows). The greatest female presence in court, however, comprised those charged with crimes—primarily fornication, bastardy, theft, or selling liquor without a license.

The following are representative entries in the records for 1675–1680 of the Suffolk County Court in Massachusetts. The jurisdiction of the court included Boston and neighboring towns. The entries convey not merely a record of charges, petitions, confessions, and decisions, but some vivid pictures of complainants and, especially, malefactors. One might wonder, for instance, about the fate of "vagabond" Quaker Joane Hyde, an unwelcome visitor from Rhode Island, or of Margaret Brewster of Barbados, who appeared at church services in sackcloth and ashes.

Carveath Fin[d] [fined] 5[l] [five pounds]

Mercy Carveath being bound over to this Court to answer for selling of liquo[rs] without licence & presenting a petition to the Court wherein Shee humbly acknowledgeth her offence therein & beggs the Courts Favour; The Court Sentenc[d] her to pay Five pound in mony as a fine to the County & Fees of Court & respit the Execucion thereof till farther order.

Langberry Fin[d] 10[s]

Elizabeth Langberry being committed to prison for her drunkenness & other misdemeano[rs] & appearing before the Court to answer for the same. She owned that shee had dranck too much & that Thomas Ockerby pulled her into his lap against her will.

The Court Sentenc^d her to pay ten Shillings in mony as a fine to the County & Fees of Court standing committ^d untill the Sentence bee perform^d.

Punnell Sentenc^d

Mary Punnell being imprisoned for her committing of Fornication & called before the Court to answer for the same, Shee appeared & confessed the Fact & brought her Childe into the Court with her chargeing one James Jarret to bee the Father thereof. The Court having considered of her offence doe Sentence her to bee whip't with Fifteen stripes & to pay Fees of Court & prison And doe Order that Shee bee returned to Milton from whence Shee came & if Shee bee not able to pay her charges nor can procure any Friend to doe it, that then the Town of Milton pay the same & entertain her according to law.

Backway Sentenc^d

William Backway & Mary his wife convict by theire own confession in Court of committing Fornication before theire marriage The Court Sentenced the s^d William to bee whip't with fifteen Stripes & Mary his wife with ten Stripes or to pay Fifty Shillings in mony as a fine to the County with Fees of Court standing committed untill the Sentence bee performed.

Amee Fined £2

Goodwife Amee being presented by the grandjury for absenting her selfe from the publique worship of God on the Lords dayes in the publique meeting places appointed by Law; which Shee owned in Court: The Court Sentenced her to pay Forty Shillings in mony as a fine to the County & Fees of Court.

Mary Wharton Sentenc^d the Wife of Phillip Wharton

Mary Wharton being complained of & imprisoned for unclean carriages with Ezekiel Gardiner The Court having heard & considered of what was proved ag^t [against] her & what Shee herselfe confessed do Sentence her to bee whip't severely with thirty Stripes at a carts tayle from her own house to the prison & then to bee committed to the house of correction there to bee kept according to the order of the house untill the next Court of this County & to pay Fees of Court standing committ^d &^a.

Gibbs Sentenc^d

Mary Gibbs being present^d for lascivious carriages & suspition of adultery. The Court having heard & considered of what was alleaged & proved ag^t her Sentenc^d her to bee whip't at the cart's tayle with twenty Stripes in comp^a [company] wth Mary Wharton from her house to the prison & to pay fees of Court standing committ^d &^a.

Hyde a Quaker Discharged

Joane Hyde being committ^d to prison as a vagabond Quaker; upon her motion to the Court & desire that Shee might return to Rhode Island whence Shee came & where Shee Saith Shee intends to Settle: The Court discharge her from the prison & grant her Liberty to return to Rhode Island.

Chelson Sentenc^d

Mary Chelson being imprisoned & called before the Court to answer for her committing of Fornication [377] & having a bastard Childe; which Shee owned in Court and charged Steven Jenkins of Piscataqua to bee the Father of it. The Court Sentenced her to bee whip't with Fifteen Stripes & to pay Fees of Court & prison standing committed untill this Sentence bee performed.

Licences

Elizabeth George, upon certificate from the Selectmen of Dorchester had her licence renewed to keepe a house of publique Entertainm^t & to Sell wine beere & Sider by retaile for the yeare ensuing; who gave in bond with Sureties for her observance of the Laws respecting Inkeepers & that Shee should not sell Sider for more then two pence a quart.

Bennet Sentenced

Mary Bennet having formerly charged her Selfe with Stealing sundry goods from her late Master Henry Thomson, the greatest part of which confession Shee retracted [395] in Court, onely some small things Shee owned Shee had Stol'n. The Court having duely considered thereof do Sentence the s^d Mary Bennet to bee whip't with Fifteen Stripes and to pay unto m^r Henry Thompson thirty Shillings in mony damage and to pay Fees of Court and prison standing committed untill the Sentence bee performed.

Order to Joyliffe

Upon the motion of Elisabeth Vicars late widdow of m^r Richard Price dec^d craving the benefit of the law respecting her thirds of a house & Land in Boston; which was alienated by her s^d husband Price in his life time unto m^r John Joyliffe Shee not having given up her thirds: The Court Orders m^r Joyliffe to Set out to the s^d Elisabeth her thirds of the s^d Estate; or else the Court will appoint a Committee for that end.

King Sentenc^d

Abigail King widdow convict in Court by the oathes of Samuel Sendall and Bartholmew Threenedle of suffering great disorders and disturbances in her house to the greife and annoyance of the neighbourhood, and for entertaining of Strangers: The Court Sentenc^d her to pay five pound in mony fine to the County charges of prosecution & Fees of Court [428] and caution her for future not to entertain any lodgers in her house without approbation of the Select men or other authority according to Law under the penalty of five pound per weeke.

Man Sentenced

John Man complained of by Judith Platts his Servant for wanton and lascivious carriages towards her & cruell beating of her: The Court having heard & considered what was alleaged and proved ag^t him Sentenced him to give in bond with Sureties of two hundred pounds for his good behavior untill the next Court of this County and to pay charges of prosecution and fees of Court standing committed &c. as also to discharge Judith Platts of the prison; and the Court declare her to bee free from her Indenture.

Miriam Negro Sentenc^d 40^s

Miriam Negro Servt to John Pynchon jun^r convict in Court by her own confession of committing Fornication & having a bastard Childe, Shee chargeing one Cornish an English man to bee the Father of it: The Court Sentenc^d her to bee whip't with ten Stripes or to pay Forty Shillings in mony fine to the County and Fees of Court standing committ^d &c.

Brewster Whip't

Margaret Brewster of Barbados convict in Court by her own confession of comming into the South meeting house in Boston upon the Sabbath day in the time of dispensing the word of God in a disguised manner with her face black^t her haire dishelved about her Shoulders, ashes on her head and sackcloth on her Shoulders, to the disturbance of the congregation and prophanation of the holy Sabbath: Sentenced to bee stripped unto the waste and to bee tied to a cart's tayle and whip't out of the Town with twenty Stripes, begining at the s^d meeting house, this to bee done upon the next Lecture day in Boston, and the Marshall is ordered to see the Execution thereof Shee standing committ^d &c.

Wharton & Gridley Bound to ye Good Behavio^r

Phillip Wharton and Mary Gridley formerly his wife being bound over to this Court to answer for theire disorderly and offensive cohabiting together having Sued out a divorce, they own^d they did live together: Sentenced to give in bond with Sureties of twenty pounds apeice for theire good abbearance untill the next Court of this County, especially to refrain the Company of each other and to pay fees of Court standing committ^d &c.

Green ag^t Jenner

Mary Green Attourny of her husband Nathanael Green of Boston Marrin^r plaint. ag^t Thomas Jenner of Charlestown Marrin^r Defend^t in an action of the case for not paying the Summe of One hundred & Ninety pounds Starling mony of Barbados due unto s^d Green from s^d Thomas Jenner in and by a bond or Obligation under his hand & Seale bearing date. 2^d of October. 1675. &c. wth other due damages. . . . The Jury . . . found for the plaint.

Auborne Fin^d £5

Rebecca Auborne convict by her own confession in Court of committing Fornication with Samuel Kemble having a bastard Childe, Sentenced to bee whip't with Fifteen Stripes and to pay fees of Court standing committ^d &c. afterwards remitted her punishm^t upon payment of five pounds in money.

Kemble Sent^a

Samuel Kemble is declared to bee the reputed Father according to Law of the Childe late born of the body of Rebecca Auborne, and ordered to pay unto the s^d Rebecca, two Shillings six pence in money per weeke weekely towards the maintenance of s^d Childe and to give in twenty pounds Security for the same untill the Court take further order and to pay fees of Court standing committ^d &c.

Phillips Sent^a

Sarah Phillips Servant unto Wm Green of Boston convict^d in Court by her own confession of Stealing mony from her Ma^r rideing away in mans Apparrell and having a bastard Childe She knoweth not (Shee Saith) by whome begotten, Sentenced to bee forthwith whip't with Fifteen Stripes and a Fortnight after to bee whip't again at Charlestown with Fifteen Stripes and to pay unto her Ma^r Green 3^{ble} damages according to Law, hee defalkeing what hee hath already received, and to pay fees of Court and prison standing committ^d &c^a and order y^t in case her Ma^r do not discharge her of the prison upon her receiving her 2^d punishm^t the keeper is ordered to dispose of her for his Satisfaction and to pay the overplus to her Master.

Waters Complaint

Upon complaint made to this Court by Elizabeth Waters that her Husband Wm Waters doth refuse to allow her victuals clothing or fireing necessary for her Support or livelihood and hath acted many unkindnesses and cruelties towards her: The Court having sent for the s^d Wm Waters and heard both partys, do Order that the s^d Waters bee admonish't for his cruelty and unkindness to his wife, and that hee forthwith provide Suitable meate drinke and apparrell for his s^d wife for future at the Judgem^t of Mr Edward Rawson and Mr Richd Collacot or allow her five Shillings per weeke.

Accusations Against Elizabeth Morse

MASSACHUSETTS, 1679–1680

Samuel G. Drake, *Annals of Witchcraft in New England* (Boston, 1869),
pp. 258–96 passim.

Women's most famous roles in colonial courtrooms were as the accusers and victims at New England witchcraft trials. The witchcraft trial of Elizabeth Morse of Newbury, Massachusetts, is one example. Morse, age sixty-five, and her husband, William, a well-off farmer, were involved in a complex series of charges and countercharges of witchcraft. At the end of 1679, many of their neighbors made depositions implicating Elizabeth. These townsfolk and others testified at her 1680 trial, where she was found guilty and sentenced to hang. When her husband persistently rebutted the charges against her, her execution was postponed several times. In the spring of 1681, Elizabeth Morse was released from prison and sentenced to an indefinite form of house arrest. Never executed, she survived her husband, who died in 1683, and lived on, claiming innocence.*

In the testimony against Elizabeth Morse, usually by deponents who had been involved in some sort of dispute with her, the townsfolk of Newbury related instances of illness and injury allegedly caused by Morse. They told of the sudden deaths of farm animals (including events that occurred years earlier); of spectral appearances of cats, rats, owls, and dogs; and of Elizabeth's apparent access to letters she had not seen and conversations she had not heard. Historian John Demos points out that the accusers in this case fell mainly into two categories. One group of accusers comprised younger men, whom Elizabeth had hired for farm work, who may have resented her authority ("Goody Morse . . . was mighty with me"), and who usually related tales about injuries to animals. The second category comprised middle-aged women, with whom Elizabeth had much more personal contact and who told about personal injuries. Sometimes their daughters supported their testimony. Among the most impressive accusations was the tale of the formidable horseshoe test, given by Esther Willson and her mother.

---

*For the complete story of the Elizabeth Morse witchcraft case, see John Demos, *Entertaining Satan: Witchcraft and the Culture of Early New England* (New York: Oxford University Press, 1982), pp. 132–52.

The following are samples of the accusations made in 1679 and
1680, when Elizabeth Morse was indicted and tried. As in other witchcraft cases, this testimony is as interesting for the window it provides
into the lives and concerns of seventeenth-century New Englanders as
it is for its bizarre—and spectral—components.

Elizabeth Titcomb, aged about fifty. After yᵉ Burning of Apples at Ensigne Greenleaf,
I was soone troubled at my House with a Noyes knocking at yᵉ Dore which did awake
mee out of a sound Sleepe: yᵉ first knocking I lay still harkening for to hear a Voice,
and none I heard: I thought Somebody did want my help knocking a second Time; but
I heard no Voyce: a third Time I heard knocking; then I went forth, and called to my
Daughter Lydia: asked her if shee did heare yᵉ Noyes. Shee said, Yes. Then I opened
my Chamber Dore, and saide, Who are you? What is your busines? But no Voyce. So
I considered yᵗ I had no Call to goe to yᵉ Dore, and begg'd of God to give mee Rest:
but I was much disturbed by the vyoulent Motion of a Creature which I did never
know before nor since. . . .

The Testemony of Caleb Moody, aged 42 Yearse, testphieth and sayeth, that I having
lived nere to Elizabeth Morse about twenty Yeers, I have lost sevrall Catell in a usiall
[usual] maner. About 16 Years a goe I had sume difrans with the seyd Morse; the next
Morning one of my best Hogs lay deed in the Yrd, and no natrial Case [natural cause],
that I know of. . . .

At another Time I had a Cowe was sudenly tacken in a very strange Maner, and
tumled ovr Logs that layd in the Yord, and strived to turne reerd upon her Heade, and
so continued a while, and rose up agayne, and went awaye. After this I sawe the same
Cowe coming doune the Hill by Wm. Morses House, and I sawe the seyed Elizabeth
Morse stand without the Doare, and my Cowe fall in to the like strange Condision, as
she did before, and tumbled into a Guter or Guly that was worne with the Runing of
the Water: after she recovred and went awaye Home. At another Time, of a Sabath
Daye Morning, one of my Cowes, great with Calfe, was turnd in to the Stale with her
Head under her, stone dead; in such a Maner that I could not thinke it posable for a
Cow to pute herself in to such a Place, but conclud the Divell by sume Instrument did
it; and sevrall that saw it did saye they were of the same Minde, or Wrds to that
Porpose.

The Deposition of Johua Richardson, aged a bought thirty Years: testifieth and saith,
that a bought five Years a goe, then I had three Sheep to drive to Hamton: and when
I came doune the Street I thought it best to cech my Sheep at good Man Morses
Barne, becase it was neare my Canue that was to carry them ovr the river; and good
Man Mors Cow House Dore stood open next the Hie Way, and I loock in and I saw
Nothing there; so I drove my Sheep into the Cowhouse, and as I was ceching the
Sheep, Gooddi Morse came out, and was mighty with mee: and said I had better aske
Leave, and I went away with my Sheep: and when I came to Hamton, abought to Ours

after, the Sheep weare all sick, and did fome at the Mouths, and one of them died presently; and they askt mee where I cecht the Sheep? and I tould them in Mors Cow Hous; and they said they did beleve they wer bewicht, and so do I to. . . .

The Testemony of Wm Faning, aged about 36 Yeers, testiphieth and sayeth, that about a Month or five Weeks agoe, living neere to Wiliam Morses, in the Evning, quickly after Sone seat [sunset], I saw John Stiles standing by Mr. Denisons Couehous and I asked him what was the best News att their House, and he tould mee that there was severall Hundreds of Divels in the Eyer, and they would be att their House by and by, and they would be att my Hous a non: and that very Night ey [I] went to Sargent Moodeys Hous, which is my Neighbor, and borrowed his Mare to go to Mill; and I went to Mill with two Bushels of Corn and got it ground; and when I came back againe, in John Hals Pasture, the Mare began to startell and snort, and rared up on End, so that I could not gett her forward; and I loocked downe upon the Mars Head I spied a great whit Cat without a Tayl upon by Brest and she had fast hold of my Neckcloth and Coat. I haveing a good Stick in my Hand, I stroock her off. And againe the Cat was a coming up upon my left Side, I toock my Stick in my left Hand and stroock her down againe; then I alighted, and as soon as I alighted the Catt came between my Legs, so that I could not well go forward; and watching my Opportunity I stroock her a very great Blow up against a Tree, and after that I stroock her another Blow which made her lay for dead, and I went presently to John Hals House, and he was abed. I caled to him and desiered him that he would go to sutch a Tree and there I thought he would find a dead Catt, and I went straight way Home and told my Wife, and tould her what I had met with all. . . .

The Deposition of Robert Earle [the jailor], aged 45 Yeeres, or thereabouts, sayth that on Twesday Night last, about to of the Cloke at Night goeing into the Camber where Elizabeth Morse was shut in, finding her setting upright in her Bed, she sayed to me that she was very glad that I was come in, for she was in great Troable, and that she thought she should dye for it now, for they were goeing to find out another Way for Blasphemye. And I went neere her Bedside, and I heard a strainge Kind of Noyse, which was like a Wheelpe sucking of the Dam, or Kittins sucking, which made me to thinke whether any of the Catts had layd any of there Kittins upon the Syde of the Bed, or wheather it might be some strainge Kind of Hissing within her. Further, I testifye, that Yesterday, when I went to fech her to ye Court, she sayd that now they say abroad I shall dye. I asking of her why she sayd soe, and whoe it was that sayd soe, she sayd, my Husband, and I have beene talking to geither of it. And she sayed that I did know what they did say, if I would speake, and such as I that doe know such Things spoke of abroad. Then I remembering there was some did ask me what I thought would be don with her. I sayd I did not know but y^t she might dye for it, which made me have the more Suspition of her calling to mind w^t I sayd abroad. . . .

The Testimony of Elizabeth Titcomb, aged about 50 Years.
    That shee being lately with Susanna Tappin, aged about 74 Years, the s^d Tappin related to her, that when Elizabeth Morse was in Examination for Witchcraft, and she being summoned gave in her Testimony among others. When she went away she sayd

Elizabeth Morse came after her and tooke her about the Wrist, as if she would enquire what was the Evidence she gave in ag^t her: who answered Nothing but what you spake your selfe. The sayd Topan went Home, and in the Night she felt a cold Damp Hand clasping her about her Wrist, wch affrighted her very much, and putt her into a very great and dropping Sweat: and from that Time she continued ill, and an itching and pricking rose upon her Body, wch afterwards came to such a dry Scurfe [incrustation], that she could scrape it off as it were Scales from an Allewife; and that Side wch she was touched in was most out of Frame; and she is smitten in the lower Parts of her Body after the same Manner that she had testifyed agt the sayd Morse what she heard her speake: and from that Time she hath continued very ill, but little from her Bed, and hath not bin able to goe abroad ever since to the publike Meeting. Who also sayth that the very Night when she being defined to goe and enquire of the sayd Topan, what her Evidence was, she had a Beast strangely hanged in a harrow and dead.

Lydia Titcomb, aged about 17 Yeares, testifyeth, that she heard the Discourse betweene her Mother and the sayd G. Morse, and the Words wch her Mother hath expressed; and also, that a little While after she and her Brother and Sister, going home from the Pond where they fetcht water, there flew somewhat out of the Bushes, in her opinion like an Owle, and it came up presently to her, and was turned into the Shape of a Catt; and quickly after turned into the Shape of a Dog: sometimes would be all black, then have a white Ring about the Neck: sometimes would have long Eares, sometimes scarce any to be discerned; sometimes a very long Taile, sometimes a very short one, scarce discernable, and in such Manner it followed us some Time, as if it would leap upon our Backs, and frighted us very much, and accompanyed us till they came neere the House: and the last Time we saw it we left it playing about a Tree, and we went in and left it.

John Chase. And as an Addition to my former Testimony, I testify and say, that yt very Day, to the best of my Knowledge, yt Kaleb Powell came to take my Testimony against Goodwife Morse yt I was taken with ye bloody Flux, and soe it held mee till I came to ye Court and charged her with itt, yt at ye very Instant of Time itt left me, and I have not been troubled with it since, and that my Wife has been sorely troubled with sore Breasts, that she have lost them both, and one of them rotted away from her.

The Testimony of Mrs. Jane Sewall, aged about 54 Yeares. Who sayth that some Yeares since Wm. Morse being at my House, began of his owne Accord to say that his Wife was accounted a Witch, but he did wonder that she should be both a healing and a destroying Witch, and gave this Instance. Thomas Wells, his Wife being come to the Time of her Delivery, was not willing (by the Motion of his Sister in whose House she was) to send for Goodwife Morse, though she were the next Neighbour, and continued a long Season in strong Labour and could not be delivered; but when they saw the Woman in such a Condition, and without any hopefull Appearance of Delivery, determined to send for the sayd G. Morse, and so Tho. Wells went to her and desired her to come; who, at first, made a Difficulty of it, as being unwilling, not being sent for sooner. Tho. Wells sayd he would have come sooner, but [his Wife's] Sister would not let him; so at last she went, and quickly after her coming the Woman was delivered. This, as she remembreth, was the Substance [of the] Discourse, though she doth not remember his very Words: and she supposeth, [that] Thomas Wells and his Wife living both at Boston can give more full Testimony concerning this Thing.

The Testimony of David Wheeler of Newberry, aged fifty five Yeares or there abouts, testifieth and saith, that haveinge lived next Neighbour to Elizabeth Morse the Wife of Wm Morse of Newberry afores^d. He tooke Nottice of many strange Actions of her ye said Eliz: Morse, more then ever hee sawe in any other Woman; Part whereof I have given in my Evedence under Oath before Mr. Woodbridge, concerneing an Heifer whereunto I would farther add that all the Rest of y^t Breed of Cattle have gennerally miscarried by strange Accedents ever since, till this present Time wch is the Space of fifteene Yeares or thereabouts; as alsoe, that ye s^d Eliz: Morse desired mee one Time to doe a smale Peece of Worke for her, wch I neglected to doe soe soone as shee desired; and I goeinge many Dayes on fowleinge, att y^t Time, always as to ye Gennerality, came Home wth lost Labour, wch my Neighbour Moody tooke Notice of as well as my selfe, and hee told mee I would gett noe Geese untill I had finished her Worke, wch accordingly I speedily did; and afterwards I had Success as I used to have formerly. Moreover, severall other Accedents have befallen mee wch I believe y^t shee, the said Morse, through the Malice and Envy of her Heart against mee might bee ye Author of by Witchcraft, and farther saith not.

The Deposicon of Margett Mirack, aged about 56. This Deponent testifieth y^t about a Letter y^t came from Puscattaq^y, by Mr. Tho: Wiggens. Wee gott Mr. Wiggens to reade ye Letter, and he went his Way; and I p^rmised to conceale ye Letter after it was read to my Husband and myselfe, and wee both did conceale it; nevertheless, in few Daijes after Goode Morse mett mee and clapt mee on ye Back, and sed, I comend you for sending such an Answerr to ye Letter. I p^rsently askt her w^t Letter? Why, s^d shee, hadst not thee such a Letter from such a Man at such a Time, and sent such and such an Answerr at such a Time? I came Home p^rsently and examined my Husband about it. My Husband s^d p^rsently, What? Is shee a Witch, or a cunning Wooman? Whereup-pon we examined our Family, and they s^d they knew Nothing of ye Letter. Afterwds I mett wth Goode Morse and askt her how shee came to know it? and desired her to tell mee any one pson [person] y^t tould her, and I should be satisfied. Shee askt mee why I was soe inquisitive, and told mee shee could not tell. My Husband testifieth that I p^rsently tould him ye same.

The Testimony of Esther Willson aged about 28. That she living with her Mother, Goodwife Chandler when she was ill, she would often cry out and complaine that G. Morse was a Witch, and had bewitched her, and every Time she came to see her she was the Worse for her. Though too meete were often forbidden, yett thay would not refraine coming. One coming to the House asked why we did not nayle a Horse-shoe on the Threshold (for that was an Experiment to try Witches). My Mother the next Morning, with her Staffe made a Shift to gett to the Doore, and nayled on a

Horseshoe, as well as she could. G. Morse, while the Horseshoe was on, would never be perswaded to come into the House; and though she were perswaded by the Deponent, and Daniel Rolfe, to goe in, she would not; and being demanded the Reason she would not tell me now, and sayd it was not her Mind to come in; but she would kneele downe by the Doore and talke and discourse, but not goe in, though she would come often Times in a Day, yett that was her practise. Wm Moody coming to the House, and understanding that there was a Horseshoe nailed on the Doore, sayd a Piece of Witchery, and knockt it off and layd it by. Very shortly after, the same Day G. Morse came in, and thrust into the Palour where my Mother lay before she was up; and my Mother complained of her, and I earnestly desired her that she would be gon, and I could very hardly with my Importunity intreat her to do it. The Horseshoe was off about a Weeke and she would very often come in that Time. About a Weeke after, my Mother, to keep her out of the House, gott Daniel Rolfe to naile on the Shooe againe, wch continued so about 7 or 8 Dayes, and at that Time she would not come over the Threshold to come in, though often importuned to do it. Then Wm Moody coming againe, tooke off the Horseshoe, and putt it in his Pockett, and carryed it away: then the sayd Goodwife Morse came as before, and would goe in as before. In a short Time after, I being at Home on a Sabbath Day, alone with my Mother, I had bin dressing her Head, and she cryed out on a Sudden, G. Morse, G. Morse is coming into the House. I sayd I could not see her, my Mother sayd I see her, there she is. Then I run to the Doore twice, but I could not see her; but my Mother cryed out, that wicked Woman would kill her, be the Death of her, she could not beare it, and fell into a grievous Fitt, and I tooke her and carryed her in and layd her on a Bed; and having so done I went out to see if any Body were coming from Meeting, and ther (though I saw her not before) she rushed in, and went into the Parlour to my Mother, and I stepping out and seeing my Father coming lift up my Hand to him to come and he made great Hast [haste], and I called in some of the Neighbours, and so my Mother continued a considerable Time before she recovered. In this Fitt, my Mother's Mouth was drawne awry, and she foamed at Mouth, and I wiped it of, but I was very much frighted to see her so till the Neighbours came in. This is all that at present she remembreth.

Widows, Wills, and Dower Rights

VIRGINIA, 1642, AND NEW YORK, 1721–1759

Susie M. Ames, ed., *County Court Records of Accomack-Northampton, Virginia, 1640–1645* (Charlottesville: University of Virginia Press, 1954), pp. 246–48; *Collections of the New York Historical Society for the Year 1896* (New York, 1897).

The colonial woman's most important legal right was probably her dower right. Under common law, a man had to leave his wife at least a life interest in one-third of his real estate, which after her death would go to his heirs, and one-third of his personal property, which belonged to his widow forever and was hers to bequeath. If a man left no will, the colonial courts ensured his widow her "thirds" in his estate. She could sue for quick access to this legacy, if the courts moved too slowly.

If a man wrote a will, he could, of course, leave his widow more than her "thirds," as was common in the early Chesapeake. Many men left all they had to their widows; after 1650, most will-writers left widows with all or most of their estates for life and made the widows executrixes of their wills. This guaranteed that a widow would control all of the family property while the estate went through probate. In the Virginia will that follows, George Travellor gave most of his land to his two children (mainly his son) but left his wife, Alice, all of the rest of his property and made her executrix. He seemed to anticipate her remarriage, which, indeed, soon occurred. Since Travellor's offspring were too young to make use of their "portions," Alice was in effect in control. In the eighteenth century, Chesapeake planters' liberality toward widows, and the custom of making wives executrixes, declined.

Even when the dower right did not come into play, it served as a guideline to men who wrote wills, as is evident in the following wills of eighteenth-century New Yorkers, mainly craftsmen and farmers. Men might still leave their widows estates that exceeded their dower right. They might also, however, limit the amount beyond the dower right in any manner, such as by specifying "while she remains my widow" or "unless she remarries." In addition, widows were less likely to become sole executrixes, as they had in the early Chesapeake. What widows lost, children tended to gain. Men who wrote wills in the eighteenth century were likely to do so at more advanced ages than did early Chesapeake will-writers, and therefore were more likely to have grown sons who could serve as executors; widows might well become dependents of these adult offspring. Eighteenth-century daughters were often beneficiaries, too. In some cases, they received only movable property such as slaves or furniture, while their brothers received land. In other instances, they shared equally with brothers in their fathers' estates.

A Virginia Will, 1642

In the Name of God Amen, [February 3, 1642]

I George Travellor being very sicke and weake of body but of perfect sence and memory blessed bee God doe make And ordayne this my last Will and Testament in manner and Forme following.

First I bequeath my soule to god That gave it and my body to the Earth from whence it was taken in sure and certayne hope of Resurrection to Eternall Life Through the merritts of Jesus Christ my only Saviour and Redeemer.

Secondly for the outward blessings which god of his mercy hath bestowed upon mee my last Will and desire is That two of my Cowes Blacke Bess and white Foote and Dazie her yearling with black Bess her Calfe shall Forthwith after my decease bee mark't and sett apart For my sonne George Travellor.

Item I give and bequeath to my sayde Sonne George one bedd with all Kinde of furniture as Blanketts, Rugg Boulster Curtaynes sheetes and Bedsteade thereunto belonging, as one Iron pott, one gunn, to bee either the same That I now use, or otherwise one as good, Three Pewter dishes, one salt, one Table and this Five hundred Acres of Land with the houseing and building Whereon I am now seated.

Item I give and bequeath unto my daughter Elizabeth Two of my Cowes call'd Dazie and Sweete lipps as alsoe blacke Bess her Yearling with one yearling more. One bedd with Furniture as to my sonn George one Table one pott, Three pewter dishes, one salt, and Two hundred Acres of Land att the Seaboard side, All the aforesaid Beding and Furniture to bee as good as the best I nowe possesse.

Item I give and bequeath to my Loveing wife Alice Travellor All the rest of my Estate wheather Cattell or Chattell, as well moveable as Immoveable goods Always Provided That shee my sayde wife makes good all the Former Legacies bequeathed to my deare Children, the Cattell with all their Female Increase, And all the rest of the forenamed goods to bee delivered to them new and good when they shall come to age, As namely to my sonne George att Eighteene yeares of Age And to my daughter Elizabeth att her day of Marriage or otherwise att Fifteene yeares of Age, And my desire is That my sayde Daughter should take the Councell of her Mother in her Match if shee bee then Liveing.

Item I doe hereby ordayne and desire my deare and Loveing wife Alice Travellor to have an Especiall care of the good Education of my tender Children That they may bee well brought upp and in the Feare of god. And if in case my sayde wife should marry and That my Children should suffer in their Estates or good Edicature, that the overseers of this my will shall hereby have full power and Authority to take my sayde Children to their or one or More of their Custody and care and to putt in good security for their Edicature as aforesaid. As alsoe with them to Receive their Portions into their possession for use of them. As to put in good security to bee Answearable therefore. As alsoe if my sayde wife should Marry That her husband put in sufficient security to my overseers for the full and Reall performance of all the promisses.

Item I ordayne and appoint That if either of my Children should dye The Survivor shall enjoye the deceaseds parte. And if it should please God to take away both, Then my wife to enjoye all, And if in case my wife should dye, shee to dispose of all her parte as shee pleaseth.

Lastly I constitute and ordayne my Loveing wife Alice Travellor my full and whole Executrix of this my Last Testament desireing my Loveing Friends Argoll Yardley Esquire, John Rosier Clerke, Capt. Frauncis Yardley and John Seaverne to bee my overseers, desireing them for gods sake (as much as in them Lyeth) to see the due performance of this my Will in manner and Forme as aforesaid. And in Testimony That this is my true Will and Testament I have hereunto Sealed and Subscribed.

Signed and Sealed in the
presence of us.
John Rosier. William Roper.

The marke of
George Travellor   The Seale.
Vera Copia cum original Concor.

Exam. per me Edwynn Conaway Clericus Curiae
Tres decimo die mensis February Anno 1642.

New York Wills, 1721–1759

In the name of God, Amen, December 15, 1753. I, Isaac Fryor, of Albany. I leave to my son John 20 shillings on account of his birth right, in full bar as eldest son and heir at law. I leave to my wife Elizabeth the use of all estate, movable and immovable, for her maintainance and support so long as she remains my widow. After the death or marriage of my wife I leave to my son John £60. To my daughter Catharine "my Great Cupboard or Kass" after my wife's decease, "or sooner if my wife should think proper." To my son Isaac my weaver's loom. I leave to my sons William and Isaac and my daughter Catharine all my now dwelling house in Albany, in the First Ward, with the lot, and all the rest of my estate. It is my will that my son Isaac and my daughter Catharine shall dwell in the house until married. I make my wife and my friend, Jacobus Hilton, executors.

Witnesses, Jacobus Hilton, Luycas Witbeck, Richard Cortwright. Proved in Albany, before Goldsbrow Banyer, October 30, 1755.

(Written in Dutch language.) In de Name Godes, Amen. I, Hendrick Kip, of Fishkill, in Duchess County, December 12, 1751. I leave to my wife Jacomintie all estate during her widowhood. If she marries she shall have £100. I leave to the son of my eldest brother Frederick £5 for his birth right. To Mathew Sledt, my oldest sister's son, £100. To Cornelius, the eldest son of Garrit Newkirk, £100. I leave to my cousin Cornelius Newkirk, son of Jan Newkirk, all my real estate after the death of my wife. I make my friend, Jacob Du Bois, and Theodorus Cornelius Van Wyck, executors.

Witnesses, Evert Brower, Alexander Schatfeld, Johanes Cooper. Proved in Court of Common Pleas, in Duchess County, before Theodorus Van Wyck and John Brinkerhoff, Judges, and Peter Montfort, Justice, December 14, 1754.

In the name of God, Amen, November 2, 1754. I, Benjamin L'Hommedieu, of Southold, being in health. I leave to my beloved wife Martha the use of all my house and lands and mills during widowhood, and a negro man and woman; and the other negro woman is to be sold by my executors, and the money paid to my eldest daughter, Elizabeth Boorn. I leave to my son, Ezra L'Hommedieu, after my wife's decease, all my houses, lands, and mills, and my negro man. I leave to my daughter, Mary L'Hommedieu, a negro girl "Hagar." All the rest of my movable estate I leave to my son Ezra and my daughter Mary. I make my wife Martha and my son Ezra and my friend, Robert Hempstead, executors.

Witnesses, John Youngs, Amasa Pike, Thomas Hempstead. Proved, November 12, 1755.

In the name of God, Amen, May 9, 1721. I, Matthew Benson, of New York, mason, being sick and weak. I leave to my son, Samson Benson, £5 in full of all claim to my estate. I leave to my wife Katie all the rest of my estate during her life if she remains my widow, and after her death to my four children, Samson, Trintie, Katalinta, and Katie. I make my brothers, Dirck Benson and Harmon Benson, executors, and they have power to sell that piece of land at the rear of the lot where I now live, from the Slip to the land of Nicholas Mathison, containing in breadth 24 feet.

Witnesses, Wynant Van Zandt, William Mastyson, Henry Rich, William Huddlestone. Proved, December 9, 1755. The executors were then dead, and Letters of administration were granted to Catharine Moore, widow of Thomas Moore, of New York, weaver, and Caroline Benson, spinster, the surviving children of Matthew Benson.

In the name of God, Amen. I, Francis Bassett, of New York, pewterer, this 16 of December, 1749. I leave to my wife, Elizabeth Mary Bassett, all my real and personal estate, to her and her heirs and assigns for ever, and I make her sole executor.

Witnesses, Christopher Roberts, Francis Foy, Simon Johnson. Proved, June 14, 1758.

In the name of God, Amen. I, Francis De Lanoy, of Beekman's Precinct, in Duchess County, being in health of body. I direct all debts and funeral charges to be paid in convenient time. I leave to my beloved wife Mary all my estate, real and personal, while she remains my widow, "But if she be married to another man, she is to have what the Law alows her." The rest to my children, Arre, Rachel, Nicholas, Lawrence, Jean, Mary, Lydia, Elizabeth, Catharine, Elias, Gershee, and Egie. I make my wife Mary, and Benjamin Hasbrouck, and Peter Vandewater, executors.

Dated May 9, 1751. Witnesses, Joseph Winslow, William Huff. Proved before Mathew Dubois, Judge of Common Pleas, Bartholemew Noxon and William Davenport, Justices, May 29, 1755.

In the name of God, Amen, April 24, 1759. I, Anthony Woodhouse, of Phillipsburgh, in Westchester County, innholder, being sick. I leave to my wife Charity all the goods that she brought to me, and a cow and cupboard. I leave to my cousin, Samuel Woodhouse, my gray horse, bridle and saddle, and my wearing clothes. After payment of all debts, I leave to my daughter, Sarah Lacey, 5 shillings and all my lands in Cumberland County, New Jersey. Of all the rest of my estate I leave one-third to my wife Charity and two-thirds to my cousin, Samuel Woodhouse. I make my wife, and Benjamin Kipp and Samuel Woodhouse, executors.

Witnesses, Joseph Townsend, Joseph Hunt, Caleb Fowler. Proved, January 15, 1760.

"The last will and Testament of Samuel Pearce, of Cow Neck, in the town of Hempstead, in Queens County," December 16, 1757. "I will that all my personal estate, that is, all my out of door movables and shop tools (household goods excepted), to be sold at public vendue." I leave to my wife Abigail, in lieu of dower, all my household goods. I leave to my daughter Elizabeth £50. "For the enabling of my wife to bring up my children in a decent manner, as well as in lieu of her dower," I give her the sole use and profit of all my farm I now live upon and all the money that I have at interest, until my son William is of age, and then my said farm is to be sold at public vendue, and the money paid to my wife Abigail and my children, Elizabeth, William, Anne, Phebe, Hannah, George, Richard, Sarah, and Freelove. My daughter Elizabeth is to have as much given her as, with what has before been given, will make her equal to the rest. I make my friends, Daniel Kissam and Adam Mott, both of Cow Neck, executors.

Witnesses, Richbell Mott, Joseph Baker, Joseph Dodge. Proved, May 8, 1758.

In the name of God, Amen, December 30, 1759. I, George Dennis, of North Castle, in Westchester County, being in a poor state of health. I leave to my wife Deborah one-third of movable estate and the use of the east end of my dwelling house, with the kitchen and small room adjoining, and one-third of my land during her widowhood. After my wife's decease, I leave all my lands to my three sons, Obadiah, Stephen, and Jesse, to be divided when my son Jesse comes of age. My sons Stephen and Jesse are to be immediately put to trades. All movable estate to be sold, and two-thirds of the money to my children and one-third to my wife. I make John Thomas, Sr., and my wife, and my son Obadiah, executors.

Witnesses, Charity Woodhouse, William Gilchrist, Anthony Woodhouse. Proved, February 19, 1760.

Women's Estates

MASSACHUSETTS, 1664, and NEW YORK, 1747–1759

Records and Files of the Quarterly Courts of Essex County, Massachusetts vol. 5, 1672–1674 (Salem, MA: The Essex Institute, 1916), pp. 203–4; *Collections of the New York Historical Society for the Year 1896* (New York, 1897).

An important impact of coverture was the remote connection between women and property, as is evident in women's wills. These wills rarely transferred real property, since few women owned real property. Most widows held only a life interest in land or homes, and when they died, this real estate went to the heirs of their deceased husbands. Still, widows could bequeath their personal property, as is evident in the wills that follow. Often, such personal property comprised household goods, clothes, and perhaps some farm animals (for instance, the will of Anne Burt of Massachusetts). By the mid-eighteenth century, as colonial wealth increased, some widows could also make bequests of cash and valuable objects.

As expected, most widows left their possessions to their children and/or other relatives. Occasionally they used their wills to express decided preferences. Jane Jones of New York, for instance, left far more to her daughters than to her sons—although perhaps the latter were the major beneficiaries of their respective fathers' estates. In some cases, women will-writers left legacies not only to their family members but to their friends or, as in the instance of well-off Anna Pritchard of New York, to a combination of friends, relatives, and charitable causes ("12 poor widows of good character"). A precise testator, widow Pritchard also made explicit plans for a funeral procession of female mourners. Unlike the widow, the married woman could write a will only with her husband's consent, since all she owned was his. See, for instance, the will of Elizabeth Sands, which conveys real estate.

A Massachusetts Will, 1664

Will of An (her mark) Bort, dated Jan. 8, 1664: "My Wil is that Willyam Bassit Juner should have won of my kowes and John bassit should have Won Cowe and Elisha bassit should have Won kowe and that samewell bassit should have the steare And it is my will that theas Children should have the proffit of theas Cattell and the prinsepell when they be eighttene yeares ould and i give to Elizebeth basset a new feather bed A boulster and a pillow and a pillow beare A blankit and a Rouge and i give to Sarah bassit my ould feather bed a boulster and pillow and A pillow beare A blankit and A tapsterri Covering and i give to meriam bassit A Copper ketel, A tabel Cloth and half A doson of napkins and a ew shep, han towel and I give to mary bassit my bigest eiorn pot a long tabel Cloth and four napkins and a han towel, a ew shep And I give to hannah bassit tow eiorn pots and a warmin pan and a pare of shetes and a pare of pillow bears and a ew shep.

"And i give to ellin bartrom A ew lam and to hanna battrom an ew lam and I give to the wife of Willyam bartrom my black brodcloth sute and one puter basson and i give to liddi Burrill five shillens or a ew lam and my will is that ther goodes should not be ewsed till the Childerren doth reseave them & that these gearls should have the proffit of theas shep & the prinsepel when thay com to age." Wit: Francis Burrill and William Crofts. "I doe desier my Brother Francis burrill and good man Craft would see that this my wil be fulfilled."

Inventory of the estate of Anne Burt, taken Mar. 18, 1672–3, by William Crofts and Francis Burrill: one petecot & wastcott, 1li. 10s.; the Remene of her wooling aperill, 5li. 12s.; too fether Beds, too Boulsters, too Pillos, three Blankits, one tapeistre Coverin, 2li. 18s.; more weareing aparill, 1li. 6s.; too cortings, 8s.; one Bibil; & one other Booke, 6s.; five peare of shets & one sheet, 3li. 11s.; a table Cloth & 8 napkins, 1li.; three pillobeares & other small things, 7s.; three shifts, 8s.; small linin, 2li. 10s. 7d.; peuter & tin, 2d.; Bras & Iron, 2li. 18s.; too yeards of Peniston, 8s.; 3 Chists, too boxes, one trunk, 1li.; too wheeles, too cheirs & other lumber, 1li.; one couw, 3li.; ten shep, 5li.; sillver, 2li. 10s.; due to her, 3li.; total, 47li. 2s. 6d.

New York Wills, 1747–1759

In the name of God, Amen. I, Rebecca Sipkins, of New York, widow, March 19, 1747. I leave to my grand child, Christina Breested, daughter of my late son, Garrett Breested, £100. I leave to my grand child, Cornelia Waldron, daughter of my late daughter, Elizabeth Griffith, deceased, £150. I leave to my three grand children, John, Rem, and Rebecca Remsen, children of my said daughter Elizabeth, deceased, each £50. To my grand child, Maria Vanderheuil, daughter of my late daughter, Johana Vanderheuil, £150. To my grand child, John Taylor, son of my daughter, Rebecca Griffith, £150. All these legacies are to be put at interest by my executors and the interest to be applied to their use for education and maintainance. I leave all the rest of my estate to every description to my daughter, Rebecca Griffith; and I make her and her husband, William Griffith, executors and guardians of my grand children.

Witnesses, William Bogert, Cornelius Boghart, Simon Johnson. Proved, December 5, 1755. Rebecca Griffith was then the surviving executor.

In the name of God, Amen. I, Catharine Bromley, of New York. After the payment of all debts and funeral charges, I leave all the remainder of my estate to my daughter, Catharine Godwin, "for the bringing of her up and placing her out to a trade during her minority, and what is left is to be paid to her when of age." My executors are to sell all personal property, except 1 bed for my daughter. I make my brother, John Van Dyck, executor.

Witnesses, Edward Man, Jean Helme, Richard R. Smith. Proved, April 22, 1756.

In the name of God, Amen. I, Ann Rapalye, of Flushing, in Queens County, widow, being now very weak and indisposed in body. I leave to my daughter Elizabeth, wife of John Hoogland, £200. To my only son, Stephen Rapalye, £100, to be paid by my son in law, John Hoogland, out of the £300 he owes to me on bond. I also leave to my son Stephen my yearling horse colt, and my son in law, John Hoogland shall furnish food for the same until my son is 14 years of age, for which I allow him the interest on the said £100. I also leave him my best bed. I leave to my daughter Elizabeth my riding chair and horse, and my cabinet and silver tea pot, and all my linnen and wearing apparell. After payment of debts and funeral charges, I leave all the rest to my children, Elizabeth and Stephen. I make my brother, Bernardus Ryder, executor.

Dated March 8, 1756. Witnesses, Elizabeth Willett, Abraham Brinkerhoff, Jr., Benjamin Hinchman. Proved, April 10, 1756.

In the name of God, Amen, July 30, 1756. I, Jane Jones, of the Parish of East Chester, being very sick. I leave to my son, John Jones, 5 shillings. I leave to my daughters, Mary and Elizabeth Weeden, all my household goods and wearing apparell, and a cow, and a horse, all to be sold and the money divided between them, and all that was left in their father's will. I leave to my daughter, Elizabeth Weeden, a bond of John Jewstead for £25. I leave to my daughter, Mary Weeden, two bonds, one for £17 from Mr. John Cromwell, and the other for £7 from Mr. Edward Griffin. I leave to my son, William Weeden, £10 "in lieu of the horse." I make Edward Griffin executor.

Witnesses, Robert Thompson, Joseph Colyer, Thomas Ward. Proved, August 11, 1756.

In the name of God, Amen, June 7, 1759. I, Anna Pritchard, of New York, widow, being at present weak in body. "My will is and I desire that my Corpse may be interred in Trinity Church yard in New York, that the Pall bearers at my funeral be men, and the followers women, excepting my relations, ministers, and doctors." I give £50 to be equally divided among 12 poor widows of good character, and who shall appear to my executors to be objects of Charity. I leave to my nephew, Peter Stuyvesant, a gold ring, a pair of gloves, and a mourning hat band. I leave to Judith Vincent, of Monmouth County, East New Jersey, and her daughter Phebe, £20. To Samson Broughton, who lives at the Raritans, in New Jersey, £10. To Sarah Southard, who now lives with me, £10 and a bed. To my nephew, Nicholas William Stuyvesant, my jewel box, a Tortoise shell box, a shell cup tipped with silver, and all my plate, 2 plain gold rings, 4 damask table cloths, and 2 dozen napkins. To John, Elias, and Hendrick Brevoort, each a gold mourning ring. To Elizabeth Skinner, of Amboy, widow, a gold mourning ring. To Cornelia Schuyler, of Albany, widow, a gold mourning ring. To Elizabeth Van Hoese, widow, and daughter of John Sydenham, a chest, table, camlet gown, and 6 shifts. I order a desk, 2 looking glasses, and a tea table to be sold. And whereas I have sundry other articles of furniture and some wearing apparell which I intend to give away, I intend to make a schedule of them and the persons to whom I intend to give them, and it is to be considered as part of my will. I leave the rest to my nephew, Nicholas William Stuyvesant, and make him executor.

Witnesses, Johanes Quackenboss, Peter Quackenboss, Whitehead Hicks. Proved, July 14, 1759.

In the name of God, Amen. I, Elizabeth Sands, of the Borroughtown of Westchester, by and with the advice and consent of my husband, Samuel Sands, and my Trustee, Elisha Barton, Jr., do make this my last will. As to my dwelling house and lot of land in the said Borrough town of Westchester, I devise the same to my sister, Keziah Glover, and her daughter, Elizabeth Lynch, during their lives, provided Elizabeth Lynch pay to my niece, Rebecca Barnes, £40, and in case of the death of Rebecca Barnes, half of this is to go to her sister Sarah, wife of Benjamin Palmer, and the other half to my three sisters, Miriam, Dorcas, and Abigail. In case of the death of my sister, Keziah Glover, then to her daughter Elizabeth I leave the house and lot, and she shall pay to my two nieces, Sarah De Lancey and Elizabeth Cleeves, £35. I leave to my sister, Keziah Glover, 2 negro women and a negro boy, "and the bed that formerly was in the Parlor," and a blue and white calico quilt, and my cow and swine. I leave to my niece, Elizabeth Lynch, a negro girl, and to my niece, Elizabeth Cleeves, my Gold chain and a bed. To Elisha Barton £10. To Thomas, son of Augustine Baxter, £5. To Charles Warner's wife Jane £5. To Dorcas, wife of Samuel Berrian, £5. To William Tippett £5. To Marcus, son of Thomas Baxter, £5. To Ann, daughter of Benjamin Palmer, £5. To Joseph Palmer £5. To Michael, son of Oliver Baxter, £5. To Bathsheba, daughter of Thomas Palmer, a set of gold buttons "to the value of a Pistole." To Mary, daughter of Oliver Baxter, half dozen silver spoons. To Keziah, daughter of Oliver Baxter, half dozen spoons, and the same to Catharine, daughter of Benjamin Baxter. Small legacies to Sarah, daughter of Theophilus Wood, Elizabeth, daughter of Edward Penney, "To Edward Penney's wife," To Edward Penney "a pair of silver shoe buckles, about 30s. price," "To George Barker's wife," To Sarah Downing, daughter of George Barker, To Benjamin Barker's wife. To my brother, Thomas Baxter, my looking glass. To my sister, Keziah Glover, my riding chair, and she is to pay to Phebe, wife of Arnot Cannon, £5. To Elizabeth, daughter of John Oakley, To Elizabeth, daughter of Cornelius Willett. I make John Oakley and Cornelius Willett executors.

June 4, 1759. Signed by Elizabeth Sands, Samuel Sands, and Elisha Barton. Witnesses, Israel Honeywell, Henry Charlick, Thomas Allen. Proved, January 15, 1760.

Chapter 5

Religious Experiences

R eligion, like law, endorsed female subjection. All religious sects in the English colonies, save the Quakers, barred women from the ministry, insisted on their silence in church, and urged their obedience outside of it. Still, for colonial women, religion represented an important outlet. First, the church provided an institutional affiliation beyond the family. Second, religion contained the enticing lure of spiritual equality. Even if subordinate in every realm of secular life, women could view their souls as equal in importance to those of men. The concept of equality of souls, and a sense of personal connection to God, sometimes thrust women into unexpectedly prominent roles.

During the seventeenth century, religious experience held special significance for women of the dissenting sects—notably Puritans and Quakers—which challenged the Church of England and indeed every other creed. In both cases, heightened religious commitment affected women's roles. Among the Puritans, women had access to the highest status in their communities, that of visible saints or members of the elect. Like men, they prepared for salvation by acquiring familiarity with biblical texts. Like men, they had to recount their conversion experiences. Like men, they were expected to exemplify their election through godly behavior. As a dissenting sect, too, the Puritans placed great emphasis on child-rearing, which raised the importance of parenthood. Puritan fathers served as spiritual heads of household and thereby played the major role in sectarian indoctrination, but mothers' influence on younger children was important, too. Early childhood was the period in which a parent had to break the child's will and establish habits of obedience that would facilitate the child's salvation in the years ahead. (See Chapter 2.)

Although female piety won approbation and acclaim, Puritans never harbored egalitarian illusions. Women, they believed, were weaker than men in brain, body, and moral fiber and therefore were more vulnerable to the devil's influence, as accusations of witchcraft during the seventeenth century suggest. Even religious fervor among women could lead to trouble, as illustrated in the episode of Anne Hutchinson. In 1636, this outspoken saint almost split the newly formed Massachusetts Bay colony in two. Holding public meetings in her home and criticizing the theology of leading clerics, Hutchinson challenged the power of men—specifically, that of the ministers and magistrates, who soon expelled her. Puritan authorities subsequently voiced suspicions about women who had acquired too much learning or expertise in theology. Still, female piety played an important—and often underrated—part in early New England history. In the late 1600s, when Puritan ministers complained of declining piety, the loss they bemoaned was mainly among men: Women had become a majority of congregants in New England churches. Female majorities would later prevail among most nineteenth-century Protestant congregations and thereby affect the development of American religion.

Unlike the Puritans, the seventeenth-century Society of Friends carried equality of souls to the furthest extreme. Among Quakers, all who had discerned their own "inner lights" could speak out at meetings or religious services. Rejecting the concept of a formal ministry, the Quakers opened to both men and women the equivalent of ministerial roles, as "Public Friends." Quaker women in England and the colonies also created their own organizational structure, or women's meetings, which monitored Quaker family life, mediated domestic disputes, regulated marriages among Friends, and kept in touch with other women's meetings. Even when Quaker zeal for proselytizing faded in the eighteenth century, women Friends retained a singular commitment to sexual equality and thereby exerted disproportionate influence in women's history well into the nineteenth century.

Compared to these dissenting sects, the Anglicans who dominated the southern and middle colonies seemed less fervent and more casual about religious affairs. But no region escaped the powerful religious revivals that tore through the colonies in the 1740s. The Great

Awakening increased male participation in churches and reduced female majorities. "The Grace of God has surprisingly . . . subdued the hardiest men, and more Males have been added here than the tenderest sex," one New England minister exclaimed. Still, religious enthusiasm—what the famous revivalist Jonathan Edwards called "heartfelt religion"—had a significant impact on women. One major import of the Great Awakening for women may have been on a private level: It provided a religious basis for female relationships, as exemplified in the correspondence of Esther Burr and Sally Prince. But the Awakening's impact also had public ramifications. Religious revivals reached new female constituencies, inspired a vocal type of enthusiasm among women, and created a mood of excitement in which they could assert themselves. Congregationalist Sarah Haggar Osborn of Newport, for instance, led a local revival in the 1760s, held religious meetings for young people and blacks in her home, and regarded religion as the "chief business" of her life.

The splintering of sects and diffusion of authority that the Great Awakening engendered increased the number of unlicensed preachers. It also spurred women's roles as religious leaders at the end of the century. Two examples are revivalist Jemima Wilkinson, who gained a reputation as the "Public Universal Friend" in the 1780s, and English immigrant Mother Ann Lee, who founded the Shakers in the 1790s and claimed to be "Jesus Christ in the form of a woman." In many ways, women of the revolutionary era seemed to channel *their* rebellious spirit into religious affairs. New dissenting sects of the late eighteenth century—Free Will Baptists, New Lights, and Methodist groups—often gave women a voice in church government. Some women adherents won local reputations as lay preachers, exhorters, and prophets. Challenging clerical titles and the need for theological education, these irregular practitioners stressed the primacy of personal religious experience. On Long Island in the 1770s, farm wife Mary Cooper recorded the impact of a congregant who led a dissenting faction and split her church, probably over the issue of a female ministry. Other examples of female defiance in religious matters sprang up throughout the Anglo-American world. One Nova Scotia woman of the 1790s made "much trouble in the church," her minister reported, with her divergent views and claims of divine visitations.

(According to the aggrieved clergyman's account, she told him that he "would not be a proper judge" because her mind "had gone farther in these things" than his.)*

This disputatious mood—and female lay preaching—ebbed as middle-class respectability took hold in the early nineteenth century. Still, the nation's founders unintentionally increased women's impact in religious life. Separation of church and state deprived the one-time established churches (Anglican in most colonies and Congregational in New England) of state revenues and created a demand for new sources of funds. Women's predominance as church members soon became significant. Throughout the early nineteenth century, women were a majority of congregants, prayer meeting participants, conversion candidates, and converts at revivals. They also became the main fundraisers for pious charities, missionary societies, and voluntary benevolent associations.[†]

The changes of the revolutionary era increased the importance of women's roles not only as congregants but as parents. A new feminine ideal that emerged in the wake of the Revolution reflected this development. When Rebeccah Sanders of Maryland died at age seventy-five in 1752, the *Maryland Gazette* offered praise for her "just sense of religion," especially because "she instilled the Principles of it thro' her numerous Family . . . having educated her children in the Paths of Virtue and Piety." Such private religiosity gained public importance at the end of the century. The "Republican Mother" of the early national period was to be a custodian and transmitter of values, including moral and spiritual values. By the early nineteenth century, although religious leadership remained beyond women's reach, piety had become in large part female property.

---

*See Louis Billington, "Female Laborers in the Church," *Journal of American Studies* 19 (1985), pp. 369–94.

[†]Mary Beth Norton, "The Evolution of White Women's Experience in Early America," *American Historical Review* 89 (June 1984), pp. 615–16.

A Spiritual Autobiography

ANNE BRADSTREET, CA. 1670

John Harvard Ellis, ed., *The Works of Anne Bradstreet in Prose and Verse* (Charlestown, MA: A. E. Cutter, 1867), pp. 3–10.

For devout Puritans, the question of salvation remained a lifelong concern that transcended gender. It also inspired personal narratives about religious experience, such as that of Anne Bradstreet (1612–1672). Bradstreet had arrived in Massachusetts Bay in 1630, with her parents and husband, on the first large shipload of Puritans to come to the colony. She was unusually well-connected. Her father, Thomas Dudley, formerly the manager of an earl's estate in England, was now deputy governor of the new colony. Anne's young husband, Simon Bradstreet, was an assistant of the Massachusetts Bay Company and, like her father, a future governor. Over the next few decades, Anne Bradstreet would raise eight children and would produce the most significant body of poetry in the seventeenth-century colonies. During her lifetime, only one book of her poems was published—in 1650 in England—and that without her knowledge.

At some undetermined point in her life, probably near the end of it, Anne Bradstreet wrote an account of her religious experience to leave for her children, who found it among her papers after her death. In this account, as in her poetry, Bradstreet was a complete professional: Her understated and apparently rapidly written spiritual autobiography was artfully composed, and full of tension and paradox. As all good Puritans knew, parents could not bring about their child's salvation, whatever their efforts. They might try to pave the way for it, but in the end, Grace came only from God, not as a result of parental concern. Nor could they hope to set an example, for their own salvation remained in question. Still, Anne Bradstreet hoped that her offspring would gain some "benefitt" or "spiritual advantage" from her narrative. What might such benefit be?

As a statement of faith, Bradstreet's narrative remains a disturbing catalog of doubts, some never resolved. Atheism and despair tempt her; "sinkings and droopings" beset her; disturbing questions plague her ("Is there faith upon the earth? . . . I have known not what to think"). Although some signs of God's favor appear, such as fertility after years of barrenness, the most consistent theme of the narrative is pain and affliction, which Bradstreet juxtaposes to a few rare moments of religious joy ("that hidden Manna"). But such pain served a function, she explained, because it corrected "a heart out of order" and therefore could be interpreted as joy. What Anne Bradstreet left her children was a typically Puritan piece of tactical advice—to find ecstasy in adversity: "If at any time you are chastened of God, take it as thankfully and Joyfully as in greatest mercyes, for if yee bee his yee shall reap the greatest benefitt by it."

My Dear Children,

I, knowing by experience that the exhortations of parents take most effect when the speakers leave to speak, and those especially sink deepest which are spoke latest—and being ignorant whether on my death bed I shall have opportunity to speak to any of you, much lesse to All—thought it the best, whilst I was able to compose some short matters (for what else to call them I know not) and bequeath to you, that when I am no more with you, yet I may bee dayly in your remembrance (Although that is the least in my aim in what I now doe) but that you may gain some spiritual Advantage by my experience. I have not studied in this you read to show my skill, but to declare the Truth—not to sett forth myself, but the Glory of God. If I had minded the former, it had been perhaps better pleasing to you, —but seing the last is the best, let it bee best pleasing to you.

The method I will observe shall bee this—I will begin with God's dealing with me from my childhood to this Day. In my young years, about 6 or 7 as I take it, I began to make conscience of my wayes, and what I knew was sinfull, as lying, disobedience to Parents, &c. I avoided it. If at any time I was overtaken with the like evills, it was a great Trouble. I could not be at rest 'till by prayer I had confest it unto God. I was also troubled at the neglect of Private Dutyes, though too often tardy that way. I also found much comfort in reading the Scriptures, especially those places I thought most concerned my Condition, and as I grew to have more understanding, so the more solace I took in them.

In a long fitt of sicknes which I had on my bed I often communed with my heart, and made my supplication to the most High who sett me free from that affliction.

But as I grew up to bee about 14 or 15 I found my heart more carnall, and sitting loose from God, vanity and the follyes of youth take hold of me.

About 16, the Lord layd his hand sore upon me and smott mee with the small pox. When I was in my affliction, I besought the Lord, and confessed my Pride and Vanity and he was entreated of me, and again restored me. But I rendered not to him according to the benefitt received.

After a short time I changed my condition and was marryed, and came into this Country, where I found a new world and new manners, at which my heart rose. But after I was convinced it was the way of God, I submitted to it and joined to the church at Boston.

After some time I fell into a lingering sicknes like a consumption, together with a lamenesse, which correction I saw the Lord sent to humble and try me and doe mee Good: and it was not altogether imeffectuall.

It pleased God to keep me a long time without a child, which was a great grief to me, and cost mee many prayers and tears before I obtaind one, and after him gave mee many more, of whom I now take the care, that as I have brought you into the world, and with great paines, weaknes, cares, and feares brought you to this, I now travail in birth again of you till Christ bee formed in you.

Among all my experiences of God's gratious Dealings with me I have constantly observed this, that he hath never suffered me long to sitt loose from him, but by one affliction or other hath made me look home, and search what was amisse—so usually thus it hath been with me that I have no sooner felt my heart out of order, but I have expected correction for it, which most commonly hath been upon my own person, in sicknesse, weaknes, paines, sometimes on my soul, in Doubts and feares of God's displeasure, and my sincerity towards him, sometimes he hath smott a child with sicknes, sometimes chasstened by losses in estate—and these Times (through his great mercy) have been the times of my greatest Getting and Advantage, yea I have found them the Times when the Lord hath manifested the most Love to me. Then have I gone to searching, and have said with David, Lord search me and try me, see what wayes of wickednes are in me, and lead me in the way everlasting: and seldome or never but I have found either some sin I lay under which God would have reformed, or some duty neglected which he would have performed. And by his help I have layd Vowes and Bonds upon my Soul to perform his righteous commands.

If at any time you are chastened of God, take it as thankfully and Joyfully as in greatest mercyes, for if yee bee his yee shall reap the greatest benefitt by it. It hath been no small support to me in times of Darknes when the Almighty hath hid his face from me, that yet I have had abundance of sweetnes and refreshment after affliction, and more circumspection in my walking after I have been afflicted. I have been with God like an untoward child, that no longer then the rod has been on my back (or at least in sight) but I have been apt to forgett him and myself too. Before I was afflicted I went astray, but now I keep thy statutes.

I have had great experience of God's hearing my Prayers, and returning comfortable Answers to me, either in granting the Thing I prayed for, or else in satisfying my mind without it; and I have been confident it hath been from him, because I have found my heart through his goodnes enlarged in Thankfullnes to him.

I have often been perplexed that I have not found that constant Joy in my Pilgrimage and refreshing which I supposed most of the servants of God have; although he hath not left me altogether without the wittnes of his holy spirit, who hath oft given mee his word and sett to his Seal that it shall bee well with me. I have sometimes tasted of that hidden Manna that the world knowes not, and have sett up my Ebenezer, and have resolved with myself that against such a promis, such tasts of sweetnes, the Gates of Hell shall never prevail. Yet have I many Times sinkings and droopings, and not enjoyed that felicity that sometimes I have done. But when I have been in darknes and seen no light, yet have I desired to stay my self upon the Lord.

And, when I have been in sicknes and pain, I have thought if the Lord would but lift up the light of his Countenance upon me, although he ground me to powder, it would bee but light to me; yea, oft have I thought were it hell itself, and could there find the Love of God toward me, it would bee a Heaven. And, could I have been in Heaven without the Love of God, it would have been a Hell to me; for, in Truth, it is the absence and presence of God that makes Heaven or Hell.

Many times hath Satan troubled me concerning the verity of the scriptures, many times by Atheisme how I could know whether there was a God; I never saw any miracles to confirm me, and those which I read of how did I know but they were feigned. That there is a God my Reason would soon tell me by the wondrous workes that I see, the vast frame of the Heaven and the Earth, the order of all things, night and day, Summer and Winter, Spring and Autumne, the dayly providing for this great houshold upon the Earth, the preserving and directing of All to its proper end. The consideration of these things would with amazement certainly resolve me that there is an Eternall Being.

But how should I know he is such a God as I worship in Trinity, and such a Saviour as I rely upon? though: this hath thousands of Times been suggested to mee, yet God hath helped me over. I have argued thus with myself. That there is a God I see. If ever this God hath revealed himself, it must bee in his word, and this must bee it or none. Have I not found that operation by it that no humane Invention can work upon the Soul? hath not Judgments befallen Diverse who have scorned and contemd it? hath it not been preserved through: All Ages maugre all the heathen Tyrants and all of the enemyes who have opposed it? Is there any story but that which showes the beginnings of Times, and how the world came to bee as wee see? Doe wee not know the prophecyes in it fulfilled which could not have been so long foretold by any but God himself?

When I have gott over this Block, then have I another putt in my way, That admitt this bee the true God whom wee worship, and that bee his word, yet why may not the Popish Religion bee the right? They have the same God, the same Christ, the same word: they only enterprett it one way, wee another.

This hath sometimes stuck with me, and more it would, but the vain fooleries that are in their Religion, together with their lying miracles and cruell persecutions of the Saints, which admitt were they as they terme them, yet not so to bee dealt withall.

The consideration of these things and many the like would soon turn me to my own Religion again.

But some new Troubles I have had since the world has been filled with Blasphemy, and Sectaries, and some who have been accounted sincere Christians have been carryed away with them, that sometimes I have said, Is there faith upon the earth? and I have not known what to think. But then I have remembred the words of Christ that so it must bee, and that, if it were possible, the very elect should bee deceived. Behold, saith our Saviour, I have told you before. That hath stayed my heart, and I can now say, Return, O my Soul, to thy Rest, upon this Rock Christ Jesus will I build my faith; and, if I perish, I perish. But I know all the Powers of Hell shall never prevail against it. I know whom I have trusted, and whom I have believed, and that he is able to keep that I have committed to his charge.

Now to the King, Immortall, Eternall, and invisible, the only wise God, bee Honoure and Glory for ever and ever! Amen.

This was written in much sicknesse and weaknes, and is very weakly and imperfectly done; but, if you can pick any Benefitt out of it, it is the marke which I aimed at.

Anne Hutchinson's Trial

MASSACHUSETTS BAY, 1637

Charles Francis Adams, *Antinomianism in the Massachusetts Bay Colony, 1636–1638*
(Boston: Prince Society, 1894), pp. 235–45, 267–70, 183–84.

John Winthrop, the Governor of Massachusetts Bay for much of the
1630s and 1640s, called Anne Hutchinson "a woman of ready wit and
bold spirit." But he believed that her influence would ruin the Puritan
experiment in his colony, which was no doubt true. Hutchinson
(1591–1643) and her family, admirers of the Puritan minister John
Cotton, had followed him to Massachusetts Bay in 1634. Anne's husband, William, was a successful merchant. By 1636, when Anne was
about fifty, they had a dozen living children. Anne also served her
Boston neighbors as a nurse and midwife. In this capacity she held
private religious conferences, which developed into weekly meetings
held at her home. Here, before some sixty to eighty people, Anne
Hutchinson discussed John Cotton's sermons and put forth her own
interpretations.

Her own views were the problem: Anne Hutchinson stressed the
overwhelming importance of the Covenant of Grace (an intuitional
experience of salvation) over the Covenant of Works (the Puritan belief
that a sanctified life was evidence of grace). Anne's beliefs were indeed
liberating, since they relieved the elect of the necessity of "good
works." Once sanctified by a mystical experience, God resided within
an individual, and "works" no longer mattered; nor did ministerial
authority. Soon, Anne had accused all of Boston's ministers, save John
Cotton and her brother-in-law John Wheelright, of preaching a "Covenant of Works." She had also divided the small community of believers into warring factions. To her critics, Anne Hutchinson and her
followers had fallen into the Antinomian heresy. Early in 1637, the
General Court condemned Wheelright, and he was banished with
some followers. In November, Anne Hutchinson too faced a civil trial.

Confronted by the magistrates and assistants of the General
Court, who served as both judges and prosecutors, Anne had no jury
or counsel. Her interrogators charged her with dishonoring the community fathers, of holding meetings at her home in a manner inappro-
priate to her sex, and of insulting ministers at a private conference by
accusing them of laboring under a Covenant of Works. In general,

Anne outwitted her questioners. John Cotton also helped her by refuting those ministers who testified against her. But just as the prosecution's case was about to crumble, Anne suddenly admitted to divine revelation: God, she said, had told her that he would destroy her persecutors ("By the voice of his own spirit to my soul"). Such a claim of "immediate" or direct revelation was heresy. Anne was sentenced to banishment and, at a church trial in 1638, was excommunicated as well.

The record of the civil trial illustrates Anne Hutchinson's successful style of disputation: When almost cornered, she made fine distinctions, logical and theological. In the segments that follow, Anne responds to Governor John Winthrop and other officials, including Deputy Governor Thomas Dudley and Assistant Simon Bradstreet (Anne Bradstreet's father and husband). The last segment includes her startling admission of revelation.

Appendix to the History of the Province of Massachusets Bay, by Mr. Hutchinson, Lieutenant Governor of the Province

November 1637

The Examination of Mrs. Anne Hutchinson at the Court at Newtown

Mr. Winthrop, governor.   Mrs. Hutchinson, you are called here as one of those that have troubled the peace of the commonwealth and the churches here; you are known to be a woman that hath had a great share in the promoting and divulging of those opinions that are causes of this trouble, and to be nearly joined not only in affinity and affection with some of those the court had taken notice of and passed censure upon, but you have spoken divers things as we have been informed very prejudicial to the honour of the churches and ministers thereof, and you have maintained a meeting and an assembly in your house that hath been condemned by the general assembly as a thing not tolerable nor comely in the sight of God nor fitting for your sex, and notwithstanding that was cried down you have continued the same, therefore we have thought good to send for you to understand how things are, that if you be in an erroneous way we may reduce you that so you may become a profitable member here among us, otherwise if you be obstinate in your course that then the court may take such course that you may trouble us no further, therefore I would intreat you to express whether you do not assent and hold in practice to those opinions and factions that have been handled in court already, that is to say, whether you do not justify Mr. Wheelwright's sermon and the petition.

Mrs. Hutchinson. I am called here to answer before you but I hear no things laid to my charge.

Gov. I have told you some already and more I can tell you. (*Mrs. H.*) Name one, Sir.

Gov. Have I not named some already?

Mrs. H. What have I said or done?

Gov. Why for your doings, this you did harbour and countenance those that are parties in this faction that you have heard of. (*Mrs. H.*) That's [a] matter of conscience, Sir.

Gov. Your conscience you must keep or it must be kept for you.

Mrs. H. Must not I then entertain the saints because I must keep my conscience.

Gov. Say that one brother should commit felony or treason and come to his brother's house, if he knows him guilty and conceals him he is guilty of the same. It is his conscience to entertain him, but if his conscience comes into act in giving countenance and entertainment to him that hath broken the law he is guilty too. So if you do countenance those that are transgressors of the law you are in the same fact.

Mrs. H. What law do they transgress?

Gov. The law of God and of the state.

Mrs. H. In what particular?

Gov. Why in this among the rest, whereas the Lord doth say honour thy father and thy mother.

Mrs. H. Ey Sir in the Lord. (*Gov.*) This honour you have broke in giving countenance to them.

Mrs. H. In entertaining those did I entertain them against any act (for there is the thing), or what God hath appointed?

Gov. You knew that Mr. Wheelwright did preach this sermon and those that countenance him in this do break a law.

Mrs. H. What law have I broken?

Gov. Why the fifth commandment.

Mrs. H. I deny that for he saith in the Lord.

Gov. You have joined with them in the faction.

Mrs. H. In what faction have I joined with them?

Gov. In presenting the petition.

Mrs. H. Suppose I had set my hand to the petition what then? (*Gov.*) You saw that case tried before.

Mrs. H. But I had not my hand to the petition.

Gov. You have councelled them. (*Mrs. H.*) Wherein?

Gov. Why in entertaining them.

Mrs. H. What breach of law is that Sir?

Gov. Why dishonouring of parents.

Mrs. H.   But put the case Sir that I do fear the Lord and my parents, may not I entertain them that fear the Lord because my parents will not give me leave?

Gov.   If they be the fathers of the commonwealth, and they of another religion, if you entertain them then you dishonour your parents and are justly punishable.

Mrs. H.   If I entertain them, as they have dishonoured their parents I do.

Gov.   No but you by countenancing them above others put honor upon them.

Mrs. H.   I may put honor upon them as the children of God and as they do honor the Lord.

Gov.   We do not mean to discourse with those of your sex but only this; you do adhere unto them and do endeavor to set forward this faction and so you do dishonour us.

Mrs. H.   I do acknowledge no such thing neither do I think that I ever put any dishonour upon you.

Gov.   Why do you keep such a meeting at your house as you do every week upon a set day?

Mrs. H.   It is lawful for me so to do, as it is all your practices and can you find a warrant for yourself and condemn me for the same thing? The ground of my taking it up was, when I first came to this land because I did not go to such meetings as those were, it was presently reported that I did not allow of such meetings but held them unlawful and therefore in that regard they said I was proud and did despise all ordinances, upon that a friend came unto me and told me of it and I to prevent such aspersions took it up, but it was in practice before I came therefore I was not the first.

Gov.   For this, that you appeal to our practice you need no confutation. If your meeting had answered to the former it had not been offensive, but I will say that there was no meeting of women alone, but your meeting is of another sort for there are sometimes men among you.

Mrs. H.   There was never any man with us.

Gov.   Well, admit there was no man at your meeting and that you was sorry for it, there is no warrant for your doings, and by what warrant do you continue such a course?

Mrs. H.   I conceive there lyes a clear rule in Titus, that the elder women should instruct the younger* and then I must have a time wherein I must do it.

Gov.   All this I grant you, I grant you a time for it, but what is this to the purpose that you, Mrs. Hutchinson, must call a company together from their callings to come to be taught of you?

Mrs. H.   Will it please you to answer me this and to give me a rule, for then I will willingly submit to any truth. If any come to my house to be instructed in the ways of God what rule have I to put them away?

Gov.   But suppose that a hundred men come unto you to be instructed will you forbear to instruct them?

---

*A reference to *Titus* ii 3–5: "Bid the older women . . . to train the young women."

Mrs. H.   As far as I conceive I cross a rule in it.

Gov.   Very well and do you not so here?

Mrs. H.   No, Sir, for my ground is they are men.

Gov.   Men and women all is one for that, but suppose that a man should come and say Mrs. Hutchinson I hear that you are a woman that God hath given his grace unto and you have knowledge in the word of God I pray instruct me a little, ought you not to instruct this man?

Mrs. H.   I think I may. Do you think it not lawful for me to teach women and why do you call me to teach the court?

Gov.   We do not call you to teach the court but to lay open yourself.

Mrs. H.   I desire you that you would then set me down a rule by which I may put them away that come unto me and so have peace in so doing.

Gov.   You must shew your rule to receive them.

Mrs. H.   I have done it.

Gov.   I deny it because I have brought more arguments than you have.

Mrs. H.   I say, to me it is a rule.

*Mr. Endicot.**   You say there are some rules unto you. I think there is a contradiction in your own words. What rule for your practice do you bring, only a custom in Boston?

Mrs. H.   No, Sir, that was no rule to me but if you look upon the rule in Titus it is a rule to me. If you convince me that it is no rule I shall yield.

Gov.   You know that there is no rule that crosses another, but this rule crosses that in the Corinthians.[†] But you must take it in this sense that elder women must instruct the younger about their business, and to love their husbands and not to make them to clash.

Mrs. H.   I do not conceive but that it is meant for some publick times.

Gov.   Well, have you no more to say but this?

Mrs. H.   I have said sufficient for my practice.

Gov.   Your course is not to be suffered for, besides that we find such a course as this to be greatly prejudicial to the state, besides the occasion that it is to seduce many honest persons that are called to those meetings and your opinions being known to be different from the word of God may seduce many simple souls that resort unto you, besides that the occasion which hath come of late hath come from none but such as have frequented your meetings, so that now they are flown off from magistrates and ministers and this since they have come to you, and besides that it will not well stand with the commonwealth that families should be neglected for so many neighbours and dames and so much time spent, we see no rule of God for this, we see not that any should have authority to set up any other exercises besides what authority hath

---

*John Endecott, an assistant in the General Court.
[†]A reference to I Corinthians 14:34,35, which states that "the women should keep silence in the churches."

already set up and so what hurt comes of this you will be guilty of and we for suffering you.

Mrs. H. Sir, I do not believe that to be so.

Gov. Well, we see how it is we must therefore put it away from you, or restrain you from maintaining this course.

Mrs. H. If you have a rule for it from God's word you may.

Gov. We are your judges, and not you ours and we must compel you to it.

Mrs. H. If it please you by authority to put it down I will freely let you for I am subject to your authority.

Mr. Bradstreet.* I would ask this question of Mrs. Hutchinson, whether you do think this is lawful? For then this will follow that all other women that do not are in a sin.

Mrs. H. I conceive this is a free will offering.

Mr. Bradstreet. If it be a free will offering you ought to forbear it because it gives offence.

Mrs. H. Sir, in regard of myself I could, but for others I do not yet see light but shall further consider of it.

Mr. Bradstreet. I am not against all women's meetings but do think them to be lawful. . . .

Dep. Gov.† I would go a little higher with Mrs. Hutchinson. About three years ago we were all in peace. Mrs. Hutchinson from that time she came hath made a disturbance, and some that came over with her in the ship did inform me what she was as soon as she was landed. I being then in place dealt with the pastor and teacher of Boston and desired them to enquire of her, and then I was satisfied that she held nothing different from us, but within half a year after, she had vented divers of her strange opinions and had made parties in the country, and at length it comes that Mr. Cotton and Mr. Vane were of her judgment, but Mr. Cotton hath cleared himself that he was not of that mind, but now it appears by this woman's meeting that Mrs. Hutchinson hath so forestalled the minds of many by their resort to her meeting that now she hath a potent party in the country. Now if all these things have endangered us as from that foundation and if she in particular hath disparaged all our ministers in the land that they have preached a convenant of works, and only Mr. Cotton a covenant of grace, why this is not to be suffered, and therefore being driven to the foundation and it being found that Mrs. Hutchinson is she that hath depraved all the ministers and hath been the cause of what is fallen out, why we must take away the foundation and the building will fall.

Mrs. H. I pray, Sir, prove it that I said they preached nothing but a convenant of works.

Dep. Gov. Nothing but a covenant of works, why a Jesuit may preach truth sometimes.

---

*Simon Bradstreet, an assistant in the General Court.
†Thomas Dudley, Deputy Governor of the colony.

Mrs. H.   Did I ever say they preached a covenant of works then?

Dep. Gov.   If they do not preach a covenant of grace clearly, then they preach a covenant of works.

Mrs. H.   No, Sir, one may preach a covenant of grace more clearly than another, so I said.

Dep. Gov.   We are not upon that now but upon position.

Mrs. H.   Prove this then, Sir, that you say I said.

Dep. Gov.   When they do preach a covenant of works do they preach truth?

Mrs. H.   Yes, Sir, but when they preach a covenant of works for salvation, that is not truth.

Dep. Gov.   I do but ask you this, when the ministers do preach a covenant of works do they preach a way of salvation?

Mrs. H.   I did not come hither to answer to questions of that sort.

Dep. Gov.   Because you will deny the thing.

Mrs. H.   Ey, but that is to be proved first.

Dep. Gov.   I will make it plain that you did say that the ministers did preach a covenant of works.

Mrs. H.   I deny that.

Dep. Gov.   And that you said they were not able ministers of the new testament, but Mr. Cotton only.

Mrs. H.   If ever I spake that I proved it by God's word.

Court.   Very well, very well.

Mrs. H.   If one shall come unto me in private, and desire me seriously to tell them what I thought of such a one, I must either speak false or true in my answer.

Dep. Gov.   Likewise I will prove this that you said the gospel in the letter and words holds forth nothing but a covenant of works and that all that do not hold as you do are in a covenant of works.

Mrs. H.   I deny this for if I should so say I should speak against my own judgment.

Mr. Endicot.   I desire to speak seeing Mrs. Hutchinson seems to lay something against them that are to witness against her.

Gov.   Only I would add this. It is well discerned to the court that Mrs. Hutchinson can tell when to speak and when to hold her tongue. Upon the answering of a question which we desire her to tell her thoughts of she desires to be pardoned.

Mrs. H.   It is one thing for me to come before a public magistracy and there to speak what they would have me to speak and another when a man comes to me in a way of friendship privately there is difference in that. . . .

[A group of ministers testifies against Anne Hutchinson, and minister John Cotton testifies in her defense. Then the proceedings continue.]

Gov. I do not see that we need their testimony any further. Mr. Cotton hath expressed what he remembered, and what took impression upon him, and so I think the other elders also did remember that which took impression upon them. . . .

Mr. Cotton. Brother Weld and Brother Shepard,* I did not then clear myself unto you that I understood her speech in expressing herself to you that you did hold forth some matter in your preaching that was not pertinent to the seal of the spirit. . . . [*Two lines defaced.*]

Dep. Gov. They affirm that Mrs. Hutchinson did say they were not able ministers of the new testament.

Mr. Cotton. I do not remember it.

Mrs. H. If you please to give me leave I shall give you the ground of what I know to be true. Being much troubled to see the falseness of the constitution of the church of England, I had like to have turned separatist; whereupon I kept a day of solemn humiliation and pondering of the thing; this scripture was brought unto me—he that denies Jesus Christ to be come in the flesh is anti-Christ—This I considered of and in considering found that the papists did not deny him to be come in the flesh, nor we did not deny him—who then was anti-Christ? Was the Turk anti-Christ only? The Lord knows that I could not open scripture; he must by his prophetical office open it unto me. So after that being unsatisfied in the thing, the Lord was pleased to bring this scripture out of the Hebrews. He that denies the testament denies the testator, and in this did open unto me and give me to see that those which did not teach the new covenant had the spirit of anti-Christ, and upon this he did discover the ministry unto me and ever since. I bless the Lord, he hath let me see which was the clear ministry and which the wrong. Since that time I confess I have been more choice and he hath left me to distinguish between the voice of my beloved and the voice of Moses, the voice of John Baptist and the voice of anti-Christ, for all those voices are spoken of in scripture. Now if you do condemn me for speaking what in my conscience I know to be truth I must commit myself unto the Lord.

Mr. Nowel.† How do you know that that was the spirit?

Mrs. H. How did Abraham know that it was God that bid him offer his son, being a breach of the sixth commandment?

Dep. Gov. By an immediate voice.

Mrs. H. So to me by an immediate revelation.‡

Dep. Gov. How! an immediate revelation.

---

*Ministers.
†Increase Nowell of Charlestown, an officer of the colony.
‡According to Puritan theology, God communicated with believers only through the Bible ("the Word"); scriptural passages were thrust into their minds. God no longer conveyed personal messages, such as those Anne Hutchinson describes: that she would come to New England and be persecuted there. The admission of immediate revelation, in the court's view, proved that Anne was deluded and therefore guilty.

Mrs. H. By the voice of his own spirit to my soul. I will give you another scripture— Jer. 46:27, 28—out of which the Lord showed me what he would do for me and the rest of his servants. But after he was pleased to reveal himself to me I did presently like Abraham run to Hagar. And after that he did let me see the atheism of my own heart, for which I begged of the Lord that it might not remain in my heart, and being thus, he did show me this (a twelvemonth after) which I told you of before. Ever since that time I have been confident of what he hath revealed unto me.

(*Obliterated*) . . . another place out of Daniel chap. 7. and he————and for us all, wherein he showed me the sitting of the judgment and the standing of all high and low before the Lord and how thrones and kingdoms were cast down before him. When our teacher came to New England it was a great trouble unto me, my brother Wheel-wright being put by also. I was then much troubled concerning the ministry under which I lived, and then that place in the 30th of Isaiah was brought to my mind. Though the Lord give thee bread of adversity and water of affliction yet shall not thy teachers be removed into corners any more, but thine eyes shall see thy teachers. The Lord giving me this promise and they being gone there was none then left that I was able to hear, and I could not be at rest but I must come hither. Yet that place of Isaiah did much follow me, though the Lord give thee the bread of adversity and water of affliction. This place lying I say upon me then this place in Daniel was brought unto me and did show me that though I should meet with affliction yet I am the same God that delivered Daniel out of the lion's den, I will also deliver thee. ————Therefore I desire you to look to it, for you see this scripture fulfilled this day and therefore I desire you that as you tender the Lord and the church and commonwealth to consider and look what you do. You have power over my body but the Lord Jesus hath power over my body and soul, and assure yourselves thus much, you do as much as in your lies to put the Lord Jesus Christ from you, and if you go on in this course you begin [began] you will bring a curse upon you and your posterity, and the mouth of the Lord hath spoken it.

Gov. The case is altered and will not stand with us now, but I see a marvellous providence of God to bring things to this pass that they are. We have been hearkening about the trial of this thing and now the mercy of God by a providence hath answered our desires and made her to lay open her self and the ground of all these disturbances to be by revelations. . . . [T]he ground work of her revelations is the immediate revelation of the spirit and not by the ministry of the word, and that is the means by which she hath very much abused the country that they shall look for revelations and are not bound to the ministry of the word, but God will teach them by immediate revelations and this hath been the ground of all these tumults and troubles. . . .

Gov. The court hath already declared themselves satisfied concerning the things you hear, and concerning the troublesomeness of her spirit and the danger of her course amongst us, which is not to be suffered. Therefore if it be the mind of the court that Mrs. Hutchinson for these things that appear before us is unfit for our society, and if it be the mind of the court that she shall be banished out of our liberties and imprisoned till she be sent away, let them hold up their hands. All but three. Those that are contrary minded hold up yours. Mr. Coddington and Mr. Colborn, only.

Mr. Jennison. * I cannot hold up my hand one way or the other, and I shall give my reason if the court require it.

Gov.   Mrs. Hutchinson, the sentence of the court you hear is that you are banished from out of our jurisdiction as being a woman not fit for our society, and are to be imprisoned till the court shall send you away.

Mrs. H.   I desire to know wherefore I am banished?

Gov.   Say no more, the court knows wherefore and is satisfied.

---

*William Jennison of Watertown, who was a deputy.

Sarah Fiske's Conversion

JOHN FISKE, 1644–1645

Robert G. Pope, ed., *The Notebook of the Reverend John Fiske, 1644–1675* (Boston: Publications of the Colonial Society of Massachusetts, 1974), pp. 25–29, 32, 34, 40–47.

In order to join a Congregational church, Puritans had to describe their experiences of religious conversion. Women sometimes did so in front of the congregation. Alternatively, a minister could question a woman in private and then present her "conversion relation" to the church members, who might ask questions. Such conversion relations followed a regular pattern. Converts told of their one-time sinful existences, of reform and relapse, and finally of the revelation of God's grace—an experience that usually was spurred by reading, hearing, or recalling a specific biblical passage.

Examples of conversion relations appear in the records of the congregational church of Wenham, Massachusetts, a town founded around 1640 by about twenty families who had migrated from nearby Salem. During the church's early years, admissions proceeded smoothly. Many applicants were former members of the Salem church. Wives of church members usually won swift acceptance, even in the case of one very shy woman who had trouble talking on any subject. Such was not the experience of Sarah Fiske, wife of congregant Phineas Fiske. Embroiled in a dispute with Phineas, Sarah Fiske went through a year-long ordeal that involved an exposé of her troubled marriage, accusations from neighbors and relatives, and unusual social pressure.

When Sarah Fiske first applied for church membership, she met two charges from congregants: that she had publicly maligned her husband, Phineas, "saying he loved another woman better than his wife &c." and that she had misbehaved during a Sabbath service. When asked to repent for these errors, Sarah accused Phineas of "false witness bearing" and further complained that he did not take her side, failed to pray for her, and behaved cruelly toward her. After congregants heard evidence on both sides, Phineas was cleared of his wife's charges. But then Sarah refused to admit the error of her accusations, and months went by. At last, she conceded some "evil in these particulars," the spouses were reconciled, and the church agreed to hear Sarah Fiske's conversion relation.*

Her testimony was unexceptional: As a young woman in England, she had been inspired by a sermon, prayed for a "sign," declared herself worse off "than any toad," experienced grace, "went forth rejoicing," and emigrated to Massachusetts. Church members, however, put Sarah through an unusually rigorous examination. They asked questions about evidence of God's will, requested citations of biblical text in support of her claims, and again demanded that she confess her mistakes in front of the congregation. Finally, Sarah Fiske was accepted as a "visible saint." Her atypical experience was recorded in the notebook of Wenham's newly ordained minister, Reverend John Fiske (by marriage, a cousin once removed), who took shorthand notes on all church proceedings.

[December 14, 1644]
14 of 12t. 44

The case of the wife of Brother Phineas Fiske considered and reduced to two heads: whether any had aught against her conversation (private offenses excepted); who had aught for her. Two things were objected against her: her carriage towards her husband in accounting him an enemy and exclaiming against him commonly and saying he loved another woman better than his wife &c., and her miscarriage one Lord's day presently after a prayer and ordinance to challenge Sister White for a debt, which it was determined she should acknowledge in the public congregation. Which, if she would promise to do and appear in some measure affected with and to speak to satisfaction to the brethren employed to acquaint her with the church's mind, the church determined to proceed no further with her. The brethren appointed by the church to show her the church's mind, and some days after she had duly considered of it to receive her answer, were Brother Read and Brother Geere.

13 of 1st. 45

This fifth day of the week the church met in the afternoon about the scandals divulged upon a brother, viz. Phineas Fiske, to inquire into the grounds of the same, his wife, known to be the person divulging them, being there present to make good her accusations. But, not finishing the work, resolved to meet again next second day.

---

*Sarah Fiske's ordeal is discussed in Charles Lloyd Cohen, *God's Caress: The Psychology of Puritan Religious Experience* (New York: Oxford University Press, 1986), pp. 154–55.

17 of 1st. 45

[Sarah Fiske's charges against Phineas Fiske are discussed at length by the congregation, and Phineas defends himself.]

These things premised, the charges or accusations considered of these two meetings were: of falsehood in our brother or false witness bearing. . . .

The second accusation: want of love towards his wife. The charge endeavored to be cleared in two or three particulars. [First,] in not using means to clear his wife wherein she was innocent. . . .

Second particular against her husband: for not praying with her and for her and not sympathizing with her condition. . . .

Third particular: for cruelty and bitterness in his carriage to her. . . .

Fourth particular: she reports that Goodwife Underwood told her that she [was] dealing with our brother for his harshness towards her [when] he said to her he would break her heart. This she stood to; her husband denied. . . .

Twas concluded by the church that our brother in the three former charges was to be quited and cleared, being judged (human frailties excepted) innocent in case of these so sad accusations. The fourth charge was left in suspension until an answer could be received from Watertown for the further clearing of it.

[Phineas Fiske's cousin, Martha Underwood of Watertown, sends a letter defending the conduct of Phineas toward Sarah.]

20 of 3d. 45

At a church meeting the wife of Brother Phineas Fiske her case spoken to. The letter from Watertown was judged to clear our brother from the imputation cast on him by his wife. Concluded touching her that she should appear convinced of the evil of her accusations against her husband before we proceeded further with her and that the whole church severally should endeavor as opportunity serve to convince her in the particulars. And as this was conceived as a way to bring her to see her evil that everyone take meet season to tell her of it plainly. So secondly to pray for her, and thirdly to walk exemplarily before her.

And the evil that she is to be convinced of is especially, publishing what she should have concealed (had this been true) to the defaming of her husband. The evil from the mind of it. First, that twas done in way of extenuating her own evil. Secondly, that she said she was provoked to it. Thirdly, that she said there were some of the church that were not dealt with withall (which was conceived meant her husband). Fourthly, that he was the cause or occasion of her trouble. And fifthly, that she still justifies herself and these and such like. Considering her relation was an aggravation of her sin.

22 of 6t. 45

. . . Our brethren returned also the message from Brother Phineas Fiske's wife that the utmost she could acknowledge wherein she had offended and if she had walked contrary to a rule she should be sorry and pray to God to forgive her, or to this effect. . . . Touching the latter, that this answer should be sent from the church to the wife of our Brother Phineas Fiske that her acknowledgement did not satisfy, but when once a manifestation of repentance was made they should joyfully proceed with her. . . .

18 of 10t. 45

A church meeting. [Sarah Fiske] hoped to speak to satisfy the church. . . . And after she acknowledged she did evil in these particulars whereas she should have kept secret and as the duty of a wife and as . . . her carriage at that time. She was asked whether . . . some reflections were cast on her husband because she said she can pass by her husband's failings. . . .

[A long church meeting is devoted to extracting apologies from Phineas and Sarah and reconciling them.]

It was asked her how she thought of the proceedings of the church toward her; she justified the church and acknowledged their faithfulness toward her and blesses God for it. So is the issue tending to put things to an end and to settle, if possible, a sweet accord betwixt them. It was asked of our brother whether he was satisfied in her acknowledgement and could pass by any offenses given on her part toward him. He answered affirmatively. It was then asked of him if he could find in his heart to desire of her to pass by his failing toward her. He answered affirmatively. Then the same things were likewise put unto her. She answered to both affirmatively. So it was agreed that we should proceed to propound her publicly for a church member. . . .

 Question: whether the wife of our Brother Phineas Fiske, having made her confession of these failings towards her husband in this church meeting, she should also acknowledge them in public. Resolved: she ought and should. . . .

[Finally, Sarah Fiske relates her conversion experience.]

30 of 11th. 45

At a church meeting. The wife of our Brother Phineas Fiske called forth to declare to the church how God hath gone along with her in bringing her soul to Christ.

 When she was a servant 22 years old, by Mr. Davis she heard there everyone gives account at the Day of Judgment for every work done in the flesh. She came to give account and said that she was guilty of two sins. . . . Then she prayed to God to show what sin was and whether the Lord spoke to her. To that answer that in John 3, the wind bloweth where it listeth &c. And if an answer to her that in Rev. 3, I counsel you to buy of me gold &c. . . . [At] once she came to see thence her one hope . . . but doubtful what effect on her. In that John 7, those that come to me I cast not away, and whereas she found that the Lord rejects not me &c. To that these words, none shall pluck them out of my hands.

[She] sought to the Lord that He show her condition. And out of Isa. 1, . . . then she saw that she is in a worse condition than any toad &c. Soon after the Lord spake to her (as twere a voice). Yet oftentimes she not resting content, but must look to God so she sought a place to pray and went trembling. And God gave her then a heart not to be satisfied till the Lord gave her some answer and given some assurance of His love in Christ. How she came out and He showed that nothing could help her but her hold of Christ and that if she has sins of 1000 worlds that was sufficient for her. And then she sought for a need of assurance and to that answered that in Rom. 8, shall I not with Him give all things. Yet she was not satisfied. . . . And then Rom. 8, neither height nor depth, things present &c., and upon that went forth rejoicing and praising God, desiring the Lord to go on further with her. . . .

When these new ordinances* came up in England &c. and she feared it a way of popery, she set upon prayer and that God would show her what to do and the more she sought God the more loathesome these things grew. And afterward . . . she essayed to go and showed it to a woman who offered to go with her to Mr. Witherall who set to praying. When she prayed that he not hide aught to any troubled soul what that soul desired to know and after she desired his counsel. He said he darst not, the times now so. She minded him of what he prayed, then he took her aside and coun-selled her. . . . Then he told her that she must refrain and then desires to come to this place &c. And when she came hither she found her heart so full of perturbation and distress and examined the cause &c. That in Heb. 10:25 by Mr. Phillips,† where-upon she was encouraged to seek to join in fellowship. . . .

Question: What evidence was there of God all this while for that time hitherto? Answer: She had a desire still continued to enjoy it, and she presumed she desired it the more. Whereupon she examined herself and found that it rested with God thus she had walked so unevenly. . . .

Question: Hath the Lord helped you to see any such failings as whereby you justly may be hindered? Answer: She would set down if hindered.

Question: But the Lord might be provoked and have occasion to glorify more-over in the knowledge of them. Answer: The Lord help you to see this failing.

It was put to the church whether they were satisfied in the relation. A brother objected. . . . Asked her how she made comfort from those words alleged in Rom. 8. She answered that the spirit bears witness with her spirit and that to holiness. And she said from the promises to her this. . . .

Question: How [do] the word and work here agree to clear this? Asked her first in what word God showed Christ to her soul. Answer: She said it twas Christ that spake to her, because love was mighty in her heart to the end &c.

Question: How came she to believe? Answer: By that first scripture &c.

Question: But how came God your soul to rest upon? Answer: John 10, he that come to me I will in no wise cast off &c.

Objection: But this scripture in order was alleged as a stay only and before the legal work was off. Answer: It was intended as that scripture and so that Matt. 11:28.

---

*Restrictions on Puritans.
†A minister from Watertown, who delivered a sermon.

It was asked here if more had aught further to query or object. It was requested that testimony should be given of a life suitable to this profession and confession. Her brother G. testified to this effect. . . . Then I replied I was condemned that twas an occasion of keeping her out hitherto for their offenses, which if but human frailties then I have done very evil in it. So her husband testified to the work his persuasion. Hereupon it was voted she should upon the Lord's day next make a public acknowledgement of her miscarriages particularly. It was moved that she show her assent to the church confession of faith. . . .

5 of 12t. 45

In the close of the day Brother Phineas Fiske's wife called and made her confession, particularly of the evil by her speeches of her husband and against the church and pastor. It was voted satisfactorily. . . .

The covenant was administered to the wife of our Brother Phineas Fiske.

An Epistle to Quaker Women

LANCASHIRE WOMEN'S MEETING, 1675

Milton D. Speizman and Jane C. Kronick, transcr., "A Seventeenth-Century Quaker Women's Declaration," *Signs: Journal of Women in Culture and Society* 1 (Autumn 1975), pp. 235–45.

The egalitarianism of seventeenth-century Quakers remains impressive. Unlike other religious groups, the Society of Friends insisted that women assume active roles in every facet of religious life. George Fox (1624–1691), founder of the sect in the 1640s, hoped "to liberate for the service of the Church the gifts of government which lay dormant in both men and women." One facet of self-government encouraged by Fox was the women's meeting, established by Quaker women in seventeenth-century England and the English colonies. Through women's meetings, which convened monthly, women Friends collectively exercised an unusual amount of authority over Quaker community life. They also kept in touch with each other through epistles, or circulating letters.

Around 1675, the women's meeting in Lancashire, England, sent out an epistle to its sister organizations that apparently crossed the Atlantic. A fragment was found among the papers of the Society of Friends in Newport, Rhode Island, and a complete copy was found in a Philadelphia meeting house. In the following excerpts from this rare document, the epistle sets forth the extensive responsibilities of women's meetings—among them, to supervise domestic life, approve marriages, prevent intermarriage (with non-Friends), help the unfortunate, and record all of their transactions, collections, and expenditures in businesslike fashion. Although the epistle acknowledges that women are "looked upon as weaker vessels," it reminds women Friends that they are equal in the eyes of God.

From our Country Women's Meeting in Lancashire to Be Dispersed Abroad, Among the Women's Meetings Everywhere

Dear Sisters,

In the blessed unity in the Spirit of grace our Souls Salute you who are sanctified in Christ Jesus, and called to be Saints, who are of the true and Royal offspring of Christ

Jesus. . . . To you that are of the true seed of the promise of God in the beginning, that was to bruise the Serpent's head, and which is fullfilled in Christ Jesus of which we are made partakers. . . . And that every particular of us, may be ready, and willing to answer what the lord requires of us; in our several places and conditions; for as many of us as are baptized into Christ, have put on Christ; for we are all the children of God by faith in Christ Jesus, where there is neither male nor female &c. but we are all one in Christ Jesus. . . .

And let us meet together, and keep our women's meetings, in the name and power, and fear of the lord Jesus, whose servants and handmaids we are, and in the good order of the Gospel meet.

And first, for the women of every . . . monthly meeting, where the men's monthly meeting is established, let the women likewise of every monthly meeting, meet together to wait upon the lord, and to hearken what the lord will say unto them, and to know his mind, and will, and be ready to obey, and answer him in every motion of his eternal spirit and power.

And also, to make inquiry into all your severall particular meetings, that belongs to your monthly meetings, if there be any that walks disorderly, as doth not become the Gospell, or lightly, or wantonly, or that is not of a good reporte: Then send to them, as you are ordered by the power of God in the meeting (which is the authority of it) to Admonish, and exhort them, and to bring them to Judge, and Condemn, what hath been by them done or acted contrary to the truth.

And if any transgression or Action that hath been done amongst women or maids, that hath been more publick, and that hath gott into the world, or that hath been a publick offence among friends; then let them bring in a paper of condemnation, to be published as far, as the offence hath gone, and then to be recorded in a booke.

And if there be any that goes out to Marry, with priests, or joineth in Marriage with the world, and does not obey the order of the Gospell as it is established amongst friends, then for the women's monthly meeting to send to them, to reprove them, and to bear their testimony against their acting Contrary to the truth, and if they come to repentance, and sorrow for their offence, and have a desire to come amongst friends again: before they can be received, they must bring in a paper of Condemnation, and repentance, and Judgment of their Action; which must be recorded in Friends Booke. . . .

And dear sisters it is duely Incumbent upon us to look into our families, and to prevent our Children of running into the world for husbands, or for wives, and so to the priests: for you know before the women's meetings were set up, many have done so, which brought dishonour, both to God, and upon his truth and people.

Therefore it is our duty and care, to prevent such things in the power, and wisdom of God: and to see that our Children are trained up in the feare of God, in the new Covenant, for the Jews were to train their Children up in the old. For you know, that we are much in our families amongst our children maids, and servants, and may see more into their inclinations; and so see that none indulge any to looseness and evill. . . .

And also all friends that keep in the power of God, and in faithfull obedience to the truth, that according to the order of the Gospell that is established, that they bring their Marriages twice to the women's meetings, and twice to the men's: the first time they are to come to the women's meetings that the women of the meeting, do examin both the man and the woman, that they be cleare and free from all other persons, and that they have their parents, and friends and Relations, Consent. . . .

And likewise, that the women of the monthly meetings, take care, and oversight of all the women that belong to their several particular meetings, that they bring in their testimonies for the lord, and his truth, against tithes, and hireling priests once every yeare. . . .

And also all friends, in their women's monthly, and particular Meetings, that they take special care for the poore, and for those that stand in need: that there be no want, nor suffering, for outward things, amongst the people of God, for the earth is the lords, and the fullness of it, and his people is his portion and the lot of his Inheritance, and he gives freely, and liberally, unto all, and upbraids none. . . .

And that all the sick, and weak, and Infirme, or Aged, and widdows, and fatherless, that they be looked after, and helped, and relieved, in every particular meeting, either with clothes, or maintainance, or what they stand in need of. So that in all things the Lord may be glorified, and honoured, so that there be no want, nor suffering in the house of God, who loves a Chearfull giver.

Also let Care be taken that every particular women's monthly meeting, have a booke to set down, and record their bussinesses and passages in, that is done or agreed upon, in every monthly meeting, or any service that any is to go upon, let the book be read, the next monthly meeting, and see that the business be performed, according to what was ordered.

And also that the collections be set downe, in the booke; and that the Receipts, and disbursments of every particular meeting, be set down in their booke, and read at their women's monthly meeting, that every particular meeting may see and know, how their collections is disbursed.

And that some faithfull honest woman, or women friends, that can Read, and write, keep the Book, and receive the Collections, and give a just and a true account, of the disbursments of them in the book. . . .

And though wee be looked upon as the weaker vessels, yet strong and powerfull is God, whose strength is made perfect in weakness, he can make us good and bold, and valliant Souldiers of Jesus Christ, if he arm us with his Armour of Light, and give unto us the sword of his Eternal Spirit which is the word of the Eternal God, and cover our hearts with the breast-plate of righteousness, and crown us with the helmet of Salvation, and give unto us the Shield of Faith, with which we can quench all the firey darts of Sathan. . . .

This is given forth for Information, Instruction, and Direction, that in the blessed unity of the spirit of grace, all friends may bee, and live in the practice of the holy order of the Gospell; if you know these things, happy are you if ye do them so.

To Fill a Larger Sphere

SARAH OSBORN, 1767

Sarah Haggar Osborn to Joseph Fish (February 28 to March 7, 1767) in Mary Beth Norton, "'My Resting Reaping Times': Sarah Osborn's Defense of Her 'Unfeminine' Activities, 1767," *Signs: Journal of Women in Culture and Society* 2 (Winter 1976), pp. 515–29.

The Great Awakening that swept the colonies in the mid-eighteenth century brought religious experience to new constituencies, including the "lower sort," the less literate, and an underclass of servants and slaves. It also diffused religious authority and created an aura of emotionalism that fostered the rise of lay preachers, among them women. Sarah Haggar Osborn of Newport, Rhode Island, who led a revival there in 1766–1767, exemplified the leadership role that women might play. But as she explained to her spiritual advisor, a local minister, she did so with considerable reluctance and only at providential insistence.

An English immigrant who came to Rhode Island as a girl, Sarah Osborn joined the Congregational church in 1737, during an early wave of revivalism. Then a young widow with a child, she ran a school to support herself. Subsequently, she continued the school in order to support her second husband, a failed merchant, and his sons. From 1741 on, Sarah Osborn also led a female prayer society—an acceptable activity for a woman, according to the scriptural injunction that older women might instruct younger women. But Osborn's religious duties gradually expanded. In 1756, she began to admit some local slaves to her home on Sunday evenings to attend family prayers. Soon she welcomed young people from the neighborhood as well. By the mid-1760s, Sarah Osborn's home had become a veritable spiritual center: Some 500 people visited it each week for religious gatherings. "Who would Ever Have Thot," she asked, "that God by such a poor Mean despiccable woman would have gathered such a number?"

Sarah Osborn's activities aroused the ire of local slaveowners, who criticized her for spreading "disturbance and disorder." Her advisor, Reverend Joseph Fish, also asked her to stop her revivalist career and to devote herself to her family and to other feminine tasks. In an impassioned response, Sarah Osborne explained that she had tried "To avoid Moving beyond my Line." Describing the strenuous schedule of evening meetings that she held each week, Osborne pointed out that she confined her services to women, children, and "servants," and had nothing to do with teenage boys, young men, or married men. Moreover, she claimed, she had asked Newport clergymen for assistance and relief, but none was forthcoming. Leadership, in short, had been thrust upon her. When forced "to fill a larger sphere," she had risen to the occasion. And once awakened to her spiritual capacity, she refused to "shut up my Mouth and doors and creep into obscurity." In the following segments of a 1767 letter to Reverend Fish, Sarah Osborn defends her divine calling.

Revd and Worthy Sir,

. . . [P]ermit me to set my self as a child in the Presence of her Father to Give you the Most Satisfactory account of my conduct as to religious affairs I am capable. I will begin with the Great one respecting the poor Blacks on Lords day Evenings, which above all the rest Has been Exercising to my Mind. And first Let me assure you Sir it would be the Joy of my Heart to commit it into Superior Hands did any arrise for their Help. My Revd Pastor and Brethren are my wittnesses that I Have earnestly Sought, yea in bitterness of Soul, for their assistance and protection. [I] would Gladly be under inspection of Pastor and church and turn things into a safe channel. O forever blessed be my Gracious God that Has Himself vouchsaft to be my protection Hithertoo by Putting His fear into My Heart and thereby Moving me as far as possible in this surprizing day. To avoid Moving beyond my Line, while I was anxiously desirous the poor creatures should be favrd with some sutable one to pray with them, I was Greatly distresst; but as I could not obtain [help] I Have Given it up and They Have not Had above one [prayer] Made with them I believe Sir Since you was here. I only read to them, talk to them, and sing a Psalm or Hymn with them, and then at Eight o clock dismiss them all by Name as upon List. They call it School and I Had rather it should be calld almost any thing that is good than Meeting. I reluct so much at being that Head of any thing that bears that Name. Pray my dear Sir don't Look upon it as a rejecting your council; that I Have not yet dismist. It is Such a tender point with me while the poor creatures attend with so Much decency and quietness you Might almost Hear as we say the shaking of a Leaf when there is More than an Hundred under the roof at onece. . . .

I know of no one in the town now that is against me. My dear Mrs. Cheseborough and Mrs Grant Have both been to see me and thank'd me for persisting Stedily in the path of duty against their discouragements, ownd they were at first uneasy but now rejoicd and wish'd a blessing. . . . And other Masters and Misstresses frequently send me presents in token of gratitude, Express their thanks Speaking of the good Effects that thro the blessing of the Lord it Has Had upon their Servants. . . .

In december I was affrighted at the throng and Greatly feard that it would indeed be as the river Jordan overflowing all the banks, and was upon the point of dismissing on that account. And I told Deacon Coggeshall, So He still insisted I ought not to do it. Then I told Him He Must Help me some way; he must take the overflowings I would send them down to Him. He concented and said I might send Him Some white Boys too for they pressd in Likewise.

The Next Lords day Evening I told them of it, that the Deacon was as willing to do them Good as I, and I would Have all go that could not find comfortable room here. I spoke to the Boys in particular and begd them to go once and again but they kept their places and would not stir. There was I think 38 of them. At Last I told them that If they would concent to give way to the poor Black folks *then*, as they could come no other Night, if they Had rather come and see me then go to play on Tusday Evening I would devote that to them. Then 26 of them and ten Blacks rose cheirfuly and went down to the Deacons, and His House is usualy full ever since, but I Have Seldom Less than 16 or 17 Boys. *Still* they will come and on Tusday Evenings upwards of 30 almost all weathers from Eight or nine years old to fifteen or sixteen. I don't pray with these because of these big ones but Mr Osborn does. . . .

As to the young Men that did in sumer visit us on Tusday Evenings and spend the Evening in religious Exercises, praying in turn etc., but as soon as time come to work on Evenings in Sept that ceasd. The Boys fills that vacancy now and the young Men Have only the priviledge of Meeting in our chamber on Sabath Evenings. I Have no thing to do with them. . . .

There is usualy 30 odd young garls every Monday Evening Except the weather is excessive bad and indeed it is surprising to see their constancy thro almost all weathers—yet I know of no Extraordinary Effects but *Here* they behave quite serious and the Pashions are sometimes toucht I think. My companies are all Voluntiers— our Society on wensday Evenings is I Hope not on the decline but rather growing. . . .

The children for catechising on Thursday afternoon Hold on with surprising chierfulness and steadiness tho not so Numerous as before winter set in, and for that reason boys and Garls come together for the winter on one day only in the week Either Thursday or Satterday, as the weather sutes. The room is usualy full consisting of all denominations. I Have Hope that God Has awakened some few of the Little Garls to a concern about their precious Souls. . . .

As to Friday Evening friends, my dear Sir I by no means Set up for their instructor. They come indeed for Mutual Edification and Sometimes condescend to direct part of conversation to me and so far I bear a part as to answer etc. but no otherway. They consist of the Brethren of our own church or congregation. . . .

That these Gatherings at our House Sir I Imagine no way tend to Separations rents or diversions but are rather a Sweet Sementing bond of union that Holds us together in this critical day. My dear Mr Osborn thro infirmity is unable to Go often to the Deacons on Thurdsdays Evenings and is very fond of this Friday Nights visit, and they are Sweet refreshing Evenings my resting reaping times and as God Has Gatherd I dare not Scatter. . . .

But I come now to answer your tender important Enquiry after approving of part of my work; viz. "Have you Strength abillity and Time consistent with other Duties to fill a Larger sphere by attending the various Exercises of other Meetings, in close succession too. A Moses May undertake More (from a tender concern of the people too) then His Shoulders was able to bear; Jethro's advice was Seasonable etc."*

As to Strength Sir it is Evident I gain by Spending; God will in no wise suffer me to be a Loser by His Service. I am much confirm'd in My belief of that work, He that will Lose His Life for My Sake Shall save it,† as I used to Lie by, unable to sit up, usualy one day in the week for years together. I have Lain by but one this winter and comparatively know nothing about weariness to what I did when I Had so Great a School and ten or more children in family to attend. I always feel stronger when my companies break up then when they come in and blessed by God I Have a Good appetite and sleep well, Except any Great pressure is on my Spirits.

As to My ability I can only say I trust Christ's Strength is Made perfect in my weakness, and at sometimes am Made open to Glory Even in my infirmities, that the Power of Christ May rest upon me and rejoice that I am nothing and can do nothing without Him. And yet tho I was born as the wild asses Colt and fit for nothing till brot too by soverign Grace, as Mr Henry Notes, yet He can Serve Himself of me and Glorifie Himself in me and in His own way too, However Misterious to me and all around me—he Has chosen the weak things of this world etc.

As to time consistent with other duties it is Most true dear Sir that I am calld by the Providence of God as well as by His word to be a redeemer of time Precious time. And Ille tell my Worthy friend How I do My wakeing time, Except unwell or weary with Exercise Generaly prevents. The dawning of the day Mr Osborn rises while it is yet dark, can Just see to dress etc. From which time I am alone as to any inturruption. . . . I do not Lie there but turn upon my knees my stomach soported with bolster and Pillows, and I am thus securd from the inclemency of all Seasons and from all inturruptions from family affairs. There I read and write almost Every thing of a religious Nature. Thus I redeem an Hour or two for retirement without which I must *starve* and this priviledge blessed by God I Have been Enabled to Hold thro all my Seeans [scenes] of business, sickness in family only Excepted. I never go down till breakfast is Near ready—after Breakfast family worship; then Giving Some orders as to family affairs, I apply to my School, to which you know Sir a kind providence Has Limited my Earning time for soport of my family. And if in this time I Educate the children of poor Neighbours who Gladly pay me in washing Ironing Mending and Making, I Imagine it is the Same thing as if I did it with my own Hands. I think my family does not Suffer thro My Neglect tho doubtless if I Had a full purse and Nothing to do but Look after them some things Might be done with more Exactness then now, but Every dear friend is ready to set a stitch or Help me in any wise and all is well Here—my fragments in the intervails I pick up for keeping and drawing out accompts etc. or what Ever my Hand finds to do besides refreshing the body.

Thursday afternoon and Evening after catechising (Except the Last Thursday in Every Month on which our Society Meets) is reserved for transient visiters business or what Ever providence allots. Satterday afternoon is my dear Miss Susa's‡

---

*In Exodus 18:18, Jethro told Moses "this thing is too heavy for thee."
†Matthew 17:25.
‡Susanna Anthony, another woman known for her piety, and a friend of Sarah Osborn.

particular time to visit me. Satterday Evening is reserv'd to ourselves. Now sir, if my Evenings were not thus improved I could not spend them to so much advantage that I know of any other way, for indeed I am not so capable after the Exercises of the day of working at my Needle; that overpowers me vastly more than the duties I am Engagd in. I could not retire the Evening as I could not Endure cold etc. nor can I Long attain to clost fixt Meditation or any Clearness of thot tho I Labour Ever so much for it; I am at that Season Much more capable of social duties then any other. These seem then to refresh recruit and enliven my Exhausted spirits, and companys Most of them are dismist before Nine o clock [so] that I have some time Left for other duties. My family Has the advantage of all these seasons, Except the Wensday Evenings *only* Mr Osborn [who] draws a Little while before they break up, I mean from the young ones. And if my Evenings were not thus filld up they doubtless would be with trancient visiters, and some chat Less to Edification Especialy in this *critical day* would break in, which is by this Means *shut out* [so] that at present I do acquiese in my time being thus taken up. Thus Sir I have given you the best account of My time I am capable of, but after all, while others are wondring, I find cause daily to bemoan before God the Misspence of precious time and oft appear to my self a very Loiterer a very snail. I fly with Haste from all my poor narrow Scanty performances and bless God I Have a perfect rightiousness to Plead and Hope to Escape to Heaven after all by the way of a free Pardon—

I would now Humbly beg leave Just to Speak a word as to Jethro's advice, which I own to be very Good, but Here my dear Sir Lies the difference. Moses was Head of the people and So Had it in His power to comply with Jethro's advice by appointing Elders etc. to take part with Him, but I am rather as a Servant that Has a Great work assignd Him and However unworthy and unequal he may think Himself, and others may think Him, and However ardently He may wish it was in Superior Hands or that His Master would at Least Help Him, yet if He declines He dares not tell Him, well if you dont do it your self it shall go undone for I will not, but rather trys to do what He can till God in his providence point out a way for it to be better done. And God did uphold Moses till He pointed out that way of relief He could comply with. Dont think me obstinate then Sir if I dont know How to Let Go these shoals of fish (to which My dear Susa compares them) that we Hope God as Gatherd ready to be caught in the Gospel Net when Ever it shall please Him to shew His dear Ministers on which side the ship to Let it down for advanight [advantage]—the Harvest truely appears to be Plenteous but the Labourers are few. O that the Lord of the Harvest may send forth Labourers into His Harvest and crown their Labours with success—

Last Summer all things were new and astonishing to me and I appeard to my self upon the very brink of ruin Except I had speedy Help, but infinite wisdom Has Hithertoo prevented all the Mischiefs I feard and brot things into so regular a way that I am quietly waiting His time and trust He will Glorifie Himself in His own way and time—but O forgive me forgive me for thus intruding upon your patience first in waiting and now by my prolixity. Cover My failings with the Mantle of Love; please to Let me know by Post if no other presents whether all comes safe to Hand. I Have dealings with the Mumfords; dont be afraid of the charge Sir, Mr Mumford is always Handsome to me and indeed Never charges me any thing but it he does all is well— Make my sincier regards acceptable to dear Mrs Fish, Mrs Noice, and all other

Enquiring friends in which Mr Osborn and Mrs Susa Joins Me etc. pray Sir accept your self from your

sincier tho unworthy friend
S Osborn
March 7 1767

PS   I Long to hear How you all do

Chapter 6

The Revolutionary Era

"**A**s every domestic enjoyment depends on the decision of the mighty contest, who can be an unconcerned and silent spectator?" wrote Mercy Warren of Massachusetts to an inquiring friend as the Revolution approached. The question that engaged these correspondents—whether women might voice political opinions—was one of several that the revolutionary era inspired. To what extent, for instance, could women be considered traitors or citizens? How would independence affect women's legal rights? What part might patriotic women play in the new republic? Compounding such questions is one that historians ask: Did the Revolution make a difference in women's lives and, if so, what was it?

From the 1760s onward, colonial women were drawn into the margins of political activity, voluntarily or inadvertently. Boycotts of English manufactured goods increased the significance of domestic work: Patriot housewives abjured tea, shunned English imports, and produced homespun cloth. The onset of war brought new disruptions. Many women facing destitution, including soldiers' widows and stranded wives of loyalists, became petitioners of legislatures and the Continental Congress. In some locales, women formed patriotic societies that raised funds for the army, contributed clothing, and issued political statements. "We cannot be indifferent," declared a group of North Carolina women, "on any occasion that appears to affect the peace and happiness of our country." In private correspondence, women commented frequently on political affairs, and in at least one instance protested the legal subordination of married women. "Remember the ladies," wrote Abigail Adams to John Adams in 1776, when she insisted—in a jesting tone—that he consider a "New Code of laws" for women, and threatened a "revolt" should such laws not materialize. "Do not put such unlimited power into the hands of the Husbands," Abigail Adams urged.

The birth of the republic, however, brought no revolutionary or legal or political changes for women. To be sure, such changes as the abolition of primogeniture and the disestablishment of churches had an impact on women's lives. But, far more important, the doctrine of coverture continued unimpeded. Married women did not gain their own legal identity or the right to own property. Married or single, women remained excluded from political life, save in New Jersey where for three decades an aberration in the state suffrage law enabled propertied unmarried women to vote. Such exclusion was neither odd nor unique. Women in general lacked property, and those persons without property—landless men, servants, slaves—expected exclusion from political life. In terms of women's political rights, the Revolution had a negligible impact. What about their rights as family members?

The late eighteenth century saw many changes in family life, changes that both preceded and followed the Revolution. Since mid-century, for instance, patriarchal bonds had been loosening, and in some cases parental power declined. Children had claimed the right to choose their own spouses, if subject to parental veto (rather than vice versa); rising premarital pregnancy rates suggested yet further escape from parental authority. After the Revolution, wives began to share in the new freedom that subordinate family members gained. The right to absolute divorce expanded, as many states enacted some type of law to terminate marriages. This important change affected the majority of petitioners for divorce, women, who thereby gained a new degree of independence. Changes in the law did not always benefit women, however. After the Revolution, legal reformers hoped to simplify and streamline the law and, in the process, discarded several women's rights. During the early national period, old equity practices like antenuptial contracts fell into disuse. So did dower rights. As historian Marylynn Salmon points out, the gradual growth of married women's property rights in the early nineteenth century was part of an evolutionary process, unconnected to the break from England, especially since courts in the United States continued to rely on English precedents.*

What, then, was the outcome for women of two decades of revolutionary agitation and of independence? The answer seems to rest less on legal change than on social upheaval and class formation. At the end of the eighteenth century, the role of women became a subject of public debate, notably within the group of well-off, educated citizens who formed the new republic's leadership class. Three signposts of the post-revolutionary concern with women's status among these pace-setters were the appearance of publications about women's rights, an outburst of interest in young women's education, and the development of a feminine ideal that infused family roles with patriotic significance.

During the Revolution, any mention of needed change in women's status had been limited to private correspondence, such as Abigail Adams's letters. In the 1790s, demands for women's rights appeared in print. The most important publication was an English import, Mary Wollstonecraft's *Vindication of the Rights of Women* (1792), which aroused antipathy on both sides of the Atlantic. All of Mary Wollstonecraft's enlightened concerns—her disgust with aristocratic frivolity, her assault on sexual inequality, her appeal for women's education—were undercut by her reputation as a free lover and radical. Still, native-born women writers voiced similar arguments. In her articles of the 1780s and 1790s, Judith Sargent Murray of Massachusetts called for the development of women's rational faculties to inculcate self-respect and celebrated "excellency in our sex." In an 1801 pamphlet, the anonymous "aged matron of Connecticut" mocked the logic that assigned women to inferior roles. Like Mary Wollstonecraft, these American proponents of women's rights urged advanced education as a panacea that would eradicate the vestiges of female inferiority.

Education, indeed, was the most concrete sign of interest in women's roles in the new nation. Starting in the 1790s, there was an

---

*Marylynn Salmon, "Republican Sentiment, Economic Change, and the Property Rights of Women in American Law," in Ronald Hoffman and Peter J. Albert, eds., *Women in the Age of the American Revolution* (Charlottesville: University Press of Virginia, 1989), pp. 447–75.

outburst of female academies catering to daughters of prospering citizens. At the Young Ladies Academy of Philadelphia, born with the nation in 1787, well-off fathers joined forces to fund an advanced curriculum that included rhetoric, foreign languages, history, geography, and science lectures. Similar enterprises emerged throughout the nation from New England to the southern states. These new schools were in part an imitation of advances in women's education in England during the late eighteenth century. Their clientele was limited to a narrow social stratum, and the training they provided boosted daughters' potential on the marriage market. Still, compared to adventure schools, they were more permanent, better-financed, and far more ambitious.

Who was to profit from such education, the students themselves or society in general? "Speaking of women at large," Mary Wollstonecraft had declared in 1792, "their first duty is to themselves as rational creatures, and the next, in point of importance as citizens, is that, which includes so many, of a mother." In the American debate, however, the needs of society took priority. When Benjamin Rush, a founder of the Philadelphia Young Ladies Academy, defended female education, he explained that it would improve women's performance as wives and mothers; the major beneficiaries apparently would be men and children. Still, the new ideal of "Republican Motherhood" was the Revolution's major legacy to women. A custodian of values, the republican mother would be educated enough to pass such values on to her children, to raise them in an atmosphere of virtue, piety, and patriotism. This ideal managed to include women in republican ideology without giving them any political rights and while keeping them in domestic roles.

The argument for republican motherhood was not unique to America. Progressive spirits of the era in England and France had similarly concluded that a woman's major role as a citizen was the raising of future citizens.* Nor was it a universally accepted argument. As historian Linda Kerber has shown, the idea that women were capable of becoming "learnd or wise" proved a subject of debate in the

---

*For a comparative analysis of republican motherhood, see Jane Rendall, *The Origins of Modern Feminism: Women in Britain, France, and the United States, 1780–1860* (Chicago: Lyceum Books, 1985), chap. 2.

new nation.* Nor is it clear how far down the social scale the impact of the republican motherhood ideal extended. The outburst of concern with women's status seems to have been limited to the post-revolutionary elite—the nucleus of the new nation's future "middle class." Still, the ideal of republican motherhood remains significant.

Members of the post-revolutionary republican elite were now in the process of finding their own identity. They wanted to distinguish themselves from foppish, idle aristocrats—degenerate and arrogant—on the one hand, as well as from the disorderly, ill-behaved mob, on the other hand. They envisioned a "republic of virtue," untainted by either aristocratic pretense or lower class liabilities. In such a republic, women might hold a place of importance. The most radical aspect of the republican motherhood ideal was that it gave women unlimited access to "virtue," which they were now supposed to absorb, preserve, and perpetuate. This was a significant concession. Beyond that, republican motherhood was not so much a revolutionary ideal as a class ideal—one on which many members of the patriotic, newborn American elite could agree.

---

*Linda K. Kerber, *Women of the Republic: Intellect and Ideology in Revolutionary America* (Chapel Hill: University of North Carolina Press, 1980), chap. 7. Kerber coins the term "Republican Mother" to refer to the body of ideas about women's roles that emerged in the wake of the Revolution.

An Address to George III

PHILLIS WHEATLEY, 1768

Phillis Wheatley, "To the King's Most Excellent Majesty," in Margaretha Matilda Odell, ed., *Memoir and Poems of Phillis Wheatley, A Native African and a Slave* (Boston: G. W. Light, 1834), pp. 43–44.

One of the first colonial women to voice political views in print was Phillis Wheatley (ca. 1753–1784), a young Boston slave. Shipped to the colonies as a child in 1761, she had been purchased by John Wheatley, a well-off tailor, and his wife, Susanna. Raised and educated by the Wheatley family, the young slave turned out to be precocious and talented. She began writing poetry at eleven years of age and won much attention as a prodigy. To opponents of slavery, Phillis Wheatley's accomplishments proved the potential of blacks for education. In 1773, the Wheatleys sent the teenage poet on a visit to England, where her first book of poems was published; on her return, the Wheatleys liberated her. Phillis died a few years later.

During Phillis Wheatley's youth in Boston, when local revolutionary fervor escalated, political sentiments appeared in her poetry. Here, she drew a parallel between hope for freedom from England and freedom from slavery. Because her first book of poetry appeared in England on the eve of the Revolution, most of the poems with political messages were omitted from the volume. One that escaped exclusion was "To the King's Most Excellent Majesty" (1768), a seemingly reverential address to George III. Like other Wheatley poems, this address was extremely conventional in form and style—Phillis Wheatley imitated the neoclassical style of Alexander Pope—and it appeared to be a poem of praise. But it also contained several subversive elements, carefully concealed in its even stanzas.

Phillis Wheatley begins her address to George III in the voice of a devoted subject and retains this respectful posture throughout. Yet, she refers to the king as "the British king," not as the ruler of the colonies. She compliments him for repealing the Stamp Act in 1766. George III is thus praised for acceding to colonial wishes and discarding an offensive measure that his representatives had attempted to enforce. The end of the poem expresses Wheatley's hope that the king will avoid further evil policies. In the last couplet, she combines the code words "free" and "equal." She also suggests that "all climes" (perhaps a reference to those whose origin was in the subtropical African clime) might appreciate the king's actions.*

To the King's Most Excellent Majesty (1768)

Your subjects hope, dread Sire, the crown upon your
   brows may flourish long,
And that your arm may in your God be strong.
Oh, may your sceptre num'rous nations sway,
And all with love and readiness obey.

But how shall we the British king reward?
Rule thou in peace, our father and our lord!
'Midst the remembrance of thy favors past,
The meanest peasants most admire the last.†
May George, beloved by all the nations round.
Live with heaven's choicest, constant blessings crowned.
Great God! direct and guard him from on high,
And from his head let every evil fly;
And may each clime with equal gladness see
A monarch's smile can set his subjects free.

---

*For a discussion of Phillis Wheatley's poetry and career, see David Grinsted, "Anglo-American Racism and Phillis Wheatley's 'Sable Veil,' 'Length'ned Chain,' and 'Knitted Heart,'" in Ronald Hoffman and Peter J. Albert, eds., *Women in the Age of the American Revolution* (Charlottesville: University Press of Virginia, 1989), pp. 338–444.
†The repeal of the Stamp Act.

A Carolina Patriot

ELIZA WILKINSON, 1782

Caroline Gilman, ed., *Letters of Eliza Wilkinson* (New York: Samuel Colman, 1839), pp. 59–62.

Before the 1760s, historian Mary Beth Norton contends, colonists of both sexes accepted "the standard dictum that political discussion, like direct political participation, fell outside the feminine sphere."* During the Revolution, when women began to voice "political" sentiments, they also asserted the legitimacy of so doing, often with considerable self-consciousness. This is evident in the comments of Eliza Wilkinson, a young widow on the Sea Islands off South Carolina, which the British invaded in 1780.

An ardent rebel, Eliza ran one of her parents' plantations during the war. She withstood confrontations with British soldiers, maintained a lively interest in military events, and claimed the right to express political opinions. "None were greater politicians than the several knots of ladies who met together," she declared. "We commenced perfect statesmen." In the following excerpt from her wartime letters to an unspecified friend, "my dear Mary," Eliza Wilkinson relates some thoughts inspired by a conversation with visiting American officers, and then an encounter with the officers' prisoners. Throughout this excerpt, as throughout the letters, Eliza Wilkinson seems to be "inventing" herself—adopting the pose appropriate to a "female patriot."

Letter 6

After various discourses, the conversation took a turn on the subject of the present war. I was proud to hear my friends express themselves in a manner not unworthy of their country. Maj. Moore† made a comparison, which, as I perfectly remember, I will give you. Your opinion is also required of the same.

"Suppose," said he, "I had a field of wheat, upon these conditions, that out of that field I was to give so much to a certain person yearly; well, I think nothing of it, I give it cheerfully, and am very punctual; it goes on thus for some years; at length

---

*Mary Beth Norton, *Liberty's Daughters: The Revolutionary Experience of American Women, 1750–1800* (Boston: Little, Brown, 1980), p. 170.

†A patriot officer.

the person sends me word I must let him have so much more, for he wants it; still I comply with cheerfulness. The next year he requires a still larger supply, and tells me he cannot do without it. This startles me! I find him encroaching, by little and little, on my property. I make some difficulty in complying; however, as he says 'he cannot do without it,' I let him have it, though I see it hurts me; but it puts me on my guard. Well, things go on so for some time; at length he begins again, and at last seems to have a design of taking my whole field. Then what am I to do?—Why, if I give it up, I am ruined, I must lie at his mercy. Is not this slavery? For my part," continued he, "I would rather explore unknown regions, blessed with liberty, than remain in my native country if to be cursed with slavery."

The land of Liberty! how sweet the sound! enough to inspire cowardice itself with a resolution to confirm the glorious title, "the land of Liberty." Let me again repeat it—how enchanting! It carries every idea of happiness in it, and raises a generous warmth in every bosom capable of discerning its blessings. O! Americans— Americans! strive to retain the glorious privilege which your virtuous ancestors left you; "it is the price of blood"; and let not the blood of your brave countrymen, who have so lately (in all the States) died to defend it, be spilt in vain. Pardon this digression, my dear Mary—my pen is inspired with sympathetic ardor, and has run away with my thoughts before I was aware. I do not love to meddle with political matters; the men say we have no business with them, it is not in our sphere! and Homer (did you ever read Homer, child?) gives us two or three broad hints to mind our domestic concerns, spinning, weaving, &c. and leave affairs of higher nature to the men; but I must beg his pardon—I won't have it thought, that because we are the weaker sex as to *bodily* strength, my dear, we are capable of nothing more than minding the dairy, visiting the poultry-house, and all such domestic concerns; our thoughts can soar aloft, we can form conceptions of things of higher nature; and have as just a sense of honor, glory, and great actions, as these "Lords of the Creation." What contemptible *earth worms* these authors make us! They won't even allow us the liberty of thought, and that is all I want. I would not wish that we should meddle in what is unbecoming female delicacy, but surely we may have sense enough to give our opinions to commend or discommend such actions as we may approve or disapprove; without being reminded of our spinning and household affairs as the only matters we are capable of thinking or speaking of with justness or propriety. I won't allow it, positively won't. Homer has a deal of morality in his works, which is worthy of imitation; his Odyssey abounds with it. But I will leave Homer to better judges, and proceed in my narration.

While the officers were there discoursing, word was brought that a party of the enemy were at a neighboring plantation, not above two miles off, carrying provisions away. In an instant the men were under arms, formed and marched away to the place. We were dreadfully alarmed at the first information, but, upon seeing with what eagerness our friends marched off, and what high spirits they were in, we were more composed, but again relapsed into our fears when we heard the discharge of firearms; they did not stay out long; but returned with seven prisoners, four whites and three blacks. When they came to the door, we looked out, and saw two of M'Girth's men* with them, who had used us so ill; my heart relented at sight of them, and I

---

*Tories.

could not forbear looking at them with an eye of pity. Ah! thought I, how fickle is fortune! but two days ago these poor wretches were riding about as if they had nothing to fear, and terrifying the weak and helpless by their appearance; now, what a humbled appearance do *they* make! But, basely as they have acted in taking up arms against their country, they have still some small sense left that they were once Americans, but now no longer so, for all who act as they do, forfeit that name; and by adopting the vices of those they join, become one with them; but these poor creatures seem to have yet remaining some token of what they once were—else why did they, last Thursday, behave so much better to us than the Britons did, when we were equally as much in their power as we were in the others'? I will let them see I have not forgot it. I arose, and went out to them. "I am sorry, my friends (I could not help calling them *friends* when they were in our power), to see you in this situation, you treated us with respect; and I cannot but be sorry to see you in distress." "It is the fortune of war, Madam, and soldiers must expect it." "Well, you need not make yourselves uneasy; I hope Americans won't treat their prisoners ill. Do, my friends (to the soldiers), use these men well—they were friendly to us." "Yes, Madam," said they; "they shall be used well if it was only for that." I asked if they would have any thing to drink. Yes, they would be glad of some water. I had some got, and as their hands were tied, I held the glass to their mouths; they bowed, and were very thankful for it. I was so busy, I did not observe the officers in the house; several of them were at the door and window, smiling at me, which, when I perceived, I went in and told them how it was. They promised that the men should be favored for their behavior to us. "Madam," said one, "you would make a bad soldier; however, if I was of the other party, and taken prisoner, I should like to fall into your hands." I smiled a reply, and the conversation took another turn.

In the meanwhile Miss Samuells* was very busy about a wounded officer who was brought to the house (one of M'Girth's); he had a ball through his arm; we could find no rag to dress his wounds, every thing in the house being thrown into such confusion by the plunderers; but (see the native tenderness of an American!) Miss Samuells took from her neck the only remaining handkerchief the Britons had left her, and with it bound up his arm! Blush, O Britons, and be confounded! your delight is cruelty and oppression; divested of all humanity, you imitate savages; neither age nor sex can move compassion; even the smiling babe suffers by your hands, and innocently smiles at its oppressor. The Americans are obliged to commit unavoidable acts of cruelty; the defence of their country requires it; you seek their lives and liberties, and they must either kill or be killed. . . . No; I cannot think we shall be overcome while we act with justice and mercy—those are the attributes of heaven. If our cause is just, as it certainly appears to be, we need not doubt success; an Almighty arm has visibly supported us; or a raw, undisciplined people, with so many disadvantages too on their side, could never have withstood, for so long a time, an army which has repeatedly fought and conquered, and who are famed for, or rather *were* famed, for their valor and determined bravery; but now their glory is fallen, and, thank heaven, we are their equals, if not their superiors in the field.

———

*A friend.

A Loyalist Wife

GRACE GALLOWAY, 1778–1779

Raymond C. Werner, ed., "Diary of Grace Growden Galloway, Kept at Philadelphia," *Pennsylvania Magazine of History and Biography* 55 (1931), pp. 41, 47–48, 50–53, 75–76.

If women could express political opinions, as patriots like Eliza Wilkinson contended, then could they be held responsible for such opinions? The question arose in regard to wives of loyalist men, who supported England. Would such wives automatically be considered traitors to the American cause? What if property they had inherited, which was legally under their husbands' control, was confiscated? Did they have any claim on such property? What if they contended that politics was beyond their domain?

A case in point was Grace Growden Galloway, daughter of a wealthy and powerful Pennsylvanian, Lawrence Growden, and wife of Joseph Galloway, speaker of the Pennsylvania assembly. After the Revolution broke out, Joseph Galloway became a Tory. When the British occupied Philadelphia in 1777, he supervised the occupation. When the Americans recaptured Philadelphia in 1778, he fled behind the British lines and took with him the Galloways's only child, their daughter Betsy. Grace Galloway remained in Philadelphia in order to claim property that she stood to inherit from her father and hoped to pass on to her daughter. She soon learned, however, that all of the Galloway property had been confiscated and that she would be evicted from her house. Throughout this ordeal, Grace Galloway kept a diary in which she recorded her loyalist sympathy, her contempt for the patriots, and her rage at her predicament. In the following segments of her diary for 1778 through 1779, Grace Galloway narrates its crucial event—the eviction from her home.

As is evident in these entries, Grace Galloway was a proud and difficult person. Unlike Eliza Wilkinson, she resented the intrusion of politics into her personal life. She found it inconvenient, if not absurd, to be held responsible for her husband's political views, or even her own. At this point in her marriage, Grace had little love for the absent Joseph Galloway. "Liberty of doing as I please makes even poverty more agreeable than any time I spent since I was married," she wrote. Her fury about her financial loss was compounded by a powerful sense of resentment. During the Revolution, the Philadelphia aristocracy, of which Grace Galloway was a part, disintegrated. Many Tory members had decamped; some Quakers, as pacifists, were linked to the loyalists by default; others shifted toward the patriot, or "Whig," camp. When the upper-crust capsized, a new group of middle-class patriots assumed leadership roles. Abandoned by former associates, shunned by the Quakers, and beset with problems, Grace Galloway seemed to find enemies everywhere. Although she remained in Philadelphia and never rejoined her husband in England, she never regained her property either. Joseph Galloway's estate was confiscated, and Grace's inheritance from her father was sequestered (seized and held by the state) for the life of her estranged husband, who outlived her.

July 22, 1778

Wednesday yᵉ 22ⁿᵈ

Was ill in yᵉ morn: . . . sent for Mr Dickison last Night & he told Me he wou'd look over yᵉ law to see if I cou'd recover My own estate & this evening he came & told Me I cou'd Not recover dower & he fear'd my income in My estate was forfeited likewise & yᵗ no tryal wou'd be of service: but advised Me to draw up a peti'on to yᵉ Chief Justice Mccean for the recovery of my estate & refused a fee in yᵉ Politest Manner but begg'd I wou'd look on him as My sincere friend & told me he would do me any service to yᵉ Utmost of his power & I think he behaves much better than Chew. So I find I am a beggar indeed I expect every hour to be turn'd out of doors & where to go I know not. No one will take me in & all yᵉ Men keeps from Me. Was I assured that My husband & child was happy nothing cou'd make me very wretched but I am fled from as a Pestilence. Mrs Jones here in the morn: sent nurse to Parson Combs to desire him to [tell] Mr G of my unhappy situation.

August 10, 1778

Monday yᵉ 10ᵗʰ

Peggy Johns & Becky Redman came in yᵉ Morn, Lewis sent Me word Smith had gave his honour not to Molest Me till the Opinion of yᵉ executive council was known but in a short time after came Peel, Will, & Shriner with a spanish Merchant & his attendants & took Possession of My house. I was taken very ill & obliged to Lay down & sent them word I cou'd not see them; they went every Where below stairs & yᵉ spaniard offer'd to let Me chuse My own bed chamber; but I sent them no Message but was very ill Up stairs. But between 2 & 3 o'clock the last went away. Peel told Nurse now they had given the spanish Gentle Man possession they had nothing More to do with it. But they took the Key out of yᵉ front parlor door & locked Me out & left the windows Open. . . .

August 16, 1778

Sunday yᵉ 16ᵗʰ

Mrs Redman & Mrs Mongomery drank tea here. I desired Mrs Mongomery to desire Mr Mccean to drank tea with me or let me know when it Wou'd be Agreeable for me to Wait on him & I find Shoemakers had been before me. The quakers all Assist her but they wou'd let me fall. I sent twice to Lewise for a sight of yᵉ pertition but he wou'd not let me see it & as I have No friends they treat me as they please. So much for Mr G [Galloway's] great friends. He has not one who will go out of yᵉ way to serve him. I am in hopes they will let me have my Estate but that will be on my own Account. No favour shown to J G [Joseph Galloway] or his Child: Nor has he a friend that will say one word in his favour. I am tired with sending after a set of men that allways keeps from me when I most need them. Am vex'd.

August 20, 1778

Thursday yᵉ 20ᵗʰ

Mrs Erwin & Sidney Howell & Peggy Johns came in yᵉ morn: but cou'd get No man to bear evidence. Lewise sent me word that I must shut my doors & windows & if they wou'd come to let them Make a forcible Entry. Accordingly I did so & a little after 10 o'clock they Knocked Violently at the door three times. The Third time I sent Nurse & call'd out myself to tell them I was in possession of my own House & wou'd keep so & that they shou'd gain No admittance Hereupon which they went round in yᵉ yard & Try'd every door but cou'd None Open. Then they went to the Kitchen door & with a scrubbing brush which they broke to pieces they forced that open, we Women standing in yᵉ Entry in yᵉ Dark. They made repeated strokes at yᵉ door & I think was 8 or 10 Minuets before they got it open. When they came in I had yᵉ windows open'd they look'd very Mad. Their was Peel, Smith, yᵉ Hatter, & a Col Will, a pewterer in second street. I spoke first & told them I was Used ill: & show'd them the Opinion of yᵉ Lawyers. Peel read it: but they all despised it & Peel said he had studyed yᵉ Law & knew they did right. I told them Nothing but force shou'd get me out of My house. Smith said they knew how to Manage that & that they wou'd throw my cloaths in yᵉ street: & told Me that Mrs Sympson & forty othere ware put out of yᵉ lines in one day: I said they had their furniture to take with them. He said that was owing to yᵉ Generosity of yᵉ british officers but yᵉ Police would let no favour be shown. I told him I knew that was not True. He told me he knew better & hinted that Mr G had treated people Cruely. I found the Villan wou'd say anything so I stop'd after hearing several insulting things & Mrs Irwin & Smith sat & Talk'd of English cruelty & Sidney Howell Whin'd out her half assent to the same. In yᵉ Mean While Peel & Will went over yᵉ House to see Nothing was Embassell'd & Locking Up the things at last Smith went away & Mrs Irwin & he sat talking [in] yᵉ Kitchen as they took my things to her House. Peel went to the generals & asked for his Chariot & then returned & told me yᵉ General was so kind as to let me have it & he, Mr Peel, was willing to Accomodate Me as well as he cou'd. I told him he Need not give himself the Trouble for if I wanted yᵉ Chariot I cou'd send to yᵉ General myself. Just after yᵉ

General sent in his Housekeeper with His compliments & to let me know that I was wellcome to His Chariot & he wou'd have it ready any hour I pleased. I then Accepted of it & told her I wou'd send after every Mortifying treatment was tiard & wanted to be turn'd out. Peel went Upstairs & brought down My Work bag & 2 bonnets & put them on the side table. At last we went in the Entry to sit & I asked yᵉ two Grays if they wou'd witness for me but they both went away. Two of yᵉ Men went out & after staying some time return'd & said they had been with the council & that they had done right & must proceed. I did not hear this myself but yᵉ rest of yᵉ Women did. Mrs Craig asked for My Bed but they wou'd let Me Have Nothing & as I told them acted entirely from Malice: after we had been in yᵉ Entry some time Smith & Will went away & Peel said yᵉ Chariot was ready but he would not hasten me. I told him I was at home & in My own House & nothing but force shou'd drive me out of it. He said it was not yᵉ first time he had taken a Lady by the Hand an insolent wretch. This speech was made some time in the room; at last he becon'd for yᵉ Chariot for yᵉ General wou'd not let it come till I wanted it & as the Chariot drew up Peel fetched My Bonnets & gave one to me yᵉ other to Mrs Craig: then with greatest air said come Mrs Galloway give me your hand. I answer'd indeed I will not nor will I go out of my house but by force. He then took hold of my arm & I rose & he took me to the door. I then Took hold on one side & Look round & said pray take Notice I do not leave my house of My own accord or with my own inclination but by force & Nothing but force shou'd have Made Me give up possession. Peel said with a sneer very well Madam & when he led me down yᵉ step I said now Mr Peel let go My Arm I want not your Assistance. He said he cou'd help me to yᵉ Carriage. I told him I cou'd go without & you Mr Peel are the last Man on earth I wou'd wish to be Obliged to. Mrs Craig then step'd into yᵉ Carriage & we drove to her house where we din'd. It was neer two o'clock. . . . Distress'd in yᵉ afternoon when I reflected on the Occurences of yᵉ day & that I was drove out of my house distitute & without any maintenance. . . . Sent for Mr. Chew. He came & told me I must sue them for a forcible Entry. I am just distracted but Glad it is over.

April 20, 1779

Tusday yᵉ 20ᵗʰ

Went to Billy Turners. The two Mrs Bonds there. yᵉ Widdow & I very sociable but Mrs Bond rather shy but did not Mind her but got My spirits at command & Laughed at yᵉ whole wig party. I told them I was yᵉ happyest woman in town for I had been stripped & Turn'd out of Doors yet I was still yᵉ same & must be Joseph Galloways Wife & Lawrence Growdons daughter & that it was Not in their power to humble Me for I shou'd be Grace Growdon Galloway to yᵉ last & as I had now suffer'd all that they can inflict Upon Me. . . .

A Republican Mother

ABIGAIL ADAMS, 1780, 1783

Charles Francis Adams, ed., *Letters of Mrs. Adams, the Wife of John Adams*, 4th ed. (Boston: Wilkins, Carter & Co., 1848), pp. 112–16, 152–55.

Exceptionally intelligent and well-read, Abigail Adams (1744–1818) seems to have exemplified the principles of patriotic womanhood for which citizens of the new republic expressed admiration. Her oft-quoted letters to John Adams during the Revolution reveal an impressive combination of ardent support, political philosophizing, and strategic advice. Abigail Adams was an impassioned patriot, with highly developed political sensibilities. "Our Country is as it were a Secondary God, and the first and greatest parent," she wrote to her friend Mercy Warren in 1776. "It is to be perferred [*sic*] to parents, to wives, children, Friends and all things the Gods only excepted."

As a republican mother, Abigail Adams was also an impressive model. This is evident in her letters to her oldest son, John Quincy Adams. During the Revolution, while Abigail was managing the family property in Braintree, Massachusetts, John Quincy Adams, then a teenager, was sent to school in Europe. The following letters were written in 1780, when young Adams was a student in Holland, and in 1783, when he accompanied John Adams on a mission to Russia. Abigail issued a formidable stream of advice. She wanted to perfect her son's character, to impart the "foundation of virtue," and to have him assume the correct political posture. He ought, for instance, to avoid "self-love" and "ungoverned passion," to achieve self-control and "dignity of character," to abhor "domination and Power," to be "superior to corruption," and to exemplify "disinterested patriotism."

To John Quincy Adams

20 March, 1780

My Dear Son,

Your letter, last evening received from Bilboa, relieved me from much anxiety; for, having a day or two before received letters from your papa, Mr. Thaxter,[1] and brother,

---

[1] This gentleman, who was a student at law in the office of Mr. Adams, at the commencement of the troubles, accompanied him in the capacity of private secretary on this mission. [C.F. Adams]

in which packet I found none from you, nor any mention made of you, my mind, ever fruitful in conjectures, was instantly alarmed. I feared you were sick, unable to write, and your papa, unwilling to give me uneasiness, had concealed it from me; and this apprehension was confirmed by every person's omitting to say how long they should continue in Bilboa.

Your father's letters came to Salem, yours to Newburyport, and soon gave ease to my anxiety, at the same time that it excited gratitude and thankfulness to Heaven, for the preservation you all experienced in the imminent dangers which threatened you. You express in both your letters a degree of thankfulness. I hope it amounts to more than words, and that you will never be insensible to the particular preservation you have experienced in both your voyages. You have seen how inadequate the aid of man would have been, if the winds and the seas had not been under the particular government of that Being, who "stretched out the heavens as a span," who "holdeth the ocean in the hollow of his hand," and "rideth upon the wings of the wind."

If you have a due sense of your preservation, your next consideration will be, for what purpose you are continued in life. It is not to rove from clime to clime, to gratify an idle curiosity; but every new mercy you receive is a new debt upon you, a new obligation to a diligent discharge of the various relations in which you stand connected; in the first place, to your great Preserver; in the next, to society in general; in particular, to your country, to your parents, and to yourself.

The only sure and permanent foundation of virtue is religion. Let this important truth be engraven upon your heart. And also, that the foundation of religion is the belief of the one only God, and a just sense of his attributes, as a being infinitely wise, just, and good, to whom you owe the highest reverence, gratitude, and adoration; who superintends and governs all nature, even to clothing the lilies of the field, and hearing the young ravens when they cry; but more particularly regards man, whom he created after his own image, and breathed into him an immortal spirit, capable of a happiness beyond the grave; for the attainment of which he is bound to the performance of certain duties, which all tend to the happiness and welfare of society, and are comprised in one short sentence, expressive of universal benevolence, "Thou shalt love thy neighbor as thyself." This is elegantly defined by Mr. Pope, in his "Essay on Man."

> Remember, man, the universal cause
> Acts not by partial, but by general laws,
> And makes what happiness we justly call,
> Subsist not in the good of one, but all.
> There's not a blessing individuals find,
> But some way leans and hearkens to the kind.

Thus has the Supreme Being made the good will of man towards his fellow-creatures an evidence of his regard to Him, and for this purpose has constituted him a dependent being and made his happiness to consist in society. Man early discovered this propensity of his nature, and found

> Eden was tasteless till an Eve was there.

Justice, humanity, and benevolence are the duties you owe to society in general. To your country the same duties are incumbent upon you, with the additional obligation of sacrificing ease, pleasure, wealth, and life itself for its defence and security. To your parents you owe love, reverence, and obedience to all just and equitable commands. To yourself—here, indeed, is a wide field to expatiate upon. To become what you ought to be, and what a fond mother wishes to see you, attend to some precepts and instructions from the pen of one, who can have no motive but your welfare and happiness, and who wishes in this way to supply to you the personal watchfulness and care, which a separation from you deprived you of at a period of life, when habits are easiest acquired and fixed; and though the advice may not be new, yet suffer it to obtain a place in your memory, for occasions may offer, and perhaps some concurring circumstances unite, to give it weight and force.

Suffer me to recommend to you one of the most useful lessons of life, the knowledge and study of yourself. There you run the greatest hazard of being deceived. Self-love and partiality cast a mist before the eyes, and there is no knowledge so hard to be acquired, nor of more benefit when once thoroughly understood. Ungoverned passions have aptly been compared to the boisterous ocean, which is known to produce the most terrible effects. "Passions are the elements of life," but elements which are subject to the control of reason. Whoever will candidly examine themselves, will find some degree of passion, peevishness, or obstinacy in their natural tempers. You will seldom find these disagreeable ingredients all united in one; but the uncontrolled indulgence of either is sufficient to render the possessor unhappy in himself, and disagreeable to all who are so unhappy as to be witnesses of it, or suffer from its effects.

You, my dear son, are formed with a constitution feelingly alive; your passions are strong and impetuous; and, though I have sometimes seen them hurry you into excesses, yet with pleasure I have observed a frankness and generosity accompany your efforts to govern and subdue them. Few persons are so subject to passion, but that they can command themselves, when they have a motive sufficiently strong; and those who are most apt to transgress will restrain themselves through respect and reverence to superiors, and even, where they wish to recommend themselves, to their equals. The due government of the passions has been considered in all ages as a most valuable acquisition. Hence an inspired writer observes, "He that is slow to anger, is better than the mighty; and he that ruleth his spirit, than he that taketh a city." This passion, coöperating with power, and unrestrained by reason, has produced the subversion of cities, the desolation of countries, the massacre of nations, and filled the world with injustice and oppression. Behold your own country, your native land, suffering from the effects of lawless power and malignant passions, and learn betimes, from your own observation and experience, to govern and control yourself. Having once obtained this self-government, you will find a foundation laid for happiness to yourself and usefulness to mankind. "Virtue alone is happiness below"; and consists in cultivating and improving every good inclination, and in checking and subduing every propensity to evil. I have been particular upon the passion of anger, as it is generally the most predominant passion at your age, the soonest excited, and the least pains are taken to subdue it;

> What composes man, can man destroy.

I do not mean, however, to have you insensible to real injuries. He who will not turn when he is trodden upon is deficient in point of spirit; yet, if you can preserve good breeding and decency of manners, you will have an advantage over the aggressor, and will maintain a dignity of character, which will always insure you respect, even from the offender.

I will not overburden your mind at this time. I mean to pursue the subject of self-knowledge in some future letter, and give you my sentiments upon your future conduct in life, when I feel disposed to resume my pen.

In the mean time, be assured, no one is more sincerely interested in your happiness, than your ever affectionate mother,

A. A.

Do not expose my letters. I would copy, but hate it.

To John Quincy Adams

Braintree, 26 December, 1783

My Dear Son,

Your letters by Mr. Thaxter, I received, and was not a little pleased with them. If you do not write with the precision of a Robertson, nor the elegance of a Voltaire, it is evident you have profited by the perusal of them. The account of your northern journey, and your observations upon the Russian government, would do credit to an older pen.

The early age at which you went abroad gave you not an opportunity of becoming acquainted with your own country. Yet the revolution, in which we were engaged, held it up in so striking and important a light, that you could not avoid being in some measure irradiated with the view. The characters with which you were connected, and the conversation you continually heard, must have impressed your mind with a sense of the laws, the liberties, and the glorious privileges, which distinguish the free, sovereign, independent States of America.

Compare them with the vassalage of the Russian government you have described, and say, were this highly favored land barren as the mountains of Switzerland, and covered ten months in the year with snow, would she not have the advantage even of Italy, with her orange groves, her breathing statues, and her melting strains of music? or of Spain, with her treasures from Mexico and Peru? not one of which can boast that first of blessings, the glory of human nature, the inestimable privilege of sitting down under their vines and fig-trees, enjoying in peace and security whatever Heaven has lent them, having none to make them afraid.

Let your observations and comparisons produce in your mind an abhorrence of domination and power, the parent of slavery, ignorance, and barbarism, which places man upon a level with his fellow tenants of the woods;

> A day, an hour, of virtuous liberty
> Is worth a whole eternity of bondage.

You have seen power in its various forms—a benign deity, when exercised in the suppression of fraud, injustice, and tyranny, but a demon, when united with unbounded ambition—a wide-wasting fury, who has destroyed her thousands. Not an age of the world but has produced characters, to which whole human hecatombs have been sacrificed.

What is the history of mighty kingdoms and nations, but a detail of the ravages and cruelties of the powerful over the weak? Yet it is instructive to trace the various causes, which produced the strength of one nation, and the decline and weakness of another; to learn by what arts one man has been able to subjugate millions of his fellow creatures, the motives which have put him upon action, and the causes of his success; sometimes driven by ambition and a lust of power; at other times swallowed up by religious enthusiasm, blind bigotry, and ignorant zeal; sometimes enervated with luxury and debauched by pleasure, until the most powerful nations have become a prey and been subdued by these Sirens, when neither the number of their enemies, nor the prowess of their arms, could conquer them. History informs us that the Assyrian empire sunk under the arms of Cyrus, with his poor but hardy Persians. The extensive and opulent empire of Persia fell an easy prey to Alexander and a handful of Macedonians; and the Macedonian empire, when enervated by the luxury of Asia, was compelled to receive the yoke of the victorious Romans. Yet even this mistress of the world, as she is proudly styled, in her turn defaced her glory, tarnished her victories, and became a prey to luxury, ambition, faction, pride, revenge, and avarice, so that Jugurtha, after having purchased an acquittance for the blackest of crimes, breaks out into an exclamation, "O city, ready for sale, if a buyer rich enough can be found!"

The history of your own country and the late revolution are striking and recent instances of the mighty things achieved by a brave, enlightened, and hardy people, determined to be free; the very yeomanry of which, in many instances, have shown themselves superior to corruption, as Britain well knows, on more occasions than the loss of her André. Glory, my son, in a country which has given birth to characters, both in the civil and military departments, which may vie with the wisdom and valor of antiquity. As an immediate descendant of one of those characters, may you be led to an imitation of that disinterested patriotism and that noble love of your country, which will teach you to despise wealth, titles, pomp, and equipage, as mere external advantages, which cannot add to the internal excellence of your mind, or compensate for the want of integrity and virtue.

May your mind be thoroughly impressed with the absolute necessity of universal virtue and goodness, as the only sure road to happiness, and may you walk therein with undeviating steps—is the sincere and most affectionate wish of

Your mother,
A. Adams

Thoughts upon Female Education

Benjamin Rush, 1787

Benjamin Rush, "Thoughts upon Female Education, Accommodated to
the Present State of Society, Manners, and Government . . ." in Frederick
Rudolph, ed., *Essays on Education in the Early Republic* (Cambridge: Harvard
University Press, 1965), pp. 27–40.

Philadelphia physician Benjamin Rush (1745–1813), a member of Benjamin Franklin's intellectual circle, was prominent as both a scientist
and a patriot. He served in the Continental Congress and signed the
Declaration of Independence. An enlightened spirit, he was also profoundly committed to education. A Princeton graduate who had studied medicine in Pennsylvania and Edinburgh, Rush taught chemistry
at the University of Pennsylvania, helped found Dickinson College,
and served as a trustee of the new Young Ladies Academy in Philadelphia, opened in 1786. There, in July of 1787, at the close of quarterly
examinations, he gave an important speech on women's education.

Decrying European models of women's education, full of aristocratic pretense, Rush posited that the women in the new American
republic demanded a new type of education—one not available in
England and France, whose influence he spurned. American women
needed a utilitarian education. They had to be trained to manage
efficient households, to be "stewards" and "guardians" of a husband's
property. As mothers, they had to raise virtuous citizens, to train their
sons "in the principles of liberty and government." Women's education, in Rush's argument, had both social value and patriotic purpose.

To achieve his goals, Benjamin Rush proposed a curriculum that
was far more academic than the offerings of adventure schools. It
included spelling, speaking, grammar, writing, arithmetic, bookkeeping, geography, history, astronomy, and some natural philosophy (science). Rush also favored instruction in singing, to lighten domestic
life; dancing, at least until Americans perfected the art of conversation;
serious reading, to replace the current passion for novels; and religion.
He rejected drawing, for which women would have no time, and, in a
final blast at deleterious European influence, the teaching of French.

This significant lecture, it should be noted, was directed toward
men ("Gentlemen"), presumably the fathers of students and trustees
of the Philadelphia Academy. At the end of the lecture, Rush shifted
briefly to the daughters ("young ladies") in his audience. But men

were his main focus, for the address on women's education was really *about* men—specifically, educated professional men like himself and the other trustees. Such men now found a multitude of obligations and "avocations" in public life. They had to work full-time for "the advancement of their fortunes." With their exodus from family life, women had to pitch in and take charge, a duty for which many were apparently at present too ignorant. Benjamin Rush, in short, directed his argument toward the male members of a specific social class—those who would assume leadership roles and set social standards in the new republic. He presented not only a plan for "a peculiar and suitable education" for women, but a response to a major social development: the emergence of an American elite.

Gentlemen,

I have yielded with diffidence to the solicitations of the Principal of the Academy, in undertaking to express my regard for the prosperity of this seminary of learning by submitting to your candor a few thoughts upon female education.

The first remark that I shall make upon this subject is that female education should be accommodated to the state of society, manners, and government of the country in which it is conducted.

This remark leads me at once to add that the education of young ladies in this country should be conducted upon principles very different from what it is in Great Britain and in some respects different from what it was when we were a part of a monarchical empire.

There are several circumstances in the situation, employments, and duties of women in America which require a peculiar mode of education.

I. The early marriages of our women, by contracting the time allowed for education, renders it necessary to contract its plan and to confine it chiefly to the more useful branches of literature.

II. The state of property in America renders it necessary for the greatest part of our citizens to employ themselves in different occupations for the advancement of their fortunes. This cannot be done without the assistance of the female members of the community. They must be the stewards and guardians of their husbands' property. That education, therefore, will be most proper for our women which teaches them to discharge the duties of those offices with the most success and reputation.

III. From the numerous avocations to which a professional life exposes gentlemen in America from their families, a principal share of the instruction of children naturally devolves upon the women. It becomes us therefore to prepare them, by a suitable education, for the discharge of this most important duty of mothers.

IV. The equal share that every citizen has in the liberty and the possible share he may have in the government of our country make it necessary that our ladies should be qualified to a certain degree, by a peculiar and suitable education, to concur in instructing their sons in the principles of liberty and government.

V. In Great Britain the business of servants is a regular occupation, but in America this humble station is the usual retreat of unexpected indigence; hence the servants in this country possess less knowledge and subordination than are required from them; and hence our ladies are obliged to attend more to the private affairs of their families than ladies generally do of the same rank in Great Britain. . . . This circumstance should have great influence upon the nature and extent of female education in America.

The branches of literature most essential for a young lady in this country appear to be:

I. A knowledge of the English language. She should not only read but speak and spell it correctly. And to enable her to do this, she should be taught the English grammar and be frequently examined in applying its rules in common conversation.

II. Pleasure and interest conspire to make the writing of a fair and legible hand a necessary branch of female education. For this purpose she should be taught not only to shape every letter properly but to pay the strictest regard to points and capitals.[1] . . .

III. Some knowledge of figures and bookkeeping is absolutely necessary to qualify a young lady for the duties which await her in this country. There are certain occupations in which she may assist her husband with this knowledge, and should she survive him and agreeably to the custom of our country be the executrix of his will, she cannot fail of deriving immense advantages from it.

IV. An acquaintance with geography and some instruction in chronology will enable a young lady to read history, biography, and travels, with advantage, and thereby qualify her not only for a general intercourse with the world but to be an agreeable companion for a sensible man. To these branches of knowledge may be added, in some instances, a general acquaintance with the first principles of astronomy and natural philosophy, particularly with such parts of them as are calculated to prevent superstition, by explaining the causes or obviating the effects of natural evil.

V. Vocal music should never be neglected in the education of a young lady in this country. Besides preparing her to join in that part of public worship which consists in psalmody, it will enable her to soothe the cares of domestic life. The distress and vexation of a husband, the noise of a nursery, and even the sorrows that will sometimes intrude into her own bosom may all be relieved by a song, where sound and sentiment unite to act upon the mind. . . .

VI. Dancing is by no means an improper branch of education for an American lady. It promotes health and renders the figure and motions of the body easy and agreeable.

---

[1]The present mode of writing among persons of taste is to use a capital letter only for the first word of a sentence, and for names of persons, places, and months, and for the first word of every line in poetry. The words should be so shaped that a straight line may be drawn between two lines without touching the extremities of the words in either of them.

I anticipate the time when the resources of conversation shall be so far multiplied that the amusement of dancing shall be wholly confined to children. But in our present state of society and knowledge, I conceive it to be an agreeable substitute for the ignoble pleasures of drinking and gaming in our assemblies of grown people.

VII. The attention of our young ladies should be directed as soon as they are prepared for it to the reading of history, travels, poetry, and moral essays. These studies are accommodated, in a peculiar manner, to the present state of society in America, and when a relish is excited for them in early life, they subdue that passion for reading novels which so generally prevails among the fair sex. I cannot dismiss this species of writing and reading without observing that the subjects of novels are by no means accommodated to our present manners. They hold up *life*, it is true, but it is not yet *life* in America.

VIII. It will be necessary to connect all these branches of education with regular instruction in the Christian religion. For this purpose the principles of the different sects of Christians should be taught and explained, and our pupils should early be furnished with some of the most simple arguments in favor of the truth of Christianity. A portion of the Bible (of late improperly banished from our schools) should be read by them every day and such questions should be asked, after reading it, as are calculated to imprint upon their minds the interesting stories contained in it. . . .

IX. If the measures that have been recommended for inspiring our pupils with a sense of religious and moral obligation be adopted, the government of them will be easy and agreeable. I shall only remark under this head that *strictness* of discipline will always render *severity* unnecessary and that there will be the most instruction in that school where there is the most order.

I have said nothing in favor of instrumental music as a branch of female education because I conceive it is by no means accommodated to the present state of society and manners in America. The price of musical instruments and the extravagant fees demanded by the teachers of instrumental music form but a small part of my objections to it. . . .

I beg leave further to bear testimony against the practice of making the French language a part of female education in America. In Britain, where company and pleasure are the principal business of ladies, where the nursery and the kitchen form no part of their care, and where a daily intercourse is maintained with Frenchmen and other foreigners who speak the French language, a knowledge of it is absolutely necessary. But the case is widely different in this country. Of the many ladies who have applied to this language, how great a proportion of them have been hurried into the cares and duties of a family before they had acquired it; of those who have acquired it, how few have retained it after they were married; and of the few who have retained it, how seldom have they had occasion to speak it in the course of their lives! It certainly comports more with female delicacy, as well as the natural politeness of the French nation, to make it necessary for Frenchmen to learn to speak our language in order to converse with our ladies than for our ladies to learn their language in order to converse with them. . . .

It is with reluctance that I object to drawing as a branch of education for an American lady. To be the mistress of a family is one of the great ends of a woman's being, and while the peculiar state of society in America imposes this station so early and renders the duties of it so numerous and difficult, I conceive that little time can be spared for the acquisition of this elegant accomplishment. . . .

It should not surprise us that British customs with respect to female education have been transplanted into our American schools and families. We see marks of the same incongruity of time and place in many other things. We behold our houses accommodated to the climate of Great Britain by eastern and western directions. We behold our ladies panting in a heat of ninety degrees, under a hat and cushion which were calculated for the temperature of a British summer. We behold our citizens condemned and punished by a criminal law which was copied from a country where maturity in corruption renders public executions a part of the amusements of the nation. It is high time to awake from this servility—to study our own character—to examine the age of our country—and to adopt manners in everything that shall be accommodated to our state of society and to the forms of our government. In particular it is incumbent upon us to make ornamental accomplishments yield to principles and knowledge in the education of our women.

A philosopher once said, "let me make all the ballads of a country and I care not who makes its laws." He might with more propriety have said, let the ladies of a country be educated properly, and they will not only make and administer its laws, but form its manners and character. It would require a lively imagination to describe, or even to comprehend, the happiness of a country where knowledge and virtue were generally diffused among the female sex. Our young men would then be restrained from vice by the terror of being banished from their company. The loud laugh and the malignant smile, at the expense of innocence or of personal infirmities—the feats of successful mimicry and the low priced wit which is borrowed from a misapplication of scripture phrases—would no more be considered as recommendations to the society of the ladies. A *double-entendre* in their presence would then exclude a gentleman forever from the company of both sexes and probably oblige him to seek an asylum from contempt in a foreign country.

The influence of female education would be still more extensive and useful in domestic life. The obligations of gentlemen to qualify themselves by knowledge and industry to discharge the duties of benevolence would be increased by marriage; and the patriot—the hero—and the legislator would find the sweetest reward of their toils in the approbation and applause of their wives. Children would discover the marks of maternal prudence and wisdom in every station of life, for it has been remarked that there have been few great or good men who have not been blessed with wife and prudent mothers. . . .

I am not enthusiastic* upon the subject of education. In the ordinary course of human affairs we shall probably too soon follow the footsteps of the nations of Europe in manners and vices. The first marks we shall perceive of our declension will appear among our women. Their idleness, ignorance, and profligacy will be the harbingers of our ruin. Then will the character and performance of a buffoon on the theater be the subject of more conversation and praise than the patriot or the minister of the gospel; then will our language and pronunciation be enfeebled and corrupted by a flood of French and Italian words; then will the history of romantic amours be preferred to

---

*By "enthusiastic," Rush means unreasonable visionary, or fanatic.

the immortal writings of Addison, Hawkesworth, and Johnson; then will our churches be neglected and the name of the Supreme Being never be called upon but in profane exclamations; then will our Sundays be appropriated only to feasts and concerts; and then will begin all that train of domestic and political calamities.

But, I forbear. The prospect is so painful that I cannot help silently imploring the great Arbiter of human affairs to interpose his almighty goodness and to deliver us from these evils that, at least, one spot of the earth may be reserved as a monument of the effects of good education, in order to show in some degree what our species was before the fall and what it shall be after its restoration. . . .

I cannot dismiss the subject of female education without remarking that the city of Philadelphia first saw a number of gentlemen associated for the purpose of directing the education of young ladies. By means of this plan the power of teachers is regulated and restrained and the objects of education are extended. By the separation of the sexes in the unformed state of their manners, female delicacy is cherished and preserved. Here the young ladies may enjoy all the literary advantages of a boarding school and at the same time live under the protection of their parents. Here emulation may be excited without jealousy, ambition without envy, and competition without strife.

The attempt to establish this new mode of education for young ladies was an experiment, and the success of it hath answered our expectations.[2] Too much praise cannot be given to our principal and his assistants, for the abilities and fidelity with which they have carried the plan into execution. The proficiency which the young ladies have discovered in reading, writing, spelling, arithmetic, grammar, geography, music, and their different catechisms since the last examination is a less equivocal mark of the merits of our teachers than anything I am able to express in their favor.

But the reputation of the academy must be suspended till the public are convinced by the future conduct and character of our pupils of the advantages of the institution. To you, therefore, young ladies, an important problem is committed for solution; and that is, whether our present plan of education be a wise one and whether it be calculated to prepare you for the duties of social and domestic life. I know that the elevation of the female mind, by means of moral, physical, and religious truth, is considered by some men as unfriendly to the domestic character of a woman. But this is the prejudice of little minds and springs from the same spirit which opposes the general diffusion of knowledge among the citizens of our republics. If men believe that ignorance is favorable to the government of the female sex, they are certainly deceived, for a weak and ignorant woman will always be governed with the greatest difficulty.

I have sometimes been led to ascribe the invention of ridiculous and expensive fashions in female dress entirely to the gentlemen[3] in order to divert the ladies from improving their minds and thereby to secure a more arbitrary and unlimited authority over them. It will be in your power, ladies, to correct the mistakes and practice of our sex upon these subjects by demonstrating that the female temper can only be governed by reason and that the cultivation of reason in women is alike friendly to the order of nature and to private as well as public happiness.

---

[2]The number of scholars in the academy at present amounts to upwards of one hundred.

[3]The very expensive prints of female dresses which are published annually in France are invented and executed wholly by gentlemen.

The Female Advocate

AN AGED MATRON OF CONNECTICUT, 1801

The Female Advocate, Written by a Lady (New Haven, CT: Thomas Green & Son, 1801), pp. 21–40 passim.

The outspoken author of *The Female Advocate* (1801), who identified herself only as "an aged matron" of Connecticut, was arguably the most impressive defender of women's rights in the new republic. In her brief but impassioned pamphlet, she assaulted sexual inequality, mocked male superiority, and demanded female empowerment. She also showed how republican ideology might be used to transform women's lives.

Asserting that both sexes had been equally endowed with "quality of genius, of talent, of morals, as well as intellectual worth," the Connecticut matron complained that "men engross all the emoluments, offices, honors, and merits of church and state." She assaulted her readers with a torrent of rhetorical questions ("Why ought the one half of mankind, to vaunt and lord it over the Other?" "But why is the fair book of knowledge hidden from our research?"). In the fashion of her day, the matron placed her faith in education as the basic prerequisite for equality. Only a "well-informed mind," she contended, would enable women—hitherto powerless, vulnerable, and demeaned—to "possess some command over ourselves." In the following excerpts, she explores some of the social inequities (from the perils of seduction to the "extreme wretchedness" of widowhood) that women's access to education might remedy.

Much and often has the world exclaimed against masculine women. Before I offer any sentiment on this exclamation, I would wish to hear the word properly and fairly defined. If by the epithet "Masculine," be meant a bold, assuming, haughty, arrogant, all sufficient, dogmatical temper and spirit, I would wish totally and entirely to discard it from the society of the fair sex. I would wish the term to be applied, where I think it is appropriate, by long established custom. I am quite willing that the other sex should share it altogether to themselves. But if by the word "Masculine," be meant a person of reading and letters, a person of science and information, one who can properly answer a question, without fear and trembling, or one who is capable of doing business, with a suitable command over self; this I believe to be a glory to the one sex, equally with the other. The sole reason why the epithet is disgraceful, in the estimation of many, is because custom, which is not infallible, has gradually introduced the habits of seeing an imaginary propriety, that all science, all public utility, all superiority, all that is intellectually great and astonishing, should be engrossed exclusively by the male half of mankind. But may I not securely say, that it is a point of great consequence, that we should have an equal share in science, of that degree of education, at least, which enables us, in some measure, to have command over ourselves, and become superior to those base artifices of the many, by which numerous females, through the want of suitable privileges in education, have been the dupes of men inferior to themselves, in every other respect but this single advantage, of education.

Are we not sensible, my female friends, and have we not often heard it observed, by the other sex, as an objection to our possessing peculiar advantages for scientific improvements, that they cannot so easily command the ascendency over us; but why should we wish them to have this dominion, if we are not sensible that that is often, and may I not say, almost always, the reason and foundation of our ruin. A young lady of the greatest purity of mind, yet uneducated, is frequently a victim to the arts of seduction: differently advantaged by knowledge, the seducer would have respected her virtues, and conducted with becoming deference. Thus, a second advantage would be the consequence of female education. It would reform the men, or at least prevent, or restrain, many of those artifices, which are now too successfully used, with innocent, uneducated, and unsuspecting females. . . .

But why is the fair book of knowledge hidden from our research? Why is it no farther disclosed to our view? Do we deserve the reproach of those men, who, in all the pride of scholastic literature, depreciate our natural talents? How different the sentiments of the worthy Burton,* in his lectures on female education. "The capacities of each sex," he justly observes, "are equal. That this is true," he continues, "may be easily perceived, by an attentive observer of children, previous to the culture of tuition. If any difference be then discernible, it is certainly in favor of girls: who in general display a greater share of vivacity, and a readier talent for conversation, than boys. Were a similar plan of education to be adopted, the women, without doubt, would be as well informed in the system of human knowledge, as the men. There are women, who have given ample testimony of the quickest genius, with a discernment and penetration equal to the ablest statesman." Plutarch,† speaking of the sexes, says, "The talents and virtues are modified by the circumstances, but the foundation is the same." . . .

Why then may not all the seeming difference between the sexes, be imputed solely to the difference of their education and subsequent advantages? Here let us draw a just and plain parallel between the education of a sister and her brother. Perhaps they are sent to the same school, till the age of ten, or twelve years. Here the advantages of their improvement are the same, and their actual augmentation of mind is equal, unless there be a real superiority of genius, in the female youth, which is a case not unusual. Behold the arbitrary distinctions where are, next, made between

---

*Robert Burton (1577–1640), English clergyman and author.
†Greek author of biography and essays.

them. The brother is taken from a common school, and transmitted to an academy, or a collegiate life; next becomes a divine, a lawyer, or physician; the whole term of time including usually from seven to nine years. But how is the time of his sister occupied, after she is taken from her early school? Immediately she is removed from every mean of literary improvement, and almost as effectually immured in a house, as a roman catholic Nun. She is admitted to walk in no road of preferment, and has before her, no incentive to aspire to public utility, by superior enlargement of mind. No! that is not the path for her to walk. Science and public utility are exclusively appropriated to the males. See the invariable sister's fate! If she be not sent to a nunnery, she is at least confined to domestic labor, and utterly secluded from all public concerns.

If not thus limited, she must have what the world calls a polite education: such as dancing, music, embroidering, altering and adjusting the fashion of her apparel. I have heard it, and I think very justly, observed, as an apology for females when frequently conversing, and being more disposed than the men, to talk of fashion, dress, amusements, and the polite customs of the fair world, that the former were precisely following the natural, and almost necessary effect of their appropriate education. A young Miss is taught to esteem it of the utmost consequence to her success in life, that she be dressed fashionably, and observe the external graces. It requires but a small share of segacity for her to discern, that unless she pay more attention to outward ornaments, than intellectual endowments, she will not be noticed by the other sex, on whom is her dependence for a partner, or, shall I say, "master," for life. For high intellectual endowments, she would rather be avoided, in the view of a connexion for life, as these would be qualities incompatible with that arbitrary sovereignty, which the man would wish to have fully established in his domestic empire. To such a man, when she is united by the dearest ties, how are the best of her days, and the prime of her life to be devoted? In a way truly, which I acknowledge to be highly beneficial; in the employments of the house and the nurturing of children, and imbruing their tender minds with the early precepts of true wisdom. But beneficial as it may be, does not this confined mode of living, and devoting our rolling years, afford sufficient arguments, why females do not advance in literary acquisitions, and the knowledge of men and manners, and the concerns of more public utility so far as the other sex. . . .

But to return from this digression to the importance and justness of admitting the idea of an equality between the sexes; how greatly doth a man of science misjudge in choosing a companion for life, if he selects one from the class of ignorant and untaught, that he may, by this mean, the more securely retain his favorite supremacy. Is it not a total blindness to the ideas of refined happiness, arising from a reciprocity of sentiments and the exchange of rational felicity, as well as an illiberal prejudice, thus to conduct? Shall the woman be kept ignorant, to render her more docile in the management of domestic concerns? How illy capable is such a person of being a companion for a man of refinement? How miserably capable of augmenting his social joys, or managing prudently the concerns of a family, or educating his children? Is it not of the utmost consequence, that the tender mind of the youth receive an early direction for future usefulness? And is it not equally true, that the first direction of a child necessarily becomes the immediate and peculiar province of the woman? And may I not add, is not a woman of a capacious and well stored mind, a better wife, a better widow, a better mother, and a better neighbor; and shall I add, a better friend in every respect? . . .

Pardon the multitude of my quotations, since they are mostly from the scriptures and men of piety, though they be adverse to the ideas entertained by many, of women's inferiority, as to intelligence, compared with the other sex. A gentleman in a late [recent] magazine observes, "Nothing conduces so much to the dignity and happiness of society, as perfect equality and frequent intercourse," in every species of information between the sexes. When women, no longer the humble dependent, or the obsequious slave, but the companion and friend, is party to an attachment founded on mutual esteem, then, and not till then, does man assume his intended rank in the scale of creation. Why should women be called the weaker sex, when it is acknowledged, that they take much more care of their reputation, than the men?

As I observed before, that a woman of information, and one viewed by her husband as a companion, made the better wife and better widow, I beg leave to state a supposition, as I imagine to the point. Suppose one who has from her youth been indoctrinated and habituated to sentiments of female inferiority, one who has never been suffered to have an opinion of her own, but on the reverse, has been taught, and accustomed to rely, and implicitly believe, right or wrong, on her parents, guardians, or husband. What will be the consequence of all this, in a situation when deprived of the counsel of either or all of them, she is necessitated to act for herself, or be exposed to the fraudulence of an unfriendly world? Perhaps she is left a widow, with a large property, and a flock of small dependent children? But where have they to look for protection, or on whom to rely, but on their insufficient, helpless mother? How poorly capable is she to fill the vacancy, and act to her tender babes and orphans, in their bereaved situation, as is absolutely necessary, both as father and mother? How incapable also is she of assisting in the settlement and adjustment of the estate; how liable to fraud, and how probable to be injured by unreal, or exaggerated debts.

But to enumerate the inconveniences, which daily attend a helpless ignorant widow, is far beyond my reach, and perhaps penetrates beyond the sensibilities of the most refined writer. No less unhappy is the consequence that follows the unfortunate wife, who has been kept in her leading strings all her days, and has no idea of taking the management of any business upon her unassisted self. Her husband views himself her guide and protector, treating her more as a child, or riper servant, than as a companion and friend. The good-hearted woman has lived all her days in ease and affluence, having never tasted the bitter cup of poverty, nor affliction. She thinks that her mountain standeth strong, and she shall never be moved. But perhaps through her ignorance, or her husband's extravagance, they live far beyond their abilities. Their neighbors are secretly whispering her unhappy situation, but the poor woman must be kept entirely ignorant, for no one is willing to be the author of such ill tidings, nor to converse with her on a subject of so delicate a nature, till the creditor makes his demand, and the officer comes, in a very unfeeling, and authoritative manner, to execute his office. The consequence is, that the unhappy family is left destitute of the comforts, yea, of the very necessaries of life. Alas, the unhappy woman! What a sudden transition from affluence to poverty, from prosperity to extreme wretchedness. All this, not infrequently ends in a state of insanity, as well as total ruin. Does not experience daily teach us, that, in this world, many things are far from what they should be; yet they must remain imperfect, in a measure, as we find them.

But modesty whispers me, and reason ratifies the admonition, that it is time to quit my subject and my pen. But before I do this, permit me to conclude by inserting a few words in the stile of personality. I candidly confess that, for a number of years, I have had a fondness, or if you please to give it a different appellation, "a mania for scribbling." Usually, when I have taken my pen in the moments of contemplative leisure, it has been devoted to the muses. Deviating from my fond love of poetic measures, I wished, for once, to exert my genius in prose. But what shall be my subject, was the next enquiry? The preceding theme occurred to me, as good, and what, if well conducted, might not be unuseful.

Perhaps these lines may chance to meet the eye of one, whose soul may yet be troubled, not withstanding all his stock of science, with spleen of criticism, and prejudiced jealousy against our sex. Surely such will say, what miserable language is this! What bad grammar! Surely she does not round her periods! She had better been at her needle work, or the distaff! Friend, I will spare you all this labor of criticism. I acknowledge all my want of literary improvement; but yet I am not willing to ascribe it to want of mental powers, but the disadvantages attending my education. I have not been brought up at the feet of Gamaliel,* but like Martha,† have been cumbered with much serving. Should any presume to say, that some man of letters has sitten, behind the curtain, to guide the movements of my pen, this I shall positively deny, and subjoin with the Authoress of the "Gleaner."‡ My "nearest friend is totally ignorant of this performance, and is an utter stranger to every line, till he may see it from the press."

Suggestions for Further Reading

James Axtell, ed., *The Indian Peoples of Eastern America: A Documentary History of the Sexes* (New York, 1981).
Emery Battis, *Saints and Sectaries: Anne Hutchinson and the Antimonian Controversy in the Massachusetts Bay Colony* (Chapel Hill, NC, 1962).
Elisabeth Potts Brown and Susan Mosher Stuard, eds., *Witness for Change: Quaker Women Over Three Centuries* (New Brunswick, NJ, 1989).
Lois Greene Carr and Lorena Walsh, "The Planter's Wife: The Experience of White Women in Seventeenth-Century Maryland," *William and Mary Quarterly*, 3rd ser., 34 (1977), 542–71.
Charles Lloyd Cohen, *God's Caress: The Psychology of Puritan Religious Experience* (New York, 1986).

---

*Teacher of Paul, Acts 22:3.
†When Jesus visited her house, Martha, the sister of Lazarus and Mary, was "cumbered about much serving," Luke 10:40.
‡Judith Sargent Murray, whose essay series, "The Gleaner," was published in the *Massachusetts Magazine*, 1792–1794, and as a book in 1798.

John Demos, *Little Commonwealth: Family Life in Plymouth Colony* (New York, 1970).

———, *Entertaining Satan: Witchcraft and the Culture of Early New England* (New York, 1982).

Mary Maples Dunn, "Women of Light," in Carol Ruth Berkin and Mary Beth Norton, eds., *Women in America: A History* (Boston, 1979), 114–36.

David Hackett Fischer, *Albion's Seed: Four British Folkways in America* (New York, 1989).

Philip Greven, *The Protestant Temperament* (New York, 1977).

Ronald Hoffman and Peter J. Albert, eds., *Women in the Age of the American Revolution* (Charlottesville, VA, 1989).

Carol F. Karlsen, *The Devil in the Shape of a Woman: Witchcraft in Colonial New England* (New York, 1987).

Carol F. Karlsen and Laurie Crumpacker, eds., *The Journal of Esther Edwards Burr: 1754–1757* (New Haven, CT, 1984).

Linda K. Kerber, *Women of the Republic: Intellect and Ideology in Revolutionary America* (Chapel Hill, NC, 1980).

Lyle Koehler, *A Search for Power: The Weaker Sex in Seventeenth-Century New England* (Urbana, IL, 1980).

Allan Kulikoff, *Tobacco and Slaves: The Development of Southern Cultures in the Chesapeake, 1680–1800* (Chapel Hill, NC, 1986).

Jan Lewis, *The Pursuit of Happiness: Family and Values in Jefferson's Virginia* (New York, 1983).

E. Jennifer Monaghan, "Literacy Instruction and Gender in Colonial New England," *American Quarterly* 40 (March 1988), 18–41.

Edmund Morgan, *The Puritan Family: Religion and Domestic Relations in Seventeenth-Century New England* (New York, 1966).

Mary Beth Norton, *Liberty's Daughters: The Revolutionary Experience of American Women, 1750–1800* (Boston, 1980).

Marylynn Salmon, *Women and the Law of Property in Early America* (Chapel Hill, NC, 1986).

Catherine M. Scholten, *Childbearing in American Society: 1650–1850* (New York, 1985).

Daniel Blake Smith, *Inside the Big House: Planter Family Life in Eighteenth-Century Chesapeake Society* (Ithaca, 1980).

Julia Cherry Spruill, *Women's Life and Work in the Southern Colonies* (New York, 1938).

Ann Taves, ed., *Religion and Domestic Violence in Early New England: The Memoir of Abigail Abbott Bailey* (Bloomington, IN, 1989).

Roger Thompson, *Sex in Middlesex: Popular Mores in a Massachusetts County, 1649–1699* (Amherst, MA, 1986).

Laurel Thatcher Ulrich, *Good Wives: Image and Reality in the Lives of Women of Northern New England, 1650–1750* (New York, 1982).

———, *A Midwife's Tale: The Life of Martha Ballard, Based on Her Diary, 1785–1812* (New York, 1990).

Alden T. Vaughan and Edward W. Clark, eds., *Puritans Among the Indians: Accounts of Captivity and Redemption, 1676–1724* (Cambridge, MA, 1981).

Lynne Withey, *Dearest Friend: A Life of Abigail Adams* (New York, 1981).

The Young Nation, 1800—1860

Americans who lived through the first half of the nineteenth century witnessed a rapid rate of change. The onset of industrialization began to shift production to workshop and factory. Railroads and canals offered new opportunities for profit in commerce and trade. The pace of immigration increased and the nation's population soared, leaping from five million in 1800 to six times that number at mid-century. The growing citizenry spread out over a larger area, pushing westward until half the continent had been settled. Simultaneously, a major surge of urbanization occurred. Migrants gravitated toward older cities and turned frontier outposts into booming river ports. The feeling of stability that once had characterized village life gave way to a sense of perpetual motion. Even for those who stood still, a host of leveling trends—broadened suffrage, educational expansion, religious revivals, and outbursts of reform—spawned an aura of promise and progress. Optimistic and patriotic, public speakers dwelt on themes of individualism and opportunity, democracy and equality.

Egalitarian rhetoric aside, early nineteenth-century Americans actually faced mounting inequality and more clearcut lines of social stratification. One important development was the emergence of a distinctive middle class, composed in part of the families of traditional community leaders—merchants, ministers, professionals—plus some newcomers who had climbed a few notches up the social ladder. In comparison to their neighbors, middle-class Americans had higher incomes, higher living standards, and greater literacy. They supported churches and schools, joined voluntary societies, bought books and periodicals, lived in well-furnished homes, and set standards of behavior toward which those of lesser means aspired. The emerging middle class, however, was concentrated in the urbanizing Northeast and comprised only ten to fifteen percent of the growing population. Most Americans lived more precarious existences. Though not mired in poverty, they had fewer resources and less resiliency in case of "vicissitudes," such as economic downswings or personal misfortunes. Some became part of the new urban working class. Many joined the throngs of transients who sought better luck in the next town or territory. Opportunity existed, but so did the risk of downward mobility.

How were women involved in the currents of change that transformed the new nation? To what extent did they share or reject the new ethos of individualism, competition, and risk? How did they respond—or contribute—to geographic expansion, the first stages of industrialization, and shifting lines of class distinction? One revelation of women's history is that every type of early nineteenth-century experience, from carving out a new western settlement to achieving a religious conversion, had a different impact on women than on men. Another revelation, perhaps contradictory, is that women's experiences were so varied—by such factors as race, class, geographic region, and individual circumstances—that few generalizations about "women's role" cover the ground.

The chapters that follow examine a variety of women's experiences between 1800 and the Civil War. Many of the documents reflect the concerns of women of the ambitious and self-conscious middle class, who dominate the written record of this era with a vengeance. Their diaries, correspondence, magazines, didactic literature, sentimental novels, and organizational reports provide a bottomless trough for nineteenth-century foragers. Other documents concern the experience of the more anonymous majority, who left less imprint on the written record: city seamstresses scrounging for subsistence, defiant daughters who went "on the town," migrants and immigrants en route to the West, or women in southwestern Hispanic communities. Some documents describe the anomalous position of women in the South, slave and free, who were excluded from many, though not all, of the developments cited above. The selections suggest the private and public roles that women assumed, the institutions with which they were involved, and the ways in which they shaped their own lives and communities.

Chapter 7

Domestic Lives

A mong members of the ambitious nineteenth-century middle class, a new type of family life emerged. Close-knit and insular, the middle-class family had distinctive hallmarks. Ideally, marriage became more egalitarian and companionate, a relationship grounded in romantic love. Spouses, bound by mutual affection, adopted complementary, specialized roles. Husbands, who worked outside the home, provided income; wives took charge of domestic affairs. Children, while fewer in number, received extended periods of nurture and attention. No longer economic assets or contributors to the family economy, they became the emotional focus of family life. Finally, as its productive function dwindled, the middle-class family cultivated a singular self-image. It was now a refuge from the commercial ethos, an antidote to the materialism and competition of the outside world.*

The advent of the middle-class family, at some point between the Revolution and the 1830s, had important consequences for women. In such families, the wife devoted herself to the domestic realm, or "woman's sphere." She ran an efficient household, provided emotional support for family members, upheld moral standards, inculcated religious values, assumed responsibility for child-rearing, and presided over her own domain. "The home is the wife's province," announced the editor of a nineteenth-century guide to manners. "It is her right to govern and direct its interior management." Paternal power, meanwhile, declined a notch. It was weakened by the companionate ethos, the affectionate domestic atmosphere, and, most important, by the

---

*Steven Mintz and Susan Kellogg, *Domestic Revolutions: A Social History of Family Life* (New York: The Free Press, 1988), chap. 3.

husband's frequent absence from home. Wives, therefore, gained a boost in authority or "influence" that they previously had lacked. To be sure, such influence was limited to what Alexis de Tocqueville called "the narrow circle of domestic interests and duties." It involved perpetual self-sacrifice and an attitude of deference toward husbands; companionate rhetoric masked the wife's subordinate, dependent role. Nonetheless, the development of a woman's "sphere" represented a net gain. What women had always done—take care of households and children—acquired new significance. Indeed, *women* acquired new significance. Not surprisingly, they welcomed celebrations of the cult of domesticity, however maudlin. "Home!" declared sentimental writer Lydia Sigourney in an 1850 essay, "Blessed bride, thou art about to enter this sanctuary, and become a priestess at its altar!"

The nineteenth-century ethos of individualism was not absent from the middle-class woman's experience but rather concentrated in a special period: courtship. The decision to marry was now both a highly personal choice, since romance was essential, and a risky one. Marriage for love required careful assessment of a man's capacity for congeniality and compatibility, the requisites for a harmonious home. Higher expectations of domestic happiness sometimes narrowed a woman's options or precluded marriage altogether. Women who married commonly preferred long engagements. Reluctant to give up the relative independence of their earlier lives, they feared awesome domestic obligations, difficult transitions to the married state, and complete separation, if not geographic then emotional, from all that they had known before. "When one marries they are so lost to their friends, as if they were miles away and we know they are gone," declared a New York state girl at mid-century.*

If courtship introduced a new level of risk, motherhood brought increased rewards: a greater degree of parental power. Child-rearing now fell under the mother's control. It was her responsibility to shape her children's values, develop their characters, ensure their piety, and

---

*Changes in middle-class courtship are described in Ellen K. Rothman, *Hands and Hearts: A History of Courtship in America* (Cambridge: Harvard University Press, 1984).

instill those habits of order and self-control that would guarantee their success in later life. Indeed, mothers had to make sure that their children would not descend from the middle-class status that their parents had either inherited or attained. Heightened maternal responsibility had some tangible repercussions. Mothers gained new influence over sons, whose upbringing they dominated for a longer time, if not, according to *The Mother's Magazine*, forever. They also made some gains in cases of separation or broken marriages, by winning—occasionally and infrequently—custody rights over their young children. Most important, mothers now played a decisive role in their offspring's spiritual destiny.

Many Protestant ministers abetted this leap in influence. The religious revivals that swept the nation, notably in the 1820s and 1830s, made clergymen increasingly dependent on female converts. Women comprised a majority of their congregants and supported the gamut of religious societies that revivals spawned. Evangelical ministers, in return, celebrated female piety on all occasions and gave mothers control over their children's souls. Salvation, they suggested, now depended primarily on upbringing. Some conservative clerics continued to support the idea of infant damnation, but mothers—and their evangelical ministers—knew better. Piety became an important bulwark to maternal power and middle-class status.

The middle-class home itself raised the status of the woman who ran it. This refuge from materialism assumed large and impressive physical proportions. At mid-century, architectural "pattern books" recommended either the flat-roofed, broad-porched, Italianate style of dwelling or the ornate gothic "cottage," with pitched roofs, ornamental gables, bay windows, and towers or cupolas. Lithographs depicted such middle-class residences in the bucolic countryside, surrounded by trees and shrubs, and away from urban corruption. The main feature of these ideal dwellings, beyond their substantial size, was the division between public and private space. Downstairs, the front hall, front parlor, sitting room, and dining room welcomed visitors and provided a center for family gatherings, from birthdays to weddings to funerals. The upstairs contained private bedrooms and perhaps a separate nursery. The middle-class home provided family members with not only a refuge from the outside world, but opportunity for refuge from each other.*

Such capacious homes, or even more modest imitations, gave middle-class women an important base of operations. They also needed attention. Even with a servant or two, another perquisite of middle-class lifestyle, housewives had to prepare meals, preserve food, clean rooms, and wash clothes, all without benefit of indoor plumbing; laundry was done in tubs heated on the stove. Standards of housekeeping rose as well. The home, its furnishings, and its upkeep symbolized the family's level of harmony, virtue, and achievement. Homemaking guides like Lydia Maria Child's *The Frugal Housewife* (1829) and Catharine Beecher's *Treatise on Domestic Economy* (1841) went through many editions and entered thousands of homes, from the eastern seaboard to the western frontier.

Such manuals served an important purpose: By mid-century, middle-class ideals extended far beyond the middle-class. As the printing industry expanded, an enormous literature emerged to define every aspect of women's domestic life. Religious tracts, books offering advice to brides, child-rearing manuals, housekeeping guides, etiquette books, women's magazines, sentimental fiction, and elaborate gift books inundated the market. This outflowing of didactic literature—much, though not all, of it written by women—reached an unprecedented audience. Rural women shared subscriptions to mother's magazines, westbound women lugged copies of *Godey's Lady's Book* across the plains, urban migrants boned up on city manners, prospective brides studied guides to marital life, and women of all classes bought the housekeeping manuals and feminine fiction that poured off the presses. The ideal of the middle-class family, and of women's new domestic role, thereby received extensive publicity and affected women's expectations and experience for decades to come.

---

*Clifford Edward Clark, Jr., *The American Family Home, 1800–1960* (Chapel Hill: University of North Carolina Press, 1986), chap. 2.

Liberty to Choose

ELIZA SOUTHGATE, 1802

Clarence Cook, ed., *A Girl's Life Eighty Years Ago: Selections from the Letters of Eliza Southgate Bowne* (New York: Charles Scribner's Sons, 1887), pp. 35–41, 138–43.

Eliza Southgate, born in 1783, came from a well-off family in Portland, Maine. Her father was a judge and her mother was a sister of Rufus King, signer of the Constitution and Federalist candidate for vice-president in 1808. First educated in a local school, Eliza moved on to Susanna Rowson's female academy in Medford, Massachusetts. After school, she accompanied family friends on an extended tour of New England and New York. During the trip, she met her future husband, Walter Bowne, whom she married in 1803.

A lively and independent teenager, Eliza engaged in a flow of correspondence to family and friends, as was the habit of well-schooled girls her age. Full of social news, messages for relatives, and requests for clothes, her letters exuded boundless enthusiasm. But Eliza also had an intellectual side, which she drew upon in a correspondence with her cousin, Moses Porter, around 1800. Here, she held forth on some crucial issues, including the awesome problem of choosing a husband and women's "inequality of privilege" in courtship. Using the political vocabulary of the day—*liberty, virtue, happiness*—Eliza applied these terms to the marriage market. Women might have "the liberty of refusing those we don't like," she declared to Moses, "but not of selecting those we do." Two years later, while touring the Northeast, Eliza exerted her "liberty" of choice. In a letter to her mother, she requested—or rather demanded—her parents' agreement to her engagement with Walter Bowne. Astutely combining deference with insistence, she encased her demands in a cloak of social trivia and travel commentary. Happily married for several years, Eliza Southgate Bowne died suddenly of an unnamed illness in 1809, after the birth of her second child.

Salem, September 9, 1802

My Dearest Mother:

Once more I am safe in Salem and my first thoughts turn toward home. I arrived last night. The attention I have received from Mr. and Mrs. Derby* has been of a kind that I shall look forward with delight to a time when I may be able to return it as I wish. I am in perfect health and spirits and have enjoyed the journey more than I can express to you. I don't know that I have had an unpleasant hour since I have been gone, and what is still more pleasing, I look back on every scene without regret or pain. At Leicester I went to Uncle Southgate's, and Cousin William helped me into the carriage when I left the tavern the next morning. We did not return thro' North-Hampton, and I consequently missed seeing Aunt Dickenson. I regret it extremely, but Mr. Derby was in such haste to return, that he left us at Worcester and took the stage. I therefore could not say a word of Hadley. I found two letters from Octavia on my return here; felt really grieved at Eliza Wait's death; she must feel it sensibly as they were such intimate friends, yet time blunts the sharp pangs of affection, and when I return she will feel that happiness has only fled for a while to make its return more delightful. I have received more attentions at the Springs than in my whole life before, I know not why it was, but I went under every advantage. Mr. Derby is so well known and respected, and they are such charming people and treated me with so much affection, it could not be otherwise! Among the many gentlemen I have become acquainted and who have been attentive, one I believe is serious, I know not, my dearest Mother, how to introduce this subject, yet as I fear you may hear it from others and feel anxious for my welfare, I consider it a duty to tell you all. At Albany, on our way to Ballston, we put up at the same house with a *Mr. Bowne* from New York; he went on to the Springs the same day we did, and from that time was particularly attentive to me; he was always of our parties to ride, went to Lake George in company with us, and came on to Lebanon when we did—for 4 weeks I saw him every day and probably had a better opportunity of knowing him than if I had seen him as a common acquaintance in town for years. I felt cautious of encouraging his attentions, tho' I did not wish to *discourage* it—there were so many *New Yorkers* at the Springs who knew him perfectly that I easily learnt his character and reputation; he is a man of *business*, uniform in his conduct and *very much respected*; all this we knew from report. Mr. and Mrs. Derby were very much pleased with him, but conducted towards me with peculiar *delicacy*, left me entirely to myself, as on a subject of so much importance they scarcely dared give an opinion. I left myself in a situation truly embarrassing. At such a distance from all my friends—my Father and Mother a perfect stranger to the person,—and prepossessed in his favor as much as so short an acquaintance would sanction—his conduct was such as I shall ever reflect on with the greatest pleasure—open, candid, generous, and delicate. He is a man in whom I could place the most unbounded confidence, nothing rash or impetuous in his disposition, but weighs maturely every circumstance; he knew I was not at liberty to

---

*Family friends with whom Eliza traveled.

encourage his addresses without the approbation of my Parents, and appeared as solicitous that I should act with strict propriety as one of my most disinterested friends. He advised me like a friend and would not have suffered me to do anything improper. He only required I would not discourage his addresses till he had an opportunity of making known to my Parents his character and wishes—this I promised and went so far as to tell him I approved him as far as I knew him, but the decision must rest with my Parents, their wishes were my law. He insisted upon coming on immediately: that I absolutely refused to consent to. But all my persuasion to wait till winter had no effect; the first of October he *will come.* I could not prevent it without a positive *refusal*; this I felt no disposition to give. And now, my dearest Mother, I submit myself wholly to the wishes of my Father and you, convinced that my happiness is your warmest wish, and to promote it has ever been your study. That I feel deeply interested in Mr. Bowne I candidly acknowledge, and from the knowledge I have of his heart and character I think him better calculated to promote my happiness than any person I have yet seen; he is a firm, steady, serious man, nothing light or trifling in his character, and I have every reason to think he has well weighed his sentiments toward me—nothing rash or premature. I have referred him wholly to you, and you, my dearest Parents, must decide. Octavia mentioned nothing about moving, but I am extremely anxious to know how soon we go into Portland and what house we shall have. Write me immediately on the subject, and let me know if you approve my conduct. Mr. Bowne wishes me to remain here until he comes on and then let him carry me home: this I objected to, but will depend on your advice. I shall be obliged to stay a few weeks longer—Harriet Howards expects me a week in Cambridge, Mrs. Sumner a week in Boston, and Mrs. Hasket Derby another week. I am now with Ellen and shall stay till Mrs. Coffin comes up, then according to promise go to Mrs. Lucy Derby's. I feel extremely anxious to hear you have moved into town, and shall most probably be here until then; write me immediately. If you wish any furniture, Mrs. Sumner will assist me in purchasing whatever you wish. I mentioned in my letter, when I set out on this journey I borrowed 15 dollars of Ellen; I wish you to send it to me immediately after receiving this, if you have not already sent it. I shall likewise stand in need of a little, as I have unavoidably incurred many expenses in this journey which I should not otherwise have done. Mr. Derby has loaded me with obligations, all my expenses he defrayed as if I was his daughter, and in such a manner as endears him more than I can express. You cannot imagine how interested they both are in the subject I have been writing you upon—my nearest friends cannot feel more, they have witnessed the whole progress, and if you knew them, would be convinced they would not have let me act improperly, they both approve my conduct. I wish my Father would write to Mr. Derby and know what he says of Mr. B.'s character. I don't know but 'tis a subject too delicate to give his opinion, but I can conceive that my Father might request it without any impropriety; and do, my Dear Mother, beg him to say any thing in his power to convince him that we all feel sensibly their great attention to me. You know not how anxious I feel for my Father to write him something of that kind, not that they appear to expect it, but on the contrary insist that they have been more obliged than I have, and really seem to think so; but this rather strengthens than lessens the obligation, nothing should have induced me to receive such from people who felt they were conferring favors. I long to hear when we move into Portland, *do* write me. My best love to Horatio and Octavia, and tell them I shall write as soon as possible. I found a large packet of 5 sheets from Martha, dated Paris, June 28th; tells me every thing, speaks almost in raptures of Buonaparte, says Uncle Rufus has a little son about 12 years old at school there, one of the finest boys she ever saw. I find most of the Southern people whom we met at the Springs, think Uncle Rufus stands as good a chance of being President as any one spoken of. I have listened for hours to his praises when not one knew how much I was interested; it was known from Mrs. Derby I was his niece, and it really gave me great conse-quence. I thought of Mrs. Dewitt and laughed. Judge Sedgwick told me had letters from him as late as June, and that he was determined on returning in the Spring. I long to hear from home. My love to all my friends, and believe me, with every sentiment of *duty* and *affection*,

> *Your daughter*
> *Eliza*

Martha sent me a most elegant Indispensable, white lutestring spangled with silver, and a beautiful bracelet for the arm made of her hair; she is too good—to love me as she says, more than ever.

Matrimonial Risks

EMMA WILLARD, 1815

"Emma Willard to Almira Hart" (1815), in John Lord, *The Life of Emma Willard* (New York: Appleton, 1873), pp. 44–45.

Marriage for love, and freedom of choice, brought risks as well as rewards. Whatever the counsel of friends and relatives, a woman now bore sole responsibility for her decision to marry; she alone would face the consequences. Such a step required extreme caution, as 28-year-old educator Emma Willard (1787–1870) suggested in a letter to her younger sister Almira Hart in 1815. Emma, who had married a much older man, physician John Willard, in 1809, was then running a female academy in Middlebury, Vermont. She had opened the school when her husband's finances collapsed. Almira lived at the sisters' parental home in Berlin, Connecticut, where she too ran a school. Her suitor was a lawyer named Simeon Lincoln.

In a hard-headed outburst of sisterly advice, Emma alerted Almira to a few of the possible disasters that lay in store in regard to "Mr. L." or presumably anyone else. What if, during courtship, he fell in love with another or revealed some defect of character? What if, after marriage, his business duties made him neglectful, gloomy, or critical? In any case, Willard warned, high hopes were likely to lead to disappointment. Almira ignored her sister's grim counsel and married her suitor in 1817. After his death she was married happily again to lawyer John Phelps. Emma Willard, ironically, eventually needed the advice she gave Almira. At age fifty, when she was a rich, successful woman, she married a much younger man who turned out to be a gambler in need of her money. The marriage disintegrated a few months later.

Middlebury, July 30, 1815

Dear Sister:

You think it strange that I should consider a period of happiness as more likely than any other to produce future misery. I know I did not sufficiently explain myself. Those tender and delicious sensations which accompany successful love, while they soothe and soften the mind, diminish its strength to bear or to conquer difficulties. It is the luxury of the soul; and luxury always enervates. A degree of cold that would but brace the nerves of the hardy peasant, would bring distress or death to him who had been pampered by ease and indulgence. This life is a life of vicissitude. A period of happiness, by softening and enervating the soul, by raising a thousand blissful images of the future, naturally prepares the mind for a greater or less degree of disappointment, and unfits us to bear it; while, on the contrary, a period of adversity often strengthens the mind, and, by destroying inordinate anticipation of the future, gives a relish to whatever pleasures may be thrown in our way. This, perhaps you may acknowledge, is generally true; but you cannot think it applies to your case—otherwise than that you acknowledge yourself liable to disappointment by death. But we will pass over that, and we will likewise pass over the possibility of your lover's seeing some object that he will consider more interesting than you, and likewise that you may hereafter discover some imperfection in his character. We will pass this over, and suppose that the sanction of the law has been passed upon your connection, and you are secured to each other for life. It will be natural that, at first, he should be much devoted to you; but, after a while, his business must occupy his attention. While absorbed in that he will perhaps neglect some of those little tokens of affection which have become necessary to your happiness. His affairs will sometimes go wrong, and perhaps he will not think proper to tell you the cause; he will appear to you reserved and gloomy, and it [will] be very natural in such a case for you to imagine that he is displeased with you, or is less attached than formerly. Possibly you may not in every instance manage a family as he has been accustomed to think was right, and he may sometimes hastily give you a harsh word or a frown. But where is the use, say you, of diminishing my present enjoyment by such gloomy apprehensions? Its use is this, that, if you enter the marriage state believing such things to be absolutely impossible, if you should meet them, they would come upon you with double force. We should endeavor to make a just estimate of our future prospects, and consider what evils, peculiar situations in which we may be placed, are most likely to beset us, and endeavor to avert them if we can; or, if we must suffer them, to do it with fortitude, and not magnify them by imagination, and think that, because we cannot enjoy all that a glowing fancy can paint, there is no enjoyment left. I hope I shall see Mr. L——. I shall be very glad to have you come and spend the winter with me, and, if he could with propriety accompany you, I should be glad to see him. I am involved in care. There [are] forty in our family and seventy in the school. I have, however, an excellent house-keeper and a very good assistant in my school. You seem to have some wise conjectures floating in your brain, but, unfortunately for your skill in guessing, they have no foundation in truth.

Little John says I must tell you he has learned a great deal. He goes to a little children's school, and is doing very well. Doctor has not yet gone to Pittsfield after mother, but expects to set out this week. We both feel very unpleasantly that he could not have gone before, but a succession of engagements made it impossible.

Yours affectionately,
Emma Willard

The Deferential Wife

CAROLINE GILMAN, 1838

Caroline Howard Gilman, *Recollections of a Southern Matron* (New York: Harper & Brothers, 1838), pp. 250–57.

Boston-born author Caroline Howard Gilman (1794–1888) married a Unitarian minister in 1819 and moved to Charleston, South Carolina. There, she had seven children and began a successful writing career. Although she disclaimed any desire for literary fame, Gilman was a striver in the field of women's literature. She ran her own periodical, *The Rose-Bud, or Youth's Gazette*, later *The Southern Rose*; contributed to leading periodicals, such as Sarah Hale's *Ladies Magazine*; and published several novels with Harper & Brothers, a New York firm that catered to the growing market of women readers.

In *Recollections of a Southern Matron*, a didactic novel, Gilman capitalized on her experience as a New Englander transplanted to a southern locale. She hoped to present as "exact a picture as possible of local habits and manners." The novel contained little local color, beyond mention of a plantation and the author's bizarre rendition of slave dialect. Instead, Gilman put forth an ideal of middle-class domestic life. In the following excerpt from a chapter called "The Planter's Bride," she counsels her readers on the value of "self-control." Deference, or at least the appearance of deference, Gilman suggests, would promote domestic harmony and preserve companionate marriage. Perhaps this was true, in the North or the South.

The planter's bride, who leaves a numerous and cheerful family in her paternal home, little imagines the change which awaits her in her own retired residence. She dreams of an independent sway over her household, devoted love and unbroken intercourse with her husband, and indeed longs to be released from the eyes of others, that she may dwell only beneath the sunbeam of his. And so it was with me. After our bustling wedding and protracted journey, I looked forward to the retirement at Bellevue as a quiet port in which I should rest with Arthur, after drifting so long on general society. The romance of our love was still in its glow, as might be inferred by the infallible sign of his springing to pick up my pocket-handkerchief whenever it fell. . . .

For several weeks all kinds of droll associations were conjured up, and we laughed at anything and nothing. What cared we for fashion and pretension? There we were together, asking for nothing but each other's presence and love. At length it was necessary for him to tear himself away to superintend his interests. I remember when his horse was brought to the door for his first absence of two hours; an observer would have thought that he was going a far journey, had he witnessed that parting; and so it continued for some days, and his return at each time was like the sun shooting through a three days' cloud.

But the period of absence was gradually protracted; then a friend sometimes came home with him, and their talk was of crops and politics, draining the fields and draining the revenue, until I (country ladies will believe me) fell off into a state as nearly approaching sleep as a straight-backed chair would allow. . . .

Arthur was a member of a social club—but he had allowed several citations to pass unnoticed, until it occurred to him that he was slighting his friends; I thought so too, and said so, without permitting the sigh to escape that lay at the bottom of my heart, at the idea of his passing an evening away from me.

"They shall not keep me long from you, my love," he said, as we parted; "I have little joy without you." . . .

This club-engagement, however, brought on others. I was not selfish, and even urged Arthur to go to hunt and to dinner-parties, although hoping that he would resist my urging. He went frequently, and a growing discomfort began to work upon my mind. I had undefined forebodings; I mused about past days; my views of life became slowly disorganized; my physical powers enfeebled; a nervous excitement followed; I nursed a moody discontent, and ceased a while to reason clearly. Wo to me had I yielded to this irritable temperament! I began immediately, on principle, to busy myself about my household. The location of Bellevue was picturesque—the dwelling airy and commodious; I had, therefore, only to exercise taste in external and internal arrangement to make it beautiful throughout. I was careful to consult my husband in those points which interested him, without annoying him with mere trifles. If the reign of romance was really waning, I resolved not to chill his noble confidence, but to make a steadier light rise on his affections. If he was absorbed in reading, I sat quietly waiting the pause when I should be rewarded by the communication of ripe ideas; if I saw that he prized a tree which interfered with my flowers, I sacrificed my preference to a more sacred feeling; if any habit of his annoyed me, I spoke of it once or twice calmly, and then bore it quietly if unreformed; I welcomed his friends with cordiality, entered into their family interests, and stopped my yawns, which, to say the truth, was sometimes an almost desperate effort, before they reached eye or ear.

This task of self-government was not easy. To repress a harsh answer, to confess a fault, and to stop (right or wrong) in the midst of self-defence, in gentle submission, sometimes requires a struggle like life and death; but these *three* efforts are the golden threads with which domestic happiness is woven; once begin the fabric with this woof, and trials shall not break or sorrow tarnish it.

Men are not often unreasonable; their difficulties lie in not understanding the moral and physical structure of our sex. They often wound through ignorance, and are surprised at having offended. How clear is it, then, that woman loses by petulance and recrimination! Her first study must be self-control, almost to hypocrisy. A good wife must smile amid a thousand perplexities, and clear her voice to tones of cheerfulness when her frame is drooping with disease, or else languish alone. Man, on the contrary, when trials beset him, expects to find her ear and heart a ready receptacle; and, when sickness assails him, her soft hand must nurse and sustain him.

I have not meant to suggest that, in ceasing to be a mere lover, Arthur was not a tender and devoted husband. I have only described the natural progress of a sensible, independent married man, desirous of fulfilling all the relations of society. Nor in these remarks would I chill the romance of some young dreamer, who is reposing her heart on another. Let her dream on. God has given this youthful, luxurious gift of trusting love, as he has given hues to the flower and sunbeams to the sky. It is a superadded charm to his lavish blessings; but let her be careful that when her husband

> Wakes from love's romantic dream,
> His eyes may open on a sweet esteem.

Let him know nothing of the struggle which follows the first chill of the affections; let no scenes of tears and apologies be acted to agitate him, until he becomes accustomed to agitation; thus shall the star of domestic peace arise in fixedness and beauty above them, and shine down in gentle light on their lives, as it has on ours.

The Mother at Home

JOHN S. C. ABBOTT, 1833

John S. C. Abbott, *The Mother at Home; or the Principles of Maternal Duty, Familiarly Illustrated* (New York: The American Tract Society, 1833), pp. 159–61.

Protestant ministers played a major role in defining woman's sphere. By expressing high regard for mothers, they enhanced the self-esteem of women parishioners and enlarged their flocks. Mothers, in turn, who held sway over other family members, could bring these relatives into the fold. Evangelical literature stressed the mother's new importance in child-rearing and gave her responsibility for religious instruction. The mother now shaped her children's destiny, temporal and eternal.

Congregationalist minister John S. C. Abbott wrote more than fifty books, but the most popular was *The Mother at Home*, a text in evangelical child-rearing. Maternal societies—local associations of mothers who met monthly to share modes of pious child-rearing—provided a receptive audience. Abbott stressed love and affection—the mother's forte—over discipline, a last resort. But with influence came obligations. Maternal neglect, Abbott warned, would lead to disobedience and self-will. So would dependence on the father, who was likely to be absent from home. The mother alone held control, and should she fail to perfect her offspring's character, she faced dire consequences: "If you are the destroyer of your child, through eternity you must bear its reproach," the minister warned. In the following excerpt, Abbott summed up his exalted and influential view of motherhood.

Mothers have as powerful an influence over the welfare of future generations, as all other earthly causes combined. Thus far the history of the world has been composed of the narrations of oppression and blood. War has scattered its unnumbered woes. The cry of the oppressed has unceasingly ascended to heaven. Where are we to look for the influence which shall change this scene, and fill the earth with the fruits of peace and benevolence? It is to the power of divine truth, to Christianity, as taught from a mother's lips. In a vast majority of cases the first six or seven years decide the character of the man. If the boy leave the paternal roof uncontrolled, turbulent and vicious, he will, in all probability, rush on in the mad career of self-indulgence. There are exceptions; but these exceptions are rare. If, on the other hand, your son goes from home accustomed to control himself, he will probably retain that habit through life. If he has been taught to make sacrifices of his own enjoyment that he may promote the happiness of those around him, it may be expected that he will continue to practise benevolence, and consequently will be respected, and useful, and happy. If he has adopted firm resolutions to be faithful in all the relations in life, he, in all probability, will be a virtuous man and an estimable citizen, and a benefactor of his race.

When our land is filled with pious and patriotic mothers, then will it be filled with virtuous and patriotic men. The world's redeeming influence, under the blessing of the Holy Spirit, must come from a mother's lips. She who was first in the transgression, must be yet the principal earthly instrument in the restoration. Other causes may greatly aid. Other influences must be ready to receive the mind as it comes from the mother's hand, and carry it onward in its improvement. But the mothers of our race must be the chief instruments in its redemption. This sentiment will bear examining; and the more it is examined, the more manifestly true will it appear. It is alike the dictate of philosophy and experience. The mother who is neglecting personal effort, and relying upon other influences for the formation of virtuous character in her children, will find, when it is too late, that she has fatally erred. The patriot, who hopes that schools, and lyceums, and the general diffusion of knowledge, will promote the good order and happiness of the community, while family government is neglected, will find that he is attempting to purify the streams which are flowing from a corrupt fountain. It is maternal influence, after all, which must be the great agent, in the hands of God, in bringing back our guilty race to duty and happiness. O that mothers could feel this responsibility as they ought! Then would the world assume a different aspect. Then should we less frequently behold unhappy families and broken-hearted parents. A new race of men would enter upon the busy scene of life, and cruelty and crime would pass away. O mothers! reflect upon the power your Maker has placed in your hands! There is no earthly influence to be compared with yours. There is no combination of causes so powerful in promoting the happiness or the misery of our race, as the instructions of home. In a most peculiar sense God has constituted you the guardians and the controllers of the human family.

System and Order

CATHARINE BEECHER, 1841

Catharine E. Beecher, *A Treatise on Domestic Economy for the Use of Young Ladies at Home, and at School* (Boston: Marsh, Capen, Lyon, and Webb, 1841), pp. 13–14, 142–54 passim.

Amidst the profusion of advice books destined for the female market, few had the impact of Catharine Beecher's *Treatise on Domestic Economy*. The oldest daughter of Lyman Beecher, a leading Congregationalist minister, Catharine Beecher (1800–1878) made her reputation as an educator. She founded the Hartford Female Seminary in 1828 and the Western Female Institute in 1833. With the publication of the *Treatise* in 1841, Beecher established a national reputation. Adopted in the classroom, the book was reprinted annually for fifteen years and revised and republished thereafter.

Catharine Beecher's housekeeping manual defined and exalted the middle-class home. It discussed every aspect of domestic existence from home design, kitchen plumbing, and house furnishings to health, hygiene, and proper meal hours. Most important, the *Treatise* presented domesticity as a female profession, comparable to the male professions of the ministry or law. It also assured readers that they were accomplishing "the greatest work that was ever committed to human responsibility." In the following excerpt, Catharine Beecher discusses the virtue of "system and order" in the home. She recommends to homemakers the same type of schedules, delegation of tasks, and habits of regularity that characterize a well-run business.

The success of democratic institutions, as is conceded by all, depends upon the intellectual and moral character of the mass of the people. If they are intelligent and virtuous, democracy is a blessing; but if they are ignorant and wicked, it is only a curse, and as much more dreadful than any other form of civil government, as a thousand tyrants are more to be dreaded than one. It is equally conceded, that the formation of the moral and intellectual character of the young is committed mainly to the female hand. The mother writes the character of the future man; the sister bends the fibres that hereafter are the forest tree; the wife sways the heart, whose energies may turn for good or for evil the destinies of a nation. Let the women of a country be made virtuous and intelligent, and the men will certainly be the same. The proper education of a man decides the welfare of an individual; but educate a woman, and the interests of a whole family are secured. . . .

The woman who is rearing a family of children; the woman who labors in the schoolroom; the woman who, in her retired chamber, earns, with her needle, the mite to contribute for the intellectual and moral elevation of her country; even the humble domestic, whose example and influence may be moulding and forming young minds, while her faithful services sustain a prosperous domestic state—each and all may be cheered by the consciousness, that they are agents in accomplishing the greatest work that ever was committed to human responsibility. It is the building of a glorious temple, whose base shall be coextensive with the bounds of the earth, whose summit shall pierce the skies, whose splendor shall beam on all lands, and those who hew the lowliest stone, as much as those who carve the highest capital, will be equally honored when its top-stone shall be laid, with new rejoicings of the morning stars, and shoutings of the sons of God. . . .

The discussion of the question of the equality of the sexes, in intellectual capacity, seems both frivolous and useless, not only because it can never be decided, but because there would be no possible advantage in the decision. But one topic, which is often drawn into this discussion, is of far more consequence; and that is, the relative importance and difficulty of the duties a woman is called to perform. . . .

There is no one thing more necessary to a housekeeper, in performing her varied duties, than *a habit of system and order*; and yet the peculiarly desultory nature of women's pursuits, and the embarrassments resulting from the state of domestic service in this Country, render it very difficult to form such a habit. But it is sometimes the case, that women, who could and would carry forward a systematic plan of domestic economy, do not attempt it, simply from a want of knowledge of the various modes of introducing it. It is with reference to such, that various modes of securing system and order, which the Writer has seen adopted, will be pointed out.

A wise economy is nowhere more conspicuous, than in the right *apportionment of time* to different pursuits. There are duties of a religious, intellectual, social, and domestic nature, each having different relative claims on attention. Unless a person has some general plan of apportioning these claims, some will intrench on others, and some, it is probable, will be entirely excluded. Thus, some find religious, social, and domestic, duties, so numerous, that no time is given to intellectual improvement. Others find either social or benevolent or religious interests excluded by the extent and variety of other engagements.

It is wise, therefore, for all persons to devise a general plan, which they will at least keep in view, and aim to accomplish, and by which, a proper proportion of time shall be secured for all the duties of life. . . .

Instead of attempting some such systematic employment of time, and carrying it out so far as they can control circumstances, most women are rather driven along by the daily occurrences of life, so that, instead of being the intelligent regulators of their own time, they are the mere sport of circumstances. There is nothing which so distinctly marks the difference between weak and strong minds, as the fact, whether they control circumstances, or circumstances control them. . . .

Some persons endeavor to systematize their pursuits, by apportioning them to particular hours of each day. For example, a certain period before breakfast is given to devotional duties; after breakfast, certain hours are devoted to exercise and domestic employments; other hours to sewing, or reading, or visiting; and others to benevolent duties. But, in most cases, it is more difficult to systematize the hours of each day, than it is to sustain some regular division of the week.

In regard to the minutiæ of domestic arrangements, the Writer has known the following methods adopted. *Monday*, with some of the best housekeepers, is devoted to preparing for the labors of the week. Any extra cooking, the purchasing of articles to be used during the week, and the assorting of clothes for the wash, and mending such as would be injured without—these and similar items belong to this day. *Tuesday* is devoted to washing, and *Wednesday* to ironing. On *Thursday*, the ironing is finished off, the clothes folded and put away, and all articles which need mending put in the mending basket, and attended to. *Friday* is devoted to sweeping and housecleaning. On *Saturday*, and especially the last Saturday of every month, every department is put in order; the castors and table furniture are regulated, the pantry and cellar inspected, the trunks, drawers, and closets arranged, and every thing about the house put in order for *Sunday*. All the cooking needed for Sunday is also prepared. By this regular recurrence of a particular time for inspecting every thing, nothing is forgotten till ruined by neglect.

Another mode of systematizing, relates to providing proper supplies of conveniences, and proper places in which to keep them. Thus, some ladies keep a large closet, in which are placed the tubs, pails, dippers, soap-dishes, starch, bluing, clothes-line, clothes-pins, and every other article used in washing; and in the same or another place are kept every convenience for ironing. In the sewing department, a trunk, with suitable partitions, is provided, in which are placed, each in its proper place, white thread of all sizes, colored thread, yarns for mending, colored and black sewing-silks and twist, tapes and bobbins of all sizes, white and colored welting-cords, silk braids and cords, needles of all sizes, papers of pins, remnants of linen and colored cambric, a supply of all kinds of buttons used in the family, black and white hooks and eyes, a yard measure, and all the patterns used in cutting and fitting. These are done up in separate parcels and labelled. In another trunk, are kept all pieces used in mending, arranged in order, so that any article can be found without loss of time. A trunk like the first mentioned, will save many steps, and often much time and perplexity; while purchasing thus by the quantity makes them come much cheaper than if bought in little portions as they are wanted. Such a trunk should be kept locked, and a smaller supply, for current use, be kept in a workbasket.

The full supply of all conveniences in the kitchen and cellar, and a place appointed for each article, very much facilitates domestic labor. For want of this, much vexation and loss of time is occasioned, while seeking vessels in use, or in cleansing those used by different persons for various purposes. It would be far better for a lady to give up some expensive article in the parlor, and apply the money, thus saved, for kitchen conveniences, than to have a stinted supply where the most labor is to be performed. If our Countrywomen would devote more to comfort and convenience, and less to show, it would be a great improvement. Mirrors and piertables [low tables] in the parlor, and an unpainted, gloomy, ill-furnished kitchen, not unfrequently are found under the same roof.

Another important item, in systematic economy, is the apportioning of *regular* employment to the various members of a family. If a housekeeper can secure the cooperation of *all* her family, she will find that "many hands make light work." There is no greater mistake, than in bringing up children to feel that they must be taken care of, and waited on, by others, without any corresponding obligations on their part. The extent to which young children can be made useful in a family, would seem surprising to those who have never seen a *systematic* and *regular* plan for securing their services. The Writer has been in a family, where a little girl of eight or nine washed and dressed herself and little brother, and made their little beds before breakfast, set and cleared all the tables at meals, with a little help from a grown person in moving tables and spreading cloths, while all the dusting of parlors and chambers was also neatly performed by her. A little brother of ten, brought in and piled all the wood used in the kitchen and parlor, brushed the boots and shoes neatly, went on errands, and took all the care of the poultry. They were children whose parents could afford to hire this service, but who chose to have their children grow up healthy and industrious, while proper instructions, system, and encouragement, made these services rather a pleasure than otherwise to the children. . . .

It is impossible for a conscientious woman to secure that peaceful mind, and cheerful enjoyment of life, which all should seek, who is constantly finding her duties jarring with each other, and much remaining undone, which she feels that she ought to do. In consequence of this, there will be a secret uneasiness, which will throw a shade over the whole current of life, never to be removed, till she so efficiently defines and regulates her duties, that she can fulfil them all.

And here the Writer would urge upon young ladies the importance of forming habits of system, while unembarrassed with multiplied cares which will make the task so much more difficult and hopeless. Every young lady can systematize her pursuits, to a certain extent. She can have a particular day for mending her wardrobe, and for arranging her trunks, closets, and drawers. She can keep her workbasket, her desk at school, and all her conveniences in proper places, and in regular order. She can have regular periods for reading, walking, visiting, study, and domestic pursuits. And by following this method, in youth, she will form a taste for regularity, and a habit of system, which will prove a blessing to her through life.

First to None

CATHARINE M. SEDGWICK, 1828

Mary E. Dewey, *The Life and Letters of Catharine M. Sedgwick* (New York: Harper & Brothers, 1871), pp. 197–99.

During the early nineteenth century, the number of unmarried women on the eastern seaboard increased. Rising expectations of marriage, plus a loss of men to western migration, helped diminish opportunities for middle-class women. Some women who never married celebrated the single state as one of "liberty." To others, such liberty was not ideal. The career of Massachusetts author Catharine M. Sedgwick (1789–1867) as a single woman embodied many contradictions. Daughter of the prominent lawyer Theodore Sedgwick—judge, congressman, senator—Catharine was one of a large brood of children, and she formed ardent attachments to her brothers. Perhaps the most talented woman author of her generation, Catharine Sedgwick claimed to write only as a sideline. Whatever her celebration of home and family life in her fiction, she never had a home of her home. Despite an inheritance plus her writing income, she lived with her adored brothers, in succession.

At mid-life, Catharine Sedgwick confided her sentiments on the single state to her private journal for 1828. Although she refers to her "happy experience" as an unmarried woman, the journal entry is permeated by muted rage about her "solitary condition" and "unnatural state." Sedgwick blames her "perfectionist" nature. She had rejected mediocre offers of marriage and never received ideal ones. In the hearts of her beloved but married brothers, she had been replaced by "others." Indeed, she had suffered a gradual loss of status within the family circle, moving downward from her one-time role as center of affection to "second place." Tormented by discontent, Catharine Sedgwick obviously was unable, if not unwilling, to feel as "grateful" and "humble" as she claimed she would like to. Significantly, her journal entry is permeated by sexual imagery, such as the arrival of verdant and voluptuous "Spring," and the coy, teasing behavior of vanishing "Hope." Such imagery was no accident. Sedgwick was, despite all of her disclaimers, an accomplished professional, even when writing solely for herself.

New York, May 18, 1828

Again the spring is here, the season of life and loveliness, the beautiful emblem of our resurrection unto life eternal. I have seen the country again arrayed in its green robe, with its budding honors thick upon it, the brimful streams, all Nature steeped in perfume, as if the gates of paradise were thrown open, and the air ringing with the wild notes of every bird upon the wing. . . . I will not say, with the ungracious poet, that I turn from what Spring brings to what she cannot bring, but alas! I find there is no longer that capacity for swelling, springing, brightening joy that I once felt. Memory has settled her shadowy curtain over too much of the space of thought, and Hope, that once to my imagination tempted me with her arch, and laughing, and promising face, to snatch away the veil with which she but half hid the future—Hope now seems to turn from me; and if I now and then catch some glimpses of her everted face, she looks so serious, so admonitory, that I almost believe that her sister Experience, with an eye of apprehension, and lips that never smile, has taken her place. All is not right with me, I know. I still build on sandy foundations; I still hope for perfection, where perfection is not given. The best sources of earthly happiness are not within my grasp—those of contentment I have neglected. I have suffered for the whole winter a sort of mental paralysis, and at times, I have feared the disease extended to my affections. It is difficult for one who began life as I did, the primary object of affection to many, to come by degrees to be first to none, and still to have my love remain in its entire strength, and craving such returns as have no substitute. How absurd, how groundless your complaints! would half a dozen voices exclaim, if I ever ventured to *make* this complaint. I do not. Each one has his own point of sight. Others are not conscious—at least I believe they are not—of any diminution in their affection for me, but others have taken my place, naturally and of right, I allow it. It is the necessity of a solitary condition, an unnatural state. He who gave us our nature has set the solitary in families, and has, by an array of motives, secured this sweet social compact to his children. From my own experience I would not advise anyone to remain unmarried, for my experience has been a singularly happy one. My feelings have never been embittered by those slights and taunts that the repulsive and neglected have to endure; there has been no period of my life to the present moment when I might not have allied myself respectably, and to those sincerely attached to me, if I would. I have always felt myself to be an object of attention, respect, and regard, and, though not *first* to any, I am, like Themistocles,* *second* to a great many. My fortune is not adequate to an independent establishment, but it is ample for ease to myself and liberality to others. In the families of all my brothers I have an agreeable home. My sisters are all kind and affectionate to me, my brothers generous and invariably kind; their children all love me. My dear Kate, my adopted child,† is, though far from perfect even in my doting eyes, yet such as to perfectly satisfy me, if I did not crave perfection for one I so tenderly love. I have troops of friends, some devotedly attached to me, and yet the result of all this very happy experience is that

---

*An Athenian statesman and naval leader whose rivals usurped the major posts of command and eventually exiled him.
†Catharine's niece.

there is no equivalent for those blessings which Providence has placed first, and ordained that they should be purchased at the dearest sacrifice. I have not set this down in a spirit of repining, but it is well, I think, honestly to expose our own feelings—they may serve for examples or beacons. While I live I do not mean this shall be read, and after, my individual experience may perhaps benefit some one of all my tribe. I ought, I know, to be grateful and humble, and I do hope, through the grace of God, to rise more above the world, to attain a higher and happier state of feeling, to order my house for that better world where self may lose something of its engrossing power.

The Widowed State

SARAH CONNELL AYER, 1832–1833

Diary of Sarah Connell Ayer (Portland, ME: Lefavor-Tower, 1910), pp. 336–52 passim.

The dependency of the married woman became clear in the plight of the widow, who faced new perils and problems. Even if middle-class and relatively young, she might lose her independent household and community position, and be forced to depend on distant relatives. Such was the case of Sarah Connell Ayer (1791–1835) of Portland, Maine, an academy-trained New England housewife whose diary of 1832–1833 recorded the trauma of her husband's death and her subsequent lurch into downward mobility. Accustomed by religious inclination to introspection and self-analysis, Sarah Connell Ayer also provided a detailed picture of her family members, social connections, and community activities.

Sarah Connell was married in 1810 to Samuel Ayer, a Dartmouth graduate and physician who had migrated from Massachusetts to Portland, Maine. After the death of her first four children, Sarah Ayer turned to religious endeavors with fervor. An extremely pious Congregationalist, she joined a women's prayer society, a maternal society, and a missionary society, and campaigned to no avail for the conversions of her husband and three new offspring. In 1821, the Ayer family moved to Eastport, Maine, where Samuel had been appointed Surveyor of the Port, and where Sarah reestablished her network of religious connections. Eleven years later, however, Ayer died, leaving his forty-year-old widow in a desperate state. Among her children (Sarah, fifteen, Samuel, thirteen, and Harriet, nine), the two teenagers were unregenerate and, in Samuel's case, unruly. Heartbroken and bereft, Sarah had to make arrangements to leave Eastport and move in with her husband's relatives in Concord, Massachusetts. During her first miserable months of widowhood, grief and loss mingled with fear of an uncertain future, and she developed a morbid interest in the sicknesses and deaths of others. Sarah Connell Ayer's widowed state proved short. Two years later, she died of scarlet fever, along with her youngest child.

Sabbath Oct. 7th, 1832. Twenty two years ago I became a wife. I was married *Oct. 7th 1810.* Since then I have experienced many changes, in this changing world; but I can say thus far, I have been enabled to say, the Lord has been my helper. I lost my first four children. The fourth was a lovely boy, who lived to be six months old, and was then removed from this world of sin and sorrow, to the Heavenly rest. I have now three living, a son and two daughters. That I may be enabled to discharge my duty in a faithful manner is my most earnest prayer. I have lost both my parents too. My Mother died in Bow, New Hampshire, fifteen years ago last May; after her death my Father came to live with me. He died here five years ago the 30th of this month. My health has for a number of years been poor. My husband too is far from being well. I often look at his changed countenance with much solicitude. O that he would no longer reject the terms of salvation, that he would no longer delay the concerns of his soul, but that he would now seek the consolations of religion. Have been to meeting all day. Mr. Gale preach'd. . . .

Sabbath November 25th, 1832. I now sit down to record the events of the last four weeks. Betsy and the children have gone to meeting, I have not felt well enough to go out, the walking being bad. But what shall I say? Is the past only a dream? No tis sad reality. I weep, my hand trembles, my heart seems ready to break; the tie which for 22 years bound me to my husband, death has severed, and though I shall ever cherish the remembrance of him with the fondest affection, I shall see his face here no more forever; no more hear his voice, or listen to hear the well known foot-step at the door, or stand ready to perform the many little offices, to which I had long been accustomed. He is no longer here, his spirit has fled, his body laid in the cold tomb. Never did I know how dear he was to my heart, till death enter'd, and I was call'd to part with him forever. And am I now a widow? Is it, can it be that my dear children have no longer a *kind father*, to watch over their childhood, and youth; to protect and guide them through this world of temptation. I would not murmur. I would hear a voice saying to me "Be still and know that I am God." I will now attempt to collect my wandering thoughts, to record the events of the trying scene, as well as I can remember. It may hereafter be read with interest by the dear, dear children. . . .

[Here, Sarah Ayer writes a long account of her husband's last illness. Although presented in diary form, the following entries for November 10th and November 12th are part of an extended flashback, in which Sarah Ayer recounts the events of the past few weeks.]

Sabbath November 10th, 1832. . . . He appear'd to be in great agony, I sat by the bed, and try'd to commit his never dying soul into the hands of the saviour, to give him up to a merciful and just God, who would do him no wrong. I then took a last look, and was led out of the room. He continued till *five* in the *afternoon*, and then expired without a groan, or a struggle. Mrs. Kimball came in to my chamber, and ask'd me if I was prepared to hear the last, I thought I was, but when she said *he is gone*, I shuddered through my whole frame, the sound went to my heart. I try'd to be composed, became more calm, and endeavoured to look to Christ for support and consolation. I did not see him that night. Thus departed the partner of my youth, the husband, with whom I had lived twenty two years. Last *August* he was *forty six years* old and last October we had been married *twenty two years.*

Monday 12th of November 1832. I went down into the parlour to look at all that was now left of my dear husband. There was a smile on his countenance, he look'd pleasant and natural. I felt as if he was conscious I was near him, that he would open his eyes once more upon me, and speak to me. I could not realize that he was dead, that he would never again look upon me, that I should never hear his voice again. I left the room, and return'd to my own chamber. Many kind friends came in to offer assistance, and to sympathize with me. Tuesday I rose and endeavoured to prepare for the last offices to be performed for my husband. I went down and took a last look, the effort was violent, it was almost more than I could bear, I look'd to God, and felt that he alone could support and comfort me. The hour came, the bell struck, minute guns were fired from the cutter, friends collected, an appropriate prayer was made by Mr. Gale, the coffin was then placed in the hearse, a carriage was brought to the door, and in it was placed myself, and children, Mr. Gale and wife; then followed the custom house officers, physicians, and friends of the family. The procession moved slowly on, it moved to the grave yard, my husband was laid in the tomb, and placed by the side of my father, the door closed upon him, and I return'd to my now solitary dwelling, with an aching heart. The scene which I had dreaded was over, I had been supported through it; I look'd into the chamber in which my early friend, my dear husband died, it look'd deserted and desolate, my soul was exceeding sorrowful, I felt forlorn, and wept. Mr. Gale wrote to Sarah, poor child! little did she dream when she left her home, that she should see her father no more in this world. . . .

Sabbath Decr. 9th, 1832. Another rainy Sabbath. All have gone to meeting but myself; I am not well, and dare not go out, to wet my feet. I have had another letter from Sarah, she had not received mine. She had heard of the death of her Father, and is very anxious to return home. Poor girl, she appears sensibly to feel her loss. She says, she feels the need of religion to support her under this heavy affliction; she now finds that this is not a place of rest. She begs Mr. Gale to remember her in his prayers. O that she would pray for herself. My children have all been given to the Lord in the ordinance of baptism, they have been taught that they were sinners, that Christ died for sinners, and that there was salvation in no other name. O that they would give up their hearts to God. Poor Sarah! she wishes to come *home* but where is to be my *home*? I must give up my house, *go* I know not where, *do* I know not what. I plan and reject, but come to no conclusion. I can determine upon nothing till I hear from my husband's friends. I have not yet had a line from one of them. I scarcely dare to think, to look back upon the past, or forward to the future. . . .

Sabbath 16th of Decr. 1832. It has been a pleasant Sabbath, and I have attended meeting all day, though I have been very unwell. A meeting this evening, all have gone but myself. Not a line yet from any of my husbands friends. I am at times anxious, my heart almost sinks, my troubles seem almost insupportable.

Sabbath 23rd of Decr. *Wednesday* was Samuel's birth-day. He was thirteen years old. This boy has caused me much anxiety. He is naturally of a rash, fiery, aspiring temper. I have endeavoured to impress upon him the importance of self-command, but as yet have not been very successful. He has talents, apply's closely to study; and has often been distinguish'd by our friends for his handsome manners, and manly deportment. It has often been injudiciously said before him, *"what a smart boy"*; such remarks though often made with no other view than to please the parents, prove most injurious to the child. I wish to see him of a humble, mild affectionate disposition; that he should have a distinct knowledge of religion, but above all that he should possess that faith, which can withstand "the temptations of the world," and despising its vanities, rise above them. My husband always gave each of the children a present on their birth-day, but Samuel had two, or three of his young friends to dine with him. Mr. Rawson had a letter from Brother Richard, they wish me to go to Concord as soon as possible. *Saturday* I received a letter from sister Charlotte and Sarah, they all wish me to go as early as I can. If I live I shall try to go on as early as April. *To day* I have been to meeting. . . .

Sabbath 30th of December, 1832. By last evening's mail I received another letter from Sarah. She wishes me not to leave Eastport. Poor girl, she is anxious to return here. She realizes not the sad change that has taken place in our family. I have been to meeting all day. Meeting this evening. I did not go out. *Alone.* . . .

Tuesday 5th [of February, 1833.] Wrote to Sarah. Mrs. Minot here to work. Mrs. Batson's little child died; this is the third death that has taken place in the same house; in less than four months.

Friday. Mr. Leavitt came up with the apprizers to apprize the things in the house. Dea. Wheeler, Gen. Peavy, and Mr. Weston, were selected by Judge Dickinson. I thought I was prepared; but when I opened my husband's chest to produce his instruments, and the door of the large book-case containing his library, when I look'd upon many relics of former days, which I must now part with. I could not keep from weeping. . . .

Sabbath 17th [of February.] The past has been a stormy week. We have had two of the most severe snow-storms I ever witnessed; our streets are almost entirely block'd up; so that it is very difficult to get out, I have not been out, but have sent the children, and am alone. The walking is so uneven, and being a little lame, I was afraid of falling. Mrs. Favour came in to dinner, it being too far for her to walk home, and back again to meeting. It is a number of weeks since I heard from Sarah and I begin to feel some anxiety. Her last letter was dated Decr. 23rd. Since then I have written to her twice. I have continued reading the Bible in course, and the more I read it, the more I am interested in it.

Tuesday 19th. I received a letter from Sarah, which relieved my anxiety respecting her. She appear'd to be in better spirits than when she wrote last. I begin to feel quite impatient to see her, never was I seperated from a child so long before.

Wednesday 20th of February. I was quite sick all day, and my spirit sunk to the lowest ebb. I have indeed of late been in a state of trial, I have had to struggle with difficulties, and my mind is enervated by indisposition, and many sorrows.

Thursday. I was much better. Why am I so cold and stupid, in regard to the subject of religion?

Monday 11th [of March, 1833.] I went up to spend a few days with Mrs. Ripley. While there, we concluded to send Samuel immediately on to Concord. Here, he was only wasting his time, and the sooner he was among his friends, and established at some school, the better. The Boundary was to sail on Tuesday, and Mr. Ripley thought it best that he should go to Boston in her, and there take the stage for Concord. I immediately set to work to prepare his things. Mr. Rawson return'd from Augusta. . . .

Saturday. I left Mrs. Ripley. Had enjoyed my visit much, and became much attached to the family. Mary-ann Mitchell came in to assist me, as I was very busy preparing Samuel for his journey. I dare not think of his leaving me. It does indeed give me pain to think of a separation. . . .

Monday. Got Samuel's things all ready, and in his trunk. His young friends all calling to bid him farewell, as he was to sail in the morning.

Tuesday 19th. Samuel left me. As he turn'd from the door he look'd round and with a sorrowful look, said *good-bye*. I could not speak, I wept, and endeavoured to commend him to the protecting care of my Heavenly Father.

Sabbath 24th. Attended meeting all day. Mr. Crosset preach'd. He was interesting as usual.

Sabbath 31st. Mr. Bond preach'd, in the afternoon Mr. Gale.

Sabbath April 7th, 1833. I have been very busily engaged the past week preparing to move. Have had a letter from Samuel; he had a long passage to Boston, but reach'd Concord in safety, in a week from leaving me. On Saturday I left the house. I walk'd round the rooms, and gave a last look, to the now desolate apartments. I wept as I gazed around the chamber, long occupied by my husband and myself, and where I took my last look of him, and from whence he was taken, to the house appointed for all living. Now it look'd dreary and deserted. I was sick at heart. I closed the door, walk'd down into the parlour, and then pass'd through the entry, out of the front door. As I closed the gate I cast one farewell look behind, and a flood of tears relieved my almost bursting heart. I went up to Mr. Ripley's, having had an invertation from him and his wife to make their house my home during my stay in Eastport. To day I have been to meeting and am quite tired, the walk being long, and feeling not quite well.

Wednesday. I went into Mrs. Bucknam's.

Friday. I wrote to the children. Return'd to Mrs. Ripley's. Found Mr. McMellan had return'd from Fryburgh, and brought Miss Webster with him. Mrs. Ripley was quite sick. I sat up with her all night.

Sabbath 14th. Did not go out. Mr. Rawson here to tea.

Monday. I spent the day with Mrs. Kimball.

Wednesday. I spent the day with Mrs. Ingols.

Friday. I went to Mrs. Gale's, and staid all night.

Saturday. I spent the day at Mrs. Balkam's, and return'd to Mrs. Ripley's at night.

Sabbath 21st. Was not at meeting in the forenoon, but went in the afternoon; took tea and spent the night at Mrs. Hawks.

Monday 22nd. After dinner I went over to Mrs. Hobbs and staid till *Wednesday*, we then went down to Mrs. Webster's.

Thursday. I left Mrs. Webster, and walk'd over to Mrs. *Witcomb's*. Mrs. Clapp had return'd from Boston, and I had a very pleasant visit. Mrs. Leavitt lives in the same house. She has been confined with an infant daughter, which she talks of calling Sarah Ayer. . . .

Saturday 4th of May. I left Doct. Balch's, and return'd to Eastport. We had a very pleasant sail over; stopt at Allen's Island and left Mr. Pennel there. Found a letter at Gen. Ripley's, from Brother Hill; and one from Sarah. Found that Mr. and Mrs. Gale had concluded to go to Boston in the Boundary, and I immediately determined to go on with them. Began to prepare for my journey.

Wednesday 8th of May. Expected to sail, but the wind was unfavourable. Mrs. Webster and several other friends call'd to bid me *good-bye*. Little Horatio was quite sick. I sat up with him till late.

Thursday 9th of May 1833. Gen. Ripley call'd me very early to go on board the Boundary; he said she would sail in the course of twenty minutes. I had to hurry on my cloaths, collect my things to send down, and leave the house, not a moment to take leave of my friends, or kiss the dear children. Gen. Ripley accompanied me down to the vessel. There Mr. Leavitt met me; my things were all on board. Dea. Wheeler, Mr. Eustis and several other friends, stood on the wharf to bid me farewell. I found Mr. and Mrs. Gale already on board, and a large number of English gentlemen. I knew none of the passengers but Mr. and Mrs. Gale. My heart was full, and I retired to the cabin as the vessel push'd from the wharf to weep in secret. I dared not take a last look at *Eastport*, which for 11 years had been my home, which contain'd many dear friends, and the tomb of my husband. Oft shall I in imagination visit the spot, where lies all that now remains of my Father, and the partner of my life; often weep over the green sod which covers them. Farewell sweet Isle, farewell ye dear departed ones; soon will the rolling waves bear me far from scenes dear to memory. I go to a distant spot, to return to the birthplace of my husband, to take my abode with his aged Mother, and again to meet his brothers and sisters, and my own children.

Saturday 11th of May 1833. Reach'd Boston [in] time enough for dinner. A carriage was provided which convey'd myself and Harriet up to Bromfield house, P. Shepard. Here I was shown into a neat little setting-room, with a small bed-chamber attach'd to it, which I was to occupy during my stay. Mr. Gale then left me. I felt alone in a crowded city. Poor little Harriet wept, because all around were strangers.

Sabbath 12th. Last Sabbath I went to meeting at Eastport, to day at Boston. This forenoon I went into the Methodist Church this afternoon to Park-Street church.

Monday 13th. Rose early and prepared to leave Boston. Set off in the stage about six o'clock. Passengers all strangers to me. Had a comfortable ride however. As I approach'd toward Concord, my spirits were much depressed. I was going to meet our dear Mother, brothers and sisters. Many years had elapsed since our last meeting, which was at the time I was sent for to attend the death-bed of my Mother; since then I had been call'd to part with my Father and my husband. I sat lost in thought, as the stage drove on, the Sun having cast his last rays on the surrounding objects. We got to Concord in the midst of a heavy shower of rain. Mother, brother James, sister Brigham, and Sarah all hurried to the door to welcome us. I scarcely knew Sarah, she has grown so much since she left me.

Sabbath 2nd of June. Another rainy Sabbath, so that I could not attend meeting. I have spent the day in my chamber, reading, writing and reflecting. As yet I have attended no prayer-meeting of any kind. I miss past religious priviledges. I long to unite in prayer with pious friends.

Monday 17th. My birth-day. I am this day 42 years old. What a change since my last birth-day. Then seated with my husband and children in my own dwelling; now far distant, alone in my chamber I am left to mourn the loss of the dear partner of my life. . . .

Sabbath 23rd of June. The Sabbath is drawing to a close. The Sun has just sank below the horizon; his last ray has set to the world; all is tranquil around me and nature seems to be settling into universal stillness. The bell begins to ring, it calls to the house of God, to close the day in united prayer and praise, and in listening to his holy word. But I am too fatigued to go. I have retired to my own little room, and here alone, I would ask myself how I have spent this holy Sabbath. O how much idle conversation, how many vain thoughts, how stupid, how cold in my devotions.

Chapter 8

The School and the Mill

W hile middle-class wives often were confined by "the narrow circle of domestic interests," a countervailing trend emerged. During the early decades of the nineteenth century, a growing number of young women found new roles outside of the home. They became, for instance, students at female academies, teachers at common schools, workers in New England textile mills, and employees in workshops and factories. The female academy and the textile mill, though obviously formed for different purposes, had much in common. Both institutions provided new types of female communities. Both imposed an ordered existence, based on discipline, schedules, and assigned tasks. Both fostered values unconnected to domesticity, such as self-reliance and achievement. The school and the mill, in short, offered the type of experience— even if temporary, as was usually the case—that separated "modern" from traditional life.

Female education evoked the fervent support of those who promoted woman's "sphere." For instance, educators Catharine Beecher and Emma Willard, and Sarah J. Hale, editor of *Godey's Lady's Book*, took conservative stances on social issues. They defended women's unique domestic mission, denigrated demands for "women's rights," and often adopted deferential postures toward men. But to such conservatives, education was a sacred cause. Women, they contended, needed special training to occupy their elevated niche at home and to excel at child-rearing, religious pursuits, and school teaching, a vocation for which they allegedly were naturally suited.

By the 1820s and 1830s, when the campaign for female education gained force, the movement to establish women's schools was well underway. Female academies, which first arose in the revolutionary era, multiplied during the early years of the new century, North and

South. Typically, they were boarding schools that offered a combination of primary and secondary education, usually with some religious training and an array of ornamentals—painting, dancing, and deportment. Attracting the daughters of the emerging middle class—the children of ministers, lawyers, merchants, and tradesmen in the North, and, in the South, of planters and professionals—the academies provided a new social experience. Attending an academy provided at least a few years in the company of peers and away from home, years that were devoted to personal achievement. An academy education also gave middle-class daughters a tangible boost on the marriage market. A Virginia father contended in 1810 that "A girl will be more respected with education than with wealth." But usually one signified at least a modicum of the other.

A more advanced institution than the academy, the antebellum female seminary sought to imitate some features of the male college curriculum. Seminaries required or taught classical languages, eschewed polite accomplishments, and admitted only older students who passed examinations. New England's prominent women educators were known for the seminaries with which they were affiliated, such as Emma Willard's Troy Seminary (1821), Catharine Beecher's Hartford Seminary (1828), Zilpah Grant's Ipswich Seminary (1828), and Mary Lyon's Mount Holyoke Seminary (1837). The very name "seminary," usually associated with the ministry, implied some type of professional training. At female seminaries, young women might be trained for missionary work or for teaching, at either the common schools or other academies and seminaries. When Oberlin College (founded in 1833) started its "female department" in 1837, graduates of the Byfield and Ipswich schools, where Zilpah Grant and Mary Lyon had taught, were involved in the department's founding.

Promotion of the woman teacher became another cause of women educators. "We have come to the conclusion that the work of teaching will never be rightly done till it passes into *female* hands," declared Harriet Beecher Stowe, an instructor at her sister Catharine's Western Female Institute, a teacher training school, in 1833. And as Catharine Beecher pointed out, women not only were naturally endowed to teach but would do so for half the pay of men. At midcentury, women dominated common school teaching in Massachusetts and had made inroads on the profession in other parts of the country as well. Although both Emma Willard and Catharine Beecher proposed ambitious schemes to fund female academies and support teacher training, respectively, neither of their plans won legislative support. But a major goal of these pioneer educators was soon fulfilled. By the end of the century, primary school teaching had become a woman's profession.

One impact of expanding educational opportunity for women was to reinforce the boundaries of class—to separate women of the ambitious middle class from those with lesser means, who might work as servants, seamstresses, or factory hands. The long-term process of industrialization had a similar impact. While enabling some women to buy goods that once had been produced within the home, the factory system deprived a larger number of women of income-producing work they once had done at home as, for instance, spinners, weavers, or brewers. But industrialization also provided some new jobs—for women typesetters, bookbinders, shoemakers, and, most notably, textile workers. New England textile mills, the nation's largest industrial establishments, depended for several decades primarily on a pool of female labor. From the 1820s through the 1840s, the underemployed daughters of New England farmers, who could no longer earn income at home from spinning, flocked to Lowell, Manchester, and other mill towns.

Like female academies, textile mills imposed new rules and regulations and taught specific skills. Unlike academies, they provided income. The young women they employed, traditionally on the margins of the labor force, could earn a substantial amount of money, at least compared to what they might have earned in the available alternative employments—as seamstresses, paid housekeepers, or even as teachers. Such income meant, in turn, the ability to support themselves, to achieve financial independence, to save for educations or dowries, to contribute to family income, or simply to have money to spend as they chose. For several decades, moreover, the experience of mill work provided a route to upward mobility. Instead of returning to their family farms, many young mill workers, especially those who managed to get some education, married enterprising local men and joined the swirl of middle-class populations in and around northeastern cities.

New England mill owners hoped to avoid the degradation of labor that characterized European manufacturing cities. They envisioned a well-behaved, efficient work force, or what one Lowell minister called "an industrious, sober, and moral class of operatives." The labor system at the mills required extensive and paternalistic supervision of employees, who lived in company-owned boarding houses. Mill work thereby provided a unique type of female community: a company town of young women workers. Memoirists sometimes stressed the similarity between the mill town and an educational institution. To author Lucy Larcom, once a teenage millhand, Lowell in its prime resembled "a rather selective industrial school for young people."

Millowners, however, hoped to maximize their profits for expansion. In the 1830s and 1840s, they imposed speed-ups and and wage cuts, which many employees protested. Capitalizing on the community spirit that mill life engendered, rebel workers refused, as one protest committee declared, "to add to the overflowing coffers of our employers." The labor protests had little impact on the textile industry. In the 1850s, when wages dropped again and working conditions further declined, young women mill workers from New England farms were gradually replaced by members of immigrant families. The female communities of young New England farm women at the early textile mills were a short-lived episode in labor history. Still, the mills remain the first industrial setting in which large numbers of women worked and in which a substantial minority organized to defend, in one millhand's words, "the common interests of all the laboring classes."

Rules of the School

ELIZA ANN MULFORD, 1814

Emily Vanderpoel, *Chronicles of a Pioneer School from 1792 to 1833, Being the History of Miss Sarah Pierce and Her Litchfield School* (Cambridge, MA: University Press, 1903), pp. 146–47.

Sarah Pierce's school in Litchfield, Connecticut, a thriving commercial center, catered to demands for female education among the aspiring middle class. Pierce started the school in 1792, in her dining room, to support herself. Local citizens later provided a building, and the school's reputation spread, attracting boarding students of all ages from New England and farther afield. The curriculum featured basic academics—reading, composition, writing, spelling, arithmetic, history, and geography—plus needlework, watercolors, dancing, drama, exercise, and a hefty dose of religion. Miss Pierce's school became the Litchfield Academy in 1827 and lasted until the 1840s.

The document that follows comes from the notebook of a young New Haven student, Eliza Ann Mulford, who attended the Litchfield school during the summer term of 1814, along with her sister and more than 100 other girls, mainly from New York, Connecticut, and Massachusetts. According to the school rules that Eliza copied, the institution stressed character building. Miss Pierce demanded neatness of appearance, courteous deportment, industrious behavior, pious routines, and, above all, orderly habits: As the school rules indicate, "Nothing can be well done without proper attention to regularity."

Rules for the School and Family
[Copied by Eliza Ann Mulford in 1814.]

It is expected that every young Lady who attends this School will be careful to observe the following rules.

1ˢᵗ To be always present at family prayers.

2ⁿᵈ It is hop'd that each young Lady will read a portion of scripture in private and regularly address her Maker Morning and evening. They who begin the day in prayer will probably find cause to end it in praise.

3ʳᵈ Let our Saviours maxim be follow'd at all times. Do unto others, as you would they should do unto you.

4ᵗʰ Avoid anger, Wrath and evil speaking. A tale bearer separates chief Friends.

5ᵗʰ It is expected public Worship be attended every sabbath except sickness or some unavoidable circumstance prevents, which you will dare to produce as a sufficient excuse at the day of Judgement.

6ᵗʰ It is expected that your outward deportment be grave and decent, while in the house of God and that you be more ready to hear, than give the sacrifice of fools.

7ᵗʰ The sabbath is to be kept holy throughout not wasted in sloth, frivolous conversation, light reading, or vain employment, but every moment must be employed in endeavoring to improve your own heart in doing good to others. Those who honour my sabbath, I will honour is the promise of the great and unchangeable God.

8ᵗʰ It is expected that every hour during the week be fully accomplish'd, either in useful employment or necessary recreation. Keep always in remembrance that time is a most invaluable blessing, and that for all our time but—particularly for the hours of youth and health you must give an account to God.

9ᵗʰ Every real Lady will treat her superior with due reverence, her companions with politeness, good humor she will always show, a sweet temper, a modest deportment on all occasions, never forgetting what is due to all persons in every situation.

10ᵗʰ Those hours appropriated for any particular study, must not be employed in other occupation. Nothing can be well done without proper attention to regularity & there is time enough to acquire every useful and elegant accomplishment provided order be observed.

11ᵗʰ Profusion in expenses, a want of Neatness and economy, a stupid inattention to instruction, are indications of a bad heart and must be avoided.

12ᵗʰ Each young lady must observe the particular rules of the family in which she resides.

Questions

Have you rose early enough for the duties of the morning. Have you read a portion of scripture by yourself. Have you prayed to that God in Whose hands your breath is.

Have you in all cases done unto others as you would be done by. Have been angry—Have spoke evil of any one. Have you attended public worship. Have you behaved in the house of God with that reverence due to his holy Character. Have you wasted any part of holy time by idle conversation, light reading, or sloth.

Have you wasted any time during the week. Have you shown decent and respectful behaviour to those who have the charge over you. Your parents, elders, Brothers and sisters, teachers, domestics, the aged, or people who are older than yourself. Have you been patient in acquiring your lessons. Have you been polite and good humored to your Companions. Have you been modest in your deportment, not boistrous or rude. Have you spoken the truth as all, tho it were to your hurt. Have you used the name of God irreverently or spoken any thing which is a brief of the third Commandmant. Have you spoken any indecent word or by any action discovered a want of true feminine delicacy. Have you been neat in your person, made no unnecessary trouble by carelessness in your chamber or with your clothes. Have you torn your clothes, books, or maps. Have you wasted paper, quills, or any other articles. Have you walked out without liberty. Have you combed your hair with a fine tooth comb, and cleaned your teeth every morning. Have you eaten any green fruit during the week.

A Rationale for Female Education

EMMA WILLARD, 1819

"An Address to the Public; Particularly to the Members of the Legislation of New York, Proposing a Plan for Improving Female Education" (1819), in John Lord, *The Life of Emma Willard* (New York: Appleton, 1873), pp. 76–84.

Emma Willard's ambition and talent made her the best-known female educator of her generation. In 1807, the twenty-year-old Connecticut teacher took a job at a female academy in Middlebury, Vermont, where she married a doctor twenty-eight years her senior (see Chapter 7). When John Willard's finances collapsed, Emma Willard opened a female seminary in her home. Her goal was advanced education for women that would include the subjects taught at men's colleges, such as classics and the sciences. Encouraged by some parents of her Middlebury students, she presented Governor Clinton of New York with her famous "plan" for improving female education (1819). Willard hoped to press the New York legislature to endow schools that would provide advanced education for women. Although the plan made no legislative headway, Emma Willard founded a female seminary in 1821 in Troy, New York, a boomtown destined to profit from the opening of the Erie canal. Within a decade the successful school attracted 300 students and became a spawning ground for teachers.

In the final segment of her 1819 plan, where Emma Willard set forth "the benefits of female seminaries," she combined deference with compelling arguments. The proper training of women, she contended, would counteract the "corruption" and "contagion" of wealth. Since educated women were value transmitters, the education of women would preserve and perpetuate republican government. By combating "the seduction of wealth and fashion," it would produce competent mothers. And it would train teachers to staff the common schools, where they would prove more qualified and less expensive than men, who could "add to the wealth of the nation" in other ways. Not least, Emma Willard explained, advanced education would provide an outlet for "master-spirits, who must have preeminence." Such spirits could "govern and improve the seminaries for their sex." Here, she was no doubt referring to herself.

The inquiry to which these remarks have conducted us is this: What is offered by the plan of female education here proposed, which may teach or preserve, among females of wealthy families, that purity of manners which is allowed to be so essential to national prosperity, and so necessary to the existence of a republican government?

1. Females, by having their understandings cultivated, their reasoning powers developed and strengthened, may be expected to act more from the dictates of reason, and less from those of fashion or caprice.

2. With minds thus strengthened they would be taught systems of morality, enforced by the sanctions of religion; and they might be expected to acquire juster and more enlarged views of their duty, and stronger and higher motives to its performance.

3. This plan of education offers all that can be done to preserve female youth from a contempt of useful labor. The pupils would become accustomed to it, in conjunction with the high objects of literature and the elegant pursuits of the fine arts; and it is to be hoped that, both from habit and association, they might in future life regard it as respectable.

To this it may be added that, if housewifery could be raised to a regular art and taught upon philosophical principles, it would become a higher and more interesting occupation; and ladies of fortune, like wealthy agriculturists, might find that to regulate their business was an agreeable employment.

4. The pupils might be expected to acquire a taste for moral and intellectual pleasures, which would buoy them above a passion for show and parade, and which would make them seek to gratify the natural love of superiority, by endeavoring to excel others in intrinsic merit, rather than in the extrinsic frivolities of dress, furniture, and equipage.

5. By being enlightened in moral philosophy, and in that which teaches the operations of the mind, females would be enabled to perceive the nature and extent of that influence which they possess over their children, and the obligation which this lays them under, to watch the formation of their characters with unceasing vigilance, to become their instructors, to devise plans for their improvement, to weed out the vices from their minds, and to implant and foster the virtues. And surely there is that in the maternal bosom which, when its pleadings shall be aided by education, will overcome the seductions of wealth and fashion, and will lead the mother to seek her happiness in commuting with her children and promoting their welfare, rather than in a heartless intercourse with the votaries of pleasure: especially when, with an expanded mind, she extends her views to futurity, and sees her care to her offspring rewarded by peace of conscience, the blessings of her family, the prosperity of her country, and finally with everlasting pleasure to herself and them.

Thus laudable objects and employments would be furnished for the great body of females who are not kept by poverty from excesses. But among these, as among the other sex, will be found master-spirits, who must have preeminence, at whatever price they acquire it. Domestic life cannot hold these, because they prefer to be infamous rather than obscure. To leave such without any virtuous road to eminence is unsafe to community; for not unfrequently are the secret springs of revolution set in motion by their intrigues. Such aspiring minds we will regulate by education; we will remove obstructions to the course of literature, which has heretofore been their only honorable way to distinction; and we offer them a new object worthy of their ambition—to govern and improve the seminaries for their sex.

In calling upon my patriotic countrymen to effect so noble an object, the consideration of national glory should not be overlooked. Ages have rolled away; barbarians have trodden the weaker sex beneath their feet; tyrants have robbed us of the present light of heaven, and fain [eagerly] would take its future. Nations calling themselves polite have made us the fancied idols of a ridiculous worship, and we have repaid them with ruin for their folly. But where is that wise and heroic country which has considered that our rights are sacred, though we cannot defend them? That though a weaker, we are an essential part of the body politic, whose corruption or improvement must affect the whole; and which, having thus considered, has sought to give us, by education, that rank in the scale of being to which our importance entitles us? History shows not that country. It shows many whose Legislatures have sought to improve their various vegetable productions and their breeds of useful brutes; but none whose public councils have made it an object of their deliberations to improve the character of their women. Yet, though history lifts not her finger to such a one, anticipation does. She points to a nation which, having thrown off the shackles of authority and precedent, shrinks not from schemes of improvement because other nations have not attempted them, but which, in its pride of independence, would rather lead than follow in the march of improvement—a nation wise and magnanimous to plan, enterprising to undertake, and rich in resources to execute. Does not every American exult that this country is his own? And who knows how great and good a race of men may yet arise from the forming hand of mothers enlightened by the bounty of that beloved country—to defend her liberties—to plan her future improvement—and to raise her to unparalleled glory?

Reports on Western Schools

LETTERS FROM TEACHERS, 1847

Catharine E. Beecher, *The True Remedy for the Wrongs of Woman* (Boston: Phillips, Sampson & Co., 1851), pp. 163–74.

By the 1840s, Catharine Beecher was well known for her *Treatise on Domestic Economy* (1841), for the two schools she had founded (the Hartford Female Seminary and the Western Female Institute), and for her promotion of teaching as a woman's profession. In 1846, Beecher created a "Board of National Popular Education" to raise funds to train teachers who would staff schools in new western communities. The next year she recruited and trained seventy young women, almost all from New England. They were sent to towns in Illinois, Indiana, Iowa, Wisconsin, Michigan, Tennessee, and Kentucky. These "missionary teachers" would serve not only as instructors of the young but as moral exemplars and religious leaders as well. To improve the home lives of their students, they would also distribute copies of Beecher's *Treatise on Domestic Economy*.

When the teachers reported back to Catharine Beecher, they described many obstacles: primitive environments, improper schoolrooms, scarcity of supplies, makeshift conditions, cold winters, incessant discomfort, local squabbles, and widespread impiety. "If I have not had discouragements here, I know not what the word means," an Iowa teacher reported, "This is hard work." The following letters, received from two teachers whom Beecher identified only as a Congregationalist and an Episcopalian, convey the writers' dedication to their students and their mission. Their locations in the West are unknown.

Letter to Catharine Beecher
From a Teacher

Dear Miss B——:

I address you with many pleasant and grateful recollections of the intercourse it was my privilege to enjoy with yourself and the other ladies associated with you at Hartford—a privilege that every day makes more precious.

We arrived safely, after a pleasant journey, and I am now located in this place, which is the county-town of a newly organized county. The only Church built here is a Catholic. Presbyterians, Campbellites, Baptists, and Methodists are the chief denominations. The last are trying to build a church, and have preaching once a fortnight. The sabbath is little regarded, and is more a day for diversion than devotion.

I board with a physician, and the house has only two rooms. One serves as the kitchen, eating and sitting room; the other, where I lodge, serves also as the doctor's office, and there is no time, night or day, when I am not liable to interruption.

My school embraces both sexes, and all ages from five to seventeen, and not one can read intelligibly. They have no idea of the proprieties of the schoolroom, or of study, and I am often at a loss to know what to do for them. Could you see them, your sympathies would be awakened, for there are few but what are ragged and dirty in the extreme. Though it is winter, some are without stockings, and one delicate little girl came with stockings and no shoes. The first day, I felt like having a thorough ablution of both the room and the occupants, they were so filthy.

I had to wait two weeks before I could get three broken panes mended, and a few poor benches brought in. My furniture consists now of these benches, a single board put up against the side of the room for a writing-desk, a few bricks for andirons, and a stick of wood for shovel and tongs. I have been promised a blackboard, but I find that promises are little to be relied on. The first week I took a severe cold by being obliged to keep both doors open to let out the smoke. The weather is much colder than I expected, and the houses are so poor, we felt the cold much more.

I am told they are abundantly able to support a minister, and pay a teacher; but could you see them grouped together on Sunday, you would think they could do neither. I learn that the place is considered not a healthy one; still I do not wish to leave on this account, if it is judged best for me to remain. I came expecting to make sacrifices, and suffer privations. When Sunday evening comes, I feel more than ever the want of some place of retirement, where I can join in concert with those who at this hour unite in prayer for this noble cause. Those seasons of social communion and prayer at Hartford I shall never forget; they come like balm to the spirit when oppressed with care. There is so much to do, and, where all are so ignorant, so much instruction to give, one can not but feel anxious to know what will be most profitable. . . .

Extract of Another Letter From the Same Teacher

Many thanks for your letter. . . . In reply to your questions, I would say that books might be loaned here to some extent with advantage. I have lent your *Domestic Economy* around, and have received applications for six copies from those who will pay.

I have a married woman and two of her children now attending my school as pupils. She is anxious to have me form a reading-circle, to meet once a week; but there are so many bickerings and so much gossip, I fear I shall not succeed, but I shall make the attempt.

I think *some money* would much promote my usefulness here, in purchasing suitable books to read in such a circle, and to loan; also to furnish schoolbooks to some of my poor children who can get none. Maps are needed much, and some simple apparatus, would greatly add to the attraction of the school, and the usefulness of the teacher. I have *four* from one family, and another of seventeen is coming, and none of them ever were in a school before. Something to interest and aid such would help me much. I need slates, pencils, and paper, and sometimes I would buy a pair of shoes for a poor child who has none.

There is work enough for *two* teachers here, if all who ought to come to school could be drawn in, and I think *two together* would accomplish more than *three* when located each alone. . . .

The people promised that, if I would stay, they would build me a schoolhouse; but since I have consented to remain, I hear nothing said about it. There is a great deal to be done here, and I can not but hope I may be the instrument of good to this people; and if it is but little, I shall not regret the privations or sacrifices I may suffer.

Letter to Catharine Beecher From Another Teacher

Dear Miss B———:

I arrived here the 17th of January, and opened school in a small log house. I now have forty-five pupils, one-half of whom are boys, and some of them grown up. They all seem anxious to please me, and I find no difficulty in governing them.

The inhabitants here are chiefly from North Carolina, Tennessee, and Germany. All are farmers, and their chief object is to make money. They seem desirous to have their children educated, but they differed so much about almost everything, that they could not build a schoolhouse. I was told, also, when I came that they would not pay a teacher for more than three months in a year. At first they were very suspicious, and watched me narrowly; but, through the blessing of my Heavenly Father, I have gained their good will and confidence, so that they have built me a good frame school-house, with writing-desks and a black-board, and promise to support me all the year round.

I commence school every day with reading the Bible and prayer; this was new to them, but they made no objections. The people here spend Sunday in hunting, fishing, and visiting. I have commenced a Sabbath-school and invited the parents to come with their children. They seem much pleased, and many come three and four miles. They never heard of a Sunday-school before. Last Sunday there were fifty present, and I proposed that we should have a Bible-class for the men, and that Mr. ———, a professor of religion near this place, should take charge of it, while I attended to the women and children. There being no church nearer than seven miles, the people think it too much trouble to go to it. I have persuaded them to invite the nearest clergyman to preach in my school-house next Sunday.

My greatest trials here are the want of religious privileges, the difficulty of sending to the distant post-office, the entire want of social sympathy, and the manner in which I am obliged to live. I board where there are eight children and the parents, and only two rooms in the house. I must do as the family do about washing, as there is but one basin and no place to go to wash but out the door. I have not enjoyed the luxury of either lamp or candle, their only light being a cup of grease with a rag for a wick. Evening is my only time to write, but this kind of light makes such a disagreeable smoke and smell I cannot bear it, and do without light except the fire. I occupy a room with three of the children and a niece who boards here. The other room serves as a kitchen, parlor, and bedroom for the rest of the family.

I have read your *Domestic Economy* through to the family, one chapter a day. They like it, and have adopted some of your suggestions in regard both to *order* and to *health*. They used to drink coffee three times a day. Now they use it only once a day. Their bread used to be heavy and half-baked, but I made yeast by the receipt [recipe] in your book, and thus made some good bread. They were much pleased with it, and I have made such ever since.

The people here are *very* ignorant; very few of them can either read or write, but they wish to have their children taught. They spend Sunday in visiting and idleness, and the fact that I kept Sunday-school for them without pay convinced them that my real object was to do good. The people in the settlements around are anxious to have more of the teachers come out. They have sent for Miss H., who came out with me, but she was engaged. I was sorry, as it would have been a comfort to have had one friend within reaching distance.

When I came here I intended to stay only one term; but the people urged me so much to remain, and have done so much in building me a school-house, that I concluded to stay longer. I did not leave my home to seek pleasure, wealth, or fame, and I do believe my Heavenly Father will bless my labors here, even if I never see the fruit. The people seem to like me, say their children never behaved so well before, were present at my examination, and like the Eastern way of keeping school.

Extract of Another Letter From the Same [Teacher]

Your kind letter was received last Thursday, and would have been immediately answered, but I was sent for to visit a sick child. The parents, being Catholic, were much alarmed lest it should die unbaptized. I explained as well as I could the nature and object of baptism, succeeded in quieting their fears, and, as they urged it, I staid all night in the cabin, with only one room, holding nine grown persons besides two children and the sick infant. There was no window, and they kept both doors shut till I persuaded them to leave a small opening to one door. In the morning I walked through the wet prairie and thus took a heavy cold, and for three weeks have been unable to use my eyes.

As soon as I could I took the draft you sent me to the nearest large town and purchased the articles you directed. Ever since I have enjoyed the luxury of bathing and candlelight, and, with my screen, I can be alone at least in a corner. I can never sufficiently thank you for your kindness in thus adding to my comfort and usefulness in a strange land. I am much pleased at the prospect of the books you have sent to me, and the children are highly delighted. Many of my scholars are now sick, and my own health is not so good as it was, as I have watched a good deal with my scholars who were sick of the scarlet and winter fevers. There is a broad field of usefulness here, large enough for all who wish to come. I have never regretted that I came, and if I am made the instrument of bringing *only one* to the knowledge of the truth, I shall be amply repaid for the sacrifices I have made in this noble cause.

A Mount Holyoke Diary

SUSAN TOLMAN, 1846–1847

Edward Hitchcock, *The Power of Christian Benevolence Illustrated in the Life and Labors of Mary Lyon* (Northampton, MA: Hopkins, Bridgeman, and Co., 1851), pp. 360–67.

Mary Lyon of Massachusetts (1797–1849) developed a passion for education early in life, when she alternated teaching terms with academy study. In 1828, she joined her friend Zilpah Grant at the latter's Ipswich Female Seminary and, five years later, discovered her life mission: the establishment of an endowed female seminary in the Connecticut River Valley. Lyon began a strenuous search for funds, canvassing among New England women. When criticized for her zeal, she responded, "I am doing a great work. I cannot come down." In 1837, Mount Holyoke Female Seminary in South Hadley welcomed eighty advanced students, ages seventeen and up, to a three-year course of study. Fees were kept low by having the students perform domestic chores.

Mount Holyoke became not only a teacher-training institute and a model for other seminaries, but a hotbed of religious zeal. Many graduates became missionaries, at home and abroad. Within the seminary, Mary Lyon assumed the role of minister and resident revivalist; the school kept careful count of "professed Christians" (those who experienced religious conversion). When teacher Susan Tolman recorded the events of the academic year 1846–1847 in a school "diary," or institutional record, she captured the reverence for Mary Lyon and the spirit of religious fervor that permeated seminary life. Like Sarah Pierce and Catharine Beecher, Lyon also urged the formation of "systematic habits" (see Tolman's entry for January 28). At the end of the school year, Susan Tolman left to become a missionary to Ceylon (now Sri Lanka). Mount Holyoke remained a seminary until 1888, when it was accredited as a women's college.

October 3, 1846.—To-day, the names of those who are professors of religion* and those who are not were taken. More than ninety, nearly half of our family, are classed with those who have no hope. May we, as a band of teachers, be faithful to these precious souls.

---

*Those who had experienced religious conversion.

October 10.—Miss Lyon is taking the Book of Proverbs in course for morning devotions, and has invited all to read it with her. She does not appear to be as well this year as last. Her extra exertion during vacation nearly exhausted her. An infirmity which must be very trying has recently fastened itself upon her, as we fear permanently. She has become so deaf that it is difficult for her to hear ordinary conversation.

October 14.—Our weekly religious meetings commenced this evening. Miss Lyon met with the Christians.* She spoke of her deep emotion in looking upon so many *professed* followers of Christ, of the possibility that some might be deceived, and then, in her own earnest, irresistible manner, urged upon each a thorough self-examination.

October 21.—We must again speak of Miss Lyon's failing health. She has taken a severe cold, which has settled upon her lungs. It is with difficulty she can speak for any length of time.

November 12.—To-day, our second missionary meeting was held. It was one of more than ordinary interest. Letters were read from several correspondents on missionary ground. The Nestorian mission was dwelt upon. A young lady was introduced dressed in Persian costume.

December 1.—Rev. Mr. H. conducted our morning devotions; we hope he will continue to do so until Miss Lyon is able to meet with us.

December 6.—Miss Lyon is so far recovered that she came into the hall this afternoon, and talked to the middle class about light reading. She urged them to lay aside entirely every thing that could be classed under this head. If they had any with them, she wished they would burn it—send it home—or seal it up and put it in the bottom of their trunks, there to remain untouched.

December 9.—To-day Miss Lyon invited to her room those whose hearts were moved by the Spirit's teachings. Nineteen were present—most seemed deeply impressed. We can but feel that God is in our midst. Christians are beginning to pray more earnestly. Many seem prostrate in the dust before the awful presence of Him who searcheth the secrets of every soul.

December 12.—Truly this has been a day of blessing. Eight are now expressing a hope in Christ. The interest appears to be deepening and extending every hour. Thus far, those who have indulged hope have been principally from the middle class. In fact, the interest seemed to commence there with a few praying hearts.

December 14.—Still the interest is increasing. It goes from heart to heart silently, yet powerfully. The whole house is as still as on the Sabbath. Every footstep is light—every voice is hushed. Several have asked to be excused from school exercises, so intense are their feelings. Many in the senior class without hope begin to inquire for Him who is the way, the truth, and the life.

December 15.—There are now more than twenty who hope they have found a Savior precious as he never was before. Five of the number are from the senior class. Some of the most careless are awakened, and anxiously inquire, "What shall I do to be saved?". . .

---

*Again, those who had experienced religious conversion.

January 4, 1847.—Day of fasting and prayer for the conversion of the world. Miss Lyon met the whole school in the hall. After some general remarks, she proceeded to suggest subjects of thought and prayer. We trust prevailing prayer has ascended here to-day from many hearts—for ourselves—for you—for our country—for a dying world.

January 28.—Miss Lyon commenced her lectures upon the subject of missions this morning. She read passages of Scripture, and remarked generally upon the duty of Christian benevolence. She then alluded to the reward to be expected in consequence of denying ourselves for Christ's sake: she differed from some who say, one is never poorer for giving to the Lord. "If," said she, "they mean poorer in a *spiritual* point of view, I agree with them, but not when they say poorer in property; for I do believe the Christian ought to give to the Lord, so as really to feel the need of what he gives—a precious reward to suffer for Christ." She seemed, if possible, more earnest and animated than ever. O that there were many more who would, in like manner, present to Christians the claims resting upon them! who would, at the same time, be themselves examples!

Our teachers' business meeting was held this evening. Miss Lyon said she had suffered much from want of systematic habits, and urged it upon us that we should accustom ourselves to a systematic division of our time and duties. She knew our interruptions were many. There were many *little* duties to be looked after, and so it must always be with ladies. "I do really think," said she, in her humorous way, "that it requires more discipline of mind to be a lady, than it does to be a gentleman. The latter has little of the minutiæ of every-day life to attend to. He can rise in the morning and drive into his business. But it is not so with the latter, nor would I have it so."

February 2.—Miss Lyon has continued her remarks upon the subject of missions for several mornings. We will try and give you the mere outline. Your own minds can supply the rest, better than our poor pen.

"*First.* We must do all Christ requires of us; because a reward is promised to him who gives a cup of cold water: if we have the means to do more, we must not think it sufficient to do this, and only this. *Secondly.* We must feel that we are as unworthy to give in the name of Christ as we are to receive. *Thirdly.* When we give the most with the most self-denial, then do we most deeply feel our unworthiness. When we do so contribute for Christ's sake, then are we brought into a blessed sympathy with his *poverty*—his sufferings. "O wonderful, wonderful," she exclaimed, "this work in which we may share! How would angels delight to have a part in it! And shall we hinder it by unwillingness to give?". . .

February 13.—Miss Lyon spoke to the young ladies upon the formation of correct habits. "I want you, young ladies," said she, "to form good habits. You have no time or strength to spare in overcoming bad ones."

February 15.—At our morning exercises, Miss Lyon addressed those who have no hope of heaven, no place to lay up their treasure. She said she had thought much of the passage, "I go to prepare a place for you." "Yes, there are many, many mansions, but to some of you none of them belong. This work of salvation is an individual work. Each must do it for herself. No friend can enter the strait gate for you. You must not only leave all behind, but enter willing to follow Christ wherever he may lead. 'If thy right hand offend thee, cut it off; if thy right eye offend thee, pluck it out.'"

March 11.—At our morning exercises, Miss Lyon has commenced the character of Christ, under the several titles applied to him in Scripture. This morning she remarked upon the passage, "I am the bread of life."

March 18.—Our spring examinations are closed. They were interesting and well sustained. To-morrow evening we are to have a social party. About fifty are invited from town. A few of Miss Lyon's friends from abroad are here. These with our own family will make quite a gathering.

March 19.—Our invited guests and young ladies assembled in the parlors about seven o'clock this evening, where we had a pleasant, social time. About nine o'clock we repaired to the seminary hall, where we had calisthenics, music, and refreshments. Miss Lyon appeared to enjoy the evening exceedingly.

March 30.—Our missionary contributions were reported to-day. Whole amount (first contribution of the year), $649.50.

May 19.—Within a short time letters have been received from correspondents in Persia, India, China, Sandwich Islands, and the far west; all of them full of glad tidings. Could you but witness, dear sisters, how much interest these journals of yours add to our missionary meetings, you would feel yourselves richly rewarded for all the labor they cost you.

June 18.—In our teachers' prayer-meeting this evening, Miss Lyon spoke of a little note received from Mrs. B. She proposed we should mention the names of those who have been connected with us, and are now on missionary ground. We each mentioned one or more of them, until all your names were repeated. We then united in prayer in your behalf. Miss Lyon led. In speaking of you afterwards, she said, "Let us each be faithful, and we may be but a step behind them in heaven." If *any one* has a bright crown there, it will be our dear Miss Lyon. Numbers in heathen lands will rise up and call her blessed.

June 22.—This afternoon, as well as every Friday afternoon, Miss Lyon claims as hers to address the young ladies upon general themes. Her subject the last time was, simplicity in dress. She spoke of different fashions, and advised that all who would dress simple and in good taste should avoid extremes. She was very animated and interesting. "Why, young ladies," said she, "what would you think to see a gentleman dressed in low neck and short sleeves?" This afternoon, her subject was, true politeness. "True politeness," said she, "consists more in avoiding than in doing many things." She dwelt particularly upon respect due to the aged.

June 29.—The subject of Miss Lyon's remarks this afternoon was conversation. She dwelt upon the importance of being able to converse with ease and propriety; mentioned some things to be observed, and some others to be avoided. "Always be observing," she remarked, "and you will always have something to say worth the saying."

July 23.—In the morning Miss Lyon said she addressed many who were soon to go out as teachers, and she did ardently desire that they might carry with them much of the spirit of Christ. "To have such a spirit," said she, "you must have clear views of the plan of salvation, of the worth of souls; must know when to speak and when to forbear."

August 5.—The scenes of our present school year have to-day closed. The anniversary occasion was one of more than ordinary interest. Nearly forty of the senior class of 1844 and 1845 met here by class appointment and invitation from Miss Lyon. She was delighted to see together so many of her former pupils. After we returned from public exercises in church, she stood in her accustomed place, and gave us a few parting words as a school. A large number of the young ladies' friends from abroad passed the evening with us. Early to-morrow morning our happy family will be scattered, no more to be united.

Rules of the Mill

LOWELL AND LANCASTER, 1820–1840

Edith Abbott, *Women in Industry* (New York: Appleton, 1910), pp. 374–77.

As the first large-scale factories in the United States, the New England textile mills depended on the imposition of order, regularity, and discipline. Female operatives, who worked twelve- to thirteen-hour days, six days a week, spent almost all of their days in a large complex of mill buildings and boarding houses. Their time was controlled not only by the factory bell but by additional regulations, such as curfews and compulsory church attendance. A rule violator might find herself without an "honorable discharge," which certified good behavior and facilitated reemployment; in effect, she was blacklisted from mill work. Surprisingly, the mill workers voiced few objections to the company or boardinghouse regulations, perhaps because they were accustomed to long working hours and supervision at home. Indeed, they seemed to appreciate a unique benefit of mill life, the company of their fellow workers.

In her 1913 history of women in industry, Edith Abbott published the Lowell Company rules of the 1830s and the regulations of a Lancaster, Massachusetts, boardinghouse in the 1820s, which follow. Labor discipline, as embodied in the Lowell rules, was intended to ensure productivity and corporate profit. Compulsory boardinghouse residence provided low-cost accommodations but, as the Lancaster regulations reveal, bound the workers in subtle ways to their jobs: the better rooms and table places were assigned according to seniority in the mill.

The Lowell Manufacturing Company's Rules and Regulations

(1830–1840)[1]

The overseers are to be punctually in their Rooms at the starting of the Mill, and not to be absent unnecessarily during working hours. They are to see that all those

---

[1] From the appendix to Seth Luther, "Address to the Working Men of New England" (pamphlet, 3rd ed., Philadelphia, 1836). [Abbott's footnote]

employed in their Rooms are in their places in due season; they may grant leave of absence to those employed under them, when there are spare hands in the Room to supply their places; otherwise they are not to grant leave of absence, except in cases of absolute necessity.

All persons in the employ of the Lowell Manufacturing Company are required to observe the Regulations of the overseer of the Room where they are employed; they are not to be absent from work without his consent, except in cases of sickness, and then they are to send him word of the cause of their absence.

They are to board in one of the Boarding-Houses belonging to the Company, and to conform to the regulations of the House where they board; they are to give information at the Counting-Room, of the place where they board, when they begin; and also give notice whenever they change their boarding-place.

The Company will not employ any one who is habitually absent from public worship on the Sabbath.

It is considered a part of the engagement that each person remains twelve months if required; and all persons intending to leave the employment of the Company are to give two weeks' notice of their intention to their Overseer, and their engagement is not considered as fulfilled unless they comply with this Regulation.

The Pay Roll will be made up to the last Saturday of every month, and the payment made to the Carpet Mill the following Saturday, and the Cotton Mill the succeeding Tuesday, when every person will be expected to pay their board.

The Company will not continue to employ any person who shall be wanting in proper respect to the females employed by the Company, or who shall smoke within the Company's premises, or be guilty of inebriety, or other improper conduct.

The Tenants of the Boarding-Houses are not to board or permit any part of their houses to be occupied by any person, except those in the employ of the Company.

They will be considered answerable for any improper conduct in their Houses, and are not to permit their Boarders to have company at unseasonable hours.

The doors must be closed at ten o'clock in the evening, and no person admitted after that time without some reasonable excuse.

The keepers of the Boarding-Houses must give an account of the number, names and employment of the Boarders when required, and report the names of such as are guilty of any improper conduct.

The Buildings, and yards about them, must be kept clean and in good order, and if they are injured otherwise than from ordinary use, all necessary repairs will be made and charged to the occupant.

It is desirable that the families of those who live in the Houses, as well as the Boarders, who have not had the Kine Pox, should be vaccinated; which will be done at the expense of the Company for such as wish it.

Some suitable chamber in the House must be reserved, and appropriated for the use of the sick, so that others may not be under the necessity of sleeping in the same room.

No one will be continued as a Tenant who shall suffer ashes to be put into any place other than the place made to receive them, or shall, by any carelessness in the use of fire, or lights, endanger the Company's property.

These regulations are considered a part of the contract with the persons entering into the employment of the Lowell Manufacturing Company.

Poignaud and Plant Boarding House at Lancaster[1]

(1820–1830)

Rules and Regulations to be attended to and followed by the Young Persons who come to Board in this House:

Rule first: Each one to enter the house without unnecessary noise or confusion, and hang up their bonnet, shawl, coat, etc., etc., in the entry.

Rule second: Each one to have their place at the table during meals, the two which have worked the greatest length of time in the Factory to sit on each side of the head of the table, so that all new hands will of course take their seats lower down, according to the length of time they have been here.

Rule third: It is expected that order and good manners will be preserved at table during meals—and at all other times either upstairs or down.

Rule fourth: There is no unnecessary dirt to be brought into the house by the Boarders, such as apple cores or peels, or nut shells, etc.

Rule fifth: Each border is to take her turn in making the bed and sweeping the chamber in which she sleeps.

Rule sixth: Those who have worked the longest in the Factory are to sleep in the North Chamber and the new hands will sleep in the South Chamber.

Rule seventh: As a lamp will be lighted every night upstairs and placed in a lanthorn, it is expected that no boarder will take a light into the chambers.

Rule eighth: The doors will be closed at ten o'clock at night, winter and summer, at which time each boarder will be expected to retire to bed.

Rule ninth: Sunday being appointed by our Creator as a Day of Rest and Religious Exercises, it is expected that all boarders will have sufficient discretion as to pay suitable attention to the day, and if they cannot attend to some place of Public Worship they will keep within doors and improve their time in reading, writing, and in other valuable and harmless employment.

---

[1]From the collection of Poignaud and Plant papers in the Lancaster Town Library. There is no date in this paper, but it clearly belongs to the decade 1820–30. [Abbott's footnote]

A Letter from Lowell

HARRIET FARLEY, 1844

The Lowell Offering, Written, Edited and Published by Female Operatives Employed in the Mills (Lowell, MA: Misses Curtis and Farley, 1844), pp. 169–72.

The *Lowell Offering*, a monthly journal full of fiction, poems, and essays, was written and produced solely by mill workers. Upbeat and appealing, the *Offering* defended the social respectability of operatives and promoted their literary achievements. The journal also served the interests of the millowners who subsidized it. It drew favorable attention to Lowell's unique labor force, boosted worker morale, denied that mill work was degrading, and defended employers against charges of exploitation. These themes appear in Harriet Farley's "Letters from Susan," a fictional correspondence between an operative and a friend at home. A minister's daughter, Harriet Farley entered the mills as a teenager. In 1842, after the *Offering* began publishing her work, a millowner paid her a stipend to take charge of the journal, along with co-editor Harriot Curtis, an author and former mill operative.

Farley's "Letters from Susan," which convey the experiences of a young New Hampshire girl as she arrives in Lowell and adjusts to mill life, give a complete account of living arrangements, social life, and work regulations. The chatty tone of "Susan"'s letters mimics that of real letters written by mill workers of the 1830s and 1840s to relatives and friends at home.* The letters also convey the *Offering*'s unstated editorial policy: to defend the reputation of employers. "Letters to Susan" appeared in 1844, just as dissident workers formed a female labor reform movement to protest speed-ups and wage decreases. In the following letter, "Susan" describes her work day and discusses a vital issue: Were mill workers content?

Lowell, April——

Dear Mary:

In my last [letter] I told you I would write again, and say more of my life here; and this I will now attempt to do.

---

*For the correspondence of mill workers, see Thomas Dublin, ed., *Farm and Factory: The Mill Experience and Women's Lives in New England 1830–1860* (New York: Columbia University Press, 1981).

I went into the mill to work a few days after I wrote to you. It looked very pleasant at first, the rooms were so light, spacious, and clean, the girls so pretty and neatly dressed, and the machinery so brightly polished or nicely painted. The plants in the windows, or on the overseer's bench or desk, gave a pleasant aspect to things. You will wish to know what work I am doing. I will tell you of the different kinds of work.

There is, first, the carding-room, where the cotton flies most, and the girls get the dirtiest. But this is easy, and the females are allowed time to go out at night before the bell rings—on Saturday night at least, if not on all other nights. Then there is the spinning-room, which is very neat and pretty. In this room are the spinners and doffers. The spinners watch the frames; keep them clean, and the threads mended if they break. The doffers take off the full bobbins, and put on the empty ones. They have nothing to do in the long intervals when the frames are in motion, and can go to their boarding-houses, or do any thing else that they like. In some of the factories the spinners do their own doffing, and when this is the case they work no harder than the weavers. These last have the hardest time of all—or can have, if they choose to take charge of three or four looms, instead of the one pair which is the allotment. And they are the most constantly confined. The spinners and dressers have but the weavers to keep supplied, and then their work can stop. The dressers never work before breakfast, and they stay out a great deal in the afternoons. The drawers-in, or girls who draw the threads through the harnesses, also work in the dressing-room, and they all have very good wages—better than the weavers who have but the usual work. The dressing-rooms are very neat, and the frames move with a gentle undulating motion which is really graceful. But these rooms are kept very warm, and are disagreeably scented with the "sizing," or starch, which stiffens the "beams," or unwoven webs. There are many plants in these rooms, and it is really a good green-house for them. The dressers are generally quite tall girls, and must have pretty tall minds too, as their work requires much care and attention.

I could have had work in the dressing-room, but chose to be a weaver; and I will tell you why. I disliked the closer air of the dressing-room, though I might have become accustomed to that. I could not learn to dress so quickly as I could to weave, nor have work of my own so soon, and should have had to stay with Mrs. C. two or three weeks before I could go in at all, and I did not like to be "lying upon my oars" so long. And, more than this, when I get well learned I can have extra work, and make double wages, which you know is quite an inducement with some.

Well, I went into the mill, and was put to learn with a very patient girl—a clever old maid. I should be willing to be one myself if I could be as good as she is. You cannot think how odd every thing seemed to me. I wanted to laugh at every thing, but did not know what to make sport of first. They set me to threading shuttles, and tying weaver's knots, and such things, and now I have improved so that I can take care of one loom. I could take care of two if I only had eyes in the back part of my head, but I have not got used to "looking two ways of a Sunday" yet.

At first the hours seemed very long, but I was so interested in learning that I endured it very well; and when I went out at night the sound of the mill was in my ears, as of crickets, frogs, and jewsharps, all mingled together in strange discord. After that it seemed as though cotton-wool was in my ears, but now I do not mind it at all. You know that people learn to sleep with the thunder of Niagara in their ears, and a cotton mill is no worse, though you wonder that we do not have to hold our breath in such a noise.

It makes my feet ache and swell to stand so much, but I suppose I shall get accustomed to that too. The girls generally wear old shoes about their work, and you know nothing is easier; but they almost all say that when they have worked here a year or two they have to procure shoes a size or two larger than before they came. The right hand, which is the one used in stopping and starting the loom, becomes larger than the left; but in other respects the factory is not detrimental to a young girl's appearance. Here they look delicate, but not sickly; they laugh at those who are much exposed, and get pretty brown; but I, for one, had rather be brown than pure white. I never saw so many pretty looking girls as there are here. Though the number of men is small in proportion there are many marriages here, and a great deal of courting. I will tell you of this last sometime.

You wish to know minutely of our hours of labor. We go in at five o'clock; at seven we come out to breakfast; at half-past seven we return to our work, and stay until half-past twelve. At one, or quarter-past one four months in the year, we return to our work, and stay until seven at night. Then the evening is all our own, which is more than some laboring girls can say, who think nothing is more tedious than a factory life.

When I first came here, which was the last of February, the girls ate their breakfast before they went to their work. The first of March they came out at the present breakfast hour, and the twentieth of March they ceased to "light up" the rooms, and come out between six and seven o'clock.

You ask if the girls are contented here: I ask you, if you know of *any one* who is perfectly contented. Do you remember the old story of the philosopher, who offered a field to the person who was contented with his lot; and, when one claimed it, he asked him why, if he was so perfectly satisfied, he wanted his field. The girls here are not contented; and there is no disadvantage in their situation which they do not perceive as quickly, and lament as loudly, as the sternest opponents of the factory system do. They would scorn to say they were contented, if asked the question; for it would compromise their Yankee spirit—their pride, penetration, independence, and love of "freedom and equality" to say that they were *contented* with such a life as this. Yet, withal, they are cheerful. I never saw a happier set of beings. They appear blithe in the mill, and out of it. If you see one of them, with a very long face, you may be sure it is because she has heard bad news from home, or because her beau has vexed her. But, if it is a Lowell trouble, it is because she has failed in getting off as many "sets" or "pieces" as she intended to have done; or because she had a sad "break-out," or "break-down," in her work, or something of that sort.

You ask if the work is not disagreeable. Not when one is accustomed to it. It tried my patience sadly at first, and does now when it does not run well; but, in general, I like it very much. It is easy to do, and does not require very violent exertion, as much of our farm work does.

You also ask how I get along with the girls here. Very well indeed; only we came near having a little flurry once. You know I told you I lodged in the "long attic." Well, a little while ago, there was a place vacated in a pleasant lower chamber. Mrs. C. said that it was my "chum's" turn to go down stairs to lodge, unless she would waive her claim in favor of me. You must know that here they get up in the world by getting down, which is what the boys in our debating society used to call a paradox.* Clara, that is the girl's name, was not at all disposed to give up her rights, but maintained them staunchly. I had nothing to do about it—the girls in the lower room liked me, and disliked Clara, and were determined that it should not be at all pleasant weather there if she did come. Mrs. C. was in a dilemma. Clara's turn came first. The other two girls in the chamber were sisters, and would not separate, so they were out of the question. I wanted to go, and knew Clara would not be happy with them. But I thought what was my duty to do. She was not happy now, and would not be if deprived of her privilege. She had looked black at me for several days, and slept with her face to the wall as many nights. I went up to her and said, "Clara, take your things down into the lower chamber, and tell the girls that *I will not come.* It is your turn now, and mine will come in good time."

Clara was mollified in an instant. "No," said she; "I will not go now. They do not wish me to come, and I had rather stay here." After this we had quite a contest—I trying to persuade Clara to go, and she trying to persuade me, and I "*got beat.*" So now I have a pleasanter room, and am quite a favorite with all the girls. They have given me some pretty plants, and they go out with me whenever I wish it, so that I feel quite happy.

You think we must live very nice here to have plum-cake, &c. The plain-cake, and crackers, and such things as the bakers bring upon the corporations, are not as nice as we have in the country, and I presume are much cheaper. I seldom eat any thing that is not cooked in the family. I should not like to tell you the stories they circulate here about the bakers, unless I *knew* that they were true. Their brown bread is the best thing that I have tasted of their baking.

You see that I have been quite *minute* in this letter, though I hardly liked your showing the former to old Deacon Gale, and 'Squire Smith, and those old men. It makes me feel afraid to write you all I should like to, when I think so many eyes are to pore over my humble sheet. But if their motives are good, and they can excuse all defects, why I will not forbid.

'Squire Smith wishes to know what sort of men our superintendents are. I know very well what he thinks of them, and what their reputation is up our way. I am not personally acquainted with any of them; but, from what I hear, I have a good opinion of them. I suppose they are not faultless, neither are those whom they superintend; but they are not the overbearing tyrants which many suppose them to be. The abuse of them, which I hear, is so very low that I think it must be unjust and untrue; and I do frequently hear them spoken of as *men*—whole-hearted full-souled men. Tell 'Squire Smith they are not what he would be in their places—that they treat their operatives better than he does his "hired girls," and associate with them on terms of as much equality. But I will tell you who are almost universally unpopular: the "runners," as they are called, or counting-room boys. I suppose they are little whipper-snappers who will grow better as they grow older.

---

*The better-paid workers labored on the lower floors of the mill. Similarly, the workers with seniority acquired the better rooms in the boardinghouse, usually those on the lower floors.

My paper is filling up, and I must close by begging your pardon for speaking of the Methodists as having lost their simplicity of attire. It was true, nevertheless, for I have not seen one of the old "Simon Pure" Methodist bonnets since I have been here. But they may be as consistent as other denominations. Had few of us follow in the steps of the primitive Christians.

Yours as ever,
Susan

A Spirit of Protest

THE *VOICE OF INDUSTRY*, 1846

The *Voice of Industry* (Lowell, Massachusetts), March 13, April 24, May 15, and September 11, 1846.

Unlike the *Lowell Offering*, the *Voice of Industry* was a voice of protest. Originally an organ of the New England Workingman's Association, the newspaper moved to Lowell in the 1840s during a period of labor unrest. Dissident mill workers had formed the Lowell Female Labor Reform Association to protest speed-ups, stretch-outs, and reduced wages, and to demand a ten-hour day. In 1846, when the Female Labor Reform Association bought its press and type, the *Voice* became the mouthpiece of the rebel mill workers—about one-third of the Lowell labor force. Like the *Offering*, the *Voice* denounced those who "looked down" on mill operatives. Unlike the *Offering*, it also denounced mill-owners, capitalists, and paternalism. The *Voice* spoke until 1848, by which time the labor reform movement had capsized.

The following pieces are a sampling of *Voice of Industry* offerings from its peak year, 1846, when labor protest raged. The letters and articles convey the workers' rising class consciousness, their pride in the labor reform movement, their commitment to the sisterhood of working women, and their hope for "unity of labor." Two pieces (May 15 and September 11) denounce the "stretch-out," a tactic of giving operatives more machines to manage and then reducing the wage paid per piece produced. The unsigned article of September 11 was probably the work of Sarah Bagley, a mill worker and labor reform leader who was part of the *Voice of Industry* publishing committee. The final selection, a reprint of a letter to a Boston newspaper, suggests the interest of the rebel workers in the oft-maligned cause of women's rights.

March 13, 1846

The Female Department

NOTICE

The Female Labor Reform Association will meet every Tuesday evening, at 8 o'clock, at their Reading Room, 76 Central Street, to transact all business pertaining to the Association, and to devise means by which to promote the common interests of all the Laboring Classes. Also to discuss all subjects which shall come before the meeting. Every *Female* who realizes the great necessity of a *Reform* and improvement in the condition of the worthy, toiling classes, and who would wish to place woman in that elevated status intellectually and morally which a bountiful Creator designed her to occupy in the scale of being, is most *cordially* invited to attend and give her influence on the side of *virtue* and *suffering humanity.*

Huldah J. Stone, Sec'y

April 24, 1846

To the Female Labor Reform Association In Manchester

SISTER OPERATIVES:

As I am now in the "City of Spindles," out of employment, I have taken the liberty to occupy a few of your leisure moments in addressing the members of your Association, and pardon me for giving you a few brief hints of my own experiences as a factory Operative, before proceeding to make some remarks upon the glorious cause in which you are so arduously engaged. It would be useless to attempt to portray the hardships and privations which are daily endured, for all that have toiled within the factory walls, must be well acquainted with the present system of labor, which can be properly termed slavery.

I am a peasant's daughter, and my lot has been cast in the society of the humble laborer. I was drawn from the home of my childhood at an early age, and necessity obliged me to seek employment in the Factory. . . . I have heard with the deepest interest, of your flourishing Association of which you are members, and it rejoices my heart to see so many of you contending for your rights, and making efforts to elevate the condition of your fellow brethren, and raising them from their oppressed and degraded condition, and seeing rights restored which god and Nature designed them to enjoy. Do you possess the principles of Christianity? Then do not remain silent; but seek to ameliorate the condition of every fellow being. Engage laboriously and earnestly in the work, until you see your desires accomplished. Let the proud aristocrat who has tyrannized over your rights with oppressive severity, see that there is ambition and enterprise among the "spindles," and show a determination to have your plans fully executed. Use prudence and discretion in all your ways; act independently and no longer be a slave to petty tyrants, who, if they have an opportunity, will encroach upon your privileges.

Some say that "Capital will take good care of labor," but don't believe it; don't trust them. Is it not plain, that they are trying to deceive the public, by telling them that your task is easy and pleasant, and that there is no need of reform? Too many are destitute of feeling and sympathy, and it is a great pity that they are not obliged to toil one year, and then they would be glad to see the "Ten Hour Petition" brought before the Legislature. This is plain, but true language.

Probably you meet with many faithless and indifferent ones. If you have a spark of philanthropy burning within your bosom, show them the errors of their ways; make them understand it; tell them that it is through the influence of the laboring community that these things are to be accomplished. . . .

Read and patronize the *Voice*, and circulate the "Ten Hour Petition" among all classes, and may God strengthen you in your efforts; may you continue on in courage and perseverence until oppression and servitude may be entirely extinguished from our land, and thus, do honor to yourselves, and good to your country.

A Lowell Factory Girl

May 15, 1846

You Cannot Unite

We are met with this argument at almost every step. But we say to you we can, we have made an experiment and it has been successful. Some two months since, a plan was proposed by the Massachusetts Corporation, to have the weavers tend four looms and reduce the wages one cent on a piece. Some of their number thought that as a protection had been given to industry, that their employers had not applied, they would take the liberty to see to the matter themselves.

A meeting was called and a President and Secretary appointed to carry out the proposed measure of "protective industry." Next in order, a Committee of three was appointed to draw up a pledge—it was presented and unanimously adopted. It reads as follows:

"In view of the rapid increase of labor without a corresponding remuneration, therefore, we the weavers of No. 2, Massachusetts Corporation, resolve, that we will not allow ourselves to be physically taxed again, to add to the already overflowing coffers of our employers—that we will not work under the proposed reduction, embracing a fourth loom and receive a cent less per piece.

Resolved, That we will not tend a fourth loom (except to oblige each other) unless we receive the same pay per piece as on three, and that we will use our influence to prevent others from pursuing a course which has always had a tendency to reduce our wages.

This we most solemnly pledge ourselves to observe, in evidence of which, we hereunto affix our names.

Resolved, That any one giving her name, and violating this pledge, shall be published in the *Voice of Industry*, as a traitor, and receive the scorn and reproach of her associates."

It has the signature of every, or nearly every job weaver on the corporation, and has been kept inviolate.

The operatives *can* unite, and they will yet give evidence to their employers, that "Union is strength."

September 11, 1846

Hints to Operatives

It has been said that this is the "age of acquisitiveness"; to learn the truth of this, we have but to take a look at our own city; here we behold in these huge piles of brick and mortar, teeming with breathing humanity, the monster avarice, with jaws distended, ready to seize his poor deluded victims and sacrifice them upon the altar of mammon.

The capitalists are not the only ones who worship at this shrine, but many of those who are helping to fill their coffers, which are now full to overflowing, are zealous devotees and blindly worship the shining dust. . . .

We frequently hear of girls who tend extra work, and, in fact, one said to us a short time since, that "she dreaded to go into the mill the next day"; upon asking her why, her reply was, "because I am to tend three looms." But why do you take the third loom?" we asked. Her answer was "I can make a little more." There you have it again, dollars and cents; and yet this same girl cannot work more than half the time, but is obliged to leave the mill and go into the country to regain her health.

But this is not all that is to be considered; should you be successful in doing this extra work, and in working by the "piece," be enabled to lay up a little more lucre in store, are you sure it will be the best policy? Your employers will, as they have ever done, take advantage of this oversight, by and by, "wages will be reduced," and you will be obliged to work harder, and perhaps take the fourth loom (as was tried by one corporation in this city) to make the same wages that you now do with two; how long will it take, in this way, to reduce yourselves to the same state of starvation and misery, which now stares in the face the sons and daughters of toil, the other side of the Atlantic? Be assured that if you do not live to witness it, the time is not far distant when those who labor in the mills will (as is the case with many now) earn barely enough to purchase the necessaries of life by working hard, thirteen hours a day; recollect that those who worked here before you did less work, and were better paid for it than you are, and there are others to come after you, whom it would be well to bear in mind. We must not live for self *altogether*, but have the good of mankind in view; it is this selfish feeling in all classes of the community that begets all the poverty and crime; the rich oppress the poor, the poor, not being able to retaliate upon the rich, oppress one another, and literally make a hell of what the Almighty intended should be a foretaste of that better land. . . .

March 13, 1846

Reprint of a Letter from Ellen Munroe To the Editor of the Boston Bee

Sir—

I have observed that it is a common practice, among Editors, to fill their papers with advice to women, and not infrequently, with ill concealed taunts of woman's weakness. . . .

It may be, that most women are so dwarfed and weakened, that they believe that dressing, cooking, and loving . . . make up the whole of life; But Nature still asserts her rights, and there will always be those too strong to be satisfied, with a dress, a pudding, or a beau, though they may take each in turn, as a portion of life. I speak not now of the distinguished of either sex; they form a bright relief in the otherwise dark picture. Neither do I suppose that there are no exceptions, perhaps many, to the general rule. But to the generality of men, let the question be put. Are you not, thousands of you, as effeminate as the veriest woman of them all? You talk of your manliness; where is it? "Alas, echo answers where." You boast of the protection you offer to women. Protection! from what? from the rude and disorderly of your own sex—reform them, and women will no longer need the protection you make such a parade of giving. Protect them, do you? let me point you to the thousands of women, doomed to lives of miserable drudgery, and receiving "a compensation which if quadrupled, would be rejected by the man-laborer, with scorn"; are they less worthy protection because they are trying to help themselves? because they have little inclination and less time to lisp soft nonsense? . . . If you would have the manliness you talk of, seek to raise those poor women from their oppressed, and too often degraded, condition; if you will not do it, go on in your old course, but prate no more of your manliness. . . .

Bad is the condition of so many women, it would be much worse if they had nothing but your boasted protection to rely upon; but they have at last learnt the lesson, which a bitter experience teaches, that not to those who style themselves their "natural" protectors," are they to look for needful help, but to the strong and resolute of their own sex. May all good fortune attend those resolute ones, and the noble cause in which they are engaged. *"She Devils"* as some of them have been elegantly termed by certain persons, calling themselves men; let them not fear such epithets, nor shrink from the path they have chosen. . . . They are breaking the way; they shall make it smoother for those that come after them, and generations yet unborn shall live to bless them for their courage and perseverance. If we choose to sit down in our indolence, and persuade ourselves that we can do nothing, let us not censure those who are wiser and stronger than we are. It has been said that men and women are "natural enemies," which I do not believe; but if a running fight must be kept up between the two, let women have half the battle-field and fair play. The time may come when both parties will learn that they can be much better friends, when they have more equal rights. . . .

Chapter 9

Western and Urban Frontiers

*E*arly nineteenth-century Americans were a people in motion. Some left the countryside for urban areas, swelling the populations of larger towns, new river ports, and older cities. Some followed the moving frontier, seeking land in the Midwest or Southwest, and later crossing the plains to the Pacific coast. Some came from abroad, settling variously in eastern cities, rural areas, and western territories. Beyond these voluntary migrants and immigrants were the involuntary ones: the remnants of eastern Indian tribes, relocated farther and farther west, and those slaves who were sent to new cotton lands in the Deep South. By mid-century, the states that had been settled earliest, Massachusetts and Virginia, had become exporters of people.

Few women escaped the consequences, for better or worse, of some type of geographic movement—whether they witnessed the depopulation of rural villages, adapted to the faster pace of city life, participated in a series of family moves, or struck out on their own, seeking sustenance or opportunity. The latter, as all noted, was elusive. For every relocation that provided upward mobility or advantage—such as those of the young women who left New Hampshire farms for Massachusetts mill towns—others seemed connected to misfortunes, like the journey of widow Sarah Ayer, who was forced to join her late husband's relatives in another state. Many women migrants fell into the "involuntary" category, since any change in family luck was likely to lead to a relocation. When her husband went bankrupt in the 1830s, author Elizabeth Oakes Smith observed that wives were obliged to "go down with the ship"—or wherever the ship might sail, which in her case meant from Maine to New York. Women whose husbands were seized by "the mania" for moving west could refuse to leave their homes, but only at the risk of being permanently left behind.

The land hunger that lured migrants to unpopulated regions was hardly new, but it now swept them over longer distances. In the 1790s, easterners had started to fill up empty spaces in western New York and Vermont. By mid-century, wagon trains crossed the plains to Oregon and California. For many migrants, western life proved a multicultural experience. A mining town of the 1850s, for instance, was likely to include transplanted easterners, Chinese, Mexican, and Indian populations, plus infusions of Canadians, English, and other Europeans. Native-born eastern women who moved west often had to adjust not only to a polyglot community but also to a leveling mixture of social classes. "It would be in vain to pretend that this state of society can ever be agreeable to those who have been accustomed to the more rational arrangement of the older world," wrote Caroline Kirkland in her popular novel about Michigan frontier life, *A New Home, Who'll Follow* (1839).

> The social character of the meals, in particular, is quite destroyed, by the constant presence of strangers, whose manners, habits of thinking, and social connections are quite different from your own. . . . I took especial care to be impartial in my own visiting habits, determined at all sacrifice to live down the impression that I felt *above* my neighbors.

Like Kirkland, a native New Yorker, many middle-class eastern women who moved west left a literary record—journals, diaries, and memoirs—of their historic experience. This literature contained many negative reviews of life in the West. Writers often criticized western materialism, disparaged rustic western cities, denounced the western lack of manners and morals, and issued warnings about the difficulties that women faced in western settlements. Many women could not "endure the sudden transition which is forced upon them by emigration to the west," claimed Eliza Farnham, who wrote about the pioneer experience in Illinois and California. They also failed to appreciate "the kind of emancipation which so endears the western country to those who have resided in it." The typical antebellum woman migrant, however, was a farmwife, often isolated in a remote outpost, and in any case a lifelong worker more than a beneficiary of emancipation. "The life she leads is one of hardship, privation, and labor," English author Frances Trollope concluded of Ohio women in the 1830s. Still, some migrants profited from the chance for independent endeavors that the West might offer: Scarcity of women and chronic labor shortages provided business opportunities that had vanished in the East.

The western frontier for antebellum Americans adjoined the northern frontier for Mexicans, who in 1821 declared their independence from Spain and established a republic. Until the mid-1840s, when the United States took over New Mexico, Arizona, California, and parts of Texas, these territories formed the northern borderland of Mexico. The experience of Mexican women in the farming and ranching communities of the Mexican frontier differed from that of their Anglo counterparts. Frontier conditions may have mitigated the tradition of female subjugation that characterized Spanish society in more settled areas, and also altered the traditional sexual division of labor. Hispanic frontierswomen, historians point out, engaged in a wide variety of paid occupations, as bakers, weavers, vendors, craftspeople, farmers, and ranchers. They also inherited a Hispanic legal tradition that enabled married women to maintain property separate from that of their husbands and gave them easy access to court, where they could and did sue and be sued. In most American frontier communities, men invariably outnumbered women. However, in Mexican communities such as Santa Fe and San Antonio, and, until the 1820s, Los Angeles, women slightly outnumbered men, although the impact of this ratio remains unclear. Overall, the distinctive lifestyle of Hispanic women in the Southwest serves as a reminder that "frontier" conditions probably had quite different impacts on different female populations.

Despite extensive celebration of the American pioneer experience, more early nineteenth-century Americans moved to cities than to the frontier. Between 1800 and 1860, the number of "urban" places—places with populations of 2,500 or more—multiplied tenfold. Rural outposts became towns, new cities such as Cincinnati and New Orleans sprang up, and older cities grew larger and larger, led by New York. For migrants with skills and education, the move to the city was a step upward—in business, the professions, and social status. More often, however, urban migration was a horizontal move by fairly poor people who were somehow dislocated: farmers who had exhausted their land or had never owned any, artisans who had been replaced by machines, single women seeking self-support. By the 1840s, immigrants from Ireland and Germany added to the urban influx. Women migrants and immigrants, including the widowed, abandoned, and deserted, joined a growing female labor pool of underpaid seamstresses, factory-hands, pieceworkers, and domestic servants. Like western communities, eastern cities needed female labor. Unlike the West, where women were scarce, eastern cities contained thousands of women. Urban working-class women were therefore crowded into the few occupations open to them. "Their work is so precarious that they are often unemployed," wrote Matthew Carey in an 1829 article about competition and low wages among Philadelphia's seamstresses, spoolers, spinners, book folders, and washerwomen. "In many cases no small portion of their time is spent seeking and waiting for work." Investigating the condition of New York seamstresses just before the Civil War, reporter Virginia Penny found a similar situation: "The supply of labor has been greater than the demand."

At mid-century, eighty percent of Americans remained in rural areas. But in the Northeast, one person out of three was an urbanite, at least according to the "2500" rule, and this development had consequences for women. First, urban residence meant a rise in the marriage age and a drop in the birth rate, at least among the striving middle-class, and subsequently among most native-born city dwellers. In addition, the combination of urbanization and westward migration created an excess of women in more places. By the start of the nineteenth century, women predominated in Massachusetts, Rhode Island, and Connecticut, and, by 1860, throughout New England and New York State. The growth of antebellum cities marked the rise of the female majority that has dominated the eastern half of the country, and urban areas throughout the nation, ever since.

Sex ratios aside, the antebellum eastern city had something in common with many new western communities along the cattle and mining frontiers. The populations of both included large concentrations of men, many of whom had been loosened from their roots and apparently severed from all sources of authority. Under such circumstances, a mood of license and instability took over. If women migrants in the West voiced dismay at violence, irreligion, prostitution, and gambling on the Sabbath, their counterparts in eastern cities seemed to share such concerns and add their own. In 1845, Massachusetts author and reformer Lydia Maria Child, then staying in New York, described the spirit of commercialism and anonymity that characterized metropolitan life:

> This is a place of rapid fluctuation, and never ceasing change. . . . The enterprising, the curious, the reckless, and the criminal, flock hither from all quarters of the world as to a common centre, whence they can diverge at pleasure. Where men are little known, they are imperfectly restrained; therefore, great numbers live here with somewhat of that wild licence which prevails in times of pestilence. Life is a reckless game and death is a business transaction. Warehouses of ready-made coffins stand beside warehouses of ready-made clothing.

To readers of the 1840s, Child's *Letter from New-York* conveyed both the energy of the city streets and some forewarnings about urban hazards.

Crossing the Plains

AMELIA STEWART KNIGHT, 1853

"Diary of Mrs. Amelia Stewart Knight, an Oregon Pioneer of 1853," *Transactions of the Fifty-Sixth Annual Reunion of the Oregon Pioneer Association, 1928* (Portland: F. W. Baites & Co., 1933), pp. 38–53 passim.

During the 1840s and 1850s, pioneers struck out for the Pacific coast along the Oregon Trail. This was a family migration, made by people who were neither well-off nor extremely poor; equipment for the journey was not inexpensive. Starting off from locations along the Missouri River, in caravans of ox-drawn wagons, they traveled up to twenty miles a day. Moving through Kansas and Nebraska, the pioneers crossed the Rockies at South Pass in Wyoming and in Idaho turned north to Oregon, ploughing over deserts and mountains for the final leg of the 2,000-mile trip.

Many of these families moved west in stages. Such was the experience of New England–born Amelia Stewart Knight. Her husband, an English immigrant, had been a student of medicine when she married him in Boston in 1834. In the late 1830s, the Knights went west to Iowa, where they remained for sixteen years. Then, in the spring of 1853, they joined a wagon train of settlers bound for Oregon. Leaving Monroe County, Iowa, they made the five-month trek across the plains to a small farm on the Columbia River, bringing with them seven children, farm hands, cattle, and a dog. Amelia Stewart Knight's journal of the voyage was in part a company log. She kept track of miles covered, rivers crossed, Indians encountered, costs of supplies, and weather conditions along the way. Yet, other details of the westward trek appear in Knight's narrative, including women's work along the trail and the sickness and antics of the various Knight children. With little time for either recreation or complaint, Amelia Stewart Knight proved an efficient and sometimes humorous record-keeper, as the excerpts below suggest. She saved a final personal note for the last entry.*

---

*For a more complete version of the end of the diary, see Margo Culley, ed., *A Day at a Time: The Diary Literature of American Women from 1764 to the Present* (New York: The Feminist Press, 1985), pp. 111–24.

Saturday, April 9th, 1853—Started from home about 11 o'clock and traveled 8 miles and camped in an old house; night cold and frosty.

Sunday, April 10th—Cool and pleasant, road hard and dusty. Evening—Came 18½ miles and camped close to the Fulkerson's house.

Monday, April 11th—Morn. Cloudy and signs of rain, about 10 o'clock it began to rain. At noon it rains so hard we turn out and camp in a school house after traveling 11½ miles; rains all the afternoon and all night, very unpleasant. Jefferson and Lucy have the mumps. Poor cattle bawled all night. . . .

Saturday, April 16th—Camped last night three miles east of Chariton Point in the prairie. Made our beds down in the tent in the wet and mud. Bed clothes nearly spoiled. Cold and cloudy this morning, and every body out of humour. Seneca is half sick. Plutarch has broke his saddle girth. Husband is scolding and hurrying all hands (and the cook), and Almira says she wished she was home, and I say ditto. "Home, Sweet Home." Evening—We passed a small town this morning called Chariton Point. The sun shone a little this afternoon. Came 24 miles today, and have pitched our tent in the prairie again, and have some hay to put under our beds. Corn one dollar per bushel, feed for our stock cost 16 dol. to night. . . .

Saturday, April 23rd—Still in camp, it rained hard all night, and blew a hurricane almost. All the tents were blown down, and some wagons capsized. Evening—It has been raining hard all day; everything is wet and muddy. One of the oxen missing; the boys have been hunting him all day. Dreary times, wet and muddy, and crowded in the tent, cold and wet and uncomfortable in the wagon. No place for the poor children. I have been busy cooking, roasting coffee, etc., today, and have come into the wagon to write this and make our bed. . . .

Friday, April 29th—Cool and pleasant; saw the first Indians today. Lucy and Almira afraid and run into the wagon to hide. Done some washing and sewing.

Saturday, April 30th—Fine weather; spent this day in washing, baking, and over-hauling the wagons. Several more wagons have camped around us.

Sunday, May 1st—Still fine weather; wash and scrub all the children.

Monday, May 2nd—Pleasant evening; have been cooking, and packing things away for an early start in the morning. Threw away several jars, some wooden buckets, and all our pickles. Too unhandy to carry. Indians came to our camp every day, begging money and something to eat. Children are getting used to them. . . .

Thursday, May 5th—We crossed the river this morning on a large steam boat called the Hindoo, after a great deal of Hurrahing and trouble to get the cattle all aboard. One ox jumped overboard and swam across the river, and came out like a drowned rat. The river is even with its banks, timber on it, which is mostly cotton-wood, is quite green. Costs us 15 dollars to cross. After bidding Iowa a kind farewell we travel about 8 miles and camp among the old ruins of the Mormon towns. We here join another company, which will make in all 24 men, 10 wagons, and a large drove of cattle. Have appointed a captain, and are now prepared to guard the stock, four men watch 2 hours and then call up four more to take their places, so by that means no person can sleep about the camp. Such a wild, noisy set was never heard. . . .

Sunday, May 8th—Sunday morning. Still in camp waiting to cross. There are three hundred or more wagons in sight and as far as the eye can reach, the bottom is covered, on each side of the river, with cattle and horses. There is no ferry here and the men will have to make one out of the tightest wagon-bed (every company should have a waterproof wagon-bed for this purpose). Everything must now be hauled out of the wagons head over heels (and he who knows where to find anything will be a smart fellow), then the wagons must be all taken to pieces, and then by means of a strong rope stretched across the river, with a tight wagon-bed attached to the middle of it, the rope must be long enough to pull from one side to the other, with men on each side of the river to pull it. In this way we have to cross everything a little at a time. Women and children last, and then swim the cattle and horses. There were three horses and some cattle drowned while crossing this place yesterday. It is quite lively and merry here this morning and the weather fine. We are camped on a large bottom, with the broad, deep river on one side of us and a high bluff on the other. . . .

Tuesday, May 17th—We had a dreadful storm of rain and hail last night and very sharp lightning. It killed two oxen for one man. We have just encamped on a large flat prairie, when the storm commenced in all its fury and in two minutes after the cattle were taken from the wagons every brute was gone out of sight, cows, calves, horses, all gone before the storm like so many wild beasts. I never saw such a storm. The wind was so high I thought it would tear the wagons to pieces. Nothing but the stoutest covers could stand it. The rain beat into the wagons so that everything was wet, in less than 2 hours the water was a foot deep all over our camp grounds. As we could have no tents pitched, all had to crowd into the wagons and sleep in wet beds, with their wet clothes on, without supper. The wind blew hard all night, and this morning presents a dreary prospect surrounded by water, and our saddles have been soaking in it all night and are almost spoiled. Our cow Rose came up to be milked; had little or nothing for breakfast. The men took the cow's tracks and found the stock about 4 miles from camp. Start on and travel about 2 miles, and come to Dry Creek, so called because it is dry most of the year. I should call it Water Creek now, as it is out of its banks and we will have to wait until it falls. No wood within 8 miles. Raining by spells. . . .

Tuesday, May 24th—Stay in camp today, to wash and cook, as we have a good camping ground, plenty of wood and water, and good grass. Weather pleasant. I had the sick headache all night, some better this morning; must do a day's work. Husband went back a piece this morning in search of our dog, which he found with some rascals who were trying to keep him. . . .

Tuesday, May 31st—Evening—Traveled 25 miles today. When we started this morning there were two large droves of cattle and about 50 wagons ahead of us, and we either had to stay poking behind them in the dust or hurry up and drive past them. It was no fool of a job to be mixed up with several hundred head of cattle, and only one road to travel in, and the drovers threatening to drive their cattle over you if you attempted to pass them. They even took out their pistols. Husband came up just as one man held his pistol at Wilson Carl and saw what the fuss was and said, "Boys, follow me," and he drove our team out of the road entirely, and the cattle seemed to understand it all, for they went into the trot most of the way. The rest of the boys followed with their teams and the rest of the stock. I had rather a rough ride, to be sure, but was glad to get away from such a lawless set, which we did by noon. The head teamster done his best by whipping and hollowing to his cattle. He found it no use and got up into his wagon to take it easy. We left some swearing men behind us. We drove a good ways ahead and stopped to rest the cattle and eat some dinner. While we were eating we saw them coming. All hands jumped for their teams, saying they had earned the road too dearly to let them pass us again, and in a few moments we were all on the go again. Had been very warm today. Thermometer at 98 in the wagon at one o'clock. Towards evening there came up a light thunderstorm which cooled the air down to 60. We are now within 100 miles of Fort Laramie.

Wednesday, June 1st—It has been raining all day long and we have been traveling in it so as to be able to keep ahead of the large droves. The men and boys are all soaking wet and look sad and comfortless. The little ones and myself are shut up in the wagons from the rain. Still it will find its way in and many things are wet; and take us all together we are a poor looking set, and all this for Oregon. I am thinking while I write, "Oh, Oregon, you must be a wonderful country." Came 18 miles today. . . .

Tuesday, June 7th—Rained some last night; quite warm today. Just passed Fort Laramie, situated on the opposite side of the river. This afternoon we passed a large village of Sioux Indians. Numbers of them came around our wagons. Some of the women had moccasins and beads, which they wanted to trade for bread. I gave the women and children all the cakes I had baked. Husband traded a big Indian a lot of hard crackers for a pair of moccasins and after we had started on he came up with us again, making a great fuss, and wanted them back (they had eaten part of the crackers). He did not seem to be satisfied, or else he wished to cause us some trouble, or perhaps get into a fight. However, we handed the moccasins to him in a hurry and drove away from them as soon as possible. Several lingered along watching our horses that were tied behind the wagons, no doubt with the view of stealing them, but our folks kept a sharp lookout till they left. We had a thunderstorm of rain and hail and a hard blow this afternoon. Have traveled 18 miles and are now camped among the Black Hills. They are covered with cedar and pine wood, sandstone, limestone and pure water. . . .

Saturday, June 11th—The last of the Black Hills we crossed this afternoon, over the roughest and most desolate piece of ground that was ever made (called by some the Devil's Crater). Not a drop of water, not a spear of grass to be seen, nothing but barren hills, bare broken rock, sand and dust. Quite a contrast to the first part of the hills. We reached Platte River about noon, and our cattle were so crazy for water that some of them plunged headlong into the river with their yokes on. Traveled 18 miles and camp. . . .

Tuesday, June 21st—We have traveled over a very rough, rocky road today; over mountains close to banks of snow. Had plenty of snow water to drink. Husband brought me a large bucket of snow and one of our hands brought me a beautiful bunch of flowers which he said was growing close to the snow, which was about 6 feet deep. Traveled 16 miles today, and have camped on the mountain about 7 miles from the summit. We are traveling through the South Pass. The Wind River Mountains are off to our right. Among them is the Fremont's Peak. They look romantic covered with snow. . . .

Monday, June 27th—Cold, cloudy and very windy— more like November than June. I am not well enough to get out of the wagon this morning. The men have just got their breakfast over and drove up the stock. It is all hurry and bustle to get things in order. It's children milk the cows, all hands help yoke these cattle, the d——l's in them. Plutarch answers, "I can't, I must hold the tent up, it is blowing away." Hurrah boys. Who tied these horses? "Seneca, don't stand there with your hands in your pocket. Get your saddles and be ready." Evening—Traveled 18 miles today and have camped on the bank of Green River and must wait our turn to cross on a ferry boat. No grass for the poor cattle. All hands discouraged. We have taken in two new hands today, which will make us full handed again. . . .

Monday, July 4th—It has been very warm today. Thermometer up to 110, and yet we can see banks of snow almost within reach. I never saw mosquitoes as bad as they are here. Chat [her son] has been sick all day with fever, partly caused by mosquitoe bites. The men have been shoeing one of the lame oxen, the first one they have tried to shoe. The other one's foot is much too swollen. . . .

Thursday, July 14th—It is dust from morning until night, with now and then a sprinkling of gnats and mosquitoes, and as far as the eye can reach it is nothing but a sandy desert, covered with wild sage brush, dried up with heat; however, it makes good firewood. Evening—I have not felt well today and the road has been very tedious to me. I have ridden in the wagon and taken care of Chatfield till I got tired, then I got out and walked in the sand and through stinking sage brush till I gave out; and I feel thankful that we are about to camp after traveling 22 miles, on the bank of Raft River, about dark; river high. . . .

Friday, July 22nd—Crossed the river before daybreak and found the smell of carrion so bad that we left as soon as possible. The dead cattle were lying in every direction. Still there were a good many getting their breakfast among all the stench. I walked off among the rocks, while the men were getting the cattle ready; then we drove a mile or so, and halted to get breakfast. Here Chat had a very narrow escape from being run over. Just as we were all getting ready to start, Chatfield, the rascal, came around the forward wheel to get into the wagon, and at that moment the cattle started and he fell under the wagon. Somehow he kept from under the wheels, and escaped with only a good, or I should say, a bad scare. I never was so much frightened in my life. I was in the wagon at the time, putting things in order, and supposed Francis was taking care of him. After traveling 6 miles, we have encamped for the day, to rest the cattle; plenty of good grass. Afternoon, rained some. . . .

Friday, August 5th—We have just bid the beautiful Boise River, with her green timber and rich currants, farewell, and are now on our way to the ferry on Snake River. Evening—Traveled 18 miles today and have just reached Fort Boise and camped. Our turn will come to cross some time tomorrow. There is one small ferry boat running here, owned by the Hudson Bay Company. Have to pay three dollars a wagon. Our worst trouble at these large rivers is swimming the stock over. Often after swimming half way over the poor things will turn and come out again. At this place, however, there are Indians who swim the river from morning till night. There is many a drove of cattle that could not be got over without their help. By paying them a small sum, they will take a horse by the bridle or halter and swim over with him. The rest of the horses all follow and by driving and hurrahing to the cattle they will almost always follow the horses, sometimes they fail and turn back. This Fort Boise is nothing more than three new buildings, its inhabitants, the Hudson's Bay Company officials, a few Frenchmen, some half-naked Indians, half breeds, etc.

Saturday, August 6th—Got all safe across the river by noon, and it being 15 miles to the next water, we are obliged to camp here, near the river, till morning. Camps all around us.

Sunday, August 7th—Traveled 15 miles, and have just reached Malheur River and camped. The roads have been very dusty, no water, nothing but dust and dead cattle all day, the air filled with the odor from dead cattle.

Monday, August 8th—We have to make a drive of 22 miles, without water today. Have our cans filled to drink. Here we left, unknowingly, our Lucy behind, not a soul had missed her until we had gone some miles, when we stopped to rest the cattle; just then another train drove up behind us with Lucy. She was terribly frightened and so were some more of us when we found out what a narrow escape she had run. She said she was sitting under the bank of the river, when we started, busy watching some wagons cross, and did not know we were ready. And I supposed she was in Mr. Carl's wagon, as he always took charge of Francis and Lucy and I took care of Myra and Chat. When starting he asked for Lucy, and Francis said "she is in Mother's Wagon," as she often went there to have her hair combed. It was a lesson to all of us. Evening—It is near dark and we are still toiling on till we find a camping place. The little ones have curled down and gone to sleep without supper. Wind high, and it is cold enough for a great coat and mittens. . . .

Wednesday, August 31st—Still in camp. It was too stormy to start out last evening, as intended. The wind was very high all the afternoon, and the dust and sand so bad we could hardly see. Thundered and rained a little in the evening. It rained and blew very hard all night. Is still raining this morning, the air cold and chilly. It blew so hard last night as to blow our buckets and pans from under the wagons, and this morning we found them (and other things which were not secured) scattered all over the valley. One or two pans came up missing. Everything is packed up ready for a start. The men folks are out hunting the cattle. The children and myself are out shivering around in the wagons, nothing for fires in these parts, and the weather is very disagreeable. Evening—Got a late start this morning. Traveled about a mile, and were obliged to stop and turn the cattle out on account of rain. At noon it cleared off. We ate dinner and started. Came up a long and awful rock hollow, in danger every moment of smashing our wagons. After traveling 7 miles, we halted in the prairie long enough to cook supper. Split up some of the deck boards of our wagons to make fire. Got supper over, and are on our way again. Cloudy and quite cold all day. . . .

Monday, September 5th—Passed a sleepless night last night as a good many of the Indians camped around us were drunk and noisy and kept up a continual racket, which made all hands uneasy and kept our poor dog on the watch all night. I say poor dog, because he is nearly worn out with traveling through the day and should rest at night; but he hates an Indian and will not let one come near the wagons if he can help it; and doubtless they would have done some mischief but for him. Ascended a long steep hill this morning, which was very hard on the cattle, and also on myself, as I thought I never should get to the top, although I rested two or three times. After traveling two or three miles over some very pretty rolling prairie, we have turned our cattle out to feed a while, as they had nothing last night. Evening—traveled about 12 miles today, and have encamped on a branch of Deschutes, and turned our cattle and horses out to tolerably good bunch grass.

Tuesday, September 6th—Still in camp, washing and overhauling the wagons to make them as light as possible to cross the mountains. Evening—After throwing away a good many things and burning up most of the deck boards of our wagons so as to lighten them, got my washing and cooking done and started on again. Crossed two branches, traveled 3 miles and have camped near the gate or foot of the Cascade Mountains (here I was sick all night caused by my washing and working too hard). . . .

Tuesday, September 13th—Ascended three steep, muddy hills this morning. Drove over some muddy, miry ground and through mud holes, and have just halted at the first farm to noon and rest awhile and buy feed for the stock. Paid $1.50 per hundred for hay. Price of fresh beef 16 and 18 cts. per pound, butter ditto, 1 dollar, eggs 1 dollar a dozen, onions 4 and 5 dollars per bushel, all too dear for poor folks, so we have treated ourselves to some small turnips at the rate of 25 cents per dozen. Got rested and are now ready to travel again. Evening—Traveled 14 miles today. Crossed Deep Creek and have encamped on the bank of it, a very dull looking place; grass very scarce. We may not call ourselves through, they say; and there we are in Oregon, making our camp in an ugly bottom, with no home, except our wagons and tent. It is drizzling and the weather looks dark and gloomy. Here old man Fuller left us and Wilson Carl remains.

Wednesday, September 14th—Still in camp. Raining and quite disagreeable.

Thursday, September 15th—Still in camp and still raining. I was sick all night.

Friday, September 16th—Still in camp. Rain in the forenoon and clear in the afternoon. Washed some this forenoon.

Saturday, September 17th—In camp yet. Still raining. Noon—It has cleared off and we are all ready for a start again, for some place we don't know where. Evening— Came 6 miles and have encamped in a fence corner by a Mr. Lambert's, about 7 miles from Milwaukie. Turn our stock out to tolerably good feed.

A few days later my eighth child was born. After this we picked up and ferried across the Columbia River, utilizing skiff, canoes and flatboat to get across, taking three days to complete. Here husband traded two yoke of oxen for a half section of land with one-half acre planted to potatoes and a small log cabin and lean-to with no windows. This is the journey's end.

(Finis)

A Norwegian Immigrant in Wisconsin

JANNICKE SAEHLE, 1847

Jannicke Saehle to Johannes Saehle, September 28, 1847, in Theodore C. Blegen, "Immigrant Women and the American Frontier: Three Early 'America Letters,'" *Norwegian American Historical Association Studies and Records* 5 (1930): 18–22.

Many immigrant women, notably Scandinavians, moved to the Great Plains before the Civil War. During the 1840s, Norwegian immigration gained momentum, propelled mainly by economic need. Increasing population and subdivision of land in Norway left many with plots too small to farm. Some 40,000 Norwegians, including farmers, laborers, and others, came to the United States before 1860, half of whom settled in Wisconsin.

Jannicke Saehle, a young, unmarried woman, arrived in America in 1847 as a servant for a Norwegian family, the Torjersens, who settled in a log cabin in Koshkonong Prairie, Wisconsin. They paid Jannicke for her services with the products of three acres of land for a three-year period. The young woman then moved on to Madison, where she worked as a servant for an American family. Undaunted by the difficulties of travel—by boat to New York and by train to Wisconsin—Jannicke Saehle was a spirited personality, ever adaptable and consistently receptive to her new environment. After a few months, she recounted her experiences to her brother in Norway, whom she was unlikely to see again.

**Koshkonong Prairie,
September 28, 1847**

Dear Brother:

It seems to me that in my last letter to you, written from my former home in the old world, I hoped that from my new home in the new world I should be able to write to you with even greater happiness and contentment, and God has fulfilled this wish. As I wrote you, we did not leave our dear native land until April 24, as we had to remain eight days at Holmen in Sandvigen waiting for a number of passengers who had not yet arrived.

We sailed in the morning at seven o'clock, with fair wind and weather, and we had lost sight of the shores of our dear fatherland by half-past three, when the pilot left us. I remained on deck until six o'clock in the evening, but as the wind was sharp and cold I was not able to stay there any longer, but had to go down to the hold, where general vomiting had been going on for a long time. And after five minutes my turn came, also, to contribute my share to the Atlantic Ocean.

Still, what can I say? Not in all eternity can I sufficiently thank God, for the America journey was not for me what it was for many others. It seems now like a faint dream to me and as if through God's providential care I had been carried in protecting arms, for I was sick only four days, and even on these I went on deck now and then. I was not afraid, but slept just as peacefully as I had in the little room that I so recently had left behind. My traveling companions were just as lucky as I, but a number of passengers had to keep to their beds nearly the whole journey, for the weather was stormy almost the entire voyage and besides, it was so cold that there were few days when we could remain on deck for the whole day. But the wind had a good effect on conditions in the hold, which was well aired, and warmer weather would have been less desirable. So, as we went steadily forward we hoped for the best, and our hopes were not disappointed. By the fourteenth of May we had already reached the Banks, where the captain and the skipper caught nine great cod, and for dinner on the Seventeenth of May we ate fish, though it was such a stormy day that we had to steady our plates with our hands, and not infrequently we were jerked backwards with our plates in our hands. In naming the skipper I can greet you from an old friend of our younger days, John Johannessen, who used to be in the service of Captain Fischer and once worked in his little fishing vessel. He is now much more alert as a seaman and looks much better than in the old days, but he is plagued by a long-standing malaria which he cannot get rid of, despite all the medicines which he is said to have used. His wife is dead. He has one married and three unmarried daughters. This was his fourth trip to this country, —and this one the fastest. As the wind continued favorable, the general opinion was that we would reach Staten Island, one mile from New York, by Whitsunday; but late in the evening before Whitsunday there came a calm, and a thick fog covered everything, so that it was necessary to keep up a constant ringing and shooting in case other sailing vessels should be in the vicinity. Later the fog lifted and we saw several vessels, and in the afternoon, about four o'clock, the captain saw a sailboat that resembled a pilot's vessel, and when he looked at it through his glass, it turned out to be so, to our delight, for the captain had not expected to get a pilot so late in the day. It was not long before the man was on board, and the next day near dinner time we anchored on American ground. The foggy weather continued and we were able to see only the delightful island, with its many lighthouses, pretty forts, and buildings, which stood out majestically among the charming stretches of woods.

After the good old doctor had come on board and we had all had the good fortune of being able to walk smartly past him, he gave his permission for the vessel to proceed immediately in to New York, where we arrived in the evening at five o'clock. The next day we made ready to go up to the town on the following day to look about, but as we had the children with us and that day was very warm, we did not get very far. The skipper accompanied us as a guide who knew the place and as an interpreter. First we came to a large and beautiful park for pedestrians, outside of which were a great number of fruit dealers, and pleasant carriages for hire. We immediately took possession of one of these and had ourselves driven for a mile through the streets, for which we paid six pennies each, about the same as six Norwegian skillings. The next day we went to the museum, which we thoroughly enjoyed. Here we saw animals and birds, from the largest to the smallest, and many things, some of which I understood, some of which I didn't, portraits of all the generals that there have been in America, and finally an old man with a richly braided uniform who stood on a table without a head. After we had looked about us at this place, we were informed that a drama was being played, and when we reached the theater there was a representation of Napoleon's funeral, which was very beautiful to see. This came to an end at half-past five. A play was to be presented again from seven to ten, but we were already satisfied. We paid about thirty skillings (Norwegian).

On May 20 we left our good ship "Juno," with its brave crew, who said goodbye to us with a three-times-repeated hurrah. The captain accompanied us on board a steamer which was to carry us to Albany. He took us about to see things. It was like a complete house four stories high, and very elegantly furnished, with beautiful rugs everywhere. He now parted from us with the best wishes. Captain Bendixen treated us more like relatives than like passengers. He was very entertaining and was courteous in every respect.

The later journey was good beyond expectation. Things went merrily on the railroads. Once in a while the passengers, when we neared some of the noteworthy sights that we rushed past on the trip, would stick their heads out of the windows so that they might see everything, but one after the other of them had the misfortune to see his straw hat go flying away with the wind caused by the speed of the train.

On the third of June, after we had passed several cities which for lack of space I cannot tell about, we reached Milwaukee, where we remained three days. We left Milwaukee on the seventh and came to Koshkonong on the ninth. Torjersen, after having made the acquaintance here of a worthy family named Homstad, from Namsen, who settled here last year and found this land the best after long travels, has now bought a little farm of forty acres of land, with a fairly livable log house and a wheat field of four and a half acres. This has brought him forty-five barrels of winter wheat, in addition to potatoes, beans, peas, more than a hundred heads of cabbage, cucumbers, onions in tremendous amounts, and many other kinds [of vegetables]. For this farm he paid $250, and with the farm followed respectfully four pigs.

After having lived here and having been in good health the whole time, I left on the sixteenth of August for Madison, the capital of Wisconsin, which is situated twenty-two miles from here. There I have worked at a hotel for five weeks, doing washing and ironing; and I enjoy the best treatment, though I cannot speak with the people. I have food and drink in abundance. A breakfast here consists of chicken, mutton, beef, or pork, warm or cold wheat bread, butter, white cheese, eggs, or small pancakes, the best coffee, tea, cream, and sugar. For dinner the best courses are served. Supper is eaten at six o'clock, with warm biscuits, and several kinds of cold wheat bread, cold meats, bacon, cakes, preserved apples, plums, and berries, which are eaten with cream, and tea and coffee—and my greatest regret here is to see the superabundance of food, much of which has to be thrown to the chickens and the swine, when I think of my dear ones in Bergen, who like so many others must at this time lack the necessaries of life.

I have received a dollar a week for the first five weeks, and hereafter shall have $1.25, and if I can stand it through the whole winter I shall get a dollar and a half a week, and I shall not have to do the washing, for I did not think I was strong enough for this work. Mrs. Morison has also asked me to remain in her service as long as she, or I, live, as she is going to leave the tavern next year and live a more quiet life with her husband and daughter, and there I also could live more peacefully and have a room by myself, and I really believe that so far as she is concerned I could enter upon this arrangement, provided such a decision is God's will for me.

I am well and so far I have not regretted my journey to this country. I have now been with the Torjersens for four days and have written to Bergen and to you, and tomorrow I shall journey up to the Morisons', where I find myself very well satisfied. I have had the honor of sitting at their daughter's marriage dinner, and I ironed her beautiful bridal gown. She was in truth a lovable bride, beautiful, and good as an angel, and she has often delighted me with her lovely singing and her playing on the piano. She was married on the sixteenth of September and left on the seventeenth for Boston with her husband to visit her parents-in-law. And now, my dear Johannes, I must say farewell for this time. God bless you. Do not forget, I shall give you Torjersen's address, so that you may write me here. I greet you affectionately. Do not forget to thank God, on my behalf, who has guided me so well. I cannot thank Him enough myself.

Jannicke

[Note in margin:]

I have now received from Torjersen for my services, three acres of land for cultivation for three years, and it is now planted with winter wheat—if God will give me something to harvest.

A Woman's View of the Gold Rush

MARY B. BALLOU, 1852

Mary B. Ballou, *"I Hear the Hogs in My Kitchen": A Woman's View of the Gold Rush*, Archibald Hanna, ed. (New Haven, CT: Beinecke Library, Yale University [350 copies printed for Fredrick W. Beinecke, Office of the Yale University Press], 1962), pp. 1–13.

Mining towns of the 1850s offered well-paid employment to women with domestic skills. Mary B. Ballou, a married woman who went to California during the gold rush with her husband, used such skills for profit as a boardinghouse cook in a mining camp. In a letter to one of her sons, she conveyed an unusual amount of information about her experiences and environment.

Much of Mary B. Ballou's letter concerned her work, which was extensive. Besides serving a large clientele three meals a day, this energetic woman lost no opportunity for paid labor. She tended children, produced soap, stitched flags, and sewed sheets and mattresses. Interspersed in her narrative are other glimpses of mining camp life— eruptions of violence, political campaigns, bouts of homesickness, chats with other women, and references to the pigs and mules who traipsed through her kitchen and dining room. Mrs. Ballou even includes a song that she made up on the spot. Despite the profits of her labor, which might have been considerable, and the preservation of her sense of humor under trying circumstances, Mary B. Ballou seems to prefer life in "the States." By this, she means the unidentified area from whence she came.

California, Negrobar
October 30, 1852

My Dear Selden:

We are about as usual in health. Well I suppose you would like to know what I am doing in this gold region. Well I will try to tell you what my work is here in this muddy Place. All the kitchen that I have is four posts stuck down into the ground and covered over the top with factory cloth no floor but the ground. This is a Boarding House kitchen. There is a floor in the dining room and my sleeping room covered with nothing but cloth. We are at work in a Boarding House.

Oct. 27: This morning I awoke and it rained in torrents. Well I got up and I thought of my House. I went and looket into my kitchen. The mud and water was over my Shoes I could not go into the kitchen to do any work to day but kept perfectly dry in the Dining [room] so I got along verry well. Your Father put on his Boots and done the work in the kitchen. I felt badly to think that I was detined [destined] to be in such a place. I wept for a while and then I commenced singing and made up a song as I went along. My song was this: To California I did come and thought I under the bed I shall have to run to shelter me from the piercing storm.

Now I will try to tell you what my work is in this Boarding House. Well somtimes I am washing and Ironing somtimes I am making mince pie and Apple pie and squash pies. Somtimes frying mince turnovers and Donuts. I make Buiscuit and now and then Indian jonny cake and then again I am making minute puding filled with rasons and Indian Bake pudings and then again a nice Plum Puding and then again I am Stuffing a Ham of pork that cost forty cents a pound. Somtimes I am . . . making gruel for the sick now and then cooking oisters sometimes making coffee for the French people strong enough for any man to walk on that has Faith as Peter had. Three times a day I set my Table which is about thirty feet in length and do all the little fixings about it such as filling pepper boxes and vinegar cruits and mustard pots and Butter cups. Somtimes I am feeding my chickens and then again I am scareing the Hogs out of my kitchen and Driving the mules out of my Dining room. You can see by the description of that I have given you of my kitchen that anything can walk into the kitchen that choeses to walk in and there being no door to shut from the kitchen into the Dining room you see that anything can walk into the kitchen and then from kitchen into the Dining room so you see the Hogs and mules can walk in any time day or night if they choose to do so. Somtimes I am up all times a night scaring the Hogs and mules out of the House. Last night there a large rat came down pounce down onto our bed in the night. Sometimes I take my fan and try to fan myself but I work so hard that my Arms pain me so severely that I kneed some one to fan me so I do not find much comfort anywhere. I made a Bluberry puding to day for Dinner. Somtimes I am making soups and cramberry tarts and Baking chicken that cost four Dollars a head and cooking Eggs at three Dollars a Dozen. Somtimes boiling cabbage and Turnips and frying fritters and Broiling stake and cooking codfish and potatoes. I often cook nice Salmon trout that weigh from ten to twenty pound apiece. Somtimes I am taking care of Babies and nursing at the rate of Fifty Dollars a week but I would not advise any Lady to come out here and suffer the toil and fatigue that I have suffered for the sake of a little gold neither do I advise any one to come. Clarks Simmon wife says if she was safe in the States she would not care if she had not one cent. She came in here last night and said, "Oh dear I am so homesick that I must die," and then again my other associate came in with tears in her eyes and said that she had cried all day. She said if she had as good a home as I had got she would not stay twenty five minutes in California. I told her that she could not pick up her duds in that time. She said she would not stop for duds nor anything else but my own heart was two sad to cheer them much.

Now I will tell you a little more about my cooking. Somtimes I am cooking rabbits and Birds that are called quails here and I cook squrrels. Occasionly I run in and have a chat with Jane and Mrs. Durphy and I often have a hearty cry. No one but my maker knows my feelings. And then I run into my little cellar which is about four feet square as I have no other place to run that is cool.

October 21: Well I have been to church to hear a methodist sermon. His Text was let us lay aside every weight and the sin that doth so easely beset us. I was the only Lady that was present and about forty gentleman. So you see that I go to church when I can.

November 2: Well it has been Lexion [election] day here to day. I have heard of strugling and tite pulling but never saw such aday as I have witnessed to day the Ballot Box was so near to me that I could hear every word that was spoken. The wind Blows verry hard here to day. I have three lights Burning and the wind blows so hard that it almost puts my lights out while I am trying to write. If you could but step in and see the inconvience that I have for writing you would not wonder that I cannot write any better you would wonder that I could write at all. Notwithstanding all the dificuty in writing I improve every leishure moment. It is quite cool here my fingers are so cold that I can hardly hold my pen. Well it is ten o'clock at night while I am writing. The people have been Declareing the votes. I hear them say Hura for the Whigs and sing Whig songs. Now I hear them say that Morman Island has gone Whig and now another time a cheering. Now I hear them say Beals Bar has gone Whig now another time cheering. Well it is getting late and I must retire soon there is so much noise I do not expect to sleep much to night. There has been a little fighting here to day and one chalenge given but the chalenge given was not accepted they got together and settled their trouble.

I will tell you a little of my bad feelings. On the 9 of September there was a little fight took place in the store. I saw them strike each other through the window in the store. One went and got a pistol and started towards the other man. I never go into the store but your mothers tender heart could not stand that so I ran into the store and Beged and plead with him not to kill him for eight or ten minutes not to take his Life for the sake of his wife and three little children to spare his life and then I ran through the Dining room into my sleeping room and Buried my Face in my bed so as not to hear the sound of the pistol and wept Biterly. Oh I thought if I had wings how quick I would fly to the States. That night at the supper table he told the Boarders if it had not been for what that Lady said to him Scheles would have been a dead man. After he got his pashion over he said that he was glad that he did not kill him so you see that your mother has saved one Human beings Life. You see that I am trying to relieve all the suffering and trying to do all the good that I can.

There I hear the Hogs in my kitchen turning the Pots and kettles upside down so I must drop my pen and run and drive them out. So you [see] this is the way that I have to write—jump up every five minutes for somthing and then again I washed out about a Dollars worth of gold dust the fourth of July in the cradle so you see that I am doing a little mining in this gold region but I think it harder to rock the cradle to wash out gold than it is to rock the cradle for the Babies in the States.

October 11: I washed in the forenoon and made a Democrat Flag in the after-noon, sewed twenty yards of splendid worsted fringe around it, and I made [a] Whig Flag. They are both swinging acrost the road but the Whig Flag is the richest. I had twelve Dollars for making them so you see that I am making Flags with all [the] rest of the various kinds of work that I am doing and then again I am scouring candle sticks and washing the floor and making soft soap. The People tell me that it is the first Soft Soap they knew made in California. Somtimes I am making mattresses and sheets. I have no windows in my room. All the light that I have shines through canvas that covers the House and my eyes are so dim that I can hardly see to make a mark so I think you will excuse me for not writing any better. I have three Lights burning now but I am so tired and Blind that I can scearcely see and here I am among the French and Duch and Scoth and Jews and Italions and Sweeds and Chineese and Indians and all manner of tongu[e]s and nations but I am treated with due respect by them all.

On the night of Election the second day of November was Burnt down and some lives lost. Adams['s] express office was Broken open by a band of robbers [and] a large quantity of money was taken. They took one man out of bed with his wife took him into the office and Bound him laid him on the floor and told him to give them the key to the safe or they would kill him. One of the robbers staid in the room [with] his wife; his face was muffled and Pistols by his side and [he] told her that if she made any noise for so long a time he would kill her. Only immagine what her feelings must be. I lived close by the office. I went in to see her the next morning [and] she told me that she nearly lost her sences she was so frigtned.

I immagine you will say what a long yarn this is from California. If you can read it at all. I must close soon for I am so tired and almost sick. Oh my Dear Selden I am so Home sick. I will say to you once more to see that Augustus has every thing that he kneeds to make him comfortable and by all means have him Dressed warm this cold winter. I worry a great deal about my Dear children. It seems as though my heart would break when I realise how far I am from my Dear Loved ones. This from your affectionate mother,

Mary B. Ballou

Notes on Women in Hispanic New Mexico

W. W. H. DAVIS, 1857

W. W. H. Davis, *El Gringo or New Mexico and Her People* (Chicago: The Rio
Grande Press, 1962 [New York, 1857]), pp. 83–85, 61–62, 64–65, 88–90,
134–40.

After Mexico became an independent republic in 1821, Americans
began to penetrate its northern territories, mainly Texas and California, and to report on the lifestyle and customs of their residents.
Relatively few Americans arrived in New Mexico until after the Mexican War, when the area became a United States territory. One early
visitor was William Watts Hart Davis, a young lawyer sent to Santa Fe
in 1848 as U.S. Attorney to the territory of New Mexico. Full of
literary ambition, Davis produced a long volume of observations on
New Mexico and its people that is still valuable to historians for the
vivid descriptions it contains.

Like many other early Anglo commentators on Mexican-Ameri-
cans in newly acquired areas, Davis was hardly an impartial observer.
He had firm convictions about the superiority of Anglo-Americans to
other peoples, took a critical stance toward Spain and its influence,
persistently objected to the Catholic church, and held a self-righteous
view of cultural differences. Still, Davis exuded praise for those New
Mexican traits that he admired, such as the courtesy, hospitality, and
generosity of his hosts and hostesses. A curious individual and an acute
observer, he also delighted in exploring his physical surroundings and
social environment, and in recounting his experiences in detail for his
readers.

Both Davis's strengths and weaknesses are illustrated in the following segments of observations about Hispanic women in New Mexico. His critical, ethnocentric characteristics are apparent in his
objections to New Mexican morals, or lack of them, which he blames
variously on the Spanish heritage and on the high fees charged by the
Catholic church for legal marriages. It should be noted here that Davis
was describing a society in which concubinage was more commonplace than marriage and out-of-wedlock births were frequent among
all classes.* Such circumstances might well have dismayed a Victorian

---

*See Janet Lecompte, "The Independent Women of Hispanic New Mexico, 1821–1846," *Western Historical Quarterly* 12 (January 1981), pp. 17–35.

American. Davis's talents for accurate reporting are evident elsewhere in his account, such as in his descriptions of the New Mexican ethnic heritage, clothing, and courtship. In the final segment of excerpts, Davis tells of his personal involvement in the process of courtship and also relates his experience at a New Mexican wedding. Despite his interest in Hispanic women's roles, Davis did not discuss—or perhaps even notice—the variety of women's occupations, nor did he comment on the traditional legal rights of Hispanic married women. Such rights disappeared or were abridged after New Mexico came under United States jurisdiction.

In some respects the New Mexicans are a peculiar and interesting people. They are of Eastern origin, and in general possess all the vices of those whose homes are washed by the blue waters of the Mediterranean Sea, whence a branch of their ancestors originally came. When the Moors were expelled from Spain, they left behind, as a legacy to the people by whom they had been conquered, many of their manners and customs, which, during their residence in the country, had become firmly ingrafted into society. They had intermarried with the Spaniards, and thus formed a mixed race, in whose veins flowed the blood of both ancestors. Among the early adventurers who came in quest of gold and fame into Mexico were many who had sprung from this union of the Moor and Spaniard, and whose manners and customs assimilated, to a considerable degree, with those of their Moslem ancestors. A portion of that gallant band of men who assisted Hernando Cortez in the subjection of the Aztec empire, or those who followed in his footsteps, in the course of time found their way into New Mexico. A thirst for the further conquest, coupled with a religious zeal, invited them thither, a distance of two thousand miles from the seat of Spanish power in America. They streamed up the valley of the Del Norte, and formed settlements upon the banks at the most favorable points that presented themselves, where they also established missions to convert the native heathen, and military posts for defense, and became themselves permanent settlers. The Good Book at well as Nature taught them that "it is not good for man to be alone," and so they considered the propriety of taking partners to share their exile and hardships. In this domestic emergency there was but one alternative; their own fair countrywomen, "the dark-eyed maids of Castile," were thousands of miles away, and could not be obtained for wives, and they were therefore compelled, by force of circumstances, to look to the daughters of their Indian neighbors for help-meets. This course was adopted, and all the settlers and gay cavaliers who were in want of the gentler sex to smooth the pathway of life and keep their houses in order took to their bed and board Indian maidens. Here was a second blending of blood and a new union of races; the Spaniard, Moor, and the aboriginal were united and made a new race, the Mexicans.

The new people who sprung from this intermarriage between the conquerors and the conquered were dark and swarthy in appearance, and so have remained, through the change of generations, for nearly three hundred years. Among the present population there is found every shade of color, from the nut-brown, which exhibits a strong preponderance of the aboriginal blood, to the pure Castilian, who is as light and fair as the sons and daughters of the Anglo-Saxon race. Of the latter there are only a few families among the *ricos* who pride themselves upon not having Indian blood in their veins. The great mass of the population are very dark, and can not claim to be more than one fourth or one eighth part Spanish. The intermixture between the peasantry and the native tribes of Indians is yet carried on, and there is no present hope of the people improving in color. The system of Indian slavery which exists in the country conduces to this state of things. The people obtain possession of their children by purchase or otherwise, whom they rear in their families as servants, and who perform a life-time servitude to hard task masters and mistresses. When they grow up to man's and woman's estate, many of them marry with the lower class of Mexicans, and thus a new stream of dark blood is constantly added to the current. Tawny skins are seen in all ranks of society, and some of the most intelligent and wealthy of the native population exhibit the most enduring traces of their Indian origin. From these causes there exists an amalgamation in color that is found in no quarter of the world except in the Spanish portions of the America continent.

In stature they are below the medium height, both male and female, but are well made, with sound constitutions, and are graceful and athletic. They have, with but few exceptions, black hair and eyes. The females exhibit, in some instances, the features of the Indian, high cheek-bones and thick lips, and many of them possess considerable personal beauty. Their fine eyes, small hands and feet, and graceful carriage, are distinguishing traits. . . .

The national costume of the Mexicans is fast disappearing among the better classes, who are learning to adopt the American style of dress. The females conform themselves to the fashions of Paris and New York with greater facility than the men, but they are so far removed from the world of dress as to be a year or two behind the times. The bonnet they discard entirely, and wear instead the *rebozo*, which appears to be a fixture in the toilet of a New Mexican lady. It consists of a long scarf, made of silk or cotton, according to the taste of the wearer, which is worn over the head, with one end thrown across the left shoulder. A lady is never seen in the street without her *rebozo*, and it is rarely laid aside within doors, when it is drawn loosely around the person. When promenading, the face is so much muffled up that not more than one eye is visible, and it is almost impossible to recognize your most intimate friend. The dress of the peasant women seldom consists of more than a chemise and *enaguas*, or petticoat of homemade flannel, generally of bright colors. They usually go barefooted, and wear the *rebozo* upon the head. . . . Among all classes, the females are extremely fond of jewelry, and when they appear in public they wear a profusion of ornaments, if they can obtain them. In dress they like bright colors, and are more fond of making a show than a neat and genteel appearance; and those who can afford it wear the most expensive articles of dress, but display little or no taste in the adornment of their persons. . . .

The standard of education in New Mexico is at a very low ebb, and there is a larger number of persons who can not read and write than in any other Territory in the Union. . . .

The education of the females has, if anything, been more neglected than that of the males, and the number of them who cannot read and write is greater. Gregg,* who wrote ten years ago, in speaking of female education in New Mexico, says, "Indeed, until very recently, to be able to read and write on the part of a woman was considered an indication of very extraordinary talent; and the fair damsel who could pen a billet-doux to her lover was looked upon as almost a prodigy." This picture is a little overdrawn, but, at the same time, except among the few wealthy families, it is a rare thing to see a woman who possesses these useful accomplishments. Those who received any education at all have been taught in the most superficial manner, and it proves of little benefit to either head or heart. . . .

[On a visit to a New Mexican home:]

We have already gone through with the hugging and kissing, and are now seated in the presence of our fair hostess. One of the first acts of courtesy of the mistress of the house is to invite you to smoke. She carries about her person a small silver tobacco-box, in which she keeps the noxious weed, and also has at hand a little package of corn-husks, one of which she fills with the fine-cut tobacco, rolls it up into a *cigarrito*, lights it, and hands it to you to smoke. The American cigar is rarely used by the men, and never by the females, both substituting the article here named. The *cigarrito* is made by each person as he requires them, who always has on hand for that purpose his box of tobacco and package of husks. . . . Smoking is habitual with all classes, not excepting the most lovely and refined females in the country. The habit is bad enough in men, but intolerable in women. The *cigarrito* seems to be an abiding presence, being handed round at the dinner-table as a refreshment, and served up in the ballroom; and it is common to see ladies smoking while they are engaged in waltzing and dancing, and some even indulge the luxury while they lie in bed. In Southern Mexico the ladies use a pair of golden tongs to hold the *cigarrito* while they light it, and the coal of fire is brought by a servant on a silver salver. . . .

In former times females were frequent visitors at gambling-houses, and lost and won their doubloons at monte and other games with a *sang froid* truly masculine. A change for the better has taken place in this particular, and the fairer portion of creation are now seldom seen at the gaming-table except at the public fairs, when they indulge a little for amusement's sake. A few years ago, quite a celebrated female, known as Señora Doña Gertrudes Barcelo, led the van in gambling in Santa Fe. She was a Taosite by birth, but extended her adventures to the capital, where she established her headquarters. Here she struck the tide that "leads on to fortune," and for a considerable time was known as the most expert monte dealer in the city. Her wealth leavened the social lump, and gained her admittance into the most fashionable and select circles, and she soon became one of the *upper tendom* of the city. She died about the year 1851, and was buried with the highest honors of the church, at an expense of upward of sixteen hundred dollars for spiritual services in the burial alone, including the grave. The bill was duly made out by the Bishop of Santa Fe, with his

---

*Josiah Gregg, a merchant who traded in Santa Fe in the 1830s and 1840s and who wrote a book about the area, *Commerce of the Prairies* (1844).

name signed thereto, and was presented to her executors and paid. Among the items were *los deréchos del obispo* (the rights of the bishop), one thousand dollars; *los posos*, each fifty dollars, which means that each time the procession halted on its way to the burial, and the bier was placed upon the ground, the Church made a charge of this amount; and the other charges were in proportion.

I regret that I am unable to speak more favorably of the morals of New Mexico, but in this particular the truth must be told. Probably there is no other country in the world, claiming to be civilized, where vice is more prevalent among all classes of the inhabitants. Their ancestors were governed in this matter by the standard of morality that prevailed in Southern Europe and along the shore of the Mediterranean, where morals were never deemed an essential to respectability and good standing in society. . . . The standard of female chastity is deplorably low, and the virtuous are far outnumbered by the vicious. Prostitution is carried to a fearful extent; and it is quite common for parents to sell their own daughters for money to gratify the lust of the purchaser, thus making a profit from their own and children's shame. It is almost a universal practice for men and women to live together as husband and wife, and rear a family of children, without having been married. One thing which has greatly conduced to this condition of life in times gone by was the high price of the marriage fee. The peasantry could not afford to be married according to the rites of the Church, and as no other ceremony was legal, they were, in a measure, driven into this unlawful and sinful intercourse. This irregular mode of life is also encouraged by the matrimonial system practiced, which results in illy-advised matches, which, in a large number of instances, drives the parties to a separation, when one or both assume an illicit connection.

It is the custom for a married man to support a wife and mistress at the same time, and but too frequently the wife also has her male friend. A gentleman of many years' residence in the country, and who had a thorough acquaintance with the people, assured me that such practices are indulged in by three fourths of the married population. The marriage vow is held sacred by a very few, and the ceremony is more a matter of convenience than any thing else. The custom of keeping mistresses appears to be part of the social system, and the feelings of society are in no manner outraged by it, because the public opinion of the country sanctions it; and what seems to argue an exceedingly liberal code of morals is the fact that the standing of neither party is injured in the community in which they live, but they seem to maintain the same degree of respectability as though they did not thus violate the rules of propriety and decency. This mode of life is practiced openly and without shame. The parties keep up a regular domestic establishment, receive their friends, and appear together in public, as though their union was sanctioned by the holy rites of marriage, and blessed by the laws of God and man. . . . In New Mexico, the *modus operandi* of winning and wooing in the court of Cupid is widely different from that practiced in the United States. . . .

One great obstacle in the way of marriage and more especially among the poorer classes is the high rate of fees the priests charge for tying the knot, which renders legal marriage almost entirely a luxury, only to be indulged in by the rich. It is said the charges in this respect have been somewhat lessened within the last few years, but they are yet much too high, and drive hundreds annually into illicit intercourse. In some instances several hundred dollars have been paid for performing the ceremony, being the regular fees of the curate, and not the voluntary gift of the party. The lowest price paid, where the parties are married in church and the simplest rites performed, is about twenty dollars. This exaction is an oppression upon the humbler classes, and injurious to that wise institution which tends, more than any other, to humanize mankind, and to make the world better, wiser, and happier. . . .

The old Spanish custom of wooing and winning is still adhered to, and, in the first place, all proposals of marriage are made to the father, or, if he be dead, to the mother, who are supposed to be the rightful keepers of their daughter's affection. In brief, the mode of procedure is simply this: If a lad becomes enamored of a lass, and desires to make her his wife, he unbosoms his troubled soul to his father, who thereupon writes a very business kind of an epistle to the father of the young lady, and, without more ado, asks the hand of his daughter in marriage for his son. The matter is then duly considered by the parents of the young lady, and if the match is viewed as an advantageous one, in nine cases out of ten the proposal is accepted without consulting the wishes of the daughter, who, as a dutiful child, is presumed, as a matter of course, to do just as pa wishes. It is beneath the pride of a Spaniard to regard the inclination or preference of the child in such matters, and if *he* is pleased with the proposed alliance, that is deemed all-sufficient. The length of time given the parents to sit in council over the proposal is generally one month, at the end of which the affair is concluded, and an answer is given in due form. It is very seldom that a young lady thinks seriously of matrimony unless it is proposed by the father, and it sometimes happens that the parties have never met until the day of marriage. This is the general custom in affairs of the heart, but there are some exceptions to the rule, and now and then love is made after our own manner of doing such things.

Here is certainly a mode very different, compared with that in which Anglo-Saxon lovers are in the habit of arranging such delicate matters, but, like most innovations, it is not wholly without its advantages. The young lady is saved a deal of trouble and anxiety, to say nothing of the jealousy which, under our system, in spite of all she can do, will now and then creep into the heart. She is relieved of the necessity of always being "fixed up," in order to be in proper trim to receive her knight, should he come at an unexpected hour. And then, under the Spanish *régime*, there are none of the heart-burnings and uncertainties as to whether her love is returned, as is often experienced under our system, and to which species of disquietude the ladies are more or less given. There is no time lost in rides and walks, nor sleep destroyed in troubled dreams, not to mention an occasional case of bona fide heart-breaking, with suit for damages. This paternal arrangement even presents more advantages for the lad than the lass: it is an immense saving of both time and money, economizes breath, otherwise expended in long-drawn sighs, and last, though not least, is a positive blessing to hired horses. This mode of procedure removes the greatest bugbear in the line matrimonial, and under it a wife can be had without the necessity of passing through the fiery ordeal of "popping the question," which is said to require more nerve than to lead a forlorn hope on the field of battle. Such is the working of the Spanish system, and the manner in which the fair sex are led willing captives in Cupid's net; but, after giving it a careful consideration, I am much inclined to the opinion that "the old way is the best, after all."

Soon after my arrival in Santa Fe, a case in point came under observation, and I had an opportunity of witnessing the practical workings of this new matrimonial arrangement. In a family in which I was an habitual visitor there was a pretty and agreeable daughter, who had inspired a *caballero* with the tender passion. He made the matter known in due season to his father, who in turn addressed a sort of diplomatic note to the mother of the young lady, proposing that the two young people should become "bone of one bone and flesh of one flesh." I chanced to call at the house the same evening the letter had been received, and the mother, feeling unusually happy in view of the proposed alliance, handed it to me to read, at the same time descanting with considerable eloquence upon the advantages to arise from such a match—that the young man was *mui rico* (very rich) and *mui buen* (very good), with many other words of praise. The letter was an ordinary business document, and couched in about the same language as would be used in the purchase of a mule or the hire of burro. The mother was quite anxious for the alliance to take place, but told me, in a semi-confidential manner, that her daughter was opposed to the arrangement—a perverseness that the old lady could not understand. The young lady sat close by, a listener to the conversation between her mother and myself, now and then giving us a meaning look from under her long eyelashes, as much as to say, "No you don't, old lady." I determined to know how the matter stood with the daughter, and at the first opportunity asked her a few leading questions touching the matter under consideration, and pretty soon found out the cause of trouble in the camp. She told me, with great frankness, that she did not love her suitor, and would not marry him. Here was the whole question in a nutshell. I counseled treason in the premises, and advised her to have her own way in a matter which was of more importance to her than any one else. She took this course, and the unromantic and unwooing swain was obliged to look elsewhere for a housekeeper. A few evenings afterward I saw the father of the young man at the house, who had come to talk the matter over with the mother; but it did no good, for the young lady had a mind of her own, and neither persuasion nor parental threats could induce her to accede to their wishes.

Notwithstanding the high rate of matrimonial fees, and the artificial restrictions placed upon love-making, people do sometimes marry in New Mexico, after all. The first winter I spent in Santa Fe I had the pleasure of attending a *bona fide* Mexican wedding, both parties being considered as belonging to the *élite* of the city. The father of the bride, Don Antonio, was a *rico*, and the happy groom was an officer of the Legislative Assembly. The ceremony took place on a Sunday evening, at the house of the bride's father, where a large number of guests were in attendance. The young lady was a comely lass, without being beautiful. The invitations specified eight o'clock as the hour when the performance was to come off, and, a short time before, in company with some friends, I wended my way to the scene of the festivities. A carriage had been provided to convey us to the house, which we found in waiting at the door of the Honorable Secretary of the Territory. Duly seated in the rickety old machine, away we rattled, and, after a drive of a few minutes, were safely deposited at the threshold.

The master of the establishment met us at the door, welcomed us in the most friendly manner, and conducted us across the court-yard into the house, passing through the *sala* into a smaller room beyond. Here were assembled some twenty ladies of all ages, and, in order to be a correct chronicler of events, I must add of all colors, from the fair skin of the pure Spanish blood to a good wholesome Indian brown. They were seated, some on benches and others upon the floor, quite after the manner of a Turk, and nearly every one of them had *cigarritos* in their mouths, which they smoked with the nonchalance of the same number of men. Upon our entrance they maintained their dignity and silence, nor presumed to salute us even with a *buenas noches*. We seated ourselves, and, in obedience to the command of Don Antonio, made ourselves as much at home as the circumstances of the case would permit. Several other ladies came in, one at a time, until the room was quite filled. Some of them were pretty and intelligent-looking, and dressed with considerable taste, but the wreaths of smoke which now and then came from the mouth and nostrils detracted considerably from their good looks, according to the American idea. In the centre of the room stood a table filled with numerous bottles of liquor, both mild and strong, supported on each side by plates of cakes and sweetmeats, which fairly formed a breastwork around the spiritual comforters. As there was no other gentleman invited to take a seat in the room with the ladies, we considered ourselves more highly honored than the rest of the company—so much for being governor, secretary, and Uncle Sam's attorney.

We had been seated some half an hour, when we were invited to walk into the *sala*, where the ceremony was about to come off. Here we found a large number of persons arranged around the room, each one holding a lighted candle. Upon our entrance candles were thrust into our hands, and we were conducted to the head of the room, where the altar was erected, and which appeared to be the post of honor. We took our position just to the left of the officiating priest, who, duly robed and book in hand, stood ready to read the service. Immediately behind us were the musicians, two with violins and the third with a harp, who were charged to discourse music upon the occasion. In a few minutes the bridal party, four in number, entered the room, and advanced in front of and near the priest. The service was performed according to the rites of the Roman Catholic Church, and in a very few minutes the affianced couple were pronounced husband and wife. When the ceremony was about half concluded, the musicians commenced their discord, which they kept up until it was finished, the leader accompanying the instruments with his voice, which sounded about as melodious as a dinner-horn out of tune. After the benediction was pronounced the ladies retired, and we saw no more of them; but the gentlemen were invited to the refreshment-room to partake of a few of the good things of life. In a short time the company bade adieu to the host and bent their steps homeward, and thus was celebrated a Mexican wedding.

Urban Employments

VIRGINIA PENNY, 1863

Virginia Penny, *The Employments of Women: A Cyclopedia of Women's Work* (Boston: Walker, Wise & Co., 1863), pp. viii, 104–5, 125, 308–10, 424–26.

Antebellum cities were centers of female employment—and of working-class women who were thrown on the job market. In 1859–1861, the indefatigable researcher Virginia Penny investigated hundreds of jobs held by New York women. She visited stores, workshops, and factories and interviewed both employers and employees. Penny's *Cyclopedia* covered every conceivable type of work: Information about snuffsellers, landscape gardeners, tea packers, junk dealers, glassblowers, book folders, hat braiders, and candlestick makers rolled off her pages. Just as impressive as Penny's research was her prose style: a rapid-fire combination of observation, digression, quotation, anecdote, analysis, commentary, and comparison—usually to Paris or London.

Virginia Penny was not an unbiased commentator. She believed, first, in the value of work. "The dignity and value of labor in the most menial occupation is superior to idleness or dependence upon others," she contended at the outset. Penny was also a most vigilant protector and supporter of women's interests as employees. In the following excerpts, Penny discusses the new and competitive field of sales work, an area in which she believed women to be very capable; the overcrowded vocation of the seamstress, for whom the recent introduction of the sewing machine had caused mounting unemployment; and the perils of domestic service, a field now filled mainly by Irish immigrant women. Interspersed at random among her bountiful sections of data are Virginia Penny's sharp analyses of trends in the female labor market.

As a friend of my sex, I have made investigations, and obtained statistics that show the business position of women at present in the United States. . . . I have made the study a specialty for three years, and spent an almost incredible amount of labor and money in doing so. I have visited factories, workshops, offices and stores, for the purpose of seeing women at their vocations. I have gone through wind and snow, cold and rain. If I could have had the time and opportunity, I would have endeavored to see, also, something of their home life. . . .

Merchants. . . . Woman has a power of adaptedness that fits her admirably for the vocation of merchant. A friend remarked to me that Mr. Stewart, of New York, she thought would employ women in his store if a large number of fashionable ladies would petition him to do so. If the retail merchants of our large cities and towns would combine and employ only saleswomen, how greatly would they promote the welfare of the nation. Young men would no longer waste their health, strength, and talents selling gloves, tapes, and dress goods, but would cultivate the soil, or find openings as traders, speculators, mechanics, and manufacturers in cities, towns, and villages of our western country. They might do something more creditable to their physical power, while they gave their half-starved sisters a chance to earn an honest livelihood. If ladies would patronize only those stores in which there were saleswomen and influence their friends to do so, employers who now engage the service of salesmen would soon learn what was to their interest, and make a change. Promptness and regularity are desirable qualifications in a shopkeeper. The business brings those engaged into intercourse with all classes of people. A lady who has lived in New York all her life said, if the merchants of the city would employ women, they could find twenty thousand tomorrow, ready and willing to enter their stores. . . .

Quick perceptive powers and judgment are also essential to the success of merchants. It is very desirable to have a good location for a store. A lady keeping a small dry goods store told me she sells $100 worth of goods a week on an average. She has been nine years in the business, and constantly gaining trade. She likes rainy Saturday evenings, as she then sells most. She said one must use judgment in the amount of profit to be made on various articles. A person must regulate her prices by others. On some goods she can make but five per cent, and on some fifty. Many of the fortunes in Boston are said to have been founded by women engaged in trade. . . .

Saleswomen. Women are quite as capable by nature to sell dry goods as men, but are not trained so thoroughly, nor from so early an age. Suavity of manner and perfect control of temper are very desirable qualifications for a clerk. Care, judgment, and taste are requisite for success. A flow of speech and ability to show goods to advantage are also desirable. Some people urge that if females are employed as attendants in stores, they will be exposed to dangerous and demoralizing influences, and something is said about the corruption of female shopkeepers in Paris, by way of warning. Now, it so happens that the corruption spoken of does not exist among the store attendants in Paris, but among sempstresses [seamstresses]. . . . "One fifth of all the female criminals in Paris are sempstresses," says Madame Mallet. Some employers complain that women are too socially inclined, too much disposed to chat, when several are employed in the same establishment. It may be true; but are they more so than men of the same age? . . .

Sempstresses. In 1845, there were in New York ten thousand sempstresses, and now there are probably many more. . . . When the times are hard, prices fall from their usually low standard. Our hearts sicken within us as we read the prices paid needle-women. The trifling remuneration and wasted health of most needlewomen is a bitter reflection on those who employ them. . . . The occupation of sempstress is crowded to overflowing in New York. In business times it is impossible to get a working person to leave New York, but in hard times they are very willing to go. One firm told me that they often have applications for operators and sempstresses in busy seasons, but then they will not leave; and when the times are dull, there is no demand, and they cannot. The supply of labor has been greater than the demand, and hence the com-petition that has arisen among clothing merchants, and the low price of made [ready-made] clothing as sold in slop shops [stores that sold cheap ready-made garments]. The use of sewing machines has to some extent done away with sewing by hand. Many a woman has been thrown out of employment by it, to which many of our newspapers can testify, and have borne witness during the past two years. We have heard of some slop shops in large cities, offering to pay the highest wages to good shirt makers, each applicant to take a shirt and make it for nothing, as a sample of her sewing. From one hundred to two hundred, perhaps, apply, and of course that many shirts are made. It meets the demands of the unprincipled shopkeeper, and he has, perhaps, employment for a dozen or more. A man that has a ladies' furnishing store, told me he pays girls that sew neatly by hand 37½ cents a day. Many clothing merchants have their work done more cheaply. . . . The majority of sempstresses have no time they can call their own. Those that sew twelve to fourteen out of the twenty-four hours, without any relatives or friends even to be protectors for them, and often in bad health, have no time for mental improvement or social intercourse. "The habits of the sempstress are indicated by the neck suddenly bending forward and the arms, even in walking, considerably bent forward, or folded more or less upward from the elbows." . . .

Sewing Machine Operators.   . . . Now that machines are more plentiful, work done by them is not so well paid. The sellers of machines say it is not unhealthy. Some people suppose the machine to be more injurious than the needle, if worked as long and as constantly. The tax on the muscles of the lower limbs and the weaker parts of the system is certainly very great. . . . I talked with a lady keeping a depository con-nected with an influential church for the supplying of poor women with work. She thinks sewing machines are very injurious—says a girl of seventeen will give out in three to five years at most. . . . The sewing machine has certainly thrown many women out of employment. Those who are able to purchase one may get along. It is in this as every other branch of labor—a capital however small, is an assistance in business. . . .

Domestics.   We think an important work of benevolence presents itself in the Free States. It is providing homes for servant girls, when they are unemployed or sick. Many of them are in a strange land, unacquainted with the language and the ways of the people. When sick, some of them are immediately sent off by their mistresses to save the trouble of waiting on them. . . . Some servants soon fail [in health], and are not fit for service more than a few years. It arises mostly from their exposure to cold and dampness without being properly clothed and fed, and sometimes from too free indulgence in the pleasures of the palate, particularly that of the consuming liquid which burns out life and sense [alcohol]. The hard work that most Irish women perform, and the large number of them in this country, have made them the most numerous domestics in the Free States. They are generally employed as maids of all work. I think the majority of American girls going into service is increasing. The majority of white female domestics in this country are single women, from sixteen to thirty-five years of age. . . . A short time ago, we counted in the New York *Herald* eight columns of situations wanted, three fourths of which were by female domestics. It shows what a surplus there is of domestics in the cities, that no doubt could find situations through the country, and in the villages. The majority of female domestics would rather starve in New York than go to the country, or even little towns around for fair wages. I think it arises from the fear that they will not find associates. . . . In 1853, domestics were receiving wages in San Francisco proportioned to the prices paid for everything else. Cooks got $100 a month, and board; house servants, from $35 to $70, and board. . . . In most towns through our country domestics get from $1.25 to $2.50 a week, and board. . . . We give the rate of wages of domestics in New York (1857) at the intelligence offices [employment agencies]. Maids of all work, very raw, $4 per month; average, $5; good, $6 to $7. Chambermaids—good, $6. Cooks—good, $7 to $8; extra, $12 to $16. . . . I have had numberless statements from different parts of Free States that it was almost impossible to obtain good domestics. I have just taken up a paper in which I read: "Female domestics are scarce in Minnesota and Wisconsin, and obtain employment readily at good prices in almost all the river towns." More particularly are female domestics scarce, where there are factories. Girls, especially American girls, prefer to work in factories to being servants, as they think it more honorable, and it secures to them more time—in short, they are their own mistresses.

New York Prostitutes

WILLIAM SANGER, 1858

William Sanger, *A History of Prostitution* (New York: The Medical Publishing Co., 1858), pp. 486–516.

As antebellum cities expanded, prostitution posed a problem for authorities. Sex was now a part of the urban economy, and a noticeable part. In New York, historian Christine Stansell points out, prostitutes could be found in all public places—near the theaters, on the waterfront, throughout the commercial district—and police statistics suggested an alarming rise in the trade. Although prostitution itself was not a statutory offense, women "on the town" might be arrested for vagrancy or keeping a disorderly house. Convictions in these areas rose precipitously during the 1850s.* The city aldermen therefore commissioned Dr. William Sanger, resident physician at the Blackwell's Island women's prison, to conduct an investigation of New York prostitutes. In 1858, Dr. Sanger presented his findings in a remarkable study that reveals both the "undercurrent," in his words, of city life and the experiences of working-class women.

According to Dr. Sanger, who interviewed a sample of 2,000 Blackwell's Island inmates, New York prostitutes were primarily young; eighty-eight percent were of ages fifteen to thirty. Over half (sixty-two percent) were immigrants, among whom the Irish were overrepresented and the Germans were underrepresented. Almost one-fourth were daughters of farmers and almost one-third were daughters of skilled workers. A majority of the interviewees had run into some sort of problem with men—or, more specifically, with financial support from men. Over half had lost their fathers as children or teenagers. Almost a quarter were married women who had been deserted or widowed. Over ten percent claimed to be "seduced and abandoned," a predicament that concerned both Dr. Sanger and those women involved in the moral reform movement (see Chapter 11). The occupations or former occupations of convicted prostitutes were also relevant, the study revealed. About half were domestic servants and a quarter held or had held jobs in manufacturing, mainly in the ill-paid needle trades.

---

*Christine Stansell, *City of Women: Sex and Class in New York, 1789–1860* (New York: Knopf, 1986), pp. 171–75.

What led these women into prostitution? Ever sympathetic, Dr. Sanger refused to issue moral condemnations of his subjects. Rather, he saw them as victims of the harsh urban environment: of family disorganization or disintegration, and especially of low wages, under-employment, and poverty. "A large number of females . . . earn so small wages that a temporary cessation of their business, or being a short time out of a situation, is sufficient to reduce them to absolute distress," the doctor observed. Still, when asked why they had become prostitutes, almost half suggested reasons other than financial hardship. Over a quarter cited "inclination"—drink, pleasure, "an easy life." Dr. Sanger distrusted such answers. Convinced that women were passionless or almost so, he contended that "inclination" was merely a product of "other and controlling influences." The following excerpts contain some of the prostitutes' responses and segments of Dr. Sanger's earnest analysis.

Question: What Was the Cause of Your Becoming a Prostitute?

CAUSES	NUMBERS
Inclination	513
Destitution	525
Seduced and abandoned	258
Drink, and the desire to drink	181
Ill-treatment of parents, relatives, or husbands	164
As an easy life	124
Bad company	84
Persuaded by prostitute	71
Too ill to work	29
Violated	27
Seduced on board emigrant ships	16
Seduced in emigrant boarding houses	8
Total	2,000

This question is probably the most important of the series, as the replies lay open to a considerable extent those hidden springs of evil which have hitherto been known only from their results. First in order stands the reply "Inclination," which can only be understood as meaning a voluntary resort to prostitution in order to gratify the sexual passions. Five hundred and thirteen women, more than one fourth of the gross number, give this as their reason. If their representations were borne out by facts, it would make the task of grappling with the vice a most arduous one, and afford very slight grounds to hope for any amelioration; but it is imagined that the circumstances which induced the ruin of most of those who gave the answer will prove that if a positive inclination to vice was the proximate cause of the fall, it was but the result of other and controlling influences. In itself such an answer would imply an innate depravity, a want of true womanly feeling, which is actually incredible. The force of desire can be neither denied nor disputed, but still in the bosoms of most females that force exists in a slumbering state until aroused by some outside influences. No woman can understand its power until some positive cause of excitement exists. . . . The full force of sexual desire is seldom known to a virtuous woman. In the male sex nature has provided a more susceptible organization than in females, apparently with the beneficent design of repressing those evils which must result from mutual appetite felt equally by both. In other words, man is the *aggressive* animal, so far as sexual desire is involved. Were it otherwise, and the passions in both sexes equal, illegitimacy and prostitution would be far more rife in our midst than at present.

Some few of the cases in which the reply "Inclination" was given are herewith submitted, with the explanation which accompanied each return. C. M: While virtuous, this girl had visited dance-houses, where she became acquainted with prostitutes, who persuaded her that they led an easy, merry life; her inclination was the result of female persuasion. E. C. left her husband, and became a prostitute willingly, in order to obtain intoxicating liquors which had been refused her at home. E. R. was deserted by her husband because she drank to excess, and became a prostitute in order to obtain liquor. In this and the preceding case, inclination was the result solely of intemperance. A. J. willingly sacrificed her virtue to a man she loved. C. L.: Her inclination was swayed by the advice of women already on the town. J. J. continued this course from inclination after having been seduced by her lover. S. C.: This girl's inclination arose from a love of liquor. Enough has been quoted to prove that in many of the cases, what is called willing prostitution is the sequel of some communication or circumstances which undermine the principles of virtue and arouse the latent passions.

Destitution is assigned as a reason in five hundred and twenty-five cases. In many of these it is unquestionably true that positive, actual want, the apparent and dreaded approach of starvation was the real cause of degradation. . . . As in all the selections already made, or that may be made hereafter, these cases are taken indiscriminately from the replies received, and might be indefinitely extended.

M. M., a widow with one child, earned $1.50 per week as a tailoress; J. Y., a servant, was taken sick while in a situation, spent all her money, and could get no employment when she recovered. M. T. (quoting her own words) "had no work, no money, and no home." S. F., a widow with three children, could earn two dollars weekly at cap-making, but could not obtain steady employment even at those prices. M. F. had been out of place for some time, and had no money. E. H. earned from two to three dollars per week as a tailoress, but had been out of employment for some time. L. C. G.: the examining officer reports in this case, "This girl (a tailoress) is a stranger without any relations. She received a dollar and a half a week, which would not maintain her." . . . E. M. G.: the captain of police in the district where this woman resides says, "This girl struggled hard with the world before she became a prostitute, sleeping in station-houses at night, and living on bread and water during the day." He adds, "In my experience of three years, I have known *over fifty cases* whose history would be similar to hers, and who are now prostitutes."

These details give some insight into the undercurrent of city life. The most prominent fact is that a large number of females, both operatives and domestics, earn so small wages that a temporary cessation of their business, or being a short time out of a situation, is sufficient to reduce them to absolute distress. . . . The struggle [that] a virtuous girl will wage against fate in such circumstances may be conceived: it is a literal battle for life, and in the result life is too often preserved only by the sacrifice of virtue.

"Seduced and abandoned." Two hundred and fifty-eight women made this reply. These numbers give but a faint idea of the actual total that should be recorded under the designation, as many who are included in other classes should doubtless have been returned in this. It has already been shown that under the answer "Inclination" are comprised the responses of many who were the victims of seduction before such inclination existed, and there can be no question that among those who assign "Drink, and the desire to drink," as the cause of their becoming prostitutes, may be found many whose first departure from the rules of sobriety was actuated by a desire to drive from their memories all recollections of their seducers' falsehoods. Of the number who were persuaded by women, themselves already fallen, to become public courtesans, it is but reasonable to conclude that many had previously yielded their honor to some lover under false protestations of attachment and fidelity. . . .

The following cases will exhibit some of the results of seduction: M. C., a native of Pennsylvania, seventeen years of age, was induced to run away from home with her lover, who promised to marry her as soon as they reached Philadelphia. Instead of keeping his word, he deserted her. She was afraid to go home, and had no means of living except by prostitution, which she practiced for eight months in Philadelphia, and then came to New York to reside. Her father, a physician, died when she was about ten years old, and her mother subsequently married a hotel-keeper, in whose house the girl was reared, and to the associations of which she probably, to some extent, owes her fall from virtue. . . .

A. B., the child of respectable parents in Germany, was seduced in her native place by a man to whom she was attached. He promised to marry her if she would accompany him to the United States. She obtained the permission and necessary funds from her parents, and two days after they landed in New York, her seducer deserted her, carrying off all the money she had brought from home. H. P., a school-girl, sixteen years of age, was seduced by a married man who now visits her occasionally. C. A. was seduced in New Jersey, brought to New York, and deserted among strangers. M. R. was seduced by her employer, a married man. A. W. was seduced while at school in Troy, N. Y., and was ashamed to return to her parents. L. H. followed a lover from England who had promised to marry her. When she arrived in New York he seduced and diseased her, and then she discovered that he was a married man. There is no necessity to multiply these cases.

"Drink, and the desire to drink." We will alter an old saying and render it, "When a woman *drinks* she is lost." It will be conceded that the habit of intoxication in woman, if not an indication of actual depravity or vice, is a sure precursor of it, for drunkenness and debauchery are inseparable companions, one almost invariably following the other. In some cases a woman living in service becomes a drunkard; she forms acquaintances among the depraved of her own sex, and willingly joins their ranks. Married women acquire the habit of drinking, and forsake their husbands and families to gratify not so much their sexual appetite as their passion for liquor. Young women are often persuaded to take one or two glasses of liquor, and then their ruin may be soon expected. Others are induced to drink spirits in which a narcotic has been infused to render them insensible to their ruin. In short, it is scarcely possible to enumerate the many temptations which can be employed when intoxicating drinks are used as the agent.

"The treatment of parent, husband, or relative" is a prolific cause of prostitution, one hundred and sixty-four women assigning it as a reason for their fall. . . .

J. M., a very well educated girl: "I was seduced at eighteen years of age, and *forced* to leave home to hide my disgrace." Admitting that this girl had been led into an error, the plain duty of her parents in every point of view was to endeavor to reform her instead of driving her from home. . . .

E. B.:   "My parents wanted me to marry an old man, and I refused. I had a very unhappy home afterward." . . .

P. G.:   "My mother ill-treated me and drove me from home. My father was very kind, but he died when I was seven years old." . . .

J. C.:   "My father accused me of being a prostitute when I was innocent. He would give me no clothes to wear. My mother was a confirmed drunkard, and used to be away from home most of the time." . . .

J. A.:   "I am the eldest of a large family. My father is a drunkard, and would not support the children. I have supported my parents, brothers, and sisters for the last five years." . . .

A. B.:   "My lover seduced and diseased me while I was working in a factory. I went home, and my parents turned me out." . . .

C. C.:   "My husband deserted me and four children. I had no means to live." In this case the husband violated the laws of God in forcibly rending the matrimonial bond, and violated the laws of his country by leaving his wife and children as burdens on society. For the former of these offenses he must answer at the bar of Infinite Justice; for the latter he is liable to punishment in this world. "Then why not punish him?" asks some one. For the very simple reason that he could not be found. . . .

J. S.:   "My husband committed adultery. I caught him with another woman, and then he left me." . . .

A. B.: "My husband accused me of infidelity, which was not true. I only lived with him five months. I was pregnant by him, and after my child was born I went on the town to support it." . . .

B. B.: "My husband brought me here (a house of ill fame). I did not know what kind of place it was. He lives with me, and I follow prostitution." . . .

L. W.: "I came to this city, from Illinois, with my husband. When we got here he deserted me. I have two children dependent on me." . . .

C. H.: "I was married when I was seventeen years old, and have had three children. The two boys are living now; the girl is dead. My oldest boy is nearly five years old, and the other one is eighteen months. My husband is a sailor. We lived very comfortably till my last child was born, and then he began to drink very hard, and did not support me, and I have not seen him or heard any thing about him for six months. After he left me I tried to keep my children by washing or going out to day's work, but I could not earn enough. I never could earn more than two or three dollars a week when I had work, which was not always. My mother and father died when I was a child. I had nobody to help me, and could not support my children, so I came to this place. My boys are now living in the city, and I support them with what I earn by prostitution. It was only to keep them that I came here." . . .

E. W.: "My husband had another wife when I married him. I left him when I found this out. I was pregnant by him, and had no other way to live than by prostitution." In point of law, this is not a married woman, the existence of the former wife rendering the second union invalid; but this is no excuse for the man's conduct; in fact, it materially aggravates his guilt. . . .

A. D.: "My parents were dead. I lived with my uncle, who treated me very unkindly." . . .

L. M.: "I was taken by my sister-in-law to a house of prostitution, and there violated." . . .

C. W.: "My parents died when I was young. I was brought up by relatives who went to California when I was sixteen years old, and left me destitute. I had no trade." . . .

C. B.: "My parents were dead. I was out of place. I had no relations but an uncle, who would not give me any shelter unless I paid him for it. I went on the town to get money to pay for my lodgings." . . .

As already stated, these cases are all facts, collected in the course of this investigation, and are believed to be substantially correct. With such disclosures as these, can any one be surprised at the continued spread of prostitution? The family circle is one of the sources whence it emanates; so is the matrimonial bond; and so are the different branches of consanguinity. When fathers, husbands, and relatives thus forget their duties, and lend their influence to swell the tide of vice, it is no matter of surprise that strangers should be found ready and eager to contribute their share to the polluted current.

But the evil is not incurable, if public opinion can be enlisted on the side of public morals, and parents are satisfied, by unmistakable demonstrations, that the voice of an indignant people will be raised against them if practices similar to those narrated continue to occur. Husbands, too, must be convinced that any infraction of their marriage vows will expose them to popular odium; and if they have contracted an ill-assorted, hasty alliance, the responsibility must be borne by themselves. The contracts they voluntarily made must be fulfilled. Relatives also must be warned that the performance of their duties will be rigidly required. There is no deficiency of legislation on this subject; all that is wanted is determination to enforce existing laws; and when this is done, some of the main causes of prostitution will be removed.

Conduct in the Street

ELIZA LESLIE, 1857

Eliza Leslie, "Conduct in the Street," *The Behaviour Book: A Manual for Ladies*, 7th ed. (Philadelphia: Willis P. Hazard, 1857), pp. 65–71.

New arrivals in antebellum cities included the upwardly mobile, who hoped to secure a place in the middle class. To women of this group, Philadelphia author Eliza Leslie (1787–1858) addressed a compendium of etiquette and social advice. *The Behaviour Book*, first published in 1853, went through many editions. Hoping "to improve her young countrywomen" who were rising on the social ladder and wanted to adjust to city life, Eliza Leslie provided a cascade of rules and tips.

Some of Leslie's advice concerned what might be called "inside" behavior. She offered, for instance, guidelines on speech and language usage, manners with gentlemen, and home entertainment. She provided tips for serving tea, excelling as a hostess, succeeding as a guest, and attending evening parties. Eliza Leslie's advice also followed women out of the house into the "outside" urban world—the world of visiting, shopping, concerts, theaters, and public transportation. It should be noted that Leslie's antebellum city was often a dangerous place. Lurking around the gutters, pavements, and trolleys were unexpected perils, such as street toughs and pickpockets. A "lady" had to show her mettle. The following excerpt concerns "conduct in the street," or manners to be followed by the upwardly mobile when out of the house. Here, Eliza Leslie captures several types of motion—the movement of people from the countryside to "town," the hustle and bustle of the city scene, and the scrambling for status with which, we can assume, her readers were concerned.

When three ladies are walking together, it is better for one to keep a little in advance of the other two, than for all three to persist in maintaining one unbroken line. They cannot all join in conversation without talking across each other—a thing that, indoors or out-of-doors, is awkward, inconvenient, ungenteel, and should always be avoided. Also, three ladies walking abreast occupy too much of the pavement and therefore incommode the other passengers [pedestrians]. Three young *men* sometimes lounge along the pavement, arm in arm. Three young gentlemen never do so.

If you meet a lady with whom you have become but slightly acquainted, and had merely a little conversation (for instance, at a party or a morning visit), and who moves in a circle somewhat higher or more fashionable than your own, it is safest to wait until she recognises you. Let her not see in you a disposition to obtrude yourself on her notice.

It is not expected that all intimacies formed at watering-places shall continue after the parties have returned to their homes. A mutual bow when meeting in the street is sufficient. But there is no interchanging of visits, unless both ladies have, before parting, testified a desire to continue the acquaintance. In this case, the lady who is the eldest, or palpably higher in station, makes the first call. It is not customary for a young lady to make the first visit to a married lady.

When meeting them in the street, always speak first to your milliner, mantua-maker, seamstress, or to any one you have been in the practice of employing. To pass without notice any servant that you know, is rude and unfeeling, as they will attribute it to pride, not presuming to speak to you themselves, unless in reply. There are persons who have accepted, when in the country, much kindness from the country-people, are ashamed to recognise them when they come to town, on account of their rustic or unfashionable dress. This is a very vulgar, contemptible, and foolish pride; and is always seen through, and despised. There is no danger of plain country-people being mistaken for vulgar city-people. In our country, there is no reason for keeping aloof from any who are respectable in character and appearance. Those to be avoided are such as wear tawdry finery, paint their faces, and leer out of the corners of their eyes, *looking* disreputable, even if they are not disreputable in reality.

When a gentleman meets a lady with whom his acquaintance is very slight (perhaps nothing more than a few words of talk at a party), he allows her the option of continuing the acquaintance or not, at her pleasure; therefore, he waits until she recognises him, and till she evinces it by a bow—he looking at her to give the opportunity. Thus, if she has no objection to numbering him among her acquaintance, she denotes it by bowing first. American ladies never curtsey in the street. If she has any reason to disapprove of his character or habits, she is perfectly justified in "cutting" him, as it is termed. Let her bow very coldly the first time, and after that, not at all. . . .

When a lady is walking between two gentlemen, she should divide her conversation equally as practicable, or address most of it to him who is most of a stranger to her. He, with whom she is least on ceremony, will excuse her.

A gentleman on escorting a lady to her own home, must not leave her till he has rung the bell, and waited till the servant has come and opened the door, and till she is actually in the house. Men who know no better, think it is sufficient to walk with her to the foot of the steps and take their departure, leaving her to get in as best she can. This we have seen—but not often, and the offenders were not Americans.

If you stop a few minutes in the street to talk to an acquaintance, draw to one side of the pavement near the wall, so as not to impede the passengers—or you may turn and walk with her as far as the next corner. And never stop to speak in the middle of a crossing. To speak loudly in the street is exceedingly ungenteel, and foolish, as what you say will be heard by all who pass by. To call across the way to an acquaintance is very unladylike. . . .

When a stranger offers to assist you across a brimming gutter, or over a puddle, or a glair of slippy ice, do not hesitate, or decline, as if you thought he was taking an unwarranted liberty. He means nothing but civility. . . .

When you see persons slip down on the ice, do not laugh at them. There is no fun in being hurt, or in being mortified by a fall in the public street; and we know not how a *lady* can see anything diverting in so painful a circumstance. It is more feminine on witnessing such a sight, to utter an involuntary scream than a shout of laughter. And still more so, to stop and ascertain if the person has been hurt.

If on stopping an omnibus, you find that a dozen people are already seated in it, draw back, and refuse to add to the number; giving no heed to the assertion of the driver that "There is plenty of room." The *passengers* will not say so, and you have no right to crowd them all, even if you are willing to be crowded yourself—a thing that is extremely uncomfortable, and very injurious to your dress, which may, in consequence, be so squeezed and rumpled as never to look well again. . . .

It is imprudent to ride in an omnibus with much money in your purse. Pickpockets of genteel appearance are too frequently among the passengers. . . . If you are obliged to have money of any consequence about you, keep your hand all the time in that pocket. . . .

No lady should venture to ride in an omnibus after dark, unless she is escorted by a gentleman whom she knows. She had better walk home, even under the protection of a servant. If alone in an omnibus at night, she is liable to meet with improper company and perhaps be insulted.

Chapter 10

Mistress and Slave

During the early nineteenth century, slavery became a larger, more severe institution. Although the nation ended legal slave importation in 1808, natural growth plus illegal arrivals swelled the slave population to more than three million by 1860. When southerners of the 1820s moved west to new cotton lands in Alabama, Mississippi, and Texas, slavery expanded over a larger area. The response to Nat Turner's rebellion in 1831 tightened restrictions on slaves in all regions, and emancipation became more difficult if not impossible. Rising slave prices, meanwhile, made slaves a repository for more and more capital. Overall, during the antebellum years, slavery became more permanent, entrenched, and intransigent.

This development affected the lives of southern women—notably the hundreds of thousands of women who *were* slaves, and the far smaller group of women who were members of slaveowning families (about one quarter of all southern families by 1860). The plantation mistress held an ironic position. Compared to her peers in the North, who might be involved in some sort of voluntary association, church organization, or reform society, the southern woman was removed from public affairs and especially isolated from politics, the domain of men. Yet, in their day-to-day lives, women of slaveowning families confronted the most important political question of the day, one they could hardly avoid. Most of their domestic responsibilities—the distribution of staples, the tending of garden and barnyard, and the supervision of household production—involved management of slaves. Although southern women traditionally lacked authority in all realms of life, including domestic affairs, they were often in a position to wield authority over slaves, especially slaves in the plantation household. How did such women feel about slavery and slaveowning?

The comments of women in slaveowning families often suggest that slave management was or had been an oppressive burden. Some postwar memoirists compared their former roles to those of slaves. "The mistress of the plantation was the most complete slave on it," declared Susan Dabney Smedes in her recollections. Myra Avery avowed that she was glad slavery ended because "I ceased to belong body and soul to my negroes." Many mistresses pointed to the detrimental impact of slavery on the morals of white men. "These fathers whose beastly passions hurry to the bed of the slave do they feel no compunction when they see their blood sold, basely bartered like horses?" asked Alabama diarist Sarah Haynesworth Gayle, "This sin is the leprosy of the earth." Miscegenation perpetrated by white men provided a recurrent theme in women's comments. "Southern women are all, I believe, abolitionists at heart," wrote Gertrude Ella Thomas of Georgia on the eve of the Civil War. "Poor women, poor slaves," observed Mary Boykin Chesnut in her famous Civil War diary.

Such comments give the misleading impression that mistress and master were locked into conflict. Yet, as recent studies of antebellum southern women contend, mistresses rarely suffered from divided loyalties or from excessive sympathy for women in slavery. Divisions of race and class far exceeded the commonality of gender. Slaves were the basis of southern wealth. White women—like white men—inherited and bequeathed slave property, reaped the benefits of slave labor, and enjoyed the status that slaveowning provided. Experienced mistresses, writes historian Catherine Clinton, were more likely to groan over "the evils of *slaves* rather than the curse of slavery."* "Class and race deeply divided Southern women," confirms historian Elizabeth Fox-Genovese, "notwithstanding their shared experience of life in rural households under the domination of men."†

Although massive data exist on slavery, provided by such sources as interviews of former slaves, slave women rarely commented on the role of gender in their lives. According to historian Deborah Gray

---

*Catherine Clinton, *The Plantation Mistress: Woman's World in the Old South* (New York: Pantheon, 1982), p. 185.
†Elizabeth Fox-Genovese, *Within the Plantation Household: Black and White Women in the Old South* (Chapel Hill: University of North Carolina Press, 1988), p. 43.

White, "The sources are silent about female status in the slave community and the bondwoman's self-perception."* The sources do, however, reveal some distinctions between the experiences of male and female slaves. Women were less likely to escape or join collective acts of resistance, because they were tied more closely to their families. They tended to work in all-women groups. They were lower in price and value, and they were more likely than men to be field-hands because they were less likely to be artisans. They were open to sexual assault by white men and, conversely, were able on occasion to manipulate a sexual relationship into some sort of privilege.

The most important and controversial distinction was the vital role of women in the slave family and the slave community. Since all relationships were subject to interference by owners, slave families never enjoyed the domestic security available to white families. Women remained the mainstay of slave family life; the family unit was mother and children. This alone provided an enormous distinction between white and black experiences. Under such circumstances, was there more "equality" among male and female slaves than among white men and women? "If the male supremacy of the Big House did not infiltrate the quarters it was in part because the jobs and services performed by slave women for the community were not peripheral but central to slave survival," writes Deborah Gray White.[†] Women's vital services to the slave community were no doubt part of the answer. Another part, perhaps, was the negative mode of sexual equality that slave status provided. No slaves owned property, all slaves did physical if not menial work, and all slaves were degraded by their condition.

Elizabeth Fox-Genovese offers an important reminder to consider when examining the roles of southern women: All were excluded from the middle-class revolution that was transforming antebellum northern society. "The history of slavery does not constitute another regional variation on the main story," Fox-Genovese contends, but rather "it constitutes another story."[‡] The following documents

---

*Deborah Gray White, *Ar'n't I a Woman? Female Slaves in the Plantation South* (New York: Norton, 1985), p. 23.
[†]White, p. 22.
[‡]Fox-Genovese, p. 42.

concern the "other" story—and some of the questions that historians have asked about women in the antebellum South. How did slave women view their condition as slaves? What can the reminiscences of former slaves reveal about gender roles? What authority did mistresses exert over slaves? How did they reconcile religion and slaveowning? In what ways did they defend or defy the slave system? Overall, how were the experiences of southern women, black and white, different from those of their northern contemporaries?

An Alabama Diary

Sarah Haynesworth Gayle, 1828, 1833

Diary of Sarah Haynesworth Gayle, 1827–1835, Special Collections, University of Alabama.

The westward expansion of slavery affected the experience of Sarah Haynesworth Gayle (1804–1835), whose parents had migrated from Sumter County in South Carolina to Alabama in the early 1800s. Sarah Haynesworth grew up on the Alabama frontier. At sixteen, she married John Gayle, the son of South Carolinians. During the years of their marriage, Gayle practiced law and worked as a judge. After Sarah Gayle's death, he served Alabama as a state legislator, governor, and congressman. The Gayles were townspeople, not planters. In the period covered in Sarah Gayle's diary, 1827–1835, they lived first in Greensboro, Alabama, and then in Tuscaloosa, the state capital. Still, they owned slaves. Sarah Gayle had inherited some twenty to thirty slaves from her parents. By the early 1830s, about half had been sold.

Sarah Gayle's diary was not about slavery. Rather, it was a record of her experience—her response to her social and physical environment—and a repository for her thoughts and dreams. The romantic rhetoric of the diary, historian Elizabeth Fox-Genovese suggests, reflected Sarah Gayle's reading of fiction. Intertwined in the diary entries are an array of themes, such as her devotion to John Gayle, her concern for her children, her preoccupation with death, and her sentimental attachment to everything having to do with her youth, such as her parents, her old friends, her girlhood memories, and indeed her slaves. The slaves were important to Sarah Gayle, Fox-Genovese points out, as a legacy from and a connection to her family of origin, and therefore part of her identity.*

In the following excerpts from the diary, Sarah Gayle mentions slavery and her role as mistress. The passages on slavery occur as the diarist's train of thought shifts rapidly from subject to subject—social news, financial worries, expected visits, feuding neighbors, local events. In an 1828 entry, Sarah Gayle complains about the deteriorating behavior of her slaves, some of whom were then sold. Among those

---

*For a lucid interpretation of the diary, see Elizabeth Fox-Genovese, *Within the Plantation Household: Black and White Women of the Old South* (Chapel Hill: University of North Carolina Press, 1988), pp. 1–28.

sold was a favorite slave, Mike, whom she had known since her child-hood and for whom she had a special concern. In a subsequent entry, five years later, she relates a fantasy about acquiring a farm where the former slaves, especially Mike and his family, could be reunited. And in the final excerpt, Sarah Gayle's troubles as a mistress resurface.

---

21 July [1828]

A little after sunrise. Mrs. Weyms stepp'd in. She has been travelling over the states to restore her health and it is improved very much. I am very fond of her she is so unaffected and free in her manner—she is a fine neighbor too, & that is an important item in a woman's character. I like her brothers too, the Mr. Pecks—they are more sincere and straightforward in their dealing as merchants—no fear of being tempted by *puffing*, to buy an article infinitely above its value. When they recommend I take with confidence, which is more than I can say of their brother merchants. Mrs. Weyms saw Nancy, who is rather inclined not to stay with me any, this summer. I feared when the time drew nigh, she would be unable to. . . . She said Mr. Gayle was uneasy to return home, & that it affected his spirits. I know he wishes to be here but I am afraid other things help to depress him. It must not continue—he must be released from his embarrassments, tho' not a cent be left. If blest with health and secure of his affection, nothing can happen (the loss of children excepted), for which I am not prepared. His profession will support us and it will not in the least mortify me, to live in the humblest situation and retrench and economize, so as to assist him in retracing the path of extravagance along which my thoughtlessness hurried him. It will not pain me now to part with the negroes, as it would a few years back—excessive indulgence has ruined them—they are idle, yet full of complaints—easy to take offence at the slightest admonition, which they frequently merit, and their attachment has weak-ened in proportion as their discipline has been slackened, so that I doubt if any of them would not believe a change of owner could benefit them. Let them try it—they will find too late their mistake. Even Mike, whom I have prized so highly, has become insolent and inattentive, anxious to leave work at every excuse, goes over the village at night, & begs every publick meeting as a holyday. The only horse left for my use he has taken to *ride* to his work, and when told that I wanted him, to send in the country for butter he answered, that "*he wanted him* too." The day has been, that he would as willingly put his hand in the fire, as use such an expression, where it might chance to come to my ears. My parents were uniform and strict in their management of the servants. I was not allowed to exercise tyranny or injustice of any sort toward them and on the other side, the most implicit submission was exacted toward me. When I used improper language to them they went to my mother for redress—and if I commanded what was proper & reasonable, they dared not hesitate. Now, when ten and fifteen years have been added to my age, I no longer feel confident that my orders will be obeyed, and often when they are the obedience is accompanied by murmuring, sour looks, and often surly language, that almost put me beside myself. As it has happened, the course pursued by my mother and father, has proved a real misfortune—I am unable to accommodate myself to the disagreeable change.

15 December 1833

I had thought to have been with Maria by this—but this hope with not a few others, has been relinquished. Indeed when the time approaches for me to leave my children, my resolution fades away. I think I never shall be able to leave them, for mere purpose of pleasure. Ten nearly ten long years have been added to my life, since I saw this friend of my early years, and if I know myself, to be with her for a short time, in the scenes of our intimacy, would bring more joy to my heart than almost any thing could. The time may come when it will not be so difficult to accomplish, and all I can do is to pray it may be hastened. . . . It is full time that we should come to some conclusion as to how we dispose of ourselves the next year. I did believe it out of the question for me to think with patience of any thing but keeping my house, but since I turn over every thing, for and against, I am reconciled to board again, if Mr. Gayle be willing. It is so much cheaper, as to make it a consideration, and beside that, I hope to leave home, after June for the rest of the year almost. The summer I should like to spend at the Springs, and the Fall in Monroe and Clarke counties. Alas! how many of these pleasant plans will come to naught.

Mr. Gayle has been so entirely engaged this winter, that the new year has almost come again, without my being able to ask him what arrangement he intends making—the subject appears to harrass him. I greatly desire to have him make a settlement somewhere to which we could retreat any time we chose. Some point upon the Alabama is greatly preferred by me, because I am anxious to live there, and because if Mobile should ever become our residence such a location must be the most convenient and advantageous. That would be our summer house where health and good spirits would be found—if we made more than the family consumed, the ready market awaits us, open at all seasons, and if we live altogether in the country, it is from Mobile we expect to receive our luxuries. But more than all, *it is the Alabama*, and on it I long to live. How happy it would make me if Mr. Gayle could go below, and on his return, tell me he had bought a rich piece of river land to which a fine . . . full of hills and springs was contiguous, and that on his way back, he called at Mr. Hobson's, and for a reasonable price bought Mike and his family, who were with the other few, to be sent to our house, there to live in comfort, and at the same time in industry, engaged in making their own support, and assisting him to pay for them. A great folly to allow my mind to dwell upon this subject as I do, for it is my employment day by day, to think of it. And will it *never* be realized? I cannot bring myself to hope no more—I should be miserable if I did, and yet, if it *cannot* be, it would be far wisest. . . .

Monday 6th July 1835

. . . Mrs. Perkins kindly offered me a seat in her carriage to the church where Mr. Davenport delivered the address and a Mr. Terrill, I think read the Declaration, prefaced by some very good remarks. Mr. Davenport blundered greatly, so that I longed to tell him to read it, like a book, and felt like running as hard as I could down the aisle and out. . . . After the conclusion, Mr. Wilson recalled the audience to announce Genl. Enoch Parsons candidate for Governor. He rose, and addressed them in a *funny* and at the same time sensible speech, well received. I have no manner of choice between the two.

Mr. and Mrs. Matheson have parted, she at Mrs. Games', he comfortable at home, having sent money, servants, horses, & carriage to her. Such as this to originate in a threat to kill a parrot—separation between the father and mother of a large family! He wrote to retain Mr. Gayle as his lawyer *in all cases*, not naming this, but meaning it doubtless.

Blake continues to have squabbles—very drunk Saturday. I believe my servants are going to craze me. ——is really unendurable, too lazy to live. Hetty appears as if she will never get well. For three of four months, she has been of no service to me.

The Cruel Mistress

ANGELINA GRIMKÉ WELD, 1839

"Testimony of Angelina Grimké Weld," *American Slavery As It Is: Testimony of a Thousand Witnesses* (New York: American Anti-Slavery Society, 1839), pp. 52–55.

In 1839, abolitionist Theodore Weld compiled a massive collection of documents to refute a major proslavery argument: that slaveowners' economic interest in the welfare of their slave property guaranteed decent treatment of slaves. *American Slavery As It Is* was intended to indict slavery through southerners' words. It comprised only southern sources (politicians' speeches, judicial decisions, items from the southern press, advertisements for runaways) and eyewitness accounts by southerners, including slaveowners. A compendium of brutality, the book reached a large audience in the United States and England.

Assisting Weld in his research project were the Grimké sisters of South Carolina: Sarah, who had left the South in 1821, and Angelina, who had followed her in 1829 and who had just married Theodore Weld in 1838. The sisters had become famous as Garrisonian abolitionists in the 1830s (see Chapter 11). Both did extensive newspaper research for Weld and, as native-born southerners and members of a slaveowning family, both contributed their first-hand "testimony" about slavery.

Writing about slavery in Charleston, South Carolina, Angelina Grimké Weld (1805–1879) discussed the impact of arbitrary power on mistress and slave. Here she deals with questions asked only by opponents of slavery. How did exertion of power affect the women of slaveowning families? How did such women reconcile slaveowning with religious convictions? To what extent did they accept the humanity of slaves? After recounting a "worst-case" scenario—the story of a cruel mistress who believes herself a paragon of religious piety—Angelina Grimké Weld turns to the injustices endured by house servants, presumably the more privileged of southern slaves.

But it is not alone for the sake of my poor brothers and sisters in bonds, or for the cause of truth, and righteousness, and humanity, that I testify; the deep yearnings of affection for the mother that bore me, who is still a slaveholder, both in fact and in heart; for my brothers and sisters (a large family circle), and for my numerous other slaveholding kindred in South Carolina, constrain me to speak: for even were slavery no curse to its victims, the exercise of arbitrary power works such fearful ruin upon the hearts of *slaveholders*, that I should feel impelled to labor and pray for its overthrow with my last energies and latest breath.

I think it important to premise, that I have seen almost nothing of slavery on *plantations*. My testimony will have respect exclusively to the treatment of "*house-servants*," and chiefly those belonging to the first families in the city of Charleston, both in the religious and in the fashionable world. And here let me say, that tho treatment of *plantation* slaves cannot be fully known, except by the poor sufferers themselves, and their drivers and overseers. In a multitude of instances, even the master can know very little of the actual condition of his own field-slaves, and his wife and daughters far less. A few facts concerning my own family will show this. Our permanent residence was in Charleston; our country-seat (Bellemont,) was 200 miles distant, in the north-western part of the state; where, for some years, our family spent a few months annually. Our *plantation* was three miles from this family mansion. There, all the field-slaves lived and worked. Occasionally, once a month, perhaps, some of the family would ride over to the plantation, but I never visited the *fields where the slaves were at work*, and knew almost nothing of their condition; but this I do know, that the overseers who had charge of them, were generally unprincipled and intemperate men. But I rejoice to know, that the general treatment of slaves in that region of country, was far milder than on the plantations in the lower country.

Throughout all the eastern and middle portions of the state, the planters very rarely reside permanently on their plantations. They have almost invariably *two* residences, and spend less than half the year on their estates. Even while spending a few months on them, politics, field-sports, races, speculations, journeys, visits, company, literary pursuits, &c., absorb so much of their time that they must, to a considerable extent, take the condition of their slaves on *trust*, from the reports of their overseers. I make this statement, because these slaveholders (the wealthier class) are, I believe, almost the only ones who visit the north with their families—and northern opinions of slavery are based chiefly on their testimony. . . .

I will first introduce the reader to a woman of the highest respectability—one who was foremost in every benevolent enterprise, and stood for many years, I may say, at the *head* of the fashionable elite of the city of Charleston, and afterwards at the head of the moral and religious female society there. It was after she had made a profession of religion, and retired from the fashionable world, that I knew her; therefore I will present her in her religious character. This lady used to keep cowhides, or small paddles, (called 'pancake sticks') in four different apartments in her house; so that when she wished to punish, or to have punished, any of her slaves, she might not have the trouble of sending for an instrument of torture. For many years, one or other, and *often* more of her slaves, were flogged *every day*; particularly the young slaves about the house, whose faces were slapped, or their hands beat with the 'pancake stick,' for every trifling offence—and often for no fault at all. But the floggings were not all; the scoldings and abuse daily heaped upon them all, were worse: 'fools' and 'liars,' 'sluts' and 'husseys,' 'hypocrites' and 'good-for-nothing creatures,' were the *common* epithets with which her mouth was filled, when addressing her slaves, adults as well as children. Very often she would take a position at her window, in an upper story, and scold at her slaves while working in the garden, at some distance from the house (a large yard intervening), and occasionally order a flogging. I have known her thus on the watch, scolding for more than an hour at a time, in so loud a voice that the whole neighborhood could hear her; and this without the least apparent feeling of shame. Indeed, it was *no disgrace among slaveholders* and did not in the least injure her standing, either as a lady or a Christian, in the aristocratic circle in which she moved. After the 'revival' in Charleston, in 1825, she opened her house to social prayer-meetings. The room in which they were held in the evening, and where the voice of prayer was heard around the family altar, and where she herself retired for private devotion thrice each day, was the very place in which, when her slaves were to be whipped with the cowhide, they were taken to receive the infliction; and the wail of the sufferer would be heard, where, perhaps only a few hours previous, rose the voices of prayer and praise. This mistress would occasionally send her slaves, male and female, to the Charleston work-house to be punished. One poor girl, whom she sent there to be flogged, and who was accordingly stripped *naked* and whipped, showed me the deep gashes on her back—I might have laid my whole finger in them—*large pieces of flesh had actually been cut out by the torturing lash.* She sent another female slave there, to be imprisoned and worked on the tread-mill. This girl was confined several days, and forced to work the mill while in a state of suffering from another cause. For ten days or two weeks after her return, she was lame, from the violent exertion necessary to enable her to keep the step on the machine. She spoke to me with intense feeling of this outrage upon her, as a *woman.* Her men servants were sometimes flogged there; and so exceedingly offensive has been the putrid flesh of their lacerated backs, for days after the infliction, that they would be kept out of the house—the smell arising from their wounds being too horrible to be endured. They were always stiff and sore for some days, and not in a condition to be seen by visitors.

This professedly Christian woman was a most awful illustration of the ruinous influence of arbitrary power upon the temper—her bursts of passion upon the heads of her victims were dreaded even by her own children, and very often, all the pleasure of social intercourse around the domestic board, was destroyed by her ordering the cook into her presence, and storming at him, when the dinner or breakfast was not prepared to her taste, and in the presence of all her children, commanding the waiter to slap his face. *Fault-finding* was with her the constant accompaniment of every meal, and banished that peace which should hover around the social board, and smile on every face. It was common for her to order brothers to whip their own sisters, and sisters their own brothers, and yet no woman visited among the poor more than she did, or gave more liberally to relieve their wants. This may seem perfectly unaccountable to a northerner, but these seeming contradictions vanish when we consider that over *them* she possessed no arbitrary power, they were always presented to her mind as unfortunate sufferers, towards whom her sympathies most freely flowed; she was ever ready to wipe the tears from *their* eyes, and open wide her purse for *their* relief, but the others were her *vassals*, thrust down by public opinion beneath her feet, to be at her beck and call, ever ready to serve in all humility, her, whom God in his providence had set over them—it was their *duty* to abide in abject submission, and hers to *compel* them to do so—*it was thus that she reasoned.* Except at family prayers, none were permitted to *sit* in her presence, but the seamstresses and waiting maids, and they, however delicate might be their circumstances, were forced to sit upon low stools, without backs, that they might be constantly reminded of their inferiority. A slave who waited in the house, was guilty on a particular occasion of going to visit his wife, and kept dinner waiting a little (his wife was the slave of a lady who lived at a little distance). When the family sat down to the table, the mistress began to scold the waiter for the offence—he attempted to excuse himself—she ordered him to hold his tongue—he ventured another apology; her son then rose from the table in a rage, and beat the face and ears of the waiter so dreadfully that the blood gushed from his mouth, and nose, and ears. This mistress was a *professor of religion*; her daughter who related the circumstance, was a *fellow member* of the Presbyterian church *with the poor outraged slave*—instead of feeling indignation at this outrageous abuse of her brother in the church, she justified the deed, and said "he got just what he deserved." I solemnly believe this to be a true picture of *slaveholding religion.* . . .

Southern mistresses sometimes flog their slaves themselves, though generally one slave is compelled to flog another. Whilst staying at a friend's house some years ago, I one day saw the mistress with a cow-hide in her hand, and heard her scolding in an under tone, her waiting man, who was about twenty-five years old. Whether she actually inflicted the blows I do not know, for I hastened out of sight and hearing. It was not the first time I had seen a mistress thus engaged. I know she was a cruel mistress, and had heard her daughters disputing, whether their mother did right or wrong, to send the slave *children* (whom she sent out to sweep chimneys) to the work house to be whipped if they did not bring in their wages regularly. This woman moved in the most fashionable circle in Charleston. The income of this family was derived mostly from the hire of their slaves, about one hundred in number. Their luxuries were blood-bought luxuries indeed. And yet what stranger would ever have inferred their cruelties from the courteous reception and bland manners of the parlor. Every thing cruel and revolting is carefully concealed from strangers, especially those from the north. Take an instance. I have known the master and mistress of a family send to their friends to *borrow* servants to wait on company, because their own slaves had been so cruelly flogged in the work house, that they could not walk without limping at every step, and their putrified flesh emitted such an intolerable smell that they were not fit to be in the presence of company. How can northerners know these things when they are hospitably received at southern tables and firesides? I repeat it, no one who has not been an *integral part* of a slaveholding community, can have any idea of its abominations. It is a whited sepulchre full of dead men's bones and all uncleanness. . . .

The utter disregard of the comfort of the slaves, in *little* things, can scarcely be conceived by those who have not been a *component part* of slaveholding communities. Take a few particulars out of hundreds that might be named. In South Carolina musketoes swarm in myriads, more than half the year—they are so excessively annoying at night, that no family thinks of sleeping without nets or "musketoe-bars" hung over their bedsteads, yet slaves are never provided with them, unless it be the favorite old domestics who get the cast-off pavilions; and yet these very masters and mistresses will be so kind to their *horses* as to provide them with *fly nets*. Bedsteads and bedding too, are rarely provided for any of the slaves—if the waiters and coachmen, waiting maids, cooks, washers, &c., have beds at all, they must generally get them for themselves. Commonly they lie down at night on the bare floor, with a small blanket wrapped round them in winter, and in summer a coarse osnaburg sheet, or nothing. Old slaves generally have beds, but it is because when younger *they have provided them for themselves.*

Only two meals a day are allowed the house slaves—the *first at twelve* o'clock. If they eat before this time, it is by stealth, and I am sure there must be a good deal of suffering among them from *hunger,* and particularly by children. Besides this, they are often kept from their meals by way of punishment. No table is provided for them to eat from. They know nothing of the comfort and pleasure of gathering round the social board—each takes his plate or tin pan and iron spoon and holds it in the hand or on the lap. I *never* saw slaves seated round a *table* to partake of any meal.

As the general rule, no lights of any kind, no firewood—no towels, basins, or soap, no tables, chairs, or other furniture, are provided. Wood for cooking and washing *for the family* is found, but when the master's work is done, the slave must find wood for himself if he has a fire. I have repeatedly known slave children kept the whole winter's evening, sitting on the staircase in a cold entry, just to be at hand to snuff candles or hand a tumbler of water from the side-board, or go on errands from one room to another. It may be asked why they were not permitted to stay in the parlor, when they would be still more at hand. I answer, because waiters are not allowed to *sit* in the presence of their owners, and as children who were kept running all day, would of course get very tired of standing for two or three hours, they were allowed to go into the entry and sit on the staircase until rung for. Another reason is, that even slaveholders at times find the presence of slaves very annoying; they cannot exercise entire freedom of speech before them on all subjects.

I have also known instances where seamstresses were kept in cold entries to work by the staircase lamps for one or two hours, every evening in winter—they could not see without standing up all the time, though the work was often too large and heavy for them to sew upon it in that position without great inconvenience, and yet they were expected to do their work as *well* with their cold fingers, and standing up, as if they had been sitting by a comfortable fire and provided with the necessary light. House slaves suffer a great deal also from not being allowed to leave the house without permission. If they wish to go even for a draught of water, they must *ask leave,* and if they stay longer than the mistress thinks necessary, they are liable to be punished, and often are scolded or slapped, or kept from going down to the next meal.

It frequently happens that relatives, among slaves, are separated for weeks or months, by the husband or brother being taken by the master on a journey, to attend on his horses and himself. When they return, the white husband seeks the wife of his love; but the black husband must wait to see *his* wife, until mistress pleases to let her chambermaid leave her room. Yes, such is the despotism of slavery, that wives and sisters dare not run to meet their husbands and brothers after such separations, and hours sometimes elapse before they are allowed to meet; and, at times, a fiendish pleasure is taken in keeping them asunder—this furnishes an opportunity to vent feelings of spite for any little neglect of "duty."

The sufferings to which slaves are subjected by separations of various kinds, cannot be imagined by those unacquainted with the working out of the system behind the curtain. Take the following instances. . . .

Persons who own plantations and yet live in cities, often take children from their parents as soon as they are weaned, and send them into the country; because they do not want the time of the mother taken up by attendance upon her own children, it being too valuable to the mistress. As a *favor*, she is, in some cases, permitted to go to see them once a year. So, on the other hand, if field slaves happen to have children of an age suitable to the convenience of the master, they are taken from their parents and brought to the city. Parents are almost never consulted as to the disposition to be made of their children; they have as little control over them, as have domestic animals over the disposal of their young. Every natural and social feeling and affection are violated with indifference; slaves are treated as though they did not possess them.

Another way in which the feelings of slaves are trifled with and often deeply wounded, is by changing their names; if, at the time they are brought into a family, there is another slave of the same name; or if the owner happens, for some other reason, not to like the name of the new comer. I have known slaves very much grieved at having the names of their children thus changed, when they had been called after a dear relation. Indeed it would be utterly impossible to recount the multitude of ways in which the *heart* of the slave is continually lacerated by the total disregard of his feelings as a social being and a human creature.

The slave suffers also greatly from being continually *watched*. The system of espionage which is constantly kept up over slaves is the most worrying and intolerable that can be imagined. Many mistresses are, in fact, during the absence of their husbands, really their drivers; and the pleasure of returning to their families often, on the part of the husband, is entirely destroyed by the complaints preferred against the slaves when he comes home to his meals.

A mistress of my acquaintance asked her servant boy, one day, what was the reason she could not get him to do his work whilst his master was away, and said to him, "Your master works a great deal harder than you do; he is at his office all day, and often has to study his law cases at night." "Master," said the boy, "is working for himself, and for you, ma'am, but I am working for *him*." The mistress turned and remarked to a friend, that she was so struck by the truth of the remark, that she could not say a word to him.

But I forbear—the sufferings of the slaves are not only innumerable, but they are *indescribable*. I may paint the agony of kindred torn from each other's arms, to meet no more in time; I may depict the inflictions of the blood-stained lash, but I *cannot describe* the daily, hourly, ceaseless torture, endured by the heart that is constantly trampled under the foot of despotic power. This is a part of the horrors of slavery which, I believe, no one has ever attempted to delineate; I wonder not at it, it mocks all power of language. Who can describe the anguish of that mind which feels itself impaled upon the iron of arbitrary power—its living, writhing, helpless victim!

every human susceptibility tortured, its sympathies torn, and stung, and bleeding—always feeling the death-weapon in its heart, and yet not so deep as to *kill* that humanity which is made the curse of its existence.

In the course of my testimony I have entered somewhat into the *minutiæ* of slavery, because this is a part of the subject often overlooked, and cannot be appreciated by any but those who have been witnesses, and entered into sympathy with the slaves as human beings. Slaveholders think nothing of them, because they regard their slaves as *property*, the mere instruments of their convenience and pleasure. *One who is a slaveholder at heart never recognizes a human being in a slave.*

As thou hast asked me to testify respecting the *physical condition* of the slaves merely, I say nothing of the awful neglect of their *minds* and *souls* and the systematic effort to imbrute them. A wrong and an impiety, in comparison with which all the other unutterable wrongs of slavery are but as the dust of the balance.

Angelina G. Weld

A Reply to Harriet Beecher Stowe

LOUISA S. CHEEVES McCORD, 1853

L. S. M., "Uncle Tom's Cabin," *The Southern Quarterly Review* 23 (January 1853), pp. 93–97, 116–19.

Louisa Susannah Cheeves McCord of South Carolina (1810–1879), a rare antebellum southern woman who established a literary reputation, had a singular career. Her father, a South Carolina politician and speaker of the U.S. House of Representatives, headed the Bank of the United States in Philadelphia from 1819 to 1829; Louisa therefore spent much of her youth in the North, where she went to school. During her twenties, when the family returned to South Carolina, Louisa Cheeves managed her own cotton plantation, with 200 slaves, near Columbia. When she was almost thirty, an advanced age for courtship in the South, she married David James McCord of Columbia, a state legislator and widower with ten children. In 1848, "L. S. M." burst into print as translator of an economic treatise. During the 1850s, Louisa McCord produced a series of articles, usually book reviews, in southern journals. In these articles she attacked abolitionists, decried women's rights advocates, put forth a conservative view of woman's sphere, supported theories of racial differentiation, and defended slavery as a humane institution.

Louisa McCord's articles were distinguished by verve, passion, and sarcasm, all of which came into play in her review of Harriet Beecher Stowe's *Uncle Tom's Cabin* (1852), the most widely read attack on slavery ever printed. Mrs. Stowe, said L. S. M., knew nothing of the South, of slaveowners, or of slavery. Moreover, she had no social standing, no grasp of manners and morals, and no comprehension of southern aristocrats. Limited by both abolitionist bias and northern middle-class ignorance, Stowe managed to get everything wrong, Louisa McCord claimed. In the following excerpts from the long and vituperative review, Louisa McCord mocks Mrs. Stowe's portrayals of two southern mistresses, Mrs. Shelby (the antislavery wife of slaveholder Shelby, Uncle Tom's master) and Mrs. St. Clare (the spoiled, selfish mother of Little Eva).

Mrs. Stowe has associated much, it would appear, with negroes, mulattoes and abolitionists; possibly, in her exalted dreams for the perfection of the race, she has forgotten the small punctilios of what, in the ordinary parlance of the world, is called decent society. She will, therefore, perhaps, excuse a hint from us, that her next dramatic sketch would be much improved by a somewhat increased decency of deportment in her performers. . . .

In the next scene, the authoress introduces us to one of her high and noble characters—one of those whose hearts, uncontaminated by the debasing effects of our system, rise above it. We will see whether she understands this class better than the gentlemanly, "good-natured and kindly":

"Mrs. Shelby was a woman of a high class, both intellectually and morally"; with "magnanimity and generosity of mind"—"high moral and religious sensibility and principles, carried out with energy and ability into practical results."

This very sensible, moral and religious lady, when made acquainted with her husband's brutal conduct, is very naturally distressed at it. But what remedy does she find? Does she consult with him as a wife should consult? Does she advise as a woman can advise? Does she suggest means and remedies for avoiding such a crisis? Does she endeavour to show her husband the folly and madness, as well as the wickedness, of his course? No. After a few remonstrances, feebly advanced, she, too (the high intellectual woman!) seems to be struck dumb with the insurmountability of that terrible debt which is to be paid by the sale of *one elderly man and a little child*; she, too, seems to think there is no imaginable way for a comfortable farmer or planter to get round that enormous sum of the one thousand dollars or thereabouts; and neither she nor her good-natured and kindly husband, seem to imagine or to care, whether it might not be possible—quite as easy, perhaps—(should they be forced to part with a negro or two) to dispose of them in families to some humane neighbour (such servants as these are described to be, seldom go begging for owners), instead of tearing them apart and selling to a brutal slave-dealer, whom Mr. Shelby himself describes as "cool and unhesitating, and unrelenting as death and the grave." No; she thinks she fulfils her Christian duty much better, by letting the "faithful, confiding, excellent creature, Tom," who is willing "to lay down his life" for his master, "be torn in a moment" from all he holds dear, the petted and delicate child, from its petted and delicate mother, while she, the magnanimous woman, who carries out her high principles with energy into practical results, bursts out into a tirade, which, if anything could, might excuse the cold brutality of her husband, by the supposition that the poor man had gone crazy under similar lectures:

"This is God's curse on slavery!—a bitter, bitter, most accursed thing!—a curse to the master and a curse to the slave! I was a fool to think I could make anything good out of such a deadly evil. It is a sin to hold a slave under laws like ours—I always felt it was." "Abolitionist! If they knew all I know about slavery they might talk!" etc., etc., etc.

Poor Mr. Shelby! perhaps we have blamed him too soon. It would not have been astonishing if, with so inspiring a sample of femininity about him, he should have gone raving mad, and after cutting, selling and slashing, wound up by a lunatic asylum. This worthy couple, however, go quietly to bed; and such was their philosophical equanimity of mind, that "they slept somewhat later than usual the ensuing morning." And so little is Mrs. Shelby troubled by the impending evil (having, we presume, set her conscience at ease by the cursing steam-burst of the preceding evening), that on waking up somewhat later than usual, she quietly lies in bed, ringing her bell to summon Eliza (the unfortunate mother of the "small quadroon," who is this morning to see her son transferred to Mr. Haley's tender mercies); and "after giving repeated pulls of her bell to no purpose," coolly exclaims: "I wonder what keeps Eliza!" Oh! blessed composure amidst life's whirl! *She* has apparently no sins upon *her* mind, nor cares either, dear, virtuous lady! She cursed them all upon her husband and slavery last night!

But enough of this incomprehensible family. This Mrs. Shelby is one of Mrs. Stowe's "first chop" ladies. Let us now look a little into the *model* gentleman slave-holder of the work, Mr. St. Clare, who is pronounced by the Westminster to be a "humane and cultivated gentleman." He is first introduced to us, joking familiarly with the fascinating Mr. Haley (who seems to have a wonderful facility in making his vulgarity acceptable to real gentlemen), concerning the purchase of "Uncle Tom," of whom, having taken possession, "soul and body" (to use a favorite expression of Mrs. Stowe, to the propriety of which we are far from prepared to accede), we follow him into the home of an elegant New Orleans family. The household consists of the master, who, having been partly educated in New England, cannot be entirely corrupted by the system of things round him; a New England cousin, with some prejudices, but very sensible of course, and

"E'en her failings lean to virtue's side";

A wife, of whom more anon; and a very angelic little daughter, who, being destined to die early, is, according to approved rule in such cases, represented as a terrible piece of precocity, and a kind of ministering, guiding angel to the whole family.

The wife "had been, from her infancy, surrounded with servants, who lived only to study her caprices; the idea that they had either feelings or rights never dawned upon her, even in distant perspective."

Heartless, selfish, foolish, and entirely corrupted by "the system," this strangely obtuse person still appears before us as an elegant woman of fortune. She seems to have no object in life, but by continued fretfulness to torment her husband, servants, and household generally, just as much as one person can well manage. Yet, as she is at the head of a princely establishment, and has been all her life accustomed to the elegancies, indulgences and luxuries of the highest style of living, we must, it is to be presumed, take it for granted that she has the manners of a lady, whatever inherent defects of character, selfish, or even cruel, might exist. Indeed, the author-ess seems anxious to impress upon us a high opinion of the elegant ease and grace of this voluptuously educated lady, whom she describes as "so graceful, so elegant, so airy and undulating in all her motions"; who has been cradled and grown up in such luxurious elegance as would become some Eastern sultana.

Such a woman, it may be well imagined, might be selfish in the extreme. Spoiled and indulged from her birth, she might snub her husband, neglect her child, be peevish and exacting with her servants; but she *could not* be the vulgar virago. We do not deny that our Southern character has its faults—faults, too, which take their stamp, in part, from our institutions and our climate, as do those of our Northern neighbours from theirs; but we do deny that any Southern woman, educated as a lady, could sit for such a portrait as Mrs. Stowe has drawn. Shrinking timidity, and an almost prudish delicacy, is perhaps a fault of our Southern women—at least, it is certainly a characteristic, which, in the opinion of many, is a fault, and which, whatever merits it may possess at a home fireside, makes them necessarily less prominent to the public gaze, less remarkable to public inspection, and gives a quietness of manner, which, when compared to the much more free and easy ways of our Northern sisters, sometimes amounts to insipidity. Such, at least, are the faults which we have heard found by Northern critics. With its disadvantages, however, this manner retains also its advantages, and a Southern lady, even in her faults—aye, term them, if you will, her vices—retains still the shadow of that delicacy which is inherent in her education, if not in her nature.

With what Southern society Mrs. Stowe and her clerk-brother have associated, we leave to be guessed by any Southern lady or gentleman who reads her description of Mrs. St. Clare. To judge from a variety of New England idiomatic expressions, such as: She asked him "to smell *of* hartshorn"; "I can't sleep nights"; "She offered to take care of me nights"; "I don't see *as* any thing ails the child"; etc., etc., we should have a shrewd suspicion that she had found her character somewhat nearer home than New Orleans. These are expressions which are almost as foreign to the idioms of our Southern tongue as Greek or Hebrew. . . .

We thought we had done; but one point more we must glance upon. Mrs. Stowe, in spite of experience, in spite of science, determines that the negro is intellectually the white man's equal. She "has lived on the frontiers of a slave State," "she has the testimony of missionaries," &c., and "her deductions, with regard to the capabilities of the race, are encouraging in the highest degree." Bravo! Mrs. Stowe! Your deductions are bold things, and override sense and reason with wonderful facility. Perhaps they would become a little more amenable to ordinary reasoning, if, instead of living "on the frontiers of a slave State," you should see fit to carry your experience, not theoretically, but practically, into the heart of one . . .

To conclude. We have undertaken the defence of slavery in no temporizing vein. We do *not* say it is a necessary evil. We do *not* allow that it is a temporary make-shift to choke the course of Providence for man's convenience. It is *not* "a sorrow and a wrong to be lived down." We proclaim it, on the contrary, a Godlike dispensation, a providential caring for the weak, and a refuge for the portionless. Nature's outcast, as for centuries he appeared to be, he—even from the dawning of tradition, the homeless, useless negro—suddenly assumes a place, suddenly becomes one of the great levers of civilization. At length the path marked out for him by Omniscience becomes plain. Unfit for all progress, so long as left to himself, the negro has hitherto appeared simply as a blot upon creation, and already the stronger races are, even in his own land, threatening him with extinction. Civilization must spread. Nature seems to require this, by a law as stringent as that through which water seeks its level. The poor negro, astounded by the torrent of progress, which, bursting over the world, now hangs menacingly (for to the wild man is not civilization always menacing?) above him, would vainly follow with the stream, and is swept away in the current. Slavery, even in his own land, is his destiny and his refuge from extinction. Beautifully has the system begun to expand itself among us. Shorn of the barbarities with which a slavery established by conquest and maintained by brute force is always accompanied, we have begun to mingle with it the graces and amenities of the highest Christian civilization. Have begun, we say, for the work is but begun. The system is far from its perfection, and at every step of its progress is retarded by a meddling fanaticism, which has in it, to borrow a quotation from Mrs. Stowe herself, "a dread, unhallowed necromancy of evil, that turns things sweetest and holiest to phantoms of horror and affright." Our system of slavery, left to itself, would rapidly develop its higher features, softening at once to servant and to master. The satanic school of arguers are far too much inclined to make capital of man's original sin, and to build upon this foundation a perfect tower of iniquitous possibilities, frightful even to imagine. Men are by no means as hopelessly wicked as Mrs. Stowe and others of this school would argue; and these would do well to remember, that when God created man, "in the image of God created he him"; and though "sin came into the world and death by sin," yet is the glorious, though clouded, image still there, and erring man is still a man, and not a devil.

Mrs. Chesnut's Complaint

MARY BOYKIN CHESNUT, 1861

C. Vann Woodward and Elisabeth Muhlenfeld, *The Private Mary Chesnut:
The Unpublished Civil War Diaries* (New York: Oxford University Press, 1984),
pp. 41–43.

Mary Boykin Chesnut (1823–1886) wrote her famous Civil War diary
while moving around the wartime South with her husband, James
Chesnut, a South Carolina lawyer, former U.S. senator, and high-level
Confederate official. Keeping this document under lock and key, she
was able to comment freely on everything and everyone, including her
husband and in-laws. The daughter of a South Carolina governor, and
related by marriage to one of the richest slaveowning families in the
state, Mary Chesnut was, like her good friend Louisa McCord, an
ardent champion of secession. Yet, on March 18, 1861, a few weeks
before the outbreak of war, she voiced in her diary a critique of slaveowners' morals that has subsequently become a subject of controversy.
According to one interpretation, this passage is the strongest indict-
ment of slavery written by a southerner. The opposing interpretation
contends that Mary Chesnut had complex views on slavery, pervasive
racist attitudes, and loyalty to the slaveowning class. Although ada-
mant about the moral evils that slavery induced, she took for granted
both the institution of slavery and the status it provided.

When Mary Chesnut revised her Civil War diary for publication
in the early 1880s, her assault on slavery became even stronger. She
retained most of the original critical passage of March 18, 1861, save
for the sentence that mentions Senator Sumner. Of whom was Mary
Chesnut thinking when she expressed her outrage in the original diary? Perhaps of her aged father-in-law, James Chesnut Sr., an extremely
wealthy South Carolinian who owned 448 slaves and whom she sus-
pected of fathering a brood of children with a woman slave, to whom
she referred elsewhere in the diary as "Rachel" (a biblical reference to
Genesis 29 and 30, in which Jacob marries his wife Leah's sister Rachel
and fathers children by both women plus their servants). It is unlikely
that Mary Chesnut was thinking of her husband. Still, at the time she
wrote the original diary entry, Mary Chesnut apparently was quarrel-
ing with James Chesnut; she refers obliquely to discord between
them—"have refused to accept overtures for peace and forgiveness";
the tears that "*scald* my cheeks & blister my heart"; and "my power to

hide trouble." Perhaps her unhappiness about this domestic quarrel—or possibly her unhappiness at her childlessness—contributed to her extraordinary outburst on adultery, miscegenation, immorality, male power, and slavery.

Mary Chesnut's artfully revised wartime diary was first published in part in 1905, after her death, by a friend to whom she entrusted it. The selection that follows is the complete entry for March 18, 1861 from the original, unrevised diary, which was published for the first time very recently.

[March 18, 1861]

Yesterday on the cars we had a mad woman raving at being separated from her daughter. It excited me so, I quickly took opium, & *that* I kept up. It enables me to retain every particle of mind or sense or brains I ever have, & so quiets my nerves that I can calmly reason & take rational views of things otherwise maddening. Then a *drunken* preacher began to console a "bereaved widow." He quoted more fluently scripture than I ever have heard it—the beast! My book (*after* the opiate) I read diligently. He misses in attempting to describe Yankee character after an elaborate trial, & his women are detestable failures. Still, it made the time *glide* rapidly for me. Here I am for Sunday & have refused to accept overtures for peace & forgiveness. After my stormy youth, I did so hope for peace & tranquil domestic happiness. There is none for me in this world. "The peace this world cannot give, which passeth all understanding."

Today the papers say peace again. Yesterday the *Telegraph* & the *Herald* were warlike to a frightful degree. I have just read that Pugh is coming down South—another woman who loved me, & I treated her so badly at first. I have written to Kate that I will go to her if she wants me—dear, dear sister. I wonder if other women shed as bitter tears as I. They *scald* my cheeks & blister my heart. Yet Edward Boykin "wondered & marvelled at my elasticity. Was I always so bright & happy, did ever woman possess such a disposition, life was one continued festival," &c, &c, & Bonham last winter *shortly* said, "it was a *bore* to see any one always in a good humour." Much they know of me—or my power to hide trouble.

> This is full of strange vicissitudes, & in nothing more remarkably than the way people are reconciled, ignore the past, & start afresh in life, to incur more disagreements, & set to bickering again.
>
> *One of Them*

This long dreary Sunday in Augusta. If I can, I will try to forget it forever.

Mr. Wright traveled with us. I found him quite pleasant. He is a *preacher* & a politician, & he was travelling Sunday, too. Last night at Atlanta I did not leave the cars. The Hotel, it seems, is kept by a Dr. Thompson who married an old school friend of mine, Elizabeth Briggs, & he came down & seemed offended that I did not go up to his house. I was amused. Said Elizabeth was his *present* wife. Whether he had had several before or meant to have several afterwards, I do not know.

I am afraid Mr. C will not please the democracy. He said aloud in the cars he wished we could have separate coaches like the English & get away from those whiskey drinking, tobacca chewing rascals & *rabble*. I was scared somebody might have taken it up, & now every body is armed. The night before we left Montgomery, a man was shot in the street for a trifle, & Mr. Browne expressed his English horror, but was answered—it was only a cropping out of the right temper! The Lord have mercy on our devoted land.

Mrs. Mary Anne Taylor continued her good offices to the last. Sent me a tray of good things to travel on.

I wonder if it be a sin to think slavery a curse to any land. Sumner said not one word of this hated institution which is not true. Men & women are punished when their masters & mistresses are brutes & not when they do wrong—& then we live surrounded by prostitutes. An abandoned woman is sent out of any decent house elsewhere. Who thinks any worse of a Negro or Mulatto woman for being a thing we can't name. God forgive *us*, but ours is a *monstrous* system & wrong & iniquity. Perhaps the rest of the world is as bad. This *only* I see: like the patriarchs of old our men live all in one house with their wives & their concubines, & the Mulattoes one sees in every family exactly resemble the white children—& every lady tells you who is the father of all the Mulatto children in every body's household, but those in her own, she seems to think drop from the clouds or pretends so to think————. Good women we have, *but* they talk of all *nastiness*—tho they never do wrong, they talk day & night of————. My disgust sometimes is boiling over—but they are, I believe, in conduct the purest women God ever made. Thank God for my countrywomen— alas for the men! No worse than men every where, but the lower their mistresses, the more degraded they must be.

My mother in law told me when I was first married not to send my female servants in the street on errands. They were there tempted, led astray—& then she said placidly, "So they told *me* when I came here—& I was very particular, *but you see with what* result." Mr. Harris said it was so patriarchal. So it is—flocks & herds & slaves—& wife Leah does not suffice. Rachel must be *added*, if not *married* & all the time they seem to think themselves patterns—models of husbands & fathers.

Mrs. Davis told me "every body described my husband's father as an odd character—a Millionaire who did nothing for his son whatever, left him to struggle with poverty," &c. I replied, "Mr. Chesnut Senior thinks himself the best of fathers— & his son thinks likewise. I have nothing to say—but it is true, he has no money but what he makes as a lawyer," &c. Again I say, my countrywomen are as pure as angels—tho surrounded by another race who are—the social evil!

Rose Williams's Story

FEDERAL WRITERS' PROJECT INTERVIEWS, 1941

Manuscript Slave Narrative Collection, Federal Writers' Project, 1941, vol. 17, Texas Narratives, pt. 4, pp. 174–78, Library of Congress, Washington, DC.

When participants in the New Deal's Federal Writers' Project interviewed aged former slaves, they faced several problems. Many of the ex-slaves had been merely children under slavery; some were extremely old, with rambling memories; and in all cases, many decades had elapsed between the events recollected and the telling of them. The interviewers' techniques also varied. Some tried to record their subjects' words verbatim in dialect, as they heard it; others edited the language and the interviews. Relatively unused by historians until the 1960s, the Federal Writers' Project interviews remain the most massive and impressive source of first-hand testimony about American slavery. They include many moving narratives, such as the testimony of Rose Williams, a ninety-year-old former slave from central Texas.

Rose Williams's story deals with an important issue: the extent to which slaveowners interfered in slave family life and encouraged slaves to reproduce. Clearly, it was in a woman slave's self-interest to have children; childbearing increased her value as a slave and thereby diminished the likelihood of her sale and separation from family members. It was even more clearly in the owner's interest to encourage reproduction and thereby increase the extent of his slave property. Such was the case with Rose Williams's master, Mr. Hawkins, who attempted to induce Rose, through offers of rewards and threats, to establish a family with another slave, Rufus. At first resisting co-residence with Rufus and then reluctantly giving way, Rose was in a difficult position, since she felt obligated to Mr. Hawkins for buying her parents.

What I say am de facts. If I's one day old, I's way over 90, and I's born in Bell County, right here in Texas, and am owned by Massa William Black. He owns mammy and pappy, too. Massa Black has a big plantation but he has more niggers dan he need for work on dat place, 'cause he am a nigger trader. He trade and buy and sell all de time.

Massa Black am awful cruel and he whip de cullud folks and works 'em hard and feed dem poorly. We'uns have for rations de cornmeal and milk and 'lasses and some beans and peas and meat once a week. We'uns have to work in de field every day from daylight till dark and on Sunday we'uns do us washin'. Church? Shucks, we'uns don't know what dat mean.

I has de correct mem'randum of when de war start. Massa Black sold we'uns right den. Mammy and pappy powerful glad to git sold, and dey and I is put on de block with 'bout ten other niggers. When we'uns gits te de tradin' block, dere lots of white folks dere what come to look us over. One man shows de intres' in pappy. Him named Hawkins. He talk to pappy and pappy talk to him and say, "Dem my woman and chiles. Please buy all of us and have mercy on we'uns." Massa Hawkins say, "Dat gal am a likely lookin' nigger, she am portly and strong, but three am more dan I wants, I guesses."

De sale start and 'fore long pappy a put on de block. Massa Hawkins wins de bid for pappy and when mammy am put on de block, he wins de bid for her. Den dere am three or four other niggers sold befo' my time comes. Den Massa Black calls me to de block and de auction man say, "What am I offer for dis portly, strong young wench. She's never been 'bused and will make de good breeder."

I wants to hear Massa Hawkins bid, but him say nothin'. Two other men am biddin' 'gainst each other and I sho' has de worryment. Dere am tears comin' down my cheeks 'cause I's bein' sold to some man dat would make sep'ration from my mammy. One man bids $500 and de auction man ask, "Do I hear more? She am gwine at $500.00." Den someone say, $525.00 and de auction man say, "She am sold for $525.00 to Massa Hawkins." Am I glad and 'cited! Why, I's quiverin' all over.

Massa Hawkins takes we'uns to his place and it am a nice plantation. Lots better am dat place dan Massa Black's. Dere is 'bout 50 niggers what is growed and lots of chillen. De first thing massa de when we'uns gits home am give we'uns rations and a cabin. You mus' believe dis nigger when I says dem rations a feast for us. Dere plenty meat and tea and coffee and white flour. I's never tasted white flour and coffee and mammy fix some biscuits and coffee. Well, de biscuits was yum, yum, yum to me, but de coffee I doesn't like.

De quarters am purty good. Dere am twelve cabins all made from logs and a table and some benches and bunks for sleepin' and a fireplace for cookin' and de heat. Dere am no floor, jus' de ground.

Massa Hawkins am good to he niggers and not force 'em work too hard. Dere am as much diff'ence 'tween him and old Massa Black in de way of treatment as 'twixt de Lawd and de devil. Massa Hawkins 'lows he niggers have reason'ble parties and go fishin', but we'uns am never tooken to church and has no books for larnin'. Dere am no edumcation for de niggers.

Dere am one thing Massa Hawkins does to me what I can't shunt from my mind. I knows he don't do it for meanness, but I allus holds it 'gainst him. What he done am force me to live with dat nigger, Rufus, 'gainst my wants.

After I been at he place 'bout a year, de massa come to me and say, "You gwine live with Rufus in dat cabin over yonder. Go fix it for livin'." I's 'bout sixteen year old and has no larnin', and I's jus' igno'mus chile. I's thought dat him mean for me to tend de cabin for Rufus and some other niggers. Well, dat am start de pestigation for me.

I's took charge of de cabin after work am done and fixes supper. Now, I don't like dat Rufus, 'cause he a bully. He am big and 'cause he so, he think everybody do what him say. We'uns has supper, den I goes here and dere talkin', till I's ready for sleep and den I gits in de bunk. After I's in, dat nigger come and crawl in de bunk with me 'fore I knows it. I says, "What you means, you fool nigger?" He say for me to hush de mouth. "Dis am my bunk too," he say.

"You's teched in de head. Git out," I's told him, and I puts de feet 'gainst him and give him a shove and out he go on de floor 'fore he know what I's doin'. Dat nigger jump up and he mad. He look like de wild bear. He starts for de bunk and I jumps quick for de poker. It am 'bout three feet long and when he comes at me I lets him have it over de head. Did dat nigger stop in he tracks? I's say he did. He looks at me steady for a minute and you's could tell he thinkin' hard. Den he go and set on de bench and say, "Jus wait. You thinks it am smart, but you's am foolish in de head. Dey's gwine larn you somethin'."

"Hush yous big mouth and stay 'way from dis nigger, dat all I wants," I say, and jus' sets and hold dat poker in de hand. He jus' sets, lookin' like de bull. Dere we'uns sets and sets for 'bout an hour and den he go out and I bars de door.

De nex' day I goes to de missy and tells her what Rufus wants and missy say dat am de massa's wishes. She say, "Yous am de portly gal and Rufus am de portly man. De massa wants you-uns fer to bring forth portly chillen."

I's thinkin' 'bout what de missy say, but say to myse'f, "I's not gwine live with dat Rufus." Dat night when him come in de cabin, I grabs de poker and sits on de bench and says, "Git 'way from me, nigger, 'fore I busts yous brains out and stomp on dem." He say nothin' and git out.

De nex' day de massa call me and tell me, "Woman, I's pay big money for you and I's done dat for de cause I wants yous to raise me chillens. I's put yous to live with Rufus for dat purpose. Now, if you doesn't want whippin' at de stake, yous do what I wants."

I thinks 'bout massa buyin' me offen de block and savin' me from bein' sep'rated from my folks and 'bout bein' whipped at de stake. Dere it am. What am I's to do? So I 'cides to do as de massa wish and so I yields.

When we'uns am given freedom, Massa Hawkins tells us we can stay and work for wages or share crop de land. Some stays and some goes. My folks and me stays. We works de land on shares for three years, den moved to other land near by. I stays with my folks till they dies.

If my mem'randum am correct, it am 'bout thirty year since I come to Fort Worth. Here I cooks for white folks till I goes blind 'bout ten year ago.

I never marries, 'cause one 'sperience am 'nough for dis nigger. After what I does for de massa, I's never wants no truck with any man. De Lawd forgive dis cullud woman, but he have to 'scuse me and look for some others for to 'plenish de earth.

Sarah Fitzpatrick's Story

TUSKEGEE INTERVIEW, 1938

John Blassingame, *Slave Testimony: Two Centuries of Letters, Speeches, Interviews, and Autobiographies* (Baton Rouge: Louisiana State University Press, 1977), pp. 639–55.

During the 1930s, when the Federal Writers' Project interviewed former slaves, so did scholars at black institutions. Ninety-year-old Sarah Fitzpatrick of Tuskegee, Alabama, who told her story in 1938 to a researcher from Tuskegee Institute, was delighted to have a black interviewer and proved a most forthcoming, if not irrepressible, subject.

Sarah Fitzpatrick was only a teenager when the Civil War ended, but she had much to tell about "de dark days." Besides relating her own family history and describing her childhood role as a house servant, she provided her recollections of courtship, religion, recreation, folklore, funerals, slave patrols, and emancipation. She recounted her experience as a free black woman in the postwar South. She also offered her current opinions on such topics as color prejudice, race relations, white people, Tuskegee Institute, and its founder, Booker T. Washington. The excerpts that follow are primarily those that concern slavery. However, Sarah Fitzpatrick moved rapidly back and forth between past and present, and her comparisons are as interesting as her memories. The complete interview, located in the Thomas Monroe Campbell Papers at Tuskegee Institute, is available in John Blassingame's *Slave Testimony*.

Sarah Fitzpatrick

Age: Ninety
b. 1847, Alabama
Enslaved: Alabama
House servant

Interviewed, 1938, Alabama, by Thomas Campbell

When I seed you drove up dere in dat big car I got kind 'o scaid. Yo' see I'm here by ma'self, an' I won't sho' at fust whudder you wuzza white man er "Nigger." I wuz born back dere in de dark days. Ma' mama wuz brought to dis here country f'om Virginya widda fam'ly ob white fo'ks name Howards. She wuz de property ob her young Mistus. Ma had a husband named Henry Haggin owned by a white man whut lived on de jining plan'ation. Dey had 3 boys an' 3 gals. Ma' mama's Mistus got mar'ied to a white man in Alabama named Fitzpatrick an' when she come down here she brung all o' her "Nigger" property wid her. Dat wuz ma' mama an' her six chillun. Dey tried to buy her husban' f'om de white man whut owned'im, but he wouldn't sell so she had to come on widdout'im. When ma' mama got down here she had to change her name. All de chilluns names den b'come Fitzpatrick. Den she mar'ied a man on de Fitzpatrick plan'ation name "Cuff" Fitzpatrick. Dey had big wed'in's in dem days too. De way dey mar'ied in dem days de Niggers dey 'cided to git mar'ied an' den dey axed dair mama an' papa, an' den dey axed de white fo'ks who dey b'long to, an' ef it wuz al'rite wid dem dey got mar'ied. Some ob'em got mar'ied at de "Big House." Uh white preacher mar'ied dem. De white preacher he read de scripture, put yo' together an' tell'ya to min'ya Mistus an' Marster an' be good "Niggers." I'se one ob 3 gals f'om de seck'on mar'iage. I'm de ollest. De Fitzpatricks lived in de town 'o Tuskegee an' owned a plan'ation in dis county knowed as de ole "Skipper Place" but de ove'seers wuz de mean fo'ks. I 'member one time de ove'seer wuz beetin' ma' brudder Mose an' mama axed'im not to kill'im, Mama wuz in de bed sick an' de white man se'd to her, "You wait till you git oudda dat bed, an' I'll double de po'tion on you." But mama never did git well, she died in chile birth.

When ma' mama died, I wuz small an' de white fo'ks tuk me in de "Big house," kep'mi dere 'tel 'mancipation. So, me, ma'self, ah hadda good time. Ma' daddy, he wuked down on de plan'ation. He use ta come to town ever 'Saddy an' come to de "Big House" to see'mi. . . .

Ma' daddy wuz'za "Nigger driver." He didn't haf'ta do no hard wurk lack de 'tothers. He ca'ied his strop jes' lack de white ove'seers, an' had po'er to whup "Niggers" jes' lack dey did. Co'se he al'ays tried to make it easy fer'um so he wouldn't haf'ta beat'em an' ma' white fo'ks didn't lack'ta have mean ove'seers needda. When dey got holt uf one, he didn't stay on de plan'ation long. De po' white fo'ks didn't own no "Niggers" an' rich white fo'ks hi'ed'im to manage dair "Niggers" an' dey didn't lack'em, an' dats whut made it so hard fer us in dem days. When de Yankees come an' seed ma' daddy wid'er big strap on his belt, drivin' "Niggers" jes' lack white fo'ks, dey made'im "hit de grit," and den dey caught'im an' tuk'im wid de Union Army. He wuz wid'em fer 4 or 5 years too. He traveled al'round de country an' ad'der de war wuz over he come back home. De white ove'seers tuk to de woods too when de Yanks come an' de Yanks went an' opuned de jail, tol' de "Niggers" to come on out, dey wuz free. Dey hadda "Nigger" man in dere who wuz to be hung an' dey turned'im loose. Dey se'd, "all uf'ya is free, come on out."

I 'member fo' de war, us chillun use'ta go out in de even'in an' watch de white fo'ks drill. Dey thought "Niggers" didn't un'erstand whut wuz gwin' on, but dey knowed whut it meant, dey wuz jes' scaid to say anythin' 'bout it.

When de Yanks come to Tuskegee de white fo'ks hist de white flag. Ma' ol' Marster hadda heeppa gold 'n silver an' wuz scaid ah tell wha' it wuz buried, he wouldn't talk to me but he made some ob de "Niggers" help'im move it an' bury it agin' an' he had de "Niggers" hide de mules at night in de swamp, but de Yankees found de mules an' tuk all de good'uns an' left deir ol' wore out mules fer de white fo'ks to plow.

Ever since I wuzza little bit'ah gal I stayed rite in de house wid ma' Mistus, played wid de white chillun, slep' in deir beds an' et' rite at deir table. In ma' case, I had jus'ta good'ah time 'fore de Yanks come as I did a'ter de war. I waited on de white chillun, set de table an' toted de food f'om de kitchen to de dinin' room. Ma' a'nt done de cookin' an' she wuz de mammy. She nu'sed de white babies f'om her own breas'. We use'ta fight a whole lot too, wid de white chillun when dey wuz comin' f'om school. We all played together an' we use'ta have rock battles. Dey'd say, "Gimme leave" an' we'd say "Take it f'om de trees," den de battle would start. 'Member one day I tho'ed a rock at a white boy, knocked'im out too. All de ud'der chillun run off an' lef'mi told'mi I dun kill dat boy. But he come too an' he didn't bodder me no mo' needda.

Yuh know 'bout de "Pattero's" [patrols]; you don't know whut dem wuz? Well, dey wuz white fo'ks whut went 'round at night an' caught "Niggers" when dey went off de place an' ef dey didn't have no pass dey'd beat'em an' run'em back home. Dats whar dat song come f'om 'bout "Run Nigger Run, de Pattero's ketch'ya." Ef dey caught a "Nigger" way f'om home an' he couldn't sho' no pass, he jes' had'ta take a beatin' or outrun'em. One time de "Niggers" wuz havin' a "Hot Sepper" at a place an' dey come dere f'om lots ob plan'ations an' de "Pattero's" got all 'round de house an' dere wuzza "Nigger" dere whut didn't have no pass an' he knowed ef he went oud'da de door de "Pattero's" wuz gwinna git'im an' whup'im, so he jes' went to de fi'place an' grab'im up two big chunks o' fi' an run'ed to de door an' jumped out in der crowd an' scat'erd dat fi' al'round an' when dem white fo'ks got through gitin' de coals oud'da deir shirts, dat "Nigger" wuz gone. Lots o' "Niggers" nuver would git a pass to go out at night. Dey jes' 'pend on outrunin' de white fo'ks. White fo'ks whut owned dem didn't mind de "Pattero's" whup'in de "Niggers," makin'em stay home an' all lack dat, but dey wouldn't 'low'em to kill'em, dey cost too much. Dere wuz a lotta mean "Niggers" in dem days too. Some "Niggers" so mean dat white fo'ks didn't bodder'em much. Ever'body knowed dey wuz mean. Will Marks wuz a bad "Nigger." He use'ta wurk at de 'Liv'ry stable. He driv'ed de omnibus. White fo'ks jes' scaid o' him. He wouldn't bodder nobody but anybody bodder him sho' would hear f'om'im. His mammy b'long to ma white fo'ks an' when he come to see his mammy, she al'ays git scaid. Ma' Marster use'ta talk 'bout killin'im an' Miss Ann, tell'im "You bedder not put your hands on dat 'Nigger,' he kill'ya." Will Marks drove de mail tell dey cot'ch'im brakin' in it, an' den dey sent'im off to de pen. He died dere.

I wuz sixteen years ol' when surrender come, but I didn't 'ceive no comp'ny tell way a'ter de war. I didn't court none tell a'ter ma daddy come back f'om de war, den de boys commence comin' to see me. Dey had'ta come up to de white fo'ks house an' dey had'ta sho' a pass. White fo'ks would ask de boys ef dey hadda pass an' ef dey had one it wuz al'rite, ef not dey had'ta go back home an' git one or stay 'way. Ya'see dis wuz always bes' coze ef de "Pattero's" come up an' axed fer er pass an' de boy didn't have it dey made'im drap his britches right dere in front ob de gals an' take a beatin'. De gals would git shame an' go in de house. De white fo'ks rudder have de boys an' gals on de same plan'ation go together cause ef dey got mar'ied it wuz al'ays unconvenient wid de wif' livin' in one place an' de husban' livin' in 'nother an' when dey couldn't buy de husban' or de wif' dey jes' had'ta stay sep'rate, de man had'ta git a pass to go see his wif'. Sho' wuz a whole lot ob trouble.

In dem times "Niggers" had'ta hav'va pass to go to church too. White fo'ks axed you whut church ya' wan'na go to an' dey issue ya a pass, write on dere de name ob de church an' de name ob de pu'son an' de time to git back home. Co'se when "Niggers" went to church wid deir white fo'ks dey didn't haf'ta have no pass. Ya'see, us "Niggers" had our meetin' in de white fo'ks Baptist Church in de town o' Tuskegee. Dere's a place up in de loft dere now dat dey built fer de "Nigger" slaves to 'tend church wid de white fo'ks. White preacher he preach to de white fo'ks an' when he git thu' wid dem he preach some to de "Niggers." Tell'em to mind deir Marster an' b'have deyself an' dey'll go to Hebben when dey die. Dey come 'round an' tell us to pray, git 'ligion, dat wuz on Sun'dy, but dey'ed beat de life out'cha de next day ef ya didn't walk de chalk line. Our white fo'ks made us go to church an' Sun'dy School too. Dey made us read de Catechism. G'ess de re'son fo' dat wuz, dey tho't it made us min' dem bedder. "Niggers" commence'ta wanna go to church by de'selves, even ef dey had'ta meet in de white church. So white fo'ks have deir service in de mornin' an' "Niggers" have deirs in de evenin', a'ter dey clean up, wash de dishes, an' look a'ter ever'thing. Den de white fo'ks come back at night an' have deir Church Service. Ya'see "Niggers" lack'ta shout a whole lot an' wid de white fo'ks al'round'em, dey couldn't shout jes' lack dey want to. My a'nt use'ta tare loose in dat white church an' shout, my! she sho' could shout. "Nigger" preachers in dem times wuz mighty-nigh free, an' we didn't have but er few uv'em. Ol' man "Doctor" Phillups an' "Rev." Henderson. "Doctor" Phillups b'long to de Phillups an' "Rev." Henderson b'long to de Hendersons, dey preached in de white church to we "Niggers." Talkin' 'bout courtin', we use'ta court by tell'in riddles. Boy set an' look at'cha an' laff an' den he'd say, "Ef ah had two strings cross de sea, one black an' one white, which one would you choose?" Co'se ya know ef de boy wuz black, de gal would say ah choose de black'un. Ef her comp'ny wuz yaller she'd say I choose de yaller'un. White fo'ks ax us, "What do yo'al say when ya court?" We tell 'em we jes' laff an talk. Dey ax' us ef de boys ever ax us to kiss 'em an' marry dem. We sey, "No Ma'am." Dey say "Yo'al don't know how to court," den dey tell us how to court. My Mistus use'ta look at my dress an' tell me when hit wuz right. Sometime she make me go back an' put on 'nother one, tell us what to wear, tell us to go back an' com' our heads. Young "Niggers" f'om sev'ral plan'ations used to git toget'er at one 'er der white fo'ks houses an' have a big time. White fo'ks lact to git 'round an' watch 'em, make 'em ring up an' play games an' things lack dat. You see de "Niggers" couldn't write in dem days an' ef a boy wanted to court a gal he had to git his Marster to write a letter fer him an' den de gal's Mistus had to read de letter to her an' write de boy back. Co'se white fo'ks had'ta no' anyway whut wuz in de letter, anytime you writ a note, white fo'ks had'ta no' whut it sed. Dat meant dey had'ta read all yer love letters. Co'se dere wuz some "Niggers" whut could read, but dey kep' dat up deir sleeve, dey played dumb lack dey couldn't read a bit tell a'ter surrender. My cousins Jim an' Jessie Fitzpatrick could read an' write too, but dey wouldn't let de white fo'ks no' it. Ma' white fo'ks didn't mine de white chillun teachin' us to read but I tell'um I didn't wanna learn how to read, too much trouble. When I commence courtin' I had plenty fellers. Co'se I didn't care nothin' 'bout 'um much, all I cared fer wuz frolicin', dancin', gwin' to big candy pullin's, an' plenty music.

We had plenty "Nigger" fiddlers; my cousin an' brudder-in-law wuz fiddlers an' my uncle wuz a banjo picker. Co'se dey wuz all nothin' but sinners, I wuz too, but we sho' had a good time. When de young fo'ks wanted to go an'wha' dey didn't have to ax deir mama an' papa, dey axed de white fo'ks an' ef de white fo'ks sed yes it wuz all right wid dem. See we b'long to de white fo'ks, not to our mamas an' papas. Ef a boy wanted to take a gal some'wha to church er to a hot se'per or frolic, both ob dem had to have passes, ef dey didn't, de "Pattero's" ketch'um an' beat'um an' run'em back home.

Now I didn't marry tell long time a'ter 'Mancipation. Ya'see a'ter de war closed all de "Niggers" wuz lookin' round fer deir own fo'ks. Husbands lookin' fer dey wives, an' wives lookin' fer dey husbands, chillun lookin' fer pa'ents, pa'ents lookin' fer chillun, ever'thing sho' wuz scrambled up in dem days. I axed my Mistus ef I could go to my gram'ma, she sed "Yes, you kin go. Go an'wha you wanna, you no' you is free now. Live wid us ef you wanna. You know we always got long here toget'er." I toll her yas'sum, but I wanted to go live wid ma' gram'ma. Den lat'ter on my papa come back f'om de war an' begin lookin' 'round fer me an' here'd I wuz wit ma' gram'ma, so he sont fer me to com an' live wid him an' his wife—ma' step'ma. I stayed wid dem 'tell I wuz good'in grown. Den I commence gwin wid a man name Willis Jackson an' got married to'im. See, a'ter surrender we got "Nigger" preachers to marry'us. White preachers married us ef we wanted dem to but we ruther a "Nigger preacher" marry'us. Jackson wuz 'bout 23 ye'rs old, leas' he said he wuz. Co'se I b'lieve he wuz older dan me. I wuz 'bout 23 or 28 ye'rs old. In dem times it wuz hard to keep up wid "Niggers" age 'cept what de white fo'ks told 'em. Me an' ma' husband didn't make out so good. Willis wont no good a'tall. He jes' wouldn't do nothin' but hunt an' fish. I told him I mar'ied him to take care 'o me, not me to take care o' him. He wuzn't mean, an' didn't run a'ter wimmen, nothin' lack dat, he wuz a Christ'un but he'd jes' do anythin' to keep f'om workin'. Tried to whup me once, but I beat'im to it. He come in one night jes' as hot as he could be; got some switches to whup me, but I cot'im, tuk his switches 'way f'om 'im an' th'owed 'im down, an' choked'im, 'tel he hollered fer ma' sister to come an' take me up off'im. I told'im, "Willie you can't whup me, you whup chillun, you don't whup grown f'oks. I'm grown." You see in dem days I wuz much uv'a 'oman, an' hit tuk a good'un to manhan'le me. Me an' Jackson jes' couldn't make it so he left home. He went way down in "Loos'ana" somewha', den he come back an' tried to git me to go wid'im, but I told'im I aint lost nothin' in "Loos'ana," den he went on back down dere somewhar an' I never did he'r f'om'im but once a'ter dat. I 'spec' he's livin' now, I never did he'r dat he wuz dead. We didn't stay together but one year.

A'ter I sep'rated f'om my husband I had a chile by a man named Jesse Ford. Dis wuz a boy an' his name wuz Jesse too. Den Jesse Ford died an' I tuk ma' chile an' moved on Lige Johnson's place to work fer him; he was a big "Nigger" landowner, run a big plan'ation, jes' lack white fo'ks, had a sto'e an' ever'thing.

Lige's wif' died a few years a'ter I went to live wid 'em, den I went to havin' chillun by him. He kept on promis'in to marry me, but he nuver did git 'round to hit, he jes' kep' puttin' off, an' puttin' off, 'tel fin'ly he married 'nother 'oman. He wuz kind'a good to de chillun dough. . . .

I had twelve chillun by Lige, an' I stayed dere 'tel ma' ol'les son, Jesse, got to be nineteen. . . .

In dem days dey didn't have no horse'pitals fer white fo'ks, much les' fer de "Niggers." When a chile wuz born de doctor brought hit in de worl' at de house. You know I nuver did he'r ob no midwif' 'tel a'ter Surrender. Dere mit'ta ben some but I didn't know nothin' 'bout 'um. Co'se a'ter dat de white doctors com'ence trainin' de "Niggers" to wait on dem an' found dat dey would do it so good dat dey giv' dem li'sens to practice as midwif's. When I git sick an' doos all I kin I b'lieve in git'in' a doctor. Back in dem days we al'ays had white doctors, I didn't have a "Nigger" doctor put his han's on me 'tel 'bout seb'en years back. I jes' thot a white doctor un'erstood ma' con'stution better dan' a "Nigger" doctor. I got a daughter livin' up in Cleveland, Ohio an' she sent fer me to come up dere an' spen' some time wid her. W'ile I wuz up dere I got sick an' dey sent fer a doctor to come in an' when I found out he wuz a "Nigger" I sho' did feel funny wid dat "Nigger" doctor waitin' on me. Den when I come back home I had a "Nigger" doctor agin so now I feel safe wid'um.

Co'se store bought medicine is all right but sometimes home rem'edies is better. I kin make some mighty good home rem'edies fer colds an' things lack dat.

When we sta'ed at de white fo'ks house dey wouldn't let us wash in deir bath tubs, dey had sep'rate tubs fer us. Dey'd make us wash all over some nights an' odder nights dey'd make us wash our feet an' legs, den we went to bed. Sho', we had to keep clean, but we didn't have no night shirts, we slep' in our under clo'es an' ever'body bathe on Sad'dy night. At de "Big House" in town de white fo'ks had toilets fer de white fo'ks an' sep'rate toilets fer de "Niggers." "Niggers" wont 'lowed to go in dey toilets a'tall. "Niggers" didn't drink out ob de white fo'ks buckets an' dippers needda. All de "Niggers" had deir own cups an' glasses to drink out uv. When a "Nigger" got a chance to live in de "Big House" wid de white fo'ks he thot he wuz somebody. Wha' I lived, we all et right at de same table wha' de white fo'ks et. When dey git thru dey'd tell us whut things to put up an' den de res' wuz lef' on de table an' we'd set right down an' eat jes' lack dey did. No sah, dey didn't fix no plates fer us an' han'em out de windows.

When ra'zen my chillun I allus' tried to bring um up in de feah ob de Lord an' not to sass no'body an' be kind to ever'body. I nuver had a chile dat sassed ole'er pur'sons in ma' lif'. I use'ta tell ole fo'ks ef ma' chillun sass dem don't wait to tell me jes' whup 'um right dere an' when I he'er 'bout it I'd whup 'um a'gin. I al'ays had de good will ob fo'ks wha' I lived.

Yo' mother an' my mother had a hard time in de ole days. You see we all b'longed to our Mistus an' Marster. Whatever dey done whuther it wuz right 'er wrong, us couldn't help ou'selves. When I got 'ligion, I tole de Lord I knowed I had dun wrong an' lived all kinds 'er lif' an' I wanted him to have 'mussy on'me, jes' so I could bring up ma' chillun in de feah ob de Lord. W'ile ma' chilluns wuz com'in' I had'ta do so much hard work in de fiel', now, I com'ence to git sick an' de Lord is de only pur'son I can look to fer he'p. I dun' so much hard work fer white fo'ks dat ef dey had paid me I could'er been rich, at leas' I'd hav'va 'nuf to take care'er me in ma' ole age.

Now, 'bout'er good 'oman an' a bad'un. You kin nuver tel 'bout'em 'tel'ya had dealin's wid'um. Ever'thing dat looks lack gold ain't gold. Er white 'oman an' cot'in is deaf' to'er darkie. Ef "Nigger" men git mixed up wid'um, white men will kill'um sho'. Tell 'dese "Nigger" boys, "Better let'um 'lone." Co'se up Nor'f maybe dey kin go wid'um, but dem is jes' de low clas'. Back in ma' er'ly days, white wimmin didn't pay much 'tention to "Nigger" men, so we didn't have many lyn'chins den. But since we got free an' "Niggers" got some ed'jucation an' all dressed up, an' look so nice, white gals lacks'um. But I tell'um dey should not pay no 'tention to dat. In dis day an' time when a "Nigger" 'oman whut takes up time wid a white man she is des'a fool, coze ef her brudder jes' looks at'er white 'oman a white man will kill'im. Cotton is whut keeps "Niggers" so po', dey wurks hard all year an' make de cotton an' white fo'ks git it all.

Yaller "Niggers" thinks dey'self better dan'er black "Niggers." I tell'em, "You may be yaller but'cha gotta take'er "Nigger" stoops jes' lack me." Dere's yaller "Niggers" right here whut thinks dey is bedder dan any blacks. Sally J——wuz'er yaller "Nigger," she dead now, her mamma had'er back in slavery time, on de plan'ation by a white ove'seer. She had seb'en chillun, all ob'em by a white man 'cept one. She put one'er her daughters in school at Tuskegee an' let'er stay dere a w'ile, den she come an' tuk'er out an' ca'ied her back down on de plan'ation an' "sold her" to a white man. Sally said she didn't want none ob her chillun to marry'er black "Nigger." De reason our race is mixed up so, is by fool'in wid 'dese white men. Co'se back in de days when I come 'long us wimmin couldn't hep'it ef a white man wanted to take up time wid us.

De "Lamp Black Nigger" is de mos' 'pendable co'se he is "honest got." But, some white fo'ks say, dat when a "Nigger" is so black he jes' natu'ly mean. I tell'em he may be so black 'tel he's slick an' shines, but he kin be honest. Sometimes "Jet Black Niggers" is 'shamed ob dey'self, 'specially when dey gits wid white fo'ks an' yaller "Niggers." Dat ain't no use co'se he's jes' as good as any o' de res' ob'em. All o' ma' chilluns is black "Niggers," ain't no mix'ures in dem. Co'se de "Niggers" gittin brighter, but dere ain't so many rail white'uns now, is dere use'ta be. Ya'see dats 'cause de white wimmin got b'hind "Nigger" wimmin an' white men an' dey jes' breakin' it up.

Love is a won'erful thing. A mother al'ays loves her chillun. Don't care whut dey do. Dey may do 'rong but it's stil' her chile. Den dere is de love uv'va 'oman fer her man, but it ain't nut'in lack a mother's love fer her chillun. I loves a man when he treats me right but I ain't never had no graveyard love fer no man. . . .

Back in de ole days we had buryin's, we didn't have no e'balmers. When a purson died, we had to hurry an' put'im in de ground right 'way. Den later on we had a big fun'el, we had big din'ers an' a whole lot'er preach'in. Dere wuz one thing I nuver did lack 'bout dem big fun'els, we had'um sometime six months a'ter de purson wuz dead, de al'ays tuk up col'leck'tion, I don't lack dat. I don't want nobody takin' up no col'leck'tion over me, 'cause Mos' times, de money dey takes up don't hep' de dead purson nor his fo'ks, de preacher takes hit his'self. Now dey dun stop'ed some'er dat. Dey kin e'balm an keep de bodies outer de groun' 'long time. Dey jes' have all de cer'mony at once.

"Niggers" didn't kill one'nudder much in dem days. Dere's mo' killin' 'mong "Niggers" now dan I ever he'red of. Back dere "Niggers" jes' had fights 'mong de'selves, ef dey got too bad white fo'ks whup'em. Co'se when white fo'ks kill darkies nothin' wuz dun 'bout it. When a "Nigger" kilt anudder "Nigger" an' run 'way, de white fo'ks sont an' got'im an' brung'im back an' beat'im an' make'im wurk dat much harder. I hadda cousin dat kilt' a "Nigger" man once 'bout some corn. Dey wuz runnin' a farm toget'er, he went in dere an' pulled mo' dan his share of ro'sin-ears, so dey hadda fight 'bout it. Ma cousin cut'im to deaf' wid a gret' big, long dirk, a'ter he kilt'im, he come to our house wid a big bloody dirk. Lack'ta scaid me to deaf' when he tol' ma papa whut he'd dun, den he left dere an' run 'way, went down b'lo Montgom'ry som'wha an' changed his name an' de white fo'ks didn't nuver ketch'im. We ain't nuver he'erd f'om 'im since. Lotta "Niggers" whut had trouble wid white fo'ks run 'way to udder states and changed dey names, som'time dey got caught, but heap o' times dey nuver could find'em. Dat wuz mos'ly a'ter surrender.

Mos' all de "Niggers" use'ta steal in Slav'ry time, co'se 'bout all dey stole f'om dey Marster 'n Mistrus wuz sum'in t'eat, steal hogs 'n kill'um an' clean'um at night den dey dig a pit an' put'um 'way in de woods, den dey go back dere an' git some uv'it when dey want it, an' cook it. Som'times de white fo'ks ketch'em wid it an' beat'em. Didn't have no cook stove in dem times. Som' uv'em cook out doors, some uv'em in fi'place. Any "Nigger" would steal when he didn't git 'nuff t'eat. Ya'fam'ly didn't git but three an' haf' pounds uv meat, one an' er haf' pecks uv meal a week, dat wont e'nuff, so "Niggers" jes' had'ta steal. He didn't steal nothin' but sump'in t'eat dough. Co'se ma' white fo'ks wuz high class, deir house gals didn't have no right to steal 'cause ma' mistrus tel' us anythin' we want, don't take it, but ax' fer it. Ef we wanna wear piece of her jewry' we ax' her fer it an' she let us wear it, to church som'time. She leave money 'roun' an' udder val'able things an' we didn't bodder it. Dey taught us not to take things. I knowed whar ma' marster kep' his money box; he kep'it right out in de sec'e'tary. He nuver did bodder 'bout lockin' it up fo'm us. We jes' didn't bodder his money. Durin' de war de white fo'ks sunt all de cot'on dey could git to de war to make gun ward'in. "Niggers" didn't think dat stealin' wuz so bad in dem times. Fak' is dey didn't call it stealin', dey called it takin'. Dey say, "I ain't takin' fo'm nobody but ma' mistrus an' Marster, an' I'm doin' dat 'cause I'se hongry." "Niggers" use'ta steal cot'on an' anything dey could sell to 'nudder white man. Co'se dats whut de whites taught'em.

"Niggers" didn't gamble tel' a'ter slav'ry time. De only thing dey did wuz pick banjos, play fiddles, have big frolic on Sad'dy night an' have big candy pullin's. In de summer white fo'ks give de "Niggers" big bar-b-ques. Invite de "Niggers" f'om udder plan'ations, dey white fo'ks come 'long an' see de "Niggers" 'njoy dey'selves. Ya'know I nuver he'erd of de "Niggers" gamblin' tel' a'ter de war. Dey tell me dey learnt dat f'om de soldiers. Ya'see de "Blue Jackets" camped at Tuskegee fer a long time a'ter de war tel' ever'thing got quiet an' peaceful den dey musted out an' lef'.

"Niggers" didn't drink much whiskey fo' de war, dey only got whiskey when de white fo'ks give it to'em. Dat wuz when dey got sick an' at Chris'mus time, dey give'em a dram. Chris'mas dey give'em all de lickker dey wanted, lot uv'em got drunk but de "Niggers" didn't make no lickker in dem times. I nuver he'erd uv'va still tel' a'ter su'render. Co'se our white fo'ks kep' whiskey in deir cellar. Dey had plen'ny in dere all de time. Dey had big demmy johns. Dey made all de wine dey needed f'om blackberry's, grapes, an' dey made plenny apple cider out'ta hoss-apples. "Niggers" made big cases uv simmon beer fer dey'selves an' dey made good simmon bread too. Fall of de year de "Nigger" git hongry dey catch possum an' cook'em. Co'se I nuver did lack possum, ma'self, but de "Nigger" cook, sho' could cook'em. Us use'ta sing a song called "I'd like de possum if it wont fer his tail."

I've lived all ma' life he'er in de South but ef I could'da gone north when I wuz young, I'd lacked it bedder, see deres mo' to be seen up dere. People is kinder up dere, dey call dat God's Country. Ain't no Mistrus's an' Marsters up dere, say yes an' no up dere. When I wuz up dere wid ma' fo'ks, dey say, "Now mama, a'ter ya cross de Mason-Dixie Line, all de pe'ple is de same up he'er." No gwin in de back door. White fo'ks an' "Niggers" go in an' out de same door up dere. Co'se ef I had'ta work out in de cold up North, I guess I'd like down here bedder but de white fo'ks up dere wuz so kind to me, I didn't know how to take it. It wuz jes' hard fer me to git use to it at fust. Den when I got all settle down, I said, "Dis sho'ly must be God's Country." Ma' daughter lived in de same buildin' wha' de white fo'ks live'. De whites lived up stairs an' ma' daughter down stairs. Ya'know it makes a heep'o dif'rense when er "Nigger" is in a country wha' he's not al'ays scaid dat sump'in gonna hap'en all de time; scaid he gwin butt into some white fo'ks an' have trouble, al'ays scaid ya' gwin do sump'in 'rong an' have de white fo'ks beat'cha up. See de "Nigger" ain't got no law, no flag, no nothin'. He lives under de white man's law, dat's whut keeps him dis'sad'isfied, an' nuverous all de time. De white man don't want de "Nigger" to have nothin' to do wid rulin'. Ya' know when white fo'ks treat "Niggers" mean hit ain't 'cause dey think it's right, dey jes' think dat de "Nigger" is nothin' mo' dan a brute. Dey don't want'cha to say yas an' naw to dem needda. Ef ya do, dey think ya crazy. Co'se up North, ef ya say yes an' naw to dem, dey think nothin' 'bout it. But down he'er hits dif'ent. De ole "Niggers" is natch'u'ly scaid uv de white man, but young ed'jucated "Niggers" ain't scaid of de white man lack de ole'uns, an' fer dat reason times is much bedder dan dey use'ta be. White fo'ks is mo' 'telligent an' mo' 'lighten dan dey use'ta be too, den de lawd's got a han' in wurkin' dis thing out, 'cause ya know it says in de Bible, "Dat de bottom rail will *become de top one fo' de end uv time.*" . . .

Tuskegee Institute is sho' a fine place, bes' thing de "Niggers" got anywha' in de worl'. Ya git up dere in som'er dem fine buildin's, ya jes think ya right up in Hebben. Co'se som'er dem up dere in dem buildin's jes'ta 'bout ne'er Hebben as dey gwin git, but hit sho' is a fine place, an' Booker Washington, he wuz de daddy uv'em all. When he passed out, we all jes' cried. He sho' wuz a good man. Booker Washington come here low down, he didn't say come one, but he say come all. He wuz a wise man too, he al'ays let de white man shine, so he could live an' wurk he'er. I use'ta go an' he'er him speak, he tole us all to git a piece uv lan' an' build a house on it, 'cause de white man is gonna ween ya to'reckly an ya ain't gwin to have no wha' to go, less ya got a little piece of lan' uv ya'own. Ma' boy come home an' said "Mama, I'se gwinna git me a house ef it's de las' thing I do, so ef I die I kin leave it he'er fer you an' de chillun." An' he bought dis he'er house whut I'se livin' in right now, fo' he died. Booker Washington an' Fred Douglass wuz de gretest "Niggers" I ever knowed 'bout. Now dere's some good white fo'ks too, in dem days in Tuskegee, dere wuz de Thompsons, Smiths, Fitzpatricks, Johnsons, an' some udders, dat b'lieved in treatin' de "Nigger" right an' givin'im a chance.

At ma age dere's very little I don' understand 'bout life, I been through it all an' it's putty clear to me now. Ef de "Niggers" wuz in power today like de white man is in charge uv dem, de white man would sho' have a hard time 'mong some uv de "Niggers," but I looks at it lack dis, I'd say, "Well ya been hard on me Mr. White-man but I ain't gonna treat ya bad, 'cause god is always 'bove de deb'el." I may never live to see it but I do b'lieve dat de "Nigger" will have mo' power dan whut he's got now. De Lawd says so in de Bible. It may take a long time but it sho' will come, you watch whut I tell you.

I he'r lot'ta fo'ks talk 'bout whut's gwinna come uv de "Niggers," but dere ain't nobody knows whut gwinna come uv de "Nigger." De only one whut knows whut gwinna come of him is de Lawd. He gwinna settle a whole lot uv our trouble fer us an' gwin make our enemies treat us right. Hebben is a good place but everbody ain't goin' to it. Lot'ta fo'ks think Hebben 'Long 'ways off but hit's right he'r an' I'm jes' strivin', so when I leave dis earf' I wanna go to a better place, whar I kin git some res' whar everyday will be Sun'dy.

Chapter 11

The Reform Impulse

E arly nineteenth-century women were firmly excluded from electoral politics and public office, but not necessarily from public life. Throughout the Northeast and the newly settled Midwest, middle-class women played active roles in benevolence and reform. Some made their marks as individuals, like the radical reformer Frances Wright, who denounced distinctions of class and sex, or the humanitarian crusader Dorothea Dix, who took up the cause of the mentally ill. Far more were involved in voluntary associations. As members of religious, charitable, and reform societies, they cultivated a habit of organization for common goals and an obligation to correct—or at least to ameliorate—an array of injustices and social ills.

The urge to build voluntary associations sprang up around the turn of the century and mushroomed thereafter. Full of pious purpose, women joined forces to save souls and perform good works. Under the auspices of their churches and ministers, they formed Bible societies, tract societies, and missionary societies. Village mothers congregated in maternal societies, where they discussed religious modes of child-rearing. Urban women united to support widows and orphans, to run houses of industry and Sunday schools, and in general to redeem or assist the worthy poor. The tradition of voluntary association provided, among other benefits, an opportunity for "horizontal" allegiances—relationships among peers—and thereby respite from "vertical" allegiances—relationships based on authority, such as those inherent in family and church.

Many factors spurred the growth of female associations. One impetus, ironically, was the doctrine of separate spheres, which uplifted woman's role within the home by granting her responsibility for child-rearing, religious concerns, and moral standards. Prizing this boost in domestic authority, women sought to extend it from home to community. Religion itself was a powerful aid. The preponderance of women in early nineteenth-century congregations gave them a special claim on ministers, who in turn supported their benevolent societies. The great revivals of the 1820s and 1830s further encouraged female association, for the Second Great Awakening left in its path, among women converts, a fervent desire for joint endeavor. In revival-swept areas, such as the western part of New York State, members of female "prayer meetings" quickly coagulated into a range of societies—maternal, missionary, and temperance societies—to demonstrate their religious commitment.

Class formation, often overlooked, also contributed to the rise of female association. Benevolence drew upon women from varied backgrounds, but all saw themselves as members of the emerging middle class. Wives of mechanics and shopkeepers, merchants and ministers, were the mainstays of female societies. They had time to participate in joint ventures, an impulse to improve the less pious, a desire to help other women and children, and a need to define, or confirm, their own social status. Those in towns and cities had yet further impetus, because urbanization broke down old-time patterns of authority and left what seemed to be a moral vacuum. It also provided new concentrations of the poor and impious among whom to work. One final factor abetted and legitimized the growth of women's associations: Female benevolence rarely defied clerical authority or encroached on male prerogatives. Indeed, many female societies began as auxiliaries to benevolent groups founded by men, such as the American Tract Society.

The reform spirit that arose in the 1830s and 1840s gave wider scope to the tradition of female association. Like benevolent causes, reform movements had evangelical roots. They often adopted perfectionist goals. Many reformers hoped to regenerate society through individual conversions, a process familiar to women congregants. Most important, reform movements that were started by men, from temperance to antislavery, needed personnel, and therefore welcomed women in the fold. Each cause had its own trajectory. The temperance movement originated with reformed drunkards, but the "Daughters of Temperance," who formed female auxiliaries, quickly found a mission of their own: They hoped to protect drunkards' victims, their impoverished or deserted wives and offspring. The female moral reform movement further explored the theme of female victimization. Inspired by the efforts of a male missionary in New York to save men from prostitutes, reform-minded women created a movement to save women from men, or at least from male depravity. Through a network of moral reform societies, they campaigned to end licentiousness, seduction, and prostitution, and to permanently eradicate vice. The abolitionist movement similarly appealed to women's moral fervor. Members of female antislavery societies, which peppered the North from New England to Ohio, wanted to liberate their "scourged sisters" in slavery from debasement and abuse. Abolitionism, however, led many female converts into political arenas of endeavor. Hundreds of women, for instance, mounted petition campaigns to Congress. Within the more radical Garrisonian wing of abolition, women became antislavery agents, addressed "mixed" audiences from public platforms, and ultimately defended women's right to participate in all facets of reform. Out of Garrisonian abolitionism came some zealous proponents of women's rights.

Antebellum reform involved only a small minority of American women. Far larger numbers of women were involved in church-related or charitable organizations, such as missionary societies, than in reform. Among women's reform movements, those that promoted restrictions, such as temperance and moral reform, attracted many more adherents than did the "ultra" reforms, such as abolition or women's rights. Indeed, the women's rights movement stood in a class by itself, in some ways more threatening than the antislavery movement from which it sprang.

When women's rights advocates gathered at Seneca Falls in 1848 to put forth a "Declaration of Sentiments," the issues they debated were hardly novelties. Since early in the century, calls for women's rights, in one form or another, had erupted in many contexts. Educators such as Emma Willard and Mary Lyon had defended women's right to advanced education. Reformers Frances Wright and Ernestine Rose promoted married women's property rights and the right to divorce. Antislavery lecturers like Abby Kelley and the Grimké sisters defended women's right to campaign for reform. Utopian ventures, like Brook Farm and other communities, promoted equal rights for women members. But before 1848 no movement had united the diffuse currents of grievances and demands. Trained in abolition, women's rights pioneers like Elizabeth Cady Stanton and Lucretia Mott brought a new perspective to their task. Capitalizing on the tradition of female association, they added the Garrisonian ideology of equality and their own familiarity with abolitionist tactics. The early women's rights adherents thereby shaped an original protest movement, midway between a perfectionist antebellum crusade and a modern political pressure group.

During the 1850s, women's rights advocates held state and national "conventions" and campaigned for legislative change, such as married women's property rights and more liberal divorce laws. But they labored under many handicaps. Limited by their close link with abolitionism, they were widely scorned as radicals and "ultras." Their most controversial demand, for the right to vote, held little appeal to their contemporaries. Unable to reach a broad constituency, they became embroiled with sister reformers, such as those in the women's temperance movement. In retrospect, however, the achievements of this hardy band of activists exceed their antebellum failures. By "breaking up the ground and sowing the seed," in Ernestine Rose's words, they created a reform movement that would long outlast its era of origin.

Seduced and Abandoned

THE ADVOCATE OF MORAL REFORM, 1838

"Is Not This a Brand Plucked from the Burning?" *The Advocate of Moral Reform*, 1 May 1838, pp. 66–67.

The moral reform movement of the 1830s and 1840s produced one of the liveliest journals of the early nineteenth century. Circulated through city and country, the New York–based *Advocate of Moral Reform* linked local moral reform societies from Pennsylvania to Vermont to Ohio. Readers learned about the sprouting of new societies and the achievements of urban "visiting committees," which ferreted out sexual misdemeanors, rescued prostitutes, and canvassed poor neighborhoods, responding to calls of distress. Anonymous articles and letters from the field related moral reformers' combat against vice and reiterated the need for eternal vigilance.

A standard *Advocate* feature was the tale of seduction, which conveyed several messages. One was the danger of cities. In many tales, a city-bred villain ruined an innocent rural girl from an upstanding family by, for instance, tricking her into marriage and exposing her to venereal disease, or, more frequently, luring her to some far-off place and then deserting her. Another message was the hazard of elopement, which moral reformers viewed as a mistaken escape from parental authority and a first step to ruin. In the tale that follows, a country girl who elopes is deserted before marriage in a distant city, where she is "decoyed" into prostitution. Fortunately, she escapes her fate through the joint efforts of a young man from her village and the local moral reform society. The tale includes brief mention of the circus, a new urban amusement for which moral reformers harbored special animosity.

Is Not This a Brand Plucked from the Burning?

Not long since, the directress of a Moral Reform Society in one of our large cities was requested to attempt the rescue of a poor deluded female under peculiarly distressing circumstances. She accordingly went to the house specified by her informant, and there, with some difficulty, and under a feigned name, found the object of her search. When questioned of her willingness to leave the abode of death, she burst into tears, and begged to be taken instantly away, though she feared she might not be permitted to leave, as she was in debt for board to the infamous keeper of the establishment. This difficulty was soon obviated by the kind friend—who, like the good Samaritan, had been touched with pity for her case—and her expenses being defrayed, she was taken by the lady to her own home, until measures could be concerted for her restoration to her friends. The particulars of her story, as related by herself, and corroborated by one who knew her, are as follows.

She was the daughter of respectable parents residing in one of our most delightful western villages. Having never been from home, she was entirely ignorant of the world and its ways, and had no suspicion that a fair exterior might cover a villain's heart. While yet young, she gave her affections to a young man whom she believed worthy of entire confidence, and her eyes were not opened when he talked of the necessity of an *elopement* previous to their intended marriage, which he assured her, should take place immediately on their arrival at A. By listening for one moment to this vile proposition, by tampering for an instant with the dangerous temptation, the ill-fated girl took the *first step* in her downward career. "Surely, in vain the net is spread in the sight of any bird." Why was she not warned by this palpable evidence of base designs on the part of her pretended lover? Could the man who truly loved, seek to degrade the object of his affections? Could he wish the woman of his choice to forfeit her own respect, and her standing in society—and trample on all filial obligations for his sake? Surely not. The very proposal stamps him with treachery and guilt, and should reveal to any young lady, the precipice on which she stands in receiving his insidious attentions. In such a case, "the woman who deliberates is lost." But the poor girl whose story I am relating, did not reason thus. She hesitated—doubted— and finally complied—taking advantage of a temporary absence of her parents, left her home for the distant city, where she expected to become the wife of her betrayer. But this was no part of *his* scheme. His object was accomplished, when he lured her from the protection of her parents, and after a few days, he departed from the city, leaving the victim of his artifice and her own imprudence, in a public house among strangers, and destitute of money to pay her expenses for one week.

When she first awoke to the consciousness of being deserted by him for whom she had sacrificed *all*, she was utterly incapable of thinking or acting for herself—but want soon stared her in the face—and compelled her to make some exertion for the relief of her immediate necessities. But where should she go, or to whom apply? She had no friend in the city, and in what way could she, a poor, ignorant, fallen girl, find employment? After some hesitation and delay, she determined to offer her services as a seamstress, and for this purpose she left the house and wandered through many streets, vainly seeking work, until night came on, when she was at a great distance from the hotel, and she knew not the way back to it again. Finding herself completely lost, she applied to a very gentlemanly looking man (as she stated), and inquired if he could direct her to ———Hotel? "Certainly," was the reply, and he very politely offered to conduct her thither, on finding that she was from the country, and a stranger. After walking some distance, and through secluded streets, she asked if they had not nearly reached the place? As it was now quite dark, he told her he did not know anything about the hotel of which she spoke, but he would take her to the house of a very kind lady of his acquaintance, as it would be utterly in vain for her to try to find employment at such a time in A. She hesitated, made many inquiries about the house, for she recollected having accidentally heard some years before, of the dangers of cities, but the villain (who, it seems, was one of those male panders, whose contemptible business it is, to cater for the vices of others) removed every objection, and succeeded in introducing her into a house of infamy, where she remained five weeks, though she never again saw the wretch who had decoyed her thither. At the end of that time, a young gentleman from her native village, and a former acquaintance, was in A. on business, and having heard of the performances of a wonderful animal at the Circus, was induced for *once* to visit that school of immorality and debauchery. Here the unhappy girl saw and recognised him, and immediately formed the determination to make herself known to him, and entreat his aid in escaping from her dreadful condition. She accordingly did so, and I am happy to say, the appeal was not in vain. Application was made to the Moral Reform Society—and, as I have before stated, the presiding officer of that Society sought and rescued her. She was sent home to her parents, by the liberality of this gentleman, and some other friends, and left the city under his protection. Those who are acquainted with the case, strongly hope she may prove a brand plucked from the burning, though from past experience, they rejoice with much trembling and many fears. She seemed truly penitent, and expressed her willingness to go on foot the whole distance (two hundred miles), if she might be again received by her injured parents. If these parents are conscious of not having done their duty, in warning their child of the evil of sin, and the snares of the wicked, how bitter must be their self-upbraiding, how grievous is their retribution! But though, if this be the case, repentance comes too late for them, there are hundreds of other parents, whose children are still innocent, still happy— *these* may be saved. Shall not these young immortals be hedged about by the prayers and counsels of the authors of their being? Or shall they be suffered to stray from the parental fold, when wolves are all about, seeking whom they may devour? If the Bible is *true*, then it is certain, that if a child is trained up in the way he should go, when he is old he will not depart from it; and what is the reason this promise is not more frequently fulfilled? We cannot, dare not say, or believe, that God has failed to accomplish his word; therefore we must come to the conclusion that the fault is in parental faithfulness and instruction.

I have already exceeded my intended limits in this communication, and must leave this subject to the *consciences* of those who are particularly concerned in it, only requesting them to take the matter into their closets, and there, alone with God, settle the course of conduct they deem advisable to pursue in relation to the instruction and guidance of their children both for time and eternity.

P. S.

A *Letter to* The Liberator

ANDOVER FEMALE ANTISLAVERY SOCIETY, 1836

The Liberator 6, 27 August 1836, p. 138.

During the 1830s, as antislavery societies spread from New England to the Midwest, William Lloyd Garrison's abolitionist newspaper, *The Liberator*, provided a forum for their views and activities. The Female Antislavery Society of Andover, Massachusetts, founded in 1836, sprang forth in the midst of abolitionist territory. It included 200 women at the outset. When society members declared their goals in the *Liberator*'s "letters" column, they cited the basic tenets of female abolitionism: (1) God intended women to be active in righteous causes, (2) women were obliged to steer men in the right moral direction ("never let him sleep again"), (3) women owed support to their enslaved sisters, and (4) women were especially justified in condemning slavery because it robbed women in slavery of virtue. Such logic was important, because when antislavery women were condemned for their political activism, they could fall back on a powerful defense: the special obligations and responsibilities of women.

Andover, Massachusetts, August 22, 1836

Mr. Editor:

In these days of women's doings, it may not be amiss to report the proceedings of some ladies in Andover. The story is now and then told of a new thing done here, as the opening of a rail-road, or the building of a factory, but we have news better than all—it is the formation of a "Female Antislavery Society."

The call of our female friends across the waters—the energetic appeal of those untiring sisters in the work of emancipation in Boston—above all, the sighs, the groans, the deathlike struggles of scourged sisters at the South—these have moved our hearts, our hands. We feel that woman has a place in this God-like work, for women's woes, and women's wrongs, are borne to us on every breeze that flows from the South—woman has a place, for she forms a part in God's created intelligent instrumentality to reform the world. God never made her to be inactive—nor in all cases to follow in the wake of man. When man proves recreant to his duty and faithless to his Maker, woman, with her feeling heart, should rouse him—should start his sympathies—should cry in his ear, and raise such a storm of generous sentiment, as shall never let him sleep again. We believe God gave woman a heart to feel—an eye to weep—a hand to work—a tongue to speak. Now let her use that tongue to speak on slavery. Is it not a curse—a heaven-daring abomination? Let her employ that hand, to labor for the slave. Does not her sister in bonds, labor night and day without reward? Let her heart grieve, and her eye fill with tears, in view of a female's body dishonored—a female's mind debased—a female's soul forever ruined! Woman nothing to do with slavery! Abhorred the thought!! We will pray to abhor it more and more. Is not woman abused—woman trampled upon—woman spoiled of her virtue, her probity, her influence, her joy! and this, not in India—not in China—not in Turkey—not in Africa—but in America—in the United States of America—in the birthplace of Washington, the father of freedom, the protector of woman, the friend of equality and human rights!

Woman out of her place, in feeling, praying, and acting for the slave! Impious idea! Her oppressed sister cries aloud for help. She tries to lift her manacled hand—to turn her bruised face—to raise her tearful eye, and by all these, to plead a remembrance in our prayers—an interest in our labors. . . . Woman then may not be dumb. Christian sisters of Boston! We gladly respond to your call. We will "leave no energy unemployed—no righteous means untried. We will grudge no expense—yield to no opposition—forget fatigue, till by the strength of prayer and sacrifice, the spirit of love shall have over come sectional jealousy—political rivalry—prejudice against color—cowardly concession of principle—wicked compromise with sin—devotion to gain, and spiritual despotism, which now bear with a mountain's weight upon the slave." As Christian women, we will do a Christian woman's duty.

The Constitution of our Society is so similar to that of other Antislavery Societies, it may not be necessary to give a copy of it. Our preamble gives our creed:

"We believe American Slavery is a sin against God—at war with the dictates of humanity, and subversive of the principles of freedom, because it regards rational beings as goods and chattels—robs them of compensation for their toil—denies to them the protection of law—disregards the relation of husband and wife, brother and sister, parent and child—shuts out from the intellect the light of knowledge—whelms hope in despair and ruins the soul—thus sinking to the level of brutes, more than one million of American females, who are created in God's image, 'a little lower than the angels' and consigns them over to degradation, physical, social, intellectual and moral: consequently, every slaveholder is bound instantly to cease from all participation in such a system. We believe that we should have no fellowship with these works of darkness, but rather reprove them—and that the truth spoken in love, is mighty to the removal of slavery, as of all other sins."

On such a creed, we base the constitution, which binds us together, and which we omit. . . .

[M]ay fearful forebodings lead the slaveholder to timely repentance.

Elizabeth Emery, President
Mary P. Abbott, Rec. Secretary

Reply to the Massachusetts Clergy

SARAH GRIMKÉ, 1837

Sarah Grimké, "Province of Women: The Pastoral Letter," *The Liberator*,
6 October 1837.

Although antislavery women stressed their prerogatives as women, their very activism, in some cases, led them to defend women's rights. A prime example was that of the Grimké sisters of South Carolina. Daughters of a slaveowning family, Sarah and Angelina Grimké left the South for Philadelphia, where they embarked on a series of conversions, first to Presbyterianism, then Quakerism, then abolitionism. In 1836, the Grimkés became abolitionist lecture agents and began speaking to mixed audiences of men and women. Such speeches evoked the ire of the Massachusetts clergy, which issued a "Pastoral Letter" of denunciation. When a woman "assumes the place and tone of man as a public reformer, our care and protection of her seem unnecessary," the ministers declared.

Responding to the clergymen, Sarah Grimké (1792–1873) set forth a passionate defense of women's rights. In the following excerpt, she attacks the ministers on their own turf, theology. Denying their "perverted" interpretation of the New Testament, Sarah Grimké mocks the contention that women should be categorized as weak and dependent, or limited to private, unobtrusive "influence." On the contrary, "men and women were CREATED EQUAL," Grimké asserts. "They are both moral and accountable beings, and whatever is right for man to do, is right for woman to do."

[The Pastoral Letter] says, "We invite your attention to the dangers which at present seem to threaten the FEMALE CHARACTER with widespread and permanent injury." I rejoice that they have called the attention of my sex to this subject, because I believe if woman investigates it, she will soon discover that danger is impending, though from a totally different source from that which the Association apprehends—danger from those who, having long held the reins of *usurped* authority, are unwilling to permit us to fill that sphere which God created us to move in, and who have entered into league to crush the immortal mind of woman. I rejoice, because I am persuaded that the rights of woman, like the rights of slaves, need only be examined, to be understood and asserted, even by some of those who are now endeavoring to smother the irrepressible desire for mental and spiritual freedom which glows in the breast of many who hardly dare to speak their sentiments.

"The appropriate duties and influence of woman are clearly stated in the New Testament. Those duties are unobtrusive and private, but the sources of *mighty power*. When the mild, *dependent*, softening influence of woman upon the sternness of man's opinions, is fully exercised, society feels the effects of it in a thousand ways." No one can desire more earnestly than I do, that woman may move exactly in the sphere which her Creator has assigned her; and I believe her having been displaced from that sphere, has introduced confusion into the world. It is therefore of vast importance to herself, and to all the rational creation, that she should ascertain what are her duties and privileges as a responsible and immortal being. The New Testament has been referred to, and I am willing to abide by its decision, and must enter my protest against the false translations of some passages by the MEN who did that work, and against the perverted interpretations by the MEN who undertook to write commentaries thereon. I am inclined to think, when we are admitted to the honor of studying Greek and Hebrew, we shall produce some various readings of the Bible, a little different from those we now have.

I find the Lord Jesus defining the duties of his followers in his sermon on the Mount, laying down grand principles by which they should be governed, without any preference to sect or condition: — "Ye are the light of the world. A city that is set on a hill cannot be hid. Neither do men light a candle and put it under a bushel, but on a candlestick, and it giveth light unto all that are in the house. Let your light so shine before men, that they may see your good works, and glorify your Father which is in heaven." I follow him through all his precepts, and find him giving the same directions to women as to men, never even referring to the distinction now so strenuously insisted upon between masculine and feminine virtues: this is one of the anti-Christian "traditions of men" which are taught instead of the "commandments of God." Men and women were CREATED EQUAL; they are both moral and accountable beings, and whatever is right for man to do, is right for woman to do.

But the influence of woman, says the Association, is to be private and unobtrusive; her light is not to shine before man like that of her brethren; but she is passively to let the lords of the creation, as they call themselves, put the bushel over it, lest peradventure it might appear that the world has been benefitted by the rays of her candle. Then her quenched light is of more use than if it were set on the candlestick: — "Her influence is the source of mighty power." This has ever been the language of man since he laid aside the whip as a means to keep woman in subjection. He spares her body, but the war he has waged against her mind, her heart, and her soul, has been no less destructive to her as a moral being. How monstrous is the doctrine that woman is to be dependent on man! Where in all the sacred scriptures is this taught? But, alas, she has too well learned the lesson which he has labored to teach her. She has surrendered her dearest RIGHTS, and been satisfied with the privileges which man has assumed to grant her, whilst he has amused her with the show of power, and absorbed all the reality into himself. He has adorned the creature, whom God gave him as a companion, with baubles and gewgaws, turned her attention to personal attractions, offered incense to her vanity, and made her the instrument of his selfish gratification, a plaything to please his eye, and amuse his hours of leisure.—"Rule by obedience, and by submission sway," or in other words, study to be a hypocrite, pretend to submit, but gain your point, has been the code of household morality which woman has been taught. The poet has sung in sickly strains the loveliness of woman's dependence upon man, and now we find it re-echoed by those who profess to teach the religion of the Bible. God says, "Cease ye from man whose breath is in his nostrils, for wherein is he to be accounted of?" Man says, depend upon me. God says, "He will teach us of his ways." Man says, believe it or not; I am to be your teacher. This doctrine of dependence upon man is utterly at variance with the doctrine of the Bible. In that book I find nothing like the softness of woman, nor the sternness of man; both are equally commanded to bring forth the fruits of the Spirit—Love, meekness, gentleness.

But we are told, "the power of woman is in her dependence, flowing from a consciousness of that weakness which God has given her for her protection." If physical weakness is alluded to, I cheerfully concede the superiority; if brute force is what my brethren are claiming, I am willing to let them have all the honor they desire: but if they mean to intimate that mental or moral weakness belongs to woman more than to man, I utterly disclaim the charge; our powers of mind have been crushed, as far as man could do it, our sense of morality has been impaired by his interpretation of our duties, but no where does God say that he made any distinction between us as moral and intelligent beings. . . .

∾

Health Reform: The Water Cure

MARY S. GOVE, 1846

Mary S. Gove, *Lectures to Women on Anatomy and Physiology with an Appendix on Water Cure* (New York: Harper & Brothers, 1846), pp. 244–50, 274–75.

Health reform attracted many middle-class women who distrusted male physicians and "heroic" medicine, which meant treatment with large doses of drugs and surgery. Seeking alternatives, women turned to homeopathic physicians, who relied on nature's curative powers, and to irregular (or unlicensed) female practitioners, often homeopaths. They also turned to health reform movements, such as diet reform, or Grahamism, and hydropathy, or water cures. Those with means might visit water-cure spas, run by hydropathic physicians. Others relied on self-help, following the advice of water-cure experts.

Mary S. Gove (1810–1884), a leading hydrotherapist of the 1840s, provided such advice. Before ending a disastrous first marriage, Gove began lecturing to women on physiology and, to cure her own tuberculosis, visited several water-cure spas. In 1845, she established a successful water-cure practice in New York City and became a frequent contributor to the *Water-Cure Journal*. In 1848, she married Thomas Nichols, a recent medical school graduate who joined her in practice. In later years, the couple moved on to new causes. They denounced matrimony, adopted spiritualism, embraced Fourierism, and then became Roman Catholics. But neither deserted hydrotherapy, in which Mary S. Gove Nichols had made her reputation.

Gove's health reform philosophy was best explained in an 1846 edition of her physiology lectures, to which she appended many of her contributions to the *Water-Cure Journal*. To preserve female health, Gove recommended commonsense preventative measures, such as sensible diet, dress, and exercise. She also urged a water-cure regimen of cold baths and wet compresses. A series of specific remedies for a gamut of ailments, from prolapsed uterus to smallpox, supported her contention that "all curable diseases can be cured by water."

Particular Directions to Females

Many women have felt the need of information upon points about which they have been unwilling to consult a physician; and when they have so far overcome their shrinking delicacy as to make inquiry, they have not always been informed as to the causes of their difficulties or the best mode of removing them. The artificial and enervating habits of society, the dissipation of fashionable life, and the destroying labor of the industrious portion of the community, have brought many difficulties upon women which are comprehended under the term "female weaknesses." . . .

Make the inquiry of yourselves, and answer it honestly, What is the cause of my disease? Is it excitement, late hours, the round of fashionable life, rich food, poisonous drinks, such as tea, coffee, wines, beer, &c.? Is the cause excessive labor, mental or bodily, as it is with many, or is it excessive indulgence of the animal nature, which last is a powerful producing cause of all the diseases mentioned above? The young are thrown upon the practice of solitary vice by having received a diseased organization from their parents, and from the structure of society, which forbids the exercise of all their powers; hence the few that can be exercised are condemned to excessive action. Now, there being a legitimate amount of activity belonging to each faculty, excess results in the waste of life, the wearing out of the organism, and consequent disease and death.

Let the sick, then, look over the catalogue of their sins; for every violation of the laws of health is sin, and comes back upon us with its penalty of pain. Let each consider whether she has clogged the wheels of life, and barred out the influx of Heaven by excessive eating, by improper food, and poisonous drinks; by neglect of healthful employment and exercise, by neglect of bathing and cleanliness, or whether she is wasting life by excessive labor, nervous abuses (which comprehend the abuses of amativeness, whether its action be social or solitary), and all the train of wrong habits which our present state of civilization produces. When you have satisfied yourself of the cause or causes of your disease, resolutely change your habits, and use the remedy which God has so abundantly given. . . .

In order to a cure, the patient should leave every evil and abuse of which she is conscious. She should eat plain food; bread, fruit, and vegetables should constitute her chief nourishment. If she eat animal food, she should eat lean, healthy flesh, that has not been fattened and diseased for the table, without gravies or other condiment than a very little salt. Pork, fat meats, and water-fowl should never be eaten by one who wishes to gain health or preserve it. She should sleep on a matress or straw, and breathe pure air at all times. The remedial treatment, by means of water, should be first a thorough cleansing of the external surface, if she has not been in the habit of daily bathing. This thorough cleansing, by which the dead, scarf skin is removed, and the pores opened, is an indispensable condition in order to the recovery of health. The skin must be daily cleansed, so that its functions may be performed in a healthy manner. In feeble persons who have not life enough to react against the cold bath and cause a glow, the vapor bath is very useful in cleansing the skin and causing it to act. Cold water should always be poured over the whole surface, or the cold sponge or plunge bath used directly on coming out of the vapor bath; this restores the tone of the skin, and prevents taking cold. Let no one fear taking cold by using cold water over the entire surface on coming out of the vapor bath; it is the one sure preventive, and no one should use the vapor bath without the cold bath after it. Persons who have strength and courage to cleanse the system wholly with cold water, will find it greatly better to do so, though they may perhaps be a longer time in obtaining their object. . . . The sitz bath should be used three times a day. The patient should continue in this bath at the least twenty or thirty minutes each time, and as much longer as is pleasant or convenient. A lady can sew or read in the sitz bath, and thus lose no time. . . .

For painful or obstructed menstruation, often quite active treatment is needed. The wet sheet, plunge, and douche may often be resorted to in this disease. But if the patient is obliged to stay at home, and can not have the benefit of the facilities for cure afforded at water-cure houses, frequent shower baths and much exercise in the open air may be resorted to. The wet bandage about the abdomen, foot and sitz baths, are also of much use, but patient must bear in mind that she must cease from all abuses, and exchange bad habits for good ones.

The Author's Case

I was born under circumstances peculiarly unfavorable to producing a firm constitution. Soon after my birth, my mother had "spotted fever" of a very malignant character, which was sufficient evidence that her system was full of morbid matter. She could not nurse me, and I was delivered over to the wise ignorance of an old nurse, who fed me in a very unhealthy manner. I was also dreadfully poisoned with opium in the first months of my life.

During all my early years I was feeble, and often ill, having scarlatina, and all the disorders incident to childhood, in a very severe form. At thirteen, in obedience to fashion, I dressed very improperly, lacing my form in the closest way, till my lungs gave signs of being diseased. In 1839 I began to bleed at the lungs. Prior to this time I had thrown off my tight dress, but I was feeble and much bent. I had been lecturing, and had been subjected to very laborious exertion and much mental suffering. Both these causes continued actively operating during the several succeeding years. I, however, lived very simply, and bathed much in cold water, and drank only water. But labor and anxiety obtained the mastery over my feeble frame and injured lungs, and in the autumn of 1843 I was attacked, while giving a course of Lectures, with severe bleeding. I attempted to go on, but was prostrated, and bled from my lungs in one week nearly three quarts. I was reduced to infantile weakness.

As soon as possible, I commenced exercise in the open air, and very active treatment with water. I used sponge and pouring baths, and wore constantly my whole chest and abdomen enveloped in wet bandages. I had my lungs examined with a stethoscope. The physician decided that there was considerable disease of the upper portion of the left lung. During the winter, I used the water very freely as above. In the mean time, I exercised much in the open air, and lived very simply, taking no animal food, except a very little butter and a little milk. In the spring, I again had my lungs examined. All traces of disease had disappeared.

I have continued the use of the water since. I have had some slight attacks of hemorrhage since, on occasions of much mental suffering and much labor. I find myself perfectly able to control the bleeding by the use of water. The cough, which I had at first, disappeared entirely under the water treatment. It returns now if I go into crowded assemblies, or in the impure air of a steam-boat, or if I am unable to get proper daily baths. I can now live in a state of comfortable health, with one bath a day, and a wet bandage about the abdomen. I am able to walk ten miles without fatigue. My lungs give me no pain or uneasiness. If I can maintain tolerable health conditions, I have no fear of further hemorrhage from the lungs. . . .

Is it not somewhat strange that man has explored all the countries of the world, and dived into the depths of the sea, and dug into the bowels of the earth, and sought to search into all of Nature's arcana of medicines wherewith to cure his diseases, when a simple, powerful, God-given medicine flows ever at his feet? Water is the panacea which shall cleanse our land from its disease and defilement.

I shall not speak of the wonderful cures wrought by the hydropathists of Europe, but tell you a few simple facts that have occurred in my own family. Some time since a terribly malignant scarlet fever overspread our town. Many children died who were seized with it; the mortality was frightful. My brother was the first person attacked. It was thought hardly possible for him to live, such was the violence of the disorder. He was deprived of rest and sleep, and reason, till after repeated bathings in cold water. A broad bandage wet in cold water was put about his chest; he then slept; and by giving him plenty of water to drink, he recovered. My daughter took the fever of her uncle, and was treated in the same way. She never wholly refrained from play any day, and remained but five days in the house. In most of the cases around us treated in the ordinary way, death was the result. A year or two after this, the same daughter, in consequence of the too free use of cream, was seized with fever. Abstinence from food, and constant bathing and drinking cold water, cured her in less than a week.

I have found the cold water wonderfully efficient in the cure of toothache. I have relieved a terrible toothache in a few hours by resolutely holding cold water in the mouth. The first effect is to aggravate the pain, but the ultimate effect is most happy. Though I believe most firmly that all curable diseases may be cured by cold water, externally and internally applied, still I think much knowledge, and judgment, and energy are needed to practice successfully with water as a curative agent. People have so long been wedded to old errors, that though they may be pretty well satisfied of the truth of simple modes of curing diseases when they fall ill, they fall back upon their old faith in drugs, give themselves up to death, and die or live, as chance may determine.

Homœopathy has paved the way for hydropathy, and homœopathic practitioners unite the two modes of practice. I have long been satisfied of the negative good of homœopathy; of its positive good I have never yet been satisfied; but any thing that takes men from the horrible dosing and drugging they have so long been guilty of, deserves our thanks.

M. S. Gove

Declaration of Sentiments

Seneca Falls Convention, 1848

Elizabeth Cady Stanton, Susan B. Anthony, and Matilda Joslyn Gage, eds., *The History of Woman Suffrage*, vol. 1 (New York: Fowler & Wells, 1881), pp. 70–73.

In the summer of 1848, five women in upstate New York placed in a local newspaper, the *Seneca County Courier*, a call to "a convention to discuss the social, civil, and religious rights of women." Two of the convention's organizers, Elizabeth Cady Stanton and Lucretia Mott, both committed abolitionists, had met eight years earlier at a World Anti-Slavery convention in London, where they had been compelled to sit in a women's gallery, excluded from the proceedings. Such exclusion was rankling, as Stanton later recounted.

> My experience at the World Anti-Slavery Convention, all I had read of the legal status of women, and the oppression I saw everywhere, together swept across my soul, intensified now by many personal experiences. It seemed as if all the elements had conspired to impel me to some onward step. I could not see what to do or how to begin—my only thought was a public meeting for protest and discussion.

Some 300 participants, including forty men, attended the two-day meeting and approved the "Declaration of Sentiments" that Elizabeth Cady Stanton (1814–1902) had prepared. Using the Declaration of Independence as a model, Stanton first itemized "repeated usurpations on the part of man," and then provided resolutions demanding equal rights in religion, education, employment, and political life. The only resolution not unanimously endorsed was the ninth, urging women to secure the vote. Many who joined the debate feared that such a demand would only defeat the others and "make the whole movement ridiculous," according to the *History of Woman Suffrage*. Even convention organizer Lucretia Mott, a zealous egalitarian, had her doubts. But two persistent advocates, Elizabeth Cady Stanton and the black abolitionist Frederick Douglass, then a newspaper editor in nearby Rochester, drummed up a small majority.

Ironically, this least favored resolution would ultimately become the pivot of the women's rights movement. Indeed, it quickly gained preeminence among antebellum women's rights advocates. As the participants at an 1851 women's rights convention declared, the right of suffrage was "the cornerstone of this enterprise, since we do not seek the protection of women, but rather to place her in a position to protect herself." In retrospect, the "Declaration of Sentiments" was a misleading title for the document approved in 1848, because the Seneca Falls participants effectively transformed "sentiments" into politics.

Declaration of Sentiments

When, in the course of human events, it becomes necessary for one portion of the family of man to assume among the people of the earth a position different from that which they have hitherto occupied, but one to which the laws of nature and of nature's God entitle them, a decent respect to the opinions of mankind requires that they should declare the causes that impel them to such a course.

We hold these truths to be self-evident: that all men and women are created equal; that they are endowed by their Creator with certain inalienable rights; that among these are life, liberty, and the pursuit of happiness; that to secure these rights governments are instituted, deriving their just powers from the consent of the governed. Whenever any form of government becomes destructive of these ends, it is the right of those who suffer from it to refuse allegiance to it, and to insist upon the institution of a new government, laying its foundation on such principles, and organizing its powers in such form, as to them shall seem most likely to effect their safety and happiness. Prudence, indeed, will dictate that governments long established should not be changed for light and transient causes; and accordingly all experience hath shown that mankind are more disposed to suffer, while evils are sufferable, than to right themselves by abolishing the forms to which they were accustomed. But when a long train of abuses and usurpations, pursuing invariably the same object evinces a design to reduce them under absolute despotism, it is their duty to throw off such government, and to provide new guards for their future security. Such has been the patient sufferance of the women under this government, and such is now the necessity which constrains them to demand the equal station to which they are entitled.

The history of mankind is a history of repeated injuries and usurpations on the part of man toward woman, having in direct object the establishment of an absolute tyranny over her. To prove this, let facts be submitted to a candid world.

He has never permitted her to exercise her inalienable right to the elective franchise.

He has compelled her to submit to laws, in the formation of which she had no voice.

He has withheld from her rights which are given to the most ignorant and degraded men—both natives and foreigners.

Having deprived her of this first right of a citizen, the elective franchise, thereby leaving her without representation in the halls of legislation, he has oppressed her on all sides.

He has made her, if married, in the eye of the law, civilly dead.

He has taken from her all right in property, even to the wages she earns.

He has made her, morally, an irresponsible being, as she can commit many crimes with impunity, provided they be done in the presence of her husband. In the covenant of marriage, she is compelled to promise obedience to her husband, he becoming, to all intents and purposes, her master—the law giving him power to deprive her of her liberty, and to administer chastisement.

He has so framed the laws of divorce, as to what shall be the proper causes, and in case of separation, to whom the guardianship of the children shall be given, as to be wholly regardless of the happiness of women—the law, in all cases, going upon a false supposition of the supremacy of man, and giving all power into his hands.

After depriving her of all rights as a married woman, if single, and the owner of property, he has taxed her to support a government which recognizes her only when her property can be made profitable to it.

He has monopolized nearly all the profitable employments, and from those she is permitted to follow, she receives but a scanty remuneration. He closes against her all the avenues to wealth and distinction which he considers most honorable to himself. As a teacher of theology, medicine, or law, she is not known.

He has denied her the facilities for obtaining a thorough education, all colleges being closed against her.

He allows her in Church, as well as State, but a subordinate position, claiming Apostolic authority for her exclusion from the ministry, and, with some exceptions, from any public participation in the affairs of the Church.

He has created a false public sentiment by giving to the world a different code of morals for men and women, by which moral delinquencies which exclude women from society, are not only tolerated, but deemed of little account in man.

He has usurped the prerogative of Jehovah himself, claiming it as his right to assign for her a sphere of action, when that belongs to her conscience and to her God.

He has endeavored, in every way that he could, to destroy her confidence in her own powers, to lessen her self-respect, and to make her willing to lead a dependent and abject life.

Now, in view of this entire disfranchisement of one-half the people of this country, their social and religious degradation—in view of the unjust laws above mentioned, and because women do feel themselves aggrieved, oppressed, and fraudulently deprived of their most sacred rights, we insist that they have immediate admission to all the rights and privileges which belong to them as citizens of the United States.

In entering upon the great work before us, we anticipate no small amount of misconception, misrepresentation, and ridicule; but we shall use every instrumentality within our power to effect our object. We shall employ agents, circulate tracts, petition the State and National legislatures, and endeavor to enlist the pulpit and the press in our behalf. We hope this Convention will be followed by a series of Conventions embracing every part of the country.

[The following resolutions were discussed by Lucretia Mott, Thomas and Mary Ann McClintock, Amy Post, Catharine A. F. Stebbins, and others, and were adopted:]

WHEREAS, The great precept of nature is conceded to be, that "man shall pursue his own true and substantial happiness." Blackstone in his Commentaries remarks, that this law of Nature being coeval with mankind, and dictated by God himself, is of course superior in obligation to any other. It is binding over all the globe, in all countries and at all times; no human laws are of any validity if contrary to this, and such of them as are valid, derive all their force, and all their validity, and all their authority, mediately and immediately, from this original; therefore:

Resolved, That such laws as conflict, in any way, with the true and substantial happiness of woman, are contrary to the great precept of nature and of no validity, for this is "superior in obligation to any other."

Resolved, That all laws which prevent woman from occupying such a station in society as her conscience shall dictate, or which place her in a position inferior to that of man, are contrary to the great precept of nature, and therefore of no force or authority.

Resolved, That woman is man's equal—was intended to be so by the Creator, and the highest good of the race demands that she should be recognized as such.

Resolved, That the women of this country ought to be enlightened in regard to the laws under which they live, that they may no longer publish their degradation by declaring themselves satisfied with their present position, nor their ignorance, by asserting that they have all the rights they want.

Resolved, That inasmuch as man, while claiming for himself intellectual superiority, does accord to woman moral superiority, it is pre-eminently his duty to encourage her to speak and teach, as she has an opportunity, in all religious assemblies.

Resolved, That the same amount of virtue, delicacy, and refinement of behavior that is required of woman in the social state, should also be required of man, and the same transgressions should be visited with equal severity on both man and woman.

Resolved, That the objection of indelicacy and impropriety, which is so often brought against woman when she addresses a public audience, comes with a very ill-grace from those who encourage, by their attendance, her appearance on the stage, in the concert, or in feats of the circus.

Resolved, That woman has too long rested satisfied in the circumscribed limits which corrupt customs and a perverted application of the Scriptures have marked out for her, and that it is time she should move in the enlarged sphere which her great Creator has assigned her.

Resolved, That it is the duty of the women of this country to secure to themselves their sacred right to the elective franchise.

Resolved, That the equality of human rights results necessarily from the fact of the identity of the race in capabilities and responsibilities.

Resolved, therefore, That, being invested by the Creator with the same capabilities, and the same consciousness of responsibility for their exercise, it is demonstrably the right and duty of woman, equally with man, to promote every righteous cause by every righteous means; and especially in regard to the great subjects of morals and religion, it is self-evidently her right to participate with her brother in teaching them, both in private and in public, by writing and by speaking, by any instrumentalities proper to be used, and in any assemblies proper to be held; and this being a self-evident truth growing out of the divinely implanted principles of human nature, any custom or authority adverse to it, whether modern or wearing the hoary sanction of antiquity, is to be regarded as a self-evident falsehood, and at war with mankind.

[At the last session Lucretia Mott offered and spoke to the following resolution:]

Resolved, That the speedy success of our cause depends upon the zealous and untiring efforts of both men and women, for the overthrow of the monopoly of the pulpit, and for the securing to woman an equal participation with men in the various trades, professions, and commerce.

A New Era in Women's History

ANTOINETTE BROWN, 1847–1848

Letters of Antoinette Brown to Lucy Stone, 1847–1848, included in type-
script of Brown's manuscript autobiography, The Schlesinger Library,
Radcliffe College.

What sort of women responded to the 1848 call for women's rights?
One answer is provided by Antoinette Brown (1825–1921), then a
student at Oberlin College, the first institution of higher education to
accept women students. Entering Oberlin in 1846, when she was
twenty-one, Brown graduated from the "literary course" in a year and
decided to pursue a theology degree. This goal evoked no support,
save from her best friend at college, Lucy Stone, a former school-
teacher from Massachusetts.

Oberlin finally allowed Brown to enter the college's theology
course, which she completed in 1850, although she was not allowed to
graduate. Brown became a lecturer on women's rights, antislavery, and
temperance, and an occasional guest speaker in pulpits. She was ordained in 1853 as a Congregational minister, the first woman minister
of a major denomination. Lucy Stone graduated from Oberlin in 1847
to become a lecturer on antislavery and women's rights. In the 1850s,
the two friends married brothers, Henry and Samuel Blackwell and, at
last, became sisters—a relationship they had long established in spirit
if not in fact.

When corresponding with Lucy Stone in 1847 and 1848, during
the time of the first women's rights convention, Brown wrote first
from Oberlin, in Ohio, and then from Michigan, where she held a
temporary teaching job, and then from Henrietta, New York, where
her family lived. The two friends were not completely in harmony, for
Stone shared none of Brown's theological interests. But both were
committed to antislavery, both hoped to become professional public
speakers, and both were extremely interested in the new cause of
women's rights, a subject they had long discussed with one another.
Of special interest in the following letters, beyond the tone of devotion
to Lucy Stone, are Antoinette Brown's embattled interchanges with
assorted acquaintances, all ministers. She takes issue with a clergyman,
Sereno Wright Streeter; with an Oberlin professor, John Morgan; and
with college president Charles G. Finney, the famous revivalist minister and leading spirit of the Second Great Awakening.

Rochester, Michigan [Winter 1847]

Dear Lucy,

. . . You tell me you do not wish to become acquainted with a very good and amiable young lady because you are afraid you will learn to love her and then she will go away and leave you. Pardon me dear Lucy, but you do need a severe rebuke. Why are you becoming so misanthropic? Do you think I feel more unhappy because I know that there are warm hearts somewhere in this bright and beautiful world, that would throb more kindly to learn of my welfare? Have I caused you more sad than happy hours, and do you regret having known me? Far different has it been in my case, and heaven send me a score of friends. . . .

I am just in the mood for telling you about my "literary society," having just returned from there. It consists of about 50 members, has been in operation several weeks and is both pleasant and profitable to all who are members. . . . There are some young ladies here of superior talent, all take a deep interest in the exercises and I must say I have never before improved so rapidly in my life in the use of the tongue. How I wish we had such a society at Oberlin, such exercises, and such fearless eagerness in the path of improvement. We are all getting to be Woman's Rights Advocates or rather the investigators of woman's duties. We are exceedingly careful in this matter and all move on together step by step, looking at principles, and entirely forgetting the conclusions we must at length come to. Some will undoubtedly shrink back when they come to find where they stand and believe they must have been mistaken, others will want moral courage to carry out what they know to be duty, and a few I hope and believe will go out into the world pioneers in the great reform which is about to revolutionize society. You see all my hoping heart in this as in everything else. . . . I have been having long discussions with my friends at home about woman's duties but I think I can do more good in some other way. But I believe there is soon to be a new era in woman's history and the means to effect this must be truth wielded in firmness, gentleness, and forbearance.

Henrietta [New York] March 1848

Dearest Lucy:

. . . You do know that I did love you a great deal, for I remember your telling me that I couldn't help it if I tried. . . . We believed no more things in common than any other of my classmates, perhaps not as many, and yet I loved you more than all the rest together. . . .

Professor Morgan* wrote to Wm.[†] a strange letter a while ago designed I suppose for my special benefit. He first assumed that if woman lectured in public then the male and the female mind must be exactly alike and then went on to talk about lilies and roses, willows and oaks, men and women, etc, and finally closed by saying, "If Antoinette will be a Mrs. Sigourney, a Mrs. Ellis, or a Mrs. Ingraham,[‡] I will say

---

*John Morgan, an abolitionist, minister, and theology professor at Oberlin.

[†]Antoinette Brown's older brother William, a Congregational minister.

[‡]Lydia Sigourney, Sarah Stickney Ellis, and Sarah R. Ingraham were popular authors of the day who won followings among women readers.

Amen, most heartily, but if she tried to be a Finney or a Webster,* I must say Alas! I hope she has too much sense to choose the latter course." For all this I like Professor Morgan; he is honest and I don't wonder at his conclusions when looking at his premises. I start for Oberlin next week. . . .

I have been examining the bible's position of woman a good deal this winter reading various commentaries, comparing them with each other and with the bible and hunting up every passage in the Scriptures that have any bearing on the subject either near or remote. My mind grows strengthened firmer on the subject and the light comes beaming in full of promise. Lately I have been writing out my thoughts to see if they will all hang together but have not finished yet. It is a hard subject and takes a long time to see through it, doesn't it. But "no cross, no crown." You have seen the account of Miss Elizabeth Blackwell.† It was a noble step, wasn't it. Truly the watchmen do bring glad tidings.

Oberlin [1848]

. . . Oh, dear Lucy I do wish we believed alike [on matters of religion]. I wished somebody believed as I do. And some people are beginning to believe so. Some people here do agree with me in sentiment enough now, only we have no tastes or heart sympathy in common, and it seems almost as bad as if we were Jews and Gentiles.

How I wish ladies would act and talk as sensibly as gentlemen! No matter what they thought if they would think sense nor what they said if there was some meaning to it. But as it is I really like the "gentlemen" better than the "ladies." Don't you feel so when you are travelling about from place to place and see women so little interested? Or do they think they must talk with you upon important subjects? . . . How many children has Lucretia Mott?‡ Please give me a brief sketch of her history. I have a particular use for it. Are her children intelligent, respectable, and well-trained? How did she manage to bring them all up and still speak so much in public? If you can tell me a few things about her I shall be much obliged. I admire her character as far as I know it. With much love. . . .

[Henrietta, New York, Winter 1848]

Dear Lucy:

Streeter§ and I have been having a talk about woman's rights and public labors—speaking in particular. He is a queer sort of man more like Professor Morgan than anyone else I can think of, but more genteel in his manners. He believes women have a right to speak in public meetings, that is, social meetings, prayer meetings, etc, but that they have no right to preach and the thought of a woman's being ordained or

---

*Oberlin president Charles G. Finney and Illinois Senator Daniel Webster were noted orators.
†Elizabeth Blackwell (1821–1910), Brown's future sister-in-law, was the first woman graduate of a licensed medical college. She received her degree in 1848.
‡Lucretia Mott (1793–1880), an organizer of the 1848 women's rights convention at Seneca Falls, New York.
§Sereno Wright Streeter, an 1836 Oberlin graduate and a Congregational minister in Henrietta, New York.

becoming a pastor over a church seemed to him perfectly absurd. When speaking of particular passages of scripture after hearing my interpretation he would sometimes give his own, but would almost always laugh and tell me I would get righted at Oberlin, that I was just beginning my theological course and he had finished his, that we would wait and have our discussion when I got through, that he thought we should not disagree so much then as now, that he hoped I would spend weeks and even years investigating the subject and if I could find my present views supported by the bible, why very well. He seemed, I think . . . glad to have women study theology, said he thought they could make it of great use to themselves in their sphere of action, etc. After all I like him better than any man I have talked to on the subject who did not believe with me. Indeed I can hardly find anyone to *talk with*. Some of them can't talk, and some of them won't talk on this question.

Associated as I have been this winter frequently with ministers, I have not found one who has been both ready and willing to talk over the matter candidly. . . . I tell you Lucy when ministers will do that way it means something—they have not examined the subject themselves and some of them around here are at least beginning to feel a little uneasy at their old position and are not quite ready to advocate that nor ready to get to a new standing point. I have a grand chance to bring the subject up almost every time I meet an old friend or a stranger for generally the first question after finding out what I am studying is, "Are you going to preach, be a minister, a public lecturer, etc," or else such remarks as "You can write sermons for your brother or for your husband" or something else of the sort and so the subject comes in without dragging. Sometimes they warn me not to be a Fanny Wright man,* sometimes believe I am joking, sometimes stare at me with amazement and sometimes seem to start back with a kind of horror. Men and women are about equal [in their responses] and seem to have their mouths opened and their tongues loosed to about the same extent. . . . The scholars [at Oberlin] have been having discussions all winter in the papers of their societies on woman's right to vote.

Oberlin [June 1848]

Lucy dearest:

. . . [M]y heart has just been called back to the time when we used to sit with our arms around each other at the sunset hour and talk and talk of our friends and our homes and of the thousand subjects of mutual interest until both our hearts felt warmer and lighter for the pure communion of spirit. . . . It will do my heart good to speak its feelings to you and you will love me no less to feel that my love towards you is still unchanged. But I am changing constantly not in looks of actions perhaps, though my classmates sometimes remind me that I am growing to look very unlike myself. . . .

The cause of woman is moving on finely here. You know the theological students are required to tell their religious experiences before Prof. Finney. Once or twice

---

*A female public speaker. The reference is to reformer Frances Wright (1795–1852), who gained notoriety in the early 1830s with her public addresses to "mixed" audiences of men and women.

when he called for those who had not done so, Tefft* mentioned Lettice† and me. He looked as though he did not know what to say, and the next time said, "Oh, we don't call upon the ladies." They had all told me we should have to speak, and I felt so badly at what he said that I just began to cry and was obliged to leave the room. It was the first and last time that I have cried about anything connected with this matter this spring, but it came so unexpectedly. After I went out they talked over the matter and it seems Professor Finney did not know we were members of the department in any other sense than the other ladies are, who go to hear the lectures. You know he was sick last fall and we are not in his class until commencement so he really did not know about it. He said he was willing any lady should speak if she wished to, and if we were members of the department he should like to know it and know about it. I went over to see him and he certainly seemed to forget that he was talking with a woman. We conversed more than an hour sometimes upon the gravest subjects of philosophy and theology and he expressed himself freely upon the true position of woman. Said he did not care how much she was educated, that her education had been fundamentally wrong, that though he did not think she was generally called upon to preach or speak in public because the circumstances did not demand it, still that there was nothing right or wrong in the thing itself and that sometimes she was specially called to speak, that he would not only permit us to take part in every exercise in his classes but would aid and encourage us in doing so, etc. . . . A week or two after Professor Finney called upon me to speak in the prayer meeting, and I did so. Told them the exercises of my mind particularly in reference to this subject, and my determination to preach and speak in public when I was prepared for this. They all seemed surprised and pleased too that I was really expecting to speak. Last week Professor Finney came along after the meeting and said he should like to have me take part in the prayer meetings at any time. . . .

So, L——, you are going to lecturing, are you? . . . Success to the Truth and to you dearest Lucy so far as you preach it and in the right spirit. I am glad you are going to lecture. You will never stop to teach if you commence talking. Be good, Lucy, be good, and don't be afraid of anybody but speak as though you had a right to.

Nette

---

*James Tefft, a fellow student at Oberlin.
†Lettice Smith Holmes, another woman theology student at Oberlin.

Sojourner Truth Speaks Out

FRANCES D. GAGE, 1881

Frances D. Gage, "Reminiscences of Sojourner Truth," *The History of Woman Suffrage*, vol. 1 (New York: Fowler and Wells, 1881), pp. 115–17.

"Sojourner Truth" was the sobriquet of a slave named Isabella Van Wagener (ca. 1797–1883), who had escaped from her owners in up-state New York in 1827, one year before the mandatory emancipation of all New York State slaves. In the 1830s and 1840s, Isabella spent part of her time working as a domestic servant in New York City, where she lived with two of her children. (Most of her children had been sold as slaves.) She was also caught up in waves of religious revivalism and mysticism. In 1843, her voices told her to call herself Sojourner Truth and to preach.

As an itinerant preacher, Sojourner Truth became a convert to abolitionism and by the time she began speaking at antislavery meetings in the 1850s, she was an experienced public personality. Tall and imposing, she would appear at abolitionist gatherings, offer startling remarks in her Dutch accent, engage in debate, sing gospel songs, and sell copies of the narrative of her life, written for her by Olive Gilbert. She also made appearances at a few women's rights conventions, notably a statewide convention in Akron, Ohio, in 1851. Here she took issue with a minister who challenged the women's rights cause. Her impromptu and oft-quoted remarks on this occasion contain considerable ambiguity. Frequently interpreted as a black woman's support for the women's rights movement, they also can be understood as a black woman's protest against exclusion from the entire category of "womanhood." Still, Sojourner Truth galvanized the meeting, as she was used to doing on other public occasions. Her unusual appearance and oratory were recorded with appreciation by author and reformer Frances D. Gage, who presided over the convention.

Akron Convention

May 28–29, 1851

The leaders of the movement trembled on seeing a tall, gaunt black woman in a gray dress and white turban, surmounted with an uncouth sun-bonnet, march deliberately into the church, walk with the air of a queen up the aisle, and take her seat upon the pulpit steps. A buzz of disapprobation was heard all over the house, and there fell on the listening ear, "An abolition affair!" "Woman's rights and niggers!" "I told you so!" "Go it, darkey!"

I chanced on that occasion to wear my first laurels in public life as president of the meeting. At my request order was restored, and the business of the Convention went on. Morning, afternoon, and evening exercises came and went. Through all these sessions old Sojourner, quiet and reticent as the "Lybian Statue," sat crouched against the wall on the corner of the pulpit stairs, her sun-bonnet shading her eyes, her elbows on her knees, her chin resting upon her broad, hard palms. At intermission she was busy selling the "Life of Sojourner Truth," a narrative of her own strange and adventurous life. Again and again, timorous and trembling ones came to me and said, with earnestness, "Don't let her speak, Mrs. Gage, it will ruin us. Every newspaper in the land will have our cause mixed up with abolition and niggers, and we shall be utterly denounced." My only answer was, "We shall see when the time comes."

The second day the work waxed warm. Methodist, Baptist, Episcopal, Presbyterian, and Universalist ministers came in to hear and discuss the resolutions presented. One claimed superior rights and privileges for man, on the ground of "superior intellect"; another, because of the "manhood of Christ; if God had desired the equality of woman, He would have given some token of His will through the birth, life, and death of the Saviour." Another gave us a theological view of the "sin of our first mother."

There were very few women in those days who dared to "speak in meeting"; and the august teachers of the people were seemingly getting the better of us, while the boys in the galleries, and the sneerers among the pews, were hugely enjoying the discomfiture, as they supposed, of the "strong-minded." Some of the tender-skinned friends were on the point of losing dignity, and the atmosphere betokened a storm. When, slowly from her seat in the corner rose Sojourner Truth, who, till now, had scarcely lifted her head. "Don't let her speak!" gasped half a dozen in my ear. She moved slowly and solemnly to the front, laid her old bonnet at her feet, and turned her great speaking eyes to me. There was a hissing sound of disapprobation above and below. I rose and announced "Sojourner Truth," and begged the audience to keep silence for a few moments.

The tumult subsided at once, and every eye was fixed on this almost Amazon form, which stood nearly six feet high, head erect, and eyes piercing the upper air like one in a dream. At her first word there was a profound hush. She spoke in deep tones, which, though not loud, reached every ear in the house, and away through the throng at the doors and windows.

"Wall, chilern, whar dar is so much racket dar must be somethin' out o' kilter. I tink dat 'twixt de niggers of de Souf and de womin at de Norf, all talkin' 'bout rights, de white men will be in a fix pretty soon. But what's all dis here talkin' 'bout?

"Dat man ober dar say dat womin needs to be helped into carriages, and lifted ober ditches, and to hab de best place everywhar. Nobody eber helps me into carriages, or ober mud-puddles, or gibs me any best place!" And raising herself to her full height, and her voice to a pitch like rolling thunder, she asked, "And a'n't I a woman? Look at me! Look at my arm! (and she bared her right arm to the shoulder, showing her tremendous muscular power). I have ploughed, and planted, and gathered into barns, and no man could head me! And a'n't I a woman? I could work as much and eat as much as a man—when I could get it—and bear de lash as well! And a'n't I a woman? I have borne thirteen chilern, and seen 'em mos' all sold off to slavery, and when I cried out with my mother's grief, none but Jesus heard me! And a'n't I a woman?

"Den dey talks 'bout dis ting in de head; what dis dey call it?" ("Intellect," whispered some one near.) "Dat's it, honey. What's dat got to do wid womin's rights or nigger's rights? If my cup won't hold but a pint, and yourn holds a quart, wouldn't ye be mean not to let me have my little half-measure full?" And she pointed her significant finger, and sent a keen glance at the minister who had made the argument. The cheering was long and loud.

"Den dat little man in black dar, he say women can't have as much rights as men, 'cause Christ wan't a woman! Whar did your Christ come from?" Rolling thunder couldn't have stilled that crowd, as did those deep, wonderful tones, as she stood there with outstetched arms and eyes of fire. Raising her voice still louder, she repeated, "Whar did your Christ come from? From God and a woman! Man had nothin' to do wid Him." Oh, what a rebuke that was to that little man.

Turning again to another objector, she took up the defense of Mother Eve. I can not follow her through it all. It was pointed, and witty, and solemn; eliciting at almost every sentence deafening applause; and she ended by asserting: "If de fust woman God ever made was strong enough to turn de world upside down all alone, dese women togedder (and she glanced her eye over the platform) ought to be able to turn it back, and get it right side up again! And now dey is asking to do it, de men better let 'em." Long-continued cheering greeted this. "'Bleeged to ye for hearin' on me, and now ole Sojourner han't got nothin' more to say."

Amid roars of applause, she returned to her corner, leaving more than one of us with streaming eyes, and hearts beating with gratitude. She had taken us up in her strong arms and carried us safely over the slough of difficulty turning the whole tide in our favor. I have never in my life seen anything like the magical influence that subdued the mobbish spirit of the day, and turned the sneers and jeers of an excited crowd into notes of respect and admiration. Hundreds rushed up to shake hands with her, and congratulate the glorious old mother, and bid her God-speed on her mission of "testifyin' agin concerning the wickedness of this 'ere people."

Suggestions for Further Reading

Norma Basch, *In the Eyes of the Law: Women, Marriage, and Property in Nineteenth-Century New York* (Ithaca, NY, 1988).

Barbara J. Berg, *The Remembered Gate: Origins of American Feminism, the Woman and the City, 1800–1860* (New York, 1978).

Carol Blesser, ed., *In Joy and in Sorrow: Women, Family, and Marriage in the Victorian South* (New York, 1991).

Jeanne Boydston, *Home and Work: Housework, Wages, and the Ideology of Labor in the Early Republic* (New York, 1990).

Jeanne Boydston, Mary Kelley, and Anne Margolis, *The Limits of Sisterhood: The Beecher Sisters on Women's Rights and Woman's Sphere* (Chapel Hill, NC, 1988).

Lee Virginia Chambers-Schiller, *Liberty, a Better Husband: Single Women in America, the Generation of 1780–1840* (New Haven, CT, 1984).

Clifford E. Clark, Jr., *The American Family Home, 1800–1960* (Chapel Hill, NC, 1986).

Catherine Clinton, *The Plantation Mistress: Woman's World in the Old South* (New York, 1982).

Nancy F. Cott, *The Bonds of Womanhood: "Woman's Sphere" in New England, 1780–1835* (New Haven, CT, 1977).

Carl Degler, *At Odds: Women and the Family in America from the Revolution to the Present* (New York, 1980).

Ann Douglas, *The Feminization of American Culture* (New York, 1977).

Thomas Dublin, *Women at Work: The Transformation of Work and Community in Lowell, Massachusetts, 1826–1860* (New York, 1979).

Faye E. Dudden, *Serving Women: Household Service in Nineteenth-Century America* (Middletown, CT, 1983).

Barbara Leslie Epstein, *The Politics of Domesticity: Women, Evangelism, and Temperance in Nineteenth-Century America* (Middletown, CT, 1981).

John Mack Faragher, *Women and Men on the Overland Trail* (New Haven, CT, 1979).

Philip S. Foner, ed., *The Factory Girls: A Collection of Writings on Life and Struggles in the New England Factories of the 1840s* (Urbana, IL, 1977).

Elizabeth Fox-Genovese, *Within the Plantation Household: Black and White Women of the Old South* (Chapel Hill, NC, 1988).

Michael K. Grossberg, *Governing the Hearth: Law and the Family in Nineteenth-Century America* (Chapel Hill, NC, 1985).

Karen Halttunen, *Confidence Men and Painted Women: A Study of Middle-Class Culture in America, 1830–1870* (New Haven, CT, 1982).

Blanche Hersh, *The Slavery of Sex: Feminist Abolitionists in Nineteenth-Century America* (Urbana, IL, 1978).

Nancy A. Hewitt, *Women's Activism and Social Change: Rochester, New York, 1822–1872* (Ithaca, NY, 1984).

Joan M. Jensen, *Loosening the Bonds: Mid-Atlantic Farm Women, 1750–1850* (New Haven, CT, 1986).

Polly Welts Kaufman, *Women Teachers on the Frontier* (New Haven, CT, 1984).

Mary Kelley, *Private Women, Public Stage: Literary Domesticity in Nineteenth-Century America* (New York, 1984).

Carol Lasser and Marlene Deahl Merrill, eds., *Friends and Sisters: Letters Between Lucy Stone and Antoinette Brown Blackwell, 1846–1893* (Urbana, IL, 1987).

Suzanne Lebsock, *The Free Women of Petersburg: Status and Culture in a Southern Town, 1784–1860* (New York, 1985).

Janet Lecompte, "The Independent Women of Hispanic New Mexico, 1821–1846," *Western Historical Quarterly* 12 (January 1981), pp. 17–35.

Gerda Lerner, *The Grimké Sisters from South Carolina: Pioneers for Women's Rights and Abolition* (New York, 1977).

Keith Melder, *Beginnings of Sisterhood: The American Women's Rights Movement, 1800–1850* (New York, 1977).

Steven Mintz and Susan Kellogg, *Domestic Revolutions: A Social History of American Family Life* (New York, 1988).

Sandra L. Myres, *Westering Women and the Frontier Experience, 1800–1915* (Albuquerque, NM, 1982).

Ellen K. Rothman, *Hands and Hearts: A History of Courtship in America* (Cambridge, MA, 1984).

Mary P. Ryan, *Cradle of the Middle Class: The Family in Oneida County, New York, 1790–1865* (New York, 1981).

Anne Firor Scott, *The Southern Lady: From Pedestal to Politics, 1830–1930* (Chicago, 1970).

Katherine Kish Sklar, *Catharine Beecher: A Study in American Domesticity* (New Haven, CT, 1973).

Carroll Smith-Rosenberg, *Disorderly Conduct: Visions of Gender in Victorian America* (New York, 1985).

Christine Stansell, *City of Women: Sex and Class in New York, 1789–1865* (New York, 1986).

Dorothy Sterling, ed., *We Are Your Sisters: Black Women in the Nineteenth Century* (New York, 1984).

Deborah Gray White, *Ar'n't I a Woman?: Female Slaves in the Plantation South* (New York, 1985).

C. Vann Woodward, ed., *Mary Chesnut's Civil War* (New Haven, CT, 1981).

Jean Fagan Yellin, *Women and Sisters: Antislavery Feminists in American Culture* (New Haven, CT, 1990).

PART III

The Late 19th Century, 1860–1900

During the last third of the nineteenth century, American women assumed new visibility outside the home—in the industrial labor force, in stores and offices, in schools and colleges, in reform organizations and settlement houses, on the lecture platform, and in leadership roles. Many of these developments had antecedents before or during the Civil War. Still, the late nineteenth century was an era of institution building and organization founding, notably among those middle-class women who dominate the documentary record. "The modern woman is capable and restless," a women's club officer declared in the 1890s. "She would enter into the competitive struggle for existence far more than she does at present."

Women's new role in public life emerged against the turbulent background of rapid industrialization. Between the Civil War and 1900, cities grew at a phenomenal pace. Immigrants arrived at unprecedented rates. Factories sprang up in rural towns. Strikes and violence erupted with regularity, and the economy swung wildly between periods of expansion and gloomy depressions. Late nineteenth-century Americans commented frequently on the pace of change and on the growing chasm between social classes—between, for instance, the new urban working class, full of recent immigrants, and the upper ranks of the professional and managerial classes. Well-off citizens tended to view lower-class contemporaries with a combination of concern and discomfort. "The main effect of the spectacle of the misery of the toiler at the rope," wrote Edward Bellamy in *Looking Backward* (1888), "was to enhance the passengers' sense of the value of their seats upon the coach."

This section is devoted to a few of the developments in women's history in the late nineteenth century. The first group of documents concerns women's responses to the Civil War, especially to the experience of emancipation and its aftermath. Subsequent documents concern some of the "new" women, especially city women, who left their marks on the post-bellum decades—wage-earners, college students, social reformers, and suffragists. These documents evoke several questions. How did women seek to redefine their "place" and expand their opportunities? How did industrialization and urbanization affect women's lives? How did the interests of middle-class women and working-class women differ? In what ways did women try to forge links across class lines? The documents provide no definitive answers. But they suggest several ways in which late nineteenth-century women shaped modern roles.

Chapter 12

The Women's War

L ate nineteenth-century women assessed the impact of the Civil War in different ways. Ardent Confederates resented the legacy of Yankee invasions. Some northerners stressed new opportunities, a quickened rate of progress, and the benefit to women of participation in national life. To others, women on both sides were the war's hapless victims—widowed, orphaned, bereaved, and unsupported. Author Elizabeth Stuart Phelps mourned the "helpless, outnumbered, unconsulted women . . . whom war trampled down without a choice or a protest." To yet others, women's unsung war service left the nation with an unpaid debt. As suffragist Matilda Joslyn Gage declared in the 1880s, "the labor women accomplished, the hardship they endured, the time and strength they sacrificed in the war . . . can never fully be appreciated." Still others judged the war in the light of what followed. Considering the oppression of southern blacks thirty years after Appomattox, former slave Susie King Taylor wondered, "Was the war in vain?"

Since few generalizations about women's experiences ever cover *all* women, it is useful to distinguish among three major groups of women in the Civil War era: Union, Confederate, and slaves or former slaves. Union women, with well-established traditions of voluntary benevolence and reform, were (compared to Confederates) both more active contributors to the war effort and greater beneficiaries of new opportunities. As the male labor supply fell, northern women took over school posts and government clerkships that men had vacated. They provided the bulk of the work force on northern farms, where productivity increased, despite a decrease in the male labor pool. When Dorothea Dix became superintendent of army nurses, the women she appointed achieved official status in the war effort. By 1865, more than 3,000 women nurses, paid and volunteer, had offered their services in hospitals and camps. Once emancipation was imminent, women's rights advocates formed the Women's Loyal League to support the president, to fan the flames of antislavery, and to petition for the Thirteenth Amendment. Other abolitionists, white and black, staffed freedmen's schools run by freedmen's aid societies, religious groups, and the Freedmen's Bureau.

The most widespread spur to female activism was undoubtedly the male-run Sanitary Commission, under whose auspices thousands of women in the North and West ran fund-raising events or "Sanitary Fairs," collected supplies and funds for the army, and provided a model of the large, national federations of women's organizations that would follow the war. Like the nursing corps and the freedmen's schools, the Sanitary Commission provided a legitimate route for women to support the war effort, while gratifying their much-voiced desire for "usefulness" and "service." As a commission agent declared, "At the first sound and threatening of war, there sprung up in my heart a concentrated impulse *to do, to act*."

Confederate women, too, formed patriotic societies to send supplies to the front and to boost morale. Many volunteered their services as nurses. But their participation in the war was as much involuntary as patriotic. Since the South was invaded, for instance, some had no choice. As the conflict progressed, Confederate disadvantages multiplied. The South had higher inflation, more severe shortages, and a far greater loss of manpower than the North experienced. Four out of five eligible southern men served in the Confederate army, as opposed to about half in the North. Confederate women were often left to manage farms, where supplies dwindled and equipment fell apart. Many women ran plantations, where productivity fell and slaves grew restive. On some wartime mistresses, left without husbands or overseers, fell the burden of maintaining slavery. "You may give your Negroes away," a Texas wife wrote to her husband in 1864. "I cannot live with them another year alone."

Wartime problems were compounded by those that followed surrender. The South suffered disproportionate casualties and economic devastation. About eighteen percent of southern white men under the age of forty-four had died in the war. Many families—and the women in them—lost their property, homes, status, security, and support. In the long run, historians have suggested, the Civil War served the interests of white southern women by dismantling, or at least impairing, the patriarchal system that had limited their options and curtailed their independence. But the benefits of this development were long in coming, since former Confederates staunchly clung to the traditions to which they were accustomed. Nor was the economic or demographic damage caused by the war quickly repaired. Many southern white women had to cope with the Civil War's impact for the rest of the century. In 1890, those states that had made up the Confederacy claimed over 60,000 war widows, some supporting themselves on farms and plantations. Only after Reconstruction did some of the former Confederate states start to supply pensions or other aid to Civil War veterans and their dependents.

For southern slaves, the implications of the Civil War were the most momentous of all. Freedom was a consequence that few had expected when the fighting began. The wartime experiences of men and women slaves often differed. About 90,000 southern black men, mainly former slaves, served in the Union army, for instance, while women remained in refugee camps or on plantations. In general, because women were tied to their families more closely than were the men, women were less likely to escape from slavery during the war. But for all slaves, emancipation, which usually occurred at the time of Confederate surrender, was the transforming wartime event. To former slaves, liberation brought monumental changes, including personal mobility, legal marriage, stable families, authority over children, and control over their own labor. As one newly freed slave declared in 1865, "I own myself."

An effective blow against compulsory labor was struck immediately after the war, when newly reconstituted black families asserted their independence. Wives and mothers refused to return to work in the fields, thereby retiring a segment of the prewar rural labor force and increasing the problems of postwar planters. The sharecropping system that evolved in the South in the late 1860s was for former slaves preferable to the wage labor systems planters had sought to impose after the war. Sharecropping meant family farms and an escape from supervision by whites. But for landowners it was also a way to reengage female workers. Until the great northward migrations of the twentieth century, the majority of black women remained southern farm workers, either on family plots or for pay. In 1870, when eighty percent of black cotton-belt households were headed by men, four out of ten black married women claimed to have jobs, mainly as field labor, and most of the rest worked on farms as well. Among the minority of former slaves who moved to southern cities, women were overrepresented. Seeking support for themselves and their families, these women eked out their livings as cooks, laundresses, seam-stresses, and domestics. In few cases did emancipation from slavery bring freedom from labor. But as one Reconstruction-era freedwoman told a northern journalist, "I've a heap better time now'n I had when I was in bondage."

A Union Nurse

LOUISA MAY ALCOTT, 1863

Ednah Dow Cheney, *Louisa May Alcott, Her Life, Letters, and Journal* (Boston: Little, Brown, 1928), pp. 115–19.

After Dorothea Dix became superintendent of nurses for the Union army in June, 1861, she issued a call for women nurses between thirty and fifty years old: single, sober, hard-working, moral, and "plain-looking women." Louisa May Alcott (1832–1888) of Concord, Massachusetts, who had been supporting herself as a seamstress, governess, teacher, and home companion, leapt at the opportunity, although she barely met the minimum age requirement. Appointed in December 1862, she took a post at the Union Hotel Hospital in the Georgetown section of Washington, D.C.

Recently a tavern, the hospital was a dark, airless pit, to which ambulances delivered mud-caked victims of nearby battles. Alcott's job was to clean and dress wounds, sew bandages, feed patients, and write letters for them. As in other wartime hospitals, the sick outnumbered the wounded. Soldiers suffered from diseases such as typhoid, pneumonia, bronchitis, and dysentery. Within three weeks, the overworked young nurse herself collapsed with typhoid pneumonia. Like her patients, she was treated with huge doses of the emetic calomel, a mercury compound that led to a multitude of ills, culminated by delirium and hallucinations. Alcott described the experience in her journal. The excerpt that follows covers November 1862 through January 1863.

The energetic and adventurous tone of Alcott's journal conceals two terrifying experiences. The first was nursing; even a lifetime of caring for others had not prepared her for the Union Hotel Hospital. A second terror was the experience of almost dying, from either the disease or its remedy. Alcott, however, made the most of her three-week wartime opportunity. *Hospital Sketches* (1863), based on her brief nursing experience, was well-received in article form and then as a book. With its publication, Louisa May Alcott began her prolific and successful career as an author.*

---

*For a first-rate study, see Martha Saxton, *Louisa May: A Modern Biography of Louisa May Alcott* (Boston: Houghton Mifflin, 1977).

November—Thirty years old. Decided to go to Washington as nurse if I could find a place. Help needed, and I love nursing, and *must* let out my pent-up energy in some new way. Winter is always a hard and a dull time, and if I am away there is one less to feed and warm and worry over.

I want new experiences, and am sure to get 'em if I go. So I've sent in my name, and bide my time writing tales, to leave all snug behind me, and mending up my old clothes—for nurses don't need nice things, thank Heaven!

December—On the 11th I received a note from Miss H. M. Stevenson telling me to start for Georgetown next day to fill a place in the Union Hotel Hospital. Mrs. Ropes of Boston was matron, and Miss Kendall of Plymouth was a nurse there, and though a hard place, help was needed. I was ready, and when my commander said "March!" I marched. Packed my trunk, and reported in B. that same evening.

We had all been full of courage till the last moment came; then we all broke down. I realized that I had taken my life in my hand, and might never see them all again. I said, "Shall I stay, Mother?" as I hugged her close. "No, go! and the Lord be with you!" answered the Spartan woman; and till I turned the corner she bravely smiled and waved her wet handkerchief on the door-step. Shall I ever see that dear old face again?

So I set forth in the December twilight, with May and Julian Hawthorne as escort, feeling as if I was the son of the house going to war.

Friday, the 12th, was a very memorable day, spent in running all over Boston to get my pass, etc., calling for parcels, getting a tooth filled, and buying a veil—my only purchase. A. C. gave me some old clothes; the dear Sewalls money for myself and boys, lots of love and help; and at 5 P. M., saying "good-by" to a group of tearful faces at the station, I started on my long journey, full of hope and sorrow, courage and plans.

A most interesting journey into a new world full of stirring sights and sounds, new adventures, and an evergrowing sense of the great task I had undertaken.

I said my prayers as I went rushing through the country white with tents, all alive with patriotism, and already red with blood.

A solemn time, but I'm glad to live in it; and am sure it will do me good whether I come out alive or dead.

All went well, and I got to Georgetown one evening very tired. Was kindly welcomed, slept in my narrow bed with two other room-mates, and on the morrow began my new life by seeing a poor man die at dawn, and sitting all day between a boy with pneumonia and a man shot through the lungs. A strange day, but I did my best; and when I put mother's little black shawl round the boy while he sat up panting for breath, he smiled and said, "You are real motherly, ma'am." I felt as if I was getting on. The man only lay and stared with his big black eyes, and made me very nervous. But all were well behaved; and I sat looking at the twenty strong faces as they looked back at me—the only new thing they had to amuse them—hoping that I looked "motherly" to them; for my thirty years made me feel old, and the suffering round me made me long to comfort every one.

January, 1863. *Union Hotel Hospital, Georgetown, D.C.*—I never began the year in a stranger place than this: five hundred miles from home, alone, among strangers, doing painful duties all day long, and leading a life of constant excitement in this great house, surrounded by three or four hundred men in all stages of suffering, disease, and death. Though often homesick, heartsick, and worn out, I like it, find real pleasure in comforting, tending, and cheering these poor souls who seem to love me, to feel my sympathy though unspoken, and acknowledge my hearty good-will, in spite of the ignorance, awkwardness, and bashfulness which I cannot help showing in so new and trying a situation. The men are docile, respectful, and affectionate, with but few exceptions; truly lovable and manly many of them. John Sulie, a Virginia blacksmith, is the prince of patients; and though what we call a common man in education and condition, to me is all I could expect or ask from the first gentleman in the land. Under his plain speech and unpolished manner I seem to see a noble character, a heart as warm and tender as a woman's, a nature fresh and frank as any child's. He is about thirty, I think, tall and handsome, mortally wounded, and dying royally without reproach, repining, or remorse. Mrs. Ropes and myself love him, and feel indignant that such a man should be so early lost; for though he might never distinguish himself before the world, his influence and example cannot be without effect, for real goodness is never wasted.

Monday, 4th—I shall record the events of a day as a sample of the days I spend.

Up at six, dress by gaslight, run through my ward and throw up the windows, though the men grumble and shiver; but the air is bad enough to breed a pestilence; and as no notice is taken of our frequent appeals for better ventilation, I must do what I can. Poke up the fire, add blankets, joke, coax, and command; but continue to open doors and windows as if life depended upon it. Mine does, and doubtless many another, for a more perfect pestilence-box than this house I never saw—cold, damp, dirty, full of vile odors from wounds, kitchens, wash-rooms, and stables. No competent head, male or female, to right matters, and a jumble of good, bad, and indifferent nurses, surgeons, and attendants, to complicate the chaos still more.

After this unwelcome progress through my stifling ward, I go to breakfast with what appetite I may; find the uninvitable fried beef, salt butter, husky bread, and washy coffee; listen to the clack of eight women and a dozen men—the first silly, stupid, or possessed of one idea; the last absorbed with their breakfast and themselves to a degree that is both ludicrous and provoking, for all the dishes are ordered down the table *full* and returned *empty*; the conversation is entirely among themselves, and each announces his opinion with an air of importance that frequently causes me to choke in my cup, or bolt my meals with undignified speed lest a laugh betray to these famous beings that a "chiel's amang them takin' notes."

Till noon I trot, trot, giving out rations, cutting up food for helpless "boys," washing faces, teaching my attendants how beds are made or floors are swept, dressing wounds, taking Dr. F. P.'s orders (privately wishing all the time that he would be more gentle with my big babies), dusting tables, sewing bandages, keeping my tray tidy, rushing up and down after pillows, bed-linen, sponges, books, and directions, till it seems as if I would joyfully pay down all I possess for fifteen minutes' rest. At twelve the big bell rings, and up comes dinner for the boys, who are always ready for it, and never entirely satisfied. Soup, meat, potatoes, and bread is the bill of fare. Charley Thayer, the attendant, travels up and down the room serving out the rations, saving little for himself, yet always thoughtful of his mates, and patient as a woman with their helplessness. When dinner is over, some sleep, many read, and others want letters written. This I like to do, for they put in such odd things, and express their ideas so comically, I have great fun interiorly, while as grave as possible exteriorly. A few of the men word their paragraphs well and make excellent letters. John's was the best of all I wrote. The answering of letters from friends after some one had died is the saddest and hardest duty a nurse has to do.

Supper at five sets every one to running that can run; and when that flurry is over, all settle down for the evening amusements, which consist of newspapers, gossip, the doctor's last round, and, for such as need them, the final doses for the night. At nine the bell rings, gas is turned down, and day nurses go to bed. Night nurses go on duty, and sleep and death have the house to themselves.

My work is changed to night watching, or half night and half day—from twelve to twelve. I like it, as it leaves me time for a morning run, which is what I need to keep well; for bad air, food, and water, work and watching, are getting to be too much for me. I trot up and down the streets in all directions, sometimes to the Heights, then half way to Washington, again to the hill, over which the long trains of army wagons are constantly vanishing and ambulances appearing. That way the fighting lies, and I long to follow.

Ordered to keep my room, being threatened with pneumonia. Sharp pain in the side, cough, fever, and dizziness. A pleasant prospect for a lonely soul five hundred miles from home! Sit and sew on the boys' clothes, write letters, sleep, and read; try to talk and keep merry, but fail decidedly, as day after day goes, and I feel no better. Dream awfully, and wake unrefreshed, think of home, and wonder if I am to die here, as Mrs. R., the matron, is likely to do. Feel too miserable to care much what becomes of me. Dr. S. creaks up twice a day to feel my pulse, gives me doses, and asks if I am at all consumptive, or some other cheering question. Dr. O. examines my lungs and looks sober. Dr. J. haunts the room, coming by day and night with wood, cologne, books, and messes, like a motherly little man as he is. Nurses, fussy and anxious, matron dying, and everything very gloomy. They want me to go home, but I *won't* yet.

January 16th—Was amazed to see Father enter the room that morning, having been telegraphed to by order of Mrs. R. without asking leave. I was very angry at first, though glad to see him, because I knew I should have to go. Mrs. D. and Miss Dix came, and pretty Miss W., to take me to Willard's to be cared for by them. I wouldn't go, preferring to keep still, being pretty ill by that time.

On the 21st I suddenly decided to go home, feeling very strangely, and dreading to be worse. Mrs. R. died, and that frightened the doctors about me; for my trouble was the same—typhoid pneumonia. Father, Miss K., and Lizzie T. went with me. Miss Dix brought a basket full of bottles of wine, tea, medicine, and cologne, besides a little blanket and pillow, a fan, and a testament. She is a kind old soul, but very queer and arbitrary.

Was very sorry to go, and "my boys" seemed sorry to have me. Quite a flock came to see me off; but I was too sick to have but a dim idea of what was going on.

Northern Women on Farms

MARY A. LIVERMORE, 1890

Mary A. Livermore, *My Story of the War: A Woman's Narrative of Four Years Personal Experience* (Hartford, CT: Worthington and Co., 1890), pp. 135–36, 145–49.

No northern organization involved more grass-roots women than the U.S. Sanitary Commission, a quasi-official group that helped the Union medical bureau. Organized in 1861 by prominent male philanthropists, the commission recorded vital statistics, tracked down the missing, evacuated the wounded, and inspected army camps. It also depended on women volunteers in 7,000 local auxiliaries, who collected supplies, raised funds, ran distribution centers, and bolstered the commission's image as—in one woman activist's words—"a great artery that bears the people's love to the army."

Mary A. Livermore (1820–1905) of Chicago, an official of the Northwestern Branch of the Sanitary Commission, took great pride in her leadership role. In the following excerpts from her hefty memoir of the war years, Livermore pays tribute to midwestern farm women, native-born and foreign-born. They not only supported the commission's efforts but made major contributions to northern agriculture, where they compensated for the absence of adult male workers. Indeed, expanded machine production and mechanization of grain farming enabled the Union to increase corn and wheat production above prewar levels and to double exports of agricultural products.

Organizations of women for the relief of sick and wounded soldiers, and for the care of soldiers' families, were formed with great spontaneity at the very beginning of the war. There were a dozen or more of them in Chicago, in less than a month after Cairo was occupied by Northern troops. They raised money, prepared and forwarded supplies of whatever was demanded, every shipment being accompanied by some one who was held responsible for the proper disbursement of the stores. Sometimes these local societies affiliated with, or became parts of, more comprehensive organizations. Most of them worked independently during the first year of the war, the Sanitary Commission of Chicago being only one of the relief agencies. But the Commission gradually grew in public confidence, and gained in scope and power; and all the local societies were eventually merged in it, or became auxiliary to it. As in

Chicago, so throughout the country. The Sanitary Commission became the great channel, through which the patriotic beneficence of the nation flowed to the army.

When the local aid society of which I was president, merged its existence in that of the Sanitary Commission, I also became identified with it. Thenceforth, until the bells rang in the joyful news of peace, my time and energy were given to its varied work. In its busy rooms I was occupied most of the time when not in the hospitals, or engaged with some of the Northwestern soldiers' aid societies. . . .

During the war I was called into the country on frequent errands. Sometimes it was to organize aid societies—sometimes to attend mass conventions, called for inspiration and instruction in the work to be done. The attendance was increased by a natural desire for social enjoyment, which the necessities of the times greatly abridged. Sometimes a meeting would be called in a large town for the double purpose of stimulating hospital supplies and enlistments—sometimes I went in charge of soldiers, too ill or enfeebled from wounds to be sent alone. On these trips I noticed a great increase of women engaged in outdoor work, and especially during the times of planting, cultivating, and harvesting.

In the early summer of 1863, frequent calls of business took me through the extensive farming districts of Wisconsin, and Eastern Iowa, when the farmers were the busiest, gathering the wheat harvest. As we dashed along the railway, let our course lead in whatever direction it might, it took us through what seemed a continuous wheat-field. The yellow grain was waving everywhere; and two-horse reapers were cutting it down in a wholesale fashion that would have astonished Eastern farmers. Hundreds of reapers could be counted in a ride of half a dozen hours. The crops were generally good, and in some instances heavy, and every man and boy was pressed into service to secure the abundant harvest while the weather was fine.

Women were in the field everywhere, driving the reapers, binding and shocking, and loading grain, until then an unusual sight. At first, it displeased me, and I turned away in aversion. Buy and by, I observed how skilfully they drove the horses round and round the wheat-field, diminishing more and more its periphery at every circuit, the glittering blades of the reaper cutting wide swaths with a rapid, clicking sound, that was pleasant to hear. Then I saw that when they followed the reapers, binding and shocking, although they did not keep up with the men, their work was done with more precision and nicety, and their sheaves had an artistic finish that those lacked made by the men. So I said to myself, "They are worthy women, and deserve praise: their husbands are probably too poor to hire help, and, like the 'helpmeets' God designed them to be, they have girt themselves to this work—and they are doing it superbly. Good wives! good women!"

One day my route took me off the railway, some twenty miles across the country. But we drove through the same golden fields of grain, and between great stretches of green waving corn. Now a river shimmered like silver through the gold of the wheat and oats, and now a growth of young timber made a dark green background for the harvest fields. Here, as everywhere, women were busy at the harvesting.

"I've got to hold up a spell, and rig up this 'ere harness," said my driver; "something's got out of kilter." And the carriage halted opposite a field where half a dozen women and two men were harvesting. Not a little curious to know what these women reapers were like, I walked over and accosted them.

"And so you are helping gather the harvest!" I said to a woman of forty-five or fifty, who sat on the reaper to drive, as she stopped her horses for a brief breathing spell. Her face was pleasant and comely although sunburned, with honest, straightforward eyes, a broad brow, and a mouth that indicated firmness and tenderness. Her dress, a strong calico, was worn without hoops, then thought essential on all occasions, and she was shod with stout boots, and wore a shaker bonnet.

"Yes ma'am," she said; "the men have all gone to the war, so that my man can't hire help at any price, and I told my girls we must turn to and give him a lift with the harvestin'."

"You are not German? You are surely one of my own countrywomen—American?"

"Yes, ma'am; we moved here from Cattaraugus county, New York state, and we've done very well since we came."

"Have you sons in the army?"

"Yes," and a shadow fell over the motherly face, and the honest eyes looked out mournfully into vacancy. "All three of 'em 'listed, and Neddy, the youngest, was killed at the battle of Stone River, the last day of last year. My man, he went down to get his body, but he came back without it. There were nine thousand of our men left dead on the field there, and our Neddy's body couldn't be found among so many. It came very hard on us to let the boys go, but we felt we'd no right to hinder 'em. The country needed 'em more'n we. We've money enough to hire help if it could be had; and my man don't like to have me and the girls a-workin' outdoors; but there don't seem no help for it now."

I stepped over where the girls were binding the fallen grain. They were fine, well-built lasses, with the honest eyes and firm mouth of the mother, brown like her, and clad in the same sensible costume.

"Well, you are like your mother, not afraid to lend a hand at the harvesting, it seems!" was my opening remark.

"No, we're willing to help outdoors in these times. Harvesting isn't any harder, if it's as hard as cooking, washing, and ironing, over a red-hot stove in July and August—only we have to do both now. My three brothers went into the army, all my cousins, most of the young men about here, and the men we used to hire. So there's no help to be got but women, and the crops must be got in all the same, you know."

"One of our German women," said another of the girls, "tells us we don't know anything about war yet. For during the last war in Germany men were so scarce that she had to work three years in a blacksmith's shop. You wouldn't think it, though, if you should see her. That would be rather tough, but I tell Annie we can do anything to help along while the country's in such trouble."

"I tell mother," said the Annie referred to, standing very erect, with flashing eyes, "that as long as the country can't get along without grain, nor the army fight without food, we're serving the country just as much here in the harvest-field as our boys are on the battle-field—and that sort o' takes the edge off from this business of doing men's work, you know." And a hearty laugh followed this statement. . . .

It was from these and similar sources, multiplied thousands of times, that the stream of supplies for the sick and weary of the army maintained its vast and constant proportions to the very close of the war. The supplies varied according to the needs of the men at the front. But whatever was the need as to quality, quantity, or cost, it was soon apparent that in the zeal and intense nationality of the women of the North there was a certainty of its being supplied systematically and bountifully. No rebuffs could chill their zeal; no reverses repress their ardor; no discouragements weaken their devotion. The women had enlisted for the war.

A Wartime Mistress

LOUTICIA JACKSON, 1863

Mrs. Louticia Jackson to Asbury H. Jackson, August 23, 1863, Edward Harden Papers, Duke University, in Clarence L. Mohr, *On the Threshold of Freedom: Masters and Slaves in Civil War Georgia* (Athens: University of Georgia Press, 1986), p. 231.

Southern women who replaced their absent husbands on farms faced more problems than did their northern counterparts: Loss of male labor, crumbling equipment, and scarcity of food and clothing proved crippling disabilities throughout the rural South. Those women who ran plantations alone had additional problems. The wartime mistress had to control an increasingly restive slave labor force, whose growing resistance sometimes became manifest in theft, malingering, absentee-ism, and sabotage. In remote rural areas, managing slaves without adult male assistance proved a formidable assignment, and one for which, historians hypothesize, southern women may have been unpre-pared. Accustomed to male dominance, they had adapted to their own subordinate status: Aggressive leadership roles were reserved for men. Habitually dependent, a plantation mistress was often forced—in the absence of husband and overseers—to depend to an extent on slaves. But her dependence arose just as the slaves were gaining in bargain-ing power.

The problems of mistresses emerge in fragments of letters to absent relatives in which women tell stories with the same double message: their own efforts to control a difficult situation and slave responses to the diminished authority of management. Louticia Jack-son, a Georgia mistress who ran a small plantation in rural Clarke County, with the help of her teenage son Johny, told of one problem she confronted. In a letter to an older son in the Confederate army, she describes her trouble with an increasingly rebellious slave, Willes, who has taken advantage of the plantation power gap. Besides his growing assertiveness and absenteeism, Willes has begun giving com-mands and influencing the other slaves.

We are doing as best we know, or as good as we can get the Servants to do. . . . [T]hey seem to feel very indepenat as no white man comes to direct or look after them, for Willes speaks shorter to Johny and orders *him* about more than any negro on the place. In consequence . . . [Johny] seldom tells him to do anything, so sure as he does . . . Willes will make some insulting reply such as thus: whats the matter with you, whats the reason you can't do it, and so on, and when I ask him why he has not done certain things he will say John never told him, and says that John will tell a story in a minute. I told him he did not have to tell me so again, but he sayed he did not care what I sayed about it. A few evenings ago I asked him where he had been all the evening; he did not make any reply. John then sayed ma's talking to you. He sayed he knew that and she's allways asking some silly question. He then commenced in such a loud harangue you might have heard him half a mile or more. It so excited me I left the door, went in the room, and lay down with the back ache. He does not suffer me to enquire in to anything without giving some insulting reply, though I tell them all together generally what must be done so as to avoid any difficulty with him.

He done as well as he knew how the first 6 months after you left. I was truly proud to see him seem to take such an intrust in the farm. But he got his own crop laid by. He then helped some in threshing the wheat, he took the fever immediately after which lasted some 5 or 6 weeks in which time I attended him closely day and night, bathed and rubbed him with my own hands fearing it would not be faithfully done [otherwise]. In 6 mounths he grew w[e]ary in well doing, [and] has been a drag ever since, and we . . . can see his evil influence in most all the others that are large enough to notice him. . . . Some person must have been lecturing him I think, for he runs about a goodeal & but seldom asks for a pass and when he does he will walk up to the door and say some of you write me a pass, rather in a commanding tone. . . . I believe he has got Johny afraid of him. . . . He does seem so wicked [that] if any one was to come upon him about his conduct I do not know what he would do afterwards.

Confronting Defeat

EVA B. JONES, 1865

Eva B. Jones to Mary Jones, letters of June 13, June 17, and July 14, 1865, in Robert Manson Myers, ed., *The Children of Pride: A True Story of Georgia and the Civil War* (New Haven, CT: Yale University Press, 1972), pp. 1273–76, 1280–81.

The postwar spirit of depression that afflicted Confederates, caused by the Union victory in 1865, emerged less in public statements than in private papers. Among educated southerners, personal correspondence was traditionally both a mode of self-definition and a form of social activity. This was all the more true in the case of women, for whom few (or no) outlets for public expression existed. When Eva B. Jones of Augusta, a young Georgia matron, expressed her feelings to her mother-in-law in the summer after surrender, she produced at once a series of private communications and some self-conscious historical documents.

An unusually literate woman, Eva B. Jones had been educated in northern schools, as had her husband, Charles Colcock Jones, a graduate of Princeton and Harvard law school. He had served as mayor of Savannah and, during the war, as an officer in the Georgia artillery. Eva B. Jones had no doubt about the historic import of the Confederate defeat: For consolation, she turned at once to her volumes of history. She also excelled as a chronicler of the current scene. Out of her letters spill the difficulties that slaveowners faced at the war's end, such as crop failure, cash shortage, property loss, lack of supplies, and the exodus of freedmen from plantations and townhouses. Above all, Eva B. Jones recounted her gnawing sense of role reversal—a suspicion that defeated Confederates would inherit the "shackles" that slaves had "abandoned."

At the end of 1865, a few months after these letters were written, Eva B. Jones and her husband moved to New York, where Charles practiced law for over a decade. They returned to Georgia only at the end of Reconstruction, in 1877.

Augusta, Tuesday, June 13th, 1865

Dear Mother,

It is with sad and heavy hearts we mark the dark, crowding events of this most disastrous year. We have seen hope after hope fall blighted and withering about us, until our country is no more—merely a heap of ruins and ashes. A joyless future of probable ignominy, poverty, and want is all that spreads before us, and God alone knowing where any of us will end a life robbed of every blessing and already becoming intolerable. You see, it is with no resigned spirit that *I* yield to the iron yoke our conqueror forges for his fallen and powerless foe. The degradation of a whole country and a proud people is indeed a mighty, an all-enveloping sorrow.

I have uninterruptedly sought forgetfulness, or rather *temporary* relief, from these present griefs in a most earnest application to study. Some fourteen volumes of history have claimed my recent attention. And yet the study of human nature from the earliest epochs affords one little comfort. How vice and wickedness, injustice and every human passion runs riot, flourishes, oftentimes going unpunished to the tomb! And how the little feeble sickly attempts of virtue struggle, and after a brief while fade away, unappreciated and unextolled! The depravity of the human heart is truly wonderful, and the moiety of virtue contained on the historic page truly deplorable. How often have these same sorrows and unmerited punishments that we are now undergoing been visited upon the brave, the deserving, the heroic, and the patient of all ages and in all climes! . . . Virtue, like the violet, modest and unnoted, blossoms in silence and fades softly away; the fragrance it threw on the morning breeze was very sweet and very rare; but the breeze died away, and the memory of the virtuous dies too. I fear you will think I am growing very allegorical, but really "the common course of events" is so out-of-date that it needs a few extra flourishes on everything we do at present to mark this most unnatural era. Had it not been for my dear books, the one comfort as yet unmolested (I do not refer to those we left in Savannah), I am inclined to believe I should have been constrained to apply for a suite of apartments in some lunatic asylum—if they too have not vanished with other national comforts!

Charles, thank Heaven, is very well and just the same immaculate darling he always was, but just now so deeply and exclusively busy at the plantation, earning his daily bread "by the sweat of his brow," that I only am occasionally enchanted with a flying visit. He received a week or two ago a letter from you which we were both rejoiced to receive, and which, by the way, he immediately answered, I enclosing a note. But after having written, some farther developments of Yankee policy being foreshadowed, he waited to see the results, and as he was suddenly called away, left me with directions "not to send the letter." I do not feel at liberty to do so until I hear more from him.

I suppose you have learned even in the more secluded portions of the country that slavery is entirely abolished—a most unprecedented robbery, and most unwise policy. So it must appear even to the ignorant. I know it is only intended for a greater humiliation and loss to *us*, but I should think that even the powerful and unconscientious conqueror would reap the ill effects of so unguarded a movement. However, it *is* done; and we, the *chained witnesses*, can only look on and draw inferences and note occurrences—"only this and nothing more." There has been a great rush of the freedmen from all families in the city and from neighboring plantations. Adeline, Grace, and Polly have all departed in search of freedom, without bidding any of us an affectionate adieu. All of Dr. Joe's servants have left save Titus and Agrippa and children, I think he told me. . . . We have lost many of our servants, but a sufficent number have remained to serve us, and as yet these appear faithful and anxious to please. On our plantation everything is "at sixes and sevens." One day they work, and the next they come to town. Of course no management of them is allowed. Our Yankee masters think that *their* term of slavery having expired, that the shackles they have abandoned, more firmly riveted, will do for us their former owners. And we meekly bow the head, receive chains and insults, and observe a mute and most submissive demeanor. Veritably like lambs we are led to the slaughter, and like sheep before the shearers we are dumb. And they *shear* ahead—in a manner most wonderful to behold.

Very shortly I will, D.V. [*deo volente*, or God willing], leave "these scenes so charming" to forget in a summer sojourning among my best-loved friends some of these present miseries. After the annual delight of a Sparta trip I hope to visit some friends in Athens; and from thence I spend the remainder of the summer in the mountain breezes of Clarkesville with my dear aunt. I trust I'll find both health and flesh in the delightful summer retreat of my aunt, for I need both sorely—although I am a little stronger for the past few days, or rather *two days*.

I fear I am quite wearying you with my unusual volubility. My dearest mother unites with me in warm love to yourself and Ruthie. I suppose the little lady is grown entirely beyond one's recollection. Kiss her for me. I know her papa would send a very affectionate one for her were he here. Dismayed at the divers accumulations of great poverty, hopeless and in the depths of an abyss of despair, faintly I reiterate:

Affectionately yours,
Eva

Augusta, Tuesday, June 27th, 1865

Your last letter to Charlie, dear Mother, reached here some few days after I had written you quite an epistle, and while he was still at Indianola. He had been hard *at work* while there, his hands hard and burnt like a common laborer's. Yet he scarcely had a breathing space before, mounting cotton bales in a wagon, he started down to Savannah to try and make a little money, which article he is totally without and greatly in need of. He begged I would write you immediately and let you know the urgency of the case and say he would try if *possible* to get out to Montevideo. The reason of this great haste was, he had invested some of his Confederate money in two bales of domestics; and hearing he could get ten cents advance on the price here in Savannah—or rather, the market being overstocked here with that sort of goods and there being a dearth of them in Savannah—he, fearing a tumble in the price in that market so soon as these flatboats now building commence to carry freight, wisely seized this probably *best* opportunity, and is now on his way to Savannah in a most primitive style.

Of course you know there is no way for him, or anybody else scarcely, to make money now. He will not be allowed to practice his profession until he is permitted to take the oath.* His wheat crop has utterly failed, and we are all as poor as church mice. The Negroes at Indianola wanted to give a little trouble during his last visit, but he soon straightened them up, and now they are behaving very well. We here have been most unfortunate, for being so near to the city, our Negroes are under all the baleful influences of the vile abolitionists (of which the worst specimens are in our midst); and they (the Negroes) work or not just as it best suits their convenience and pleasure. We have only a third-crop planted (that not worked); and our most promising fields are now under water.

Besides this, the Negroes and Yankees have broken into our smokehouse and swept it of *every piece* of meat. Not content with this great and to us terrible robbery, they have even entered with false keys our storeroom here, and have not left us a single ham. So we are now dependent on the market, and have to purchase every bit of meat we eat. Constant depredations are being made on the place, and we can obtain no *redress*, and are entirely at the mercy of the merciless.

I grow so wearied with all these troubles that I long so for the quiet of the up country, where I trust before long to be. I will now wait until my cousin, Miss Casey, is strong enough to accompany me. She has been dangerously ill with typhoid fever, which is spreading all over the city. I have heard that the Yankee surgeon mentioned a few days since a case of black vomit, which sounds something like yellow fever. Indeed, I should be surprised at nothing, for the city is kept fearfully filthy, and the cellars (many of them) continue filling with water from the springs in them caused by last month's great freshet.

Charlie will go to Atlanta so soon as he returns from Savannah. Another great reason for his going so immediately was that a friend had written us if he would go down *directly* he might be able to save *some* of his furniture, which was a great consideration to people who have now to earn their daily bread. It is pitiable the state in which we all find ourselves.

I saw the Doctor yesterday; he said Carrie and the children were quite well. All of their servants but Titus left them.

Do give my warm love to Mr. and Mrs. Mallard and the children. I trust they are all quite well. I know the pleasant climate of Atlanta will invigorate you all. Mother sends kind remembrances. We both send a warm kiss to Ruthie. I saw her aunt, Philo Neely, the other day. She came up for some *new things*, having just received from her father-in-law forty thousand greenbacks. But tell Ruthie she did not remember her, I fear.

Affectionately yours,
Eva

I directed my last letter to Atlanta. I think it, however, reached that city before you did.

Have you taken the oath yet?

---

*Under Presidential (Johnsonian) Reconstruction, the plan for restoration of the South that President Andrew Johnson announced in May of 1865, southerners who took an oath of allegiance to the Union would receive a pardon and amnesty, and restoration of all property save slaves. The more stringent Reconstruction acts that Congress passed in 1867 replaced the Johnsonian plan.

Augusta, Friday, July 14th, 1865

How very much have I been surprised, my dear mother, to learn that so few of our letters to you have been received! I have within the last three weeks written you two long letters.

In the last I told you of Charlie's going to Savannah in order to make a little money before leaving for Atlanta; for of funds we *too* were utterly *destitute.* He went down in a most primitive style, mounted upon some bales of cotton, of which our estate owned *six*—a mere pittance. But we were glad to have even that forlorn quantity. Charlie returned from Savannah on yesterday, and left this morning for his plantation to attend some urgent business. He will return very soon in order to go to Atlanta. I suppose he will leave the first of next week. I assure you he would have gone to see you and get Ruthie two weeks since but that we have *not* a *greenback.* And strange to say, the Yankees won't take our Confederate money!

Well, we are all down here as poor as poverty can make us. Besides the freeing of our Negroes (which deprives us of the greater part of our property, of course), the Yankees and Negroes together have stolen every piece of meat we had (about one hundred and seventy pieces), and we have not a *ham* even left. Then a variety of mules, sheep, and hogs; so altogether we are in a forlorn condition. I expect before long to become a very efficient chambermaid and seamstress, though the latter comes very hard to my poor unused fingers. Our ménage has been frightfully reduced; and of our numerous throng there remains a seamstress (who has had to lay aside her old calling to become cook, washer, and chambermaid) and one who attends to everything else about this unfortunate establishment. Adeline, Grace, and Polly were the first to assume freedom. To crown my misfortunes, which persistently attack me from all sides, Charlie and I had been laying aside carefully every few cents of specie that we could gather; and most tenderly did I keep it locked and laid away. To no one would I breathe of my few gold and silver dollars, when what was my surprise and despair the other day to find that my wardrobe had been *entered with a false key* and my forty-three dollars in specie gone—vanished, abstracted!

> 'Twas ever thus from childhood's hour:
> I've seen my fondest hopes decay.

One of our freedwomen expects shortly to enter the holy state of matrimony, and has therefore indulged in some extravagancies and petty fineries. The question arises: Whence came the "filthy lucre" to purchase these indulgences? And my empty wardrobe echoes emphatically: *"Where?"*

Charlie will soon be with you and tell you all the news of Augusta and Savannah; also Indianola. I have been expecting to go up the country this whole summer, and my friends have been writing constantly for me; but I fear my recent loss will preclude my traveling to any extent. . . . I have some pretty little dresses for Ruthie, but will send nothing I have for her, as you say Charlie will bring her back with him, and it will be merely giving you additional trouble and take up more room in her trunk. I will try to get a servant to attend her, but I suppose as she is growing so fast I will *almost* be able to attend her myself.

Your letters coming this way have been more fortunate in reaching their destination than ours. Both of my last had Yankee stamps and were put in the post office.

I saw Dr. Joe this morning; he told me he would try to find some reliable person who would see that you received this.

Charlie never looked better than he does now, and is if anything more adorable than ever. I fear I have spoiled him a little bit, though for *my life* I can't see that I have! We are both going to hard work and try to gain a livelihood some way.

My poor brother Edgeworth feels his glory departed, and lays aside the captaincy with a sigh as he opens an up-country store. He goes bravely to work, and says he'll gain an honest livelihood; and many of his best friends here are delighted with his independence and energy. But these times try men's souls—and women's too!

Tell Ruthie I have sent word to her "new mama," Sallie Casey, that I would wait until she came and carry her up to see her at her sweet cool country home.

Augusta is very unhealthy just now; there is a great deal of typhoid fever here. . . . Sallie Casey came quite near leaving this terrestrial a few weeks since; she had merely come down on a visit. . . . There were twelve Negroes interred yesterday; the city is crowded with them.

Do give my warm love to Mr. and Mrs. Mallard and the children. My mother sends her kind regards to all of you. With love for yourself and Ruthie,

Affectionately yours,
Eva

Moments of Emancipation

ACCOUNTS OF FORMER SLAVES, 1865–1937

Emancipation was an erratic process. How and when it occurred (whether during the war, at its end, or after) depended on many factors: where slaves lived, how mobile they were, the proximity of the Union army, or, in some cases, whether their masters announced their liberation. Slave experiences of emancipation therefore vary widely. Some slaves declared themselves free when northern troops approached, and fled behind Union lines. Some were liberated by successive Yankee invasions and reenslaved in their intervals between invasions. Some were transferred to interior locations, away from enemy encroachment. For most slaves, the moment of freedom occurred at Confederate surrender, but in some cases it occurred as long as months or years after.

No sampling can do justice to the variety of former slaves' accounts of the moment of emancipation, or their responses to it. Some of the following accounts were told to and written down by others, either during the war or after. Harriet Tubman's description of a gunboat exodus was recorded by her biographer, Sarah H. Bradford; the story of a woman who experienced the fall of Richmond was told to abolitionist Laura S. Haviland; the experience of Clarissa Burdett, a Kentucky slave, was dictated to a notary in a nearby Union army camp. The other stories that follow appear in the extensive twentieth-century interviews of aged former slaves, who responded to freedom in different ways. Some took quick advantage of their postwar mobility, some stayed on where they had always lived, and some waited for the right opportunity—like the Texas bondswoman who, after three years with her former owners, declared that she was "free as the birds in the air."

A Virginia Woman

Laura S. Haviland, *A Woman's Life-Work: Labors and Experiences* (Chicago: Waite and Co., 1887), pp. 412, 414–15.

Abolitionist Laura S. Haviland (1808–1898) of Michigan traveled around the postwar South doing philanthropic work among former slaves. In 1866, a Virginia woman described to Haviland her first taste of freedom at the fall of Richmond the previous year.

During my three weeks' stay in Williamsburg, Fort Magruder, and vicinity, I had a number of meetings with these newly freed slaves, three of them in those old slave-pens in which were large schools taught. . . .

I found many of these people in trouble, because they saw plainly the old slave spirit reviving, and they were trembling with fear; but others had stronger faith. There was one poor woman, whose husband and four children were sold to a trader, to be taken down the river in a gang. When the news came to her master's home that Richmond had fallen, she said:

"Missus an' all was cryin', and say da catch Jeff. Davis. An' I hurried de supper on de table; an' I say, 'Missus, can Dilla wait on table till I go to de bush-spring an' git a bucket o' cool water?' She say, 'Hurry, Mill'; an' I seed 'em all down to table afore I starts. Den I walks slow till I git out o' sight, when I runn'd wid all my might till I git to de spring, an' look all 'round, an' I jump up an' scream, 'Glory, glory, hallelujah to Jesus! I's free! I's free! Glory to God, you come down an' free us; no big man could do it.' An' I got sort o' scared, afeared somebody hear me, an' I takes another good look, an' fall on de groun', an' roll over, an' kiss de groun' fo' de Lord's sake, I's so full o' praise to Massar Jesus. He do all dis great work. De soul buyers can neber take my two chillen lef' me; no, neber can take 'em from me no no'"; and the tears fell thick and fast as she told me how she clung to her husband, then to her children, as the trader took them to the slave-pen to lock up till they were ready to start for the river. Her mistress ordered her to be whipped because she cried so long for her husband and children. I did not wonder at her ecstasy.

Harriet Tubman

Sarah H. Bradford, *Harriet Tubman, the Moses of Her People* (Secaucus, NJ: Citadel Press, 1974 [1886]), pp. 99–102.

Former slave Harriet Tubman (ca. 1820–1913) of Maryland, who had escaped to the North as a young woman in 1849, made several hundred trips south to lead other slaves to freedom. During the Civil War, when she worked as a scout for the Union army, her rescue work continued. She told her biographer, Sarah H. Bradford, about a gunboat expedition in South Carolina that culminated in the liberation of hundreds of plantation slaves, men, women, and children.

General Hunter asked her at one time if she would go with several gun-boats up the Combahee River, the object of the expedition being to take up the torpedoes placed by the rebels in the river, to destroy railroads and bridges, and to cut off supplies from the rebel troops. . . . Harriet describes in the most graphic manner the appearance of the plantations as they passed up the river; the frightened negroes leaving their work and taking to the woods, at sight of the gun-boats; then coming to peer out like startled deer, and scudding away like the wind at the sound of the steam-whistle. "Well," said one old negro, "Mas'r said de Yankees had horns and tails, but I nebber beliebed it till now." But the word was passed along by the mysterious telegraphic communication existing among these simple people, that these were "Lincoln's gun-boats come to set them free." In vain, then, the drivers used their whips in their efforts to hurry the poor creatures back to their quarters; they all turned and ran for the gun-boats. They came down every road, across every field, just as they had left their work and their cabins; women with children clinging around their necks, hanging to their dresses, running behind, all making at full speed for "Lincoln's gun-boats." Eight hundred poor wretches at one time crowded the banks, with their hands extended toward their deliverers, and they were all taken off upon the gun-boats, and carried down to Beaufort.

"I nebber see such a sight," said Harriet; "we laughed, an' laughed, an' laughed. Here you'd see a woman wid a pail on her head, rice a smokin' in it jus' as she'd taken it from de fire, young one hangin' on behind, one han' roun' her forehead to hold on, 'tother han' diggin' into de rice-pot, eatin' wid all its might; hold of her dress two or three more; down her back a bag wid a pig in it. One woman brought two pigs, a white one an' a black one; we took 'em all on board; named de white pig Beauregard, and de black pig Jeff Davis. Sometimes de women would come wid twins hangin' roun' der necks; 'pears like I nebber see so many twins in my life; bags on der shoulders, baskets on der heads, and young ones taggin' behin', all loaded; pigs squealin', chickens screamin', young ones squallin'." And so they came pouring down to the gun-boats. When they stood on the shore, and the small boats put out to take them off, they all wanted to get in at once. After the boats were crowded, they would hold on to them so that they could not leave the shore. The oarsmen would beat them on their hands, but they would not let go; they were afraid the gun-boats would go off and leave them, and all wanted to make sure of one of these arks of refuge. At length Colonel Montgomery shouted from the upper deck, above the clamor of appealing tones, "Moses, you'll have to give 'em a song." Then Harriet lifted up her voice, and sang:

> Of all the whole creation in the East or in the West,
> The glorious Yankee nation is the greatest and the best.
> Come along! Come along! don't be alarmed,
> Uncle Sam is rich enough to give you all a farm.

At the end of every verse, the negroes in their enthusiasm would throw up their hands and shout "Glory," and the row-boats would take that opportunity to push off; and so at last they were all brought on board. The masters fled; houses and barns and railroad bridges were burned, tracks torn up, torpedoes destroyed, and the object of the expedition was fully accomplished.

Clarissa Burdett

Ira Berlin et. al., *Freedom: A Documentary History of Emancipation, 1861–1867*, ser. 1, vol. 1 (Cambridge: Cambridge University Press, 1986), pp. 615–16.

One month before the Confederate surrender, Clarissa Burdett, a Kentucky fugitive whose husband had joined the Union army, filed a complaint at a nearby federal camp about her former master's ill-treatment and her desire to regain the children she had left behind. Kentucky was a loyal border state, whose citizens fought on both sides during the war. Legal emancipation did not occur in Kentucky until the ratification of the Thirteenth Amendment, eight months after the end of the war.

Affidavit of Clarissa Burdett, A Black Soldier's Wife

Camp Nelson, Ky., 27th of March 1865

Personally appeared before me J M Kelley Notary Public in and for the County of Jessamine State of Kentucky Clarissa Burdett a woman of color who being duly sworn according to law doth despose and say:

I am a married woman and have four children. My husband Elijah Burdett is a soldier in the 12th U.S.C.H. Arty. I and my children belonged to Smith Alford, Garrard County Ky. When my husband enlisted my master beat me over the head with an axe handle saying as he did so that he beat me for letting Ely Burdett go off. He bruised my head so that I could not lay it against a pillow without the greatest pain. Last week my niece who lived with me went to Camp Nelson. This made my master very angry and last Monday March 20th 1865 he asked me where the girl had gone. I could not tell him. He then whipped me over the head and said he would give me two hundred lashes if I did not get the girl back before the next day. On Wednesday last March 22nd he said that he had not time to beat me on Tuesday but now he had some and he would give it to me. He then tied my hands threw the rope over a joist stripped me entirely naked and gave me about three hundred lashes. I cried out. He then caught me by the throat and almost choked me then continued to lash me with switches until my back was all cut up. The marks of the switches are now very visible and my back is still very sore. My master was a very cruel man and strongly sympathizes with the rebels. He went with the Rebel General Bragg when the latter retreated from the State. He took me and my children to Beans Station and sent the parents and two sisters of my niece to Knoxville where he sold them. After he whipped me on Wednesday last he said he would give me until next morning to bring the girl back, and if I did not get her back by that time he would give me as much more. I knew that I would be whipped so I ran away. My master frequently said that he would be jailed before one of his niggers woul[d] go to Camp. I therefore knew he would not permit any of my children to come with me. So when I ran away I had to leave my children with my master. I have four children there at present and I want to get them but I cannot go there for them knowing that master who would whip me would not let any of my children go nor would he suffer me to get away.

(Signed)
Clarissa Burdett
her mark

Fanny Berry

Charles L. Perdue, Thomas E. Barden, and Robert K. Phillips, *Weevils in the Wheat: Interviews with Virginia Ex-Slaves* (Charlottesville: University of Virginia Press, 1976), pp. 36–38.

Fanny Berry, a Virginia slave born in 1841, told her life story—not necessarily in chronological order—to Susie R. C. Boyd, an interviewer for the Virginia Federal Writers' Project, in 1937. The segments below deal with Fanny Berry's experience of emancipation.

Now Miss Sue, take up. I jes like to talk to you, honey, 'bout dem days ob slavery 'cause you look like you wan' ta hear all 'bout 'em—all 'bout de ol' Rebels—an' dem niggers who left wid de Yankees and were sot free but, poor things, dey had no place to go after dey got freed. Baby, all us wuz helpless an' ain't had nothing.

I wuz free a long time fo' I knew it. My mistess still hired me out 'till one day, in talkin' to de woman she hired me to, she—God bless her soul—she told me, "Fannie, yo' ar' free an' I don't have to pay your master for you now. You stay with me." She didn't give me no money but let me stay there an' work for vitals an' clothes 'cause I ain't had no where to go. Jesus! Jesus! God help us! Um, um, um! You chillun don't know! I didn't say nothing when she wuz telling me but done 'cided to leave her and go back to the white folks dat furst own me.

I was at Pamplin and de Yankees and Rebels were fighting and dey were waving the bloody flag an' a Confederate soldier was up on a post and they were shooting terribly. Guns were firing everywhere. All of a sudden dey struck up Yankee Doodle song. A soldier came along, called me and said softly, close to me, "How far is it to the Rebels?" An' I honey, wuz feared to tell him. So I said, I didn't know. He called me again. Scared to death, I recollect, gitting behind the house and pointed in the direction. You see, ef de Rebels knew dat I told the soldier, they would have killed me. These were the Union men going after Lee's army which had don' bin 'fore dem to Appomattox.

The colored regiment came up behind and when they saw the colored regiment they put up the white flag—Yo' 'member fo' dis red or bloody flag was up—Now, do you know why dey raised dat white flag? (No, tell me why.) Well, honey, dat white flag wuz a token dat Lee had surrendered.

Glory, glory! Yes, child, the Negroes are free, an' when they knew dat dey were free dey—oh baby!—began to sing:

> Mammy don't yo' cook no mo',
> Yo ar' free, yo' ar' free.
>
> Rooster don't yo' crow no mo',
> Yo' ar' free, yo' ar' free.
>
> Ol' hen don't yo' lay no mo' eggs,
> Yo' free, yo' free.

Sech rejoicing and shoutin' you never he'rd in your life.

A Tennessee Woman

Unwritten History of Slavery: Autobiographical Accounts of Negro Ex-Slaves (Washington, DC: Microcard Editions, 1968), p. 135.

A Mississippi slave, who had been moved by her owners to Tennessee when the Civil War began, remained attached to the white children she had cared for while in slavery. She told her story in 1929 and 1930 to Ophelia Settle, a member of the research staff of the new Social Science Institute at Fisk University, a major center of black scholarship.

I stayed with my white folks three years after freedom, and they tried to make me think I wasn't free. And I'll tell you I made it hot for them when they tried to bother the chillen (master's children). When he'd start to whip them I'd say, "You just let these chillen alone. Miss Janie (first wife) said you was gonna marry some other woman and be mean to her chillen," and he'd say, "Lu, don't tell me that," and I would say, "Yes I is, too; I'm gonna tell you every time you hit one of these chillen." One Sunday I wanted to go to a meeting in Franklin, and I didn't ask; I just told this woman I was going, and she said, "I say you can't go," and I said, "Oh, yes, I'm going," and she called Marse Tom and I told him I was going, and he said, "I say you can't go." So I said, "You look right here, Marse Tom, I'm free, just as free as the birds in the air; you didn't tell me, but I know it," and he didn't say another word. You see, they thought that 'cause I stayed there I was fool enough not to know I was free; but I knowed it; and I went on to Franklin. I was nine miles from town, but I walked there to the meeting.

Later on, they wanted me to go down to Mississippi to live, but I said, "I never 'spect to go to old Sip again long as I live." The chillen kissed me and told me goodbye, and they cried and cried. Later on he bought here, and they moved back and I would go up there every month to see how my chillen was getting along. They would meet me down at a big tree and tell me, "She's (stepmother) just as mean to us as she can be," and they would take me up to the house and give me lots of things to carry home with me. I would tell Marse Tom I come after some money and some clothes, too, and he'd give me a dollar and tell them to give me what I wanted, and they would go to the smokehouse and give me some meat and anything else I wanted. I still can get anything I want if I go to them, but it is hard for me to get way up there now. . . .

I used to make the chillen cry during the War. I would say, "I'm going to the Yankees; Miss Maggie's getting just so mean to me," and the youngest child would say, "We'll go too; I'll tell you which-a-way to go." And she woulda went with me, too; all of them chillen woulda went if I'd run away then. I had a hard time, I tell you.

I married 'reckly after the War ceasted. My old boss married his own niggers in Mississippi; he'd just get the Bible and marry them, and he had the 'surance to marry me after the War, and he had to pay ten dollars for it, too, 'cause he wasn't no officer that could marry me. . . .

When the War was coming up, I would hear the white folks reading the papers about it, and I would run in the kitchen and tell Aunt Harriet. She would say, "Don't let the white folks hear you talk; they'll kill you," and if I would be going too far she would stop me, and wouldn't let me finish telling it to her.

Mary Anderson

Norman R. Yetman, *Life Under the "Peculiar Institution": Selections from the Slave Narrative Collection* (New York: Holt, Rinehart & Winston, 1970), pp. 17–18.

Mary Anderson, born in 1851, had learned "to talk like white folks" as a favored slave child on a large plantation in Wade County, North Carolina. When the Union army invaded, her master and mistress told the slaves they were free. Many slaves left with the Union soldiers, but some returned to their former owners, including Mary Anderson.

The War was begun and there were stories of fights and freedom. The news went from plantation to plantation and while the slaves acted natural and some even more polite than usual, they prayed for freedom.

Then one day I heard something that sounded like thunder and Marster and Missus began to walk around and act queer. The grown slaves were whispering to each other. Sometimes they gathered in little gangs in the grove. Next day I heard it again, boom, boom, boom. I went and asked Missus, "Is it going to rain?" She said, "Mary, go to the icehouse and bring me some pickles and preserves." I went and got them. She ate a little and gave me some. Then she said, "You run along and play."

In a day or two everybody on the plantation seemed to be disturbed and Marster and Missus were crying. Marster ordered all the slaves to come to the Great House at nine o'clock. Nobody was working and slaves were walking over the grove in every direction. At nine o'clock all the slaves gathered at the Great House and Marster and Missus came out on the porch and stood side by side. You could hear a pin drop everything was so quiet. Then Marster said, "Good morning," and Missus said,

"Good morning, children." They were both crying. Then Marster said, "Men, women, and children, you are free. You are no longer my slaves. The Yankees will soon be here." Marster and Missus then went into the house; got two large arm chairs and put them on the porch facing the avenue and sat down side by side and remained there watching.

[In] about an hour there was one of the blackest clouds coming up the avenue from the main road. It was the Yankee soldiers. They finally filled the mile long avenue reaching from Marster's house to the main Louisburg road and spread out over the mile square grove. The mounted men dismounted. The footmen stacked their shining guns and began to build fires and cook. They called the slaves, saying, "You are free."

Slaves were whooping and laughing and acting like they were crazy. Yankee soldiers were shaking hands with the Negroes and calling them Sam, Dinah, Sarah, and asking them questions. They busted the door to the smokehouse and got all the hams. They went to the icehouse and got several barrels of brandy: such a time! The Negroes and Yankees were cooking and eating together. The Yankees told them to come and join them, they were free. Marster and Missus sat on the porch and they were so humble no Yankee bothered anything in the Great House.

The slaves were awfully excited. The Yankees stayed there, cooked, ate, drank, and played music until about night. Then a bugle began to blow and you never saw such getting on horses and lining up in your life. In a few minutes they began to march, leaving the grove which was soon silent as a graveyard. They took Marster's horses and cattle with them and joined the main army and camped just across Cypress Creek one and one-half miles from my marster's place on the Louisburg Road.

When they left the county, lot of the slaves went with them and soon there were none of Marster's slaves left. They wandered around for a year from place to place, fed and working most of the time at some other slave owner's plantation and getting more homesick every day.

The second year after the surrender our Marster and Missus got on their carriage and went and looked up all the Negroes they heard of who ever belonged to them. Some who went off with the Yankees were never heard from again. When Marster and Missus found any of theirs they would say, "Well, come on back home." My father and mother, two uncles and their families moved back. Also Lorenze Brodie and John Brodie and their families moved back. Several of the young men and women who once belonged to him came back. Some were so glad to get back they cried 'cause fare had been mighty bad part of the time they were rambling around and they were hungry.

Since the surrender I married James Anderson. I had four children, one boy and three girls.

Katie Darling

Norman R. Yetman, *Life Under the "Peculiar Institution": Selections from the Slave Narrative Collection* (New York: Holt, Rinehart & Winston, 1970), pp. 70–71.

Katie Darling, of Texas, was born in 1849. As a teenager she was nurse for her owner's six children during the Civil War. She remained in servitude for six years after emancipation, until she was rescued by her brother.

I 'member that fight at Mansfield like it [was] yesterday. Massa's field am all tore up with cannon holes and every time a cannon fire, Missy go off in rage. One time when a cannon fire, she say to me, "You li'l black wench, you niggers ain't gwine be free. You's made to work for white folks." 'Bout that time she look up and see a Yankee soldier standin' in the door with a pistol. She say, "Katie, I didn't say nothing, did I?" I say, "I ain't tellin' no lie, you say niggers ain't gwine get free." That day you couldn't get 'round the place for the Yankees and they stays for weeks at a time.

When Massa come home from the War he wants [to] let us loose, but Missy wouldn't do it. I stays on and works for them six years after the War and Missy whip me after the War just like she did before. She has a hundred lashes laid up for me now, and this how it am. My brudders done left Massa after the War and move next door to the Ware place, and one Saturday some niggers come and tell me my brudder Peter am comin' to get me away from old Missy Sunday night. That night the cows and calves got together and Missy say it my fault. She say, "I' gwine give you one hun'erd lashes in the mornin', now go pen them calves."

I don't know whether them calves was ever penned or not, 'cause Peter was waitin' for me at the lot and takes me to live with him on the Ware place. I'se so happy to get away from that old devil Missy, I don't know what to do, and I stays there several years and works out here and there for money. Then I marries and moves here and me and my man farms and nothin' exciting done happened.

Teaching the Freedmen

SARAH CHASE AND LUCY CHASE, 1866–1868

Letters of Sarah and Lucy Chase, 1866–1868, in Henry Swint, ed., *Dear Ones at Home: Letters from Contraband Camps* (Nashville: Vanderbilt University Press, 1966), pp. 193–95, 202–3, 233–37, 242–43.

During the Civil War, Freedmen's Aid Societies in northern cities began to sponsor relief work and education among former slaves, in areas of the South that had fallen under Union control. After the war, the northern aid societies enlarged their efforts. By the end of Reconstruction, several thousand northern teachers, black and white, were at work in southern freedmen's schools. Three-quarters of these teachers were women, primarily New England women. They were among the first northerners, beyond army personnel, to have extensive contact with the newly freed blacks. Once fervent abolitionists, they now endorsed the goals of Reconstruction. This meant not only restoration of the South to the Union but also the integration of blacks into southern life—through education, male suffrage, industry, and self-discipline. These hard-working educators, in short, hoped to regenerate the South and transform it into something like the North. They were, in a sense, the last regiment of the Union war effort.

Sarah and Lucy Chase of Worcester, Massachusetts, the daughters of a wealthy Quaker businessman, had been ardent opponents of slavery before the war. They moved South in 1862 to a captured island near Norfolk, Virginia, to work among some 20,000 former slaves in contraband camps. Lucy Chase was then about forty-one years old, and Sarah was fourteen years younger. Teaching in varied occupied locations throughout the war, the Chase sisters remained in the South until 1869. Throughout these years, they sent detailed commentary on their experiences to family and friends in New England.

The two years immediately after the war were especially crucial in the process of emancipation. Former slaves sought to reconstitute their families, join or form churches, educate their children, and support themselves. In the following correspondence of 1866–1868 from Columbus, Georgia, and Richmond, Virginia, the Chase sisters describe their students and their communities. They also reveal their commitment to Reconstruction, their opposition to racial prejudice, and their interest in all facets of the freedmen's lives, including language, religious habits, and domestic relations. The last letter in this excerpt contains the story of Laura Spicer. Here, Lucy Chase presents the poignant history of a couple that had been separated during slavery. The letters are in the collection of the American Antiquarian Society, Worcester, Massachusetts.

Letters from Sarah Chase to the Mays

Columbus, Georgia
Feb. 5th 1866

Dear Mrs. May;*

When I last wrote we had just opened a school at Savannah. There were already several schools opened there and Col. Sickles was administering the affairs of the [Freedmen's] Bureau in a most admirable manner, so it did not seem right to tarry in that charming city, though we could have found enough important work to fill every moment. Wishing to work where there was the most need (there being so many places where nothing has been done for the Freedmen, and where they are sorely persecuted), we came here, where a school house, built by the soldiers, had just been destroyed by the citizens and the feeling is intensely bitter against *anything* Northern. The affairs of the Bureau have been [f]rightfully mismanaged here; and our Govt has been disgraced by the troops who were stationed here. Now the troops are withdrawn, and the people are chafing at the presence of the Bureau and "a few pious and enthusiastic N.E. school marms": "both must be cleared out of the place," says the daily press.

We have never seen any discourtesy in any of the citizens, but we know that we are generally *discussed* in circles; and many plans are proposed for "getting rid" of us.——We have glorious schools in full blast——. And I am so satisfied with the work here that nothing in the world could make me wish to be in another place, or doing anything else. In my own day school and night school, I have 140 pupils, who have made truly wonderful progress, in the five weeks I have been teaching.

How much I wish you could see my school! A more earnest, fine looking set of scholars could not be found—than I could show. Wouldn't I like to grace your Academy Halls with their presence, giving the good people a chance to talk with them and hear their varied experiences. I find the people here more tidy and thrifty than in any place I am acquainted with—though many are intensely poor—and there has been nothing given them from the North, they are always tidy, cheerful and hopeful, ever anxious to *improve*. "How I wish I were rich!" For the first time in my life I say it, for I have so much need of money here. We are too far from the North to make it worth while to send any boxes here—the expense is so great—but I ought to have a purse to get an occasional flannel, or drug or splint for a broken limb or piece of bedding for

---

*The wife of Fred W. G. May of Boston, a member of the clothing and supplies committee of the New England Freedmen's Aid Society.

some good old soul, who has "raised eight children for missus, as if they were my own; and nussed master so well, the Dr. said I saved his life—and am now too old to work—I'se turned out to die like a dog." Though I have a liberal allowance from home—the expense of living is very great; and no individual purse is long enough for the absolute needs. . . .

There are a number of colored people in this place who are very well off—and they cheerfully bear their burden of the new dispensation, but in a population of about 8 thousand they can do little. I shall organize mutual relief societies in the Negro churches (Baptist and Methodist) as soon as possible. Large numbers are working for their food alone; and the white people tell them that they are not free yet. Across the river, in Alabama, several Negroes have been shot *because* they were free!

Union! I can more easily conceive of the Lion and Lambs lying down together, than of a union of the North and South. In all the counties around here, the Union familys are suffering shameful persecution, and the people do not hesitate to say that those who favor the North, shall not live in their communities. We have now with us a family who fled for their lives from their plantation—fourteen miles out———. They have never owned slaves & always been loyal; and consequently the neighbors have been killing their cattle and taking their farming utensils and doing many things to make them leave their place. A few nights ago, a regular armed force from the county round threw out guards around their house, and surrounded it for the purpose of killing the whole family—but finding one of the sons absent, withdrew to decide whether to postpone it for another time or not—in the delay a part of the family escaped to the woods.

Such things are occurring the whole time; but it does not do to write North about them; for if they get in print, it gives encouragement to many communities who are ready to go and do likewise. Now the military courts are withdrawn I see no alternative for Southern Unionists, in many parts of the South, between constant persecution, and going North. . . .

With ever best wishes—singing at the plough.

S.E.C.

Monday April 2d (1866)

Dear Mr. May,

Your welcome letter, *and* the money, came duly to hand. . . . In regard to "mixed schools" [desegregated schools], I regret that I am obliged to say, not what I *think*, but what I *know*; id est, they are an impossibility. I feel confident they would be of no benefit to the blacks in Md. Va. N.C. S.C. Ga. and Ala., consequently I cannot see how they will work well, in any part of the South.

No one is more anxious than I that the Southern whites should be elevated; but my life is consecrated to the blacks.

Since all are friendly to the whites, there is a certainty that their cause will not suffer. If the few friends of the Freedmen continue in their special field, I think they will be far better satisfied, in the end. Enough will be done for the whites, *without* the combination, and *far less* for the blacks, will be accomplished *through* it than is now. I think no one who has been in the field could differ from me. How long it took the enlightened North to make the experiment of mixed schools a success! I am not sure that they could yet be pronounced successful except in a few districts. Think how much the South is behind the North in civilization, and how much worse the feeling is between the whites and blacks! Wishing well to *all* mankind, I have much desired to see a movement for the elevation of the Southern whites: (though I feel it no duty to take part in the work, [there] being plenty of people for it) and have had this matter on my mind throughout my Southern life and have talked Education and Industry to them whenever I have met them; and on my own responsibility urged them to go to the "Yankee Schools," knowing what a benefit it would be to the *blacks*, to be thus associated with the whites they are to have dealings with in the future. But though the parents were "wishing their children had the advantages the Niggers were enjoying" they usually "would rather they'd die than go to school with the Niggers" or they said: "I never will get so low as to have my children learnin with nigs."

No matter how strict the rules, and wise and kind the teachers plans, for the comfort, and rights of the black scholar; the *feeling* of the whites expressed or not— *will* keep the sensitive African away; though he would willingly bear cold, hunger, and whippings if need be—to "get a little larnin." I know L. agrees with me, for she made no dissent, when I was talking on the subject last eve. . . .

With best wishes,
S.E.C.

Excerpt of Letter from Lucy Chase to Anna Lowell Of the New England Freedmen's Aid Society

Howard Grove Hospital
Richmond, Virginia
June 1868

. . . Still, we see all around us the demoralizing influence of idleness, and the depressing influence of unsuccessful clamor for remunerative work. Not a few hardworkers are growing thin and weak by trying to live on promises to pay. Still, here—as elsewhere, people with ready money leave their washing-bills unpaid; and I visit many women stooping over their washtubs, weak in body and hopeless in mind, who say, "I keeps on washin for em, for if I leave em they'll never pay me what they owe me." So wearing care and scanty food unite with their task-masters in grinding them very small. It is astonishing what light food sustains *men hard-working*. I have seen a coal-heaver sit down to a dinner of half-baked corn-bread and coffee. I have seldom seen a greedy colored child, and I have never seen one who would not give up his dinner for almost anything that would bring him pleasure.

Children of the poorest and most distracted mothers seem to pick up certain general all-pervading ideas of neatness. In all my schools a general cry would be raised if a child should return an undrained dipper to the water-bucket. And until taught economy by the teachers few children would pass a school-mate a dipper of water to which he had put his own lips. Anything like an oath sets a whole schoolroom on fire, and if it is heard at recess, the children rush to their teacher with Oh's! and Ah's! and staring eyeballs.

I have often told you how rare it is to find a dirty colored house. A curiosity-hunter from the North might think the neat houses the rare ones; but to one unfamiliar with the homes of the poor, simple barreness and poverty express filth. . . .

I today attended a monster baptism of two hundred and thirty persons (colored). But few of them lost their self-control. Now and then a woman would "Thank God! thank God!" with exultant emphasis. And two or three gave way to physical excitement. The officiating minister (a colored man) and the deacons checked all such demonstrations. And the minister said, after some shouting, "We shall expect that all who shout, will fall back into the ways of the world again." Thousands crowded the church as spectators, and, at times, the buzz of tongues was heard. But the vast multitude was under the ready control of the quiet, dignified preacher, when he said, "My friends, remember that this is the house of God. We are not in a theatre. Let us have *quiet*." . . .

I saw in her home, today, a very interesting colored woman, who reads the Anti-Slavery Standard with great readiness, and with understanding. She was sold from her father at five years of age, and he was her sole teacher. Miss Canedy found two of her boys lying on the grass the other day—reading Wendell Phillips' and Sumner's speeches. One of them asked what Charles Sumner meant when he said, "The God of Christianity is not the God of battles." "Why," said the young man, "we *always* said after a successful battle, *God* gave us the victory." . . .

Oh, I must decline for you the verb "Dun" as I hear it daily used.

PRESENT

I dun it
You dun it
He dun it
We uns dun it
They uns dun it
You uns dun it

IMPERFECT

I dun dun it
You dun dun it
He dun dun it
We uns dun dun it
They uns dun dun it
You uns dun dun it

PERFECT

I gone dun dun it
You gone dun dun it
He gone dun dun it
We uns gone dun dun it
You uns gone dun dun it
They uns gone dun dun it

PLUPERFECT

I dun gone done it
You dun gone done it
He dun gone done it
We uns dun gone done it
You uns dun gone done it
They uns dun gone done it

FIRST FUTURE

I gwine dun it
You gwine dun it
He gwine dun it
We uns gwine dun it
You uns gwine dun it
They uns gwine dun it

SECOND FUTURE

I dun gwine dun it
You dun gwine dun it
He dun gwine dun it
We uns dun gwine dun it
They uns dun gwine dun it
You uns dun gwine dun it

One of our teachers asked a child the meaning of *forget*. "When you are sent for a thing to fergit fur to git it," the child replied. I wonder if I ever told you a Norfolk child's definition of irrational————: "It's rational when you have rations, and irrational when you do not." I had a little imp in my school early in the winter who was known as Moses Propkins Juice. After careful inquiry, his name was found to be, "Moses, the prophet, the King of the Jews." I had in my night school, a man who persistently read Abercrombies philosophy, until I happened to think of the "Freedmen's Book," as a most refreshing substitute. He was deep in its pages when the ladies from Roxbury accidentally found their way into my school. Let me beg you to thank them for looking there again for me. . . .

Excerpt of Letter from Lucy Chase To an Unknown Correspondent

[1868]

. . . I don't know whether I have told you Laura Spicers story. She was sold from her husband some years ago, and he, hearing she was dead, married again. He has had a wavering inclination to again unite his fortunes with hers; and she has been persistent in urging him to do so. A few days ago she received a letter from him in which he said, "I read your letters over and over again. I keep them always in my pocket. If you are married I don't ever want to see you again." And yet, in some of his letters, he says, "I would much rather you would get married to some good man, for every time I gits a letter from you it tears me all to pieces. The reason why I have not written you before, in a long time, is because your letters disturbed me so very much. You know I love my children. I treats them good as a Father can treat his children; and I do a good deal of it for you. I was very sorry to hear that Lewellyn, my poor little son, have had such bad health. I would come and see you but I know you could not bear it. I want to see you and I don't want to see you. I love you just as well as I did the last day I saw you, and it will not do for you and I to meet. I am married, and my wife have two children, and if you and I meets it would make a very dissatisfied family."

Some of the children are with the mother, and the father writes, "Send me some of the children's hair in a separate paper with their names on the paper. Will you please git married, as long as I am married. My dear, you know the Lord know both of our hearts. You know it never was our wishes to be separated from each other, and it never was our fault. Oh, I can see you so plain, at any-time, I had rather anything to had happened to me most that ever have been parted from you and the children. As I am, I do not know which I love best, you or Anna. If I was to die, today or tomorrow, I do not think I would die satisfied till you tell me you will try and marry some good, smart man that will take good care of you and the children; and do it because you love me; and not because I think more of the wife I have got than I do of you. The woman is not born that feels as near to me as you do. You feel this day like myself. Tell them they must remember they have a good father and one that cares for them and one that thinks about them every day————. My very heart did ache when reading your very kind and interesting letter. Laura I do not think that I have change[d] any at all since I saw you last. ———I thinks of you and my children every day of my life. Laura I do love you the same. My love to you *never* have failed. Laura, truly, I have got another wife, and I am very sorry, that I am. You feels and seems to me as much like my dear loving wife, as you ever did Laura. You know my treatment to a wife and you know how I am about my children. You know I am one man that do love my children. You will please make a———of the thing."

Remembering the War

SUSIE KING TAYLOR, 1902

Susie King Taylor, "Thoughts on Present Conditions," in *Reminiscences of My Life in Camp* (New York: Arno Press, 1968 [n.p., 1902]), pp. 61–68 passim.

Susie King Taylor (1848– ?) was born a slave on one of the Georgia Sea Islands and grew up in Savannah, where she learned to read and write at a clandestine school run by a free black woman. When Union troops invaded and occupied the Sea Islands in the Spring of 1862, Taylor, then fourteen, escaped to freedom, volunteered to teach in a freedmen's school, and went to Port Royal Island, off the South Carolina coast, where she married. When her husband joined the First South Carolina Volunteers, the first black unit in the Union army, Taylor worked in the Union army camp, teaching reading, cleaning weapons, and nursing the wounded. Her first husband died in 1866.

After the war, Taylor taught school near Savannah. In the 1870s, she remarried and moved to Boston. While living in Boston, she maintained contact with members of her regiment, and wrote an account of her wartime experience. At the end of this account, Susie King Taylor looked back on the war years from a turn-of-the-century vantage point. Considering the increase of lynching, the disfranchisement of black voters, and the spread of Jim Crow laws, Taylor asked, "Was the war in vain?"

Living here in Boston where the black man is given equal justice, I must say a word on the general treatment of my race, both in the North and South, in this twentieth century. I wonder if our white fellow men realize the true sense or meaning of brotherhood? For two hundred years we had toiled for them; the war of 1861 came and was ended, and we thought our race was forever freed from bondage, and that the two races could live in unity with each other, but when we read almost every day of what is being done to my race by some whites in the South, I sometimes ask, "Was the war in vain? Has it brought freedom, in the full sense of the word, or has it not made our condition more hopeless?"

In this "land of the free" we are burned, tortured, and denied a fair trial, murdered for any imaginary wrong conceived in the brain of the negro-hating white man. There is no redress for us from a government which promised to protect all under its flag. It seems a mystery to me. They say, "One flag, one nation, one country indivisible." Is this true? Can we say this truthfully, when one race is allowed to burn, hang, and inflict the most horrible torture weekly, monthly, on another? No, we cannot sing, "My country, 't is of thee, Sweet land of Liberty"! It is hollow mockery. The Southland laws are all on the side of the white, and they do just as they like to the negro, whether in the right or not. . . . I may not live to see it, but the time is approaching when the South will again have cause to repent for the blood it has shed of innocent black men, for their blood cries out for vengeance. For the South still cherishes a hatred toward the blacks, although there are some true Southern gentlemen left who abhor the stigma brought upon them, and feel it very keenly, and I hope the day is not far distant when the two races will reside in peace in the Southland, and we will sing with sincere and truthful hearts, "My country, 't is of thee, Sweet land of Liberty, of the I sing."

I have been in many States and cities, and in each I have looked for liberty and justice, equal for the black as for the white; but it was not until I was within the borders of New England, and reached old Massachusetts, that I found it. Here is found liberty in the full sense of the word, liberty for the stranger within her gates, irrespective of race or creed, liberty and justice for all. . . .

I read an article, which said the ex-Confederate Daughters had sent a petition to the managers of the local theatres in Tennessee to prohibit the performance of "Uncle Tom's Cabin," claiming it was exaggerated (that is, the treatment of the slaves), and would have a very bad effect on the children who might see the drama. I paused and thought back a few years of the heart-rending scenes I have witnessed; I have seen many times, when I was a mere girl, thirty or forty men, handcuffed, and as many women and children, come every first Tuesday of each month from Mr. Wiley's trade office to the auction blocks, one of them being situated on Drayton Street and Court Lane, the other on Bryant Street, near the Pulaski House. The route was down our principal street, Bull Street, to the court-house, which was only a block from where I resided.

All people in those days got all their water from the city pumps, which stood about a block apart throughout the city. The one we used to get water from was opposite the court-house, on Bull Street. I remember, as if it were yesterday, seeing droves of negroes going to be sold, and I often went to look at them, and I could hear the auctioneer very plainly from my house, auctioning these poor people off.

Do these Confederate Daughters ever send petitions to prohibit the atrocious lynchings and wholesale murdering and torture of the negro? Do you ever hear of them fearing this would have a bad effect on the children? Which of these two, the drama or the present state of affairs, makes a degrading impression upon the minds of our young generation? In my opinion it is not "Uncle Tom's Cabin," but it should be the one that has caused the world to cry "Shame!" It does not seem as if our land is yet civilized. It is like times long past, when rulers and high officers had to flee for their lives, and the negro has been dealt with in the same way since the war by those he lived with and toiled for two hundred years or more. I do not condemn all the Caucasian race because the negro is badly treated by a few of the race. No! for had it not been for the true whites, assisted by God and the prayers of our forefathers, I should not be here to-day.

There are still good friends to the negro. Why, there are still thousands that have not bowed to Baal. So it is with us. Man thinks two hundred years is a long time, and it is, too; but it is only as a week to God, and in his own time—I know I shall not live to see the day, but it will come—the South will be like the North, and when it comes it will be prized higher than we prize the North to-day. God is just; when he created man he made him in his image, and never intended one should misuse the other. All men are born free and equal in his sight.

I am pleased to know at this writing that the officers and comrades of my regiment stand ready to render me assistance whenever required. It seems like "bread cast upon the water," and it has returned after many days, when it is most needed. I have received letters from some of the comrades, since we parted in 1866, with expressions of gratitude and thanks to me for teaching them their first letters. One of them, Peter Waggall, is a minister in Jacksonville, Fla. Another is in the government service at Washington, D.C. Others are in Darien and Savannah, Ga., and all are doing well.

There are many people who do not know what some of the colored women did during the war. There were hundreds of them who assisted the Union soldiers by hiding them and helping them to escape. Many were punished for taking food to the prison stockades for the prisoners. When I went into Savannah, in 1865, I was told of one of these stockades which was in the suburbs of the city, and they said it was an awful place. The Union soldiers were in it, worse than pigs, without any shelter from sun or storm, and the colored women would take food there at night and pass it to them, through the holes in the fence. The soldiers were starving, and these women did all they could towards relieving those men, although they knew the penalty, should they be caught giving them aid. Others assisted in various ways the Union army. These things should be kept in history before the people. There has never been a greater war in the United States than the one of 1861, where so many lives were lost—not men alone but noble women as well.

Let us not forget that terrible war, or our brave soldiers who were thrown into Andersonville and Libby prisons, the awful agony they went through, and the most brutal treatment they received in those loathsome dens, the worst ever given human beings; and if the white soldiers were subjected to such treatment, what must have been the horrors inflicted on the negro soldiers in their prison pens? Can we forget those cruelties? No, though we try to forgive and say, "No North, no South," and hope to see it in reality before the last comrade passes away.

Chapter 13

Urban Wage Earners

A fter the Civil War, a growing economy provided new jobs for women
workers—in factories, stores, offices, and schools. Simultaneously, a
quickened pace of migration and immigration brought more women
to where the jobs were: cities. Between 1870 and 1900, when urban
populations doubled every decade, the number of women wage earners tripled, and the proportion of women who worked for pay rose
from fourteen percent to twenty-one percent. To late nineteenth-
century city dwellers, the female wage earner—the "working girl"—
personified the swift rate of industrialization and urbanization that
transformed American life.

Despite the rapid growth of the female work force, many traditional patterns in women's employment persisted. The vast majority
of married women, for instance, continued to work at home for no
pay, or in home-based enterprises—for instance, taking in boarders.
Such women did not count as wage earners. The largest single category
of wage earning among women remained domestic service. In 1900,
one quarter of women workers were household help. Even within
manufacturing, an area that absorbed millions of new employees, new
male workers far outnumbered new women workers. Indeed, women
lost the dominant role they had held in manufacturing before the Civil
War, when textile workers formed the bulk of the industrial labor
force. Finally, despite rapid growth, the *nature* of the female work force
remained fairly constant. Although the numbers of married, widowed,
and older women employees kept rising, the majority of women workers continued to be single, young, and poor. A study of urban wage
earners in the 1880s suggested most women who worked were eighteen to twenty-six years old, unmarried, and immigrants or daughters

of immigrants. Although many women might work at some point in their lives, the typical working girl was expected to be—and usually was—only a temporary participant in the paid labor force.

Few young women who sought jobs had much choice about what sort of work they would do. Limited by local options and often by their race, nationality, or lack of skills, they also faced sex-segregation in the job market. Women continued to form a separate labor pool, concentrated in certain types of work—typically, work that was un-skilled or semi-skilled, indoors, and poorly paid. At the bottom of the late nineteenth-century female labor scale were domestic workers, including household servants, laundresses, and waitresses. They were usually immigrant or black. Within the growing industrial sector, women worked in hundreds of trades, but primarily in the production of cloth, clothing, and food products. They formed a separate labor reserve in this sector. (Blacks were excluded from industrial work except in menial capacities.) Native-born women with some skills might move on to new white collar jobs—as shop girls, sales clerks, or even office clerks, the new elite of the female labor force. By the end of the century, women stenographers and typists had forced out male competition. At the upper end of the female employment scale, edu-cated job seekers entered women's fields, such as teaching or library work. They were likely to work in the growing public sector, rather than as self-employed, freelance professionals.

Sex-segregation in employment sometimes protected women workers from unemployment. Domestic work, however undesirable, remained fairly stable, even during depressions, since expanding de-mand exceeded the shrinking supply. Office work, too, was usually secure. However, industrial workers—the new armies of spoolers and reelers, packers and pieceworkers—were subject to seasonal shifts in their trades, plus vagaries of the business cycle and drastic fluctuations of the economy. Irregularly paid and underemployed, they were often out of work. As a report on Boston women workers in 1880 declared, "It is the constant occurrence of waiting spells which makes the lives of working girls so hard."

The growing labor movement had little impact on most women workers. Local actions organized by women operatives were relatively few. On the national scene, the Knights of Labor (K of L) strove to include women workers, though mainly after 1886 when K of L fortunes were in decline. But the wave of the future was the trade union, which represented skilled craftsmen, a category that exempted most women employees. Trade unionists regarded women workers as a threat to male jobs. As a Massachusetts mill worker contended in the 1880s, lower paid female competition led to "the extinction of the male operative." To an extent, the craftsmen's fears were justified. Technological change could wipe out a skilled craft and bring in lower paid female labor to run machines. More often, technological change provided more male jobs in female fields, as in garment production, where the sewing machine increased competition among poorly paid seamstresses *and* attracted male competitors. Moreover, most women workers were crowded into separate segments of the work force, where they took newly created jobs and did not replace male workers. Nonetheless, to the skilled workingman, the "working girl" was not an ally but a hazard.

The public at large also viewed the growing ranks of urban working women as a source of concern. The young female wage earner seemed not merely a new phenomenon but a new problem. So did all facets of her environment—the crowded boardinghouse, dismal tenement, unsafe factory, poorly lighted sweatshop, and the proximity of these places to vice-ridden neighborhoods. Of special concern were "women adrift," the term used to describe women wage earners who lived apart from their families or employers. Often migrants to urban areas, these truants from the family economy—about one-fifth of women wage earners by 1900—seemed an ominous trend. Concern over the working woman's plight fed into a larger set of anxieties, such as the visible gulf between social classes and the unknown social consequences of continued industrial growth.

These concerns led to an outpouring of reports. During the 1880s, state governments, the federal government, and urban journalists all explored the status of the woman wage earner—her working conditions, living arrangements, character, and morals. In the 1890s, the first wave of progressive reformers joined the fray with their own surveys and exposés. The documents that follow include some samples of these late nineteenth-century investigations.

The Character of Working Women

CARROLL D. WRIGHT, 1888

Carroll D. Wright, *Fourth Annual Report of the Commissioner of Labor, 1888: Working Women in Large Cities* (Washington, DC: Government Printing Office, 1889), pp. 73–77.

In 1888, Commissioner of Labor Carroll D. Wright (1840–1909), an expert statistician, surveyed the working and living conditions of women in twenty-two major cities. Using women agents of the labor department, who conducted 17,427 interviews, Wright reached a major segment of the female labor force: shop clerks and factory workers. Excluded from the study were domestic servants, office clerks, and professionals, as well as textile workers (who were not to be found in large cities, the commissioner pointed out). Wright's research yielded a statistical gold mine and a composite portrait: three-fourths of the workers surveyed were fourteen to twenty-five years of age, more than 14,000 were native-born, and the vast majority were single—save for 745 who were married and 1,038 who were widowed.

In the narrative section of his report, Wright commented frequently on the good moral character of the young working women, many of whom lived at home with their families, especially in the South and Midwest. (The "alert and worldly wise" working girls of New York, in contrast, were installed in boardinghouses, which the commissioner distrusted.) To defend the virtue of the average working girl and to dispel the reputed link between wage work and lives of sin, Wright made a survey of prostitutes in major cities. This survey was not executed by women agents. Wright denied that low wages (even "ridiculously low or dangerously low") led to prostitution or that factories were recruiting grounds for prostitutes or that employers' treatment of workers pushed them into the profession. On the contrary, Wright concluded, many prostitutes entered their trade directly from home. These conclusions differed from those of physician William Sanger in 1858 (see Chapter 9). Surveying 2,000 inmates at New York's Blackwell Island prison, Sanger had found that low wages contributed directly to prostitution. Among the prostitutes surveyed in the 1850s, about half had been servants, one-fourth had lived with friends or family, and the bulk of the remainder were seamstresses, a trade that Sanger judged "prejudicial to virtue."

In some ways, Carroll D. Wright's conclusions agree with recent research on prostitution in the progressive era, which suggests that a disturbed home life was an important factor leading women into prostitution. On the other hand, recent research also reveals that the financial lure of prostitution was important: The turn-of-the-century prostitute could earn five times as much as the young woman who became a factory worker.*

The Character of Working Women

. . . It is often flippantly asserted that the shop girls, those comprising the class under investigation, recruit the ranks of prostitution. It would be a relief, of course, to all honest citizens to have this charge removed entirely, and further, to have the facts warrant its removal. Of course, such a charge can not be entirely removed when applied to any class. The only question here is, Does it apply to the class against which it is brought? . . .

Original investigation was made in the following cities: Brooklyn, Buffalo, Chicago, Cincinnati, Cleveland, Indianapolis, Louisville, Newark, New Orleans, New York, Philadelphia, Richmond, Saint Louis, and San Francisco.

In 1884 the Massachusetts Bureau of Statistics of Labor made a report as to the previous occupations of one hundred and seventy professional prostitutes in the city of Boston, and the facts then given have been incorporated in this report.

The number of prostitutes as stated in the following table, for any one of the cities named, falls far below the total number of prostitutes in that city, but the number and variety of those from whom information has been received are sufficient to insure representative results. Thus in Chicago, for example, there are, or were at the time of the investigation of the Department, 302 houses of ill-fame, assignation houses, and "rooming" houses, known to the police, containing 1,097 inmates. This investigation involved 557 of this number. In some of the other cities, Philadelphia and Brooklyn notably, the proportion of prostitutes interviewed was not so large as in Chicago, but a sufficient number of reports were obtained to afford a basis for a fair conclusion as to the part played, if any, by the working women in swelling the ranks of these unfortunates.

In certain of the cities in which this subject was investigated return was made of the number of women who had been married before entering on a life of shame. Some of these women were married before engaging in industrial work, some between periods of industrial employment; some after working at various employments were married, and then entered upon a life of prostitution, and some of the married prostitutes had never been industrially employed.

---

*See Ruth Rosen, *The Lost Sisterhood: Prostitution in America, 1900–1918* (Baltimore: Johns Hopkins University Press, 1982), chap. 8.

The facts as to marriage are shown by the following brief table, which gives the number of prostitutes furnishing information in the cities referred to, the number reporting themselves as having been married, and the per cent of the total number who were married:

City	Number of Prostitutes Furnishing Information	Number of Prostitutes Reported as Having Been Married	Percent of Married of Total Number
Boston	170	13	7.65
Chicago	557	143	25.67
Cincinnati	382	77	20.16
Louisville	263	70	26.62
New Orleans	167	4	2.40
Philadelphia	100	3	3.00
San Francisco	323	81	25.08

It is hardly worth while to take space at this time to give the occupations of all those who have entered prostitution from the different cities involved.

The number of prostitutes giving information was 3,866, and the following summary exhibits the occupations of this number preceding their entry upon their present life. For this purpose, occupations similar in character have been grouped, and no occupation or group containing less than ten persons has been included in the classification—those numbering under ten being put into the general classification of "various occupations":

Actresses, ballet girls, circus performers, singers, etc.	52
Bead-trimming makers, embroiderers, lace workers	21
Bookbinderies	18
Bookkeepers, clerks, copyists, stenographers, typewriters, etc.	31
Candy factories	10
Cigarette, cigar, and tobacco factories	78
Corset factories	16
Dressmakers, seamstresses, employés of cloak and shirt factories, button-hole makers, etc.	505
Hairdressers and hair workers	15
House work, hotel work, table work, and cooking	1,155
Laundry work	70
Milliners and hat trimmers	71

No previous occupation (home)	1,236
Nurses (hospitals and house), and nurse girls	22
Paper box factories	32
Rope and cordage factories	12
Saleswomen and cashiers	126
Shoe factories	43
Students (at schools or convents)	14
Teachers, governesses, etc.	23
Telegraph and telephone operators	11
Textile factories	94
Various occupations	211

The following list shows the character of the more important occupations omitted from the foregoing summary, with the number of women who had been employed in each, and which are included under "various occupations":

Artificial flower makers, 9; button factories, 9; farm work, 9; canning establishments, 8; necktie makers, 8; housekeepers, 7; straw sewers, 7; hat and cap factories, 6; bag factories, 5; canvassers, 5; clock and watch factories, 5; box factories (wooden), 4; chewing-gum factories, 4; florists, 4; feather curlers and sewers, 4; restaurant, 4.

The preceding figures are exceedingly instructive. By them it will be seen that the largest number coming from any occupation has been taken from those doing house work, hotel work, and cooking; this number, 1,155, being 29.88 per cent of the whole number comprehended in the statement.

The next largest number, so far as occupation is concerned, ranks with the seamstresses, including the dressmakers, employés of cloak and shirt factories, etc., this number being 505.

A fact which strikes one sadly is the large number who enter prostitution directly from their homes. This number is 1,236, being 31.97 per cent of the whole number comprehended.

It can not be said, therefore, so far as this investigation shows, that the employés in workshops are to be burdened with the charge of furnishing the chief source whence the ranks of prostitution are recruited. . . .

Nor does the investigation show that employers of labor are guilty of reducing their employés to a condition of prostitution, as is often alleged. Only in the rarest cases can one meet with a whisper that this is the case. And these whispers, followed to their source, have rarely disclosed any facts which would lead to the conclusion that employers make bargains based on the loss of character of their employés.

From all that can be learned one need not hesitate in asserting that the working women of the country are as honest and as virtuous as any class of our citizens.

All the facts are against the idea that they are not virtuous women. The statistics given show that a very large percentage of them are living at home. They are living in whatever moral atmosphere there is in their homes.

And it is true that they are not corrupted by their employers, nor do their employers seek to corrupt them. All such impressions originate in the idea that girls can not dress well upon the small wages they receive unless they lead immoral lives, in which they receive pecuniary assistance. But all the testimony that the writer has ever been able to collect upon this point is against such a sentiment, which prevails in too great a degree. The testimony of capable and honest women—of the heads of departments in great stores and millinery establishments and shops, forewomen of shops, the matrons of homes, and of all those best informed and in the best positions to give testimony on this point—is that the working women are as respectable, as moral, and as virtuous as any class of women in the country.

Of course there are exceptions in this class, as in all, but the grand fact must stand out plainly that the working women are not to be burdened with a charge that belongs to others as well as to them, so far as it lies at all.

Working women are not street-walkers. They could not carry on their daily toil and walk the streets too. A captain of police[1] expressed the matter well when he said that people who charge the working women with walking the streets at night for evil purposes do not know what they are talking about. Night-walkers are all of them hardened convicts. The prostitutes, some of them, may have been hard-working women, but no working woman ever walks the streets as a prostitute. This captain said that when a girl falls from virtue she has first to graduate as a "parlor" girl, and then serve some time in a still lower house, before she is hardened enough to take to the streets.

The fact that here and there a case of depravity comes to public attention can not be considered as conclusive evidence that the class to which the depraved case belongs is the cause of the depravity, or that the class itself is depraved.

Virtue and integrity belong to the individual. Either may be stimulated by surroundings, or destroyed by them. But when it is known that women are willing to work from morning till night for the paltry sum of $5 per week, out of which they must, and do, assist their friends, contribute, as a rule, to the general expenses of the household, to a large extent pay for their own sewing, and in various ways help on the family, it can not be assumed, with any reasonableness, that they enter lives of prostitution, even in that private way which it is alleged often accompanies their lives. Certainly the houses of prostitution do not contain them.

Many professional prostitutes, when finding a new acquaintance, are very apt to state that they are saleswomen in this or that well-known house. This attracts the victim, and gives him to understand that he is in company with some half-respectable woman, and not in company with a professional prostitute. His conscience, what little he has left, might rebel at associating with a professional prostitute, when it would allow him to continue in the company of a woman in a respectable calling.

The virtuous character of our working women is all the more attractive when the cost of their virtue is recognized. With their poor pay, if they continue virtuous they are the more entitled to our applause, and certainly one must recognize the

---

[1] During the investigation in Boston in 1883. (Fifteenth Annual Report, Massachusetts Bureau of Labor.)

heroic struggle they make to sustain life, to appear fairly well, and to remove what every honorable-minded man and woman seeks to remove, the appearance of poverty.

All the helps that are thrown around them in our great cities, all the kindness and the care of benevolent employers, all the influences of church and school, must be increased, and these, joined with the heroic efforts of the women themselves, must gradually deepen their characters, strengthen their purposes, and help them to gain a more generous livelihood.

Shop Girls and Piece Workers

HELEN CAMPBELL, 1893

Mrs. Helen Campbell, *Darkness and Daylight: Lights and Shadows of New York Life* (Hartford, CT: Worthington and Co., 1893), pp. 255–56, 259–65, 276–78.

Author and reformer Helen Campbell (1839–1918) began investigating urban poverty in the early 1880s by joining a "mission" on the New York waterfront. In 1886 she wrote a series of articles for the New York *Tribune* on women workers in stores and the garment trade. The articles led to a book, *Prisoners of Poverty* (1887), and a prize-winning study of women wage earners (1891). After her success as an investigator, Campbell lectured at the University of Wisconsin, served as head resident of a Chicago settlement, became an expert in home economics, and published a major text in that field, *Household Economics* (1897). In her later years, Campbell lived with feminist author Charlotte Perkins Gilman (see Chapter 17). Twenty-one years younger than Campbell, Gilman referred to her as "one of my adopted 'mothers.'"

The following excerpts from one of her books, published in 1893, distill Campbell's observations as a reporter and mission worker in the 1880s. Like her *Tribune* articles, these passages are intended to convey to readers the evils of poverty. Campbell and Commissioner of Labor Carroll D. Wright apparently agreed that female wage earning in New York often meant, in Wright's words, "struggling beyond belief." Unlike Wright, however, Campbell does not focus on the young, single wage earner; the shop clerk receives brief mention, but her youth and her longing for upward mobility seem to disqualify her, in Campbell's view, from the ranks of the truly oppressed. Instead, Campbell devotes most of her attention to the older pieceworker, who labored at home, supported a family, and bore the brunt of industrialization's inequities.

A quarter of a million women, and this exclusive of domestic service! Three hundred and forty-three trades open to them, and each one thronged with eager learners! This is the beginning of the story of New York working-women, and day by day the number grows. What the three hundred and forty trades specified in the last United States Labor Bureau Report are, no man knows save only the census-taker and the newspaper reporter, who must know all things. Many of them are simply subdivisions of old trades which include many processes, each one so thoroughly separated from all the rest as to form a trade in itself. Whatever they are, and however little reward the knowledge of their intricacies may bring, it is certain that a row of applicants are always in waiting, and that an advertisement for one often brings a hundred.

Before sketching the life of the worker in trades of all orders, let us see how it fares with the shop-girl. Often she begins as a cash-girl, leaving school at twelve or thirteen, and making one of the long list of applicants always on file in the great retail dry-goods establishments. It is a favorable ambition with the public-school girl from the better class of tenement-house, where one finds chiefly Irish and Germans. The children are quick and bright; apt to be ready reckoners, and look upon the great stores as the high road to fortune. That she must be on her feet most of the day and work for $1.50 or at most $2.00 a week, and may not be counted worth more than this for two or three years, does not deter hundreds from applying if any vacancy occurs. Certain things are learned that at home would probably have been impossible. They find that punctuality is the first essential, learning the lesson perhaps through the fines over which they cry. To them nothing can be better than to be a full-fledged "saleslady," and it may be, even, in time, the head of a department. If wages are a pittance, hours exhausting, and an army always waiting to fill their places if they in any way forfeit them, the fact of companionship and of the constant interest and excitement of watching the throng in shop and street seems sufficient to satisfy all longings and prevent much complaint. Their quickness and aptness to learn, their honesty and general faithfulness, and their cheapness, are essentials in their work; and this combination of qualities—cheapness dominating all—has given them a permanent place in the modern system of trade. The shop-girl has no thought of permanence for herself. The cheaper daily papers record in fullest detail the doings of that fashionable world toward which many a weak girl or woman looks with unspeakable longing; and the weekly "story papers" feed the flame with details of the rich marriage that lifted the poor girl into the luxury which stands to her empty mind as the sole thing to be desired in earth or heaven. Hope is strong. She expects to marry, and in many a silly little head there is hidden away the conviction that it will probably be some rich and handsome customer, who will woo her over the counter to the admiration and desperation of all the other girls, and place her at once where she really belongs.

She knows far better what constitutes the life of the rich than the rich ever know of the life of the poor. From her post behind the counter the shop-girl examines every detail of costume, every air and grace of the women she so often despises, even when longing most to be one of them. She imitates where she can, and her cheap shoe has its French heel, her neck its tin dog-collar. Gilt rings, bracelets and bangles, frizzes, bangs and cheap trimmings of every order, swallow up her earnings. The imitation is often more effective than the real, and the girl knows it. She aspires to a "manicure" set, to an opera glass, to anything that will simulate the life daily paraded before her and most passionately desired. . . .

And what about the workers in trades? Why are they at work? There are as many motives as trades. For the most part the answer is simple. They must earn because there is no one to earn for them, and this is the great majority. Outside of this army is another—the large class of women already provided for in homes of their own, but who want more pin-money, and hosts of married women who want means for more stylish living or dress, and who work at home to accomplish this very end, often underbidding their poorer sisters by working at half price or even less. With them we have nothing to do. It is the life of the average working-woman wholly dependent on her own resources that we must know; its struggles, its resources, its outlook as a whole.

Naturally the great mass are needlewomen of all orders. It is this one employment toward which every woman left to fight her own battle turns instinctively, unless she has had a training that fits her for something better. Either she enters a factory, where the intelligence demanded is of the lowest order, as in bag-making and kindred industries, or she takes home slopwork [piecework] of all sorts, from overalls and jumpers to coarser or finer work. For such work a sewing-machine must be owned, and as to get one even on installments is often quite beyond the power of the worker, this fact is taken advantage of by numbers of "sweaters," who rent cellars called by courtesy "basements," and act as "middlemen," taking the work in great packages from the cutter of the manufacturing house, and paying the women so much a dozen for the work done. The making of underclothing and cheap jackets and cloaks is managed in the same way. Everything, in short, that makes up the cheaper forms of clothing falls largely into the hands of these "middlemen," and often the women prefer this form of employment, since working with numbers has a more exhilarating effect than the same task alone, and heat and machine are both furnished. But every order of work goes on also in the tenement-houses, where the woman who owns a machine can take work direct from the factory.

The division of labor, which is one of the marked features of all modern work, rules here no less than elsewhere. Many a woman spends month after month in stitching fells till she has acquired a purely mechanical accuracy, who could by no possibility either cut, fit, or make an entire garment. There is always a dearth of trained seamstresses, who understand all forms of sewing, and for whom there is a demand that is yet to be fully met.

There is another class, helpless through no fault of theirs, though often powerless through lack of training. It is the hundreds—yes, thousands—of women, widows or worse than widows, who must care for little children often more fortunate without a father than with one. Drunken husbands, who not only furnish nothing toward the family support, but demand support themselves, are worked for with a patience that is a constant miracle to all who watch. Sewing in some of its myriad forms is the first thought, and often in the wretched dens of these down-town tenements one sees embroideries destined for happy children in sunny homes, or rich cloaks whose velvet and silk seem a mockery. Poverty is not infectious, yet strange germs must go with the garments into which these women have stitched all the want and pain born of hunger and cold and nakedness, of endurance and final despair. . . .

Cloakmakers generally earn from sixty to seventy cents a day, but even this means comfort and profusion compared with the facts that were revealed in a Fourth Ward rookery. Here in an old wooden house given over to the lowest uses, in a room ten feet square, low-ceiled, and lighted only by a single window, whose panes were crusted with the dirt of a generation, seven women sat at work. Three machines were the principal furniture. A small stove burned fiercely, the close smell of red-hot iron hardly dominating the fouler one of sinks and reeking sewer-gas. Piles of cloaks were on the floor, and the women, white and wan, with cavernous eyes and hands more akin to a skeleton's than to flesh and blood, bent over the garments that would pass from this loathsome place saturated with the invisible filth furnished as air. They were handsome cloaks, lined with quilted silk or satin, trimmed with fur or sealskin, and retailing at prices from thirty to seventy-five dollars. A teapot stood at the back of the stove; some cups and a loaf of bread, with a lump of streaky butter, were on a small table, absorbing their portion also of filth. An inner room, a mere closet, dark and even fouler than the outer one, held the bed; a mattress, black with age, lying on the floor. Here such rest as might be had was taken when the sixteen hours of work ended—sixteen hours of toil unrelieved by one gleam of hope or cheer, the net result of this accumulated and ever-accumulating misery being $3.50 a week. Two women, using their utmost diligence, could finish one cloak per day, receiving from the "sweater," through whose hands all work must come, fifty cents each for a toil unequalled by any form of labor under the sun, unless it be that of the haggard wretches dressed in men's clothes but counted as female laborers in Belgian mines. They cannot stop, they dare not stop, to think of other methods of earning. They are what is left of untrained, hopelessly ignorant lives, clinging to these lives with a tenacity hardly higher in intelligence than that of the limpet on the rock, but turning to one with lustreless eyes and blank faces, asking only the one question—"Lord, how long?" . . .

Outside of the army of needlewomen come the washers and ironers, who [launder] shirts and underwear, whose work is of the most exhausting order, who "lean hard" on the iron and in time become the victims of diseases resulting from ten hours a day of this "leaning hard." . . . There is a constantly increasing army of scrub women who clean the floors of offices and public buildings at night for a pittance, whose life is of the hardest. . . .

I turn at last from these women, whose eyes still follow me, filled with mute questions of what can be done. Of all ages and nations and creeds; of all degrees of ignorance and prejudice and stupidity; hampered by every condition of birth and training; powerless to rise beyond them till obstacles are removed—the great city holds them all. . . .

It is as student, not as professional philanthropist, that I write; and the years that have brought experience have also brought a conviction, sharpened by every fresh series of facts, that no words, no matter what fire of fervor may lie behind, can make plain the sorrow of the poor.

Objections to Domestic Service

LUCY MAYNARD SALMON, 1897

Lucy Maynard Salmon, *Domestic Service* (New York: Macmillan, 1897), pp. 140–50.

Vassar historian Lucy Salmon (1853–1927) began her inquiry into domestic service in 1889 by preparing questionnaires for thousands of employers and servants, to be distributed by college alumnae and members of women's clubs. The questionnaire method had its drawbacks: Salmon's survey was limited to those willing to submit written responses, and these were mainly employers. Still, she reached some 700 servants or former servants, who submitted data on their wages and work histories, along with personal comments.

Lucy Salmon used the servants' responses to assess the advantages and liabilities of domestic service, from the servant's viewpoint. The advantages (for instance, steady work and the ability to save wages) were far outweighed by drawbacks. Beyond the major disadvantage—the social degradation of servitude—Salmon's respondents voiced a range of objections to their work and working conditions. The servants' views were elicited by the following questions: (1) Why do you choose housework as your regular employment? (2) What reasons can you give why more women do not choose housework as a regular employment? (3) Would you give up housework if you could find another occupation that would pay you as well? Some of the responses to these questions appear in the footnotes that follow.

No one occupation includes every advantage and no disadvantages. There must always be a balancing of the pros and cons, and domestic service has its industrial disadvantages, which are as patent as its advantages, and like them are independent of the personal relationship existing between the employer and the employee.

The question was asked of employees, "What reasons can you give why more women do not choose housework as a regular employment?" The reasons assigned may be classified as follows:

Pride, social condition, and unwillingness to be called servants	157
Confinement evenings and Sundays	75
More independence in other occupations	60

Too hard and confining	42
Other work pays better	42
Lack of consideration by mistresses	38
Hours too long	38
Do not like housework	19
Do not know how to do housework	12
Can live at home by working in shops	11
Girls are too lazy	8
Health considerations	8
Girls are too restless	6
Too few privileges	6
Hard work, little pay	5
Other occupations easier	4
Different tastes	4
Bad character of some reflects on others	3
Receive no encouragement	3
Too lonely and meals alone	3
Constant change in work	3
Shop work cleaner	2
No chance for promotion	2
Miscellaneous reasons, one each	11
Total	562

Some of these and other reasons demand a more detailed explanation.

The first industrial disadvantage is the fact that there is little or no opportunity for promotion in the service nor are there opening out from it kindred occupations. An ambitious and capable seamstress becomes a dressmaker and mistress of a shop, a successful clerk sets up a small fancy store, the trained nurse by further study develops into a physician, the teacher becomes the head of a school; but there are no similar openings in household employments. Success means a slight increase in wages, possibly an easier place, or service in a more aristocratic neighborhood, but the differences are only slight ones of degree, never those of kind. "Once a cook, always a cook" may be applied in principle to every branch of the service. . . . Those women who would become the most efficient domestics are the ones who see most clearly this drawback to the occupation.

The second disadvantage is the paradoxical one that it is possible for a capable woman to reach in this employment comparative perfection in a reasonably short time. Table service is a fine art which many waitresses never learn, but it is easily mastered by one who "mixes it with brains." One illustration of this is the superior service given at summer resorts by college students without special training. The proper care of a room is understood by few maids, but the comprehension of a few simple principles enables an intelligent woman soon to become an expert. The work of a cook involves much more, but because many persons cook for years without learning how to provide a single palatable and nourishing dish, it does not follow that the art cannot be readily acquired. This fact taken in connection with the previous one unconsciously operates to prevent a large number of ambitious women from becoming domestics.

A third disadvantage is the fact that "housework is never done." In no other occupation involving the same amount of intelligent work do the results seem so literally ephemeral. This indeed is not the true statement of the case—mistresses are learning slowly that cooking is a moral and scientific question, that neatness in caring for a room is a matter of hygiene, and that table service has æsthetic possibilities. But if it has taken long for the most intelligent part of society to understand that the results of housework are not transient, but as far-reaching in their effects as are the products of any other form of labor, it cannot be deemed strange that domestics as a class and those in other occupations complain "in housework there's nothing to show for your work."

A fourth disadvantage is the lack of organization in domestic work. The verdict from the standpoint of the statistician has been quoted. A domestic employee sums up the question from her point of view when she says, "Most women like to follow one particular branch of industry, such as cooking, or chamber work, or laundry work, because it enables one to be thorough and experienced; but when these are combined, as a general thing the work is hard and never done."

A fifth disadvantage is the irregularity of working hours. This is a most serious one, since the question is complicated not only by the irregularity that exists in every family, but also by the varying customs in different families. The actual working hours of a general servant may vary from one instance of five hours in Kansas to another of eighteen hours in Georgia. They sometimes vary in the same city from seven to seventeen hours. It is a difficult matter to ascertain with the utmost definiteness, but a careful examination of all statements made seems to show that the actual working hours are ten in the case of thirty-eight per cent of women employees, thirty-seven per cent averaging more than ten hours, and twenty-five per cent less than this. The working hours for men average somewhat longer than the hours for women, while there are slight differences in the various classes of servants; but they are of too indefinite a character to be specially noted. . . .

A sixth disadvantage closely connected with the preceding is the matter of free time evenings and Sundays. This objection to housework is frequently made[1]; it is one that can never be wholly obviated, since the household machinery cannot stop at six o'clock and must be kept in order seven days in the week, but were society so inclined the objection could be lessened.

---

[1] "Women want the free use of their time evenings and Sundays."

"If I could bear the confinement I would go into a mill where I could have evenings and Sundays."

"Sunday in a private family is usually anything but a day of rest to the domestic, for on that day there are usually guests to dinner or tea or both, which means extra work."

"I wouldn't mind working Sundays if it wasn't for the extra work."

"I suppose the reason why more women choose other work is, they would rather work all day and be done with it, and have evenings for themselves."

"Some families have dinner at three o'clock Sundays and lunch at eight or nine, and that makes it very hard for girls."

A seventh difficulty is presented to the American born girl when she realizes that she must come into competition with the foreign born and colored element.[2] Although much of this feeling is undoubtedly unreasonable, it is not peculiar to domestic service. The fact must be accepted, with or without excuse for it.

Another disadvantage that weighs with many is the feeling that in other occupations there is more personal independence. This includes not only the matter of time [during] evenings and Sundays, which they can seldom call unconditionally their own, but there is a dislike of interference on the part of the employer, either with their work or with their personal habits and tastes. This interference is often hard to bear when the employer is an experienced housekeeper—it is intolerable in the case of an inexperienced one. The "boss" carpenter who himself knew nothing about the carpenter's trade would soon have all his workmen arrayed against him; in every occupation an employee is unwilling to be directed except by his superior in knowledge and ability.[3] It seems unreasonable to expect domestic service to be an exception to this universal rule. . . .

The industrial disadvantages of the occupation are best summed up by a young factory operative who was for a time in domestic service. In answer to the question, "Why do girls dislike domestic service?" she writes:

> "In the first place, I don't like the idea of only one evening a week and every other Sunday. I like to feel that I have just so many hours' work to do and do them, and come home and dress up and go out or sit down and sew if I feel like it, and when a girl is in service she has very little time for herself, she is a servant. In the second place, a shop or factory girl knows just what she has to do and can go ahead and do it. I also think going out makes a girl stupid in time. She gets out of style, so to speak. She never reads and does not know what is going on in the world. I don't mean to say they all get stupid, but it makes gossips of

---

[2]"A great many very ignorant girls can get housework to do, and a girl who has been used to neatness and the refinement of a good home does not like to room with a girl who has just come from Ireland and does not know what neatness means."

"In ———— they have much colored help and do not have white help, so the white girls think any other work is better than housework."

"In California self-respecting girls do not like to work with Chinamen—they do not know how to treat women."

"Before the introduction of Chinese labor a young girl never lost social caste by doing housework; but since this element came, household service as an occupation has fallen in the social scale."—*Employer*

"When a native American girl goes out to housework she loses caste at once, and can hardly find pleasure in the foreign immigrants that form the majority of servants, and who make most of the trouble from their ignorance and preconceived notions of America."—*Employer*

[3]"The reason for dislike of housework is the want of liberty, and the submission which girls have to submit to when they have to comply with whatever rules a mistress may deem necessary. Therefore many girls go into mechanical pursuits, that some of their life may be their own."

"Girls in housework are bossed too much."

"There are too many mistresses in the house when the mother and grown-up daughters are all at home."

"Most of us would like a little more independence, and to do our work as we please."

"In housework you receive orders from half a dozen persons, in a shop or factory from but one."

"A man doesn't let his wife and daughters and sons interfere in the management of his mill or factory—why does a housekeeper let everybody in the house boss?"

girls that if they worked in shops or factories [they] would be smart girls. Then I think shop or factory girls make the best wives. Now I don't mean all, but the biggest part of them, and the cleanest housekeepers. The domestic after she gets married gets careless. She don't take the pride in her home that the shop-girl does. She has lived in such fine houses that her small tenement has no beauty for her after the first glow of married life is over. She don't try either to make her home attractive or herself, and gets discouraged, and is apt to make a man disheartened with her, and then I think she is extravagant. She has so much to do with before she is married and so little to do with after she don't know how to manage. She can't have tenderloin steak for her breakfast and rump roast for her dinner, and pay the rent and all other bills out of $12 a week—and that is the average man's pay, the kind of man we girls that work for a living get. Of course I don't mean to say the domestics don't have a good time, they do; some of them have lovely places and lay up money, but after all, what is life if a body is always trying to see just how much money he or she can save?"

The industrial disadvantages of the occupation certainly are many, including as they do the lack of all opportunity for promotion, the great amount of mere mechanical repetition involved, the lack of organization in the service, irregularity in working hours, the limitation of free time evenings and Sundays, competition with the foreign born and the negro element that seems objectionable to the American born, and the interference with work often by those less skilled than the workers themselves.

Black Servants in Philadelphia

ISABEL EATON, 1899

Isabel Eaton, "Special Report on Negro Domestic Service in the Seventh
Ward, Philadelphia," in W. E. B. Du Bois, *The Philadelphia Negro: A Social Study*
(New York: Benjamin Bloom, 1899), pp. 464–67.

Black women workers in late nineteenth-century America had little
choice of occupation. In 1890, thirty-seven percent were agricultural
laborers, fifteen percent were laundresses, and thirty-one percent
were domestic servants. Those who lived in cities found few opportunities for jobs in factories, stores, or offices. Compared to white
women workers, black wage earners were more likely to be older,
married, and major contributors to family income.

In 1896, settlement worker Isabel Eaton, a Smith alumna and
graduate student at Columbia, began research on domestic servants as
part of the scholar W. E. B. Du Bois's massive 1899 study of the black
residents of Philadelphia's Seventh Ward. Unlike the servants surveyed by Lucy Salmon, Eaton's black subjects were both male and
female. Like Salmon's respondents, they voiced objections to servitude: Social stigma and monotony were the main complaints. But most
of Eaton's subjects were unable to find any preferable type of work,
even if they had been trained as teachers or typists or if they were
college graduates. In the following excerpt from her report, Eaton
examines the opinions that black servants voiced about domestic work
and their desire to find alternate employment.

The dullness and monotony of a domestic servant's life seems to be the most generally
pressing question. The demand is for more Sundays and evenings out and a monthly
holiday. . . . Careful mistresses assert that they find that even quite young girls fresh
from the country chafe under any restriction as to the manner in which they shall
spend their leisure, or as to being out late alone.

The same tendencies are noticeable throughout American domestic service,
both with native whites, foreign whites, and colored domestics. This dissatisfaction is
shown by the restless attempts of domestics to enter other occupations. Among
American domestic employees the country over, 28 per cent are found to have been
engaged in other occupations, such as hop-picking, grape and cotton-picking and
factory work. That these people are now employed in domestic work, Miss Salmon*

---

*Lucy Maynard Salmon.

believes, means not so much a preference for service as that it is a sort of *derniere ressort* to be taken up only when no better paid or more popular work offers. . . .

Among the colored people in the city of Philadelphia, 524 domestics report in regard to other occupations. Of this number 91, or 17.4 per cent, have done, or attempted to get the opportunity to do, other work than domestic service, and it is noticeable that the employment which has occupied this 17.4 per cent of colored domestics has been very different in character from the field and factory work attracting young domestics in general. Among colored city domestics, the work done by the women before entering service has very generally been dressmaking, typewriting or teaching, while the men have worked as porters, or drug clerks, or have practiced trades or even professions. One man was encountered who had graduated from Hampton and from a law school as well, while several stonecutters, brick masons and carpenters were found who had drifted or been forced into the ranks of domestic service. . . .

[T]he colored city employees who attempt to get other work wish to leave domestic service permanently. They wish to do this partly because they consider that service savors of slavery and that they are degraded by it, and being ambitious of achieving respectability, they attempt to better their social standing by becoming teachers or dressmakers; partly also because they hope for higher wages from teaching and other work than they receive as domestics. The difference between the proportion of servants the country over who have done other work and the proportion of colored domestics in Philadelphia who have done or attempted to do other work is a large one. Twenty-eight per cent of general domestic service as contrasted with 17.4 per cent of colored domestic service shows a difference which is almost in the ratio of five to three. And also it must be remembered—and this accentuates the difference still further—that the colored servants who have tried to get other work and failed have also been counted, since the attempt showed their restlessness in service and their desire to leave it. There must be some reason for this apparent willingness to remain in service on the part of the colored people. In answer to the schedule question, "Have you ever tried to do other work?" a large number of domestics replied, "I never go any place I'm not sure of—I won't give them a chance to refuse me." One girl who had taught for four years and who thinks she lost her place at the end of that time from prejudice on the part of the school-committee, says, without the slightest apparent touch of resentment, "The reason I don't try to teach is because I know I'd have trouble, and I can save as much this way." Another ex-teacher has now been a chambermaid for several years for the same reason. One Philadelphia carpenter and builder says, "We have five granddaughters—my son's children—from twenty-three years old to fourteen; and what can we do with them? They can't get teachers' places, though they are good students. Dressmaking is about played out. Service? They don't want to do *that*. Typewriting is about the only hope, and the oldest one was refused that the other day." . . .

When colored domestics are refused it appears to be generally with the simple statement that white help is preferred. It should be said here that among those who said that they had never attempted anything except domestic employment, fifty-two, or about 10 per cent, have even been refused domestic work when applying for it. Some of these were inclined to charge the refusal to race prejudice; some attribute it to the fact that unintelligent employers class all colored people together; or, to put it in their own words, "If the mistresses has bad luck with one colored girl they won't never have another. They think all colored is alike." Still others think it is not a race question at all, but merely one of supply and demand. As one man put it, "There isn't work enough or places enough to go round; that's it." There are many well-authenticated cases also of "light" colored people who have retained their places from two to fifteen years, under the impression, on the part of the employer, that they were white people; but on the discovery of the slight tincture of African blood, although it could not be detected, and although the work had been entirely satisfactory, their situations were immediately forfeited. Such instances might be multiplied indefinitely, as they were encountered upon every hand.

In consideration of all this, it appears highly probable that the Negroes are deterred in many cases from attempting to obtain other work, from unwillingness to run the risk of insult or failure. The moral certainty of "having trouble" is probably sufficient to account for the comparatively low percentage of colored domestics who have attempted to leave service, while the well-known fact that so many industries are closed against the race would account in large measure for the scarcity of those who have actually been engaged in other employments. These facts are sufficient to explain the 10.6 per cent difference in the two percentages compared.

Judging by the character of the work sought by the domestics who have left or attempted to leave service, it seems fair to conclude that while the monotony of service and the low pay, as compared with harvest wages, are the chief things that rural American servants have against it, probably the chief objection of colored city domestics against service is the social stigma which rightly or wrongly attaches to it. It savors to them of the degradation of their slavery days, while they believe that to be a teacher, is to achieve immediate social position and become a respected member of the community. Colored city domestics seek other work, therefore, from the desire to escape social degradation first, from the desire for greater personal freedom next, and finally from the hope of higher remuneration.

The Office Clerk

CLARA LANZA, 1891

Clara Lanza, "Women Clerks in New York," *Cosmopolitan* 10 (1891),
pp. 487–92.

The late nineteenth-century office worker—white, middle-class, and
native-born—saw herself as a pioneer in the business world. Trained
stenographers and "typewriters" were in demand. Within only a few
decades, they almost replaced male office clerks; by 1900, women
formed seventy-five percent of office personnel. Such rapid success
evoked a backlash. Male critics charged in the press that business work
imperiled femininity and disqualified women for marriage and motherhood. Women's higher moral status, they asserted, was unsuited to
the office world. Critics also contended, in a second barrage of arguments, that women were incapable of office work: They were flighty,
temperamental, and unsystematic; they lacked steadfastness, energy,
and purpose; and they tended to giggle, talk back, or sulk on the job.

Journalist Clara Lanza, who wrote about women's employment,
responded directly to criticism of the female office worker. She
claimed that women's higher moral calibre would improve the business world, that male workers were less reliable than female ones, and
that women would preserve their femininity in the office. In fact, she
concluded, office work made them superior candidates for marriage.

To her credit be it said that woman, in striving to attain in certain lines of action the
eminence already occupied by man, has not proved herself by any means a failure.
She has shown herself to be fully his equal in physical endurance and mental capacity.
Among the woman workers in New York there are none who afford a more interesting
study than the vast army of clerks, the work of a clerk being admirably adapted to the
sex. You may count almost on the fingers of one hand the number of years that have
elapsed since the women clerks appeared. Yet so prevalent have they become in all
our large cities, that one might say they have entirely superseded the men in this
particular department. Nine employers out of ten prefer women as clerks. If this
statement appears to be a sweeping one, it can be verified by the fact that the demand
for women as clerical workers is steadily on the increase, while men stand a comparatively poor chance of securing positions. The circumstance is amply justified by many
reasons, not the least of these being the superior quality of the work performed
by women.

Speaking, not long ago, to the head of a large publishing house where women were employed as cashiers and book-keepers, I ventured to ask whether the women compared favorably with men in the fulfilment of their respective duties.

"Women," was the answer, "are much to be preferred for a number of reasons. They are capable and industrious, and, so far as my personal experience goes, absolutely reliable. Besides, a woman is more conscientious about her work. Mathematical exactness in small things is a virtue not often accredited to women, but it can be cultivated as well as anything else. Double-entry book-keeping is just as much an exact science as differential calculus. Do you see that fair-haired girl yonder?" pointing to a quiet-looking figure seated before a tall desk and a formidable ledger, "well, she is one of the most accomplished book-keepers in New York. There is not one man in a hundred who can compare with her. She has the whole thing at her fingers' ends. She never makes a mistake and she never misses a day here from January to December. She comes at half-past eight and remains till six. None of my women clerks are irregular in their attendance. There is the cashier. She handles every penny that comes into the business, and I trust her implicitly. Her accounts are beautifully kept and always perfectly accurate. I wouldn't take men in place of these girls in any circumstances. Men are troublesome. They complain about trifles that a woman wouldn't notice. The office boys don't suit, or the temperature of the building is too hot or too cold, or the light is not properly adjusted. Then, if they have a slight headache, they stay at home. Most of them are married, and their wives fall ill, or their mother-in-law comes on a visit, and all these things are made an excuse for absence. The women come whether they have headaches or not. They never want a day off to attend a baseball match. They undertake the work with a full understanding of what is required of them, and they are steadfast in the performance of their duties. We treat them well and never refuse to grant them any trifling favor. There is only one thing we exact over and above their business qualifications. We do not employ a woman unless she lives at home with her family.

"This has the appearance of injustice, but if you reflect a moment you will recollect that the temptations to which a woman living by herself is exposed in a great city are manifold and dangerous, and for our own sake we find it necessary that our clerks, like Cæsar's wife, should be above suspicion as to character and antecedents. We must know all about them and their families. The cashier who is here now did not take a regular course of instruction at a business college. She had a relative, an uncle or a cousin, well established in business, and who trained her privately for the position she occupies. She has been accustomed to office work ever since she was a child."

The above proved conclusively that capability and a readiness to work did not in every instance insure a desirable occupation to the woman who sought it. A girl who had no "family," and who was obliged to depend upon her individual exertions for the food she ate and the clothes she wore, could not hope to get any position of trust. A woman who handles large sums of money that do not belong to her must be surrounded on all sides by a definite respectability; and while it sounds a bit quixotic to insist that she must have family connections over and above all her other virtues, it is perfectly just in the abstract. Unfortunately, respectable relations cannot be manufactured to order; therefore she who has them not would better become a typewriter, a stenographer, or a telegraph operator.

The large schools of stenography and typewriting turn out annually hundreds of women who rank easily with the most accomplished men clerks. Typewriting, being in great demand, is perhaps the most lucrative of the minor employments open to women. It is claimed that the market is decidedly overstocked with typewriters, and that there are not half enough positions for the largely increasing number of candidates. But this is a mistake. The market may be overcrowded with women who claim to be typewriters and stenographers, but in reality there is not a sufficient number of well-trained and capable clerks to supply the demand.

"By far the greatest difficulty I have to contend with," says Miss Seymour,* who presides over the Union School of stenography and typewriting, "is to keep my best operators with me. Although I pay them liberal salaries and do everything I can to secure their services permanently, they are in constant receipt of offers that men would be glad to receive. Many pupils of the school receive offers of positions at salaries varying from eight to twelve dollars a week before they have finished the six months' course of instruction. I mention this for the purpose of showing how popular the employment of women clerks has become, that is, if they are properly trained for the work. It is positive that an intelligent woman is especially fitted for clerical work. If she does not succeed her failure is due to faulty training. Business men tell me they prefer women as shorthand amanuenses for one particular reason. It is because, contrary to accepted tradition, women are less likely than men to disclose the business secrets of their employers. Then, too, they are more faithful and more apt to remain for a long period in the service of one employer.

"Of course, a number of employers engage women under the prevailing impression that they will work for lower wages; but while this is true in the majority of cases, it is equally true that efficient women can command as high salaries as men, particularly if they refuse to work for less, which is usually the case."

Typewriting and stenography are not of themselves very difficult of comprehension or execution, and it does not take long in order to familiarize one's self with either; but a clerk who wishes to succeed must know many more things. She must possess a ready knowledge of English composition and orthography. She must be able to punctuate properly, and above all, be quick to grasp an idea. Large numbers of girls spend their last penny in an attempt to fit themselves for clerical work, only to discover that, owing to their rudimentary education and total inaptitude, it is impossible for them to fill any responsible position. . . .

Telegraph operators, insurance clerks, shorthand reporters and proof-readers command wages in proportion to the proficiency with which their work is accomplished. A great number of these girls have relatives dependent upon them for support, so that it is hard very often to make both ends meet. I have in mind at this moment a girl of twenty, a telegraph operator, who supports not only herself but a crippled and semi-imbecile brother. There is something pathetic about this little household—a couple of rooms in a westside boarding house where the sun illumines fitfully the dreary interior. There is a gas stove in the corner and an easy chair by the

---

*Mary Foot Seymour (1846–1893) opened the Union School of Stenography in downtown New York in 1879. She subsequently ran four stenography schools, a stenography company, an employment bureau for stenographers, a publication called *The Business Woman's Journal*, and her own publishing company.

window. Here, beside a row of potted geraniums, the invalid brother sits all day—sits and looks with vacant eyes into the street, while the sister works and earns the money that pays the doctor and buys medicine, that this useless existence may be prolonged.

It must not be supposed that this dull-tinted vignette is by any means typical of a woman clerk's life. Quite the contrary. Most clerks have comfortable homes with their parents, and numbers of them enjoy not only the ordinary necessaries of life, but a considerable portion of its luxuries. As a rule, the clerk's entire salary is at her disposal for her personal requirements. She must dress neatly, and then there are petty vanities that every woman likes to indulge, no matter what her station may be. The woman clerk is rarely frivolous in her demeanor. She cannot afford frivolity; the mere fact of her self-dependence invests her with a certain outward dignity that one sees seldom displaced even when brought into collision with the powerful exuberance of youthful animal spirits. Not that she is prim and puritanical. She does not eschew legitimate pleasure nor regard amusement as superfluous. But she seems impressed by the consciousness that being forced to trust her mental resources for whatever she now has and is destined to enjoy in the future constitutes an inspiring duty that is not the less evident or sacred because it happens to devolve entirely upon herself. . . .

So much for the actual conditions that surround women clerks in New York. But what of the future? In what special line of life and thought are these women casting their destiny? The majority are, undoubtedly, worthy and enterprising. Indeed, it stands to reason that a dying ambition or a sudden relaxation of the working stimulus would create a rapid decadence in the ranks. As this does not make itself anywhere apparent we must infer that the existing relations between the employer and the employees are, on the whole, satisfactorily maintained on both sides. A woman dismissed from a profitable situation for laziness or raw inexperience would find her career practically ended. Where a man would in all probability secure other work to take the place of what he had lost, a woman would be more likely to remain inactive and lukewarm, a victim to her femininity.

The matrimonial achievements of women clerks have become a species of national pleasantry. So many women employed in offices and mercantile houses have married men with whom they would hardly have come in contact in another sphere, that the subject has long ceased to be a matter of speculation, and has gradually drifted from witty comment to the more sober attention that bespeaks a recognized fact.

"It is curious," said not long ago the chief partner in a large insurance firm, "but during the past year five of our best women clerks have married men of means and are now living in ease and leisure. How did they manage it? Well, it happened naturally enough, chiefly through business correspondence. It is very romantic, though one would not expect romance to be mixed up with insurance policies. Every insurance company has of course a policy department where all business connected with policies and their holders is transacted. At the head of this department is a forewoman who gets from forty to sixty dollars a week, and who is in direct correspondence with the president and other officers. The policy department is divided into geographical sections; each of these sections has a special room provided for its own business.

These rooms are superintended by a head clerk with an assistant. The head clerk gets about sixteen dollars a week and conducts all the necessary correspondence with agents. The letters are dictated to a stenographer. The correspondence is a long one very often. The agents come to New York from the North, South or West as the case may be, visit the company offices, see all the girls at work, and, of course, ask which ones have been conducting special correspondences. If a girl happens to be pretty and modest, an acquaintance springs up, and at last Miss Blank announces to the forewoman that she intends to leave and get married. This happens again and again. Then, too, the girls are often brought into business relations with our men clerks and marry them."

From all I am able to gather the girls make good wives. There is nothing in clerical training that detracts from the finest womanly qualities, and men have outgrown their admiration for feminine helplessness and have come to look upon independence as something worth having. Clerical training educates the mind to accuracy in details, punctuality in the daily affairs of life, economy in the adjustment of time and quickness of perception. Perhaps this is the reason why so many men choose a wife amid the deft-fingered clerks in preference to the society misses. The woman clerk has studied the value of concentration, learned the lesson that incites to work when a burden bears heavily upon her strength. She knows the worth of self-reliance, and the fine courage that springs from the consciousness that a good result has been accomplished by a well-directed effort.

The Public Sector:
A Police Matron

MARY A. JENKS, 1893, 1898

Mary A. Jenks, "The Matron's Report to the Chief of Police" (City of Pawtucket, Rhode Island), *Annual Report* (1893), pp. 51–54, *Annual Report* (1898),
pp. 38–41.

Throughout the late nineteenth century, urban women with skills
found jobs in the rapidly growing public sector. They worked in government offices and in state or local institutions such as public schools,
libraries, asylums, and prisons. Most female jobs in these institutions
involved work with other women, children, the sick, the insane, or
persons who for various reasons needed care. Such was the experience
of a Rhode Island widow, Mary A. Jenks, who became a police matron.
Hired in 1893 by the Pawtucket Police Department, Jenks took up
residence in the city jail where she ran an eight-bed ward. There she
supervised a mixed clientele of women and children, including va-
grants, the deranged, the injured, the homeless, and lost youngsters.
She also supervised women who had been indicted for or convicted of
crimes—mainly drunks and prostitutes awaiting trial or sentencing.

Jenks's duties were both managerial and domestic. She sewed
sheets for her charges, distributed cast-off clothing, cared for un-
tended infants, welcomed temperance agents, resolved family disputes
in the community, and attempted to reform her female inmates,
though with little success. Mary Jenks, however, was an unqualified
success, since she won the approval of the police officers with whom
she worked. The following documents are Mary Jenks's reports to her
superior, the Chief of Police, in 1893 and 1898. The reports suggest
Jenks's responsibilities and convey her compassionate view of "fallen
humanity." They also provide a window through which we can glimpse
the problems of extremely poor women—those who at best eked out
an existence on the margins of the urban economy. At worst, they
tumbled afoul of the law or into need of public assistance.

The Matron's Report to the Chief of Police

Pawtucket, R.I., November 30, 1893

Entering upon my duties as Police Matron August 15th, 1893, I found three women in custody. These were soon disposed of, and I proceeded to adapt myself to the pleasant, comfortable apartments that had been provided for me, and to take into consideration the best possible manner of employing my time pending intervals between arrests.

At first I shrank from stepping out of my cosy room, fearing lest I should seem intrusive. But the cordiality of the superior officers, and the courtesy and gentlemanly manner of all the other officers, dispelled every hesitancy, and assured me that I was a welcome addition to their number. Consequently I assumed the role of housekeeper in downright earnest. The first important need that claimed my attention was the neglected and unwholesome appearance that the bed linen and towels presented from want of proper washing. Upon interviewing the laundress, we were not surprised that the clothes had been thus improperly laundered, for the woman had grown old in her service, and was no longer strong enough for her task. Consulting with Chief Perry in regard to the matter, it was suggested that we make an entire change. This resulted in taking the most worn and unsavory looking sheets and pillow slips for bandages and cloths in case of accident or emergency, and replacing them with new ones. Chief Perry kindly gave me an order to get the required material, which I did, and immediately set about the work. Have made eleven towels, twenty-five sheets, twenty-two pairs of pillow slips, six bedspreads, two excelsior pillows for the accident room, besides repairing many articles of bedding and finding numerous other things that required attention. Have cared for nine lost children until claimed by their friends. In two cases of arrests the mothers have had young babes that have been given proper care while the mother was held in charge. As also in cases where mothers are in court as witnesses, infants have been left for hours in my care. Several homeless and motherless children have received our special care pending the disposition of them by the authorities. Four insane women have been placed in my care while arrangements were being made for their commitment in some institution.

I have endeavored in every possible way to drop a word of advice or admonition to the unfortunate persons of whom our sympathy and labor have been given.

Of the pleasant things I here record is the number of visitors. One hundred and eighty-four different ones have given us their good cheer and "God bless you" in our work, manifesting interest and appreciation of the efforts to make the experiment of "Police Matron" in the city of Pawtucket a veritable success. One of the needs of the work I found to be a want of wearing apparal for those unfortunate women who are often brought in half clad, and in some cases nothing but a single undergarment on, many times with no hat, shoes or wrap. They can tell us nothing about them. We suppose they are pawned for drink, and it becomes necessary to supply their needs for humanity's sake. To do this I have, through the gratuity of the Times, made a call for cast-off garments. For the prompt and liberal responses that I have received I wish to express my heartfelt gratitude, as it has in every case enabled me to discharge or commit my prisoners comfortably and respectably clad; which not only gives credence to our work, but gives credit where credit is due, viz: to the ladies of the city of Pawtucket.

Among other duties we have quite an extensive correspondence. Persons from different parts of the state writing for information concerning this branch of women's work and the practical good resulting from it. Of the latter I cannot speak very encouragingly. In one way it is discouraging indeed. In but two instances only, out of the seventy that have come under my charge, are we sure that genuine reformations have been the reward of our efforts. Two young girls have been persuaded to leave the questionable boarding houses and return to their respective homes and parents. Some few have refrained from drinking for a few weeks under our watchful care, but have at length spurned advice and gone back to their cups. Many persons have sought servants or children for adoption through this channel. Others call from time to time to "have a talk with the matron" concerning some real or imaginary domestic trouble that threatens to break up the home and scatter the little ones—as the vase is broken and the fragments scattered, to be gathered into the waste box as lost. There are too many broken homes, too much human waste. Fortunately in a few instances we have been able to calm the troubled waters, and a reconciliation was the happy result of our weak efforts. Many, indeed, are the unfortunate cases and heart-stirring scenes that have been brought to bear upon our sympathies and call for entire consecration to this work for fallen humanity. There is something more in this work—this labor of love—than simply work for fallen women. Police matron work may truly be compared to the Banyan tree.* Enough cannot be said in praise of Chief Perry and his staff of superior officers, who have in every way co-operated with and given me their best endeavors to aid me in making a grand success of this new department of police work. So that I can truly say, "our lines have fallen in pleasant places." The kind and gentlemanly consideration that I have received from every member of the police force has given a gleam of the bright side, else our work would all be on the dark side of life.

Of the sixty-six females that have been committed to my charge during the three months ending November 30th, 1893,

> Twenty-three paid fines and costs were discharged.
> Sixteen were committed to Providence County Jail.
> Sixteen have been lodgers.
> Three have been turned over to Agent Thurber of the S. P. C. C.[†]
> Three committed to Butler Insane Asylum.
> Two appealed to the Common Pleas division of the Supreme Court.

> *Mary A. Jenks,*
> *Police Matron*

---

*An East Indian fig tree with branches that send out roots to the ground.
[†]The Society for the Prevention of Cruelty to Children.

Matron's Report to Chief of Police

Year Ending October 1, 1898

The labor in this department has been but a repetition of the preceding years in which I have been in charge. If there is any change worthy of note, it is that fewer cases of what we call the "Old-timers" have been brought in, and not as many young girls, or girls under twenty. The majority of young girls have been brought in for protection or safe keeping. All boys under sixteen are placed in my care according to the law respecting juveniles. I find the same courteous co-operation and ready assistance from the superior officers, and in no wise have I ever had cause to think that a "police matron" was not duly appreciated by the entire force; as all are obliging, kind and forbearing, thus making my duties less arduous and wearing upon me. There is, however, some assistance solicited from the women of the W. C. T. U.* and other charitably inclined persons. Many of the women are brought in with tattered, bedraggled garments on, scarce enough to cover them. I cannot take them before the Court, until I have them decently clad. The city makes no appropriation for this need; therefore I must either supply from my own wardrobe—or buy. I have bought underwear, shoes, rubbers, stockings, shirtwaists, etc, to make them respectably clothed for their journey to the State institution, as this is not only in credit to the city I represent, but out of respect to the sex, and for humanity's sake. One cannot imagine the condition of some of these cases, unless they have witnessed them. If a few cast-off garments could be sent in for this purpose, it would not only save trouble but expense. Thirty-nine lost children have been brought in during the past year; some of them have been kept for half a day before they were claimed by their friends. These little ones must be fed, amused, tended, and quieted, requiring patience, tact and ability, to assure the little strangers that they have fallen into motherly hands. When once convinced of this fact, they are often reluctant to leave. A few pence to be spent for cookies, bananas, milk or crackers, would not come amiss; and we doubt not, there are childless parents in the city who would be glad to contribute to the needs along this line. 174 women and girls have been in my care this year. Of that number 19 have been "lodgers"; these are women who are travelling and looking for employment. Many of them are in very destitute circumstances, with scarce a decent garment on them. One old woman had but one shoe on, and on one foot had two stockings, both ragged and worn out, an old dress waist for underwear, and a thin, much worn black alpaca dress comprised her entire outfit when she came to the station to seek shelter for the night in a pouring rain last spring. After making her comfortable with food, rest and clothing, the next day she was sent to the Rescue Home in Providence, and from a letter received later from the matron, we learned that she proved herself worthy of our labor and expense.

Another line of work in this department, worthy of mention and solicitation, is the work leading to the S. P. C. C. Many times the little child whom we have in

---

*Women's Christian Temperance Union.

charge, has scarce a garment on that will cover them; especially is a little girl the most needy. These children have all to be taken to Providence. To make them comfortable or respectably clad, the matron has to go to her own resources.

With all the societies in the city whose aim and efforts are for charity and humanity's sake, it seems quite fitting that the police matron's work, ways and means, should be considered. While the drink habit is not on the increase among the women, the vice and immoral atmosphere is unchanged, as far as the "Matron's Record" of the past year shows. Therefore, there is no less duty, no fewer needs; and in fact new avenues of work are opening every day, that bring their own needs, as well as rewards. Though ours is often said to be a "thankless task," yet we would do it well, and wherein we have failed, it has been the fault of the head, and not the heart.

The laundry is still under my supervision. All articles are numbered when sent out, and renumbered when returned, and a book account kept of the same, so that not an article can be lost. All articles of bedding promptly repaired, as need requires, or new ones made if more necessary. I have made all the sheets, pillow cases and towels, that have been used in the station during my five years in office. There are eight beds, beside the accident beds, made up in the station. The care of the bedding is a small item; yet the neglect of it would mean much in the city's finances.

In all cases I have endeavored to alleviate suffering among the sick, insane or injured as they have been brought to my care.

My sincere thanks are due the officers and members of the department, for their courteous and kindly assistance, always so willingly rendered.

Respectfully submitted,
Mary A. Jenks, M.D.,
Police Matron

A Labor Organizer

LEONORA BARRY, 1888

Leonora Barry, "What the Knights of Labor Are Doing for Women," *Report of the International Council of Women, Assembled by the National Woman Suffrage Association* (Washington, DC: Rufus H. Darby, 1888), pp. 153–56.

The Knights of Labor (K of L), a labor organization started by Philadelphia tailors in 1869, grew rapidly in the early 1880s when it discarded its former policy of secrecy. During the 1880s, the K of L formed local assemblies that welcomed all types of working people, skilled and unskilled, save lawyers, bankers, and other alleged pawns of capitalism who, it was believed, did no productive work. The Knights also recruited women members, started women's assemblies, and welcomed women delegates to their conventions. Finally, they urged that women receive equal pay for equal work. This was the first "pay equity" demand made by an American labor organization. In 1886, the Knights set up a women's department. Leonora Barry (1849–1930), an Irish-born hosiery worker from upstate New York, led the new women's department until her retirement in 1890, when she married a fellow Knight. The women's department then capsized, as did, a few years later, the entire organization. Most of the K of L's female recruitment coincided with its period of decline, when the organization's membership and reputation dwindled.

During the late 1880s, Barry proved an impressive organizer. She formed new assemblies and lectured widely on women's issues. In 1888, Barry spoke to the International Council of Women, a gathering of representatives from many middle-class women's organizations. Addressing those "at the top of the ladder," Barry explained the Knights of Labor philosophy, her mission as a labor organizer, and her concern for the woman worker. Her speech follows.

What the Knights of Labor Are Doing for Women

The Knights of Labor are a body of men organized for protection and education, that they may be the better able to cope with the scheming means resorted to by those who live upon the proceeds of their toil, and subtract from labor so large a portion of labor's rights. The Knights of Labor were organized openly in 1879. For several years they existed in secrecy, because they feared that terrible weapon so unmercifully used upon the employees—the black list. Fearing that, they kept many years in secret; but after having become so compact and strong, after having the gospel of the Knights of Labor taught from Maine to Oregon, from the Atlantic to the Pacific, and over in the Old World, they then made known their aims, which were to abolish poverty, to demand that moral and industrial worth and not wealth be made the standard of national and individual greatness. Those poor working men, the tin-pail brigade, the seventy-two thousand miners of Pennsylvania, the hundreds and thousands of unskilled workmen, those people recognized what your legislators, what your pulpits, what your press have failed to recognize within all the years of your agitation—woman's right to equitable consideration by the side of men in the nation's government. Having recognized this, they inserted in the platform of principles that plank which demands equal pay for equal work; and ere many more years have passed over our heads, there will be another plank inserted not only in the platform of the Knights of Labor, but upon the statute-books of our country, making it a criminal offense for any man to dare employ a woman at less remuneration for labor than will enable her to procure the comforts of life without necessitating temptation to sin. The Knights of Labor are elevating the conditions of men; teaching them self-respect; their duty to themselves and each other. We are building around our working girls a wall of protection to defend them from the indignities which heretofore they have been subjected to, such as making the price of their honor the possibility of a place to earn their livelihood.

We are trying to teach the outside world that the working woman has feelings, has sensitiveness, has her heart's longings and desires for the better things of life, and any social or industrial system or environment that prevents woman from enjoying those gifts of a common Father must be broken, because it is utterly false. Any condition of society that prevents woman or child from cultivating the three elements of which humanity is composed—the moral, physical, and mental—that state of society is false, and it becomes the duty of every honest man and woman, I care not what their station in life, to try to overturn it. There are no better law supporters, no more loyal citizens true to the laws of their country and their country's flag than the organized working men and women of to-day. They do not demand revolution, but they do demand reform; they do not ask it by the power of physical force; they do not ask it by the destruction of life or property; they simply ask it at the hands of the law-making bodies of their nation. And as we, the people, are the law-making bodies, and those whom we send to the legislative halls are but our servants, we, the women in the Knights of Labor, are educating our men to know what the ballot means, not only for the working man, but for the working man's wife and sister.

Seven years ago I was left without knowledge of business, without knowledge of work, without knowledge of what the world was, with three fatherless children looking to me for bread. To support these children it became my duty to go out in the army of the employed and in one of the largest factories in central New York. I went, and for four years and seven months remained a factory woman for the support of my little ones. Four years ago this spring I became a Knight of Labor. I became a member of an assembly of 1,500 women. Of those 1,500 women from the withdrawing of what is called trades assembly—women of one particular trade or calling—I became the master workman of an assembly of 927 women, ranging from 14 years of age to 60. And let me say to you here that although there was not one amongst them could boast of more than a minor part of a common school education, yet in that body of women there was more executive ability, more tact, more shrewdness, more keen, calculating power than could be found in twice that number of men in the United States.

I was sent from my assembly, composed entirely of women, to the District Assembly, No. 65, which met in the city of Albany; from that district I was sent to Richmond, Va., a delegate to the General Assembly, and from there I was sent into the world to educate my sister working women and the public generally as to their needs and necessities. We are instituting co-operative industries throughout the breadth and length of our land—the industries in which women are engaged—taking those we find in the most helpless condition, and from becoming operatives in those factories they eventually become shareholders. In the city of Chicago, a tailoring establishment was started. A few girls were locked out because they went to a labor parade. It was a breach of discipline, but they did not deserve so severe a punishment. They came back, and by soliciting subscriptions by every means in their power they raised $400, with $100 of which they paid a month's rent and started with $300 capital. Inside of nine months those few men and women in that co-operative tailoring estab-lishment at 882 Fifth avenue, Chicago, Ill., have done $36,000 worth of business. We have our co-operative shirt factories in Baltimore and New York, conducted solely by women; we have our collar and cuff factories in Waterford, N. Y.; we have our co-operative knitting mill at Little Falls, N. Y., and many other industries. And I am at this time negotiating with Nashville, Tenn., for the institution of co-operative industry for the manufacture of women's and children's underwear, at which our poor unfortu-nate sisters in New York suffer more than can be imagined any human being might suffer under a slop-shop system of work in New York city.

I have, during my connection with the organization, instituted what is known as the Working Women's National Beneficial Fund. This gives to women in sickness not less than $3 nor more than $5 per week, and in case of death not less than $75 nor more than $100. It gives protection to every woman, whether she be a Knight of Labor or not, for it is the duty, the aim, and the object of Knights of Labor to elevate woman, no matter what her nationality, her creed, her color, or her position in life. The Knights of Labor are taking the little girls from the factory, the workshop, and the mines, and educating them, because we know that the little child of to-day is the mother of the future. As these are the children of to-day, and as these shall be the working women of the future, we demand that they shall be taken from the workshop, factory, and the mine and put into the schoolrooms to be educated. If there is any one State for which I might make a special plea it is that monopoly-bound State of Penn-sylvania, with her 125,000 children under the age of fifteen employed in the work-shops, factories and mines.

While you are looking to the literary attainments of these women*; while you are mounting to your position at the top of the ladder, do not, I ask you, in the name

---

*Delegates to the International Council of Women.

of justice, in the name of humanity, do not forget to give your attention and some of your assistance to the root of all evil, the industrial and social system that is so oppressive, which has wrought the chain of circumstances in which so many have become entangled, and which has brought the once tenderly-cherished and protected wife, the once fondly-loved mother to the position of the twelve or fourteen-hour toiler of to-day. If you would protect the wives and mothers of the future from this terrible condition we find these in to-day, give them your assistance. The Knights of Labor may have made mistakes, but they are the mistakes of those who started out with a dim knowledge of their object before their eyes and do not see their way clear to reach it, but by education and by help, the black list, the boycott, the strike, and the lock-out shall soon be swept away into the dark ages where they belong, and no longer be found under the stars and stripes of our American flag.

Chapter 14

College Women

E xpanding opportunity for higher education was the greatest advance
made by late nineteenth-century women. Between 1870 and 1900,
when the number of colleges doubled, the number of women students
skyrocketed. In 1870, only 11,000 women attended colleges and seminaries, mainly the latter. By 1900, 85,000 women students were enrolled in institutions of higher learning. From 1870 to 1900, the
proportion of women among college students leapt from twenty-one
percent to thirty-five percent. At the turn of the century, at least one
out of three college students was a woman.

The college-bound woman of the late nineteenth century could
choose among a variety of schools. At the outset, a majority of women
students flocked to the new women's colleges: Vassar, opened in 1865,
was followed by Smith and Wellesley (1875), Bryn Mawr (1885), and,
in 1888, Mount Holyoke, which gained collegiate status. Other single-
sex schools were established, too. By the 1890s, women also enrolled
in coordinate colleges like Barnard and Radcliffe, the "annexes" of
elite, all-male universities. Most women students of the 1890s, however, attended coeducational schools, especially those state institutions
that profited from the Morrill Land Grant Act of 1862. Between 1855
and 1870, the universities of Iowa, Wisconsin, Kansas, Indiana, Minnesota, Missouri, Michigan, and California welcomed women students. So did a range of private coeducational schools, from Oberlin
(founded in 1833; women admitted in 1837), Antioch (1852), and
Swarthmore (1864) to newcomers like Boston University (1873), Stan-
ford (1885), and the University of Chicago (1892).

Considering the degree of prejudice against women in the late
nineteenth century—based on their limited part in public life, their
exclusion from politics, the widespread anxiety about their role in the

work force, and the tacit belief that they had limited capacities—their rapid progress in higher education remains astounding. One explanation lies in academe's marginal status. Higher education was, at the time, a small albeit growing enterprise. Only one percent of college-age students attended college in 1870, for instance, and only four percent attended in 1900. Nor was the scholar's realm an especially prestigious one. Most professors lived in genteel poverty, had little influence, and were seen by others as forgetful bumblers. Higher education was also in a state of flux. Many questioned the utility of the classical college for *men*, and a range of competing institutions, like the land-grant colleges, sprang up. Under such chaotic circumstances, higher education was singularly vulnerable to female invasion. An early Vassar president put the case succinctly: "While education for men has outgrown the old college system, that for women has just grown up to it."

Women reacted to collegiate status with unbounded exuberance—no matter that Vassar regarded itself as an "experiment," or that state universities viewed the influx of coeds with suspicion. "Entering College was for me almost a Sacramental experience," declared reformer Florence Kelley, who attended Cornell in the 1870s. Pride ran especially high at the innovative women's schools, where, as Bryn Mawr president M. Carey Thomas explained, "Everything is done for the woman student." The founders of women's colleges hoped to prove that women could fulfill the highest academic requirements without losing their health, minds, or femininity. Women students, meanwhile, created a distinctive type of "college life," one that often fostered qualities associated with men—qualities such as leadership, independence, and self-confidence.

The rapid female invasion of higher learning did not go unchallenged. In 1873, Dr. Edward Clarke, a former professor at Harvard Medical School and a member of the Harvard Board of Overseers, launched a major attack. In his book, *Sex in Education*, Clarke contended that exposing young women to the rigors of a higher education intended for men overtaxed their capacities, drew blood away from the reproductive system, and thereby led to invalidism, mental collapse, infertility, and worse. Dr. Clarke's treatise evoked a hostile response. Students decried it, reformers denounced it, and women professionals refuted it. In a prize-winning essay of 1876, physician Mary Putnam Jacobi disproved some of Clarke's contentions; and the Association of Collegiate Alumnae, which surveyed women students in the 1880s, declared their health unimpaired by higher education.

Since growing numbers of women survived their college years without breakdowns, Dr. Clarke's alarmist cry soon faded. But the gist of his attack—that higher education for women had dire potential—resurfaced in the 1890s when a new threat arose: Higher education might not ruin women's health but it seemed to limit their chances of—or inclination toward—marriage. Surveys of women graduates all led to the same conclusions: Less than half of college alumnae married, and those who did so married later and tended to have fewer children. Marriage rates were lowest, moreover, among alumnae of the elite single-sex schools, whose academic standards were highest. To be sure, as researchers often explained, their samples were swollen by crowds of younger (and unmarried) alumnae, since colleges produced larger groups of women graduates each year. Moreover, as investigators pointed out, college men of the late nineteenth century seemed averse to marriage too; almost a quarter of Harvard and Yale graduates remained single. But the "marriage question" among college alumnae was a real one, and it revived the shadow that Dr. Clarke's treatise cast over education for women. Whether college caused infertility or decreased marriageability, it seemed to be abetting what was called "race suicide" among the educated classes. This fear would not be calmed until well into the twentieth century, when college populations again expanded exponentially.

A third response to female progress in higher education directly reflected its success. By the end of the century, enrollment of women students had increased so rapidly that they seemed to be feminizing the entire realm of academe. Here the coed was to blame. In the 1870s, most female students attended women's schools; after 1880, however, a majority enrolled in "mixed" schools; and by 1900, coeds outnumbered other women college students two to one. As the twentieth century began, so did a movement of backlash against the female invasion. Educators at universities feared that a large presence of women students would simultaneously repel male applicants and distract those who were already enrolled from serious endeavor. Such fears led to pressure for separatism in higher education, quotas on female admissions in coeducational schools, and the segregation of women students in universities in special programs and divisions. Meanwhile, psychologist G. Stanley Hall incited antipathy to women students in 1904, when he predicted that educated women would become "unwilling to accept the limitations of married life" and would become resentful of "the functions peculiar to their sex."

Yet, despite critics' continued attacks, the influx of women students, especially coeds, continued unabated and indeed accelerated. Advocates of women's education in the late nineteenth century had proved their original contentions: Women could meet the rigors of collegiate training, at whatever schools they chose to attend, without risk of collapse. When overstating the case, as did M. Carey Thomas, they might even claim that college women formed better marriages and raised healthier children. By 1900, the college alumna emerged as a leading "new woman" of the twentieth century.

Miss D. and Miss E.

EDWARD H. CLARKE, 1873

Edward H. Clarke, M.D., *Sex in Education; or, a Fair Chance for the Girls* (Boston: James R. Osgood and Co., 1873), pp. 78–87.

Supporters of college training for women were alarmed in 1872 when Dr. Edward Clarke, an eminent physician, declared that higher education posed grave dangers for young women students. Addressing a meeting of the Boston Women's City Club, Dr. Clarke contended that the rigors of higher learning threatened female reproductive capacity. Women's physiology, accordingly, limited their educational potential. Clarke explained his case more fully in 1873 in *Sex in Education*, in which he declared that "identical education of sexes is a crime before God and humanity." To subject women students to "the regimen of a college arranged for boys," would deprive their reproductive organs of nourishment and lead to a host of ailments, including "those grievous maladies which torture a woman's earthly existence: leuchorrhœa, amenorrhœa, dysmenorrhœa, chronic and acute ovaritus, prolapsus uturi, hysteria, neuralgia, and the like." If not turned into invalids, those young women exposed to the rigors of higher study would become masculine in nature and "hermaphrodite of mind." To prevent such disasters, Clarke recommended that women study one-third less than men, and not at all during menstruation, when complete rest was indicated.

   In support of his argument, Dr. Clarke offered the case studies of seven afflicted young women. The following excerpts concern two cases that aroused great controversy: that of Miss D., whose reproductive organs and health were ruined allegedly by four years at Vassar, and that of Miss E., a young woman of intellectual background, whose intense studies caused a wide range of ailments and led to her institutionalization.

Miss D—— entered Vassar College at the age of fourteen. Up to that age, she had been a healthy girl, judged by the standard of American girls. Her parents were apparently strong enough to yield her a fair dower of force. The catamenial function first showed signs of activity in her Sophomore Year, when she was fifteen years old.

Its appearance at this age[1] is confirmatory evidence of the normal state of her health at that period of her college career. Its commencement was normal, without pain or excess. She performed all her college duties regularly and steadily. She studied, recited, stood at the blackboard, walked, and went through her gymnastic exercises, from the beginning to the end of the term, just as boys do. Her account of her regimen there was so nearly that of a boy's regimen, that it would puzzle a physiologist to determine, from the account alone, whether the subject of it was male or female. She was an average scholar, who maintained a fair position in her class, not one of the anxious sort, that are ambitious of leading all the rest. Her first warning was fainting away, while exercising in the gymnasium, at a time when she should have been comparatively quiet, both mentally and physically. This warning was repeated several times, under the same circumstances. Finally she was compelled to renounce gymnastic exercises altogether. In her Junior Year, the organism's periodical function began to be performed with pain, moderate at first, but more and more severe with each returning month. When between seventeen and eighteen years old, dysmenorrhœa was established as the order of that function. Coincident with the appearance of pain, there was a diminution of excretion; and, as the former increased, the latter became more marked. In other respects she was well; and, in all respects, she appeared to be well to her companions and to the faculty of the college. She graduated before nineteen, with fair honors and a poor physique. The year succeeding her graduation was one of steadily-advancing invalidism. She was tortured for two or three days out of every month; and, for two or three days after each season of torture, was weak and miserable, so that about one sixth or fifth of her time was consumed in this way. The excretion from the blood, which had been gradually lessening, after a time substantially stopped, though a periodical effort to keep it up was made. She now suffered from what is called amenorrhœa. At the same time she became pale, hysterical, nervous in the ordinary sense, and almost constantly complained of headache. Physicians were applied to for aid: drugs were administered; travelling, with consequent change of air and scene, was undertaken; and all with little apparent avail. After this experience, she was brought to Boston for advice, when the writer first saw her, and learned all these details. She presented no evidence of local uterine congestion, inflammation, ulceration, or displacement. The evidence was altogether in favor of an arrest of the development of the reproductive apparatus, at a stage when the development was nearly complete. Confirmatory proof of such an arrest was found in examining her breast, where the milliner had supplied the organs Nature should have grown. It is unnecessary for our present purpose to detail what treatment was advised. It is sufficient to say, that she probably never will become physically what she would have been had her education [been] physiologically guided.

This case needs very little comment: its teachings are obvious. Miss D——— went to college in good physical condition. During the four years of her college life, her parents and the college faculty required her to get what is popularly called an

---

[1]It appears, from the researches of Mr. Whitehead on this point, that an examination of four thousand cases gave fifteen years six and three-quarter months as the average age in England for the appearance of the catamenia. —WHITEHEAD, *on Abortion, &c.*

education. Nature required her, during the same period, to build and put in working-order a large and complicated reproductive mechanism, a matter that is popularly ignored—shoved out of sight like a disgrace. She naturally obeyed the requirements of the faculty, which she could see, rather than the requirements of the mechanism within her, that she could not see. Subjected to the college regimen, she worked four years in getting a liberal education. Her way of work was sustained and continuous, and out of harmony with the rhythmical periodicity of the female organization. The stream of vital and constructive force evolved within her was turned steadily to the brain, and away from the ovaries and their accessories. The result of this sort of education was, that these last-mentioned organs, deprived of sufficient opportunity and nutriment, first began to perform their functions with pain, a warning of error that was unheeded; then, to cease to grow[2]; next, to set up once a month a grumbling torture that made life miserable; and, lastly, the brain and the whole nervous system, disturbed, in obedience to the law, that, if one member suffers, all the members suffer, became neuralgic and hysterical. And so Miss D—— spent the few years next succeeding her graduation in conflict with dysmenorrhœa, headache, neuralgia, and hysteria. Her parents marvelled at her ill-health; and she furnished another text for the often-repeated sermon on the delicacy of American girls.

It may not be unprofitable to give the history of one more case of this sort. Miss E—— had an hereditary right to a good brain and to the best cultivation of it. Her father was one of our ripest and broadest American scholars, and her mother one of our most accomplished American women. They both enjoyed excellent health. Their daughter had a literary training—an intellectual, moral, and æsthetic half of education, such as their supervision would be likely to give, and one that few young men of her age receive. Her health did not seem to suffer at first. She studied, recited, walked, worked, stood, and the like, in the steady and sustained way that is normal to the male organization. She *seemed* to evolve force enough to acquire a number of languages, to become familiar with the natural sciences, to take hold of philosophy and mathematics, and to keep in good physical case while doing all this. At the age of twenty-one she might have been presented to the public, on Commencement Day, by the president of Vassar College or of Antioch College or of Michigan University, as the wished-for result of American liberal female culture. Just at this time, however, the catamenial function began to show signs of failure of power. No severe or even moderate illness overtook her. She was subjected to no unusual strain. She was only following the regimen of continued and sustained work, regardless of Nature's periodical demands for a portion of her time and force, when, without any apparent cause, the failure of power was manifested by moderate dysmenorrhœa and diminished excretion. Soon after this the function ceased altogether; and up to this present

---

[2] The arrest of development of the uterus, in connection with amenorrhœa, is sometimes very marked. In the New York Medical Journal for June, 1873, three such cases are recorded, that came under the eye of those excellent observers, Dr. E. R. Peaslee and Dr. T. G. Thomas. In one of these cases, the uterine cavity measured one and a half inches; in another, one and seven-eighths inches; and, in a third, one and a quarter inches. Recollecting that the normal measurement is from two and a half to three inches, it appears that the arrest of development in these cases occurred when the uterus was half or less than half grown. Liberal education should avoid such errors.

writing, a period of six or eight years, it has shown no more signs of activity than an amputated arm. In the course of a year or so after the cessation of the function, her head began to trouble her. First there was headache, then a frequent congested condition, which she described as a "rush of blood" to her head; and, by and by, vagaries and forebodings and despondent feelings began to crop out. Coincident with this mental state, her skin became rough and coarse, and an inveterate acne covered her face. She retained her appetite, ability to exercise and sleep. A careful local examination of the pelvic organs, by an expert, disclosed no lesion or displacement there, no ovaritis or other inflammation. Appropriate treatment faithfully persevered in was unsuccessful in recovering the lost function. I was finally obliged to consign her to an asylum.

Sex in Education *Attacked*

JULIA WARD HOWE ET AL., 1874

Julia Ward Howe, ed., *Sex and Education: A Reply to Dr. E. H. Clarke's* Sex in Education (Cambridge, MA: Roberts Brothers, 1874), pp. 14–16, 27–29, 34, 45–51, 197–99.

Dr. Clarke's attack unleashed a storm of rebuttal. Opponents at once contributed their denunciations to *A Reply*, edited by Julia Ward Howe and to which were appended testimonials from many colleges with evidence that Clarke was wrong. Dr. Clarke's detractors usually accepted at least one of his contentions—that evolution had led to "differentiation" between the sexes. But they rejected his argument that women's capacity for higher learning was thereby decreased. Instead, they asserted (among other arguments), that Dr. Clarke's evidence was faulty, that the physical damage inflicted by intense social life and improper clothing exceeded that imposed by study, and that women college students were supremely healthy. Overall, it is probable that the implicit accusation against Dr. Clarke was one of misogyny; some of his critics almost stated such a charge. He seemed to harbor both dislike of, and contempt for, women.

The following selections from the replies to Dr. Clarke were written by editor Julia Ward Howe (1819–1910), well-known author, clubwoman, and suffragist; liberal minister and reformer Thomas Wentworth Higginson (1823–1911), an advocate of woman suffrage and coeducation; and pioneer Universalist minister Olympia Brown (1835–1926), a graduate of Antioch.

Julia Ward Howe

Dr. Clarke supports his side of the argument by a statement of facts insufficient for his purpose, and by reasonings and inferences irrelevant to the true lesson of these facts. He makes in the first place a strange confusion between things present, past, and future, and in the terror of the identical education to come sees identical education of the sexes in the past and present as the cause of all the ills that female flesh is heir to. He asserts the fact of an ascertained and ever increasing deterioration in the persons of American women from the true womanly standard. He finds them tending ever more and more towards a monstrous type, sterile and sexless; and these facts, which some of us may strongly doubt, he considers accounted for by the corresponding fact that boys and girls receive the same intellectual education. According to him, you cannot feed a woman's brain without starving her body. Brain and body are set in antagonism over against each other, and what is one organ's meat is another's poison. . . .

The Doctor's prognosis is even more dismal and unpromising. Open the doors of your colleges to women, and you will accomplish the ruin of the Commonwealth. Disease—already, according to him, the rule among them—will become without exception. Your girls will lose their physical stature, and your boys their mental stature, since the tasks set for the latter would be limited by the periodical disability of the girls. The result will be a physical and sexual chaos, out of which the Doctor sees no escape. . . .

It may occur to some that the assumed identity of the intellectual education given to girls and boys in America may have less to do with the ill-health of the former than the dissimilarity of their physical training. Boys are much in the open air. Girls are much in the house. Boys wear a dress which follows and allows their natural movements. Girls wear clothes which impede and almost paralyze their limbs. Boys have, moreover, the healthful hope held out to them of being able to pursue their own objects, and to choose and follow the business or profession of their choice. Girls have the dispiriting prospect of a secondary and derivative existence, with only so much room allowed them as may not cramp the full sweep of the other sex. The circumstances first named directly affect health, the last exerts a strong reflex action upon it. "We are only women, and it does not matter," passes from mother to daughter. A very estimable young lady said to me the other day, in answer to a plea for dress-reform, "It is better to look handsome, even if it does shorten life a little." Her care of herself probably does not go beyond that indicated by this saying. Dr. Clarke cites a few instances of functional derangement. But by far the most frequent difficulty with our women arises from uterine displacement, and this in turn comes partly from the utter disuse of the muscles which should keep the uterus in place, but which are kept inactive by the corset, weighed upon by the heavy skirt, and drawn upon by the violent and unnatural motion of the dancing at present in vogue. Is it any wonder that these ill-educated, over-burthened muscles give way, like other ill-trained, overpowered things? Some instances of remarkable robustness in women have been the result of a physical education identical with that usually given to boys. In these cases, the parents, after repeated losses of children through much cherishing, have at last determined to give the girls a chance through athletic sports and unrestricted exercise in the open air. And this has again and again proved successful.

Much in Dr. Clarke's treatment of his subject is objectionable. We are left in doubt whether his book was written for men or for women, and we conclude that his method of statement is not good for either.

Thomas Wentworth Higginson

I have visited Vassar College, where I found a good deal of dissatisfaction to exist among the authorities, over one of those five cases, as stated by Dr. Clarke. He mentions a certain Miss D. who entered Vassar College at fourteen. The President and the Resident Physician assured me that no pupil had ever entered that institution at that age. Dr. Clarke says of this young lady that "she studied, recited, stood at the blackboard, walked, and went through her gymnastic exercises, from the beginning to the end of the term, just as boys do." The same authorities told me that this statement, taken as a whole, was an absolute untruth; the gymnastic exercises being absolutely forbidden to the students at certain periods, and the greatest care being enjoined upon them in all respects. The President and the Resident Physician also expressed some surprise that, in a case of such importance, their testimony should not have been at least called for, instead of relying solely on that of the patient. I believe that it is customary among physicians to show some consideration or courtesy to each other in such matters, before putting cases in print which seem to reflect on the professional fidelity of any one. Be this as it may, this denial of fundamental facts leaves this instance at least open to suspicion; and reduces Dr. Clarke's yet undisputed cases of injury to the health of girls, through schooling, to four.

But suppose the instances were four thousand. Grant all his premises. What is his conclusion? All that he demands of an educational establishment for girls is that "the organization of studies and instruction must be flexible enough to admit of the periodical and temporary absence of each pupil, without loss of rank, or necessity of making up work, from recitation and exercise of all sorts." And yet he goes on to declare that for Harvard College, for instance, to adapt itself for the introduction of young women, would be a thing so enormously difficult that it would cost two millions of dollars!

This is what is so inexplicable to me in the conclusions of the book. Grant all Dr. Clarke's facts, and all his demands—what follows? Of course, in that case, those grammar schools and high schools to which girls are admitted must be essentially remodelled. These I waive. But, so far as our leading colleges are concerned—and Harvard in particular—I not only do not see why the remodelling for the admission of women should cost two millions, but I do not see why it should cost a cent. I do not see, indeed, why there is needed at Harvard any remodelling at all: only a quiet carrying out of what is already the marked tendency in that institution—to substitute elective for required studies, voluntary attendance on exercises for required atten- dance, and examinations as tests of scholarship in place of daily marks. Surely it cannot have escaped Dr. Clarke's notice that if he were having Harvard College arranged on purpose to suit girls, according to his formula just quoted, it could hardly be done by a more effectual process than is actually going on at this moment, without any reference to women at all. If this be so, why not extend this new system to women and let them have the benefit of it?

When Dr. Clarke and I were in Harvard College, every absence from daily prayers or recitation counted as an offence. Now each student is allowed sixty ab- sences from prayers—almost one-fourth of the whole number—and no questions are asked until that number is exceeded. Then almost all rank turned on marks given at the daily recitation. Now there are departments in which no daily marks are given, and the question of scholarship is determined by occasional examinations. To these, it would seem, Dr. Clarke does not object, for he says "it is easy to frame a theoretical emulation, in which results only are compared and tested, that would be healthy and invigorating." Yet such emulation as this is all that seems likely to be left at Harvard in the way of dangerous rivalry, when the present system shall have been fully developed. "The steady, untiring, day-by-day competition" that Dr. Clarke deprecates is being utterly laid aside; and a more flexible system is being introduced for young men, which turns out to have also the incidental advantage of being precisely what young women need.

It is a valuable discovery that, the more you transform a college into a University, the better it is adapted for both sexes. . . .

Nor do I see why, even if we admit all Dr. Clarke's facts, he has given a single valid reason why our colleges should not admit girls to-morrow—making, as many of them have already made on other grounds, the necessary changes to secure sufficient flexibility of system.

It therefore seems to me that, as his facts are not worked out with sufficient thoroughness to justify any general conclusions whatever, so his conclusion that our present colleges, and particularly Harvard College, cannot, except at a vast expense, admit women, is utterly unsustained by his facts.

Reverend Olympia Brown

All the time I was at Antioch College I never heard of a young lady in the college requiring a physician's advice. Among the seven girls in my class I never remember an instance of illness: they were always at recitations, and always had their lessons. I spent four years at Antioch—two at the theological school; and I have been over ten years a settled pastor, and I never yet was absent from an engagement or suspended labor on account of sickness. When in Kansas, I spoke every day from the first of July to the fifth of November, besides travelling to my appointments each day, some days giving two lectures and preaching Sundays, making in all two hundred and five speeches, averaging more than an hour in length, and came home just as well as I went; and this moment I am as well as ever, and could walk ten miles a day with ease. To me such statements as Dr. Clarke's seem absurd, and contrary to everybody's experience. . . .

The ill-health of the women of our time is not due to study or regularity in study: it is due to the want of regularity, and want of aim and purpose, and want of discipline. If you should take the whole number of women in this country who have graduated from a regular college with men, and place them side by side with the same number of women who have not had that course of study, select them where you will, the college graduates will be stronger in mind and body, able to endure more and work harder than the others. This I am sure of, as I am acquainted with many of the somewhat small number of women graduates; and I know something of other women, having belonged to various female seminaries at different times.

A Debate over Coeducation

OLIVE ANDERSON, 1878

Olive Anderson, *An American Girl and Her Four Years at a Boy's College* (New York: Appleton & Co., 1878), pp. 120–21, 129–36.

Among those who accepted women's capacity for college training, a new question loomed: What setting was most appropriate for the female "experiment" in higher learning? Should women attend single-sex colleges or coeducational ones? Each had its defenders. Advocates of coeducation, male and female, argued that the "mixed" school provided the healthiest setting for students of both sexes, and that coeducation would improve relations between the sexes. But since women were excluded from the elite male colleges, defenders of the single-sex college hardly needed an argument. Not only did the women's college cater to the female student, but educated women had a vested interest in it: The single-sex school provided a prestigious place under women's control, as well as opportunities for women academics.

In the following chapter from an autobiographical novel of 1878, two college students of the 1870s—a young woman at a coeducational university and her friend at Vassar—compare their experiences. Although they disagree on the ideal mode of education for women, the two young women students agree on the irrelevance of Dr. Clarke's concerns. Author Olive Anderson was an 1875 graduate of the University of Michigan, where women had been admitted since 1870. Presumably, it is her alma mater that is represented in her novel as "Ortonville." And, presumably, the lively protagonist, Wilhelmine, or "Will," represents the author. Will's college class is made up of 150 boys and seven girls.

Ortonville versus Vassar

Ortonville, February 24, 187——

Dear Mame:

You have asked me, ever since I came here, to write you a descriptive letter telling all about the university, the professors, the boys and girls, and so on. I've never found time to do it until now, so here goes. I must begin with our faculty, of course, as they are the crowning glory of the whole, and may Jove hurl one of his ever-ready thunder-bolts at me if I do not deal justly with them! There are more than forty men in our faculty, including our president, senior professors, assistant professors, emeritus professors, and "toots," as the boys call them. Our Prex's name is Hannaford, and we all dote on him. It is a hard position to fill, that of president of an institution of this size. He has to be all things to all men, and to women, too, now, under the new dispensation. He is a perfect Chrysostom in eloquence, and the baccalaureate addresses delivered by him will be long remembered by the classes who heard them. To be sure, our class owes him a little grudge for expelling one of our boys for hazing, but then we know it was just, for he almost killed a freshman by holding him under the pump one freezing night, so that he had convulsions and meningitis afterward. Then comes lovely Prof. Atkins, who occupies the chair of Latin Language and Literature. There is an air of refinement and culture about his every movement, and in every line of his sensitive face. He has spent many years in Europe, and is as familiar with the city on the Tiber as with his own native town. There is some talk of his resigning, on account of poor health, while young Prof. Lathrop will take his place; he is engaged to Prof. Atkins's daughter, and bids fair to become a giant in the world of learning. Dear, old, sour Prof. Borck comes next, who is our exponent of Greek language and customs. His sourness is mostly on the outside, for under his frowning exterior there beats a heart as tender as a woman's. They say he has domestic trouble. Poor man! Do you notice that many of our great men are unfortunate in their selection of companions for life? . . .

[The letter writer devotes considerable space to descriptions of her professors. Most, she claims, are harmless, lovable gentlemen with esoteric interests who seem well-suited to the noncompetitive haven of academic life.]

Now, you wanted to know about the boys—whether they pay us much attention. You old girl, don't I know what a flirt you are? What clover you would be in here, where there are thirty boys for every girl! Well, I'll just tell you that you could not carry on many flirtations, and keep up your standing in class too. Some of the girls tried it, but found they must give up one or the other; and, with remarkable good sense, they chose their books instead of the boys. Yet, from the way the wind blows, I should not wonder if one or two matches were made in our class. Well, what could be more natural and fitting? Where can men and women learn to know each other better than by reciting in the same classes? Why did not your father let you come here with me, instead of sending you off to an old boarding-school, where you don't see a fellow once a month, and are always watched by some old corridor-spy?

I never could stand such a system of espionage as that, and would, no doubt, be expelled before one term was out; while here, where we have the most unbounded liberty, I am a pattern of decorum.

I see that you shy at the word "club," and say some pretty things about home-life, and I want to set you right on one or two points. I have not tried club-life yet, though I expect to next year; but I know what it is from those who have tried it. It is simply this: a company of students, boys and girls, club together and get a woman to cook for them, and have a steward to attend to marketing. In this way they can make their expenses as much or little as they choose. It is just going out to meals. Next year we will have our rooms at Mr. Lewis's, just the same, but they cannot board us, so we are going to club it. We have the best motherly woman to cook for us, and our company is very select—made up of boys from our class (the best ones, of course), ourselves, and some freshman girls. That is a great beauty of clubbing; you admit those only whom you want, and make your club just like a family. The only difference between your table and ours is, that instead of a lot of girls, with a pair of spectacles at each end of the table looking to see that you eat what is digestible, and that you behave decorously in the mean time, we have a jolly set of girls and boys, and flatter ourselves that we behave a great deal better than if some one were watching us. You want to know, then, what I would have in place of boarding-schools for girls. I would have the girls distributed around into as many good families where it is taken for granted that they will conduct themselves properly without surveillance, and have the college provide for nothing but their intellectual wants. For those who cannot stand such liberty, if they must be sent from home to learn something, I'd send them to the house of correction. But I am growing too didactic, and I hope you will not consider my comparisons odious, since you asked for everything in full. You ask if all the boys are reconciled to our being here yet? Most of them, I think, are willing, now that we are really established, to "give the thing a trial." It is very amusing to hear a boy of nineteen or twenty years define woman's sphere, and mark the line which she shall walk or ought to walk.

Boys know a great deal from fifteen to twenty-one. Of course, the boys here do a great many silly things for our benefit—for example: when we have experiments in physics, the room is often darkened, so that there is not a ray of light for some minutes; then some boy makes the sound of a loud kiss, which will pass round the room. It is suggestive, but harmless; so we pay no attention to it. They do lots of outlandish things, and go to a great deal of trouble to tear up sidewalks and move gates, and, don't you think, one day they managed to get a live donkey up-stairs and set him on the platform in the chapel, and, when we came to prayers, he stood looking over the Bible as solemn as if he were reading a funeral-service instead of eating the hay they provided for him. It is the Fresh and Sophs who do such things. Juniors and Seniors are too elegant and dignified to engage in that kind of sport, and they generally have flirtations enough on hand, with the girls in the city, to occupy their extra time. You want to know if there are still "disagreeable" things that we have to encounter. We have outlived the most of them, I guess. There is one disagreeable thing, though, that I must speak of. I hope that, before I have a daughter old enough to go to college, they will have expunged from the classical course some of the selections from authors to which they now cling, and it will be well for them to use a little carbolic acid as a disinfectant in the process. I know they say people ought to be pure-minded enough to read those things and still not have any definite idea of wrong suggested by them; but I want to know where the good is in trailing classes along, year after year, through the indelicate thoughts of certain authors because they are considered good examples of the idiomatic use of the language when there are plenty of other selections that might be taken, and that would illustrate just as well.

Now, my dear, if you will pardon this ridiculously long letter, you will give an illustration of your usual amiability. If you do not have time to read it all at one sitting, you can keep it by you for light reading. Tell me all about your life there at Vassar, and forgive me if I have been too hard on boarding-schools, but I can't believe in any of your one-sided institutions, Matthew Vassar to the contrary notwithstanding. Write to me very soon, and believe me, ever yours,

Wilhelmine Elliot

P. S.—What do you think of Dr. Clarke's book? The way he makes you Vassar girls faint and lop around on all occasions is perfectly funny. In my opinion he makes a great ado about nothing, and fails to hit the point. "It's flat burglary, and I [am going] to prove it."

W. E.

Vassar College, March 15, 187——

My Dear Will:

I received your splendid long letter more than two weeks ago. If it were any person but you, I vow I would resent some of the things you said, but you always have a way of saying what you please, and everybody lets you. Some of your assertions are based on ignorance; therefore you are, to an extent, excusable; for, when you speak of this institution as nothing more than a "boarding-school," it simply shows that you know nothing about it.

Your theory about having the girls put out in families to board might be a good one, but it is exceedingly unpractical. You are so carried away, dear, with the idea of co-education that you only see one side. Well, you know that I never was radical in anything, and least of all on this subject. I do not believe in mixed schools, for, as you yourself admit, both the boys and girls might be tempted to neglect their work by being together. For all you protest that you are a "pattern of decorum," I can't imagine it; and I doubt not a little judicious watching would be good for you.

But we are as free here as it is possible to be in an institution of the kind. I'd like to see you put four hundred girls together, and leave no particular rules and no one in particular to see that they behave! I would not trust even "patterns of decorum" in such a case. Oh, no; with all your fine talk you cannot make me believe in your precious hobby. You can't make me believe that it is a good thing for a few stray girls to be mixed up with such a tremendous crowd of boys as you have there, and the unequal proportion will exist for a long time, and maybe always. Their "refining influence upon the ruder sex" is purchased at too great a cost to themselves. How preposterous to think of seven girls in a class of one hundred and fifty boys! As to the competition between the male and female mind being the best incentive to study, that, again, is all talk, for you can't find more competition and enthusiasm in study than we have here among the girls. Again, you say that, since we have to live all our lives with them, it is absurd to be separated in education.

Bless me! that's just an argument in favor of one-sided institutions, as you are pleased to term them; when we are destined inevitably by the Fates to eat three meals a day with some John, George, or Thomas, the four years of college when we see nothing of them ought to be counted clear gain, and I prefer to put off the comparison of the relative merits of the male and female intellect until my education is finished. I'm glad to be informed about "clubs," though I can't help shivering a little at the word yet, but hope to get over it.

I feel tolerably safe about you now; but at one time I expected to hear that you girls at Ortonville were playing foot and base ball, hazing freshmen, and engaging in other manly sports. I'm glad there is one thing we can agree on—Dr. Clarke's book. A lady-physician, who lectured for us the other night, said that he had drawn very sweeping conclusions from very narrow premises, and that most of the evil he lays at the door of the school could better be traced to the improper training and habits of young children; in other words, that it is in the nursery where the foundations are laid for failing health in womanhood. I don't dare to say a word to the folks at home, though, against Dr. Clarke; for, you know, he was our family physician when we lived in Boston, and mother and Aunt Jane swear by him in everything.

Don't stop telling me things because I scold you, for that is one of my privileges.

Ever your loving friend,
Mary Palmer

A College Romance

M. CAREY THOMAS, 1877

Marjorie Housepian Dobkin, *The Making of a Feminist: Early Journals and Letters of M. Carey Thomas* (Kent, OH: Kent State University Press, 1979), pp. 116–19.

During the 1870s, concern arose over the intense, demonstrative, and romantic friendships that might evolve between young women at single-sex boarding schools and colleges. Such "smashes" might occur as well in the early coeducational setting, where women students were few and depended upon other women for company. This was the experience of Martha Carey Thomas (1857–1935), who attended Cornell from 1875 to 1877. Thomas's social predicament at Cornell was unusual, since her Quaker parents told her to avoid "all company among the gentlemen," and to stay away from college events, such as dances. On occasion, Thomas complained about this "sacrifice" ("I stand *absolutely alone*"). But she seemed to comply with her parents' wishes, obligingly "barricaded" herself from male company, and counted on what few women students there were for friendship and affection. In her journal entries at graduation time, Thomas summed up her Cornell experience and her major romantic friendship with a "Miss Hicks."

In 1884, M. Carey Thomas became the first dean of Bryn Mawr College, and a decade later its president, a post she held until 1922. The forthright, outspoken style that characterized her later speeches and essays is evident in the journal entries of her youth.

June 12, 1877

Sage College, Cornell University. It is almost two years since I have made an entry. I have now finished all my senior examinations and have nothing to do for the next nine days except wait for my degree. . . .

At last the object of my ambition—the one purpose that runs through my journals has been attained. I have graduated at a university. I have a degree that represents more than a Vassar one.

I wish I had kept a slight, at least, record of my experience here and now it is too late to recall it. The first two years I had a difficult time to get into the new methods of study and especially in Latin I entered behind.

Altogether I have learned a great deal and it has been thoroughly profitable to be here—it has given me a new outlook. Though I feel very far from a good Latin and

Greek scholar, yet I do see light somewhat. My life here has been very hermit like, except seven girls. I have seen very few people, half the men here are uncultivated and Cornell misses all that glorious culture that one reads of in college books. The girls are for the most part of a different social station and I have seen very little of them as they have nothing to counterbalance that fact.

I want to write about my fifth friendship, for in spite of myself I have one. When I came here I made up my mind that at Howland I had wasted a great deal of time with friends and that it amounted to very little except pleasure and that especially away from home the pain of being separated more than overbalanced the other.

The first girl I saw was a young lady in Algebra examination—lace-dressed, in gray with a brown hat with a wing in it. She was up at Pres. White's to tea and we had a little talk. I thought she was smart and well prepared in the examinations next day. I "rather hoped" I should see her again next fall. Next fall came—she was the first person I saw as I drove up to the Sage College. Her mother was with her and together we chose our rooms on the same corridor third hall. Miss Mills was to room with Miss Hicks and would not unpack until she had heard from her examinations. Miss Putnam whom I had met at Prof. Russel's chose a room on the same floor. It was lonely at first—my only consolation was going down to Howland every other Friday and seeing Carrie [Ladd]. At first I rather looked down on the girls in our hall. Miss Hicks, Miss Putnam, Miss Mills, Miss Head and Miss Mitchell—they seemed more interested in fun than anything else. And not one of them was smart except Miss Hicks; the other girls in the Sage were good enough students but not ladies, and the gentlemen, except Prof. Boyesen, were second rate, "half cut" Bessie would say.

Well, I began to see more and more of Miss Hicks. She got in the habit of coming and reading me her mother's letters and of bidding me good night. We used to go and study some time in Casquadilla woods and when it would get dark we would sit under her blue shawl and talk. Then we came across Swinburne's "Atalanta in Calydon" and Miss Hicks would come in her wrapper after I was in bed and we would read it out loud and we learned several of the choruses. One night we had stopped reading later than usual and obeying a sudden impulse I turned to her and asked, "Do you love me?" She threw her arms around me and whispered, "I love you passionately." She did not go home that night and we talked and talked. She told me she had been praying that I might care for her.

That was the beginning and from that time, it was the fall of '75, till June '77 we have been inseparable. I put this all down because I cannot understand it. I am sure it is not best for people to care about each other so much. In the first place it wasted my time—it was a pleasure to be with Miss Hicks and as I cared to be with no one else, I would have spent all that time in reading. It was different with her—as she likes a great many people and liked the other girls and would have wasted her time anyway. In the second place it was almost more pain than pleasure because we quarreled so. All our ideas were opposite. Miss Hicks' mother I think is rising in society and there is not the least bit of fastidiousness in Miss Hicks' nature. She likes everyone. She cares for everyone's opinion. She would do a great many things I did not think suitable. I would object and say more than I ought to and Miss Hicks would fling herself on the lounge in a passion of tears and sometimes we would both cry— altogether it was dreadful—yet all the time we cared about each other so much that we could not give up our friendship. Again and again we gave up in despair and then we would care and have such lovely times that we began again and the whole thing was over again. Often I prayed that I might stop loving her.

This high tragedy seems ridiculous written but I know I shall forget the possibility of such things unless I do. It seems rather too bad when one goes to college to study to be distracted by such things. It was not Miss Hicks' fault but I know I did not study as well because of her, but I could not help it. I was mastered by it—one thing that made our friendship as unpleasant as it sometimes was was my feeling that I ought not to give way to it. Miss Hicks has no generous abandon in study—her companionship did not help me, I think, in an intellectual way. I tell her she ought to be obliged to me. I taught her to love passionately and to be passionately angry. Neither of which she had experienced before.

She is lovely in many ways. She has a sweet simplicity and straightforwardness about her, an utter faithfulness—I would trust her absolutely with any secret—she is naturally very smart but I think, at least until she came to Cornell, she studies because she had nothing else to do and because of her love of approbation. She wants to be an architect and seems very fond of it but I do not feel as if she would make a success. She seems to me to be easily turned aside by people. It is hard to talk to her—I never feel except when she is angry as if she were really saying what she feels with all her heart. In her manners she wants a certain quiet self assurance. I think she will probably get married. These are almost all unfavorable things but I leave out all her prettiness and her traits of character that attract me—in fact I just fell in love with her and I did it gradually too (not that adoring worship I had for Libbie [Conkey], nor the equal fun and earnest loving devoted friendship Carrie and I have) but, that Atalanta night I knew I did not care as much as she did and so it went on, I getting fonder and fonder of her until it was as I say—all the time against my better judgment and yet I cannot tell why it was. She is lovely, in many many ways much better than I am.

A Father's Advice

WILLIAM BRECKINRIDGE, 1884–1885

Sophonisba Preston Breckinridge Papers, Library of Congress, published in Helen Lefkowitz Horowitz, "With More Love Than I Can Write: A Nineteenth Century Father to His Daughter," *Wellesley* 65 (Fall 1980), pp. 16–20.

According to members of the first generation of women college students, many derived inspiration and support from their mothers—who often were women of ambition, talent, and academy training. Fathers, however, may also have been important. When Sophonisba Breckinridge (1866–1948) of Lexington, Kentucky, entered Wellesley in 1884, her mother sent her news from home, but her father took a more active role in her college experience. William Breckinridge, a former Confederate colonel, was a lawyer and soon-to-be congressman. Devoted to his gifted daughter, he sent letters full of solicitous advice, ardent admiration, and high expectations.

After her graduation from Wellesley in 1888, Sophonisba Breckinridge had an illustrious career. She studied law with her father, was admitted to the Kentucky Bar, received a Ph.D. in Political Science in 1901 and a J.D. in law in 1904 from the University of Chicago, worked as a resident at the Hull House settlement, participated in the founding of the Graduate School of Social Service Administration at the University of Chicago, and became a leading figure in the emerging field of social work.* The following letters from her father were written during her freshman year, 1884–1885, as she sought to adjust to college life and, later, to win the post of president of her class.

Sept. 20, 1884

We are sorry that you are so home-sick. I feared it very much. You have been tenderly reared & always treated with rather peculiar & affectionate esteem. Dutiful, loving & unselfish; you were appreciated & perhaps a little spoilt in our not very large circle. At Wellesley you are but one of five hundred—a new, unknown one at that, from a distant state, &, so far as Wellesley is concerned, an uninfluential connection.

---

*For the career of Sophonisba Breckinridge, see Ellen Fitzpatrick, *Endless Crusade: Women Social Scientists and Progressive Reform* (New York: Oxford University Press, 1990).

However kind & pleasant every one may be—the difference is immense; & you will continue to feel it in a certain degree. When you establish for yourself—as you will—your own position; this will diminish.

It is a double & a very hard lesson you are unconsciously learning—the individual insignificance of each of us when put out of our circle & our own peculiar surroundings; and the difference between our home, & any place else. I dreaded this for you— far more than I ever told you; for I knew that you could not appreciate & would not understand my fear; and as you had your heart set on going & had been good & dutiful; I yielded to your wishes. But now that you are there, my darling girl; you must conquer. We miss you very much. . . .

With more love than I can put in words.

Your Father
Wm C.P. Breckinridge

Oct. 8, 1884

It is sometimes sad to think how the years separate families and weaken if not destroy these tender ties. And at times it is a little gloomy to me that we have three absent children who are forming new ties that are absolutely dissimilar. One of the best results of education at home is common friends—that all the members of a family have in a certain sense mutual friendships & common associations. It has been both a great pleasure & I think a source of real strength that my ties & friendships have been at home—educated wholly in Kentucky schools, serving in the war with Kentucky troops & living in Kentucky—I have inherited the old friendships & created new ones. This you & Desha [Sophonisba's brother] may either lose or have in impaired strength; & I doubt if what you gain compensates for this.

Your Sunday letter has given us great joy as it shows you are happy as well as at work; & your letters are very pleasant in that they tell us all about yourself & your work & your school-mates.

I trust you will like Chemistry & the sciences. I have a notion that in Chemistry & its cognate sciences—such as pharmacy—& in electricity, botany & such sciences there is a great field of profitable & honorable work for women—less onerous & more attractive than the needle, the school-room & the store—but I am not going to inflict another essay on you to-day.

Goodbye—my precious girl—

Your Father
Wm C.P. Breckinridge

Dec. 12, 1884

I wrote to you to let me know what money you would need for your stay in Boston. Make it as pleasant & profitable as you can. See the libraries, museums, galleries & stores; & become as familiar as in so short a time is practicable with Boston. The most wonderful thing in a Great City is the City itself—this is always a marvel to me. The rows of houses; the endless variety of house, business & store; the tide of people

& ever changing scene with yet unchanging surroundings. Boston is in & of itself worth a study, & ten days or two weeks spent in it with persons who are pleasant companions & know the city ought to be more profitable than any two weeks of school.

While we will miss you—how it will be Xmas without you I cannot imagine—it will gratify us to know that you are enjoying your holiday. And my daughter please don't spend any money on Xmas gifts for any home folks. You have not the money to spare from what I can send you this Xmas; & all at home know this; & I really mean it when I ask you this. . . .

Good night, my sweet daughter—God be with you.

Your Father
Wm C.P. Breckinridge

Dec. 17, 1884

I am not surprized at the girls wanting to make you President of their class; & while I would do nothing whatever to seek it, I would not avoid it, nor try to elect another. Situated as you are, it is not only a personal compliment that you must regard it—it is more & is a compliment to your people. It may also do you good—character is developed by responsibility, & power to do something by having power to exercise. I do not know what I can do to help you, but if you will tell me I will do my best. As other classes preceeding yours have had such organizations, there ought to be a good many models to form your constitution after. I never doubted what impression you would make on any body of teachers & associates as they learnt to know you, nor the permanency of that impression; nor the generous disposition you would show to have others preferred. I sympathize with & love you more for that unselfish disposition. My anxiety was only for your health.

As to what your Ann Arbor friend said about Southern girls, you will find it is a common thing in the North. It is in part the product of the same feeling that actuated our Pharissee in the Temple with the Publican; in part the result of provincial ignorance, for as a rule the ordinary educated Northern man or woman is provincial. It is in part the feud of an old jealousy growing out of the old contests. But like all prejudices it also has a foundation in truth. The culture of the South has always tended to elegance of manners, gem of conversation, polish of the lighter accomplishments; & our ladies as a rule have not sought a severer training. In olden times there were good reasons for all this—our ladies were called to be housewives, & entertainers— not breadwinners. It was their vocation to know how to be in its high sense agreeable & house-wifely; and thank God they were—pure, chaste, brave, attractive, elegant— as we say, *Ladies*. They were "lacking" in some qualities necessary to a severer climate, the harder life & a different society.

In all essentials the true ladies are alike everywhere; in the accidentals, in the mere mode of development, in the subtle influences of environment there were differences.

You can yet distinguish them in your school. A thoroughbred lady from Boston, is full sister to one from Lexington a scrub, even if she has the "gift of tongues" is precisely like all other scrubs—whether from Vermont or Georgia. And underneath the accidental differences the essentials will reveal themselves. You will find that to a lady like you, there will never be trouble in looking over & beyond these differences, & rising above such prejudices; & having a good natured contempt for their exhibition in others. It is a fashion in some of our good Northern kinsmen & kinswomen to speak thus of us: it tickles the bone of their auditors & is an indirect way of lauding themselves. Treat it with the same good natured forbearance that you do the pretensions of the blacksmith's daughter—when rich—in *condescending* to associate with the preacher's daughter. . . .

With more love than I can write.

Your Father
Wm C.P. Breckinridge

Jan 16, 1885

About your class—I would be careful to do nothing to seek any place by suffrage, nor on the hand to seem above my classmates & careless of their good opinion. You will in the end win the esteem & confidence of all the better ones. I hardly know exactly how to express the thought—of cultivating pleasant relations with your own classmates. This is both a duty & will also be profitable. In colleges there is of necessity a certain amount of *caste*—of *class feeling;* each class in a certain sense & to a certain extent form a caste; & caste feeling is one of the most remarkable things in mankind. As you study history philosophically you may become interested in this phase of humanity. Now you are a Freshman—You belong to that caste & will for four years; & it will resent your failure to recognize or your refusal to acknowledge, or your neglect of this: Therefore in your pleasant association with seniors & others, you must be careful to treat your classmates *as* classmates—as full equals; & form ties that will be pleasant for four years.

I do not know what your scheme is, but whatever it is, I know that it is all right. My only caution is—don't increase your work.

To keep the devil out of your pocket I enclose $5.

With more love than I can write.

Your Father
Wm C.P. Breckinridge

Feb. 11, 1885

Your Sunday letter just came; & I write to congratulate you, my precious daughter, on your election: not because of the office but because of the evidence of respect & affection that it affords.

We know that you deserve it—knew that you would win it as they grew to know you. But it gratifies us that such evidence is given. It may be some day a gratification to you to know that I felt that you had always been a loving, truthful & unselfish girl—dutiful, earnest and affectionate.

And it adds to my pleasure to know how much it will gratify your Mother; and will please not only the family but your teachers. I know that you will bear the honors gracefully & perform the duties worthily. It is something to me that my child has made the name known creditably in a new circle & among a new generation; & that the first Southern girl thus honored is my girl. But my baby take care of your health— this is the first consideration.

I am writing in the Courtroom with a buzz around me.

God bless you, my sweet daughter & preserve your life to those who love you.

With love & pride and kisses.

Your Father
Wm C.P. Breckinridge

The Changing College Population

VIRGINIA C. GILDERSLEEVE, 1899

"The Change in the Spirit of Barnard" (Undergraduate Essay), 25 April 1899,
Virginia C. Gildersleeve Collection, Columbia University.

In their early years, the women's colleges attracted a distinct clientele: studious middle-class daughters who intended to teach. During the 1890s, a new wave of students arrived: young women from wealthier families, with few scholarly goals, no career plans, and the desire to have a good time. The growing presence of the well-off changed the tenor of college life by adding a spirit of revelry and an emphasis on clubs, parties, teams, theatrical performances, and sororities. One college senior, Virginia C. Gildersleeve (1877–1965), class of 1899, noted the changes that transformed Barnard as a new type of student entered.

Although she herself was upper class, Gildersleeve represented the "old" type of "sober-minded" student. As class president and leading scholar, she took college life very seriously. At the start of this formal essay, Gildersleeve seems quite dismayed at the frivolity of the most recent entrants, who appear to be "drifting" into college without any purpose. At the end, however, she applauds—or at least accepts—their arrival. At least, she suggests, Barnard's democratic spirit might improve the newcomers. Caught up in a spirit of rivalry among the elite women's colleges, Gildersleeve also seems somewhat pleased that Barnard was keeping up with social changes at its sister schools.

Virginia C. Gildersleeve became Dean of Barnard in 1911 and held the position for almost four decades. As an administrator, she oversaw many changes, including the recruitment of leading scholars to the faculty and the imposition of distribution requirements. She pressured Columbia to welcome women to its graduate and professional schools. And she played up the advantages of "college life" in order to attract applicants and to maintain Barnard's social prestige among the seven sisters.

Overwhelming, truly, is the change which four years have brought in the outward aspect of Barnard life, in her material surroundings. Yet scarcely less striking, and certainly no less important, is the change in the spirit of our college world—in the character of the students who make the college spirit what it is. During Barnard's early years her classes were made up almost wholly of women who entered for no other reason than a desire for knowledge, for mental training, or for the university degree which they could obtain from the annex of Columbia. A large majority hoped to fit themselves for teacher's careers; the others came, as a rule, from love of learning, and they, too, felt a determination to extract from their four years all the intellectual improvement possible. The result was a college life where study absolutely overshadowed all other interests. . . .

Many factors have rendered impossible the continuance of such a state of affairs. Of primary influence has been the marked change in the attitudes of society toward college education for women. No longer is a college course considered nearly so unusual an experience for a woman as it was ten, or even five years ago. No longer does determined ambition alone bring girls to academic life. They come now more as the majority of men enter—drifting direct from school, largely as a matter of course, because it seems a natural thing to do, because their families wish it, or because they themselves have a notion that four years at college is an amusing experience. The present Freshman is younger, and far less sober-minded than the students who entered women's colleges during the early years of this establishment; she is willing to accomplish, even to enjoy a certain amount of learning, but far more eagerly, as is natural enough, does she seek that indefinable thing called "college life."

It was to be expected that this new attitude towards a collegiate course should affect Barnard much later than it did Vassar, Bryn Mawr, and most of our other sister colleges. Certainly nothing, as a rule, but a strong desire for study could have attracted girls to a place in all other respects so little like a college as was the old Barnard. It was not until the infinitely more attractive home on the heights* made us resemble more nearly the average girl's idea of what a college should be that we began to feel decidedly the influx of the younger, pleasure-seeking element—in the main, that portion of it prevented by home ties from seeking the college experience at the more attractive institutions outside the city. Within the space of our college course the change has been marked. The majority of the class of Ninety-eight, for instance, have already entered the teacher's career. Not quite so large a proportion of Ninety-nine, probably, will follow this example; but the present Senior class is nevertheless, in general character, a typical exponent of the studious attitude, the much-abused "earnest spirit" of former Barnard days—the last, as I often feel, of the old classes. Our average mark has been unusually high; indeed, it seems higher as succeeding classes are posted on the bulletin board. We have never presented a play, nor have we put in the field a basketball team. The younger classes attribute to our festivities a sober-mindedness which occasionally arouses their derision. Our immediate successor, Nineteen-hundred, seems to be a transition class, made up of both the old and the new types; but the present Sophomores—the first class to enter the new Barnard—and the Freshmen as well, represent distinctly the element which has so changed the spirit of the college.

Amid the favorable conditions of the present site, the new type of student is developing a "college life" which is already, for a city institution, a decidedly creditable achievement. The serious tone of the old days is giving way to a gayer spirit. The literary associations of former years have been displaced by dancing-classes and

---

*Barnard had recently moved from a downtown building to an uptown campus.

basketball teams. (The "under class-men" can scarcely appreciate the strange emotions with which a member of Ninety-nine first gazed upon a notice requesting "candidates for the Varsity Team" to present themselves in the gymnasium.) The "Barnard teas," too, stimulated by class rivalry under the new plan of management, have developed into functions far gayer and more pretentious than we ever dreamed of in the old days. The fraternities,* while fortunately avoiding the acute rivalry from which many of the western universities suffer, have added a very noticeable element to our college life. It is more than interesting to watch, in other fields as well, the evolution and establishment of traditions and customs. Three plays at least, for instance, are apparently to be enjoyed by the college every year—one presented by the fraternities and one by each of the lower classes. And these productions, with the aid of the new theatre, and the richer treasuries of classes strong in numbers, seem likely to develop into fair rivals of the famous plays performed in some of the other women's colleges.

Needless to say, the time and the interest devoted to these varied amusements means just so much less expended on books. It is inevitable, under the new conditions, that the average mark of scholarship should decidedly fall. For study is no longer the all-important object of life in college. It is a thing to be taken lightly, to be accomplished only so far as will insure creditable standing or at least passing. Save where special interest leads her on, the average student is very apt, indeed, to regard the mental work merely as the necessary but rather painful price which she must pay for the privilege of enjoying the other side of college life.

. . . [T]he change, though not absolutely sweeping, is nevertheless a very real and striking one. Is it to be welcomed or lamented? In spite of one's natural inclination to regard the past as the "good old times," welcomed, I think, by all means. The average scholarship must fall, it is true; but there is little danger that it will fall too low. . . . There is much, moreover, to compensate for the lower attainments in scholarship, much training of another sort—in the management of affairs and of people in the far larger and more complicated college world of today. . . . We have preserved unharmed, I think, one thing which was in the old days and still is the most precious of our endowments, as indeed it must be to any college. I mean the frank, democratic spirit, the absence of snobbery and prejudice, the necessity for valuing a girl solely for what she is in herself, ignorant as one must generally be of her family, friends, and circumstances. Men can experience in other relations of life this free and frank intercourse with the most varied types of people. But to most women college alone affords such an opportunity for broadening their sympathies, eradicating prejudices, rubbing, so to speak, the corners off their characters.

. . . [W]hat Barnard has experienced has come, in greater or lesser degree, to most colleges. A collegiate course is merely coming to mean for the average woman more and more what it means for the average man. Barnard is but growing more like Bryn Mawr, Vassar, and her other sister colleges. . . . The Barnard graduate of the years to come will, I think, go forth better fitted for the life the average woman leads than was the graduate of past years.

---

*The "fraternities" to which Gildersleeve refers were in fact sororities, which began at Barnard in 1894—when an entire class banded together in a sorority. Sororities at Barnard ended in 1912, after a campaign by student Frieda Kirchwey, who assaulted the sororities as reactionary bastions of snobbery and secrecy.

The Marriage Question

MILICENT WASHBURN SHINN, 1895

Milicent Washburn Shinn, "The Marriage Rate of College Women," *The Century Magazine* 50 (October 1895), pp. 946–48.

By the 1890s, a trend had emerged that to some was disconcerting: College graduates were marrying at far lower rates than other women. To analyze the "marriage question" in 1895, Milicent Shinn (1858–1940) examined the careers of 1,805 members of the Association of the Collegiate Alumnae (ACA), of whom 28.2 percent were married—compared to eighty percent of women over twenty in the general population. The disparity, however, was misleading, Shinn pointed out. The ACA membership was weighted toward younger graduates (women in their twenties), and college women married later than other women. Also, a high proportion of ACA members were alumnae of women's colleges, whose graduates married at the very lowest rate. Finally, most ACA members came from the Northeast, whereas educated women from the Midwest seemed to have the best marriage prospects. But of most interest are Shinn's hypotheses as to *why* the marriage rates were lower among college women. She contended that college women had higher standards, and that "the bent toward congenial marriage may lessen the actual probability of marriage." Her analysis concludes with some revealing comments on the marriage question by two college graduates, a male and a female.

At the time Milicent Shinn wrote this article, she was a graduate student in psychology at the University of California, where she had earned a B.A. in 1880, and where she became the first woman to receive a Ph.D. She made her reputation as a psychologist with a widely admired study of infant development and was active in the California branch of the Association of Collegiate Alumnae. She never married.

If it be asked why college women marry less than others, it may very safely be answered, to begin with, that it is *not* because they crave a more exciting and public life; for the majority of them are school-teachers. In the register of the Association, *

---

*The Association of Collegiate Alumnae.

address after address is at some school; nearly 63 per cent of the California branch are teachers. The Association includes but thirty-four physicians, and a half-dozen lawyers, preachers, and journalists. A few members are librarians, or employees of some scientific staff; a very few are in independent business. The women that write striking books, that lead in public movements, that address great audiences, that explore and venture, are rarely among them. The conspicuous exceptions—notably Lucy Stone and Frances Willard—were among the earliest graduates; the present type of college woman is conservative, retiring, and more apt to disappoint expectation by differing too little than too much from other respectable, conventional folk— exactly as college men do.

It is probable that in the very general employment of college women as teachers in girls' schools lies one effective cause of celibacy. There is no station in life (save that of a nun) so inimical to marriage as that of resident teacher in a girls' school. The graduates of women's colleges usually prefer teaching in private girls' schools, while co-educational graduates seek the public high schools; and this may have something to do with the difference in their marriage rates. It is probable, too, that the private girls' school is a more frequent institution in the Atlantic States than in the West.

No one who has any extended acquaintance with college women doubts that the quiet and even pursuits of college, during years that might else have gone to social gaieties, increase rather than lessen the disposition to congenial home life; that the danger to unselfish affection from a student's ambition is slight compared to the danger from the ambition of social display; that in women as in men the emotional nature grows with intellectual growth, while becoming at the same time more even and controlled. That they are highly maternal as a class, a more conspicuous success as mothers than in any other calling they have tried, is now evident; it is doubtless here, and not in the learned professions, in letters, or in public life, that the main effect of the higher education of women is to be looked for.

But the bent toward congenial marriage may lessen the actual probability of marriage. It is not the ardent woman, but the cold woman, for whom one marriage will do as well as another. And the college woman is not only more exacting in her standards of marriage, but under less pressure to accept what falls below her standard than the average woman, because she can better support and occupy herself alone. As a matter of fact, unhappy marriages are virtually unknown among college women.

I have no doubt that the remaining cause of the low marriage rate is that many men dislike intellectual women,—whether because such women are really disagreeable or because men's taste is at fault, I shall not try to determine. And even among those who like them as friends, many feel as the young man did who made this confession:

"I never expected to marry the sort of girl I did. You know I always believed in intellectual equality and all that, and had good friendships with the college girls. But you see, you girls hadn't any illusions about us. After you had seen us hanging at the board on problems you could work, and had taken the same degrees yourselves, you couldn't imagine us wonders just because we had gone through college; and when I met a dear little girl that thought I knew everything—why, it just keeled me right over; it was a feeling I had no idea of."

And the college woman answered:

"I will betray something to you. Lots of us are just as unreformed as you: we want just as much to look up to our husbands as you want to be looked up to. Only, of course, the more we know, the harder it is to find somebody to meet the want. Probably the equal marriage is really the ideal one, and everybody will come to prefer it some day. But personally, *I* like men to be superior to me: only I'll tell you what I don't like in them: the wish to keep ahead of us by holding us back, like spoiled children that want to be *given* the game, and then admired for their skill. If men would encourage us to do our very best, and then do still better themselves, it ought to be good for civilization."

I am not here discussing the significance, but only the facts, of celibacy among college women: it does not seem to me, however, as important a social phenomenon as some have considered. It may be a temporary one, a small sign among others of a movement toward higher standards of marriage and parenthood. If not, it is not a matter for regret that the unmarried women of the country should be largely of a class that can be more contented and useful in single life than others might. And in any case, we need not doubt that all good knowledge is safe in the long run for all men and women.

A Georgia Seminary

CATALOG FROM SPELMAN SEMINARY, 1901

Spelman Catalog of 1901, in Beverly Guy-Sheftall and Jo Moore Stewart,
Spelman: A Centennial Celebration, 1881–1981 (Atlanta: Spelman College, 1981),
pp. 36–37.

A small number of southern black women also profited from new educational institutions in the late nineteenth century. During the 1860s and 1870s, northern missionaries and philanthropists founded the first colleges for blacks, such as Howard University in Washington, D.C., which was funded by the Freedmen's Bureau. Northern philanthropy and missionary zeal also led to the founding of single-sex schools. A leading example was Spelman Female Seminary in Atlanta, Georgia, started in 1881 by Sophia B. Packard, a middle-aged New England teacher who was committed to the education of southern freedwomen. With her friend, Harriet E. Giles, Packard went to Atlanta in 1880 to start a school. The women's efforts were supported by a group of Massachusetts churchwomen that Packard had helped to organize, the Women's American Baptist Home Missionary Society, which raised funds. In 1884, while on a fundraising tour for the new institution, Packard evoked the interest of John D. Rockefeller, who made a substantial contribution. In return, the seminary took the family name of Rockefeller's wife, whose relatives had been abolitionists.

Within a year of its founding, 150 women were enrolled in the new school, and, by the end of 1883, 400 were enrolled. The first students were primarily middle-aged former slaves who sought literacy and who constituted a large portion of the student body through the 1890s. Although primary education remained Spelman's major focus in its early decades, the school also organized courses of study in teaching, nursing, and missionary work. The first graduating class, in 1887, comprised five young women who became teachers (see the photograph on page 365). In 1888, the seminary received a state charter as an "institution of learning for young colored women" that would instill "industrial habits and Christian character."

Under the leadership of Packard and Giles, and with continued financing from contributors, enrollment mounted. The following statistics from the Spelman catalog in 1901 suggest the seminary's development by the turn of the century. The student body and courses of study reflect the school's origins and the needs of its constituency. Of the 669 students, half of them boarders, the majority were young women under twenty-five years of age. Foreign students came from Central and South America and Africa. The seminary continued to provide a combination of academic and vocational training. Most students were enrolled in the "English Preparatory" course, a primary program whose graduates might enter high school. Degrees were awarded to a small number of academic students, teachers, nurses, and missionaries. Those who studied printing, dressmaking, and domestic arts won certificates. Following the trend of other southern female secondary schools that became women's colleges, the seminary became Spelman College in 1924.

From the Spelman Seminary Catalog, 1901

Statistical

Average Enrolment, 1883–1901... 618
Different Pupils, Boarders, 1881–1901........................... 2671
Different Pupils, Day Scholars (est. 1881–1901)............. 3000
Conversions Pupils, 1881–1901.................................... 1200

Enrolment, 1900–1901

Teachers............................42
Students...........................669
Boarders..........................336
Day-Scholars.................... 333
Under 16 years................. 250
Between 16 and 25 years.. 362
Over 25 years.....................57

College Students...........................5
Christian Worker Students.......... 13
Teachers Professional Students....19
College Preparatory Students.........9
Academic Students...................... 88
English Preparatory Students.... 503
Nurse Training Students..............16
Dress-Making only
Students.................................... 16

Students Geographically Considered

From Georgia................... 82%
From States adjacent
to Georgia....................... 13%
From other regions.............5%

Total from Congo............................5
Total from Colombia.................... 13
Total from Honduras......................2
Total from Jamaica....................... 2

Diplomas Given

Academic (since 1887).......137
Missionary (since 1893)...... 18
Teachers Professional
(since 1894)........................ 29
College Preparatory
(since 1899)........................ 13

Total...............................197

Certificates Given

Domestic Arts (since 1886)......... 186
Nurse Training (since 1888)..........65
Printing (since 1892).................... 68
Dress-Making (since 1899).............5

Total...324

Degrees of Bachelor of Arts given...............2

Courses of Instruction

Literary

English Preparatory—Nine years, leading to..............High School Courses
Academic—(English High), four years, leading to a......................Diploma
College Preparatory—(Classical High), four years, leading to a......Diploma
Christian Workers'—Two years, leading to a................................Diploma
Teachers' Professional—Open to High School Graduates,
one to three years, leading to a.. Diploma
*College—Four years, leading to the.................Degree of Bachelor of Arts

Industrial

Nurse Training—Three years, leading to a....................................Diploma
Printing—Two or three years, leading to a............................... Certificate
Sewing—Seven years, leading to a..Certificate
Dress-Making—Three years, leading to a..................................Certificate
Cooking and Domestic Arts—Three years, leading to a............. Certificate
Laundry Work—Leading to a...Certificate

Musical

Vocal Music
Instrumental Music—Piano and Organ

*In connection with Atlanta Baptist College.

Equipment

Each Department has a limited working equipment;
there are still pressing needs

Chapter 15

Clubs, Causes, and Reform

D uring the last decades of the nineteenth century, a contagious fever of organization swept middle-class women into clubs, societies, and national associations. The impulse to organize was scarcely new. Throughout the century, women had been involved in church-related charity groups and missionary societies, which continued to boast huge female enrollments. A smaller number had been drawn into antebellum reform movements, usually in league with male allies. But the new women's organizations of the late nineteenth century differed from their predecessors. National in scope, formal in organization, and secular in goals, they were founded and led solely by women. Male authority, including ministerial authority, was discarded. Carving out a separate realm of female activism, major women's associations provided stepping stones between the domestic world and public life.

Temperance locals and women's clubs were the pivots of this organizational upsurge. The women's temperance crusade erupted in the early 1870s, when pious midwestern women joined forces to close saloons. The temperance movement mushroomed quickly to national scope. By the 1890s, 150,000 members of the Women's Christian Temperance Union (WCTU), founded in 1873, not only were battling drink but were engaged in a gamut of related causes—such as peace, social purity, and urban welfare work. No jail, asylum, or school was safe from their efforts. Simultaneously, the women's club movement sped forward, drawing upon a less combative if more selective clientele. The first women's club, Sorosis, formed in New York in 1868 by journalists and other professionals, inspired thousands of imitators nationwide. At first, clubwomen met to discuss literary topics. After the founding of the General Federation of Women's Clubs (GFWC) in 1892, club members shifted their focus from cultural uplift to civic issues and social reform. Still, the women's club continued to serve as a self-education center, or, in one club leader's words, "a mutual improvement society, which should educate [women] and lead them out into better hope, nobler aspiration, and larger life."

If temperance formed the more potent political force, the women's club model was more easily replicated. During the 1880s and 1890s, the club world expanded at a rapid pace, reaching not only all regions of the country but diverse constituencies. Black women, for instance, who rarely were accepted in white women's clubs, organized a separate club movement, devoted primarily to educational and philanthropic work in black communities. College graduates joined the Association of Collegiate Alumnae, to discuss the role of educated women and to foster women's acceptance in higher education. Well-off city women founded working girls clubs, to enhance the lives of young urban wage earners and to instill middle-class habits. At the end of the century, networks of mothers' clubs formed the National Congress of Mothers, which, like the GFWC, embarked on pressure group politics. Whatever the membership or goals of a specific group, club work involved the same type of activities—parliamentary-style meetings, formal minutes, public speaking, committee reports, annual conventions, and national federations—all the trappings of contemporary public affairs. Even the WCTU, with its Christian fervor and revivalist style, was more of a political party than a religious crusade. Those drawn into the world of women's organizations spoke of the "exhilaration" of collective effort, of "joyful, useful activities."

At the turn of the century, yet another wave of organizations emerged with more specific goals: to solve urban problems and bridge the gulf between social classes. The National Consumer's League (1899), an outgrowth of working women's societies of the 1880s, focused on women's working conditions in department stores. The National Women's Trade Union League, founded in 1903, encouraged the formation of women's trade unions. The most innovative type of association in which women were involved was the settlement house, which capitalized on the experience of both clubwomen and college women. In 1889, when Jane Addams and Ellen Gates Starr founded Hull House in Chicago, and a group of recent graduates started the College Settlement in New York, they provided both a promising solution to urban problems and a novel way for educated women to assert themselves in civic affairs. Located in urban ghettoes, the settlements gratified, in one resident's words, "a thirst to know how the other half lived." Settlement residents not only provided services to immigrant communities, but depended on a wide range of clubs to involve neighborhood denizens in settlement affairs and expose them to "the best" in American life.

Women often felt the need to defend the existence of their organizations, especially during the 1870s and 1880s, when the club world was new. To justify their exertions, members promoted their "mission" as women. Temperance workers asserted the need for "home protection." Clubwomen proclaimed their commitment to higher feminine standards. Other associations announced their allegiance, variously, to working women and children, to neighborhood and community, or in the case of social settlements, to the study of "industrial and social problems." Unlike the woman suffrage movement, which directly challenged male power, most women's organizations favored a more covert brand of aggression. Both their causes and their modus operandi enabled them collectively to feminize a portion of public space and establish a tradition of female activism outside the home.

Women and Politics

FRANCES A. WILLARD, 1885

"President's Annual Address," *Minutes of the National Christian Temperance Union, Twelfth Annual Meeting in Philadelphia, Pa.* (Brooklyn: Martin and Niper, 1885), pp. 62, 89–91.

Temperance leader Frances A. Willard (1839–1898), who served as president of the Women's Christian Temperance Union (WCTU) from 1879 to 1898, was arguably the nineteenth century's most successful woman politician. With managerial genius and contagious zeal, she transformed the WCTU from a midwestern prayer society into a militant pressure group of unparalleled size. Unafraid of taking a controversial stand, she risked her leadership role to endorse woman suffrage in 1880. Adept at making contacts throughout the world of women's organizations (she belonged to almost all of them), Willard also excelled at the public address—or the political harangue.

When white-ribboned temperance delegates gathered for their annual conventions, Willard customarily opened the meeting with a long, inspirational speech. Crafting slogans and maxims, distributing credit far and wide, and summarizing the achievements of the WCTU's many departments, she exhorted the delegates to further effort. At the end of her 1885 speech, Willard turned to a major problem: Should women temperance advocates become involved in politics? Should they, for instance, endorse the efforts of the all-male Prohibition Party, which ran candidates for national office? Should they take a stand in state and national political campaigns? The answer, of course, was yes. Willard explained that temperance advocates should avoid "entangling alliances" with other groups and should cling to their own brand of "gospel politics." She contended, however, that the sacred nature of their cause justified—indeed demanded—any foray they might make into the male realm of politics.

President's Annual Address

Beloved Sisters:

Very sacred seems the comradeship of the Woman's Christian Temperance Union. Nothing in life has so satisfied some of our hearts. It is a high and holy calling. As I have long believed, it is God's way out of the wilderness for half the human race. In its glowing crucible, the dross of sectional enmity is being rapidly dissolved; the trifling occupations, the narrow aims, the paralyzing indolence of women, are barriers burned away by its all-conquering heat; while their once impoverished lives are expanding into wide areas of gracious strength and heavenly magnanimity. Beloved, this is our testing time. The fiery ordeal is upon us. "The fire shall declare it." Can we not bear and forbear with each other? Can we not disagree down to the eyebrows, but agree in the heart?

We now come directly to the question, what has the National W. C. T. U. actually done this year, in the realm of politics? Let us carefully separate in our thought, what the newspapers and the great, thoughtless, outside public, in their ignorance and inattention say we have done, from what we actually have. "Why," says one, "the Ohio women helped the Prohibition campaign." True, but we believe in "State rights"; if we had passed a non-partisan resolution at St. Louis it would not have bound Ohio, and she would probably have felt it her duty, with a license candidate on one side and a tax candidate on the other, to do just what she has done now, and we could not have hindered her, even had we wished to do so. "But the national officers have talked politics." Yes, some of us have, not as a specialty, however. For myself, I have spoken less than half a dozen times in my whole life under the auspices of a Prohibition Party, Club or Committee. But I judge that every National officer is free to speak when and what she thinks best, and would do so or resign, no matter what resolution we might here adopt. Scan the records of the National W. C. T. U. in 1885, and no allusion to politics can be found. Analyze the Treasurer's Report; not a penny has been paid out for any political purpose. Listen to the year's summary of a work vast as the continent, and many sided as a great character; you will find that philanthropy, not politics, comprises the sublime and holy task to which the W. C. T. U. has set itself.

But surely, where so much smoke is, there must be a little fire. We must have done something more or less terrible to have called down such unlooked-for reprobation in quarters where we, in our simplicity, had looked for sympathy. What was it? Why, in the heat of a presidential campaign, that was bitter as gall and relentless as death, when the two great parties had failed us, one by open declaration, the other by scornful silence, we dared, within ten days of election, to reaffirm our loyalty to the party* that gave the best embodiment of prohibition principles, and whose triumph—for it surely will triumph some day—would most surely protect our homes. But nay, this was not the head and front of our offending. Had "the plumed knight" been chosen one week later, only good-natured wit would have aimed at us its harmless shafts. But on the 4th of November last, a great party, long accustomed to the bewildering prerogatives of power, was hurled from its high place, and seeking for a scapegoat, turned in the fierceness of its baffled rage, and poured out its vials of wrath upon the devoted heads of women, who, up to that hour, had been accounted thoughtful, trustworthy, and patriotic.†

---

*The Prohibition Party.
†In the election of 1884, the Democratic presidential candidate, Grover Cleveland, defeated Republican James G. Blaine by very small margin. During the campaign, a clergyman at a Republican rally referred to the Democrats as the party of "rum, Romanism, and rebellion," and Blaine refused to retract this description.

What have we done since then as a National Society? What could we do but go quietly along the even tenor of our way, each individual officer frankly stating her own opinions, and *The Union-Signal* carefully and moderately setting forth the view of the majority, while by no means refusing to the minority a fair and courteous hearing? Have we done more? Could we do less? And yet, how often have the changes been rung upon the words, "The women have joined the Prohibition party; the W. C. T. U. is now nothing but a political annex."

Sisters, none would deplore the situation more than I if this were true. The strength and glory of the W. C. T. U. is its organic independence and separateness from every other form of organization. Entangling alliances would work its downfall, and that right speedily. Some of you can remember that the cry of our enemies was constantly reiterated: "They have gone over to the suffragists; the next you know the two societies will be merged, for the leaders are in secret council." To prove the falsity of this, how careful some of us have been to advocate the ballot only from our own platform and the Temperance point of view. That "fright" is over. The public is now convinced that no such purpose was ever cherished, and in a year or two, if we go quietly on with our own work, they will be equally at rest concerning our "political alliances."

Sisters, here we are once more, as we shall often be again, face to face with this great question and its ominous decision—ominous either way, for we can by no means escape the strongest and the sternest criticism. It will hurl its missiles remorselessly down on our devoted heads, no matter what we do. The battle has become too fierce for us to hold the position of neutrals. Neither has it been our "call" to do this, from the beginning. We are outspoken and quietly aggressive in our spirit, and no less so in our methods. At first we assailed the saloon itself with a directness and courage unparalleled in history. Later, when we found the saloon to be intrenched in law, we followed it straight to city council room and legislative hall; and last, when its hidings of power were discovered to be in politics, we followed it there, as brave soldiers always pursue their enemy, even to his forts and fastnesses. We are crusaders as truly as when the outward and visible saloon itself was our objective point; only now we have grown wiser, and carry our crusade straight to the brain, the heart, and the conscience of the *individual voter*, praying him to represent his home constituency, and to stand at the ballot-box for *prohibition* first, last, and always. What the women of this nation earnestly desire and devotedly strive to attain, is as sure to succeed as to-morrow's sun is sure to rise. The stream cannot rise higher than the fountain, we are told, but its tendency always is to rise as high. The mother-heart is the world's fount of healing; what it pours forth in prayer to God and pleading with mankind is the best prophecy of what shall be. . . .

Great wars live in history under great names. . . . Everywhere, in England and in Canada, in the Sandwich Islands and Australia, in Asia and the isles of the sea, ours will be known as the *Home Protection War*. We all remember that famous utterance of a great statesman in America who said: "Where liberty is, there is my country." It is time for a new motto, that shall mean to this age what that did in a struggle now fought out to its inevitable and righteous end. Let us inscribe on our white banner, "*Wherever the liquor power is marshalled*, there is our battlefield."

A Temperance Tale

MARY CLEMENT LEAVITT, 1888

Frances E. Willard, *Women and Temperance; or the Work and Workers of the Women's Christian Temperance Union* (Hartford, CT: Park Publishing Co., 1888), pp. 95–98.

The temperance advocate's influence depended not only on the collective efforts of the local organization to which she belonged but on her individual powers of persuasion. Mary Clement Leavitt (1830–1912), a leading protégé of Frances Willard, was an inveterate lecturer and the WCTU's "ambassador at large" to the world. In her speeches, she often used the following story of "The Shoemaker and the Little White Shoes." This story showed how a persistent temperance worker could succeed in a personal confrontation with a habitual drunkard. Significantly, in the story, Mary Clement Leavitt assumes a quasi-ministerial role as she leads the sinning shoemaker to the point of conversion. Significantly, too, Mrs. Leavitt depicts herself as a person of considerable authority in relation to her working-class target.

One morning during the Crusade, a drunkard's wife came to my door. She carried in her arms a baby six weeks old. Her pale, pinched face was sad to see, and she told me this sorrowful story: "My husband is drinking himself to death; he is lost to all human feeling; our rent is unpaid, and we are liable to be put into the street, and there is no food in the house for me and the children. He has a good trade, but his earnings all go into the saloon on the corner near us; he is becoming more and more brutal and abusive. We seem to be on the verge of ruin. How can I, feeble as I am, with a babe in my arms, earn bread for myself and children?"

Quick as thought the question came to me, and I asked it: "Why not have that husband of yours converted?"

But she answered hopelessly, "Oh, there's no hope of such a thing. He cares for nothing but strong drink."

"I'll come and see him this afternoon," said I.

"He'll insult you," she replied.

"No matter," said I; "my Saviour was insulted, and the servant is not above his Lord."

That very afternoon I called at the little tenement house. The husband was at work at his trade in a back room, and his little girl was sent to tell him that a lady wished to see him. The child, however, soon returned with the message: "My pa says he won't see anyone."

But I sent him a message proving that I was indeed in earnest. I said, "Go back and tell your pa that a lady wishes to see him on important business, and she must see him if she has to stay till after supper."

I knew very well that there was nothing in the house to eat. A moment afterward a poor, bloated, besotted wreck of a man stood before me.

"What do you want?" he demanded as he came shuffling into the room.

"Please be seated and look at this paper," I answered, pointing to a vacant chair at the other end of the table where I was sitting, and handing a printed pledge to him.

He read it slowly, and then, throwing it down upon the table, broke out violently: "Do you think I'm a fool? I drink when I please, and let it alone when I please. I'm not going to sign away my personal liberty."

"Do you think you can stop drinking?"

"Yes, I could if I wanted to."

"On the contrary, *I* think you're a slave to the rum-shop down on the corner."

"No, I ain't any such thing."

"I think, too, that you love the saloon-keeper's daughter better than you do your own little girl."

"No, I don't, either."

"Well, let us see about that. When I passed the saloon-keeper's house I saw his little girl coming down the steps, and she had on white shoes, and a white dress, and a blue sash. Your money helped to buy them. I come here, and your little girl, more beautiful than she, has on a faded, ragged dress, and her feet are bare."

"That's so, madam."

"And you love the saloon-keeper's wife better than you love your own wife."

"Never; no, never!"

"When I passed the saloon-keeper's house, I saw his wife come out with the little girl, and she was dressed in silks and laces, and a carriage waited for her. Your money helped to buy the silks and laces, and the horses and the carriage. I come here and I find your wife in a faded calico gown, doing her own work; if she goes any where, she must walk."

"You speak the truth, madam."

"You love the saloon-keeper better than you love yourself. You say you can keep from drinking if you choose; but you helped the saloon-keeper to build himself a fine brick house, and you live in this poor, tumble-down old house yourself."

"I never saw it in that light before." Then, holding out his hand, that shook like an aspen leaf, he continued, "You speak the truth, madam—I am a slave. Do you see that hand? I've got a piece of work to finish, and I must have a mug of beer to steady my nerves, or I cannot do it; but to-morrow, if you'll call, I'll sign the pledge."

"That's a temptation of the devil; I did not ask you to sign the pledge. You are a slave, and cannot help it. But I do want to tell you this: *There is One who can break your chains and set you free.*"

"I want to be free."

"Well, Christ can set you free, if you'll submit to Him, and let him break the chains of sin and appetite that bind you."

"It's been many a long year since I prayed."

"No matter; the sooner you begin the better for you."

He threw himself at once upon his knees, and while I prayed I heard him sobbing out the cry of his soul to God.

His wife knelt beside me and followed me in earnest prayer. The words were simple and broken with sobs, but somehow they went straight up from her crushed heart to God, and the poor man began to cry in earnest for mercy.

"O God! break these chains that are burning into my soul! Pity me, and pity my wife and children, and break the chains that are dragging me down to hell. O God! be merciful to me a sinner." And thus out of the depths he cried to God, and He heard him and had compassion upon him, and broke every chain and lifted every burden; and he arose a free, redeemed man.

When he arose from his knees he said: "Now I will sign the pledge, and keep it."

And he did. A family altar was established, the comforts of life were soon secured—for he had a good trade—and two weeks after this scene his little girl came into my husband's Sunday-school with *white shoes and white dress and blue sash on*, as a token that her father's money no longer went into the saloon-keeper's till.

But what struck me most of all was that it took less than *two hours* of my time thus to be an ambassador for Christ in declaring the terms of heaven's great treaty whereby a soul was saved from death, a multitude of sins were covered, and a home restored to purity and peace.

The Woman's Club

CLEVELAND SOROSIS, 1893

Cleveland Sorosis Annual (Cleveland, OH: Examiner Publishing Co., 1893), pp. 51–54.

Less militant and more exclusive than the WCTU, the women's club paved another route from domestic affairs to public life. Women's clubs offered a combination of conviviality, self-education, and philanthropy. After the General Federation of Women's Clubs (GFWC) was formed in 1892, clubwomen shifted their focus to public affairs and social reform. But on the grass-roots level, much of the club's function remained the same: to provide a "school after school" for its members.

The following documents concern the 272-member Cleveland Sorosis Club in 1893: first, the club's organizational chart, which shows the many committees in which clubwomen were involved, from "Ceramic Art" to "Parliamentary Law"; second, a paper, given at a club luncheon, that provides the standard rationale for women's clubs. Denying any impetus to "usurp the place of man," the speaker stresses women's need for elevation, self-respect, individualism, and a stimulating mental atmosphere. The odd ending reflects GFWC leader Jennie C. Croly's dictum that "club life ends in uniting the sexes, and creating a better understanding between men and women."

CLEVELAND SOROSIS

OFFICIAL ORGANIZATION 1893–94

PRESIDENT
MRS. WILLIAM G. ROSE

VICE PRESIDENTS
1ST.— MRS. N. COE STEWART
2D. — MRS. H. E. HAMMOND
3D. — MRS. C. E. WYMAN
4TH.— MRS. L. A BENTON
5TH.— MRS. S. E. STOCKWELL

EXECUTIVE BOARD

Mrs. J. M. P. Phelps, Chairman	Mrs. C. W. Loomis
Mrs. T. D. Crocker	Mrs. J. H. Paine
Mrs. C. C. Burnett	Mrs. Mary B. Ingham
Mrs. J. K. Hord	Mrs. W. S. Kerruish
Mrs. Arthur E. Hatch	Mrs. A. T. Anderson

The President, Recording and Corresponding Secretaries, and Treasurer, *ex-officio* members.

RECORDING SECRETARY
MRS. S. P. CHURCHILL

CORRESPONDING SECRETARY
MRS. GEORGE A. ROBERTSON

TREASURER
MRS. C. S. SELOVER

AUDITOR OF ACCOUNTS
MRS. M. A. REILLY

CHAIRMEN OF DEPARTMENTS

June—Suffrage...Mrs. S. M. Perkins
July—Philanthropy..Mrs. C. E. Wyman
August—Science.......................Mrs. A. D. Davidson and Mrs. E. M. Avery
September—Physical Culture and Dress Reform............ Mrs. M. J. Caton
October—Ceramic Art..Mrs. B. D. Babcock
November—Business Women.......................................Mrs. W. A. Ingham
December—Drama..Mrs. Anna P. Tucker
January—Home Making as a Profession.....................Mrs. N. Coe Stewart
February—Literature..Mrs. Sidney H. Short
March—Temperance... Mrs. D. W. Gage
April—Parliamentary Law.. Mrs. H. E. Hammond
May—House and Home... Mrs. J. M. P. Phelps

STANDING COMMITTEES

CUSTODIANS

Mrs. C. H. Seymour, Chairman
Mrs. X. X. Crum, Secretary
Mrs. Arthur Hatch, Cor. Secretary
Mrs. Rose M. Anderson, Treasurer
Mrs. J. M. Wilcox
Mrs. E. W. Doan
Mrs. C. E. Wyman

Mrs. J. K Hord
Mrs. J. H. Paine
Mrs. N. Coe Stewart
Mrs. C. S. Selover
Mrs. M. H. Barlett
Mrs. M. A. Reilly
Mrs. C. E. Tillinghast

MUSIC

Mrs. S. P. Churchill, Chairman
Mrs. C. A. Christie
Mrs. Olga Sturm

Miss Ethel Seymour
Miss Susie Stockwell
Miss G. Browne

LITERATURE

Mrs. Sidney H. Short, Chairman

Miss Mary C. Quintrell
Mrs. C. E. Tilllnghast
Mrs. L. H. Winch
Mrs. M. J. Caton

Miss Dorothy Paine
Mrs. Frank Houghton
Mrs. W. R. Rose
Mrs. M. A. Reilly

ART

Mrs. Georgia Norton, Chairman
Mrs. C. C. Ruthrauff
Mrs. N. A. Gilbert
Mrs. W. J. Hilands
Miss Mary C. Quintrell

Mrs. H. French
Mrs. J. M. P. Phelps
Miss M. L. Morigon
Mrs. A. M. Searles
Mrs. Cornwall

DRAMA

Mrs. Anna P. Tucker, Chairman
Mrs. Arthur E. Hatch
Mrs. A. E. Campbell
Mrs. C. Feil
Mrs. W. R. Rose
Miss Dorothy Paine
Miss Florence Drake

Mrs. Olga Sturm
Mrs. O. C. Lawrence
Miss Clara Blandin
Miss Ida Brown
Miss Augusta Wilcox
Miss Nellie Gunn
Mrs. H. B. Roosa

PHILANTHROPY

Mrs. C. E. Wyman, Chairman
Mrs. M. J. Caton
Mrs. J. S. White
Mrs. W. J. Fuller

Mrs. B. D. Babcock
Mrs. L. A. Benton
Mrs. G. P. Needham
Mrs. E. A. Wilson

SCIENCE

Mrs. A. D. Davidson, Chairman

Mrs. S. M. Perkins
Mrs. N. Coe Stewart
Miss M. C. Quintrell
Mrs. James Shipherd
Mrs. S. L Wrlght
Mrs. Thomas Wilson
Mrs. W. G. Rose
Mrs. B. D. Babcock
Miss Axtell

Mrs. Crossley
Mrs. W. S. Kerruish
Mrs. J. H. Thomas
Mrs. Dr. Gerould
Mrs. Theresa Jenkins
Mrs. James H. Paine
Mrs. Elroy M. Avery
Mrs. Arthur Adams
Mrs. M. J. Caton

Mrs. C.E. Wyman

HOUSE AND HOME

Mrs J. M. P. Phelps, Chairman

Mrs. S. P. Churchill
Mrs. E. J. Blandin
Mrs. L. H. Winch

Mrs. John Freeman
Mrs. J. K Hord
Mrs. X X Crum

BUSINESS WOMEN

Mrs. Mary B. Ingham, Chairman
Mrs. A E. Macomber
Mrs. M. E. Beckwith
Mrs. J. S. Wood

Mrs. Mary Spargo-Fraser
Miss Nellie Horton
Mrs. J. H. Paine
Mrs. L. C. Seymour

TEMPERANCE

Mrs. D. W. Gage, Chairman
Mrs. S. M. Perkins

Mrs. H. E. Hammond
Mrs. Esther T. Silver

SUFFRAGE

Mrs. S. M. Perkins, Chairman

PHYSICAL CULTURE AND DRESS REFORM

Mrs. M. J. Caton, Chairman
Mrs. B. F. Taylor
Miss Mary C. Quintrell

Mrs. W. G. Rose
Mrs. Olga Sturm
Mrs. C. E. Tillinghast

HOME MAKING AS A PROFESSION

Mrs. N. Coe Stewart, Chairman
Mrs. James McIntyre
Mrs. L. O. Jones
Mrs. E. A. Wilson
Mrs. William Christie

Mrs. Frank Houghton
Mrs. W. B. Swlft
Mrs. Frank Reilly
Mrs. Frank Stockton
Mrs. J. M. P. Phelps

CERAMIC ART

Mrs. B. D. Babcock, Chairman

PARLIAMENTARY LAW

Mrs. H. E. Hammond, Chairman

Mrs. E. T. Silver

Mrs. Ella Grant Wilson

ANNUAL AND PRINTING

Mrs. J. H. Paine, Chairman

Mrs. Rose Anderson
Mrs. Sidney Short

Mrs. Frank Houghton
Mrs. J. S. Wood

REVIEWERS

Mrs. Rose Anderson
Mrs. J. H. Paine

Mrs. H. E. Hammond
Mrs. C. E. Wyman

USHERS

Miss Gabrielle Stewart
Miss Grace Felton
Miss Nellie Brewer

Miss Nellie Gunn
Miss Susie Stockwell
Miss Augusta Wilcox

The Woman's Club

Paper Read by Mrs. Leo Dautel,
At Myrtle Luncheon, April 27, 1893

The old chivalrous ideas in regard to woman are fast disappearing. In making this assertion, I do not wish to be understood as introducing a plea for the self-assertive, unwomanly woman. A woman's greatest power consists in her femininity. Her aesthetic sense, her spirituality, her innate refinement, which expresses itself even in the dainty belongings with which she chooses to surround herself, have an influence for good in the world not to be measured by words. Gœthe made Faust give expression to this sentiment, when, in the absence of Margherita, he gained access to her chamber. Overcome by the sentiment that expressed itself everywhere, from the flowers in the tiny vase in the lattice window to the books of devotion on the table, in a momentary, at least, state of contrition he exclaimed, "This is the abode of purity."

But with all this in view, woman still recognizes the fact that if she has to wrestle with the problems of life successfully she must first understand them. This knowledge she can only gain by hearing them discussed intelligently by others and by calm reasoning upon them herself. In other words, by having the same advantages that her husband, her father and her brother possess! Woman's intuitions have stood her instead of reason about long enough. Let us hope the day is not far distant when a woman's reason will no longer be—"because." She has come into the knowledge of her weakness in many things, her ignorance of many more, and is aware that the great problems of life, whether of religion, politics, charities, literary or artistic culture, political or domestic economy, require the same solution of her undisciplined and inexperienced mind that they do of that of man, with centuries of discipline and experience behind him. It is the expert against the novice. It is a wonder that man has accomplished as much as he has, yoked to so unequal a partner.

It is the desire on the part of woman to level these inequalities and to better fit herself for her responsibilities, that prompts her to this onward movement. It is that she may better fill her own place in life, rather than that she has any desire to usurp that of man. Thus, with the cobwebs brushed from her eyes, imbued with the idea that if she is to be more than a man's shadow while he lives, and his relict at death, in short to be his true helpmeet and companion, she must be up and doing.

With her little hand she has cut the Gordian knot that bound her. The pent-up eloquence and long dormant talent which have accumulated to such extent in the brain of the active nineteenth-century woman, have at last found vent in Woman's Clubs.

The first Woman's Club was formed by Sappho, a Greek poetess, who was wont to gather her friends around her for intellectual intercourse.

That was early in the Christian era, but the club idea did not seem to take very well until this latter end of the nineteenth century, when the blind struggle after union and co-operation in organized societies is beginning to crystalize. The Woman's Club has taken definite form and has proved its right to existence, its helpfulness to women, and through her to society. The early steps were slow. Mountains had to be overcome, ridicule being the worst among them, perhaps. The pioneers in advanced education for women were called "short-haired women," "emancipated females," etc.

Perhaps they were too busy making the rough places smooth to give due consideration to the amenities of life. The pioneers in a new country do not clear the forests in dress suits. And we who are enjoying the fruits of the labors of the women who have borne the brunt of the battle in the advancement of their sex, are just as little justified in criticising their so-called radical methods as the modern fine gentleman would be in ridiculing the manners and methods of the men who, centuries before, had cleared forests and built roadways.

The claims of a woman's club are manifold. To begin with, it is elevating, and it inspires her with self-respect. It is broadening. It dispels the old idea of exclusiveness in its narrow sense. It is a refreshment, a change of the mental atmosphere just as necessary as a change of air in the material world. It is a school after school—a place where women will learn to accept honest opposition, goodnaturedly. Here she may get in an hour the result of many hours, study and research, condensed in the various papers read before the club. Here she may learn that there is another point of view besides her own.

In the ideal woman's club, the interests of the club will be greater than that of any member in it. The nobility of true womanhood, not the aristocracy of wealth or position, should be the "open sesame" to its privileges. Character, intellect and attainments—these should be the credentials necessary for membership. It should be broader than any creed, and wider than any sect.

The object of a woman's club should be to develop those traits that belong to the ideal woman, and teach her the requirements of a perfect life. It should imbue her with the idea that housekeeping is not all of homekeeping—that art, religion, music and literature are as necessary to a perfect home as good bread, perfect ventilation and good cooking. It is the ideal that endures—material things are only transitory. They only have their place as they minister to the comfort of the individual or convey some idea of beauty to his soul.

A club that does its work properly would lead its members to prefer to be judged as individuals, rather than to have any degree of praise or blame on account of sex. Let it be in this line of thought that they may strive to leave their impress on the world, having endeavored to ennoble and enrich the day and generation in which they have lived. Do you ask me where this ideal club exists? "In my mind's eye, Horatio," and in it are women—and men.

The Black Club Movement

FANNIE BARRIER WILLIAMS, CA. 1900

Fannie Barrier Williams, "The Club Movement Among Colored Women of America," in J. E. McBrady, ed., *A New Negro for a New Century* (Chicago: American Publishing House, ca. 1900), pp. 379–84.

The black women's club movement developed in the 1890s, led by such groups as the Colored Women's League of Washington, D.C., founded in 1892, and the New Era Club of Boston, founded in 1893. In 1896, a large federation, the National Association of Colored Women, was formed. Although a few blacks were accepted in white women's clubs, and the National Council of Women (an umbrella group of women's organizations) included representatives of the black clubs, the GFWC rejected black delegates. Black clubwomen therefore took pride in their separate identity. Beyond fulfilling the traditional functions of women's clubs, they hoped to inculcate racial self-respect, combat race prejudice, and improve the "social condition of the race." Indeed, self-interest dictated a primary concern with racial issues and racial uplift. As historian Paula Giddings points out, black activist women "understood that their fate was bound with that of the masses."*

In the excerpts that follow, clubwoman Fannie Barrier Williams (1855–1944), the sole black member of the prestigious Chicago Woman's Club and a leader in the black club movement, describes the goals and interests of black women's clubs. A native of New York State, Williams was an 1870 graduate of the State Normal School at Brockport, New York. With her husband, a successful lawyer, she settled in Chicago. Prominent as a lecturer and in a variety of philanthropic projects and settlement work, Fannie Barrier Williams often served as a spokesperson for black women, whose interests she championed. Of special interest in the following essay is her comparison of the black women's clubs with those of the "more favored race."

---

*Paula Giddings, *When and Where I Enter: The Impact of Black Women on Race and Sex in America* (New York: William Morrow and Co., 1984), p. 97.

Afro-American women of the United States have never had the benefit of a discriminating judgment concerning their worth as women made up of the good and bad of human nature. What they have been made to be and not what they are, seldom enters into the best or worst opinion concerning them.

In studying the status of Afro-American women as revealed in their club organizations, it ought to be borne in mind that such social differentiations as "women's interests, children's interests, and men's interests" that are so finely worked out in the social development of the more favored races are but recent recognitions in the progressive life of the negro race. Such specializing had no economic value in slavery days, and the degrading habit of regarding the negro race as an unclassified people has not yet wholly faded into a memory.

The negro as an "alien" race, as a "problem," as an "industrial factor," as "ex-slaves," as "ignorant" etc., are well known and instantly recognized; but colored women as mothers, as home-makers, as the center and source of the social life of the race have received little or no attention. These women have been left to grope their way unassisted toward a realization of those domestic virtues, moral impulses and standards of family and social life that are the badges of race respectability. They have had no special teachers to instruct them. No conventions of distinguished women of the more favored race have met to consider their peculiar needs. There has been no fixed public opinion to which they could appeal; no protection against the libelous attacks upon their characters, and no chivalry generous enough to guarantee their safety against man's inhumanity to woman. Certain it is that colored women have been the least known, and the most ill-favored class of women in this country.

Thirty-five years ago they were unsocialized, unclassed and unrecognized as either maids or matrons. They were simply women whose character and personality excited no interest. If within thirty-five years they have become sufficiently important to be studied apart from the general race problem and have come to be recognized as an integral part of the general womanhood of American civilization, that fact is a gratifying evidence of real progress.

In considering the social advancement of these women, it is important to keep in mind the point from which progress began, and the fact that they have been mainly self-taught in all those precious things that make for social order, purity and character. They have gradually become conscious of the fact that progress includes a great deal more than what is generally meant by the terms culture, education and contact.

The club movement among colored women reaches into the sub-social condition of the entire race. Among white women clubs mean the forward movement of the best women in the interest of the best womanhood. Among colored women the club is the effort of the few competent in behalf of the many incompetent; that is to say that the club is only one of many means for the social uplift of a race. Among white women the club is the onward movement of the already uplifted.

The consciousness of being fully free has not yet come to the great masses of the colored women in this country. The emancipation of the mind and spirit of the race could not be accomplished by legislation. More time, more patience, more suffering and more charity are still needed to complete the work of emancipation.

The training which first enabled colored women to organize and successfully carry on club work was originally obtained in church work. These churches have been and still are the great preparatory schools in which the primary lessons of social order, mutual trustfulness and united effort have been taught. The churches have been sustained, enlarged and beautified principally through the organized efforts of their women members. The meaning of unity of effort for the common good, the development of social sympathies grew into woman's consciousness through the privileges of church work.

Still another school of preparation for colored women has been their secret societies. "The ritual of these secret societies is not without a certain social value." They demand a higher order of intelligence than is required for church membership. Care for the sick, provisions for the decent burial of the indigent dead, the care for orphans and the enlarging sense of sisterhood all contributed to the development of the very conditions of heart that qualify women for the more inclusive work of those social reforms that are the aim of women's clubs. The churches and secret societies have helped to make colored women acquainted with the general social condition of the race and the possibilities of social improvement.

With this training the more intelligent women of the race could not fail to follow the example and be inspired by the larger club movement of the white women. The need of social reconstruction became more and more apparent as they studied the results of women's organizations. Better homes, better schools, better protection for girls of scant home training, better sanitary conditions, better opportunities for competent young women to gain employment, and the need of being better known to the American people appealed to the conscience of progressive colored women from many communities.

The clubs and leagues organized among colored women have all been more or less in direct response to these appeals. Seriousness of purpose has thus been the main characteristic of all these organizations. While the National Federation of Woman's Clubs has served as a guide and inspiration to colored women, the club movement among them is something deeper than a mere imitation of white women. It is nothing less than the organized anxiety of women who have become intelligent enough to recognize their own low social condition and strong enough to initiate the forces of reform.

Working Girls' Societies

GRACE H. DODGE, 1889

Grace H. Dodge, "Working Girls' Societies," *Chautauquan* 9 (January 1889), pp. 223–25.

During the 1880s, well-off urban women founded clubs to improve the lives of young women wage earners. Working girls' clubs were in no way unions, nor were they concerned with the nature of the labor that their members—shop girls and factory employees—performed. Their purpose, instead, was to supply a wholesome environment and useful instruction, to cultivate industrious habits and genteel manners, and to offer the same experience in democratic organization and self-improvement that women's clubs enjoyed, through lectures, discussions, committee reports, election of officers, and so on. The clubs, which formed a national association in 1894, attracted a membership of native-born young women workers.

Philanthropist Grace H. Dodge (1856–1914), who founded the first working girls' club in 1884—for New York silk mill workers—served as spokeswoman for the working girls' club movement. In an 1889 article, Dodge presented her view of the working girls, their need for uplift, and the clubs' efforts to provide it. These efforts were not totally successful, because the club movement capsized around the mid-1890s. Suspicious of middle-class patronage, some young club members apparently preferred social activities that brought them into the company of men. Others abandoned the clubs for trade unions or other labor associations. By the turn of the century, Grace H. Dodge had resigned from the club movement. Economic problems, she now believed, were the major problems that working women confronted. Working girls' clubs, in the end, represented a failed effort to establish gender bonds across class lines, to bridge—in Dodge's words—"the chasm between the leisure and working classes."

Working girls! How these words suggest a grand army of toilers who are bravely struggling against great odds to support themselves! Some of them are scarcely more than children, taken from school to earn a weekly pittance, because the mother feels she cannot longer afford to forego their aid; some, looking worn and tired after years of factory or shop life, yet with nothing ahead but the same weary work; others, tenderly brought up, who have been suddenly thrown upon the world to care for themselves. . . .

These girls have left school early and have had little instruction. Few of them know anything of housework, and some can scarcely sew, yet what noble, true women hundreds of them become. They are filled with longings for higher things, but unaided they do not know how to attain them. They are self-reliant and independent, and would resent being considered in any sense objects of charity. Bright and observant, they quickly read the characters of those they meet. Trade unions and labor organizations have influenced many of them; weekly and daily papers give them certain ideas and knowledge; cheap novels present false sentiments, and put wrong estimates on the purpose and scope of life. Money is squandered because never properly valued, and the science of saving and using not understood, and health is thrown away by improper living and eating. Thoughts of marriage are constantly in their minds, and meeting with men and boys considered the great excitement of their life, while the duties of wifehood and motherhood are utterly unknown to them.

These girls are our sisters; they are like ourselves. They need us and we need them. I am addressing women and girls who have had advantages of education and culture. The question arises, how can we help one another. In cooperation there is strength—as societies, clubs, and associations have proved, and such organizations have been formed by working women and girls with great success. Let us look back and see how some of these have started, and with what objects.

Several years ago for three successive winters, a young lady in New York met every Tuesday evening a number of factory girls to talk over with them the practical things of life. They discussed household matters, health, morals, books, how to use and how to keep money, and kindred topics. One night the question arose, "Can we not do more?" and it was arranged that a meeting should be held to decide, "How can working girls have a good, useful time in the evening?" This meeting soon took place at the home of one of the girls, and twelve were present. After a talk of two hours, they adjourned to meet again in a few nights. At this gathering the Working Girls' Society received its name, and its first officers were elected. For six weeks they met in various rooms offered to them, and by that time the society numbered sixty members, each pledged to pay twenty-five cents per month; then a constitution was adopted, and a small floor rented for twenty-five dollars a month. The fees and dues of the one hundred members—and soon there were more than this—met the rent, and a few donations helped with other necessary expenses.

We must now turn to the principles and ideas elaborated by the society and sum up the results of nearly six years of its existence.

The society has its rooms open every evening but Saturday from half past seven to half past nine throughout the year. It has a library of several hundred volumes, a table for writing letters, illustrated books, and games, etc., in one room. It also has a large room for general use where lectures or classes are held nightly, a small reception room which serves as an office for its woman physician, and the use of a kitchen where the cooking classes are held. It is *home* to all its members. It is a joyous place, fun and laughter being nightly visitors, even in the numerous classes. These are not such as try to fit the members for work that will never come to them, but are planned to help them in practical, every day living, and to make them better women. The dress-making classes teach how to cut and fit, and it is a proud evening when a class finishes with a "dress parade," each girl wearing a dress made by herself. In the millinery class, ideas are given for making hats and bonnets out of almost nothing—costing very little, and yet with pretty results. The cutting-out class teaches how underclothes should be cut and made. The cooking and housekeeping classes make good housewives, while the embroidery and reading classes instruct and cheer. The doctor makes them thoughtful for their health, and stronger members are the result.

To many the pleasantest evening of all is the one for "practical talk." About forty or fifty girls cluster around the leader, and bright, yet earnest, solemn talks follow on every topic interesting to girls and young women. "Womanhood," "Purity," "Men Friends," "How to get a Husband," "Money, How to get it, and How to keep it," "Accounts," "Books," "Characteristics," "Home Life," and similar subjects are always popular. Lectures are given to the members by prominent people, and mothers and friends are invited to these.

In this society there is an inside organization whose object is to help others poorer than themselves. The Harry Wadsworth motto has been adopted, and the girls learn the great pleasure of helping others, by sacrificing themselves in order to bring cheer and gladness to the suffering. Flowers, fruits, and fresh eggs are sent to the Resolve Club—for that is its name—by country friends, and then taken out to sick and dying members, or to others who need them. At Christmas time poor children are rendered happy in various ways, garments are made and carried to destitute people, and by numerous methods the suggestive motto "Lend-a-Hand" is carried out.

Upon the first Monday night of each month is held the business meeting, which is conducted upon strictly parliamentary rules. At this meeting dues are collected, committees report, and new work is discussed. . . . A class is not started with less than fifteen members, the teacher receiving fifteen dollars for the course. Donations are accepted from interested friends, and upon vote of the whole society, applied to special objects. Certain incidental outlays are met by the officers, but appear on the treasurer's monthly statement. The members feel that they are self-supporting as to rent and the main expenses, but like other societies and clubs they do not refuse donations, though all public begging is forbidden. Last year, besides the $485.50 from fees and dues, the members themselves paid $88.90 for classes, and $391.15 toward the expenses of the vacation fund.

The attendance at the rooms for the past year was 9,364, an average of 180 weekly. The class membership was 386 in the following classes: dress-making 70; cooking 15; millinery 50; writing and arithmetic 12; elocution 30; first aid to the injured 30; practical talks 80; embroidery and sewing 75; French 12; German 12.

The occupations of the members are varied. A large majority work in carpet and silk factories; others at corsets, cigarettes, and trimmings; a percentage are in stores and dress-making establishments; others are telegraph operators or stenographers; a few are teachers; and there are single representatives of other pursuits. Catholics, Protestants, and Jews meet together.

From this first society have sprung many others of similar character. There are eighteen in New York and its immediate vicinity, all started and carried on after the pattern of the parent society. As societies multiplied it seemed wise for them to co-operate, so an Association of the Working Girls' Societies was formed with the following objects:

(1) To strengthen, to knit together, and to protect, the interests of the several societies. (2) To hold meetings, when the reports of the societies shall be presented, and to make more generally known their aims and advantages. (3) To promote the general adoption of the principles upon which the societies have been formed. (4) To secure the services, by co-operation, of good teachers, lady physicians, and lecturers. (5) To keep the several societies informed of such classes and schemes as are proved valuable. (6) To encourage and assist in the establishment of new societies.

This Association is governed by a General Council, composed of representatives appointed by each club. This Council elects from its body five directresses and two secretaries, who act for the Association between its meetings.

While alike in the main, the individual societies differ in certain particulars. One of them has a house built especially for its use; another has a literary evening, when men friends are invited to share in the discussions and exercises. Rambling parties have been instituted by a small society, and thus the Saturday half holidays are enjoyed together.

The meetings of all are business-like, a general vote deciding questions. Habits of saving are inculcated. One society says in its annual report: "Special attention has been paid this year to the study of economy. We have found the envelope system very satisfactory in helping the girls to save money against the coming summer vacation expenses. Little envelopes properly labeled are given out each week, and returned to the treasurer the week following, by each girl who saves, with the money she has been able to put by." In the same society it is becoming the fashion to study how a woman may dress tastefully, and yet spend only the right proportion of her income on her clothes. A very pretty woolen dress was made in the dress-making class, the total cost of which was $3.72.

The interests, occupations, and responsibility which have come to the members from the societies, give new meaning and impulse to their lives. Difficulties arising from waste, mismanagement, neglect, and ignorance are overcome by their enlarged knowledge and opportunities.

Simply coming into a bright room where books and papers are easily read, where laughter and singing are heard, cheers and strengthens the girl, and makes the next day's toil easier. Then the chasm between the leisure and working classes is bridged in the happiest way, by bringing out the fact that women who are not obliged to work, often do understand many kinds of work from choice, and these in turn, when they come to know the busy working girls, learn to understand and admire them. . . .

This is a little outline of what is being done. Why should not hundreds of such societies be started? They will start when we women learn more and more to think of each other, not in a narrow, pharisaical spirit, but in one of sisterly love.

The Clubs of Hull House

JANE ADDAMS AND ELLEN GATES STARR, 1895

Jane Addams and Ellen Gates Starr, "Hull House: A Social Settlement," *Hull House Maps and Papers* (Boston: Thomas Y. Crowell & Co., 1895), pp. 207–30 passim.

No institution applied the "club principle" more avidly than the social settlement. Although settlements had many purposes, a major goal was to introduce immigrants and their families to the "best" of American life. Toward this goal, clubs—made up of neighborhood residents—were essential. They taught order and regularity, manners and skills, democratic principles, and good citizenship. As Jane Addams (1860–1935), a founder of Hull House in Chicago, later explained, the settlement club was valuable as "an instrument of companionship through which many may be led from a sense of isolation to one of civic responsibility."

When Addams and co-founder Ellen Gates Starr (1859–1940) summarized Hull House's functions in 1895, after a mere six years of operation, they outlined a huge array of services, classes, and especially clubs. The club descriptions appear in the following reading. Designed to reach all age groups and cater to all interests, the Hull House clubs obviously were not limited to women. Most, however, involved women and children, who, residents hoped, would transmit what they learned to other family members. The overwhelming majority of the twenty Hull House residents of 1895, similarly, were women. Of the seventeen long-term residents (in residence for six months or more), only two were men.

The thriving institution that Jane Addams and Ellen Gates Starr portray continued to expand. By 1910, Hull House buildings covered a city block and the settlement boasted some seventy residents. Jane Addams, who in 1893 described herself as the "grandmother of settlements," presided over Hull House for the rest of her life. She summarized her experience in a famous autobiography, *Twenty Years at Hull-House* (1910), and in a sequel published twenty years later.

Hull-House: A Social Settlement

The two original residents of Hull-House are entering upon their sixth year of settlement in the nineteenth ward. They publish this outline that the questions daily asked by neighbors and visitors may be succinctly answered. . . . It aims not so much to give an account of what has been accomplished, as to suggest what may be done by and through a neighborhood of working-people, when they are touched by a common stimulus, and possess an intellectual and social centre about which they may group their various organizations and enterprises.

The original residents came to Hull-House with a conviction that social intercourse could best express the growing sense of the economic unity of society. They wished the social spirit to be the undercurrent of the life of Hull-House, whatever direction the stream might take. All the details were left for the demands of the neighborhood to determine, and each department has grown from a discovery made through natural and reciprocal social relations. . . .

The Jane Club

The Jane Club, a co-operative boarding-club for young working-women, had the advice and assistance of Hull-House in its establishment. The original members of the club, seven in number, were a group of trades-union girls accustomed to organized and co-operative action. The club has been from the beginning self-governing, without a matron or outside control, the officers being elected by the members from their own number, and serving for six months gratuitously. . . .

The club now numbers fifty members, and the one flat is increased to five. The members do such share of the housework as does not interfere with their daily occupations. There are various circles within the club for social and intellectual purposes; and while the members are glad to procure the comforts of life at a rate within their means, the atmosphere of the club is one of comradeship rather than thrift. The club holds a monthly reception in the Hull-House gymnasium.

The Phalanx Club

A similar co-operative club has been started by nine young men at 245 West Polk Street, most of the members of which are members of the Typographical Union. The club has made a most promising beginning.

The Labor Movement

The connection of the House with the labor movement may be said to have begun on the same social basis as its other relations. Of its standing with labor unions, which is now "good and regular," it owes the foundation to personal relations with the organizer of the Bindery Girls' Union, who lived for some months in the House as a guest. It is now generally understood that Hull-House is "on the side of unions." Several of the women's unions have held their regular meetings at the House, two have been organized there, and in four instances men and women on strike against reduction in wages met there while the strike lasted. In one case a strike was successfully arbitrated by the House. It is most interesting to note that a number of small and feeble unions have, from the very fact of their weakness, been compelled to a policy which has been their strength, and has made for the strength of their cause. In this policy it has been the privilege of Hull-House to be of service to them.

Eight-Hour Club

After the passage of the factory and workshop bill, which includes a clause limiting women's labor to eight hours a day, the young women employees in a large factory in the near neighborhood of Hull-House formed an Eight-Hour Club for the purpose of encouraging women in factories and workshops to obey the eight-hour law.

The Working-People's Social Science Club

was formed during the first year of residence at Hull-House, and has met weekly ever since, with the exception of the two summer months. In the summer of 1893, however, owing to the number of interesting speakers to be secured from the World's Fair Congresses, the club met without interruption. The purpose of the club is the discussion of social and economic topics.

The Arnold Toynbee Club Meets at Hull-House. The objects of the club are: (1) To offer lectures upon economic subjects, (2) to ascertain and make known facts of interest to working-people in the fields of economics and legislation, (3) to promote legislation for economic and social reform, especially to secure greater public control over natural monopolies.

The Chicago Question Club

meets in the Hull-House Art Gallery at two o'clock every Sunday afternoon. The club was fully formed before it asked for the hospitality of Hull-House. It is well organized, and each meeting is opened by presentation of two sides of a question. Occasionally the various economic clubs meet for a common discussion. One of the most successful was led by Father Huntington, on the subject, "Can a Freethinker believe in Christ?" An audience of four hundred people followed closely the two hours' discussion, which was closed by Mr. Henry George.

The Nineteenth Ward Improvement Club

The Nineteenth Ward Improvement Club meets at Hull-House the second Saturday evening of each month. The president is the district representative in the Illinois State Legislature, and one of the ward aldermen is an active member. The club is pledged to the improvement of its ward in all directions. It has standing-committees on street-cleaning, etc., and was much interested in the efforts of the Municipal Order League to secure public baths.

The Hull-House Women's Club

which now numbers ninety of the most able women in the ward, developed from a social meeting for purposes of tea-drinking and friendly chat. Several members of this club have done good work in street and alley inspecting through the Municipal Order

League. The club has also presented to a public school in the neighborhood a fine autotype of Millet's Knitting Shepherdess, and hopes to do more in future for the art-in-schools movement. They have been active in the visiting and relief work which has taken so large a share of the energies of the settlement during the hard times. One winter they purchased a ticket to the lectures given to mothers in the Kindergarten College. One member attended each week, and reported to the club. They are in touch with some of the vigorous movements of the city, and have frequent lectures on philanthropic and reform questions.

Children's Clubs

Since its foundation, Hull-House has had numerous classes and clubs for children. The fortunes and value of the clubs have varied, depending very much upon the spirit of the leaders. An effort has always been made to avoid the school atmosphere. The children are received and trusted as guests, and the initiative and control have come from them as far as possible. Their favorite occupation is listening to stories. One club has had a consecutive course of legends and tales of chivalry. There is no doubt that the more imaginative children learn to look upon the house as a gateway into a magic land, and get a genuine taste of the delights of literature. One boy, after a winter of Charlemagne stories, flung himself half-crying, from the house, and said that "there was no good in coming any more now that Prince Roland was dead." The boys' clubs meet every Tuesday afternoon at four o'clock, and clubs of little girls come on Friday. The latter are the Schoolgirls' Club and the Pansy Club, the Story-Telling Club and the Kindergarten Club. They sew, paint, or make paper chains during the story-telling, and play games in the gymnasium together before they go home at five o'clock. A club of Bohemian girls, called "Libuse," meets every Monday, and studies the heroic women in history. The little children meet one afternoon in the week for advanced kindergarten work. There are various children's classes for gymnastics and dancing; and two children's choruses, of two hundred and fifty each, meet weekly under the direction of Mr. William Tomlins. Dinners are served to schoolchildren upon presentation of tickets which have been sold to their mothers for five cents each. Those children are first selected whose mothers are necessarily at work during the middle of the day; and the dinner started with children formerly in the Hull-House *crèche*. While it is desired to give the children nutritious food, the little diners care much more for the toys and books and the general good time than they do for the dinners. It has been found, too, that the general attractiveness performs the function of the truant-officer in keeping them at school; for no school implies no dinner. The House has had the sympathetic and enthusiastic co-operation of the principal of the Polk Street public school.

The Paderewski Club

A club of twenty children, calling themselves the Paderewski Club, has had a year of instruction on the piano, together with Sunday afternoon talks by their teacher on the lives of the great musicians. Six of the most proficient have obtained scholarships in the Chicago Conservatory.

The Hull-House Men's Club

holds a reception there [at Hull House] once a month, and an occasional banquet. This club, which rents a room in the front of the building, is composed of one hundred and fifty of the abler citizens and more enterprising young men of the vicinity. Their constitution commits them, among other things, to the "cultivation of sobriety and good-fellowship."

Young People's Clubs

The Lincoln Club is a debating-society of young men, whose occasional public debates are always heard by a large and enthusiastic audience. In their weekly meeting they have a carefully prepared debate, usually upon current political events. They meet once a month with the Hull-House Social Club. This is composed of young women of the neighborhood, many of whom have met every week for four years. Their programmes are literary and social. They give an occasional play. The last one presented was the court scene from the "Merchant of Venice."

Among the other clubs of young people, the Young Citizens boasts the oldest club-life. Their programmes alternate between discussions and readings. An effort is made in both for civic and municipal education.

The Anfreda Club of thirty young girls meets the same evening. After the literary programme is concluded, the two clubs have half an hour of dancing or games together before going home.

Henry Learned Club, Hull-House Glee Club, Jolly Boys' Club, Good-Fellowship Club, Lexington Club, Bohemian Garnet Club, Longfellow Club, Laurel Club, Harrison Club, and others, are composed of young people from fourteen to twenty-five years of age. Alumni associations of the neighboring public schools hold their meetings at the House. An effort is being made toward school extension.

The Hull-House Coffee-House and Kitchen

The Hull-House coffee-house was opened July 1, 1893. The room itself is an attractive copy of an English inn, with low, dark rafters, diamond windows, and large fireplace. It is open every day from six in the morning to ten at night. An effort has been made to combine the convenience of a lunch-room, where well-cooked food can be sold at a reasonable rate, with cosiness and attractiveness. The residents believe that substitution is the only remedy against the evils of the saloon. The large kitchen has been carefully equipped, under the direction of Mrs. Ellen Richards,* with a New England kitchen outfit, including a number of Aladdin ovens.

Residents

No university or college qualification has ever been made for residence, although the majority of residents have been college people. The organization of the settlement

---

*M. I. T. chemist Ellen Swallow Richards (1842–1911) developed the New England Kitchen, a public facility in which nourishing meals could be prepared at low cost and cooking techniques demonstrated.

has been extremely informal; but an attempt has been made during the last winter to limit the number of residents to twenty. The household, augmented by visitors, has occasionally exceeded that number. Applicants for residence are received for six weeks, during which time they have all privileges, save a vote, at residents' meetings. At the end of that period, if they have proved valuable to the work of the House, they are invited to remain, if it is probable that they can be in residence for six months. The expenses of the residents are defrayed by themselves on the plan of a cooperative club under the direction of a house committee. A limited number of fellowships has been established, one of them by the Chicago branch of the Inter-Collegiate Alumnæ Association.

All the residents of Hull-House for the first three years were women, though much valuable work has always been done by non-resident men. During the last year men have come into residence in a cottage on Polk Street, dining at Hull-House, and giving such part of their time to the work of the settlement as is consistent with their professional or business life.

It is estimated that two thousand people come to Hull-House each week, either as members of clubs or organizations, or as parts of an audience. One hundred of these come as teachers, lecturers, or directors of clubs. The house has always had much valuable assistance from the citizens of Chicago. This voluntary response to its needs perhaps accounts for the fact that it has never found it necessary to form an association with chapters in colleges, as other settlements have done.

Chapter 16

The Suffrage Movement

*T*he woman suffrage movement had much in common with the wider world of women's organizations, of which it was a part. Arising in the decade after the Civil War, at the same time as women's clubs and the women's temperance crusade, the suffrage movement recruited among middle-class women. Like other women's pressure groups, it held conventions, published journals, and formed federations of local clubs, or suffrage leagues. But woman suffrage was distinctive. The early suffragists—a small group of veterans from the antebellum abolitionist and women's rights campaigns—sought equality with men and chose the vote as a tool to obtain it. By demanding the ballot, they challenged male power directly. They also threatened traditional ideas of woman's place, and therefore had difficulty attracting a female constituency. Compared to the rest of the late nineteenth-century "woman movement," as it was often called, woman suffrage was more radical and more marginal. During the last decade of the nineteenth century, suffragists began a pilgrimage from the periphery of women's politics to the mainstream.

The quest of suffragists started in the early years of Reconstruction, when a national issue, black political rights, transformed the women's rights movement. Hoping that the Republicans would support woman suffrage along with black male suffrage, the small contingent of women's rights activists concentrated their efforts on one right—the vote. Defending suffrage as a "natural right," they formed an Equal Rights Association in 1866 to promote enfranchisement of blacks and women. But former allies in antislavery proved resistant. The "negro's hour" would not be the woman's hour. One turning point was an 1867 referendum campaign in Kansas, where abolitionists deserted the women's cause, and voters defeated both black suffrage and woman suffrage. Another turning point was the campaign for the Fifteenth Amendment (ensuring black suffrage), which divided adherents of women's rights. Rejecting the prospect of black suffrage without woman suffrage, the more defiant women reformers—Elizabeth Cady Stanton, Susan B. Anthony, and their colleagues—used their journal, *Revolution*, to denounce Republicans, abolitionists, and the proposed amendment. Extending the franchise while excluding women from it, Stanton argued, further debased them. In 1869, the early suffragists split into factions. The Stanton-Anthony group formed the all-female National Woman Suffrage Association (NWSA). Suffragists who accepted the Fifteenth Amendment as a first step in the right direction joined with abolitionist men to form the Boston-based American Woman Suffrage Association (AWSA). Lucy Stone and Julia Ward Howe were prominent members of this organization.

In the election of 1872, several women affiliated with the NWSA—Susan B. Anthony, Victoria Woodhull, and Virginia Minor—attempted to achieve the vote by casting ballots, though with no success. Anthony was convicted of illegal voting. Virginia Minor and her husband, who sued a Missouri registrar, lost their case in 1875, when the Supreme Court declared that the Fourteenth Amendment did not entitle women to vote. The "equal rights" argument was stymied and so was the suffrage movement. Until 1890 it followed a divided course. The NWSA called for a constitutional amendment, and the AWSA campaigned on a state-by-state basis. Neither made headway. While the wildly successful women's temperance movement flourished and women's clubs multiplied, suffragists won a comparatively small following. Sometimes mutual support was possible, as when temperance leader Frances Willard endorsed woman suffrage. Other attempts at outreach fizzled. In 1888, the NWSA organized a large International Council of Women, with delegates from many women's reform organizations, that met in Washington for a round of speeches. But the NWSA appeal for support failed. Woman suffrage was still too extreme a cause to win endorsement, even among other women reformers.

In 1890, as rivalry between their two factions faded, suffragists united in the National American Woman Suffrage Association (NAWSA), and agreed on a common strategy: state campaigns. Although almost all of these campaigns failed (by 1910, only four western states enfranchised women), they provided a forum for suffragist views. During the 1890s, moreover, the tenor of suffragist arguments shifted from an emphasis on "equal rights," or the justice of female enfranchisement, to an emphasis on the desirability of woman suffrage—the special qualities that women would bring to the polls and the good they would do if enfranchised. The new arguments, geared to attract a larger base of support, made woman suffrage seem less radical, threatening, and challenging. Such an appeal was effective, at least in drawing new members to the NAWSA. But the search for constituency was not without casualties. One was Elizabeth Cady Stanton, whose unquenchable radicalism had permeated the suffrage movement's early years. Although she served briefly as president of the new NAWSA, Stanton was too outrageous for its enlarged membership. She offended many by her calls for liberal divorce laws and by her emancipated, free-thinking *Women's Bible*, which the NAWSA rejected.

By the end of the century, women had made many gains for which early women's rights advocates had campaigned. They had won the opportunity for higher education and entry into the professions. Many states had granted married women property rights and equal guardianship rights over children. Many states also had granted women a limited form of suffrage, as in local elections or school-board elections. But complete woman suffrage remained the last hold-out. "Men have granted us . . . everything, but the pivotal right, the one that underlies all the other rights," Susan B. Anthony claimed. Not until around 1910 would woman suffrage gain centrality in the larger "woman movement." Real momentum toward victory materialized only in the World War I era. During the late nineteenth century, the suffrage movement succeeded by surviving, and by offering its participants a political education. It also provided activists with a sense of participating in the nation's history. This historical consciousness emerged in suffragists' memoirs and recollections, in their speeches and arguments, and in their own documentary record, the massive *History of Woman Suffrage*.

The Joys of Activism

JULIA WARD HOWE, 1899

Julia Ward Howe, *Reminiscences, 1819–1899* (Boston: Houghton Mifflin, 1899), pp. 372–77.

The appeal of the late nineteenth-century woman's movement lay in the benefit of association with other women, the freedom to participate in public life, and the sense of commitment to a noble cause. Looking back at the end of the century, Julia Ward Howe (1819–1910) summarized the joy of collective action that she and her colleagues experienced in the late 1860s. At this juncture Howe was one of the most famous women in the nation. During the Civil War, Union troops had marched off to the front singing her "Battle Hymn of the Republic." A founding member of the New England Woman's Club, and of the American Woman Suffrage Association (AWSA), Howe brought her considerable prestige to both organizations.

Howe's recollections were of course partisan ones. She sought to pay tribute to her own wing of the suffrage movement, the AWSA; to her colleagues Lucy Stone and Mary Livermore; and to the group of male reformers who allied themselves with this faction. Still, she eloquently describes the process of "politicization" that many members of the early suffrage movement experienced.

I sometimes feel as if words could not express the comfort and instruction which have come to me in the later years of my life from two sources. One of these has been the better acquaintance with my own sex; the other, the experience of the power resulting from associated action in behalf of worthy objects.

During the first two thirds of my life I looked to the masculine ideal of character as the only true one. I sought its inspiration, and referred my merits and demerits to its judicial verdict. In an unexpected hour a new light came to me, showing me a world of thought and of character quite beyond the limits within which I had hitherto been content to abide. The new domain now made clear to me was that of true womanhood—woman no longer in her ancillary relation to her opposite, man, but in her direct relation to the divine plan and purpose, as a free agent, fully sharing with man every human right and every human responsibility. This discovery was like the addition of a new continent to the map of the world, or of a new testament to the old ordinances.

"Oh, had I earlier known the power, the nobility, the intelligence which lie within the range of true womanhood, I had surely lived more wisely and to better purpose." Such were my reflections; yet I must think that the great Lord of all reserved this new revelation as the crown of a wonderful period of the world's emancipation and progress.

It did not come to me all at once. In my attempts at philosophizing I at length reached the conclusion that woman must be the moral and spiritual equivalent of man. How, otherwise, could she be entrusted with the awful and inevitable responsibilities of maternity? The quasi-adoration that true lovers feel, was it an illusion partly of sense, partly of imagination? or did it symbolize a sacred truth?

While my mind was engaged with these questions, the Civil War came to an end, leaving the slave not only emancipated, but endowed with the full dignity of citizenship. The women of the North had greatly helped to open the door which admitted him to freedom and its safeguard, the ballot. Was this door to be shut in their face?

While I followed, rather unwillingly, this train of thought, an invitation was sent me to attend a parlor meeting to be held with the view of forming a woman's club in Boston. I presented myself at this meeting, and gave a languid assent to the measures proposed. These were to hire a parlor or parlors in some convenient locality, and to furnish and keep them open for the convenience of ladies residing in the city and its suburbs. Out of this small and modest beginning was gradually developed the plan of the New England Woman's Club,* a strong and stately association destined, I believe, to last for many years, and leaving behind it, at this time of my writing, a record of three decades of happy and acceptable service.

While our club life was still in its beginning, I was invited and induced to attend a meeting in behalf of woman suffrage. Indeed, I had given my name to the call for this meeting, relying upon the assurance given me by Colonel Thomas Wentworth Higginson,[†] that it would be conducted in a very liberal and friendly spirit, without bitterness or extravagance. The place appointed was Horticultural Hall. The morning was inclement; and as I strayed into the hall in my rainy-day suit, nothing was further from my mind than the thought that I should take any part in the day's proceedings.

I had hoped not to be noticed by the officers of the meeting, and was rather disconcerted when a message reached me requesting me to come up and take a seat on the platform. This I did very reluctantly. I was now face to face with a new order of things. Here, indeed, were some whom I had long known and honored: Garrison, Wendell Phillips, Colonel Higginson, and my dear pastor, James Freeman Clarke. But here was also Lucy Stone, who had long been the object of one of my imaginary dislikes. As I looked into her sweet, womanly face and heard her earnest voice, I felt that the object of my distaste had been a mere phantom, conjured up by silly and senseless misrepresentations. Here stood the true woman, pure, noble, great-hearted, with the light of her good life shining in every feature of her face. Here, too, I saw the husband whose devotion so ably seconded her life-work.[‡]

---

*A pioneer woman's club, formed in 1868.

[†]An abolitionist and fund-raiser for John Brown, Higginson had led a regiment of black soldiers, the First Regiment of South Carolina Volunteers, during the Civil War. After the war, he supported the American Woman Suffrage Association.

[‡]Henry Blackwell.

The arguments to which I now listened were simple, strong, and convincing. These champions, who had fought so long and so valiantly for the slave, now turned the searchlight of their intelligence upon the condition of woman, and demanded for the mothers of the community the civil rights which had recently been accorded to the negro. They asked for nothing more and nothing less than the administration of that impartial justice for which, if for anything, a Republican government should stand.

When they requested me to speak, which they did presently, I could only say, "I am with you." I have been with them ever since, and have never seen any reason to go back from the pledge then given. Strangely, as it then seemed to me, the arguments which I had stored up in my mind against the political enfranchisement of women were really so many reasons in its favor. All that I had felt regarding the sacredness and importance of the woman's part in private life now appeared to me equally applicable to the part which she should bear in public life.

One of the comforts which I found in the new association was the relief which it afforded me from a sense of isolation and eccentricity. For years past I had felt strongly impelled to lend my voice to the convictions of my heart. I had done this in a way, from time to time, always with the feeling that my course in so doing was held to call for apology and explanation by the men and women with whose opinions I had hitherto been familiar. I now found a sphere of action in which this mode of expression no longer appeared singular or eccentric, but simple, natural, and, under the circumstances, inevitable.

In the little band of workers which I had joined, I was soon called upon to perform yeoman's service. I was expected to attend meetings and to address audiences, at first in the neighborhood of Boston, afterwards in many remote places, Cleveland, Chicago, St. Louis. Among those who led or followed the new movement, I naturally encountered some individuals in whom vanity and personal ambition were conspicuous. But I found mostly among my new associates a great heart of religious conviction and a genuine spirit of self-sacrifice.

My own contributions to the work appeared to me less valuable than I had hoped to find them. I had at first everything to learn with regard to public speaking, and Lucy Stone and Mrs. Livermore* were much more at home on the platform than I was. I was called upon to preside over conventions, having never learned the rules of debate. I was obliged to address large audiences, having been accustomed to use my voice only in parlors. Gradually all this bettered itself. I became familiar with the order of proceedings, and learned to modulate my voice. More important even than these things, I learned something of the range of popular sympathies, and of the power of apprehension to be found in average audiences. All of these experiences, the failures, the effort, and the final achievement, were most useful to me.

In years that followed I gave what I could to the cause, but all that I gave was repaid to me a thousandfold.

---

*Mary A. Livermore.

Political Lessons

ELIZABETH CADY STANTON AND SUSAN B. ANTHONY, 1882

Elizabeth Cady Stanton, Susan B. Anthony, and Matilda Joslyn Gage, eds., *History of Woman Suffrage*, vol. 2 (New York: Fowler and Wells, 1882), pp. 264–68.

When NWSA leaders Elizabeth Cady Stanton (1815–1902) and Susan B. Anthony (1820–1906) looked back at the early days of the woman suffrage crusade, their recollections were less sanguine than those of Julia Ward Howe. Compared to Howe, Stanton and Anthony had much more political experience. They had been leaders of the antebellum women's rights movement and of the wartime Women's Loyal League. For them, the conflicts of the late 1860s provided another sort of political lesson.

After the failed Kansas campaign of 1867, when voters rejected both black suffrage and woman suffrage, the Stanton/Anthony faction had been thrown back on their own resources. Rejected by their former abolitionist allies, who found the women's cause to be a liability, Stanton and Anthony in turn rejected "liberal men" who could not grasp the "humiliation" and "degradation" of women's disfranchisement, nor the legitimacy of the women's cause. In retrospect, this rejection was in fact an advantage, for it extricated the NWSA leaders from their dependence on abolitionist men. Isolated but independent, if only by default, they moved on to experiment with new alliances and strategies.

So utterly had the women been deserted in the Kansas campaign by those they had the strongest reason to look to for help, that at times all effort seemed hopeless. The editors of the New York *Tribune* and the *Independent* can never know how wistfully, from day to day, their papers were searched for some inspiring editorials on the woman's amendment, but naught was there; there were no words of hope and encouragement, no eloquent letters from an Eastern man that could be read to the people; all were silent. Yet these two papers, extensively taken all over Kansas, had they been as true to woman as to the negro, could have revolutionized the State. But with arms folded, Greeley, Curtis, Tilton, Beecher, Higginson, Phillips, Garrison, Frederick Douglass, all calmly watched the struggle from afar, and when defeat came to both propositions, no consoling words were offered for woman's loss, but the women who spoke in the campaign were reproached for having "killed negro suffrage."

We wondered then at the general indifference to that first opportunity of realizing what all those gentlemen had advocated so long; and, in looking back over the many intervening years, we still wonder at the stolid incapacity of all men to understand that woman feels the invidious distinctions of sex exactly as the black man does those of color, or the white man the more transient distinctions of wealth, family, position, place, and power; that she feels as keenly as man the injustice of disfranchisement. Of the old abolitionists who stood true to woman's cause in this crisis, Robert Purvis, Parker Pillsbury, and Rev. Samuel J. May were the only Eastern men.* Through all the hot debates during the period of reconstruction, again and again, Mr. Purvis arose and declared, that he would rather his son should never be enfranchised, unless his daughter could be also, that, as she bore the double curse of sex and color, on every principle of justice she should first be protected. These were the only men who felt and understood as women themselves do the degradation of disfranchisement. . . .

And here is the secret of the infinite sadness of women of genius; of their dissatisfaction with life, in exact proportion to their development. A woman who occupies the same realm of thought with man, who can explore with him the depths of science, comprehend the steps of progress through the long past and prophesy those of the momentous future, must ever be surprised and aggravated with his assumptions of headship and superiority, a superiority she never concedes, an authority she utterly repudiates. Words can not describe the indignation, the humiliation a proud woman feels for her sex in disfranchisement.

In a republic where all are declared equal an ostracised class of one half of the people, on the ground of a distinction founded in nature, is an anomalous position, as harassing to its victims as it is unjust, and as contradictory as it is unsafe to the fundamental principles of a free government. When we remember that out of this degraded political status, spring all the special wrongs that have blocked woman's success in the world of work, and degraded her labor everywhere to one half its value; closed to her the college doors and all opportunities for higher education, forbade her to practice in the professions, made her a cipher in the church, and her sex, her motherhood a curse in all religions; her subjection a text for bibles, a target for the priesthood; seeing all this, we wonder now as then at the indifference and injustice of our best men when the first opportunity offered in which the women of any State might have secured their enfranchisement.

It was not from ignorance of the unequal laws, and false public sentiment against woman, that our best men stood silent in this Kansas campaign; it was not from lack of chivalry that they thundered forth no protests, when they saw noble women, who had been foremost in every reform, hounded through the State by foul mouthed politicians; it was not from lack of money and power, of eloquence of pen and tongue, nor of an intellectual conviction that our cause was just, that they came not to the rescue, but because in their heart of hearts they did not grasp the imperative necessity of woman's demand for that protection which the ballot alone can give; they did not feel for *her* the degradation of disfranchisement.

---

*An organizer of the American Antislavery Society, Robert Purvis was one of the prominent black men in abolitionist circles. Parker Pillsbury had been editor of *The National Anti-Slavery Standard*. Unitarian minister Samuel J. May was another active participant in the Garrisonian wing of the antislavery movement.

The fact of their silence deeply grieved us, but the philosophy of their indifference we thoroughly comprehended for the first time and saw as never before, that only from woman's standpoint could the battle be successfully fought, and victory secured. "It is wonderful," says Swift, "with what patience some folks can endure the sufferings of others." Our liberal men counseled us to silence during the war, and we were silent on our own wrongs; they counseled us again to silence in Kansas and New York, lest we should defeat "negro suffrage," and threatened if we were not, we might fight the battle alone. We chose the latter, and were defeated. But standing alone we learned our power; we repudiated man's counsels forevermore; and solemnly vowed that there should never be another season of silence until woman had the same rights everywhere on this green earth, as man.

While we hold in loving reverence the names of such men as Charles Sumner, Horace Greeley, William Lloyd Garrison, Gerrit Smith, Wendell Phillips and Frederick Douglass, and would urge the rising generation of young men to emulate their virtues, we would warn the young women of the coming generation against man's advice as to their best interests, their highest development. We would point for them the moral of our experiences: that woman must lead the way to her own enfranchisement, and work out her own salvation with a hopeful courage and determination that knows no fear nor trembling. She must not put her trust in man in this transition period, since, while regarded as his subject, his inferior, his slave, their interests must be antagonistic.

But when at last woman stands on an even platform with man, his acknowledged equal everywhere, with the same freedom to express herself in the religion and government of the country, then, and not till then, can she safely take counsel with him in regard to her most sacred rights, privileges, and immunities; for not till then will he be able to legislate as wisely and generously for her as for himself.

If Women Could Vote

ISABELLA BEECHER HOOKER, 1868

[Isabella Beecher Hooker] "Two Letters on Woman Suffrage," *Putnam's Magazine* 2 (November 1868), pp. 603–06.

Isabella Beecher Hooker (1822–1907), younger sister of educator Catharine Beecher and author Harriet Beecher Stowe, was the wife of a Hartford lawyer and the mother of four children. A convert to the women's rights campaign during the Civil War, Hooker participated in the founding of the New England Woman Suffrage Association in 1868. Two years later, she became an active member of the NWSA and remained committed to the cause for the rest of her life.

One of the problems of the early suffrage movement was that women did not seem to be particularly interested in gaining the vote. In two anonymous magazine articles of 1868, Isabella Beecher Hooker tried to make the radical idea of equal suffrage acceptable to women by anticipating—and invalidating—all possible objections to it. To persuade her readers that woman suffrage was both desirable and just, Hooker adopted the pose of a mother writing to a recently married young daughter. In the first letter, which follows, she deals with a hypothetical question: Are women capable of holding political office? In response, Hooker presents a vision of a model officeholder—a middle-aged mother of ten who is more than competent to cope with the decisions faced by a state legislator. She also assures her readers that women would not be corrupted by politics or the ballot.

———

———, ———, 1868

My Dear Daughter:

You ask me what I think of the modesty and sense of a woman who can insist, in these days, that she is not sufficiently cared for in public and in private, and who wishes to add the duties of a politician to those of a mother and housekeeper.

This is a large question to ask, and a still larger one to answer by letter; but since you have a clear and thoughtful head of your own, and we are widely separated just now and unable to converse together as in times past, I will see what can be said by pen and paper for just the woman you have described.

And let me begin by asking you the meaning of the word *politician*. Having consulted your dictionary, you reply, "One who is versed in the science of government and the art of governing." Very well. Now who is thus versed in the science and art of governing, so far as the family is concerned, more than the mother of it? In this country, certainly, the manners, the habits, the laws of a household, are determined in great part by the mother; so much so, that when we see lying and disobedient children, or coarse, untidy, and ill-mannered ones, we instinctively make our comments on the mother of that brood, and declare her more or less incompetent to her place.

Now let me suppose her to be one of the competent ones who, like your Aunt E., has helped six stout boys and four of their quick-witted sisters all the way from babyhood up to manhood and womanhood, with a wisdom and gentleness and patience that have been the wonder of all beholders—and let us think of her as sitting down now in her half-forsaken nest, calm, thoughtful, and matured, but fresh in her feeling as ever she was, and stretching out by her sympathies in many directions after the younglings who have gone each to a special toil, and what wonder if she finds it hard to realize that she is unfitted either by nature or education for the work of law making, on a broader and larger scale than she has ever yet tried.

Her youngest boy, the privileged, saucy one of the crowd, has just attained his majority, we will say, and declaims in her hearing on the incompetence of women to vote—the superiority of the masculine element in politics, and the danger to society if women are not carefully guarded from contact with its rougher elements—and I seem to see her quiet smile and slightly curling lip, while in memory she runs back to the years when said stripling gathered all he knew of laws, country, home, heaven, and earth, at her knee—"and as for soiling contacts, oh! my son, who taught you to avoid these, and first put it into your curly little head, that evil communications corrupt good manners, and that a man cannot *touch* pitch, except he be defiled."

I have taken the bull by the horns, you perceive, in thus taking our mother from her quiet country home and setting her by imagination among the legislators of the land—but it is just as well, because the practical end of suffrage is, not *eligibility* to office merely, but a larger *use* of this privilege than most women have ever yet dreamed of, much less desired. . . .

And now she is there, we will say, in the legislature of our State—a high-minded, well-bred woman; one who, amid all her cares, has never failed to read the newspapers more or less, and to keep alive her interest in the prosperity of her country, whatever the claims of her numerous family. She is one, too, who has not had the assistance of wealth in doing all this; she is, as you know, straight from the rural districts, a genuine farmer's wife. But she has more leisure now than she once had, and with it there comes a longing for change, for more cultivated society, for recreations and diversions such as her busy hours have seldom afforded her; and just now, by the unanimous vote of her townspeople, she is sent to our glorious old Hub, to spend the winter in considering what the Commonwealth of Massachusetts shall do this year, by legislation, for the public good. . . .

Having secured a home not far from the old State House, she seeks the Assembly Room and meets there gentlemen from all parts of the State—farmers, merchants and mechanics, physicians, teachers and ministers, lawyers and bankers, and they go into debate on such questions as these: Shall our deaf mutes be educated at home, or in the Institution at Hartford, as heretofore? What of the economies of our past practice, and are there better methods of training than those instituted there? State Prison—shall the discipline be penal merely, or reformatory? the institution self-supporting by a system of rigid tasks, or partially supported by the State? What punishment shall be allowed, what religious and moral instruction furnished, and what sanitary regulations enforced? The prohibitory law—has it proved itself adapted to the suppression of intemperance? Are its provisions enforced, and why not? Is a special license law better adapted to the desired end, or is there any thing which human ingenuity can devise that shall arrest the spread of intemperance over the land? The school for juvenile offenders—is that managed judiciously? Here obviously the great aim should be reformation. Is a system of rewards or punishments, or both together, best adapted to that end? Should boys and girls be associated in the same buildings and classes, and for what length of time should they be retained for improvement before sending them out again into society? Endowments for colleges and other educational institutions supported in whole or in part by the State: Shall these be confined to institutions designed exclusively for men, or shall they be applied equally to the education of both sexes? Taxation—how apportioned? What interests can best bear heavy taxation, and is any further legislation needed to secure the right of representation to all who are taxed? Prostitution—shall it be licensed as in the old countries, or left to itself, or subjected to severe penalties? Divorces—by whom granted, and for what cause, and upon what conditions? Common schools, and high schools, and the whole system of State education; insane asylums, poor-houses, jails, and many other institutions of modern civilization—in all these objects, you will perceive, our mother has a deep and intelligent interest, and it is not difficult to imagine the warm, even enthusiastic energy with which she will give herself to the discussion of the questions involved—some of them the highest that can come before a human tribunal.

If you say, There are other State interests with which she is less familiar, I reply, No one legislator understands the detail of all the business that comes before the House, or is expected to; committees are appointed for specialties, as you know, and composed, or they ought to be, of those whose education and training have fitted them for that special investigation.

Our mother will have her hands full if she should serve on the Committee of Charitable Institutions alone; and none can do better service there than such a wise, prudent, affectionate care-taker as she has ever been. . . . She need not necessarily perfect herself in the technicalities of a legal education, though some would like well to do that, no doubt; professional gentlemen are generally called upon now by committees at their need; but she can bring a clear, practical, and experienced head and sound heart to the help of many a vexed question. And as to railroad bills and management—would that she might have a voice there; you may be sure that all charters would contain provisions for the comfort and safety of passengers, and the holding of all officials to a strict responsibility for neglect of duty.

And so in all matters pertaining to merchandise and business, which fairly come under state jurisdiction; it is late in the day to assert that women know nothing of those things, and could not learn if they should try. There are too many honest and successful women-traders, artists, and littérateurs in every city of the land, and too many men dependent in whole or in part upon their earnings, to give a show of color to such assertions. . . .

On the whole, then, my dear, you begin to perceive that my mind receives no shock when I am charged with the crime of desiring to meddle with politics, and to educate my daughters as well as my sons to take an intelligent, and, if need be, an active part in the government of their country; though I begin to fear, since the receipt of your letter, that my efforts in your behalf have not been crowned with the success I had much reason to hope. However, there is a gallant young husband in the case now, and I am very much mistaken if this is not the chief cause of your present difficulty; so I wish to say further, that I owe my young son-in-law no grudge whatever for this counter influence, nor do I abate one jot my confidence in him as a man of intelligence, integrity, and true nobility. The truth is, that one chief reason why your husband, and so many like him, oppose the extension of suffrage is, that their sense of true gallantry, their desire to shield and protect, is violated by *their conception* of the probable result of a woman's going to the polls. This is certainly a misconception. Every woman knows in her own heart that she does not hold her purity and delicacy subject to injury by such cause. We know that we have never entered any precinct, however vile and debased, without carrying something of that God-given power of womanhood—of motherhood—with us, which is a greater protection against insult and contamination than all the shields that man can devise. But we ought not to blame men too severely for their reluctance to relinquish this office of protector and guardian, which custom has so long laid upon them as a high duty and privilege.

In the days when physical forces ruled the world, men might naturally offer, and women receive with thankfulness, the protection of a strong arm, and become greatly dependent upon it, without serious harm to either sex; but in the day of moral forces it is quite otherwise. This day has come upon us, however, so silently, so gradually, that we ourselves have scarcely recognized that we are now near its noon-tide: how then can our fathers, brothers, and husbands be expected to feel its quickening glow and inspiration? It may seem to them a consuming heat though to me it is delicious warmth, pure air, God's own blue sky, and His benignant smile over all.

But I must stop here and wait your reply, since on your acceptance of my views thus far stated will depend the courage and enthusiasm with which I shall proceed to develop further my thought on the whole matter of the relation of the sexes to each other and to government. . . . I am persuaded, contrary to the judgment of many earnest advocates of equal suffrage, that women are quite as much responsible for the present condition of affairs as men, and that they, as a body, will be the last to be convinced of their duty in the matter of good citizenship; so I am seriously anxious to make converts to my faith from the young mothers, rather than from any other class. I know, of course, that the power of regulating suffrage now lies wholly with men; that not a single vote can be given, save by them; but I know as well that the minds of all honest, earnest thinkers among them are turned to this subject, and that they are inclined to give it an impartial hearing; and I am convinced that the indifference, not to say opposition, of their wives, mothers, and sisters, stands in the way of their coming to a right solution of the problem before them, beyond anything or all things else.

I beg you, therefore, to give my argument so far a candid consideration, and let me hear from you in reply.

I am always your affectionate

Mother

Social Purity

SUSAN B. ANTHONY, 1875

Ida Husted Harper, *The Life and Work of Susan B. Anthony*, vol. 2 (Indianapolis: Bowen-Merrill, 1899), pp. 1004–12 passim.

During the 1870s and 1880s, NWSA continued to voice concern about a broad range of women's rights. Elizabeth Cady Stanton, an advocate of divorce reform, lectured nationwide to women's audiences on such topics as marriage, home life, and "self-ownership." Susan B. Anthony, a tireless organizer and crusader, was more single-mindedly committed to the goal of woman suffrage. But she too spoke often on related causes, such as labor reform and moral reform.

In a Chicago speech of 1875, Anthony presented some of the sexual themes that had always been present in the women's rights crusade—and with which she long had been familiar, from her early days as a member of the moral reform and temperance movements. Women's dependent status, Anthony contended, fostered male vices: immorality, drunkenness, and prostitution. These could be remedied, she asserted, only by women's economic independence and enfranchisement. Although some of Anthony's concerns may seem dated, or peculiar to the nineteenth century, similar concerns have been resurrected by contemporary feminists.

Though women, as a class, are much less addicted to drunkenness and licentiousness than men, it is universally conceded that they are by far the greater sufferers from these evils. Compelled by their position in society to depend on men for subsistence, for food, clothes, shelter, for every chance even to earn a dollar, they have no way of escape from the besotted victims of appetite and passion with whom their lot is cast. They must endure, if not endorse, these twin vices, embodied, as they so often are, in the person of father, brother, husband, son, employer. No one can doubt that the sufferings of the sober, virtuous woman, in legal subjection to the mastership of a drunken, immoral husband and father over herself and children, not only from physical abuse, but from spiritual shame and humiliation, must be such as the man himself can not possibly comprehend.

It is not my purpose to harrow your feelings by any attempt at depicting the horrible agonies of mind and body that grow out of these monster social evils. They are already but too well known. Scarce a family throughout our broad land but has had its peace and happiness marred by one or the other, or both. That these evils exist, we all know; that something must be done, we as well know; that the old methods have failed, that man, alone, has proved himself incompetent to eradicate, or even regulate them, is equally evident. It shall be my endeavor, therefore, to prove to you that we must now adopt new measures and bring to our aid new forces to accomplish the desired end.

Forty years' efforts by men alone to suppress the evil of intemperance give us the following appalling figures: 600,000 common drunkards! Which, reckoning our population to be 40,000,000, gives us one drunkard to every seventeen moderate drinking and total-abstinence men. Granting to each of these 600,000 drunkards a wife and four children, we have 3,000,000 of the women and children of this nation helplessly, hopelessly bound to this vast army of irresponsible victims of appetite. . . .

The prosecutions in our courts for breach of promise, divorce, adultery, bigamy, seduction, rape; the newspaper reports every day of every year of scandals and outrages, of wife murders and paramour shootings, of abortions and infanticides, are perpetual reminders of men's incapacity to cope successfully with this monster evil of society.

The statistics of New York show the number of professional prostitutes in that city to be over twenty thousand. Add to these the thousands and tens of thousands of Boston, Philadelphia, Washington, New Orleans, St. Louis, Chicago, San Francisco, and all our cities, great and small, from ocean to ocean, and what a holocaust of the womanhood of this nation is sacrificed to the insatiate Moloch of lust. And yet more: those myriads of wretched women, publicly known as prostitutes, constitute but a small portion of the numbers who actually tread the paths of vice and crime. For, as the oft-broken ranks of the vast army of common drunkards are steadily filled by the boasted moderate drinkers, so are the ranks of professional prostitution continually replenished by discouraged, seduced, deserted unfortunates, who can no longer hide the terrible secret of their lives. . . .

The work of woman is not to lessen the severity or the certainty of the penalty for the violation of the moral law, but to prevent this violation by the removal of the causes which lead to it. These causes are said to be wholly different with the sexes. The acknowledged incentive to this vice on the part of man is his own abnormal passion; while on the part of woman, in the great majority of cases, it is conceded to be destitution—absolute want of the necessaries of life. . . . [T]here is no escape from the conclusion that, while woman's want of bread induces her to pursue this vice, man's love of the vice itself leads him into it and holds him there. While statistics show no lessening of the passional demand on the part of man, they reveal a most frightful increase of the temptations, the necessities, on the part of woman.

In the olden times, when the daughters of the family, as well as the wife, were occupied with useful and profitable work in the household, getting the meals and washing the dishes three times in every day of every year, doing the baking, the brewing, the washing and the ironing, the whitewashing, the butter and cheese and soap making, the mending and the making of clothes for the entire family, the carding, spinning and weaving of the cloth—when everything to eat, to drink and to wear was manufactured in the home, almost no young women "went out to work." But now, when nearly all these handicrafts are turned over to men and to machinery, tens of thousands, nay, millions, of the women of both hemispheres are thrust into the world's outer market of work to earn their own subsistence. Society, ever slow to change its conditions, presents to these millions but few and meager chances. Only the barest necessaries, and oftentimes not even those, can be purchased with the proceeds of the most excessive and exhausting labor. . . .

Clearly, then, the first step toward solving this problem is to lift this vast army of poverty-stricken women who now crowd our cities, above the temptation, the necessity, to sell themselves, in marriage or out, for bread and shelter. To do that, girls, like boys, must be educated to some lucrative employment; women, like men, must have equal chances to earn a living. If the plea that poverty is the cause of woman's prostitution be not true, perfect equality of chances to earn honest bread will demonstrate the falsehood by removing that pretext and placing her on the same plane with man. Then, if she is found in the ranks of vice and crime, she will be there for the same reason that man is and, from an object of pity, she, like him, will become a fit subject of contempt. From being the party sinned against, she will become an equal sinner, if not the greater of the two. Women, like men, must not only have "fair play" in the world of work and self-support, but, like men, must be eligible to all the honors and emoluments of society and government. Marriage, to women as to men, must be a luxury, not a necessity; an incident of life, not all of it. And the only possible way to accomplish this great change is to accord to women equal power in the making, shaping and controlling of the circumstances of life. That equality of rights and privileges is vested in the ballot, the symbol of power in a republic. Hence, our first and most urgent demand—that women shall be protected in the exercise of their inherent, personal, citizen's right to a voice in the government, municipal, state, national. . . .

Whoever controls work and wages, controls morals. Therefore, we must have women employers, superintendents, committees, legislators; wherever girls go to seek the means of subsistence, there must be some woman. Nay, more; we must have women preachers, lawyers, doctors—that wherever women go to seek counsel—spiritual, legal, physical—there, too, they will be sure to find the best and noblest of their own sex to minister to them. . . .

Marriage never will cease to be a wholly unequal partnership until the law recognizes the equal ownership in the joint earnings and possessions. The true relation of the sexes never can be attained until woman is free and equal with man. Neither in the making nor executing of the laws regulating these relations has woman ever had the slightest voice. The statutes for marriage and divorce, for adultery, breach of promise, seduction, rape, bigamy, abortion, infanticide—all were made by men. They, alone, decide who are guilty of violating these laws and what shall be their punishment, with judge, jury and advocate all men, with no woman's voice heard in our courts, save as accused or witness, and in many cases the married woman is denied the poor privilege of testifying as to her own guilt or innocence of the crime charged against her. . . .

In answer to my proposal to speak in one of the cities of Iowa, an earnest woman replied, "It is impossible to get you an audience; all of our best women are at present engaged in an effort to establish a 'Home for the Friendless.' All the churches are calling for the entire time of their members to get up fairs, dinners, concerts, etc., to raise money. In fact, even our woman suffragists are losing themselves in devotion to some institution."

Thus, wherever you go, you find the best women, in and out of the churches, all absorbed in establishing or maintaining benevolent or reform institutions; charitable societies, soup-houses, ragged schools, industrial schools, mite societies, mission schools—at home and abroad—homes and hospitals for the sick, the aged, the friendless, the foundling, the fallen; asylums for the orphans, the blind, the deaf and dumb, the insane, the inebriate, the idiot. The women of this century are neither idle nor indifferent. They are working with might and main to mitigate the evils which stare them in the face on every side, but much of their work is without knowledge. It is aimed at the effects, not the cause; it is plucking the spoiled fruit; it is lopping off the poisonous branches of the deadly upas tree, which but makes the root more vigorous in sending out new shoots in every direction. A right understanding of physiological law teaches us that the cause must be removed; the tree must be girdled; the tap-root must be severed.

The tap-root of our social upas lies deep down at the very foundations of society. It is woman's dependence. It is woman's subjection. Hence, the first and only efficient work must be to emancipate woman from her enslavement. . . .

I am a full and firm believer in the revelation that it is through woman that the race is to be redeemed. And it is because of this faith that I ask for her immediate and unconditional emancipation from all political, industrial, social and religious subjection.

Seeking a Constituency

ELIZABETH CADY STANTON, 1888

Report of the International Council of Women, Assembled by the National Woman Suffrage Association (Washington, DC: Rufus H. Darby, 1888), pp. 31–37.

In 1888, the NWSA convened an "International Council of Women," a one-time meeting of representatives of many women's organizations. Intending to create a spirit of sisterhood and unity, the suffragists hoped to win support for the vote. When Elizabeth Cady Stanton welcomed the delegates, she tried to tone down her radicalism to appeal to a larger constituency and to bring diverse women's groups into the suffrage camp. She told the delegates that all of women's recent gains in education, employment, and legal rights were "the natural result of suffrage agitation." Celebrating the growing legitimacy of the suffrage movement, she invited the delegates to forget disagreements and join in "future combined action." In the last paragraph of this excerpt from her speech, Stanton turned to the theme of a speech she would give in 1892, "The Solitude of Self." Stanton asserted that life makes the same demands on women and men—that each stands alone and each deserves "self-sovereignty."

The NWSA's aims for the International Council of Women failed; when the week-long council summed up its goals, woman suffrage was ignored. Two years later, however, the two suffrage factions joined forces and formed the National American Woman Suffrage Association. The merger was a first step toward converting the rest of the "woman movement."

Address of Welcome

Mrs. Stanton:

We are assembled here to-day to celebrate the fortieth anniversary of the first organized demand made by women for the right of suffrage. The initiative steps were taken in my native State. In 1848 two conventions were held in Central New York, and the same year the Married Women's Property Bill passed the legislature. Other conventions were soon called in Ohio, Indiana, Massachusetts, Pennsylvania, and other States, one after another, adopted New York's advance legislation. This started the greatest movement for human liberty recorded on the pages of history—a demand for freedom to one-half the entire race; the key-note struck in this country in '48 has been echoed round the world. . . .

In the great National and State conventions for education, temperance, and religion, even thirty years ago, woman's voice was never heard. . . . Half a century ago the women of America were bond slaves, under the old common law of England. Their rights of person and property were under the absolute control of fathers and husbands. They were shut out of the schools and colleges, the trades and professions, and all offices under government; paid the most meager wages in the ordinary industries of life, and denied everywhere the necessary opportunities for their best development. Worse still, women had no proper appreciation of themselves as factors in civilization. Believing self-denial a higher virtue than self-development, they ignorantly made ladders of themselves by which fathers, husbands, brothers, and sons reached their highest ambitions, creating an impassable gulf between them and those they loved that no magnetic chords of affection or gratitude could span. Nothing was more common forty years ago than to see the sons of a family educated, while the daughters remained in ignorance; husbands at ease in the higher circles, in which their wives were unprepared to move. . . .

Whether our feet are compressed in iron shoes, our faces hidden with veils and masks, whether yoked with cows to draw the plow through its furrows, or classed with idiots, lunatics, and criminals in the laws and constitutions of the state, the principle is the same, for the humiliations of spirit are as real as the visible badges of servitude. A difference in government, religion, laws, and social customs makes but little change in the relative status of woman to the self-constituted governing classes, so long as subordination in all nations is the rule of her being. Through suffering we have learned the open sesame to the hearts of each other. There is a language of universal significance, more subtle than that used in the busy marts of trade, that should be called the mother-tongue, by which with a sigh or a tear, a gesture, a glance of the eye, we know the experiences of each other in the varied forms of slavery. With the spirit forever in bondage, it is the same whether housed in golden cages, with every want supplied, or wandering in dreary deserts of life friendless and forsaken. Now that our globe is girdled with railroads, steamships, and electric wires, every pulsation of your hearts is known to us. Long ago we heard the deep yearnings of your souls for freedom responsive to our own. Mary Wolstonecraft, Mesdames de Stael and Roland, George Sand, Frederica Bremer, Elizabeth Barrett Browning, Frances Wright, and George Eliot have pictured alike the wrongs of woman in poetry and prose. Though divided by vast mountain ranges, boundless oceans and plains yet the psalms of our lives have been in the same strain, too long, alas in the minor key; for hopes deferred have made the bravest hearts sometimes despairing. But the same great over-soul has been our hope and inspiration. The steps of progress already achieved in many countries should encourage us to tune our harps anew to songs of victory. . . .

Experience has fully proved, that sympathy as a civil agent is vague and powerless until caught and chained in logical propositions and coined into law. When every prayer and tear represents a ballot, the mothers of the race will no longer weep in vain over the miseries of their children. The active interest women are taking in all the great questions of the day is in strong contrast with the apathy and indifference in which we found them half a century ago, and the contrast in their condition between now and then is equally marked. . . .

Now even married women enjoy, in a measure, their rights of person and property. They can make contracts, sue and be sued, testify in courts of justice, and with honor dissolve the marriage relation when it becomes intolerable. Now most of the colleges are open to girls, and they are rapidly taking their places in all the profitable industries, and in many of the offices under Government. They are in the professions, too, as lawyers, doctors, editors, professors in colleges, and ministers in the pulpits. Their political status is so far advanced that they enjoy all the rights of citizens in two Territories, municipal suffrage in one State, and school suffrage in half the States of the Union. Here is a good record of the work achieved in the past half-century; but we do not intend to rest our case until all our rights are secured, and, noting the steps of progress in other countries, on which their various representatives are here to report, we behold with satisfaction everywhere a general uprising of women, demanding higher education and an equal place in the industries of the world. Our gathering here to-day is highly significant, in its promises of future combined action. When, in the history of the world, was there ever before such an assemblage of able, educated women, celebrated in so many varied walks of life, and feeling their right and ability to discuss the vital questions of social life, religion, and government? When we think of the vantage-ground woman holds to-day, in spite of all the artificial obstacles she has surmounted, we are filled with wonder as to what the future mother of the race will be when free to seek her complete development. . . .

Above all things that women need to-day in their reform work is thorough organization, and to this end we must cultivate some *esprit de corps* of sex, a generous trust in each other. A difference of opinion on one question must not prevent us from working unitedly in those on which we agree. Above all things, let us hold our theological speculations of a future life in abeyance to the practical work of the present existence, recognizing all sects alike and all religions—Jew and Gentile, Catholic and Protestant—to be held equally sacred in their honest opinions. . . . We trust this interchange of sentiments and opinions may be a fresh inspiration to us all in our future work, and that this Convention may be long remembered as among the most pleasant and profitable days of our lives. As the character of this Convention must depend in a large measure on what those who call it may do and say, it would be well for us to keep in mind the responsibility that rests on each and all. If it be true that we can judge of the civilization of a nation by the status of its women, we may do much during this Convention to elevate our institutions in the estimation of the world. . . .

Under a government and religion recognizing in rational beings the rights of conscience and judgment in matters pertaining to their own interests, above all authority of church and state, it needs no argument to prove the sacredness of individual rights, the dignity of individual responsibilities. The solitude of every human soul, alike in our moments of exaltation and humiliation, in our highest joys and deepest sorrows, into which no other one can ever fully enter, proves our birthright to supreme self-sovereignty. As in all the great emergencies of life, we must stand alone, and for final judgment rely upon ourselves, we can not overestimate the necessity for that liberty by which we attain our highest development and that knowledge that fits us for self-reliance and self-protection.

An "Anti" Speaks Out

AMELIA BARR, 1896

Mrs. Amelia Barr, "Discontented Women," *North American Review* 162 (February 1896), pp. 201, 205–07, 209.

When state suffrage campaigns of the 1890s gained force, so did the movement against suffrage. Opponents, male and female, joined anti-suffrage societies, and voiced their objections in speech and in print. According to the "anti" arguments, women were (variously): already represented by a "household" vote; too pure to be contaminated by the mire of politics; unfit to use the vote wisely; and, above all, disinterested in gaining it. Female enfranchisement, the antisuffragists claimed, would lead to household discord, confusion of gender roles, disintegration of the family, and a state of anarchy.

Most of those who denounced woman suffrage in print were men, especially ministers. But women had something to add to the "anti" armory, as novelist Amelia Barr showed. In her analysis of various "discontented" women, Barr saved particular scorn for those who harbored political grievances. If enfranchised, she contended, women would become tools of others, such as priests. They would make irrational policy decisions, refuse to defend the nation by force, and drive the men they outvoted to armed rebellion. (The last charge was, indeed, an original one.) Like all "anti" arguments of the 1890s, Barr's contentions were grounded in the conservative doctrine of "woman's sphere."

Discontent is a vice six thousand years old, and it will be eternal; because it is in the race. Every human being has a complaining side, but discontent is bound up in the heart of woman; it is her original sin. For if the first woman had been satisfied with her conditions, if she had not aspired to be "as gods," and hankered after unlawful knowledge, Satan would hardly have thought it worth his while to discuss her rights and wrongs with her. That unhappy controversy has never ceased; and, with or without reason, woman has been perpetually subject to discontent with her conditions and, according to her nature, has been moved by its influence. Some, it has made peevish, some plaintive, some ambitious, some reckless, while a noble majority have found in its very control that serene composure and cheerfulness which is granted to those who conquer, rather than to those who inherit.

But with all its variations of influence and activity there has never been a time in the world's history, when female discontent has assumed so much, and demanded so much, as at the present day; and both the satisfied and the dissatisfied woman may well pause to consider, whether the fierce fever of unrest which has possessed so large a number of the sex is not rather a delirium than a conviction; whether indeed they are not just as foolishly impatient to get out of their Eden, as was the woman Eve six thousand years ago. . . .

The discontent of working women is understandable, but it is a wide jump from the woman discontented about her work or wages to the woman discontented about her political position. Of all the shrill complainers that vex the ears of mortals there are none so foolish as the women who have discovered that the Founders of our Republic left their work half finished, and that the better half remains for them to do. While more practical and sensible women are trying to put their kitchens, nurseries and drawing-rooms in order, and to clothe themselves rationally, this class of Discontents are dabbling in the gravest national and economic questions. Possessed by a restless discontent with their appointed sphere and its duties, and forcing themselves to the front in order to ventilate their theories and show the quality of their brains, they demand the right of suffrage as the symbol and guarantee of all other rights.

This is their cardinal point, though it naturally follows that the right to elect contains the right to be elected. If this result be gained, even women whose minds are not taken up with the things of the state, but who are simply housewives and mothers, may easily predicate a few of such results as are particularly plain to the feminine intellect and observation. The first of these would be an entirely new set of agitators, who would use means quite foreign to male intelligence. For instance, every favorite priest and preacher would gain enormously in influence and power; for the ecclesiastical zeal which now expends itself in fairs and testimonials would then expend itself in the securing of votes in whatever direction they were instructed to secure them. It might even end in the introduction of the clerical element into our great political Council Chambers—the Bishops in the House of Lords would be a sufficient precedent—and a great many women would really believe that the charming rhetoric of the pulpit would infuse a higher tone in legislative assemblies.

Again, most women would be in favor of helping any picturesque nationality, without regard to the Monroe doctrine, or the state of finances, or the needs of the market. Most women would think it a good action to sacrifice their party for a friend. Most women would change their politics, if they saw it to be their interest to do so, without a moment's hesitation. Most women would refuse the primary obligation on which all franchises rest—that is, to defend their country by force of arms, if necessary. And if a majority of women passed a law which the majority of men felt themselves justified in resisting by physical force, what would women do? Such a position in sequence of female suffrage is not beyond probability, and yet if it happened, not only one law, but *all* law would be in danger. No one denies that women have suffered, and do yet suffer, from grave political and social disabilities, but during the last fifty years much has been continually done for their relief, and there is no question but that the future will give all that can be reasonably desired. . . . Development, growth, completion, is the natural and best advancement. We do not progress by going over precipices, nor re-model and improve our houses by digging under the foundations.

Finally, women cannot get behind or beyond their nature, and their nature is to substitute sentiment for reason—a sweet and not unlovely characteristic in womanly ways and places; yet reason, on the whole, is considered a desirable necessity in politics. . . . Women may cease to be women, but they can never learn to be men, and feminine softness and grace can never do the work of the virile virtues of men. Very fortunately this class of discontented women have not yet been able to endanger existing conditions by combinations analagous to trades-unions; nor is it likely they ever will; because it is doubtful if women, under any circumstances, could combine at all. Certain qualities are necessary for combination, and these qualities are represented in women by their opposites. . . .

The one unanswerable excuse for woman's entrance into active public life of any kind, is *need*, and alas ! need is growing daily, as marriage becomes continually rarer, and more women are left adrift in the world without helpers and protectors. But this is a subject too large to enter on here, though in the beginning it sprung from discontented women, preferring the work and duties of men to their own work and duties. Have they found the battle of life any more ennobling in masculine professions, than in their old feminine household ways? Is work done in the world for strangers, any less tiresome and monotonous, than work done in the house for father and mother, husband and children? If they answer truly, they will reply "the home duties were the easiest, the safest, and the happiest."

Of course all discontented women will be indignant at any criticism of their conduct. They expect every one to consider their feelings without examining their motives. Paddling in the turbid maelstrom of life, and dabbling in politics and the most unsavory social questions, they still think men, at least, ought to regard them as the Sacred Sex. But women are not sacred by grace of sex, if they voluntarily abdicate its limitations and its modesties, and make a public display of unsexed sensibilities, and unabashed familiarity with subjects they have nothing to do with. If men criticize such women with asperity it is not to be wondered at; they have so long idealized women, that they find it hard to speak moderately. They excuse them too much, or else they are too indignant at their follies, and unjust and angry in their denunciation. Women must be criticized by women; then they will hear the bare uncompromizing truth, and be the better for it.

The Social Housekeeping Response

ANNA GARLIN SPENCER, 1898

Anna Garlin Spencer, "The Fitness of Women to Become Citizens from the Standpoint of Moral Development," in Susan B. Anthony, ed., *History of Woman Suffrage*, vol. 4 (Indianapolis: Hollenbeck Press, 1902), pp. 308–09.

Suffragists of the 1890s responded to antisuffrage attacks by taking the offensive. Their arguments emphasized the distinctive virtues that women would bring to the polls and the social benefits that would result. Minister Anna Garlin Spencer (1851–1931), a frequent speaker on moral issues, presented several major points of the "expediency" argument in an address to the National American Woman Suffrage Association convention in 1898. Women's special moral traits were now vital in politics, Spencer contended. Since government had expanded its power into education and welfare, it had "entered the area of distinctive feminine training and power" and therefore needed the contribution of women. Jane Addams would forcefully present a similar argument in the early twentieth century.

Government is not now merely the coarse and clumsy instrument by which military and police forces are directed; it is the flexible, changing and delicately adjusted instrument of many and varied educative, charitable and supervisory functions, and the tendency to increase the functions of government is a growing one. Prof. Lester F. Ward* says: "Government is becoming more and more the organ of the social consciousness and more and more the servant of the social will." The truth of this is shown in the modern public school system; in the humane and educative care of dependent, defective and wayward children; in the increasingly discriminating and wise treatment of the insane, the pauper, the tramp and the poverty-bound; in the provisions for public parks, baths and amusement places; in the bureaus of investigation and control and the appointment of officers of inspection to secure better sanitary and moral conditions; in the board of arbitration for the settlement of political and labor difficulties; and in the almost innumerable committees and bills, national, State and local, to secure higher social welfare for all classes, especially for the weaker and more ignorant. Government can never again shrink and harden into a mere mechanism of military and penal control.

It is, moreover, increasingly apparent that for these wider and more delicate functions a higher order of electorate, ethically as well as intellectually advanced, is

---

*Sociologist Lester Frank Ward (1841–1913), a liberal social Darwinist.

necessary. Democracy can succeed only by securing for its public service, through the rule of the majority, the best leadership and administration the State affords. Only a wise electorate will know how to select such leadership, and only a highly moral one will authoritatively choose such. . . .

When the State took the place of family bonds and tribal relationships, and the social consciousness was born and began its long travel toward the doctrine of "equality of human rights" in government and the principle of human brotherhood in social organization, man, as the family and tribal organizer and ruler, of course took command of the march. It was inevitable, natural and beneficent so long as the State concerned itself with only the most external and mechanical of social interests. The instant, however, the State took upon itself any form of educative, charitable or personally helpful work, it entered the area of distinctive feminine training and power, and therefore became in need of the service of woman. Wherever the State touches the personal life of the infant, the child, the youth, or the aged, helpless, defective in mind, body or moral nature, there the State enters "woman's peculiar sphere," her sphere of motherly succor and training, her sphere of sympathetic and self-sacrificing ministration to individual lives. If the service of women is not won to such governmental action (not only through "influence or the shaping of public opinion," but through definite and authoritative exercise), the mother-office of the State, now so widely adopted, will be too often planned and administered as though it were an external, mechanical and abstract function, instead of the personal, organic and practical service which all right helping of individuals must be.

In so far as motherhood has given to women a distinctive ethical development, it is that of sympathetic personal insight respecting the needs of the weak and helpless, and of quick-witted, flexible adjustment of means to ends in the physical, mental and moral training of the undeveloped. And thus far has motherhood fitted women to give a service to the modern State which men can not altogether duplicate. . . .

Whatever problems might have been involved in the question of woman's place in the State when government was purely military, legal and punitive have long since been antedated. Whatever problems might have inhered in that question when women were personally subject to their families or their husbands are well-nigh outgrown in all civilized countries, and entirely so in the most advanced. Woman's nonentity in the political department of the State is now an anachronism and inconsistent with the prevailing tendencies of social growth. . . .

The earth is ready, the time is ripe, for the authoritative expression of the feminine as well as the masculine interpretation of that common social consciousness which is slowly writing justice in the State and fraternity in the social order.

Chapter 17

New Woman/New Century

*I*n the 1890s, journalists revealed the "New Woman," a dynamic, independent character who left her imprint on metropolitan life well into the twentieth century. Urban and sophisticated, the New Woman might be college-educated. After school, she was likely to be self-supporting, and probably single. If married, she anticipated a small family, a life beyond the home, and perhaps a career. Her manner was forthright, frank, and energetic. Among men she sought "equality" and "fellowship." Self-sufficient and self-confident, she conveyed a spirit of rebellion. As a young woman in a magazine story of the mid-1890s declared, "The question now is, not 'What does man like?' but 'What does woman prefer?'"

A protean composite, the New Woman of 1900 took many forms. As a college student, she read Charlotte Perkin Gilman's *Women and Economics* (1898), a tirade against traditional femininity, and Thorstein Veblen's critique of conspicuous consumption in *Theory of the Leisure Class* (1899). As a settlement worker, she immersed herself in progressive ideals and explored "social and industrial problems." As an academic, she specialized in the latest trends in "social science" or behavioral psychology. Though likely to support votes for women, she was probably less interested in amending the constitution than in changing social relations. She held new ideas about marriage and divorce, childbearing and child-rearing, women's rights and women's roles. By the pre–World War I era, the New Woman was usually a careerist. "They were all social workers or magazine writers in a small way," journalist Randolph Bourne wrote to a woman friend in 1913. "They are decidedly emancipated and advanced, and so thoroughly healthy and zestful. . . . They are all of course self-supporting and independent, and they enjoy the adventure of life."

From the moment that she was first mentioned in the press, discussion of the New Woman revived the "woman question" that had permeated the late nineteenth century, when concern centered around the potentially dire effects of advanced education, excessive club meetings, or the ballot. By the turn of the century, 85,000 women were attending college, social reformers had won acceptance, and the enlarged suffrage movement was inching its way toward respectability. But the New Woman complicated the "woman question," because she embodied some of the ambiguities that characterize modern feminism. On the one hand, she hoped to transform all aspects of public life, by adding her feminine influence to the professions, politics, and the "outside world." On the other hand, in her inveterate quest for independence, she seemed ready to discard most trappings of femininity, such as deference, domesticity, and subordination. "Does she wish to be a woman or a modified man?" asked a writer in the *Outlook* in the early 1900s. This question was not resolved, either at the turn of the century or thereafter, although the answer probably was "both." The excerpts that follow depict some aspects of the New Woman around 1900, from a variety of perspectives.

The Ills of the Home

CHARLOTTE PERKINS GILMAN, 1903

Charlotte Perkins Gilman, *The Home* (New York: McClure, Phillips & Co., 1903), pp. 97–102, 315.

Charlotte Perkins Gilman's *Woman and Economics* (1898), an argument for women's economic independence, was the most influential feminist text at the turn of the century. Centuries of dependence on man, said Gilman (1860–1935), had transformed woman into a purely sexual being, trapped in the home, and unable to make a contribution outside it. As a nonproductive consumer, she had become deformed, defective, and pathological. Only when she participated in the larger society, would she become "humanly developed, civilized, and socialized." To emancipate women from the home, Gilman proposed arrangements for communal living, housekeeping, and child-rearing. As a socialist, she admired Edward Bellamy's utopian schemes and attempted to apply his collectivist vision to domestic life.

 In subsequent lectures, books, and articles, Gilman elaborated on the basic theme set forth in *Woman and Economics*. The home, she contended, kept woman a "social idiot." The following excerpts from *The Home* (1903) disparage household labor as wasteful, nonspecialized, and primitive. They also anticipate Betty Friedan's condemnation of the 1950s "housewife-heroine." Finally, they include one of Gilman's favorite argumentative techniques, role reversal. What if society believed that men's contributions should be made solely as lone individuals within the confines of the home?

The initial purpose of the home is the care of children. The initial purpose of motherhood is the care of children. How are the duties of the mother compatible with the duties of the housewife?* How can child-culture, as a branch of human progress, rise to any degree of proficiency in this swarming heap of rudimentary trades?

 Nothing is asked—here—as to how the housewife, doing all these things together her life long, can herself find time for culture and development; or how can she catch any glimmer of civic duty or public service beyond this towering pile of domestic duty and household service. The particular point herein advanced is that the conditions

---

*The duties of the housewife, Gilman had just pointed out, were cooking, cleaning, washing, ironing, baking, mending, and so on.

of home industry *as such* forever limit the growth of the industry so practised; forever limit the growth of the persons so practising them; and also tend to limit the growth of the society which is content to leave any of its essential functions in this distorted state.

Our efforts to "lift the standard of household industry" ignore the laws of industry. We seek by talking and writing, by poetising and sermonising, and playing on every tender sentiment and devout aspiration, to convince the housewife that there is something particularly exalted and beautiful, as well as useful, in her occupation. This shows our deep-rooted error of sex-distinction in industry. We consider the work of the woman in the house as essentially feminine, and fail to see that, as work, it is exactly like any other kind of human activity, having the same limitations and the same possibilities.

Suppose we change the sex and consider for a while the status of a house-husband. He could be a tall, strong, fine-looking person—man-servants often are. He could love his wife and his children—industrial status does not affect these primal instincts. He could toil from morning to night, manfully, to meet their needs.

Suppose we are visiting in such a family. We should find a very rude small hut—no one man could build much of a house, but, ah! the tender love, the pride, the intimate emotion he would put into that hut! For his heart's dearest—for his precious little ones—he had dragged together the fallen logs—chipped them smooth with his flint-ax (there could have been no metal work while every man was a house-husband), and piled them together. With patient, loving hands he had daubed the chinks with clay, made beds of leaves, hung hides upon the walls. Even some rude stools he might have contrived—though furniture really belongs to a later period. But over all comes the incessant demand for food. His cherished family must eat, often and often, and under that imperative necessity all others wait.

So he goes forth to the hunt, brave, subtle, fiercely ingenious; and, actuated by his ceaseless love for his family he performs wonders. He brings home the food—day after day—even sometimes enough for several days, though meat does not keep very long. The family would have food of a sort, shelter of a sort, and love. But try to point out to the house-husband what other things he could obtain for them, create for them, provide for them, if he learned to combine with other men, to exchange labour, to organise industry. See his virtuous horror!

What! Give up his duty to his family! Let another man hunt for them!—another man build their home—another man make their garments! He will not hear of it. "It is my duty as a husband," he will tell you, "to serve my wife. It is my duty as a father to serve my children. No other person could love them as I do, and without that love the work would not be done as well." Strong in this conviction, the house-husband would remain intrenched in his home, serving his family with might and main, having no time, no strength, no brain capacity for undertaking larger methods; and there he and his family would all be, immovable in the Stone Age.

Never was any such idiot on earth as this hypothetical home-husband. It was not in him to stay in such primitive restrictions. But he has been quite willing to leave his wife in that interestingly remote period.

The permanent error of the housewife lies in that assumption that her love for her family makes her service satisfactory. Family affection has nothing to do with the specialist's skill; nor with the specialist's love of his work for the pleasure of doing it. That is the kind of love that makes good work; and that is the kind of work the world needs and the families within it. Men, specialised, give to their families all that we know of modern comforts, of scientific appliances, of works of art, of the complex necessities and conveniences of modern life. Women, unspecialised, refuse to benefit their families in like proportion; but offer to them only the grade of service which was proper enough in the Stone Age, but is a historic disgrace to-day.

A house does not need a wife any more than it does a husband. Are we never to have a man-wife? A really suitable and profitable companion for a man instead of the bond-slave of a house? There is nothing in the work of a house which requires marital or maternal affection. It does require highly developed skill and business sense—but these it fails to get.

Would any amount of love on the part of that inconceivable house-husband justify him in depriving his family of all the fruits of progress? What a colossal charge of malfeasance in office could be brought against such a husband—such a father; who, under the name of love, should so fail in his great first duty—Progress.

How does the woman escape this charge? Why is not she responsible for progress, too? By that strange assumption does she justify this refusal to keep step with the world? She will tell you, perhaps, that she cannot do more than she does—she has neither time nor strength nor ambition for any more work. So might the house-husband have defended himself—as honestly and as reasonably. It is true. While every man had to spend all his time providing for his own family, no man ever had, or ever could have, time, strength, or ambition to do more.

It is not *more* work that is asked of women, but less. It is *a different method* of work. Human progress rests upon the interchange of labour; upon work done humanly for each other, not, like the efforts of the savage or the brute, done only for one's own. The housewife, blinded by her ancient duty, fails in her modern duty. . . .

The home, in its arbitrary position of arrested development, does not properly fulfil its own essential functions—much less promote the social ones. Among the splendid activities of our age it lingers on, inert and blind, like a clam in a horse-race.

It hinders, by keeping woman a social idiot, by keeping the modern child under the tutelage of the primeval mother, by keeping the social conscience of the man crippled and stultified in the clinging grip of the domestic conscience of the woman. It hinders by its enormous expense; making the physical details of daily life a heavy burden to mankind; whereas, in our stage of civilisation, they should have been long since reduced to a minor incident.

Small versus Large Families

IDA HUSTED HARPER, 1901

Ida Husted Harper, "Small vs. Large Families," *The Independent* 53 (December 26, 1901), pp. 3055–59.

Throughout the late nineteenth century, advocates of women's rights like Elizabeth Cady Stanton defended the principle of "voluntary motherhood," the right of women to have children when they wanted. By the end of the century, the voluntary motherhood ideal collided with the roadblock of "race suicide": a mounting fear among the well-off that the native-born middle and upper classes, with their dwindling birthrates, would soon be outnumbered by prolific immigrant hordes. The impulse toward "race suicide," critics charged, could be blamed on women, especially educated women, who were selfishly avoiding the duties of motherhood and perhaps marriage as well.

Turn-of-the-century feminists continued to defend voluntary motherhood by arguing that "unwanted" children were inferior, or even that all women might not be suited to marriage and motherhood. In a 1901 magazine article, long-time suffragist Ira Husted Harper (1851–1931), a friend and biographer of Susan B. Anthony and editor of the *History of Woman Suffrage*, defended all those whom "race suicide" theorists sought to attack—the educated woman, the woman who chose not to marry, the childless wife who pursued a profession instead of procreating, and the woman who wanted a small family. Indeed, Harper defended the small family itself. Most important, she shifted the blame for the small family, placing it upon well-off professional men, who did not want to be saddled with the burden of many children. Significantly, Harper refrained from any mention of contraception, a controversial subject at the turn of the century, and one that suffragists usually tried to avoid.

Two little children were playing together in the hall. Finally the girl began climbing the stairs. "Come down," said the boy, but she kept on creeping up the steps. "Come down," he cried again, but the climber ignored the cry. "Come down," he commanded, savagely, at last. "I want you." Then, without turning her head, the little girl answered calmly, "I want myself"—and continued her upward course. This is a true story.

Now the central force in the whole progressive movement on the part of woman to-day is simply that she "wants herself." In the long history of the human race woman has been considered almost wholly in her relation to man—the wife entirely so. The man is educated, trained and developed as an individual—the woman solely as a correlative of man. . . .

The point for consideration is simply this—that, in all this protest against the higher education, woman is not considered as an individual, but solely in relation to wifehood and motherhood. There is no recognition of the great pleasure and benefit she will derive from it, and no anxiety in regard to her health as it will affect her own comfort and happiness, but only as it may interfere with her becoming the wife of some man and the mother of his children. Woman never has attempted one advanced step which has not been blocked by these two words—wifehood and motherhood. In olden times the position of the "spinster" was so intolerable that she was glad to find refuge behind this barrier, but in the new freedom which has come to the unmarried woman she is ordering her own life according to her own ideas. When men would deprive her of a university education lest it should interfere with the functions of marriage, she says, "Very well; if I must choose I will take the education and remain single;" and in books, writing, art, music, travel, cultured friends and, perhaps, a profession, she finds a very acceptable substitute. Marriage, nowadays, is by no means so necessary to women as men are apt to think; and while, if all the conditions were favorable, the average woman might prefer to be married, she may not consider it worth the sacrifices which are oftentimes required. The number of educated women who take this position is apt to increase so long as men continue to insist on a certain amount of ignorance and a strong constitution as the essentials of matrimony. After a while, when they become liberal enough and wise enough to make intellectual companionship, sympathy of thought and congeniality in tastes the prominent features, they may be able to convince such women of its great advantages.

There is another phase of this question which is being continually obtruded by men, viz.: The disinclination of women who do marry to have a number of children, or, in some cases, to have any, but in all of this one-sided discussion, for women themselves take no part in it, one indisputable fact is wholly ignored—that where there are one hundred wives who desire few or no children, there can be found one hundred husbands of the same mind. There could be no greater injustice than to hold wives alone responsible for the failure to have a family. The mother instinct is much stronger in woman than is the father instinct in man, and, notwithstanding the far greater liabilities incurred by the wife, there is no hesitation in saying that as a rule she would be willing to assume them if there was a great desire for children on the part of the husband. But there is not. The average man does not want the burden of a large family, and there are many husbands who object for other reasons. With an apology for being personal the writer will mention several examples among her own acquaintances.

One man, a banker, with an only son, in speaking on this subject, said: "I should be very glad, indeed, to have a few more children, but I am not willing for my wife or myself to make the sacrifices which would be necessary. We are perfectly alike in our tastes; we love music and art, good lectures, the theater and society in moderation;

we like to take long walks and to travel. We married so that we might enjoy these things together. For the most of a year before our boy was born all these things had to be given up, and for two or three years afterward he was very delicate and required practically her whole time. I would not go out to find pleasure, leaving her alone, so we were both deprived of what we most liked. If every few years there had been another child we would simply have had to settle down to a humdrum and common-place existence which would have been unendurable. While we will help our boy to make as fine a man as possible we will also try to get something out of life for ourselves."

Another, the wealthy president of a corporation, also with one son, declared: "I would give half I am worth for a daughter, but when I saw what my wife endured before our boy was born, at the time and afterward, I thought, 'Not for ten times what I am worth would I ever allow this again.'"

A professional man of much refinement and sensibility said with emotion: "I would be willing to give my own life to save my wife from pain and sorrow and, much as I love children, I will do without them forever rather than permit her to pass through the necessary ordeal."

Still another, with a beautiful home and spacious grounds which would be a paradise for children, said, when some one suggested this: "My first wife died in childbirth. When I married the second I resolved that there should not be another sacrifice."

These instances might be multiplied. They will touch a responsive chord in the heart of more than one man who reads them, and all who are honest will admit that it is husbands as well as wives who are responsible for the small families of the present day.

When men criticise women so severely for avoiding maternity do they ever stop to consider what they themselves would do in her place? A man in New York, not long ago, sent the writer of this a letter regarding something which she had published, in which, in a burst of rage, he declared that all the "crimes against women," for which men are punished, are offset by the refusal of women to bear children, for which they are not punished. He would like a law to punish them.

It is only in recent years, since there has been a decrease in the number of children, that the life insurance companies will insure women. They refused on account of the terrible mortality in childbirth, which, as the ages go by, counts more victims than all the wars. Is it not asking a great deal of a woman to face death deliberately every few years from youth to middle age? We laud the soldier to the skies who risks his life in battle, but we take it as a matter of course that women should be continually putting their lives in peril, year after year, mother, daughter, granddaughter, from generation to generation, for all time.

Putting aside, however, the danger, the suffering and all the immediate inconveniences, think what it means for a woman to give the core of her life, the beautiful years between twenty and forty-five, the time when the mental powers are at their best, when enjoyment in the pleasant things of the world is keenest, to the exacting demands of the nursery. The society of little children has much in it that is sweet, but it is not mentally stimulating, and there is nothing that so wears on the nerves as to have their constant care. It would drive a man insane, and he would welcome a change to mining coal or excavating the New York tunnel. There never was a mother of a large family who was willing that her daughters should have a similar experience.

Women are encouraged with the assurance that "motherhood is regarded as the most sacred office in the world." That is not true. Motherhood is only considered sacred when it is preceded by wifehood. Without this it is looked upon as a disgrace. The unmarried mother is repudiated by the whole world, including the father of her child. It is only when a woman has been consecrated to the one man and bears children who are to perpetuate his name and family that her "motherhood" becomes sacred either to the Church, the State, or the man himself. The most sacred thing about maternity is the divine love of the mother for her child, and in this she needs no instruction. There is no human being, however, who has the right to dictate to her the number of children she shall bear. The vast majority of women gladly devote the years necessary to rearing two or three, but when there is a demand that they shall give up their entire life they object. . . .

The question arises, also, to what extent individuals are under obligations to sacrifice themselves, their ambitions, their desires, their hopes, for the sake of society at large? A man with a keen love of books and order and quiet went home every night from his large and exacting business to a house full of little ones, a tired, nervous wife and inevitable noise and confusion. One evening he called on a friend who had been married at the same time but had no family. The house was in exquisite order, his friend was stretched out in an easy chair and, by a shaded lamp, his wife, daintily dressed, rested and fresh, was reading aloud. Looking about, he said with a sigh: "No man could love his children more than I do, but this was my dream of marriage."

Must the sweetest dreams be prevented from fulfilment because of an alleged duty to the public when life is so short and contains at best so little of happiness? It is shown by statistics that of college women who marry over sixty per cent marry college men. These marriages are founded almost wholly on congeniality of tastes, which find expression in a purely literary life. If this is to be broken up by a constantly increasing family of children, driving the father to the lonely seclusion of his study and depriving the mother entirely of any share in pursuits which are just as dear to her as to him, can there be any real happiness for either? And would it help matters if the wife had been debarred from the college education in order that she might be contented simply to raise children and have nothing else in common with the husband?

With the requirements of modern life the expense and responsibility of bringing up children are out of all proportion to what they were a century ago. Where the family is large it means for parents in moderate circumstances a lifetime of self-denial in the companionship of each other and in the development which comes through means and leisure, as there must be a never-ending outlay of time and money in properly clothing, educating and training the many children. They are deprived also of rendering such service in civic affairs as might have been possible had they not been necessarily absorbed in rearing their numerous progeny. By what authority has the State a right to exact such self-abnegation, and how much more is it benefited by these many new citizens than it would have been with a smaller number and more assistance from the older ones?

In the pioneer days of our country the need of large families was greater than any other, but that need no longer exists. We are already increasing more rapidly than necessity requires. . . . There are already more workers than there is employment for them, and hundreds of thousands are coming in every year full grown. In every large city there are thousands of children for whom no school privileges can be furnished. The charitable institutions everywhere are overflowing with them. Why, then, this continual cry that women must be barred from the colleges and the industries lest it affect their capacity as mothers? Instead of insisting upon larger families it should be urged that they become smaller.

It is said that the present increase is not of a desirable nature and that large families of the better classes are necessary for the welfare of the Government. The supremacy of the future is not to be a matter of numbers, but of intellect. There is no hope of a decrease in the undesirable population, and the remedy lies not so much in more children among the better classes as in a careful training of the present number and the applying of the surplus time, money and effort to the improvement of those whose parents are wholly unequal to it. For both of these purposes there is the most urgent need of highly educated, well disciplined and thoroughly progressive women.

A Voice from the South

ANNA J. COOPER, 1892

Bert James Loewenberg and Ruth Bogin, eds., *Black Women in Nineteenth-Century American Life: Their Words, Their Thoughts, Their Feelings* (University Park, PA: Pennsylvania State University Press, 1976), pp. 324–28.

Black educator Anna J. Cooper (ca. 1859–1964) expressed the spirit of ambition that characterized the New Woman. The daughter of a North Carolina slave and a white father, Cooper attended and later taught at a freedman's school near Raleigh. In 1877, she married a former slave who had become an Episcopal minister. After he died, two years later, she attended Oberlin, graduated in 1884, and earned a master's degree there four years later. In 1887, Cooper became a teacher at a black preparatory school, later the Dunbar School, in Washington, D.C. As an educator, she promoted higher education for blacks, a goal that diverged from Booker T. Washington's emphasis on vocational education at Tuskegee Institute. In 1901, Cooper became principal of her school but lost her post five years later, perhaps due to opposition from Washington supporters. Eventually, she returned to the teaching of Latin, earned an advanced degree from the Sorbonne at age sixty-five, and founded an evening school in Washington for employed blacks.

Over the course of her life, Anna J. Cooper published several studies in French, including her Sorbonne thesis on French attitudes toward slavery in Saint Domingue (Haiti) in the era of the French Revolution. Late in life, she wrote a book about the South Carolina Grimké family, which had both black and white descendants. Her first book, *A Voice from the South* (1892), however, holds most significance for women's history. Here, Cooper conveyed her conviction that neither race nor sex should disqualify able students from higher education. In the following excerpts, she expresses her views about the importance of advanced education for women, discusses the "marriage question" that plagued educated women, and voices her ambitions for black women in the new century. In the spirit of the New Woman, she also takes issue with men—in this case, black men—who fail to appreciate women's aspirations. Her views reflect her own life of achievement, her success as a scholar and teacher, and her combination of race pride and feminism.

The men of our time have asked with Emerson, "that woman only show us how she can best be served"; and woman has replied: the chance of the seedling and of the animalcule is all I ask—the chance for growth and self development, the permission to be true to the aspirations of my soul without incurring the blight of your censure and ridicule. . . .

Matthew Arnold during his last visit to America in '82 or '83, lectured before a certain co-educational college in the West. After the lecture he remarked, with some surprise, to a lady professor, that the young women in his audience, he noticed, paid as close attention as the men, *"all the way through."* This led, of course, to a spirited discussion of the higher education for women, during which he said to his enthusiastic interlocutor, eyeing her philosophically through his English eyeglass: "But—eh—don't you think it—eh—spoils their *chawnces*, you know!"

Now, as to the result to women, this is the most serious argument ever used against the higher education. If it interferes with marriage, classical training has a grave objection to weigh and answer. . . .

I grant you that intellectual development, with the self-reliance and capacity for earning a livelihood which it gives, renders woman less dependent on the marriage relation for physical support (which, by the way, does not always accompany it). Neither is she compelled to look to sexual love as the one sensation capable of giving tone and relish, movement and vim to the life she leads. Her horizon is extended. Her sympathies are broadened and deepened and multiplied. She is in closer touch with nature. Not a bud that opens, not a dew drop, not a ray of light, not a cloud-burst or a thunderbolt, but adds to the expansiveness and zest of her soul. And if the sun of an absorbing passion be gone down, still 'tis night that brings the stars. She has remaining the mellow, less obtrusive, but none the less enchanting and inspiring light of friendship, and into its charmed circle she may gather the best the world has known. She can commune with Socrates about the *daimon* he knew and to which she too can bear witness; she can revel in the majesty of Dante, the sweetness of Virgil, the simplicity of Homer, the strength of Milton. She can listen to the pulsing heart throbs of passionate Sappho's encaged soul, as she beats her bruised wings against her prison bars and struggles to flutter out into Heaven's aether, and the fires of her own soul cry back as she listens. "Yes; Sappho, I know it all; I know it all." Here, at last, can be communion without suspicion; friendship without misunderstanding; love without jealousy. . . .

Now, then, does it destroy or diminish her capacity for loving?

Her standards have undoubtedly gone up. The necessity of speculating in 'chawnces' has probably shifted. The question is not now with the woman "How shall I so cramp, stunt, simplify and nullify myself as to make me eligible to the honor of being swallowed up into some little man?" but the problem, I trow, now rests with the man as to how he can so develop his God-given powers as to reach the ideal of a generation of women who demand the noblest, grandest and best achievements of which he is capable; and this surely is the only fair and natural adjustment of the chances. Nature never meant that the ideals and standards of the world should be dwarfing and minimizing ones, and the men should thank us for requiring of them the richest fruits which they can grow. If it makes them work, all the better for them.

As to the adaptability of the educated woman to the marriage relation, I shall simply quote from that excellent symposium of learned women that appeared recently. . . . "Admitting no longer any question as to their intellectual equality with the men whom they meet, with the simplicity of conscious strength, they take their place beside the men who challenge them, and fearlessly face the result of their actions. They deny that their education in any way unfits them for the duty of wifehood and maternity or primarily renders these conditions any less attractive to them than to the domestic type of woman. On the contrary, they hold that their knowledge of physiology makes them better mothers and housekeepers; their knowledge of chemistry makes them better cooks; while from their training in other natural sciences and in mathematics, they obtain an accuracy and fair-mindedness which is of great value to them in dealing with their children or employees."

So much for their willingness. Now the apple may be good for food and pleasant to the eyes, and a fruit to be desired to make one wise. Nay, it may even assure you that it has no aversion whatever to being tasted. Still, if you do not like the flavor all these recommendations are nothing. Is the intellectual woman *desirable* in the matrimonial market?

This I cannot answer. I confess my ignorance. I am no judge of such things. I have been told that strong-minded women could be, when they thought it worth their while, quite endurable, and, judging from the number of female names I find in college catalogues among the alumnae with double patronymics, I surmise that quite a number of men are willing to put up with them.

Now I would that my task ended here. Having shown that a great want of the world in the past has been a feminine force; that that force can have its full effect only through the untrammelled development of woman; that such development, while it gives her to the world and to civilization, does not necessarily remove her from the home and fireside; finally, that while past centuries have witnessed sporadic instances of this higher growth, still it was reserved for the latter half of the nineteenth century to render it common and general enough to be effective; I might close with a glowing prediction of what the twentieth century may expect from this heritage of twin forces—the masculine battered and toil-worn as a grim veteran after centuries of warfare, but still strong, active and vigorous, ready to help with his hard-won experience the young recruit rejoicing in her newly found freedom, who so confidently places her hand in his with mutual pledges to redeem the ages.

> And so the twain upon the skirts of Time,
> Sit side by side, full-summed in all their powers,
> Dispensing harvest, sowing the To-be,
> Self-reverent each and reverencing each.

Fain would I follow them, but duty is nearer home. The high ground of generalities is alluring but my pen is devoted to a special cause: and with a view to further enlightenment on the achievements of the century for THE HIGHER EDUCATION OF COLORED WOMEN, I wrote a few days ago to the colleges which admit women and asked how many colored women had completed the B.A. course in each during its entire history. These are the figures returned: Fisk leads the way with twelve; Oberlin next with five; Wilberforce, four; Ann Arbor and Wellesley, three each; Livingstone, two; Atlanta, one; Howard, as yet, none.

I then asked the principal of the Washington High School* how many out of a large number of female graduates from his school had chosen to go forward and take a collegiate course. He replied that but one had ever done so, and she was then in Cornell.[1]

Others ask questions too, sometimes, and I was asked a few years ago by a white friend, "How is it that the men of your race seem to outstrip the women in mental attainment?" "Oh," I said, "so far as it is true, the men, I suppose, from the life they lead, gain more by contact; and so far as it is only apparent, I think the women are more quiet. They don't feel called to mount a barrel and harangue by the hour every time they imagine they have produced an idea."

But I am sure there is another reason which I did not at that time see fit to give. The atmosphere, the standards, the requirements of our little world do not afford any special stimulus to female development.

It seems hardly a gracious thing to say, but it strikes me as true, that while our men seem thoroughly abreast of the times on almost every other subject, when they strike the woman question they drop back into sixteenth century logic. They leave nothing to be desired generally in regard to gallantry and chivalry, but they actually do not seem sometimes to have outgrown that old contemporary of chivalry—the idea that women may stand on pedestals or live in doll houses (if they happen to have them), but they must not furrow their brows with thought or attempt to help men tug at the great questions of the world. I fear the majority of colored men do not yet think it worth while that women aspire to higher education. . . . The three R's, a little music and a good deal of dancing, a first rate dress-maker and a bottle of magnolia balm, are quite enough generally to render charming any woman possessed of tact and the capacity for worshipping masculinity.

My readers will pardon my illustrating my point and also giving a reason for the fear that is in me, by a little bit of personal experience. When a child I was put into a school near home that professed to be normal and collegiate, i. e. to prepare teachers for colored youth, furnish candidates for the ministry, and offer collegiate training for those who should be ready for it. Well, I found after a while that I had a good deal of time on my hands. I had devoured what was put before me, and, like Oliver Twist, was looking around to ask for more. I constantly felt (as I suppose many an ambitious girl has felt) a thumping from within unanswered by any beckoning from without. Class after class was organized for these ministerial candidates (many of them men who had been preaching before I was born). . . .

Finally a Greek class was to be formed. My inspiring preceptor informed me that Greek had never been taught in the school, but that he was going to form a class *for the candidates for the ministry,* and if I liked I might join it. I replied—humbly I hope, as became a female of the human species—that I would like very much to study

---

*The school at which Anna J. Cooper taught.
[1]Graduated from Scientific Course, June, 1890, the first colored woman to graduate from Cornell. [Cooper's note]

Greek, and that I was thankful for the opportunity, and so it went on. A boy, however meager his equipment and shallow his pretentions, had only to declare a floating intention to study theology and he could get all the support, encouragement and stimulus he needed, be absolved from work and invested beforehand with all the dignity of his far away office. While a self-supporting girl had to struggle on by teaching in the summer and working after school hours to keep up with her board bills, and actually to fight her way against positive discouragements to the higher education; till one such girl one day flared out and told the principal "the only mission opening before a girl in his school was to marry one of those candidates." He said he didn't know but it was. And when at last that same girl announced her desire and intention to go to college it was received with about the same incredulity and dismay as if a brass button on one of those candidate's coats had propounded a new method for squaring the circle or trisecting the arc.

Now this is not fancy. It is a simple unvarnished photograph, and what I believe was not in those days exceptional in colored schools, and I ask the men and women who are teachers and co-workers for the highest interests of the race, that they give the girls a chance! We might as well expect to grow trees from leaves as hope to build up a civilization or a manhood without taking into consideration our women and the home life made by them, which must be the root and ground of the whole matter. Let us insist then on special encouragement for the education of our women and special care in their training. Let our girls feel that we expect something more of them than that they merely look pretty and appear well in society. Teach them that there is a race with special needs which they and only they can help; that the world needs and is already asking for their trained, efficient forces. Finally, if there is an ambitious girl with pluck and brain to take the higher education, encourage her to make the most of it. Let there be the same flourish of trumpets and clapping of hands as when a boy announces his determination to enter the lists; and then, as you know that she is physically the weaker of the two, don't stand from under and leave her to buffet the waves alone. Let her know that your heart is following her, that your hand, though she sees it not, is ready to support her. To be plain, I mean let money be raised and scholarships be founded in our colleges and universities for self-supporting, worthy young women, to offset and balance the aid that can always be found for boys who will take theology.

The earnest well trained Christian young woman, as a teacher, as a home-maker, as wife, mother, or silent influence even, is as potent a missionary agency among our people as is the theologian; and I claim that at the present stage of our development in the South she is even more important and necessary.

Let us then, here and now, recognize this force and resolve to make the most of it—not the boys less, but the girls more.

A Sweatshop Girl's Story

SADIE FROWNE, 1902

Sadie Frowne, "The Story of a Sweatshop Girl," *Independent* 54 (September 25, 1902), pp. 2279–82.

Although the New Woman described in the press was a middle-class phenomenon, working-class daughters in big cities similarly demonstrated an innovative spirit of independence. This spirit emerges in the story of a teenage garment worker, as told to a reporter in 1902. A Polish immigrant, Sadie Frowne had arrived in New York with her mother in 1899 when she was thirteen. She worked first as a servant, as she had in Poland. After her mother, a garment worker, died of tuberculosis—an ailment that spread rapidly in the overcrowded lower east side—Sadie Frowne found work in a sweatshop. Within a very brief period of time, and with the assistance of the aunt who had paid her passage to America, she established an independent lifestyle.

Sadie Frowne's narrative conveys not only the experience of an enterprising new immigrant, but a working-class variant of the New Woman. Employment, income, independent residence, leisure-time activities, and a hefty measure of ambition—all were factors in the lifestyle that Sadie Frowne created. After her initial sweatshop experience on the lower east side, she obtained a stable job in a small garment shop in Brownsville, Brooklyn, a more desirable location. Her modest wages of $5.50 a week were not the lowest in the shop; they covered her expenses and enabled her to save. During her first venture in her own residence in Manhattan, when she roomed with a co-worker, Ella, Sadie Frowne took pride in managing her housekeeping expenses. Her new residence, in a home of some Brownsville friends, was even less expensive. In the workplace, Sadie Frowne joined a union, although she was "not a Socialist or an Anarchist." She attended night classes at a local public school, read English newspapers and romantic fiction, and appreciated her opportunity for education ("It makes you feel higher"). She enjoyed clothes and her ability to buy them ("A girl who does not dress well is stuck in a corner"). She took advantage of the city's opportunities for inexpensive recreation—dancing, theatre, Coney Island—usually in the company of her boyfriend, Henry.

Despite Henry's importuning, Sadie Frowne—who was not yet seventeen—resisted marriage, at least for the moment. Undoubtedly, she viewed her sweatshop career as temporary ("I will keep on working in the factory for a time"). But undoubtedly, too, she was proud of her achievements and appreciated her independence.

My mother was a tall, handsome, dark complexioned woman with red cheeks, large brown eyes and a great quantity of jet black, wavy hair. She was well educated, being able to talk in Russian, German, Polish and French, and even to read English print, tho, of course, she did not know what it meant. She kept a little grocer's shop in the little village where we lived at first. That was in Poland, somewhere on the frontier, and mother had charge of a gate between the countries, so that everybody who came through the gate had to show her a pass. She was much looked up to by the people, who used to come and ask her for advice. Her word was like law among them.

She had a wagon in which she used to drive about the country, selling her groceries, and sometimes she worked in the fields with my father.

The grocer's shop was only one story high, and had one window, with very small panes of glass. We had two rooms behind it, and were happy while my father lived, altho we had to work very hard. By the time I was six years of age I was able to wash dishes and scrub floors, and by the time I was eight I attended to the shop while my mother was away driving her wagon or working in the fields with my father. She was strong and could work like a man.

When I was a little more than ten years of age my father died. He was a good man and a steady worker, and we never knew what it was to be hungry while he lived. After he died troubles began, for the rent of our shop was about $6 a month and then there were food and clothes to provide. We needed little, it is true, but even soup, black bread and onions we could not always get.

We struggled along till I was nearly thirteen years of age and quite handy at housework and shop keeping, so far as I could learn them there. But we fell behind in the rent and mother kept thinking more and more that we should have to leave Poland and go across the sea to America where we heard it was much easier to make money. Mother wrote to Aunt Fanny, who lived in New York, and told her how hard it was to live in Poland, and Aunt Fanny advised her to come and bring me. I was out at service at this time and mother thought she would leave me—as I had a good place—and come to this country alone, sending for me afterward. But Aunt Fanny would not hear of this. She said we should both come at once, and she went around among our relatives in New York and took up a subscription for our passage.

We came by steerage on a steamship in a very dark place that smelt dreadfully. There were hundreds of other people packed in with us, men, women and children, and almost all of them were sick. It took us twelve days to cross the sea, and we thought we should die, but at last the voyage was over, and we came up and saw the beautiful bay and the big woman with the spikes on her head and the lamp that is lighted at night in her hand.*

---

*The Statue of Liberty, or, as the editor of *The Independent* calls it, the Goddess of Liberty.

Aunt Fanny and her husband met us at the gate of this country and were very good to us, and soon I had a place to live out,* while my mother got work in a factory making white goods.

I was only a little over thirteen years of age and a greenhorn, so I received $9 a month and board and lodging, which I thought was doing well. Mother, who, as I have said, was very clever, made $9 a week on white goods, which means all sorts of underclothing, and is high class work.

But mother had a very gay disposition. She liked to go around and see everything, and friends took her about New York at night and she caught a bad cold and coughed and coughed. She really had hasty consumption, but she didn't know it, and I didn't know it, and she tried to keep on working, but it was no use. She had not the strength. Two doctors attended her, but they could do nothing, and at last she died and I was left alone. I had saved money while out at service, but mother's sickness and funeral swept it all away and now I had to begin all over again.

Aunt Fanny had always been anxious for me to get an education, as I did not know how to read or write, and she thought that was wrong. Schools are different in Poland from what they are in this country, and I was always too busy to learn to read and write. So when mother died I thought I would try to learn a trade and then I could go to school at night and learn to speak the English language well.

So I went to work in Allen street [in Manhattan] in what they call a sweatshop, making skirts by machine. I was new at the work and the foreman scolded me a great deal.

"Now, then," he would say, "this place is not for you to be looking around in. Attend to your work. That is what you have to do."

I did not know at first that you must not look around and talk, and I made many mistakes with the sewing, so that I was often called a "stupid animal." But I made $4 a week by working six days in the week. For there are two Sabbaths here—our own Sabbath, that comes on a Saturday, and the Christian Sabbath that comes on Sunday. It is against our law to work on our own Sabbath, so we work on their Sabbath.

In Poland I and my father and mother used to go to the synagogue on the Sabbath, but here the women don't go to the synagogue much, tho the men do. They are shut up working hard all the week long and when the Sabbath comes they like to sleep long in bed and afterward they must go out where they can breathe the air. The rabbis are strict here, but not so strict as in the old country.

I lived at this time with a girl named Ella, who worked in the same factory and made $5 a week. We had the room all to ourselves, paying $1.50 a week for it, and doing light housekeeping. It was in Allen street, and the window looked out of the back, which was good, because there was an elevated railroad in front, and in summer time a great deal of dust and dirt came in at the front windows. We were on the fourth story and could see all that was going on in the back rooms of the houses behind us, and early in the morning the sun used to come in our window.

We did our cooking on an oil stove, and lived well, as this list of our expenses for one week will show:

---

*As a domestic servant.

Ella and Sadie for Food (One Week)

Tea	$0.06
Cocoa	.10
Bread and rolls	.40
Canned vegetables	.20
Potatoes	.10
Milk	.21
Fruit	.20
Butter	.15
Meat	.60
Fish	.15
Laundry	.25
Total	$2.42
Add rent	1.50
Grand total	$3.92

Of course, we could have lived cheaper, but we are both fond of good things and felt that we could afford them.

We paid 18 cents for a half pound of tea so as to get it good, and it lasted us three weeks, because we had cocoa for breakfast. We paid 5 cents for six rolls and 5 cents a loaf for bread, which was the best quality. Oatmeal cost us 10 cents for three and one-half pounds, and we often had it in the morning, or Indian meal porridge in the place of it, costing about the same. Half a dozen eggs cost about 13 cents on an average, and we could get all the meat we wanted for a good hearty meal for 20 cents—two pounds of chops, or a steak, or a bit of veal, or a neck of lamb—something like that. Fish included butter fish, porgies, codfish and smelts, averaging about 8 cents a pound.

Some people who buy at the last of the market, when the men with the carts want to go home, can get things very cheap, but they are likely to be stale, and we did not often do that with fish, fresh vegetables, fruit, milk or meat. Things that kept well we did buy that way and got good bargains. I got thirty potatoes for 10 cents one time, tho generally I could not get more than 15 of them for that amount. Tomatoes, onions and cabbages, too, we bought that way and did well, and we found a factory where we could buy the finest broken crackers for 3 cents a pound, and another place where we got broken candy for 10 cents a pound. Our cooking was done on an oil stove, and the oil for the stove and the lamp cost us 10 cents a week.

It cost me $2 a week to live, and I had a dollar a week to spend on clothing and pleasure, and saved the other dollar. I went to night school, but it was hard work learning at first as I did not know much English.

Two years ago I came to this place, Brownsville, where so many of my people are, and where I have friends. I got work in a factory making underskirts—all sorts of cheap underskirts, like cotton and calico for the summer and woolen for the winter, but never the silk, satin or velvet underskirts. I earned $4.50 a week and lived on $2 a week, the same as before.

I got a room in the house of some friends who lived near the factory. I pay $1 a week for the room and am allowed to do light housekeeping—that is, cook my meals in it. I get my own breakfast in the morning, just a cup of coffee and a roll, and at noon time I come home to dinner and take a plate of soup and a slice of bread with the lady of the house. My food for a week costs a dollar, just as it did in Allen street, and I have the rest of my money to do as I like with. I am earning $5.50 a week now, and will probably get another increase soon.

It isn't piecework in our factory, but one is paid by the amount of work done just the same. So it is like piecework. All the hands get different amounts, some as low as $3.50 and some of the men as high as $16 a week. The factory is in the third story of a brick building. It is in a room twenty feet long and fourteen broad. There are fourteen machines in it. I and the daughter of the people with whom I live work two of these machines. The other operators are all men, some young and some old.

At first a few of the young men were rude. When they passed me they would touch my hair and talk about my eyes and my red cheeks, and make jokes. I cried and said that if they did not stop I would leave the place. The boss said that that should not be, that no one must annoy me. Some of the other men stood up for me, too, especially Henry, who said two or three times that he wanted to fight. Now the men all treat me very nicely. It was just that some of them did not know better, not being educated.

Henry is tall and dark, and he has a small mustache. His eyes are brown and large. He is pale and much educated, having been to school. He knows a great many things and has some money saved. I think nearly $400. He is not going to be in a sweatshop all the time, but will soon be in the real estate business, for a lawyer that knows him well has promised to open an office and pay him to manage it.

Henry has seen me home every night for a long time and makes love to me. He wants me to marry him, but I am not seventeen yet, and I think that is too young. He is only nineteen, so we can wait.

I have been to the fortune teller's three or four times, and she always tells me that tho I have had such a lot of trouble I am to be very rich and happy. I believe her because she has told so many things that have come true. So I will keep on working in the factory for a time. Of course it is hard, but I would have to work hard even if I was married.

I get up at half-past five o'clock every morning and make myself a cup of coffee on the oil stove. I eat a bit of bread and perhaps some fruit and then go to work. Often I get there soon after six o'clock so as to be in good time, tho the factory does not open till seven. I have heard that there is a sort of clock that calls you at the very time you want to get up, but I can't believe that because I don't see how the clock would know.

At seven o'clock we all sit down to our machines and the boss brings to each one the pile of work that he or she is to finish during the day, what they call in English their "stint." This pile is put down beside the machine and as soon as a skirt is done it is laid on the other side of the machine. Sometimes the work is not all finished by six o'clock and then the one who is behind must work overtime. Sometimes one is finished ahead of time and gets away at four or five o'clock, but generally we are not done till six o'clock.

The machines go like mad all day, because the faster you work the more money you get. Sometimes in my haste I get my finger caught and the needle goes right through it. It goes so quick, tho, that it does not hurt much. I bind the finger up with a piece of cotton and go on working. We all have accidents like that. Where the needle goes through the nail it makes a sore finger, or where it splinters a bone it does much harm. Sometimes a finger has to come off. Generally, tho, one can be cured by a salve.

All the time we are working the boss walks about examining the finished garments and making us do them over again if they are not just right. So we have to be careful as well as swift. But I am getting so good at the work that within a year I will be making $7 a week, and then I can save at least $3.50 a week. I have over $200 saved now.

The machines are all run by foot power, and at the end of the day one feels so weak that there is a great temptation to lie right down and sleep. But you must go out and get air, and have some pleasure. So instead of lying down I go out, generally with Henry. Sometimes we go to Coney Island, where there are good dancing places, and sometimes we go to Ulmer Park to picnics. I am very fond of dancing, and, in fact, all sorts of pleasure. I go to the theater quite often, and like those plays that make you cry a great deal. "The Two Orphans" is good. Last time I saw it I cried all night because of the hard times that the children had in the play. I am going to see it again when it comes here.

For the last two winters I have been going to night school at Public School 84 on Glenmore avenue. I have learned reading, writing and arithmetic. I can read quite well in English now and I look at the newspapers every day. I read English books, too, sometimes. The last one that I read was "A Mad Marriage," by Charlotte Braeme. She's a grand writer and makes things just like real to you. You feel as if you were the poor girl yourself going to get married to a rich duke.

I am going back to night school again this winter. Plenty of my friends go there. Some of the women in my class are more than forty years of age. Like me, they did not have a chance to learn anything in the old country. It is good to have an education; it makes you feel higher. Ignorant people are all low. People say now that I am clever and fine in conversation.

We have just finished a strike in our business. It spread all over and the United Brotherhood of Garment Workers was in it. That takes in the cloakmakers, coatmakers, and all the others. We struck for shorter hours, and after being out four weeks won the fight. We only have to work nine and a half hours a day and we get the same pay as before. So the union does good after all in spite of what some people say against it—that it just takes our money and does nothing.

I pay 25 cents a month to the union, but I do not begrudge that because it is for our benefit. The next strike is going to be for a raise of wages, which we all ought to have. But tho I belong to the Union I am not a Socialist or an Anarchist. I don't know exactly what those things mean. There is a little expense for charity, too. If any worker is injured or sick we all give money to help.

Some of the women blame me very much because I spend so much money on clothes. They say that instead of a dollar a week I ought not to spend more than twenty-five cents a week on clothes, and that I should save the rest. But a girl must have clothes if she is to go into high society at Ulmer Park or Coney Island or the theatre. Those who blame me are the old country people who have old-fashioned notions, but the people who have been here a long time know better. A girl who does not dress well is stuck in a corner, even if she is pretty, and Aunt Fanny says that I do just right to put on plenty of style.

I have many friends and we often have jolly parties. Many of the young men like to talk to me, but I don't go out with any except Henry.

Lately he has been urging me more and more to get married—but I think I'll wait.

Women Bachelors

MARY GAY HUMPHREYS, 1896

Mary Gay Humphreys, "Women Bachelors in New York," *Scribner's Magazine* 20 (November 1896), pp. 626–36.

Late nineteenth-century reformers often voiced concern about single female wage earners who lived apart from their families or employers. Typically migrants to cities, such "women adrift" eked out livings in stores or factories or in some form of sexual service. As fugitives from family control, they struck contemporaries, variously, as victims or threats.* In the twentieth century, however, the single, independent working woman gained legitimacy. Near the turn of the century, journalist Mary Gay Humphreys described a middle-class version of the "woman adrift."

The enterprising New York wage earners whom Humphreys observed exemplified the independence of the New Woman. They ran their own households, sometimes teaming up with another "woman bachelor." They established "a new order of female friendship," based on camaraderie and mutual respect. Spunky and confident, they boasted active social lives, and even ventured forth at night alone to pursue their business interests or recreation. Most important, the "women bachelors" sought not "separatism" but "wholesome commingling among men." Entering the business world, they gained a "clearer sight of men among men," and indeed, through their very independence, *became* more like men. As the new century approached, in short, journalist Humphreys identified some forerunners of twentieth-century "career women."

The exodus of women, for one reason or another, to the cities in the last ten years parallels that of men. They have come from the West in regiments, and from the South in brigades. Each year they come younger and younger. They have ameliorated the customs and diversified the streets; nor are they to be confused with any of the better-known types. . . .

---

*See Joanne J. Meyerowitz, *Women Adrift: Independent Wage Earners in Chicago, 1880–1930* (Chicago: University of Chicago Press, 1988).

New York and perhaps city women in general, when they are suddenly called upon to earn their livings, are much more independent about it, and more original in their methods than women in smaller places, where womanly pursuits, as they are called, follow more closely prescribed lines. The New York woman has more knowledge of the world, and she knows that one can do pretty much what one pleases, if it is done with a certain dash, *élan*, carrying-all-before-it air. When she comes to work for her living she profits by this knowledge. Instead of becoming a governess or a teacher of music, she tries to get hold of something original that will excite interest. When she has found it she holds it up, as it were, on a blazoned banner, inscribed with this legend, "I have not a penny to my name, and I'm going to work." She accepts the situation with the greatest good-humor and makes herself more acceptable to the old set by relating her discouragements, trials, and mistakes so comically that she is better company than before. If her story is not bad enough she embroiders it to the proper point of attractiveness. . . .

In the measure that women are determining their own lives, they want their own homes. The desire is entirely reasonable. The woman who is occupied with daily work needs greater freedom of movement, more isolation, more personal comforts, and the exemption, moreover, from being agreeable at all times and places. She wants to be able to shut her doors against all the world, and not to be confined within four walls herself; and she wants to open her doors when it pleases her, and to exercise the rites of hospitality unquestioned. In fact, she wants many things that cannot be had except in her own home. It is an interesting fact in natural history that women in their first breathing-spell should revert to constructing homes as their natural background, to which is added the male realization that the home is the proper stimulus to achievement.

The first woman bachelor establishment in this city was in 1881, coexistent with the first woman's apartment-house in London. With a gay fillip of the finger at consequences, it was set up in the most expensive part of the town. It was easy to argue that it would be a material saving in car-fares, city rent being merely one of the natural incentives to hard work; in any case, in a fashionable area poverty glorified by gilded Japanese cottons and unframed etchings might well be endured. So novel an undertaking did not fail to excite attention. . . . To turn the necessity of earning a living into a co-operative lark was a new and captivating idea. Thus was the enterprise mistakenly regarded. It was, in fact, the serious effort on the part of four women to find some way of living in which, at the least expense, the greatest comfort and independence could be obtained, and the social instincts gratified. . . .

Since the initial effort tiny households having sprung up all over town. These are as well ordered and the rent as promptly paid as that of other and older households. These women rarely live alone. They combine against burglars, out of congeniality, and to save expense. But their domestic lives are neither adhesive nor entangled. They have common points of interest, but these are surrounded by large areas of unencumbered space, in which each moves freely and without interruption. In its best aspect this new development in women's lives is worthy of admiration. Out of it has arisen a new order of feminine friendship that combines independence, *camaraderie*, frank disagreement, wise reticence, large patience, mutual respect, amiable blindness, consideration in illness, sympathy in joy and sorrow, and the possibility of borrowing money from one another when necessary. . . .

Meanwhile, significant changes have taken place in every part of town. Instead of hiving,* women bachelors in braces and alone are encountered everywhere. Some of the older apartment-houses have found it more profitable to divide their space to accommodate them than to rent to orthodox families. There are few apartment-houses so dignified that women bachelors are not received as are other tenants. For the woman bachelor is not now essentially a person who puts on her bonnet and goes out in all sorts of weather. There are feminine Mæcenases who have establishments, boxes at the opera, and who fulfil social exactions in the most prominent manner. As was intimated before, in the ability to gratify the social instinct there is a tendency to finality much more important than in the ability to earn money.

To be the mistress of a home, to extend hospitalities, briefly to be within the circumference of a social circle, instead of gliding with uneasy foot on the periphery, is the reasonable desire of every woman. When this is achieved many temptations, so freely recognized that nobody disputes them, are eliminated. It is a noticeable fact in all women-bachelor households, no matter how humble, that the rugs are scarcely down and the curtains up, until the kettle is lighted and the reign of hospitality has begun. It is interesting to observe how soon the shyest novice over the tea-cups loses her timidity, and assumes that air of confidence that once was the enviable property of only married women.

George Eliot has remarked that sense of promotion that married women seem to carry in their demeanor toward other women. So discriminating an observer, if she had lived longer, could not have failed to notice in the bachelor maid its counterpart, slightly differentiated to be sure. The mystery of men's lives in the world, out of which illusions are spun, has always had a greater influence in determining the fate of women than is readily admitted. To feel transmitted through the ring-finger the electric thrill of business, of politics, of clubs, of the stirring movements in the life of men, gives any woman vantage-ground over others of her sex. But in the actual commerce of business, the community of affairs, the wear and tear of daily life in offices and elevators, this mystery vanishes. A couple of type-writers at luncheon will illustrate badly a situation yet too new to be fairly reckoned up. Over knife and fork they will match employers as small boys do pennies.

Out of hours the boss is only a man of whose necktie they may disapprove, or of the way he wears his hair, or perhaps of his grammar, and it may be he appears greatly to the advantage of some young man at a neighboring machine.

The type-writer of this estate always marries, and is consequently not a woman bachelor. But this one, too, arrives at something of the same knowledge of the strength of men and of their weaknesses; this is apt to be considered a not undesirable exchange for the will-o'-the-wisps that dance before the eyes of the home-keeping women. With these franker relations, the community of outside interests, the wider exchange of opinions, the clearer sight of men among men, and of men as they are, come also larger sympathy, a better appreciation of their difficulties, of their larger needs, of the greater leeway required by them that even wives can scarcely arrive at.

---

*Living in a group residence with other women.

These inevitably form the basis for social intercourse and a newer comradeship that have hardly yet been taken into account, but are plainly reflected in the frank, unapologetic manner of the woman bachelor that has replaced the hesitating, graceful timidity of the old maid.

Science came in opportunely as their handmaid and messenger-boy. When Mr. Edison was experimenting with the subdivision of the electric light, it seemed to have no special bearings on the evolution of the woman bachelor. The brilliancy of the streets at night has been so conspicuous a factor that the latest goddess, Electra, may well be adopted as the patron and guardian of the sex. The duties of legions of women take them out at night. Duty is its own excuse; accompanied by the chivalrous umbrella, many a woman has braved the powers of night and not unfrequently done battle. The woman who must be escorted home from a newspaper office at midnight limits her value to the extent of the bother she makes; the doctor who cannot respond to a night-call without a cab or a messenger-boy is handicapped beyond the possibility of success. Ease of movement is essential in the competitive struggle for a livelihood. But amusement and recreation have recognized places in all these later schemes of life. The increase in the number of women abroad at night, with no other protector than the benign beams of the electric light, afford a new and interesting manifestation of the streets. They are found in the streetcars at hours that once would have been called unseemly. . . .

The women bachelors of New York have nothing that corresponds to the London women's clubs. It has been plainly demonstrated that similarity of pursuits does not form the best basis on which to found a club in the repeated failures and timid successes of such efforts. It is not separatism, it appears, that attracts the woman bachelor in her moments of dearly bought and dearly prized leisure, but the more wholesome commingling among men and women as a recognized part of the social structure.

The Steel-Engraving Lady and the Gibson Girl

CAROLINE TICKNOR, 1901

Caroline Ticknor, "The Steel-Engraving Lady and the Gibson Girl," *The Atlantic Monthly* 88 (July 1901), pp. 105–08.

Journalist Caroline Ticknor presented the New Woman to *Atlantic* readers by inventing a dialogue between two fashion plates, the Steel-Engraving Lady and the Gibson Girl. Her turn-of-the-century audience could immediately visualize these protagonists. The Steel-Engraving Lady was a familiar image in nineteenth-century lithographs, such as those in *Godey's Lady's Book* and in Currier and Ives reproductions. Contemporaries described her as "etherialized"; she exuded fragility. The Gibson Girl, created by commercial artist Charles Dana Gibson, first appeared in *Life* magazine in 1890, and soon became a sensation. Throughout the nineties, her stylish, tailored figure, clad in shirtwaists and long, swinging skirts, graced advertisements and magazine covers. Discarding fragility, the Gibson Girl conveyed a sportive aura and radiated energy and self-confidence.*

As the dialogue proceeds, and as Ticknor's fashion plates spring to life, the Gibson Girl voices the note of independence that typified the New Woman. Active, healthy, modern, and "advanced," she appears to have less in common with her Victorian forerunner than with the yet-to-come flapper, who inherited some of her salient characteristics. These include her "companionate" relationship with her young man, her insistence on equality, and her defiance of tradition.

The Steel-Engraving Lady sat by the open casement, upon which rested one slender arm. Her drapery sleeve fell back, revealing the alabaster whiteness of her hand and wrist. Her glossy, abundant hair was smoothly drawn over her ears, and one rose nestled in the coil of her dark locks.

Her eyes were dreamy, and her embroidery frame lay idly upon the little stand beside her. An air of quiet repose pervaded the apartment, which, in its decorations, bespoke the lady's industry. Under a glass, upon a gleaming mirror, floated some waxen pond lilies, modeled by her slim fingers. A large elaborate sampler told of her

---

*For an illuminating discussion of the two fashion plates, see Lois W. Banner, *American Beauty* (New York: Knopf, 1983), chaps. 3 and 8.

early efforts with her needle, and gorgeous mottoes on the walls suggested the pleasing combination of household ornamentation with Scriptural advice.

Suddenly a heavy step was heard upon the stair. A slight blush mantled the Steel-Engraving Lady's cheek.

"Can that be Reginald?" she murmured.

The door flew open, and on the threshold stood the Gibson Girl.

"Excuse me for dropping in upon you," she said, with a slight nod, tossing a golf club down upon the sofa near by. "You see I've been appointed to write a paper on Extinct Types, and I am anxious to scrape acquaintance with you."

The Steel-Engraving Lady bowed a trifle stiffly. "Won't you be seated?" she said, with dignity.

The Gibson Girl dropped into a low chair, and crossed one knee over the other; then she proceeded to inspect the room, whistling meanwhile a snatch from the last comic opera. She wore a short skirt and heavy square-toed shoes, a mannish collar, cravat, and vest, and a broad-brimmed felt hat tipped jauntily upon one side.

She stared quite fixedly at the fair occupant of the apartment, who could with difficulty conceal her annoyance.

"Dear me! you're just as slender and ethereal as any of your pictures," she remarked speculatively. "You need fresh air and exercise; and see the color of my hands and face beside your own."

The Steel-Engraving Lady glanced at her vis-à-vis, and shrugged her shoulders.

"I like a healthy coat of tan upon a woman," the Gibson Girl announced, in a loud voice. "I never wear a hat throughout the hottest summer weather. The day is past when one deplores a sunburned nose and a few freckles."

"And is a browned and sunburned neck admired in the ballroom?" the other queried. "Perhaps your artists of to-day prefer studies in black and white entirely, and scoff at coloring such as that ivory exhibits?" She pointed to a dainty miniature upon the mantel.

"No wonder you can't walk in those slim, tiny slippers!" the Gibson Girl exclaimed.

"And can you walk in those heavy men's shoes?" the Steel-Engraving Lady questioned. "Methinks my slippers would carry me with greater ease. Are they your own, or have you possibly put on your brother's shoes for an experiment? If they were only hidden beneath an ample length of skirt, they might seem less obtrusive. And is it true you walk the streets in such an abridged petticoat? You surely cannot realize it actually displays six inches of your stockings. I blush to think of any lady upon the street in such a guise."

"Blushing is out of style." The Gibson Girl laughed heartily.

"Nor would it show through such a coat of sunburn," the other suggested archly.

"It very likely seems odd to you," the visitor continued, "who are so far behind the times; but we are so imbued with modern thought that we have done away with all the oversensitiveness and overwhelming modesty in which you are enveloped. We have progressed in every way. When a man approaches, we do not tremble and droop our eyelids, or gaze adoringly while he lays down the law. We meet him on a ground of perfect fellowship, and converse freely on every topic."

The Steel-Engraving Lady caught her breath. "And does he like this method?" she queried.

"Whether he *likes* it or not makes little difference; *he* is no longer the one whose pleasure is to be consulted. The question now is, not 'What does man like?' but 'What does woman prefer?' That is the keynote of modern thought. You see, I've had a liberal education. I can do everything my brothers do; and do it rather better, I fancy. I am an athlete and a college graduate, with a wide, universal outlook. My point of view is free from narrow influences, and quite outside of the home boundaries."

"So I should have imagined by your dress and manner," the Steel-Engraving Lady said, under her breath.

"I am prepared to enter a profession," the visitor announced. "I believe thoroughly in every woman's having a distinct vocation."

The Steel-Engraving Lady gasped. "Doesn't a woman's home furnish her ample employment and occupation?"

"Undoubtedly it keeps her busy," the other said; "but what is she *accomplishing*, shut in, walled up from the world's work and interests? In my profession I shall be brought in contact with universal problems."

"A public character! Perhaps you're going on the stage?"

"Oh no. I'm to become a lawyer."

"Perhaps your home is not a happy one?" the Steel-Engraving Lady said, with much perplexity.

"Indeed it is, but I have little time to stay there."

"Have you no parents?"

"Parents? Why, to be sure; but when a woman is capable of a career, she can't sit down at home just to amuse her parents. Each woman owes a duty to herself, to make the most of her Heaven-given talents. Why, I've a theory for the entire reorganization of our faulty public school system."

"And does it touch upon the influence at home, which is felt in the nursery as well as in the drawing-room?"

"It is outside of all minor considerations," the Gibson Girl went on. "I think we women should do our utmost to purify the world of politics. Could I be content to sit down at home, and be a toy and a mere ornament"—here she glanced scornfully at her companion—"when the great public needs my individual aid?"

"And can no woman serve the public at home?" the other said gently. Her voice was very sweet and low. "I have been educated to think that our best service was"—

"To stand and wait," the Gibson Girl broke in. "Ah, but we all know better nowadays. You see the motto 'Heaven helps her who helps herself' suits the 'new woman.' We're not a shy, retiring, uncomplaining generation. We're up to date and up to snuff, and every one of us is self-supporting."

"Dear me!" the Steel-Engraving Lady sighed. "I never realized I had aught to complain of; and why should woman not be *ornamental* as well as useful? Beauty of person and manner and spirit is surely worthy of our attainment."

"It was all well enough in your day, but this is a utilitarian age. We cannot sit down to be admired; we must be 'up and doing'; we must leave 'footprints on the sands of time.'"

The Steel-Engraving Lady glanced speculatively at her companion's shoes. "Ah, but such great big footprints!" she gasped; "they make me shudder. And do your brothers approve of having you so clever that you compete with them in everything, and are there business places enough for you and them?"

"We don't require their approval. Man has been catered to for ages past, while woman was a patient, subservient slave. To-day she assumes her rightful place, and man accepts the lot assigned him. And as for business chances, if there is but one place, and I am smarter than my brother, why, it is fair that I should take it, and let him go without. But tell me," the Gibson Girl said condescendingly, "what did your so-called education consist of?"

"The theory of my education is utterly opposed to yours, I fear," the other answered. "Mine was designed to fit me for my home; yours is calculated to unfit you for yours. You are equipped for contact with the outside world, for competition with your brothers in business; my training merely taught me to make my brother's home a place which he should find a source of pleasure and inspiration. I was taught grace of motion, drilled in a school of manners, made to enter a room properly, and told how to sit gracefully, to modulate my voice, to preside at the table with fitting dignity. In place of your higher education, I had my music and languages and my embroidery frame. I was persuaded there was no worthier ambition than to bring life and joy and beauty into a household, no duty higher than that I owed my parents. Your public aspirations, your independent views, your discontent, are something I cannot understand."

The Steel-Engraving Lady rose from her chair with grace and dignity; she crossed the room, and paused a moment on the threshold, where she bowed with the air of a princess who would dismiss her courtiers; then she was gone.

"She surely is an extinct type!" the Gibson Girl exclaimed. "I realize now what higher education has done toward freeing woman from chains of prejudice. I must be off. I'm due at the golf links at three-fifteen."

When the sun set, the Steel-Engraving Lady might have been seen again seated beside the open casement. Her taper fingers lightly touched the strings of her guitar as she hummed a low lullaby. Once more she heard a step upon the stair, and once again the color mantled her damask cheek, and as she breathed the word "Reginald" a tall and ardent figure came swiftly toward her. He dropped upon one knee, as if to pay due homage to his fair one, and, raising her white hand to his lips, whispered, "My queen, my lady love."

And at this moment the Gibson Girl was seated upon a fence, swinging her heavy boots, while an athletic youth beside her busied himself with filling a corn-cob pipe.

"I say, Joe," he said, with friendly accent, "just you hop down and stand in front of me to keep the wind off, while I light this pipe."

And the sun dropped behind the woods, and the pink afterglow illumined the same old world that it had beautified for countless ages.

Its pink light fell upon the Steel-Engraving Lady as she played gently on her guitar and sang a quaint old ballad, while her fond lover held to his lips the rose that had been twined in her dark locks.

The sunset's glow lighted the Gibson Girl upon her homeward path as she strode on beside the athletic youth, carrying her golf clubs, while he puffed his corn-cob pipe. They stopped at a turn in the road, and he touched his cap, remarking: "I guess I'll leave you here, as I am late to dinner. I'll try to be out at the links to-morrow; but if I don't show up, you'll know I've had a chance to join that hunting trip. Ta-ta!"

And the night breeze sprang up, and murmured: "Hail the new woman—behold she comes apace! Woman, once man's superior, now his equal!"

Suggestions for Further Reading

Lois Banner, *Elizabeth Cady Stanton: A Radical for Women's Rights* (Boston, 1980).

Rosalyn Baxandall, Linda Gordon, and Susan Reverby, eds., *America's Working Women: A Documentary History, 1600 to the Present* (New York, 1976).

Karen J. Blair, *The Clubwoman as Feminist: True Womanhood Redefined, 1868–1914* (New York, 1980).

Ruth Bordin, *Women and Temperance: The Quest for Power and Liberty, 1873–1900* (Philadelphia, 1980).

W. Elliott Brownlee and Mary N. Brownlee, eds., *Women and the American Economy: A Documentary History* (New York, 1976).

Steven M. Buechler, *The Transformation of the Woman Suffrage Movement: The Case of Illinois, 1850–1920* (New Brunswick, NJ, 1986).

Mary Jo Buhle and Paul Buhle, eds., *The Concise History of Woman Suffrage: Selections from the Classic Work of Stanton, Anthony, Gage, and Harper* (Urbana, IL, 1981).

Margery W. Davies, *Woman's Place Is at the Typewriter: Office Work and Office Workers, 1870–1930* (Philadelphia, 1983).

Allen F. Davis, *American Heroine: The Life and Legend of Jane Addams* (New York, 1973).

Sarah Deutsch, *No Separate Refuge: Culture, Class, and Gender on an Anglo-Hispanic Frontier in the American Southwest, 1880–1940* (New York, 1987).

Hasia R. Diner, *Erin's Daughters in America: Irish Immigrant Women in the Nineteenth Century* (Baltimore, 1983).

Ellen Dubois, *Feminism and Suffrage: The Emergence of an Independent Women's Movement, 1848–1869* (Ithaca, NY, 1978).

———, ed., *Elizabeth Cady Stanton/Susan B. Anthony: Correspondence, Writings, Speeches* (New York, 1981).

Mario T. Garcia, "The Chicana in American History: The Mexican Women of El Paso, 1880–1920: A Case Study," *Pacific Historical Review* 49 (May 1980), pp. 315–37.

Paula Giddings, *When and Where I Enter: The Impact of Black Women on Race and Sex in America* (New York, 1984).

Linda Gordon, *Women's Body, Women's Right: A History of Birth Control in America* (New York, 1976).

Lynn D. Gordon, *Gender and Higher Education in the Progressive Era* (New Haven, CT, 1990).

Herbert Gutman, *The Black Family in Slavery and Freedom, 1750–1925* (New York, 1976).

Barbara Meil Hobson, *Uneasy Virtue: The Politics of Prostitution and the American Reform Tradition* (New York, 1987).

Helen Lefkowitz Horowitz, *Alma Mater: Design and Experience in the Women's Colleges from their Nineteenth-Century Beginnings to the 1930s* (New York, 1984).

Jacqueline Jones, *Labor of Love, Labor of Sorrow: Black Women, Work, and the Family, from Slavery to the Present* (New York, 1985).

David M. Katzman, *Seven Days a Week: Women and Domestic Service in Industrializing America* (New York, 1978).

Alice Kessler-Harris, *Out to Work: A History of Wage-Earning Women in America* (New York, 1982).

Alexander Keyssar, *Out of Work: The First Century of Unemployment in Massachusetts* (New York, 1986), chapter 4.

Aileen Kraditor, *Ideas of the Woman Suffrage Movement, 1890–1920* (New York, 1965).

William Leach, *True Love and Perfect Union: The Feminist Reform of Sex and Society* (New York, 1980).

Leon F. Litwack, *Been in the Storm So Long: The Aftermath of Slavery* (New York, 1979).

Joanne J. Meyerowitz, *Women Adrift: Independent Female Wage Earners in Chicago, 1880–1930* (Chicago, 1988).

Regina Markell Morantz-Sanchez, *Sympathy and Science: Women Physicians in American Medicine* (New York, 1985).

William L. O'Neill, *Feminism in America: A History*, Second Revised Edition (New Brunswick, NJ, 1989).

Kathy Peiss, *Cheap Amusements: Working Women and Leisure in Turn-of-the-Century New York* (Philadelphia, 1986).

Rosalind Rosenberg, *Beyond Separate Spheres: Intellectual Roots of Modern Feminism* (New Haven, CT, 1982).

Sheila M. Rothman, *Woman's Proper Place: A History of Changing Ideals and Practices, 1870 to the Present* (New York, 1978).

Cynthia Eagle Russett, *Sexual Science: The Victorian Construction of Womanhood* (Cambridge, MA, 1989).

Ann F. Scott and Andrew Scott, *One Half the People: The Fight for Women Suffrage* (Philadelphia, 1975).

Maxine Schwartz Seller, ed., *Immigrant Women* (Philadelphia, 1981).

Barbara Miller Solomon, *In the Company of Educated Women: A History of Women and Higher Education in America* (New Haven, CT, 1983).

Nancy Woloch, *Women and the American Experience* (New York, 1984).